East Coast Australia

The landscape is so immense, hot and huge like nothing on earth, that I fear it might swallow me.

Tom Flood, Oceana Fine (1989)

Don't miss...

1. The remarkable architecture of Federation Square, Melbourne ▸▸ p60.

2. Soaking up the atmosphere around Circular Quay, Sydney ▸▸ p109.

3. The viewpoints of the Blue Mountains National Park ▸▸ p158.

4. Basic camping in and around the Myall Lakes National Park ▸▸ p194.

5. The hype and buzz of Byron Bay ▸▸ p216.

6. South Bank Lagoon, Brisbane ▸▸ p253.

7. A swim in idyllic Lake McKenzie on Fraser Island ▸▸ p278.

8. Laying or hatching time at the Mon Repos turtle rookery, near Bundaberg ▸▸ p294.

9. Exploring the Whitsunday Islands under sail ▸▸ p317.

10. Diving or snorkelling on the Great Barrier Reef ▸▸ p351.

It's easy to see why they call Australia the 'Lucky Country'. You only have to look at its East Coast. Here, on the edge of the world's largest and driest island, a remarkable biodiversity and range of habitats combines to form one of the most exceptional environments on earth. Where else would you find two completely different and accessible World Heritage parks – Daintree and the Great Barrier Reef – separated only by the tide? And these are just two examples of Australia's embarrassing wealth of natural assets. There are over 580 national parks and nature reserves in New South Wales alone, including the majestic Blue Mountains near Sydney.

These beautiful envirnoments are populated by an amazing variety of wildlife, from the cuddly koala to the duckbilled platypus, a bizarre creature that looks like it was designed by committee. Another bizarre design is that of the country's greatest man-made icon, the Sydney Opera House. The Melbourne to Cairns route includes Australia's two biggest cities: both equally absorbing; both as rich and varied as the country's wildlife. Melbourne's urbane, sophisticated residents contrast sharply with Sydney's brash, fun-loving population.

Contents

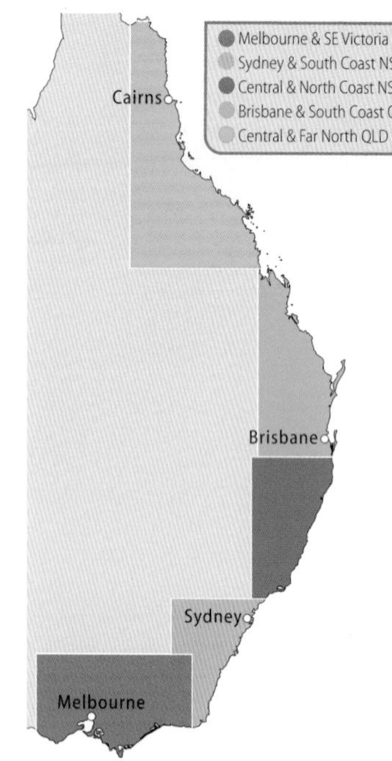
Melbourne & SE Victoria
Sydney & South Coast NSW
Central & North Coast NSW
Brisbane & South Coast QLD
Central & Far North QLD
Cairns
Brisbane
Sydney
Melbourne

Sydney & South Coast NSW 103

Brisbane & South Coast QLD 237

Central and North Coast NSW 185

Central & Far North QLD 309

About the guide

Until recently, backpacking was the preserve of the impecunious student, stretching their pesos/baht/rupees as far as possible, sleeping in cockroach-infested, cell-like rooms and risking food poisoning by eating at the cheapest market stalls they could find. Today's backpackers, however, are different. They still have the same adventurous spirit but they probably don't have endless months to swan around the globe; they're interested in the people, culture, wildlife and history of a region and they're willing to splash out occasionally to ensure that their trip is truly memorable.

Footprint's discover guides are designed precisely for this new breed of traveller. We've selected the best sights, sleeping options, restaurants and a range of adventure activities so that you can have the experience of a lifetime. With over 80 years' experience of writing about travel, we hope that you find this guide easy to use, enjoyable to read and good to look at.

Essentials, the first chapter, deals with practicalities: introducing the region and suggesting where and when to go, what to do and how to get around; we give the lowdown on visas, money, health and transport, and provide overviews of history, culture and wildlife. The rest of the guide is divided into area-based chapters, colour-coded for convenience. At the start of each chapter, a highlights map gives an instant overview of the area and its attractions. A star rating system also gives each area marks out of five for Landscape, Activities, Culture etc. The Costs category refers to value for money in relation to Europe and North America, where **$$$$$** is expensive and **$** is very cheap. Follow the cross references to the district that interests you to find a more detailed map, together with a snapshot of the area, showing the amount of time you will need, how to get there and move around, and what to expect in terms of weather, accommodation and restaurants. **Special features** include expert tips, inspiring travellers' tales, suggestions for busting your budget and ideas for going that little bit further.

We use a range of symbols throughout the guide to indicate the following information:

- Sleeping
- Eating
- Entertainment
- Festivals
- Shopping
- Activities and tours
- Transport
- Directory

Please note that hotel and restaurant codes, pages 29 and 32, should only be used as a guide to the prices and facilities offered by the establishment. It is at the discretion of the owners to vary them from time to time.

Footprint feedback We try as hard as we can to make each Footprint guide as up to date as possible but, of course, things always change. If you want to let us know about your experiences – good, bad or ugly – then don't delay, go to www.footprintbooks.com and send in your comments.

Essentials

Diver passing an enormous soft coral tree on Osprey reef

Where to go

With a combined landmass of over 2.7 million sq km, Victoria, New South Wales and Queensland form an area 11 times the size of the UK. Although the interior does not possess the same diverse scenery as the UK and is certainly far less populated (14% of the UK's and 7% of the USA's), it is obvious that if you have no more than one or two weeks for a visit, you can dismiss the idea of trying to see too much of all three states, and certainly of attempting to see very much of the outback – unless you intend to fly.

This is why the route from Sydney to Cairns in particular is so popular: a 2,685-km journey along the world's favourite coastline. The entire journey covered in this guide, from Melbourne to Cairns via the coast (approximately 3,725-km), stopping only to sleep, takes six days by car (Sydney to Cairns, four). To give US residents some idea of scale, the distance between Seattle and San Diego (essentially the entire western seaboard of the USA) is just over 2000-km.

Where you choose to visit will primarily be determined by the time of year. Broadly speaking, the far north from October to April is extremely hot, humid and monsoonal. Cairns still gets visitors who want to see the Great Barrier Reef, but most people will want to enjoy the glorious summer weather in the southern regions and avoid the humidity up north. A visit during May to September not only opens up the north, but also allows an itinerary to range almost anywhere within the two states. See also Climate, page 14.

One- to two-week trip

A trip of one or two weeks could only ever sample a specific area between Sydney and Cairns with perhaps a flying visit (literally) to Melbourne. The following tips suggest making the most out of Sydney, Brisbane, the Gold Coast and Cairns with your own transport. Other specific recommended destinations en route include the **Myall Lakes National Park**, **Byron Bay**, **Fraser Island**, **Magnetic Island** (off Townsville) and the **Whitsunday Islands**.

If you visit **Sydney**, allow at least three days to do it justice. Add to that a three-day trip to the **Blue Mountains**, a two-day trip to the **Hunter Valley** vineyards or, alternatively, the Myall Lakes National Park. **Brisbane** will require at least two days and the **Gold Coast** at least three days with added exploration of

The iconic and unmistakable architecture of the Sydney Opera House and Harbour Bridge

Steep sandstone escarpments, typical of the Blue Mountains near Sydney

Coolangatta, the Gold Coast hinterland national parks and (from Brisbane) Moreton or North Stradbroke Islands or Noosa also being recommended. **Cairns and the Barrier Reef** could occupy anyone for months, never mind a week or two. However, the 'must see and do's' include a reef island trip with snorkelling or a dive (you can do an introductory dive even if you are not certified), **Kuranda** and the rainforest gondola, **Daintree**, **Cape Tribulation** and the perfect retreat from the coastal heat, the **Atherton Tablelands**.

Three- to four-week trip

Ideally, this is the minimum amount of time a visitor from Europe or the USA should spend in the region. A three to four week trip could comfortably involve a few days in Sydney, then a trip north to Byron Bay, or the lesser visited Port Macquarie, or alternatively a visit to Brisbane and the Gold Coast then a rather hurried drive to Cairns. The route south of Sydney to Melbourne has lots to offer but, if pushed for time, the New South Wales and Queensland

How big is your footprint?

One of Australia's main attractions is the natural environment and its wildlife and there are many opportunities for ecotourism. **CALM** promote a minimal impact bushwalking code aimed at protecting the environment, which is also a useful guide for minimizing your footprint in other natural environments. Fire is a critical issue in Australia's hot, dry environments where only a spark is needed to create a fire that can get out of control and destroy an area the size of a small European country in a day or two, perhaps threatening lives and property. The national parks around Sydney have been particularly badly hit in the last decade. For this reason, in some areas, there are total fire bans, either for a seasonal period or on days when a high risk of fire is predicted. In extreme circumstances a national park, scenic attraction or walking trail may be closed because the risk of fire is so high. Fire bans or restrictions usually apply in summer (November to March) in the south and during the late dry season in the north (July to November). Check fire restrictions before travel with the nearest parks, shire, police or tourist office as they may affect your preparations; on days of Total Fire Ban you will have to take food that doesn't need cooking.

If you want to know more about environmental issues or get involved in conservation, contact **Australian Conservation Foundation**, T02 9212 6600, www.acfonline.org.au, or **The Wilderness Society**, T03 6234 9799, www.wilderness.org.au. Other organizations include: **Parks Victoria**, T03 8627 4699, www.parkweb.vic.gov.au; **NSW National Parks and Wildlife Service**, T02 9247 5033, www.nationalparks.nsw.gov.au; **Queensland Parks and Wildlife Service**, T07 3227 8186, www.env.qld.gov.au; **National Trust of Australia**, T07 3229 1788, www.nationaltrustqld.org. The quarterly wilderness adventure magazine *Wild* is also a good source of information on current environmental issues and campaigns.

- Campers should always carry a fuel stove for cooking as many national parks or public reserves forbid campfires or the collection of wood or both. It is also good practice to keep your walking or camping gear clean between different environments.

- Travellers in Australia will also come across 'sacred sites', areas of religious importance to indigenous people, and naturally it is important to respect any restrictions that may apply to these areas. Permission is usually required to enter an Aboriginal community and you may be asked to comply with restrictions, such as a ban on alcohol. If you visit a community, or travel through Aboriginal land, respect the privacy of Aboriginal people and never take photographs without asking first.

(Clockwise from top left) A rainbow sweeps across Port Phillip Bay towards Melbourne city centre; the pool at the Dunk Island Resort, Queensland; a patchwork quilt adds some colour to the weekly market in Port Douglas, Queensland; Sugarloaf Point Lighthouse, Myall Lakes National Park.

coasts undoubtedly take precedence. That said, a flight to Melbourne is recommended to explore Australia's 'second city'. The one-way 2,685-km trip between Sydney and Cairns in four weeks by car is possible, but pushing it, so you may like to consider doing one of the sections below, then flying from Brisbane to Sydney or Brisbane to Cairns and perhaps from there to Melbourne. Although there is not much in it, of the two coastal sections the Queensland trip (Brisbane to Cairns) is the best. Added to the city-based suggestions in the one-to-two week section above, you should consider the following itineraries:

Sydney to Brisbane Between Sydney (5 days) and Brisbane you can visit Port Stephens (2 days), Myall Lakes National Park (3 days), Hunter Valley (2 days), Port Macquarie (3 days), South West Rocks (2 days), Bellingen including the Dorrigo and New England National Parks (2-3 days), Coffs Harbour (2 days), Iluka and Woody Head (2 days) and Byron Bay (4 days). All are recommended.
Brisbane to Cairns Between Brisbane (3 days) and Cairns the Sunshine Coast and Noosa (3 days) are excellent locations for a short break along with an additional day trip along the hinterland Blackall Range. Fraser Island (3 days) is, of course, a major highlight, while Bundaberg (especially the turtle rookery) and the twin towns of 1770 and Agnes Waters are both great venues off the beaten track (2 days each). Around Rockhampton (1 day) try to take in Yeppoon and Great Keppel Island (2-3 days) and around Mackay the Eungella National Park (1-2 days). In and around Townsville don't miss Magnetic Island (3 days) and Charters Towers (1 day). Airlie Beach (2 days) and the Whitsunday Islands (2-3 days) are almost obligatory while just south of Cairns, Mission Beach (2 days) and Dunk Island (1-2 days) are also well worth visiting. With all that to consider, make sure you leave at least 5 days in and around Cairns and the Great Barrier Reef.

Over one month

To make the trip by car or campervan between Melbourne and Cairns, taking in the cities, the prime destinations mentioned above and other recommended side trips comfortably will require 10-15 weeks one way. You can then fly back to Sydney or Melbourne, or, if you own a vehicle, endure the 4-6 day drive. Of course provided you have the time you should aim to arrive in Melbourne as opposed to Sydney, then do the entire trip from Melbourne to Cairns, using Sydney and Brisbane as the two main city stops along the way. As well as the locations mentioned above other recommended short-stay destinations (with an emphasis on ecology and camping) include:
Melbourne to Sydney Ben Boyd National Park, Batemans Bay (Murramarang National Park), Jervis Bay (Booderee National Park).
Sydney to Brisbane Barrington Tops National Park, Yuraygir National Park and Byron Bay Hinterland national parks.
Brisbane to Cairns Cooloola Coast (Great Sandy National Park), Lady Musgrave Island (from Town of 1770), Heron Island (from Gladstone), Hinchinbrook Island (from Cardwell), Lizard Island (Great Barrier Reef from Cairns or Cooktown), Undara Lava Tubes (from Cairns), Cooktown and 4WD tour to Cape York.

When to go

One of the joys of the East Coast is that at any time of year there is always some section where the weather is just right. The converse, of course, is that those particular about their destination need good timing. Due to its southerly position Victoria is the coldest and wettest state, especially in winter. However, that said, inland areas of the state (including Melbourne) can get very hot in summer (hotter than Sydney) with much of its interior currently sharing New South Wales and Queensland's protracted drought issues. The heightened variance in Victoria's climate is due to the influence of northerly winds from the interior and the ocean borne influences from the south and west. The former ,known as the 'southerly change', is essentially Victorian for 'put the fire on and find the umbrella'. Melbourne is famous for its 'four seasons in one day' with a southerly change from a northerly influence seeing the temperature drop dramatically by over 20°C, often with lively thunderstorms.

Broadly speaking, the peak season between Sydney and Brisbane is from mid-December through to the end of January. Conversely autumn, winter and spring (March to October) is considered the peak season north of Rockhampton (Tropic of Capricorn), when dry, warm

Snow gums, a species common at high altitudes within the Kosciuszko National Park, NSW

weather is the norm. The 'stinger season' between October and May also presents its own dangers. See box, page 37. Generally, accommodation and tourist sites in all three states stay open year-round, the main exceptions being in the far north in mid-summer (December to March).

Watch out for school holidays and peak seasons, when some areas get completely booked out months in advance (particularly between Sydney and Brisbane). School holidays tend to take place from mid-December to late January, a week or two around Easter, a couple of weeks in June and July and another couple during September and October. If planning a long trip, say three months or more, try to make spring or autumn the core of your time. Also note that during big sporting events such as cricket (summer) and rugby tests (winter) as well as the Aussie Rules Football finals (again in winter, especially in Victoria), you are strongly advised to book transport tickets and accommodation as far ahead as possible.

Climate

As a general rule of thumb, the further north you travel, and the further in time from July, the hotter it gets. And hot means very hot: days over 40°C (104°F) regularly occur in summer in the arid regions, and even cities as far south as Melbourne average around 25°C. In the north of the country summer (November to April) is synonymous with 'the wet', a period characterized by high humidity, heat, tremendous monsoonal rainfall and occasional, powerful cyclones. Periods of prolonged showers, particularly late in the wet season, are also common. Australia is the driest inhabited continent, and virtually nowhere further than 250 km inland gets more than an average of 600 mm (24 in) of rain a year. About half the continent, in a band across the south and west, gets less than 300 mm and much of it is desert. Naturally, the East Coast and elevated areas along the Great Divide see much higher rainfall. For weather forecasts: T1196, www.bom.gov.au.

Sport and activities

Australia is one of the world's great adventure countries and the East Coast can offer a tremendous range of activities. Many of the best experiences are offered by specialist tour and hire operators along the coast, and if you have some specific goals it is essential to check out your options carefully in advance as the time of year and availability of spaces can make a big difference to what is possible. *Wild* magazine has a good website, www.wild.com.au, and publishes quite a few walking and adventure guides.

Canoeing, kayaking, rafting

Australia may be the driest continent but there are a few opportunities for river rafting. Tropical Queensland rivers can generate quite a bit of white water in winter and the Snowy Mountains of New South Wales are another top destination for those after a rough and exciting ride.

★ **Head for**
Snowy Mountains (NSW) » *p179*
Whitsunday Islands (QLD) » *p317*
Great Barrier Reef (QLD) » *p351*

Sea kayaking is obviously huge and there are numerous operators in almost every major coastal town along the coast. The Australian canoeing website, www.canoe.org.au, concentrates on competitive canoeing, but some of the state links have good river descriptions and links to commercial operators. White-water rafting companies are mentioned in the text and predominate in Cairns, Mission Beach and Airlie Beach (QLD).

Climbing and abseiling

Although much of Australia is flat as a tack there are a few fabulous climbing spots. Most of the recognized routes are in the eastern half of the country in the Great Dividing Range. To find out more get hold of **Climbing Australia: The Essential Guide** by Greg Pritchard, or see www.climbing.com.au, which picks out abseiling operators.

★ **Head for**
Blue Mountains (NSW) » *p158*
Glasshouse Mountains (QLD) » *p272*

Canyoning is a sport almost exclusively restricted to the Great Dividing Range of New South Wales and involves a combination of climbing, abseiling, wading and swimming through the canyons and gorges of the Blue Mountains and Manning Valley.

Cycling and mountain biking

Bicycles are commonly available for hire in cities and major towns but facilities are scarce otherwise. Huge as the country is, cycling around it is a popular pastime and some states, notably Victoria with its Rail Trails, are actively promoting the activity.

★ **Head for**
Cairns (QLD) » *p346* **Melbourne (VIC)** » *p58* **Hunter Valley (NSW)** » *p189*

If you plan to do most of your touring on a bike you will need to either bring your own or buy in Australia, as long-term hire facilities are virtually non-existent. One alternative is to join a cycle-based tour, such as those organized by **Boomerang Bicycle Tours**, T02 9890 1996, ozbike@ozemail.com.au. Sydney-based companies are also an excellent source of information. See page 153.

Diving

From the very tip of Queensland to the very bottom of Australia's east coast, there are unlimited scuba diving possibilities. What makes this coast so interesting for divers is that the huge expanse covers several different climatic zones. The far north is tropical, then as you head south it goes to subtropical, eventually becoming temperate and the sheer variety of marine species is vast. The undoubted highlight is The Great Barrier Reef, the planet's longest coral reef system. Stretching for 2,000 km, it has 3,000 individual reefs, 1,500 species of fish, 400 corals and 4,000 molluscs. One of the major attractions across all regions though is sharks and, following hot on their heals, would be marine mammals.

(Top) The Napoleon wrasse, aka, humphead or maori; (Bottom left) One of Australia's most colourful marine residents, the harlequin tuskfish; (Bottom right) Swimming with the fishies! A school of rainbow runners

★ Head for
The Great Barrier Reef (QLD) »» p351 **Whitsundays (QLD)** »» p317 **Great Keppel** »» p300 **Lady Musgrave Island (QLD)** »» p294 **Byron Bay (NSW)** »» p218 **Sydney (NSW)** »» p106 **Jervis Bay (NSW)** »» p174

Australia's oceans are known for as many rare and indigenous marine species as land ones. www.diveoz.com.au and www.scubaaustralia.com.au both have some very useful general information as well as fairly comprehensive, though not qualitative, state-by-state directories including sites, dive centres and charter boats. Details of several multi-day diving trips can be found on www.divedirectory.net.

Aggressive if hunting, the bronze whaler can also be inquisitive

Fishing

One of Australia's favourite hobbies, fishing, is in some areas the only recreational activity available to locals and is pursued with an almost religious obsession. As you head north, surfboards begin to disappear from vehicle roof racks, only to be replaced by the 'tinnies', short aluminium boats that allow the fishing family to go where they please. Inland fishing, mostly for barramundi in the north and the feral trout in the south, requires a licence in some states, though beach and sea fishing do not.

Head for
Cairns (QLD) ➡ *p346* **Snowy Mts (NSW)** ➡ *p179* **Port Macquarie to Byron Bay coast (NSW)** ➡ *p206* **Sydney and around (NSW)** ➡ *p106*

Whatever your requirements, tour operators and hire companies will usually organize it for you. Excellent offshore sports fishing is widely available as a day tour, usually for around $150-200. There are several excellent websites on recreational fishing in Eastern Australia, including www.fishnet.com.au and www.sportsfishaustralia.com.au.

Gliding and hang-gliding

Gliding is particularly popular in inland towns, often bordering the wheatbelts, where there is a rich harvest of sunny days and strong thermals and most commonly out on the plains of inland New South Wales. For a comprehensive list of gliding clubs see www.gfa.org.au.

Hang-gliding, while still requiring thermals for extended flights, makes use of elevated areas for take-off and so is most popular in upland and coastal cliff areas. A few operators offer hang-gliding and para-gliding lessons and some one-off flights. You'll find a listing of top sites at www.hgfa.asn.au, the website of the Hang Gliding Federation of Australia, T02 6947 2888.

Head for
Central QLD Coast ➡ *p312*
Byron Bay (NSW) ➡ *p218*

Flying in microlights, effectively hang gliders with engines and wheels and also known as 'trikes', and ultralights, similar but more airplane-like, is a fast-growing activity in Australia where weather and space make it an ideal sport, or simply a way of getting around. A few operators around the country offer scenic flights in 2-seat versions but if you're interested

Surfers reading the waves, Gold Coast

in getting more involved contact one of the local clubs listed at www.members.ozemail.com.au/~aerial.

Horse riding

Australia has a great number of horse-riding schools and station stays, both offering recreational rides and you can't travel far in the more populated regions without finding one. Rides can be from 30 minutes to several days' duration.

Head for
Cairns (QLD) ›› *p346* **Airlie Beach (QLD)** ›› *p316* **Snowy Mountains (NSW)** ›› *p179*

The high country, between Mansfield, in Victoria, and Canberra, is where the most awesome Australian horse riding can be experienced but there are many places along the East Coast that offer fine scenic trails or multi-day treks and these are listed under the relevant destination.

Parachuting/bungee jumping

Many of the several dozen skydiving clubs in Australia offer short, usually one-day courses in parachuting (also known as 'skydiving'), including a jump or two and some cut out much of the training by organizing tandem jumps where you're strapped, facing forward, to the chest of the instructor. If a quick thrill is all you're after then the latter is the better option as it usually involves 30-60 secs of freefall, by far the most exhilarating part of the experience, and costs around $280-320.

Head for
Cairns (QLD) ›› *p346*
Sydney (NSW) ›› *p106*

A list of skydiving clubs affiliated to the Australian Parachute Federation, T02 62816830, can be found at www.apf.asn.au, and there are numerous opportunities to make the big leap all along the East Coast and around Sydney. If you fancy jumping out into thin air without a parachute then bungee jumping is just about the safest option going and available from a site just north of Cairns. A list of bungee operators can be found at www.bungee-experience.com.

The Murray River marks the border between New South Wales and Victoria

Skiing and snowboarding

Australia boasts some world-class resorts, though these are mostly confined to the Snowy Mountains in NSW, with some notable slopes also in the Victorian Alps. The peak season is, of course, winter, from June to September.

★ **Head for**
Thredbo (NSW) » p179
Perisher Valley (NSW) » p179

Surfing and waterskiing

If an Aussie lives near the beach there's a fair bet they'll be a surfer; if they're inland and anywhere near water then it'll be waterskiing. This makes for a great many local clubs, tuition and equipment hire. Surfing is generally best in the southern half of the country, from Sydney north to the QLD border.

★ **Head for**
Newcastle (NSW) » p189
Port Macquarie (NSW) » p207
Byron Bay (NSW) » p218 **Coolangatta (QLD)** » p244 **Noosa (QLD)** » p270

There are quite a few websites dedicated to surfing, including www.surfinfo.com.au, which links to a great many surfie retail and travel businesses, and www.real surf.com, which has condition reports from all the major spots around the country. You can make surfing the core activity on your travels with a number of companies offering specialist surf tours up and down the East Coast. A four-night trip between Sydney and Byron Bay will cost around $479, www.surfaris.com.au. Windsurfing and kitesurfing are also widespread, with Noosa (QLD) being a good place to learn the new art of kitesurfing. Information can be found at www.windsurfing.org, with club, holiday and tuition details on the state pages.

Walking and trekking

Australia boasts a great range of short, day and overnight walks, mostly in the many national parks and even a few multi-day treks that rank alongside the best in the world.

★ **Head for**
Thorsborne Trail on Hinchinbrook Island (QLD) » p325
Blue Mountains (NSW) » p158
Snowy Mountains (NSW) » p179

Many of Australia's natural ecologies are particularly sensitive to human activity and you should take care to disturb as little as possible. All the state conservation authorities have a minimal impact bushwalking code, published on their websites and printed on the park notes for all the national parks. Most of the longer walks, and some even as short as two hours, have a walker registration system in place – essentially ensuring that if you get lost or injured someone will come looking. If there is no such system in place make sure someone (it can be the local park ranger or the police) knows where you are going and how long you plan to be.

Bushwalking clubs are a good source of local advice and often welcome visitors on their regular expeditions. For a comprehensive list of clubs see www.bushwalking.org.au. The best series of books on walking in Australia has been penned by the indefatigable Tyrone T Thomas, see www.members.ozemail.com.au/~tyronet.

Getting there and flying around

There are international flights direct to Melbourne, Sydney, Brisbane and Cairns and it is quite possible to have different points of arrival and departure that complement your intended itinerary. If there is not a direct flight to your primary choice there will usually be a same-day connection from Sydney or Melbourne. It is usually possible to book internal Australian flights when booking your international ticket, at lower prices than on arrival. Some do not even require a stated departure and arrival point. If you have any plans to fly within New South Wales or Queensland check this out prior to booking.

Fares will depend on the season, with prices much higher during December and January unless booked well in advance. Mid-year tends to see the cheapest fares. **Qantas**, www.qantas.com.au, is Australia's main international airline and flies from most international capitals and major cities. Most other major airlines have flights to Australia from their home countries or Europe capitals.

Airport information

Melbourne, Sydney, Brisbane and Cairns are the main airports and all have excellent services. All the main airlines fly to these airports with regular connections from international and national destinations. Facilities are good and include banks, ATMs and tourist offices where help is on hand with accommodation booking and organizing tours and transport. They offer regular and efficient connections with the city centres either by coach or rail. See the respective sections for further details.

From Europe

The main route, and the cheapest, is via Asia, though fares will also be quoted via North America or Africa. The Asia route usually takes 20-30 hours including stops. There are no non-stop routes so it's worth checking out which stopovers are on offer. Stopovers of a few nights do not usually increase the cost of the ticket appreciably. The cheapest return flights, off-season, will be around £650 (€960), with stand-by prices rising to at least £850 (€1,255) around Christmas.

From North and South America

There are direct **Qantas** flights from Los Angeles to Brisbane and Sydney, and from Vancouver and New York to Sydney. Connections to Melbourne and Cairns are available from Auckland. The cost of a standard return in the high season from Vancouver starts from around US$2,200, from New York from US$2,000 and from Los Angeles from US$1,700. Flights take around 11 hours. There are also direct flights from Buenos Aires to Sydney.

Departure tax

There are currently a number of departure taxes levied by individual airports (ie, noise tax) and the government. All taxes are included in the cost of a ticket.

Discount flight agents

Ebookers, www.ebookers.com. Comprehensive travel ticket booking website.
Expedia, www.expedia.com. Another travel site based only on the internet, with lots of background information.
STA Travel, 86 Old Brompton Rd, London SW7 3LH, T0870 1600599, www.statravel.co.uk. Specialists in student discount fares, IDs and other travel services. Also branches in most major cities and many college campuses.
In Australia: **STA**, T131776, www.statravel.com.
Trailfinders, 194 Kensington High St, London W8 6FT, T0845 058 5858, www.trailfinders.com. Particularly good on personalized itineraries and adventure travel.
Flight Centre, T131600, www.flightcentre.com.au.
Harvey World Travel, T132757, www.harveyworld.com.au.
JetSet, T136384, www.jetset.com.au.

Regional flights

Qantas, www.qantas.com.au, **Regional Express (REX)**, www. regionalexpress.com.au, **Jetstar**, www.jetstar.com.au, and **Virgin Blue**, www.virginblue.com.au, link most of the state capitals to each other and to many of the larger provisional towns and main tourist destinations. There are also several regional airways operating smaller planes on specialist routes. Domestic fares have dropped dramatically in recent years. In 2005 a one-way fare between Sydney and Cairns for example was available for as little as AUS$150. For up-to-date information on whether a destination is served by a scheduled or charter flight, contact your destination's tourist office or each airline direct.

Getting around by land

Public transport is generally good and efficient and often easier than driving. Most cities have good metropolitan bus services, though some are curiously unaware of tourist traffic and there is many an important outlying attraction poorly served by public transport, or even missed off the bus routes completely. Some cities are compact enough for this to be a minor irritation, others are so spread out that the visitor must invest in an expensive tourist bus service or taxis. In such places staying at a hostel or B&B with free or low-cost bike hire can save a lot of money.

By far the best way of seeing the East Coast is under your own steam, or with a tour operator with an in-depth itinerary. See Tours and tour operators, page 41, and individual town and city sections for details. The further from the cities you go, the more patchy and irregular public transport becomes. All the states have networks based on a combination of air, bus and train. Some of these services connect up at border towns but you are advised to check first. If short on time and long on funds, flying can save a lot of time and effort, both interstate and within New South Wales and Queensland. In some cases it is the only real option. Most other interstate options involve long-distance buses, and on a few routes, trains.

Bus

State and interstate bus services offer the most cost-effective way of constructing an itinerary for a single traveller. The main operator throughout New South Wales and Queensland is **Greyhound Pioneer**, T131499, www.greyhound.com.au (referred to simply as Greyhound throughout this guide) while in Victoria the principal service provider is **V-Line**, T136196, www.vlinepassenger.com.au. Their networks follows all the main interstate highways up and down the coast with offshoots including the Blue Mountains, New England (Hunter Valley), Armidale, Charters Towers, the Atherton Tablelands and so on. As well as scheduled routes and fares, they offer a range of passes. There are also many other smaller regional companies.

Most are listed under the relevant destinations. **Countrylink**, T132232, www.countrylink.nsw.gov.au, also offer coach services to some centres in conjunction with rail schedules between New South Wales and Queensland. In Victoria rail is also covered by **V-Line**.

Greyhound offer two varieties of jump-on, jump-off passes. The **Explorer Pass** commits you to a set one-way or circular route and is valid for between 30 and 365 days. There are a couple of dozen options including **Sydney-Cairns** at around $325 and an **All Australian** ($2,458). Slightly more expensive per km is the more flexible **Kilometre Pass**. This allows you to travel anywhere on the network over the course of a year, with a maximum total of kilometres agreed and paid for in advance. A 2,000 km pass is $300, concessions $270, with each extra 1,000 km costing around $100.

Backpacker buses There are now several operators who make the assumption that the most important part of your trip is the journey. These companies combine the roles of travel operator and tour guide, taking from two to five times longer than scheduled services (a good indicator of just how much they get off the highway). They are worth considering, especially if you are travelling alone. In terms of style, price ($75-150 per day) and what is included, they vary greatly and it is important to clarify this prior to booking. Some offer transport and commentary only, others include accommodation and some meals, a few specialize in 4WD and bush camping. A few, including **Oz Experience** (see below) offer jump-on, jump-off packages and are priced more on distance. The popular option of flying Sydney to Cairns and returning by bus is $665. The main backpacker bus companies in NSW and Queensland are **Oz Experience**, T1300 300028, www.ozexperience.com, and **Travelabout**, T08 9244 1200, www.travelabout.au.com.

Car

If you live in a small and populous country travelling by car in Australia will be an enlightening experience, as well as an enervating one. Distances are huge and travelling times between the major cities, towns and sights can seem endless, so put on some tunes and make driving part of the whole holiday experience.

You should consider buying a car if you are travelling for more than three months. Consider a campervan if hiring or buying a car. Traffic congestion is rarely an issue on the East Coast route-only Sydney has anything like the traffic of many other countries, so driving

Despite their love of trees, koalas are often killed crossing Australian roads

Top tips

Buying a vehicle

Buying a vehicle in Australia is a relatively simple process, provided you have somewhere you can give as an address. Bona fide cars and vans can be picked up for as little as $2,500, or $6,000 for a 4WD. Paying more increases peace of mind but obviously increases possible losses when you sell it. If you're negotiating with a second-hand car dealer you may be able to agree a 'buy-back' price, saving considerable hassle, and usually you will be offered some sort of warranty. Alternatively, you can acquire a vehicle from fellow travellers, or through hostel notice boards and the classifieds. Buying privately is usually cheaper and real bargains can be had from travellers in a hurry to close a deal before returning home. But get it checked out before parting with your cash and scrutinize service records. State motoring organizations offer vehicle checks for around $150. An older vehicle may need a little 'tlc' so the availability of spares is a consideration. Fords and Holdens are best but Toyota parts are also common.

Every car is registered within the state where it is first purchased and the registration papers must be transferred at each sale. If a car is resold in a different state it has first to be re-registered in that state. It must also have an Australian Compliance Plate. You will need to formally complete the transfer of registration with the transport department, presenting them with the papers, a receipt (there is a stamp duty tax of about 5%), plus in some states a certificate of roadworthiness. The seller may provide the latter or you may have to get a suitable garage to check the vehicle. Registration must be renewed in the state the vehicle was last sold, every six or 12 months. Do not, if you can possibly avoid it, let your vehicle registration run out in New South Wales. The best option is to ensure the car you purchase has a registration covering the entire period of your stay and preferably longer to make a resale more viable. Third-party personal injury insurance is included in the registration. You are advised, however, to invest in third-party vehicle and property insurance, or even comprehensive cover if you cannot afford to lose the value of your vehicle.

itineraries can be based on covering a planned distance each day. Up to, say, 100 km for each solid hour's driving. The key factor in planning is distance. It is pretty stress-free and as the distances can be huge, drivers can get bored and sleepy. There are a lot of single-vehicle accidents in Australia, many the result of driver fatigue.

The other major factor when planning is the type of roads you may need to use. Almost all the main interstate highways between Sydney and Cairns are 'sealed', though there are a few exceptions. Many country roads are unsealed, usually meaning a stony or sand surface. When recently graded (levelled and compacted) they can be almost as pleasant to drive on as sealed roads, but even then there are reduced levels of handling. After grading, unsealed roads deteriorate over time. Potholes form, they can become impassable when wet, and corrugations

Driving safely

- If you stray from the coast and 'go outback', watch out for large animals such as kangaroos and emus. Hitting a kangaroo, emu or sheep can write off the vehicle and cause injury.
- On country and outback roads you will also meet road trains. Overtake them with great care.
- If you're on a single-track bitumen road or an unsealed road pull right over when a road train comes the other way. Not only can dust cause zero visibility but you will also minimise the possibility of stones pinging up and damaging your windows.
- Drive only in full daylight if possible.
- Always check with the hire company where you can and cannot take your 4WD vehicle (some will not allow them off graded roads or on sand, like Fraser Island) and also what your liability will be in the case of an accident.
- To minimize costs on long journeys: ensure correct tyre pressures, avoid using a/c if possible, pack luggage in the car rather than on the roof, check the oil regularly and stick to 90-100 kph (56-62 mph).
- Some hire companies will offer one-way hire on certain models and under certain conditions.
- The general breakdown number for all associations is T131111.
- For excellent travel route planning along the East Coast consult the Travel Planner section on the RACQ website, www.racq.com.au.

usually develop, especially on national park roads, with heavy usage. These are regular ripples in the road surface, at right angles to the road direction that can go on for tens of kilometres. Small ones simply cause an irritating judder, large ones can reduce tolerable driving speeds to 10-20 kph. Generally, the bigger the wheel size and the longer the wheel-base, the more comfortable the journey over corrugations will be. Many unsealed roads can be negotiated with a two wheel-drive (2WD) low-clearance vehicle but the ride will be a lot more comfortable, and safer, in a four wheel-drive (4WD) high-clearance one. Most 2WD hire cars are uninsured if driven on unsealed roads. Some unsealed roads (especially in the outback) are designated as 4WD-only or tracks, though individual definitions of some differ according to the map or authority you consult. If in doubt, stick to the roads you are certain are safe for your vehicle and you are sufficiently prepared for. With careful preparation, however, and the right vehicles (convoys are recommended), traversing the major outback tracks is an awesome experience.

If you stray far from the coast, and certainly anywhere outback, prepare carefully. Carry essential spares and tools such as fan belts, hoses, gaffer tape, a tyre repair kit, extra car jack, extra spare wheel and tyre, spade, decent tool kit, oil and coolant and a fuel can. Membership of the NRMA (NSW) or the RACQ (QLD) is recommended (see below), as is informing someone of your intended itinerary. Above all carry plenty of spare water, at least 10 litres per person, 20 if possible.

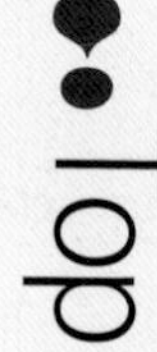

Top tips

Getting around the region

- Many provincial airports may not be staffed when you arrive. Check with the local tourist office regarding transport from the airport to the town.
- If travelling by bus in Australia, always check the journey duration and time of arrival. Some routes can literally take days, with just a couple of short meal stops.
- Many coaches are equipped with videos but you may want a book to hand. It's also a good idea to take warm clothing, socks, a pillow, toothbrush and ear-plugs. There's a good chance you will arrive in the late evening or the early hours of the morning. If it is the case, book accommodation ahead and, if possible, transfer transportation.
- Road and street maps for all the major Australian regions, cities and towns can be found at www.arta.com.au.
- A large selection of bus services can be found at www.buslines.com.au.
- Train fares be considerably cheaper if booked in advance.

Rules and regulations To drive in Australia you must have a current driving licence. Foreign nationals also need an international drivers licence, available from your national motoring organization. In Australia you drive on the left. Speed limits vary between states, with maximum urban limits of 50-60 kph and maximum country limits of 100-120 kph. Speeding penalties include a fine and police allow little leeway. Seatbelts are compulsory for drivers and passengers. Driving under the influence of alcohol is illegal over certain (very small) limits and penalties are severe.

Petrol costs Fuel costs are approximately half that in Britain twice that in the US – but due to the recent increase in the price of crude are following the global trend and rising rapidly. In late 2005 they were fluctuating between $1.10 and $1.30 a litre in city centres and marginally more in the outback. When budgeting allow at least $12 for every estimated 100 km (62 miles). A trip around the eastern circuit can easily involve driving 20,000+ km. Picking an economical vehicle and conserving fuel can save hundreds of dollars.

Motoring organizations Every state has a breakdown service affiliated to the **Australian Automobile Association (AAA)**, www.aaa.asn.au, with which your home country organization may have a reciprocal link. You need to join one of the state associations: in New South Wales **NRMA**, T132132, www.nrma.com.au, in Victoria **RACV**, T131329, www.racv.com.au, and in Queensland **RACQ**, T131905, www.racq.com.au. Note also that you may only be covered for about 100 km (depending on the scheme) of towing distance and that without cover towing services are very expensive. Given the sheer distances you are likely to cover by car, joining an automobile organization is highly recommended but read the fine print with regard to levels of membership in relation to coverage outside metropolitan areas and the outback. Several publishers produce countrywide and state **maps**. Regional maps are also available and the most useful for general travel. The best and cheapest of these are generally published by the above motoring organizations.

A traditional sign with a traditional message

Vehicle hire Car rental costs vary considerably according to where you hire from (it's cheaper in the big cities, though small local companies can have good deals), what you hire and the mileage/insurance terms. You may be better off making arrangements in your own country for a fly/drive deal. Watch out for kilometre caps: some can be as low as 100 km per day. The minimum you can expect to pay in Australia is around $200 a week for a small car. Drivers need to be over 21. At peak times it can be impossible to get a car at short notice and some companies may dispose of a booked car within as little as half an hour of you not showing up for an agreed pick-up time. If you've booked a car but are going to be late, ensure that you let them know before the pick-up time.

Cycling

Long-term bicycle hire is rarely available and touring cyclists should plan to bring their own bike or buy in Australia. Bicycle hire is available in most towns and cities and companies are listed in the book in the relevant sections. See also Sport and activities, page 16. If you do plan on touring the coast by bicycle, the website www.aussiecycling.com.au is recommended.

Hitch-hiking

Hitch-hiking, while not strictly illegal in New South Wales and Queensland, is not advised by anyone. The tragic events near Barrow Creek in 2001 demonstrate that there will always be twisted souls who will assault or abduct people for their own evil ends. This is not to say that hitching is more dangerous in Australia than elsewhere else.

Train

Train travel up and down the east coast is a viable mode of transport and can be a delightful way to get from A to B, especially if you are short of time. Given the distances between the main centres, Australia lends itself to rail travel and you may find routes with such evocative names as *Sunlander*, *Spirit of Capricorn* and *Savannahlander* irresistible. That said, a car or coach is a better option if you wish to explore or get off the beaten track. The east coast offers endless beaches and numerous national parks that are well away from any railway stations. Also bear in mind the track gauges differ in NSW and Queensland so the crossing between the two takes in an intriguing transition by road. Also note that overnight travel by rail is possible but often

5 Best

Resorts, lodges and retreats

Kingfisher Bay Resort, Fraser Island » p282
Hinchinbrook Island Wilderness Lodge » p331
Whitsunday Wilderness Lodge » p331
Sanctuary Retreat, Mission Beach » p335
Lizard Island Resort, Northern Great Barrier Reef » p367

expensive if you wish to find comfort in your own compartment and to do it in style. One thing well worth considering is a jaunt into the outback from Rockhampton to Longreach on board the *Spirit of the Outback*, or from Cairns to Forsayth on the *Savannahlander*.

In New South Wales **Countrylink**, T132232, www.countrylink.nsw.gov.au, offer rail and rail/coach services state-wide and to Brisbane. The main *Countrylink Travel Centre* in Sydney is at the Central Railway Station, Eddy Avenue, T9955 4237. A useful website for general travel throughout New South Wales is www.webwombat.com.au/transport/nsw.htm.

In Queensland **Queensland Rail**, T132232, www.qr.com.au, offer a range of rail services up and down the coast and into the outback. Roma Street Transit Centre in Brisbane, T3236 3035, hosts offices for most major coach and rail service providers and is a fine source of general travel information. **Outback Queensland** is also well served by all of the above but stopovers and less frequent travel schedules are obviously the norm.

In Victoria **V-Line**, T136196, www. vlinepassenger.com.au, are the main service provider.

Sleeping

East Coast Australia presents a diverse and attractive range of accommodation options, from cheap national park campsites to luxurious Great Barrier island retreats. The real beauty here, given the weather and the environment, is that travelling on a budget does not in any way detract from the enjoyment of the trip. On the contrary, this is a place where a night under canvas in national parks is an absolute delight.

Hotels, motels and resorts

At the top end of the scale, especially in the state capitals, the Gold Coast, Moreton Bay Islands, Fraser Island, Whitsunday Islands, Cairns and the Great Barrier Reef Islands there are some impressive international-standard hotels and resorts with luxurious surroundings and facilities, attentive service and often outstanding locations. Rooms will typically start in our **L** range. In the main cities are a few less expensive hotels in the **A-B** range. Most 'hotels' outside of the major towns are pubs with upstairs or external accommodation. If upstairs, a room is likely to have access to shared bathroom facilities, while external rooms are usually standard en suite motel units. The quality of pub-hotel accommodation varies considerably but is usually a budget option (**C-D**). Linen is almost always supplied.

Motels in Australia are usually depressingly anonymous but dependably clean and safe and offer the cheapest en suite rooms. Most have dining facilities and free, secure parking. Some fall into our **D** range, most will be a **B-C**. Linen is always supplied.

B&Bs and self-catering

Bed and Breakfast (B&B) is in some ways quite different from the British model. Not expensive, but rarely a budget option, most fall into our **B-C** ranges. They offer very comfortable accommodation in usually upmarket, sometimes historic houses. Rooms are usually en suite

Sleeping categories explained

Accommodation price-grades in this guide are based on the cost per night for two people sharing a double room in the high season, with breakfast where included. Many places offer discounts during low season or for long stays.

LL	$300 or over for a double or twin
L	$200-299 for a double or twin
A	$150-199 for a double or twin
B	$110-149 for a double or twin
C	$80-109 for a double or twin
D	$50-79 for a double or twin
E	$31-49 for a double or twin
F	$15 or under for a single or dorm

or have access to a private bathroom. Hosts are usually friendly and informative. Some B&Bs are actually a semi or fully self-contained cottage or cabin with breakfast provisions supplied. Larger ones may have full kitchens. As well as private houses, self-contained, self-catering options are provided by caravan parks and hostels and some resorts and motels with apartment-style units. Linen may not be supplied in self-catering accommodation. A couple of good websites are www.bedandbreakfastnsw.com (NSW) and www.bnb.au.com (QLD).

National parks, farms and stations

Some national parks and rural cattle and sheep stations have old settlers' or workers' homes that have been converted into tourist accommodation, usually self-contained. They are often magical places to stay and include many old lighthouse keepers' cottages and shearers' quarters. Stations may also invite guests to see, or even get involved in, the day's activities. Transport to them can be difficult if you don't have your own vehicle. Linen is often not supplied in this sort of accommodation. For a few examples in QLD, see page 328.

Hostels

For those travelling on a tight budget there is a large network of hostels offering cheap accommodation (**D-F**). These are also popular centres for backpackers and provide a great opportunity for meeting fellow travellers. All hostels have kitchen and common room facilities, almost all now have internet and some have considerably more. A few, particularly in cities, will offer freebies including breakfast and pick-ups. Many are now open 24-hours, even if the front desk is closed at night. Standards vary considerably and it's well worth asking the opinions of other travellers. Most are effectively independent, even most **YHAs** are simply affiliates, but the best tend to be those that are owner-managed. Of several hostel associations **YHA** (www.yha.org.au) and **NOMADS** (T0883-637633, www.nomadsworld.com, no membership fee) seem to keep the closest eye on their hostels, ensuring a consistency of quality. The **YMCA** (T03 9699 7655, www.ymca.org.au) and **YWCA** (T02 6230 5150, www.ywca.org.au), are usually a clean and quiet choice in the major cities. The list of hostels on www.bpf.com.au also offers dependably good choices. International visitors can obtain a **Hostelling International Card** (HIC) from any **YHA** hostel or travel centre. For this you get a handbook to *YHA* hostels nationwide and around $3 off

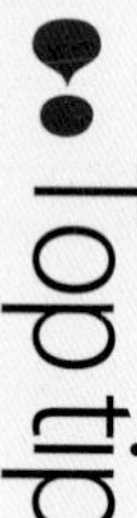

Sleeping

- Booking accommodation in advance is highly recommended, especially in peak seasons.
- Check if your accommodation has air-conditioning (a/c) when booking. Rooms without a/c are almost impossible to sleep in during hot weather.
- Note that single rooms are relatively scarce. Twin or double rooms let to a single occupant are rarely half the price, and you may even be charged the full cost for two people.

every night's *YHA* accommodation. Some transport and tourist establishments will also offer discounts to HIC holders.

Caravan and tourist parks

Almost every town will have at least one caravan park with unpowered and powered sites, varying from $10-20 for campers, caravans and campervans, an ablution block and usually a camp kitchen or BBQs. Some will have permanently sited caravans (on-site vans) and cabins. On-site vans are usually the cheapest option (**E-F**) for families or small groups wanting to self-cater. Cabins are usually more expensive (**C-D**). Some will have televisions, en suite bathrooms, separate bedrooms with linen and well-equipped kitchens. Power is rated at the domestic level (240/250v AC) which is very convenient for budget travellers. Some useful organizations are: **Big 4**, T03 9811 9300, www.big4.com.au; **Family Parks of Australia**, T02 6021 0977, www.familyparks.com.au; **Top Tourist Parks**, T08 8363 1901, www.toptourist.contact.com.au. Joining a park association will get you a discount in all parks that are association members.

Camping

Bush camping is the best way to experience the natural environment in Australia. Some national parks allow camping, mostly in designated areas only, with a few allowing limited bush camping. Facilities are usually minimal, with basic toilets, fireplaces and perhaps tank water; a few have BBQs and shower blocks. Payment is often by self-registration (around $3-10 per person) and BBQs often require $0.20, $0.50 or $1 coins, so have small notes and change ready. In many parks you will need a gas stove. If there are fireplaces you must bring your own wood as collecting wood within parks is prohibited. No fires may be lit, even stoves, during a Total Fire Ban. Even if water is supposedly available it is not guaranteed so take a supply, as well as your own toilet paper. Camping in the national parks is strictly regulated. For details of the various rules, contact the National Parks Wildlife Service (NPWS) and Queensland Parks and Wildlife Service (QPWS) or Parks Victoria. See box on page 48 for details and for park fees.

Campervans

A popular choice for many visitors is to hire or buy a vehicle that can be slept in, combining the costs of accommodation and transport (although you will still need to book into caravan parks for power and ablutions). Ranging from the popular VW Kombi to enormous vans with integral bathrooms, they can be hired from as little as $40 per day to a deluxe 4WD model for as much as $750. A van for two people at around $100 per day compares well with hiring a car and staying in hostels and allows greater freedom. High-clearance, 4WD campervans are also available and increase travel possibilities yet further. Kombis can usually be bought from

Hostels

Bellingen YHA Backpackers, Bellingen ►► *p223*
Arts Factory, Byron Bay ►► *p225*
Woolshed, Hervey Bay ►► *p282*
Platypus Bush Camp, Eungella ►► *p330*
Cape Trib Beach House, Cape Tribulation ►► *p368*

about $2,500. An even cheaper, though less comfortable alternative is to buy a van or station wagon (estate car) from anywhere between $1,000 and $5,000 that is big enough to lay out a sleeping mat and bag in.

Sales outlets Apollo, T1800 732001, www.australiancarhire.com/apollo; **Backpacker**, T1800 670232, www.backpackercampervans.com; **Britz**, T1800 331454, www.britz.com; **Getabout**, T1800 656 899, www.getaboutoz.com; **Maui**, T1300 363800, www.maui-rentals.com; **NQ**, T1800 079529, www.nqrentals.com. **Wicked**, T1800 246869, www.wickedcampers.com.au, are proving immensely popular with the backpacker set and you will see their vivid, arty vans all over the country. However, they may not suit everybody (you'll see what we mean).

Eating and drinking

The quintessential image of Australian cooking may be of throwing some meat on the barbie but Australia actually has a dynamic and vibrant cuisine all its own. Freed from the bland English 'meat and three veg' straitjacket in the 1980s by the skills and cuisines of Chinese, Thai, Vietnamese, Italian, Greek, Lebanese and other immigrants, Australia has developed a fusion cuisine that takes elements from their cultures and mixes them into something new and original.

Asian ingredients are easily found in major cities because of the country's high Asian population. Australia makes its own dairy products so cheese or cream may come from Tasmania's King Island, Western Australia's Margaret River or the Atherton Tablelands in Far North Queensland. There is plenty of seafood, including some unfamiliar creatures such as the delicious Moreton bugs (crabs), yabbies and crayfish. Mussels, oysters and abalone are all also harvested locally. Fish is a treat too: snapper, dhufish, coral trout and red emperor or the dense, flavoursome flesh of freshwater fish such as barramundi and Murray cod. Freshness is a major feature of Modern Australian cuisine, using local produce and cooking it simply to preserve the intrinsic flavour. Native animals are used, such as kangaroo, emu and crocodile and native plants that Aboriginal people have been eating for thousands of years such as quandong, wattle seed or lemon myrtle leaf. A word of warning, however. This gourmet experience is mostly restricted to cities and large towns. There are pockets of foodie heaven in the country but these are usually associated with wine regions and are the exception rather than the rule.

Eating out

Eating habits in Australia are essentially the same as in most Western countries and are of course affected by the climate. The BBQ on the beach or in the back garden is an Aussie classic but you will find that most eating out during daylight hours takes place outdoors. Weekend brunch is hugely popular, especially in the cities and often takes up the whole morning. Sydney and Melbourne are the undisputed gourmet capitals, where you will find the very best of Modern Australian as well as everything from Mexican to Mongolian, Jamaican to Japanese. Brisbane also boasts some fine eateries. Restaurants are common even in smallest towns but the smaller

Top tips

Eating categories

In this guide places to eat are divided into the following three categories. Prices are based on two-course meal (entrée plus main course) without drinks.

TTT expensive (over $35 a head)
TT mid-range ($25-35 a head)
T cheap ($15-25 a head)

the town the lower the quality, though not usually the price. Chinese and Thai restaurants are very common, with most other cuisines appearing only in the larger towns and cities. Corporate hotels and motels almost all have attached restaurants as do traditional pubs, which also serve counter meals. Some may have a more imaginative menu or better quality fare than the local restaurants. Most restaurants are licensed, others BYO only, in which case you provide wine or beer and the restaurant provides glasses. Despite the corkage fee this still makes for a better deal than paying the huge mark up on alcohol. Sadly, Australians have taken to fast food as enthusiastically as anywhere else in the world. Alongside these are food courts, found in the shopping malls of cities and larger towns. Also in the budget bracket are the delis and milk bars, also serving hot takeaways, together with sandwiches, cakes and snacks.

Drinks

Australian **wine** will need no introduction to most readers. Many of the best-known labels, including *Penfolds* and *Jacob's Creek*, are produced in South Australia but there are dozens of recognized wine regions right across the southern third of Australia, where the climate is favourable for grape-growing and the soil sufficient to produce a high-standard grape. The industry has a creditable history in such a young country, with several wineries boasting a tradition of a century or more but it is only in the last 25 years that Australia has become one of the major players on the international scene, due, in part to its variety and quality. There are no restrictions, as there are in parts of Europe, on what grape varieties are grown where, when they are harvested and how they are blended.

Visiting a winery is an essential part of any visit to the country and a day or two's tasting expedition is a scenic and cultural as well as an epicurean delight. Cellar doors range from modern marble, and glass temples to venerable, century-old former barns of stone and wood, often boasting some of the best restaurants in the country. In New South Wales the Hunter Valley provides one of the best vineyard experiences in the world with over 100 wineries, world-class B&Bs and a range of tours from cycling to horse-drawn carriage.

Australians themselves drink more and more wine and less beer. The average rate of consumption is now 20 litres per person per year, compared to 8 litres in 1970. Beer has dropped from an annual 135 litres per person in 1980 to 95 litres now. The price of wine, however, is unexpectedly high given the relatively low cost of food and beer. Even those from Britain will find Australian wines hardly any cheaper at the very cellar door than back home in the supermarket.

The vast majority of **beer** drunk by Australians is lager, despite many being called 'ale' or 'bitter'. The big brands such as *VB* (VIC), *Tooheys* (NSW) and *Castlemaine* XXXX (QLD) are fairly homogenous but refreshing on a hot day. If your palate is just a touch more refined, hunt out some of the imported beers on tap which are predominantly found in the pseudo Irish pubs found in almost all the main coastal towns. Beer tends to be around 4-5% alcohol, with the

The didgeridoo is made from a tree trunk that has been hollowed out by termites

popular and surprisingly pleasant tasting 'mid' varieties about 3½%, and 'light' beers about 2-2½%. Drink driving laws are strict and the best bet is to not drink alcohol at all if you are driving. As well as being available on draught in pubs, beer is also available from bottleshops (or 'bottle-o's') in cases (or 'slabs') of 24-36 cans ('tinnies' or 'tubes') or bottles ('stubbies') of 375 ml each. This is by far the cheapest way of buying beer (often under $2 per can or bottle).

Shopping

Most tourist merchandise seems to consist of soft toy kangaroos and koalas, or brightly coloured clothing featuring the same creatures. Another typical item which perpetuates the Australian stereotypes is the hat strung with corks. Don't even think about it.

Corkless hats, however, are a popular and practical souvenir, particularly the distinctive Akubras, made from felt in muddy colours. Along the same lines, stockman's clothing made by *RM Williams* is also popular and very good quality. Two of the company's best sellers are elastic-sided boots and moleskins. The *Driza-bone* long oilskin raincoat is also an Aussie classic. Australian surfwear is sought after worldwide and is a good buy while in the country. Look for labels such as *Ripcurl*, *Quiksilver*, *Mambo* and *Billabong*. Australia is also a good place to buy **jewellery**. Sydney in particular offers plenty of choice for precious gems such as opal, pearl and diamonds. The widest range will be available in the cities but, as in most countries, products are often cheapest at the source and a wonderful memento of a particular place.

Aboriginal designs are as ubiquitous as cuddly toys and printed on everything from t-shirts to tea towels. Some of these designs can be beautiful but be aware that many have no link to Aboriginal people and do not benefit them directly – check the label. *Desert Designs* is a successful label printing the stunning designs of the Great Sandy Desert artist Jimmy Pike on silk scarves and sarongs. It is possible to buy genuine Aboriginal arts and crafts but it is more commonly available in country areas close to Aboriginal communities or from Aboriginal-owned or -operated enterprises. Buying arts and crafts from reputable sources ensures that the money ends up in the artist's pocket and supports Aboriginal culture, skills and self-reliance.

Many people are keen to buy an Aboriginal **dot painting**, usually acrylic on canvas, and there are different styles, depending on the region the artist comes from. The best paintings sell for many thousands of dollars but simple works on canvas can be as little as $100. A good painting will cost at least $800-1500. Take your time and have a good look around. Visit public and private galleries where you can see work of the highest quality – you may not be able to afford it but you'll learn something of what makes a good piece of Aboriginal art. Sydney has a number of excellent commercial galleries selling Aboriginal arts and crafts, see page 143.

Accident & emergency

Dial 000 for the emergency services. The three main professional emergency services are supported by several others, including the **State Emergency Service (SES)**, **Country Fire Service (CFS)**, **Surf Life Saving Australia (SLSA)**, **Sea-search and Rescue**, and **St John Ambulance**. The SES is prominent in co-ordinating search and rescue operations. The CFS provides invaluable support in fighting and controlling bush fires. These services, though professionally trained, are mostly provided by volunteers.

Children

Australia is a wonderful place to take children. Far-fetched stories and rumours about poisonous snakes and insects, man-eating sharks and crocs can put parents off but they shouldn't. If children are aware and sufficiently supervised, Australia will provide a memorable holiday experience for all the right reasons.

As far as accommodation is concerned the vast majority of establishments welcome kids and offer reasonable financial concessions. Tourist based attractions and activities, many of which are directed at the children's market, usually offer reduced rates for children and family concessions. When it comes to eating out some places welcome children while others don't. In general you are advised to stick to eateries that are obviously child-friendly or ask before making a booking.

Customs & duty free

The limits for duty-free goods brought into the country include: 1,125 ml of any alcoholic drink (beer, wine or spirits) and 250 cigarettes, or 250 g of cigars or tobacco. There are various import restrictions, many to help protect Australia's fragile ecology. These primarily involve live plants and animals, plant and animal materials (including all items made from wood) and foodstuffs. If in doubt, bring processed food only, though even this may be confiscated. Even muddy walking boots may attract attention. Declare any such items for inspection on arrival if you are unsure.

There are strict prohibitions when exiting Australia. Plant and animal life, including derivative articles and seeds, cannot be taken from the country. Australia's cultural heritage is also protected and though a dot painting or didgeridoo are fine to take home, some art works and archaeological items are definitely not. See www.dcita.gov.au, or call T02 6271 1610 for details.

Almost all goods in Australia are subject to a Goods and Services Tax (GST) of 10%. Visitors from outside Australia will find certain shops can deduct the GST if you have a valid departure ticket. See www.customs.gov.au, for more details.

Disabled

Facilities for disabled travellers are spread quite thinly, especially outside the major cities, but high-profile sights and attractions and even parks generally have good access. **Qantas**, T1800 652660 (TTY), has considerable experience with disabled passengers and offers passengers with a nominated carer a 50% discount. The interstate railways generally have facilities for the disabled but public transport is not always well designed for disabled travel without assistance. The major car hire companies have adapted vehicles available. The website www.babs.com.au has a list of particularly well set up B&Bs. **WeCare Tours and Travel**, T02 9670 6668, wecaretours@fastmail.fm, are a New South Wales-based tour company specializing in tours for the disabled and elderly. Also see www.disabilityworld.org, and state sections.

For more information, the following organizations are helpful: **Access Foundation**, Suite 33, 61 Marlborough St, Surry Hills, NSW, T02 9310 5732, www.accessibility.com.au, provide information, resource contacts and links; **ACROD**, PO Box 60, Curtin, ACT 2600, T02 6283 3200, www.acrod.org.au, is the industry association for disability services; and **NICAN**, PO Box 407, Curtin, ACT 2605, T02 6285 3713, info@nican.com.au, provide information on recreation, tourism, sport and the arts. In Sydney the free leaflet 'CBD Access Map Sydney', available from the VICs or information booths, is a very useful map and guide for the disabled. For more detailed information contact **Disability Services Australia**, T02 9791 6599, www.dsa.org.au.

Electricity

The current in Australia is 240/250v AC. Plugs have 2- or 3-blade pins and adaptors are widely available.

Gay & lesbian travellers

The gay community in Australia is vibrant, vocal and visible. Sydney is the undoubted capital of gay and lesbian Australia, hosting in February the annual **Gay and Lesbian Mardi Gras** (see page 141), www.mardigras.org.au, the biggest event of its kind in the world and, incidentally, one of the biggest and most watched events in the country. Melbourne also has a very active gay and lesbian scene. Outside of the major cities, however, discrimination is not unknown and public displays of affection may not be enthusiastically received by the locals. The **International Gay & Lesbian Travel Association** (IGLTA), T02 9818 6669, www.iglta.com, has several members in Australia happy to help with travel and accommodation advice. There are several national magazines keeping lesbians and gays in touch with what's going on, including **Lesbians on the Loose**, www.lotl.com.au, **DNA** and **The Sydney Star Observer**, www.ssonet.com.au. One of the most comprehensive websites is **www.gayaustraliaguide.com**, T02 4787 7905. Dedicated to lesbian and gay friendly accommodation is **www.qbeds.com**. See also www.gayaustralia guide.com. For counseling and support services contact the **Gay and Lesbian Counselling Service**, T1800 184527.

Health

Ideally, you should see your GP or travel clinic at least six weeks before your departure for general advice on travel risks, malaria and vaccinations. No vaccinations are required or recommended for travel to Australia unless travelling from a yellow-fever-infected country in Africa or South America. Check with your local Australian Embassy for further advice. A tetanus booster is advisable, however, if you have one due. Make sure you have travel insurance, get a dental check (especially if you are going to be away for more than a month), know your own blood group and, if you suffer a long-term condition such as diabetes or epilepsy, make sure someone knows or that you have a Medic Alert bracelet/necklace with this information on it. There are three main threats to health in Australia: **dengue fever**, **poisonous snakes** and **spiders** and the powerful **sun**.

Top tips

Keeping safe in the bush

✔ The main dangers while bushwalking are dehydration, heat-stroke and getting lost. Before setting out seek advice about how to access the start and finish of the track, the terrain you are planning to traverse, how long it will take given your party's minimum fitness level, the likely weather conditions and prepare accordingly. Park rangers and the police are good sources of information.

✔ Take a decent map of the area, a compass and a first-aid kit. Take full precautions for the sun, but also be prepared for wet or cold weather. Take plenty of water, in hot weather at least one litre for every hour you plan to walk (a frozen plastic bottle will ensure cold water for hours). On long-distance walks take something to purify stream and standing water as giardia is present in some areas.

✔ Wear stout walking shoes and socks. Tell someone where you are going and when you plan to get back. Plan, if possible, to walk in the early morning or late afternoon when the sun is at its least powerful. These are also the best times for viewing wildlife.

✔ Learn about the various local poisonous snakes, their seasonal habits, tell-tale wound-marks and symptoms and the correct procedure for treatment.

✖ Avoid striding through long grass and try to keep to tracks. If the path is obscured, make plenty of noise as you walk.

✖ If you do see a snake, give it a wide berth. If you need to squat to go to the toilet, or are collecting firewood, bash the undergrowth around your position.

✔ If you do get bitten by either a spider or snake stay calm and still, apply pressure to the bite area and wind a compression bandage around it (except for redback bites). Remain as still as possible and keep the limb immobile. Seek urgent medical attention. A description of the creature and residual venom on the victim's skin will help with swift identification and therefore treatment. Anti-venom is available for most spider and snake bites.

For the latter, a decent wide-brimmed hat and factor 30 sun-cream (cheap in Australian supermarkets) are essential. Follow the Australians with their Slip, Slap, Slop campaign. Slip on a shirt, Slap on a hat and Slop on the sun screen.

Dengue can be contracted throughout Australia. In travellers this can cause a severe flu-like illness which includes symptoms of fever, lethargy, enlarged lymph glands and muscle pains. It starts suddenly, lasts for 2-3 days, seems to get better for 2-3 days and then kicks in again for another 2-3 days. It is usually all over in an unpleasant week. The mosquitoes that carry the dengue virus bite during the day, unlike the malaria mosquitoes, which sadly means that repellent application and covered limbs are a 24-hour issue. Check your accommodation for flower pots and shallow pools of water since these are where the dengue-carrying mosquitoes breed.

In the case of snakes and spiders, check loo seats, boots and the area around you if you're visiting the bush. A bite itself

Keeping safe in the water

- When swimming in the sea, keep between the patrolled flags and beware of the rip, a strong, off-shore undertow that can sweep even waders off their feet, submerge them and drown them astonishingly quickly. Always look out for signs indicating common rip areas, and ask locals if at all unsure. See the Surf Life Saving Australia website, www.slsa.asn.au, for more information.
- While snorkelling or diving, do not touch either creatures or coral. Even minor coral scratches can lead to infections and it doesn't do the coral any good either. Wear a wetsuit or t-shirt and shorts even if the water is warm. This will lessen the effect of any sting and help protect against the sun.
- If you are bitten or stung, get out of the water, carefully remove and keep any spine or tissue, seek advice as to appropriate immediate treatment and apply it and quickly seek medical help.
- The biggest danger in the water is from Estuarine crocodiles ('salties') in northern Queensland. Always check whether a waterhole or river is likely to be a crocodilian home, and if in doubt assume it is.
- Beware the box jellyfish, whose highly poisonous tentacles trail several metres behind it. They pose a significant threat between October and May.
- If you are stung, your blood pressure triples, CPR is administered and an ambulance is duly called to the scene.

An antivenin is widely available at hospitals.

Take these simple precautions:

- Do not swim in the sea (outside the 'stinger nets' provided at most major beaches) during the 'stinger season' (October to May).
- Do not swim alone during the stinger season.
- Be aware of the effectiveness of vinegar for immediate treatment and call the emergency services as soon as possible.
- Seek local knowledge as to the best locations to swim.

does not mean that anything has been injected into you. However, a commonsense approach is to clean the area of the bite (never have it sutured early on) and get someone to take you to a medical facility fast.The most common poisonous spider is the tiny, shy redback, which has a shiny black body with distinct red markings. It regularly hides under rocks or in garden sheds and garages. Outside toilets are also a favourite. Far more dangerous, though restricted to the Sydney area only, is the Sydney funnel-web, a larger and more aggressive customer, often found in outdoor loos. There are dozens of venomous snake species in Australia. Few are actively aggressive and even those only during certain key times of year, such as mating season, but all are easily provoked and for many an untreated bite can be fatal (see box above).

Australia has some reciprocal arrangements with a few countries allowing citizens of those countries to receive free emergency treatment under the *Medicare* scheme. Citizens of New Zealand and the Republic of Ireland are entitled to free care as a public patient in public hospitals and subsidized medicines under the Pharmaceutical Benefits Scheme. Visitors from Finland, Italy, Malta, the Netherlands, Sweden and the UK also enjoy subsidized out-of-hospital treatment (ie visiting a doctor). If you qualify, contact your own national health scheme to check what documents you will require in Australia to claim *Medicare*. All visitors are, however, strongly advised to take out medical insurance for the duration of their visit.

Insurance

It is essential to take out some form of travel insurance, wherever you're travelling from. This should cover you for theft or loss of possessions and money, the cost of medical and dental treatment, cancellation of flights, delays in travel arrangements, accidents, missed departures, lost baggage, lost passport and personal liability and legal expenses. Also check on inclusion of 'dangerous activities' such as climbing, diving, skiing, horse riding, even trekking, if you plan on doing any. Always read the small print carefully. Not all policies cover ambulance, helicopter rescue or emergency flights home. Find out if your policy pays medical expenses direct to the hospital or doctor, or if you have to pay and then claim the money back later. If the latter applies, make sure you keep all records. If you have something stolen, get a copy of the police report – you will need this to substantiate your claim. There are a variety of policies to choose from, so it's best to shop around. Your travel agent can advise on the best deals available.

Internet

Internet access, and thus email, is widely available in hostels, hotels and cafés. Expect to pay about $3-6 for 30 mins. State governments are keen for their citizens to have access to the internet and some have set up schemes to allow cheap or even free access. Based either in libraries or dedicated centres, they are usually also accessible to visitors. One of the best ways to source information from abroad is on the web. The Australian Tourism Commission website (www.australia.com) is a good place to start, but almost all the regions have excellent, informative websites and these are listed in the relevant areas in the text. The national and regional tourist boards and local information centres (VICs) are generally good at replying to specific enquiries, especially by email, and of course are usually willing to send heaps of useful information by snail mail.

Media

The Australian, www.theaustralian.news.com.au, is the only national paper and has the biggest readership of them all (453,000). It is generally popular, politically 'middle of the road' and publishes a good glossy magazine with the weekend edition. *Sydney Morning Herald*, considered by many to be the unofficial national tabloid 'voice'. *Courier Mail* is the main newspaper in Brisbane and southern Queensland. *'The Age'* is the main newspaper in Melbourne and Victoria.

Foreign newspapers and magazines are widely available in the main urban centres. It is also possible to buy special weekly editions of British papers such as *The Guardian*. There are Asian editions of *Time* and *The Economist*.

There are five main television channels in New South Wales and Queensland; the publicly funded *ABC* and *SBS*, and the independent, commercial stations,

Channel 7, *Channel 9*, and *Channel 10*. *ABC* aims for Australian high quality content including many BBC programmes. *SBS* focuses on multi-national culture, current affairs, sport and film. It has the best world news, shown daily at 1830.

Money

The Australian dollar ($) is divided into 100 cents (c). Coins come in denominations of 5c, 10c, 20c, 50c, $1 and $2. Banknotes come in denominations of $5, $10, $20, $50 and $100. **Exchange rates** as of September 2005 were as follows: US$1 = A$ 1.33; £1 = A$2.38; €1 = A$1.61. **All dollars quoted in this guide are Australian unless specified otherwise.**

Banks, ATMs, credit and cash cards

The four major banks, the Challenge/ Westpac, Commonwealth, National and ANZ are usually the best places to change money and traveller's cheques, though bureaux de change tend to have slightly longer opening hours and often open at weekends. You can withdraw cash from ATMs (cashpoints) with a cash card or credit card issued by most international banks and they can also be used at banks, post offices and bureaux de change. Most hotels, shops, tourist operators and restaurants in Australia accept the major credit cards, though some places may charge for using them. When booking always check if an operator accepts them. EFTPOS (the equivalent of Switch in the UK) is a way of paying for goods and services with a cash card. Unfortunately EFTPOS only works with cards linked directly to an Australian bank account. Bank opening hours are Mon-Fri, from around 0930 to 1630.

Traveller's cheques

The safest way to carry money is in traveller's cheques, though they are fast becoming superseded by the prevalence of credit cards and ATMs. *American Express*, *Thomas Cook* and *Visa* are the cheques most commonly accepted. Remember to keep a record of the cheque numbers and the cheques you've cashed separate from the cheques themselves. Traveller's cheques are accepted for exchange in banks, large hotels, post offices and large gift shops. Some insist that at least a portion of the amount be in exchange for goods or services. Commission when cashing traveller's cheques is usually 1% or a flat rate. Avoid changing money or cheques in hotels as rates are often poor.

Money transfers

If you need money urgently, the quickest way to have it sent is to have it wired to the nearest bank via Western Union, T1800 337377, www.travelex.com.au. Charges apply but on a sliding scale. Money can also be wired by Amex or Thomas Cook, but may take a day or two, or transferred direct from bank to bank, but again can take several days. Within Australia money orders can be used to send money. See www.auspost.com.au.

Cost of travelling

By European, North American and Japanese standards Australia is an inexpensive place to visit. Accommodation, particularly outside the main centres, is good value, though prices can rise uncomfortably in peak seasons. Eating out can be indecently cheap. There are some restaurants in Sydney, comparable with the world's best, where $175 is enough to cover dinner for two. The bill at many excellent establishments can be half that. Transport varies considerably in price and can be a major factor in your travelling budget. Australian beer is about $4-6 and imported about $5-7 in most pubs and bars, as is a neat spirit or glass of wine. Wine will generally be around 1½ times to double the price in restaurants than it would be from a bottleshop. The minimum budget required, if staying in hostels or campsites, cooking for yourself, not drinking much and travelling relatively slowly, is about $70 per person per day, but this isn't going to be a lot of fun. Going on the odd tour, travelling faster and eating out occasionally will raise this to a more realistic $85-110. Those staying in modest B&Bs, hotels and motels as couples, eating out most nights and taking a few tours will need to reckon on about $200 per person per day. Costs in the major cities will be 20-50% higher. Non-hostelling single travellers should budget on spending around 60-70% of what a couple would spend.

Opening hours

Generally 0830-1700 Mon-Fri. Many convenience stores and supermarkets are open daily. Late night shopping is generally either Thu or Fri. For banks, see previous page.

Post

Most post offices are open Mon-Fri 0900-1700, and Sat 0900-1230. Airmail for postcards and greetings cards is $1 anywhere in the world, small letters (under 50 g) are $1.10 to southeast Asia and the Pacific, $1.65 beyond. Parcels can be sent either by sea, economy air or air. Most of the principal or main offices in regional centres or cities offer *Post Restante* for those peripatetic souls with no fixed address, open Mon-Fri 0900-1700. For more information contact *Australia Post* on T131318, www.auspost.com.au.

Public holidays

New Years Day; **Australia Day** (26 Jan 2005); **Good Friday** (25 Mar 2005); **Easter Monday** (28 Mar 2005); **Anzac Day** (25 Apr 2005); **Queen's Birthday** (13 Jun 2005); **Labour Day** (3 Oct 2005 in NSW, 2 May 2005 in QLD); **Christmas Day** (25 Dec); **Boxing (Proclamation) Day** (26 Dec).

Safety

Australia certainly has its dangers, but with a little common sense and basic precautions they are relatively easy to minimize. The most basic but important are the effects of the **sun**, see Health above. In **urban areas**, as in almost any city in the world, there is always the possibility of muggings, alcohol-induced harassment or worse. The usual simple precautions apply, like keeping a careful eye and hand on belongings, not venturing out alone at night and avoiding dark, lonely areas. For information on road safety see page 25, or contact one of the AAA associations, see page 26.

Smoking

Not permitted in restaurants, cafés or pubs where eating is a primary activity, and on any public transport.

Student travellers

There are various official youth/student ID cards available, including the widely recognized **International Student ID Card** (ISIC), www.isic.org/www.isiccard.com. **Federation of International Youth Travel Organisations (FIYTO)** card, **Euro 26 Card** and **Go-25 Card**. Each also conveys benefits from simply getting discounts to emergency medical coverage and 24-hr hotlines. The cards are issued by student travel agencies and hostelling organizations. Backpackers will find a YHA or VIP membership card just as useful. Students are also eligible for discounts on many forms of transport and most tourist sites and tours.

Taxes

Most goods are subject to a **Goods and Services Tax** (GST) of 10%. Some shops can deduct the GST if you have a valid departure ticket. GST on goods over $300 purchased (per store) within 30 days before you leave are refundable on presentation of receipts and purchases at the GST refund booth at Sydney International Airport (boarding pass and passport are also required). For more information T1300 363 263.

Telephone

Most public payphones are operated by nationally-owned *Telstra*, www.telstra.com.au. Some take phonecards, available from newsagents and post offices, and credit cards. A payphone call within Australia requires $0.40 or $0.50. If you are calling locally (within approximately 50 km) this lasts indefinitely but only a few seconds outwith the local area. Well worth considering if you are in Australia for any length of time is a pre-paid mobile phone. Telstra and *Vodafone* give the best coverage and their phones are widely available from as little as $50, including some call time. There are also some smaller companies like *'3'* and *Optus* offering attractive deals. By far the cheapest way of calling overseas is to use an international pre-paid phonecard (though they cannot be used from a mobile phone, or some of the blue and orange public phones). Available from city post offices and newsagents, every call made with them initially costs about $1 (a local call plus connection) but subsequent per minute costs are a fraction of *Telstra* or mobile phone charges.

There are no area phone codes. Instead, you need to use a state code if calling outside the state you are in. These are: 02 for ACT/NSW (08 for Broken Hill); 03 for VIC; 07 for QLD. To call Eastern Australia from overseas, dial the international prefix followed by 61, then the state phone code minus the first 0, then the 8-digit number. To call overseas from Australia dial 0011 followed by the country code. Country codes include: Republic of Ireland 353; New Zealand 64; South Africa 27; the USA and Canada 1; the UK 44. Directory enquiries: 1223. International Directory enquiries: 1225.

Time

Australia covers three time zones: Queensland and New South Wales are in Eastern Standard GMT+10 hrs. NSW operate daylight saving, which means that clocks go forward one hour from Oct and Mar.

Tipping

Tipping is not the norm in Australia, but a discretionary 5-10% tip for particularly good service will be appreciated.

Tourist information

Tourist offices, or **Visitor Information Centres** (VICs), can be found in all but the smallest Australian towns. Generally speaking you are advised to stick with accredited VICs for the best, non-biased advice. Their locations, phone numbers, website or email addresses and opening hours are listed in the relevant sections of this guide. In larger towns they have met certain criteria to be officially accredited. This usually means that they have some paid staff and should be open daily 0900-1700. Smaller offices may close at weekends. All offices will provide information on accommodation, local sights and tours. Many will also have information on eating out, local history and the environment and sell souvenirs, guides and maps. Most will provide a free town map. Some in high density tourist destinations like Airlie Beach and Cairns in Queensland also double as privately run booking agencies, but may simply promote those that pay a booking commission to the office.

Tour operators

There are a host of companies offering general or special interest tours. Most are district, state or multi-centre based.
See individual town and city sections for details. There are several companies

offering 1- to 10-day trips along parts of the coast and many others venturing inland from the main centres. Most involve coach travel or some degree of 4WD manoeuvring and adventure activities.

In UK and Ireland

Australia Travel Centre, 43-45 Middle Abbey St, Dublin, Ireland, T01-8047188, australia@abbeytravel.ie. Good source of general advice for those travelling from Ireland.
Contiki Wells House, 15 Elmfield Rd, Bromley, Kent BR1 1LS, T1300 188635, www.contiki.com. One of the world's largest travel companies catering primarily for the 18-35's market with numerous affordable Australian options.
Travelbag, T0870 8146614, www.travelbag.co.uk. Reputable UK based firm offering a good range of general and tailor-made trips to Eastern Australia at reasonable prices.
Wildlife Worldwide Chameleon House, 162 Selsdon Rd, T020 8667 9158, www.wildlifeworldwide.com. One of the best wildlife oriented global operators offering tailor-made, mainly small group trips to Australia including Queensland's Lamington National Park and the Great Barrier Reef.

In North America

Abercrombie and Kent, 1520 Kensington Rd, Suite 212, Oak Brook, Illinois, 60523-2156, T800-5547016, www.abercrombiekent.com. Well-established US company offering a diverse range of luxury, locally guided global trips to Australia.
Earthwatch Research and Exploration, PO Box 75, Maynard, MA 01754 USA, T978 461 0081, www.earthwatch.org. Excellent ecotourism trips to Eastern Australia in combination with conservation research on Australian wildlife. Offices in USA, UK and Australia.
Wilderness Travel, 1102 Ninth St, Berkeley, CA, 94710, T1800-368-2794, www.wilderness travel.com. 10 or 12-day cultural, wildlife and hiking trips to Australia from $5,000.

Visas and immigration

Visas are subject to change, so check with your local Australian Embassy or High Commission. All travellers to Australia, except New Zealand citizens, must have a valid visa to enter Australia. These must be arranged prior to travel (allow two months) and cannot be organized at Australian airports. Tourist visas are free and are available from your local Australian Embassy or High Commission, or in some countries, in electronic format (an Electronic Travel Authority or ETA) from their websites and from selected travel agents and airlines. Passport holders eligible to apply for an ETA include those from Austria, Belgium, Canada, Denmark, France, Germany, Irish Republic, Italy, Japan, Netherlands, Norway, Spain, Sweden, Switzerland, the UK and the USA. Tourist visas allow visits of up to three months within the year after the visa is issued. Six-month, multiple entry tourist visas are also available to visitors from certain countries. Application forms can be downloaded from the embassy website or from www.immi.gov.au. Tourist visas do not allow the holder to work in Australia. See also www.immi.gov.au/visitors.

Weights and measures

The metric system is universally used.

A sprint through history

1606	Spaniard Luis de Torres negotiates his way through the strait between Australia and New Guinea, becoming the first European to glimpse the Australian mainland.
1642	Dutchman Abel Tasman charts the northwest coast of what is now called New Holland. He also finds Tasmania before heading west to 'discover' New Zealand.
1770	Captain James Cook charts the hitherto unexplored east coast of New Holland. He names the 'new territory' New South Wales.
1786	Following the loss of the American colonies, the British Government decides to transport felons instead to New South Wales. The following year Arthur Phillip's 'first fleet' sets out.
1787-1788	Botany Bay is not to Phillip's liking so he explores the harbour just to the north, Port Jackson. Sydney Cove is duly named as the site for the new penal colony.
1801-1803	Matthew Flinders charts the unknown southern coasts and circumnavigates the whole continent in 1801-03, proving it at last to be one vast island. He also suggests the name 'Australia' for this new continent.
1830-	Numbers of new settlers steadily increases as New South Wales slowly comes to be seen as a land of opportunity. Wool becomes the single most important industry and the Australian sheep population explodes. This is the catalyst for the Murray steamboats, the railways and new, non-penal towns.
1850	Aboriginal population decimated by various infectious diseases against which the native Australians have little defence. Meanwhile, wool and grain industries are booming and coal and copper are being profitably mined.
1850-1860	Gold is first publicly found in New South Wales and soon after in Victoria, leading to a mass influx of would-be prospectors.
1860	Transportation of convicts ended. Nearly 160,000 had made the enforced trip over the previous 60-odd years, with few returning to their homelands.
1860-1890	Australia's own industrial revolution is in full flow and urbanization of the country continues apace. The indigenous population meanwhile are driven to the margins of society.
1889	NSW Prime Minister suggests political federation. Two years later a draft constitution is drawn up.

1893	Falling prices leads to an economic crash of unprecedented proportions. Victoria suffers worst and state government revives the idea of federation.
1897	Queensland Aborigines Act introduced. Aboriginal people in the state can be forced to move to a reserve, denied alcohol and the vote, and are paid for work under conditions and wages stipulated by the act.
1898-1900	Colonies vote for federation.
1901	The Commonwealth officially comes into existence on 1 January. Melbourne is the first capital, remaining so until 1927 when Canberra is built.
1902	Women given the vote.
1914-1918	First World War breaks out. Australian (and NZ) troops feature in many campaigns, most famously at Gallipoli, in 1915. Of the 300,000 who went to war over 50,000 were killed, a greater number than was lost by the USA.
1927	Canberra's Parliament House opened.
1932	Sydney Harbour Bridge completed.
1933-1939	Aboriginal Act passed in QLD permits marriage and sexual relations between Aboriginal people and Europeans, with the aim of ultimately 'breeding out' the Aboriginal race.
1939-1945	Second World War. Australia sends troops to Europe. In 1942 Japanese bombers and warships shell Darwin, Sydney and Newcastle. In the same year, Australian troops help prevent occupation of Port Moresby in New Guinea. Out of a population of around seven million in 1939, a little under one million are enlisted or conscripted, of which nearly 40,000 are killed. Over 2,000 Aborigines fight in the defence of their country.
1945-	Government pursues a vigorous population programme. Tens of thousands of European economic migrants pour into the country. Many form ghettos in suburbs of Sydney and Melbourne.
1949	Robert Menzies leads his new Liberal party to election victory. A staunch monarchist, he welcomes Queen Elizabeth II to Australia in 1954, the first reigning monarch to make the trip. Immigration policies continue apace. Between 1945 and 1973 about three and a half million people arrive.
1956	Melbourne hosts the Olympic Games.
1960s	Australia sends 8000 troops to fight with the USA in Vietnam, marking a growing shift from British influence. Protest movement against the war broadened to include Aboriginal people. In the early 1960s new legislation largely removes the paternalistic and restrictive laws relating to Aboriginal people. In 1967 Australians vote in a referendum to allow the federal government to legislate for Aboriginal people.

1972	Labor Party elected under charismatic and energetic Gough Whitlam. Within days the troops are recalled from Vietnam and conscription ended, women legally granted an equal wage structure, 'White Australia' formally abandoned, a Ministry of Aboriginal Affairs created and 'God Save the Queen' scrapped as the National Anthem.
1970s/80s	Whitlam sacked in controversial circumstances but he has permanently altered the mood of the nation. The fledgling Green movement begins to make its mark, and 1978 sees Sydney's first Gay and Lesbian march in 1978, which will become the Mardi Gras, the biggest event of its kind in the world. The country opens its doors to thousands of Vietnamese 'boat people'.
1988	Australia celebrates the Bicentennial – 200 years of white settlement. Aboriginal people do not join the celebrations.
1992	High Court rules that native title (or prior indigenous ownership of land) not extinguished by the Crown's claim of possession in the Murray Islands of Torres Strait. This is enshrined in the Native Title Act of 1993.
1996-1998	The High Court rules that pastoral leases and native title can co-exist but government of John Howard is opposed. A compromise, the Native Title Amendment Bill, is passed in 1998. In 1997, the Human Rights and Equal Opportunity Commission produces a damning report into the separation of Aboriginal and Torres Strait Islander children from their families and recommends compensation, counselling and an official apology.
1999	'No' vote in national referendum for an Australian Republic, despite polls showing a majority in favour.
2000	The Council for Aboriginal Reconciliation presents a Declaration of Reconciliation to the government. In the same year there are large reconciliation marches all over the country. The Olympics are held in Sydney. The Aboriginal athlete Kathy Freeman wins gold in the women's 400 m track sprint.
2001-2002	Bush fires ravage the surrounding national parks and the fringes of Sydney, destroying numerous properties, taking several lives. In 2002, exacerbated by severe drought conditions, Victoria suffers its worst fires for years.
2001	The Liberal-National coalition government of John Howard is returned to power. In the same year, a Norwegian vessel, the *Tampa*, rescues boat people claiming to be refugees from Afghanistan but the Australian government refuses to allow the 'illegal immigrants' to land on the mainland. This not only diminishes Australia's international standing but also polarises society.
2002	Two nightclubs bombed in Bali, killing around 200 people, almost half of whom are Australian. Prime Minister Howard continues to support US invasion of Iraq, despite majority public opposition domestically.
2005	A second terrorist bomb in Bali kills 19.

Aboriginal Australia

When the First Fleet arrived with its cargo of convicts in 1788 there were between 300,000 and 750,000 Aboriginal people living in Australia, belonging to about 500 tribes or groups, each of which had its own territory, its own language or dialect and its own culture. Naturally, neighbouring groups were more similar to each other; perhaps speaking dialects of the same language and sharing some 'Dreamtime' myths linked to territory borders such as rivers and mountains. However, if a man from Cape York had found himself transported to the Western Desert he would have been unable to communicate with the desert people. He would have found them eating unfamiliar food and using different methods to obtain it. Their art would have been incomprehensible to him and their ceremonies meaningless. If he had been able to speak their language he would have found that they had a different explanation of how they came into existence and his own creation ancestors would have been unknown to them. Each group was almost like a small state or nation.

Dreaming

Every traveller in Australia will encounter the concept of the 'Dreaming' or the 'Dreamtime', a complex idea at the heart of Aboriginal culture. Most Aboriginal groups believe that in the beginning the world was featureless. Ancestral beings emerged from the earth and as they moved about the landscape they began to shape it. They could be in any form – humans, animals, rocks, trees or stars – and could transform from one shape to another. Nor were they limited by their form (kangaroos could talk, fish could swim out of water). Wherever these beings went and whatever they did left its mark on the landscape. A mountain might be the fallen body of an ancestor speared to death, a waterhole the place a spirit emerged from the earth, or yellow ochre the fat of an ancestral kangaroo. In this way the entire continent is mapped with the tracks of the ancestor beings.

Although the time of creation and shaping of the landscape is associated with the temporal notion of 'beginning', it is important to understand that Dreaming is not part of the past. It lies within the present and will determine the future. The ancestral beings have a permanent presence in spiritual or physical form. Ancestor snakes and serpents still live in the waterholes that they created; this is why visitors are sometimes asked not to swim in certain pools, so that these ancestors will not be disturbed. This is also why mining or similar development can cause great distress to Aboriginal people if the area targeted is the home of an ancestral being. The ancestors are also still involved in creation. Sexual intercourse is seen as being part of conception but new life can only be created if a conception spirit enters a woman's body. The place where this happens, near a waterhole, spring or sacred site, will determine the child's identification with a particular totem or ancestor. In this way Aboriginal people are directly connected to their ancestral world.

Ceremonies

Aboriginal people belonged to a territory because they were descended from the ancestors who formed and shaped that territory. The ancestral beings were sources of life and powerful performers of great deeds but were also capable of being capricious, amoral and dangerous. Yet in their actions they laid down the rules for life. They created ceremony, song and designs to commemorate their deeds or journeys, established marriage and kinship rules and explained how to look after the land. In the simple forms related to outsiders, Dreaming stories often sound like moral fables. They were passed on from generation to generation, increasing in complexity or sacredness as an individual aged. With knowledge came the responsibility to look after sacred creation or resting places. Ceremonies were conducted to ensure the continuation of life forces and fertility. Aboriginal people had no concept of land

Aboriginal protest sign in the shadow of Old Parliament House, Canberra

ownership, because they believe that humans, animals and spirits are inseparable from the land; one and the same. Consequently, Aboriginal people of one group had no interest in possessing the land of another group. A different and strange country was meaningless to them. To leave your country was to leave your world.

Ceremony and art were at the very heart of life for these were the ways in which Aboriginal people maintained their connection with the ancestors. During ceremonies the actions and movements of the ancestors would be recalled in songs and dances that the ancestors themselves had performed and handed down to each clan or group. Not only did the ancestral beings leave a physical record of their travels in the form of the landscape but also in paintings, sacred objects and sculptures. Ceremonies maintained the power and life force of the ancestors thus replenishing the natural environment. Some ceremonies, such as those performed at initiation, brought the individual closer to his or her ancestors. Ceremonies performed at death made sure that a person's spirit would rejoin the spiritual world.

Art

The most immediately obvious feature of Aboriginal art is its symbolic nature. Geometric designs such as circles, lines, dots, squares or abstract designs are used in all art forms and often combine to form what seems to be little more than an attractive pattern. Even when figures are used they are also symbolic representations; an emu may be prey or an ancestral being. The symbols do not have a fixed meaning; a circle may represent a waterhole, a camping place or an event. In Aboriginal art symbols are put together to form a map of the landscape. This is not a literal map where the 'key' relates to the topography of a piece of countryside, but rather a mythological map. Features of the landscape are depicted but only in their relation to the creation myth that is the subject of the painting. A wavy line terminating in a circle might represent the journey of the Rainbow Serpent to a waterhole. That landscape may also contain a hill behind the waterhole but if it is not relevant to the serpent's journey it will not be represented, although it may feature in other paintings related to different ancestral beings. Unlike a conventional map, scale is not consistent. The size of a feature is more likely to reflect its importance rather than its actual size or there may be several scales within a painting. Nor is orientation fixed.

Background

Park life

Australia's national parks generally constitute natural areas of ecological, cultural or simply aesthetic importance (often a combination of all three) and can claim to encompass almost all of Australia's most jaw-dropping and sublime natural attractions. In New South Wales alone there are over 580 national parks and reserves, ranging from a few hectares to the size of small countries and the degree of public access allowed is as variable. Many have excellent basic camping facilities and the experience is highly recommended.

National parks are generally managed by the state in which they are situated. In New South Wales they are managed by the **National Parks and Wildlife Service (NPWS)**, www.nationalparks.nsw.gov.au/, in Queensland, national parks are run by the **Queensland Parks and Wildlife Service (QPWS)**, www.env.qld.gov.au, and in Victoria by **Parks Victoria**, www.parkweb.vic.gov.au. Fees vary from state to state and from park to park. Some parks in NSW, for example, charge $7 a day vehicle entry fee, while other, more high profile parks such as Kosciuszko cost $14, and in Victoria a day pass for Wilson's Promontory costs $9.50 and Mornington Peninsula only $4. Where entry fees are charged it is usually possible to obtain an annual state-wide pass. This costs $85 in NSW and $66 in VIC. If you intend to visit many parks and are in the country for a while, this is often a sensible way to go, but bear in mind camping fees are generally extra. Passes can be purchased at park visitors centres and some major VICs. There is no national pass. Full details for each state are given on the websites listed above.

To many people Aboriginal art is recognized by its style – dots, X-ray or cross hatching – but what is painted is just as important as how it is painted. Aboriginal people working in traditional forms simply do not paint landscapes, figures or people that they are not spiritually connected to. The idea of painting a landscape simply because it is pretty is utterly foreign to Aboriginal art. Also because of the use of symbols and the fact that Dreaming stories are only known to the ancestral descendants, only the painter and perhaps his or her close relatives will be able to fully understand the meaning of a painting. Those interested should read the excellent *Aboriginal Art* by Howard Morphy.

Wildlife

Wildlife is very much a part of the Australian holiday experience. Living icons like the koala and kangaroo are just as ingrained in our psyche as the famous Opera House or Uluru (Ayers Rock). The list of species reads like a who's who of the marvellous, bizarre and highly unlikely. There are over 750 bird species alone. The following is a very brief description of the species you are most likely to encounter on your travels.

Resident roos at the Capricorn Caves near Rockhampton

Marsupials

Marsupials (derived from the Latin word marsupium meaning 'pouch') can be described as mammals that have substituted the uterus for the teat. Their reproductive system is complex, the females have not one, but three vaginas and there is a short gestation and a long lactation. It is a specialist system, developed to meet harsh environmental demands.

The most famous of the marsupials are of course the kangaroos and wallabies. There are over 50 species of kangaroos, wallabies and tree kangaroos in Australia. The most commonly seen are the eastern grey and the red. The eastern grey can be seen almost anywhere in NSW, Queensland and Victoria, especially in the wildlife and national parks along the coast. Sadly in the outback most of the red kangaroos you see will be road kill. Tree kangaroos, meanwhile, live deep in the bush and are notoriously shy and are therefore very seldom seen.

Equally famous is the koala (which is not a bear). Koalas are well adapted to the harsh Australian environment, surviving quite happily on one of the most toxic of leaves – eucalyptus. Koalas are easily encountered in the many wildlife parks throughout the country and while cuddling one of these impossibly cute bundles of fur is the most seminal Australian experience, do bear in mind that the wild variety may take exception to being manhandled and attempt to rip your arms to shreds. Sadly, koalas are on the decline in most regions of Australia and over 80% of their natural habitat has been destroyed since white settlement began.

There are three species of wombat: the common, northern and southern hairy-nosed variety. Like the koala, they are very well adapted to the Australian environment and spend much of their time asleep. They are also nocturnal. Campsites are the best places to see them where burrows and small piles of dung will provide testimony to their presence. Sadly, like kangaroos and koalas, they are far more commonly seen as road kill. Another very familiar family member of the marsupials is the possum. There are numerous species with the most commonly encountered being the doe-eyed brushtail possum and the smaller ring-tailed possum. Both are common in urban areas and regularly show up after dusk in campsites. Another magnificent little possum that may be seen is the squirrel-sized feather tailed glider, which as the name suggests can glide from tree to tree. All the possum species are nocturnal hence the huge eyes. The best way to see them is by joining a night spotting tour, especially in Queensland, where in only a few acres of bush there may be as many as 18 different species. Other marsupials include the rare and meat-eating tiger quoll, which is about the size

(Left) A wild koala perched high in a eucalyptus tree, outback NSW; (Right) Tawny frogmouth, a species common throughout Australia

of a cat with a brownish coat dotted with attractive white spots, the delightful quokka (like a miniature wallaby), bandicoots, the numbat (endangered) and the bilby.

Monotremes

There are only three living species of monotremes in the world: the duck-billed platypus and the short-beaked echidna, both of which are endemic to Australia, and the long-beaked echidna, which is found only on the islands of New Guinea. Aside from meaning 'one hole', their most remarkable feature is that they are mammals that lay eggs.

The duck-billed platypus is only found in rivers and freshwater lakes in eastern Australia. They live in burrows, are excellent swimmers and can stay submerged for up to 10 minutes. The duck-like bill is not hard like the beak of a bird, but soft and covered in sensitive nerve endings that help to locate food. The males have sharp spurs on both hind leg ankles that can deliver venom strong enough to cause excruciating pain in humans and even kill a dog. Platypuses are best seen just before dawn. The echidna is not related to the hedgehog but looks decidedly like one. You will almost certainly encounter the echidna all over Australia, even in urban areas, where they belligerently go about their business and are a delight to watch. They are immensely powerful creatures not dissimilar to small spiny tanks. They are mainly nocturnal and hunt for insects by emanating electrical signals from the long snout, before catching them with a long sticky tongue.

Eutherians

Eutherians are placental mammals. Perhaps the best-known is the dingo. Although not strictly endemic to Australia, having being introduced, most probably by Aboriginals over 3-4,000 years ago and derived from an Asian wild dog, they are now seen to be as Australian as Fosters lager. Found everywhere on the continent, but absent in Tasmania, they are highly adaptable, opportunist carnivores, which makes them very unpopular with farmers. The best place to see dingoes is on Frazer Island, off Queensland, where sadly they have come into conflict with humans due to scavenging. The mighty fruit bat is another placental mammal and a remarkable creature you will almost certainly see (or smell) on your travels. You can even see them flying around at dusk on the fringes of Sydney's CBD (especially the Botanical Gardens).

The dwarf minke whale is nearly 8 m long

Birds

With one of the most impressive bird lists in the world, Australia is a bird watchers' paradise and even the most indifferent cannot fail to be impressed by their diversity, their colour and their calls. The most famous of Australian birds is the Kookaburra which is related to the kingfisher. Other than their prevalence, their fearlessness and their extrovert behaviour, it is their laughing call that marks them out. A much stranger looking specimen is the tawny frogmouth, a kind of cross between an owl and a frog, with camouflaged plumage, fiery orange eyes and a mouth the size of the Channel Tunnel. Due to its nocturnal lifestyle it is hard to observe in the wild and is best seen in zoos and wildlife parks.

Australia is famous for its psittacines – the parrot family – including parakeets, lorikeets, cockatiels, rosellas and budgerigars, which can be seen at their most impressive in the outback, in huge flocks against the vast blue sky. The rainbow lorikeet is a common sight (and sound) in urban areas, while in rural areas and forests the graceful red, white and yellow tailed black cockatoos are also a pleasure to behold. Others include the pink galah, the breathtaking king parrot and the evocatively named gang-gang.

Almost as colourful are the bowerbirds. There are several species in Australia with the most notable being the beautiful but endangered, regent bowerbird, with its startling gold and black plumage, and the satin bowerbird. Another member of the bowerbird family is the catbird, which once heard, proves to be very aptly named.

In the bush one of the commonest of birds is the brush-turkey, about the size of a chicken, with a bare head and powerful legs and feet. Another well-known bird of the bush is the lyrebird, of which there are two species in Australia. Unremarkable in appearance (rather like a bantam) though truly remarkable in their behaviour, they are expert mimics often fooling other birds into thinking there are others present protecting territory. Their name derives from the shape of their tail (males only) which when spread out looks like the ancient Greek musical instrument.

A far larger, rarer bird of the tropical rainforest is the cassowary, a large flightless relative of the emu with a mantle of black hair-like plumage, colourful wattles and a strange, blunt horn on its head. It is a highly specialist feeder of forest fruits and seeds. Tragically, road kills

Places to spot wildlife

Sydney Harbour (whales, fairy penguins, flying foxes) » p110
Hervey Bay (whales) » p274
Mon Repos near Bundaberg (turtles) » p294
Eungella National Park (platypus) » p314
Hinchinbrook Island National Park (dugong) » p325

are common. Their last remaining stronghold in Australia is in Far North Queensland, especially around Mission Beach, where they are keenly protected. They are well worth seeing but your best chance of doing so remains in wildlife sanctuaries and zoos.

Almost as large, yet flighted, and more often seen around lakes and wetlands, are the brolga and the black-necked stork, or jaribu. The brolga is a distinctly leggy, grey character with a dewlap (flap of skin under the chin) and a lovely splash of red confined to its head. The brolga is equally leggy but has a lovely iridescent purple-green neck set off with a daffodil-yellow eye and rapier-like beak. One of the most impressive birds is the white-breasted sea eagle, which is a glorious sight almost anywhere along the coast, or around inland lakes and waterways. They are consummate predators and highly adept at catching fish with their incredibly powerful talons.

The fairy penguin, found all along the southern coastline of Australia, is the smallest penguin in the world. The largest colony is on Phillip Islands near Melbourne, where over 20,000 are known to breed in a vast warren of burrows. The emu, with its long powerful legs, is prevalent yet quite shy, unlike that other giant of the outback, the huge wedge-tailed eagle (or 'wedgie'). Wedgies are most commonly sighted feeding on road kills, especially kangaroos.

Reptiles, amphibians and insects

The range of reptile, amphibian and insect species is, not surprisingly, as diverse as any other in Australia. First up is the crocodile. There are two species in Australia, the saltwater crocodile (or 'saltie' as they are known) found throughout the Indo-Australian region, and the smaller freshwater crocodile, which is endemic. There is no doubt the mighty 'saltie' is, along with the great white shark, the most feared creature on earth and perhaps deservingly so. Although you will undoubtedly encounter crocodiles in zoos, wildlife parks and farms throughout the country, you may also be lucky (or unlucky) enough to spot one in the wild in the northern regions. Note that in Queensland the many warning signs next to rivers and estuaries are there for a good reason.

The goanna, or monitor, is a common sight, especially in campsites, where their belligerence is legendary. There are actually many species of goanna in Australia. They can reach up to 2 m in length, are carnivores and if threatened, run towards anything upright to escape. Of course, this is usually a tree, but not always, so be warned!

There are many species of frogs and toads in Australia including the commonly seen green tree frog. They are a beautiful lime-green colour. If you find one do not handle them since the grease on our hands can damage their sensitive skin. Another character worth mentioning is the banjo frog. If you are ever in the bush and are convinced you can hear someone plucking the strings of a banjo, it is probably a banjo frog singing to its mate.

Insects are well beyond the scope of this handbook, but there are two, that once encountered, will almost certainly never be forgotten. The first is the huntsman spider, a very common species seen almost anywhere in Australia, especially indoors. Although not the largest spider on the continent, they can grow to a size that would comfortably cover the palm of your hand. Blessed with the propensity to shock, they are an impressive sight, do bite, but only when provoked and are not venomous. Of the huge variety of glorious butterflies and moths in Australia perhaps the most beautiful is the Ulysses blue, found in the tropics, especially in Far North Queensland.

Marine mammals and turtles

Along both the eastern and western seaboards of Australia humpback whales are commonly sighted on their passage to and from the tropics to Antarctica between the months of July and October. Occasionally they are even seen wallowing in Sydney Harbour or breaching in the waters off the famous Bondi Beach. The southern right whale is another species regularly seen in Australian waters; likewise the orca, or killer whale. Several species of dolphin are present including the bottlenose dolphin, which are a common sight off almost any beach surfing the waves with as much skill and delight as any human on a surfboard.

Another less well-known sea mammal clinging precariously to a few locales around the coast is the dugong or sea cow. Cardwell and the waters surrounding Hinchinbrook Island, in Queensland, remains one of the best places to see them. Australia is also a very important breeding ground for turtles. The Mon Repos turtle rookery, near Bundaberg, Queensland, is one of the largest and most important loggerhead turtle rookeries in the world. A visit during the nesting season from October to May, when the females haul themselves up at night to lay their eggs, or the hatchlings emerge to make a mad dash for the waves, is a truly unforgettable experience.

The region today

In the run up to the October 2004 election campaigning bore a striking similarity to that of the U.S. just prior to it and the UK early the following year. The opposition tactic was to focus primarily on the issues of trust and the folly of the 2003 invasion of Iraq and the ruling party the experience of its leader and the strength of the economy. Predictably perhaps the efforts of maverick Labour MP Mark Latham, although stoic was not enough and like the US and the UK the majority of the electorate voted through their own pockets and firmly on domestic issues. As a result Howard won the day convincingly and his victory made him the second longest serving Prime Minister in Australia. It is clear he and the Liberals saw the clear victory as vindication of his policies and despite the tide of world and domestic opinion turning against the United States and its allies on the issue of Iraq he remains loyal and steadfast in his actions and his opinions with Australian troops remaining. Many however are now predicting that this denial and such overt loyalty to the Bush Administration has made Australia a primary terrorist target as the Bali bombings clearly demonstrated. To meet that threat the Howard government has, like the US, introduced controversial domestic terrorism laws and, like the UK government, is struggling in its relationship with the domestic Muslim community. Now it seems that whatever the Howard government does it does with a level of impunity that like Bush and Blair has earned 'Johnny Howard' the status of an 'either love him, or hate him' figure both in Australia and abroad. Some see him as a great politician while others merely as a gutless puppet of the Bush Administration. Yet others would argue that the opinion depends entirely how much money you have in the bank. Also, with the resignation of Mark Latham and the reinstatement of former opposition Labour leader Kim Beazley – who has consistently been ineffectual against John Howard for almost a decade – the trend of the Liberal domination with 'Johnny' firmly at the helm looks set to continue.

Melbourne
YOU ARE HERE

Melbourne & SE Victoria

The Flinders Street Station entrance is perhaps the most famous meeting place in Melbourne

Don't miss...
1 The remarkable architecture of **Federation Square, Melbourne** ▶▶ p60.
2 Where twelve Apostles became eleven along the **Great Ocean Road** ▶▶ p68.
3 A parade of penguins on **Phillip Island** ▶▶ p72.
4 The bush and beaches at **Wilson's Promontory** ▶▶ p93.
5 Wildlife watching in the **Croajingolong National Park** ▶▶ p95.
CANBERRA
AUSTRALIAN CAPITAL TERRITORY
NEW SOUTH WALES
VICTORIA
Southern Ocean
p58
30 km
N
Curyo
Kerang
Quambatook
Cohuna
Mathoura
Finlay
Henty
Rand
Culcairn
Walbundrie
Holbrook
Carabost
Batlow
Tumbarumba
Queanbeyan
Bungendore
Captains Flat
Hume Highway
Monaro Highway
Echuca
Cobram
Corowa
Howlong
Albury
Murray River
Murray Valley Highway
Yarrawonga
Numurkah
Rutherglen
Wodonga
Jingellic
Cabramurra
Snowy Mountains Highway
Bredbo
Moruya
Wyuna
Rochester
Stanhope
Midland Highway
Shepparton
Wangaratta
Glenrowan
Chiltern
Kiewa
Beechworth
Tallangatta
Khancoban
Kosciuszko National Park
Cooma
Wadbilliga National Park
Central Tilba
Elmore
Bendigo
Rushworth
Murchison
Benalla
Dederang
Mytleford
Omeo Highway
Perisher
Thredbo
Jindabyne
Berridale
Nimmitabel
Violet Town
Euroa
Hume Freeway
Heathcote
Castlemaine
Seymour
Northern Highway
Bright
Mt Beauty
Falls Creek
Glen Valley
Anglers Rest
Omeo
Bemboka
Bega
Tathra
Bournda National Park
Sapphire Coast
Mansfield
Harrietville
Mt Buller
Hotham
Mackillop Ridge
Bombala
Merimbula
Kyneton
Trentham
Lancefield
Woodend
Wallen
Yea
Alexandra
To Grampians National Park
Gelantipy
Snowy River National Park
Delegate
Bonang
Twofold Bay
Eden
Marysville
Bacchus Marsh
Melton
Melbourne
Werribee
Yarra Valley
Healesville
Dandenong Ranges
Warburton
Dargo
Great Alpine Road
Buchan
Snowy River
Ben Boyd National Park
Cann River
Genoa
Gipsy Point
Cape Howe
Mallacoota
Gabo Island
Port Phillip Bay
Geelong
Queenscliff
Cranbourne
Pakenham
Bairnsdale
Orbost
Princes Highway
Bemm River
Croajingolong National Park
Point Hicks
Cape Conran
Marlo
Lakes Entrance
Metung
Paynesville
Stratford
Heyfield
Maffra
Sale
Terang
Camperdown
Inverleigh
Colac
Warrnambool
Bay of Islands Coastal Park
Angahook-Lorne State Park
Forrest
Torquay
Anglesea
Lorne
Great Ocean Road
Port Campbell
Port Campbell National Park
Lavers Hill
Princetown
Apollo Bay
Otway National Park
Cape Otway
Hastings
French Is
Phillip Is
Drouin
Warragul
Moe
Traralgon
Morwell
Mirbo North
Balook
Leongatha
Gippsland Lakes Coastal Park
Ninety Mile Beach
Wonthaggi
Inverloch
Foster
Welshpool
Yarram
Woodside Beach
Port Albert
Fish Creek
Port Welshpool
Sandy Point
Wilson's Promontory

Introduction

Victoria is Australia's smallest and most populous mainland state. By Australian standards, you could almost say it is crowded. Despite its size, however, it is incredibly diverse: mountains, deserts, rainforest, beaches and plains make up the landscape. The state also has a rich historical heritage, multicultural people and a large sophisticated city.

The state revolves around Melbourne, a city which combines the gracious character of its Victorian past with style, innovation and energy. Within just an hour or two of Australia's second largest city, you can swim with dolphins or try local wines in the Yarra Valley. To the west are the popular coastal towns of the Great Ocean Road. Inland is one of the state's best national parks, the magnificent Grampians, where craggy sandstone rock faces tower above swathes of forest. Towards the coast the foothills run down to the moist green fields of Gippsland and come to an end in the perfect sandy coves of Wilson's Promontory and the series of tranquil lakes, lagoons and inlets further east.

Ratings

Landscape
★★★★

Relaxation
★★★

Activities
★★★

Wildlife
★

Costs
$$$

Melbourne and around

Melbourne has always been 'marvellous, right from its earliest days when it was the largest, wealthiest and most refined city in the country. This former wealth, reflected in the ornate 19th-century architecture and spacious public gardens, has also bred an innate confidence and serious sophistication that gets right up the noses of Sydneysiders. By the same token, Melbournians see their New South Wales cousins as insufferably brash and hedonsitic. The Victorian capital is the most European of Australia's cities. Its theatres, bookshops and galleries all vibrate with the chatter of cosmopolitan urbanites, and its famously damp, grey weather lends the city an air of introspection lacking in other state capitals.

Getting there International and interstate flights; interstate and regional buses.

Getting around Tram and train networks.

Time required 2-3 days in the city, 4-6 days exploring Mornington Peninsula, Dandenongs, Wilsons Promontory and Great Ocean Road.

Weather Changeable.

Sleeping Huge range across the board.

Eating Eclectic and cosmopolitan cuisine.

Activities and tours Wine tasting in the Yarra Valley, penguin-viewing tours on Phillip Island and sightseeing tours along the Great Ocean Road.

★ **Don't miss** Federation Square » *p60*.

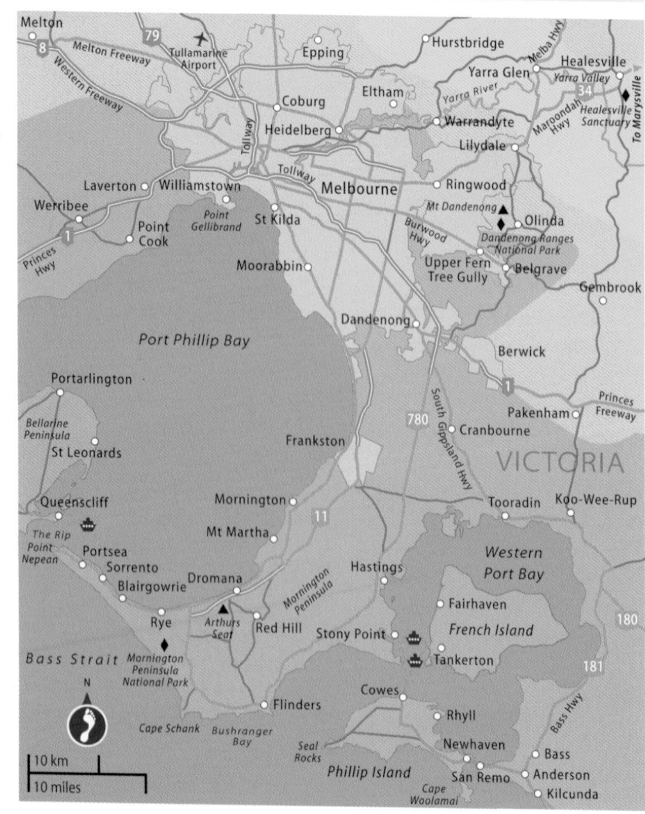

Ins and outs

Getting there

Melbourne's Tullamarine airport is 20 km northwest of the city and services both domestic and international flights, www.melair.com.au. Terminal facilities include car hire, bank ATMs, currency exchange and a Travellers Information Desk, T9297 1805, open almost 24 hours, which provides accommodation and tour bookings as well as general information. From the airport, the **Skybus**, T9335 2811, runs every 15 minutes 0600-2130 and half hourly or hourly 2130-0600 between the International terminal and the Spencer Street Coach Station ($13) in the city centre, also stopping near the YHAs in Abbotsford Street, North Melbourne and Courtney Street, Carlton. Tickets can be purchased on board or from the information desk. A taxi between the airport and the city will cost around $40.

Bus Transit Centre, Franklin Street, is the terminal and ticket office for interstate operators **Greyhound**, T131499. The Spencer St Coach Station is the terminus for all **V~Line** services, T136196, and the **Firefly Express Coaches** service, T9670 7500, from Adelaide and Sydney.

Flinders St Station is the main terminus for metropolitan **Connex** and **M-Train** services, but is also the station for V~Line Gippsland services. Spencer St Station is the main terminus for all other state V~Line services. All interstate trains, *The Overland*, *Ghan* and *XPT* also operate from Spencer Street. » *p89*.

Getting around

All metropolitan services are operated by the Met and if intending to use public transport it's a good idea to head for the **Met Shop** ⓘ *103 Elizabeth St, 0830-1655 Mon-Fri, 0900-1300 Sat*. The shop has useful maps of tram, bus and train routes and timetables. For all train, bus and tram information, T131638 or www.victrip.com.au. A single Metcard fare system covers trains, trams and buses. Three zones cover greater Melbourne, but you will rarely need anything other than a Zone 1 ticket as this covers everything within about 10 km of the city centre. The city operates a system of saver cards, see box page 153. Most services operate every day, from early morning to around midnight. » *p89*.

Tourist information

Melbourne Visitors Centre ⓘ *Federation Sq, corner of Flinders St and St Kilda Rd, T9658 9658, www.visitmelbourne.com.au, 0900-1800*, offers information, brochures and bookings for Melbourne and the rest of the state. Also event ticketing, multi-lingual information and an ATM. The VIC runs one of the world's few **Greeter Services**, T9658 9658, greeter@melbourne.vic.gov.au, where local volunteers take visitors on a free sightseeing walk of the city centre. Greeters and visitors are matched by interests and language (over 30 languages spoken). Three days notice is required. There are also information booths in the Bourke St Mall and Flinders St Station. Melbourne has a useful telephone interpreting service, offering assistance in communication in over 100 languages, T131450 (24 hours).

City centre » *pp75-91*.

Melbourne has some of the best museums, galleries, gardens and architecture in the country and recent developments will ensure that the city continues to possess the most impressive spread of cultural and sporting facilities in Australia. The recent development of Federation Square has spruced things up. Encompassing an entire city block next to Flinders Street Station, it is a major arts and tourism venue in the heart of Melbourne. The central plaza contains space for 10,000 people, and the square buzzes with restaurants, galleries and shops. In addition, the new Melbourne Museum and the redevelopment of the National Gallery of Victoria highlight the importance of arts to this city.

Federation Square and the NGV

Whether by design or location, or indeed both, Federation Square has become the main focus for visitors to Melbourne and no matter what your movements around the city centre it always seems to draw you back. Initiated as an international architectural design competition in 1996, and finally opened in October 2002 at the mind-boggling cost of $450 mn, it is one of the most ambitious construction projects ever undertaken in Australia. Covering an entire block, the ultra

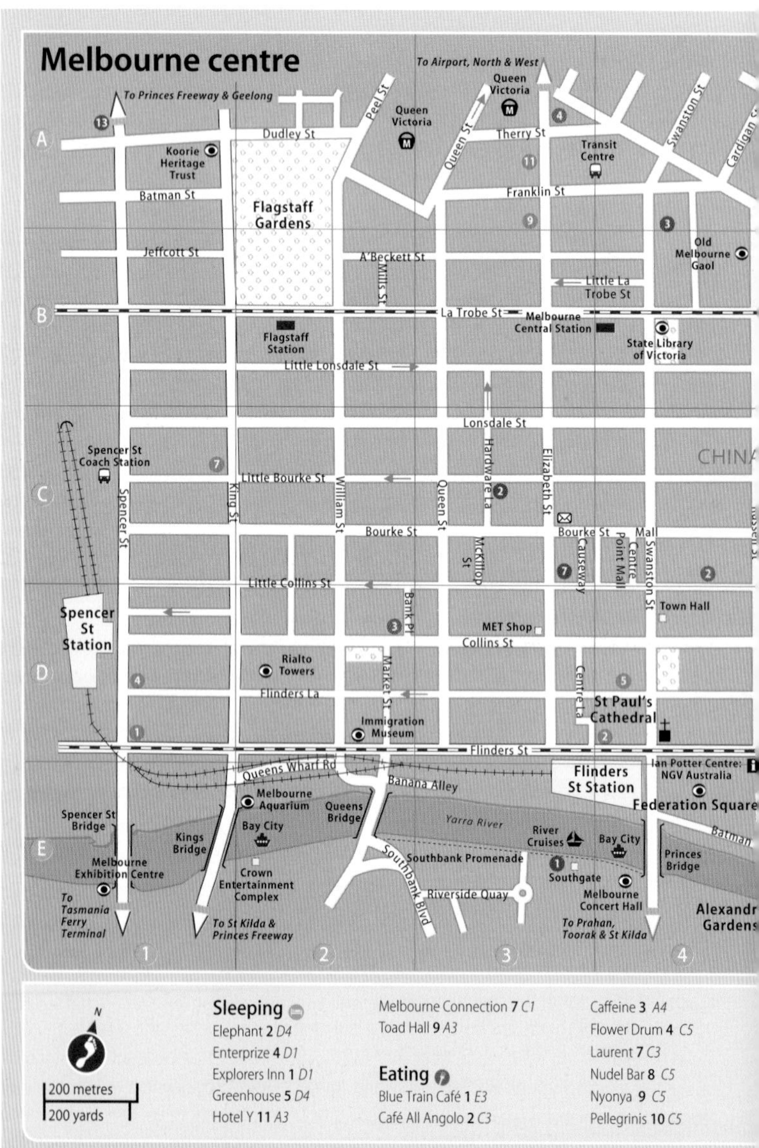

modern city square is an intriguing combination of angular plates, steel girders and plate glass, all cleverly housing restaurants, cafes, performance spaces, the main VIC and the supremely well-endowed **Ian Potter Centre: NGV Australia** ⓘ *T8620 2222, www.ngv.vic.gov.au, daily 1000-1700, free except for special exhibitions*, which is one of two sites of the National Gallery of Victoria. This site houses the largest collection of Australian art in the world. Across the river, at 180 St Kilda Road, is the revamped **NGV International** (same details as NGV Australia), where the international collections are displayed. Especially impressive is the 19th-century European section, purchased during Melbourne's boom period.

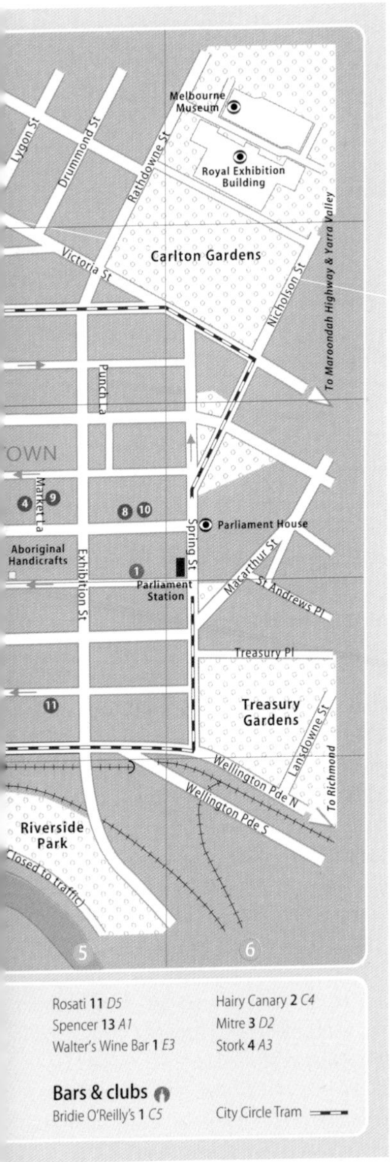

Rosati **11** *D5*
Spencer **13** *A1*
Walter's Wine Bar **1** *E3*
Hairy Canary **2** *C4*
Mitre **3** *D2*
Stork **4** *A3*

Bars & clubs
Bridie O'Reilly's **1** *C5*

City Circle Tram

Immigration Museum

ⓘ *Corner of William St and Flinders St, T9927 2700, www.immigration.museum.vic.gov.au, 1000-1700. $6, children and concessions free.*

A few blocks west of Fed Square is the late 19th century former Customs House which seems an appropriate spot for an immigration museum due to the relationship between this part of the riverbank and the city's earliest immigrants. Melbourne's culture has been heavily influenced by immigration but this museum focuses on the how the experience affected the migrants. Personal stories are told using photographs, recordings and letters and there is even a mock ship to illustrate voyage conditions. Regular travelling exhibitions also explore the history and culture of migrants. Should you start suffering from information overload then you can always migrate to the on-site. café.

Rialto Towers

ⓘ *525 Collins St, T9629 8222, Sun-Thu 1000-2200, Fri-Sat 1000-2300. $13.50, children $7.80, concessions $9.50-8.*

At 253 m, Rialto Towers is Australia's tallest building and the public have access to an observation deck, 236 m up on the 55th floor, with as good a view as you would expect. There's also a small café up there. There are also great views from the **Sofitel Hotel** which takes up floors 35 to 50. The rooms are suitably impressive, but there is also an excellent, if expensive, café and restaurant up on the 50th. If the budget doesn't allow for a sky-high meal then catch the lift up anyway for a brief glimpse, and make sure you pop to the toilet when you do.

Interior of Melbourne Central Shopping Mall

Melbourne Aquarium

ⓘ *Yarra riverbank, T1300-882392, bookings T9510 9081, www.melbourneaquarium.com.au, 0930-1800, $23, children $13, concessions $15.*

The Aquarium features the creatures of the Southern Ocean and offers the chance to get as close to those creatures as most people would wish to. By entering a glass tunnel, visitors step into the Oceanarium, a large circular room with thick perspex walls. Sharks, stingrays, turtles and fish swim around and above you, so close that you can count the rows of teeth in the mouth of a 3 m long shark. Several times a day divers get into the tank and feed the fish and visitors can do the same (the sharks are kept well fed so they don't eat their tank mates). It is pricey, however: certified divers pay $184 and non-divers (who must complete a two-day resort dive course) $264. The Aquarium also has a simulated rollercoaster ride, café and shop.

Melbourne Museum and the Royal Exhibition Building

ⓘ *Carlton Gardens, T131102, www.melbourne.museum.vic.gov.au, 1000-1700, $6, children/concessions free.*

Due north of Fed Square is the vast and striking Melbourne Museum. Opened in 2000, it uses the most advanced display techniques to make the museum experience lively and interesting. The **Bunjilaka Aboriginal Centre** looks at the history of Aboriginal people since white invasion and the politics of displaying their possessions and artefacts. **Koorie Voices**, a photo gallery of Victorian Aboriginal people, is particularly fascinating for its contemporary recording of individual life stories. The **Mind and Body Gallery** examines humans in exhaustive detail, perhaps more than is palatable for the squeamish. Other highlights include the **Australia Gallery**, with its focus on the social history of Melbourne and Victoria and the **Children's Museum**, where the little darlings can check out their weight and height in 'wombats'. The museum also has an excellent shop and lots of eating choices.

Facing the Melbourne Museum, and in striking architectural contrast, is the Royal Exhibition Building, a Victorian confection built for the International Exhibition of 1880. At the time it was Australia's largest building and grand enough to be used for the opening of the first Federal Parliament. The Victorian parliament sat here for 26 years until it was able to move back into the Victorian Parliament House (see below). The building is still run as an exhibition centre, and the museum occasionally runs tours.

The striking architecture of Federation Square

Old Melbourne Gaol

ⓘ *Russell St, T9663 7228, www.nattrust.com.au, 0930-1700, $12.50, children $7.50, concessions $9.50; night tours Wed and Sun, sometimes Fri and Sat $20, children $13, 1½ hrs (bookings essential).*

Near Carlton Gardens is Melbourne Gaol, built in the 1850s when Victoria was in the grip of a gold rush. Like Tasmania's Port Arthur, the design was based on the Model Prison at Pentonville, a system of correction that was based on isolation and silence. The three levels of cells now contain stories and death masks of female prisoners, hangmen, and of some of the 135 people hanged here. Visitors can also see the scaffold on which bushranger Ned Kelly was hanged in 1880, as well as his death mask and a set of Kelly Gang armour. The gaol comes alive on night tours when a tour guide acts as a prisoner from 1901 to explain the history of the gaol.

State Library of Victoria

ⓘ *328 Swanston St, corner of La Trobe St, T8664 7000, www.slv.vic.gov.au, Mon-Thu 1000-2100, Fri-Sun 1000-1800.*

Designed by Joseph Reed, who also designed the Town Hall and Exhibition Building, the doors behind the grand classical portico opened in 1856 with 3,800 books personally chosen by the philanthropist Sir Redmond Barry. In 1913 a domed reading room was added, modelled on London's British Museum Library and the Library of Congress in Washington. The library exhibits some of the treasures in its collection, such Audubon's 'Birds of America' (the library's most valuable book) and Ned Kelly's armour. The grassy forecourt is a popular meeting place and also serves as a sculpture garden.

Koorie Heritage Trust

ⓘ *295 King St, T8622 2600, www.koorieheritagetrust.com, Tue-Sun 1000-1600, entry by donation.*

On the northwestern fringes of the CBD is the Koorie Heritage Trust. Koorie is the collective name given to the Aboriginal people of southeastern Australia. The trust preserves and celebrates the 60,000 year-old history and culture of the Koorie people of Victoria from their own viewpoint. The centre has some hard-hitting history displays on the shocking results of the arrival of Europeans in 1835. There are also exhibitions of contemporary art and crafts by

Melbourne inner suburbs

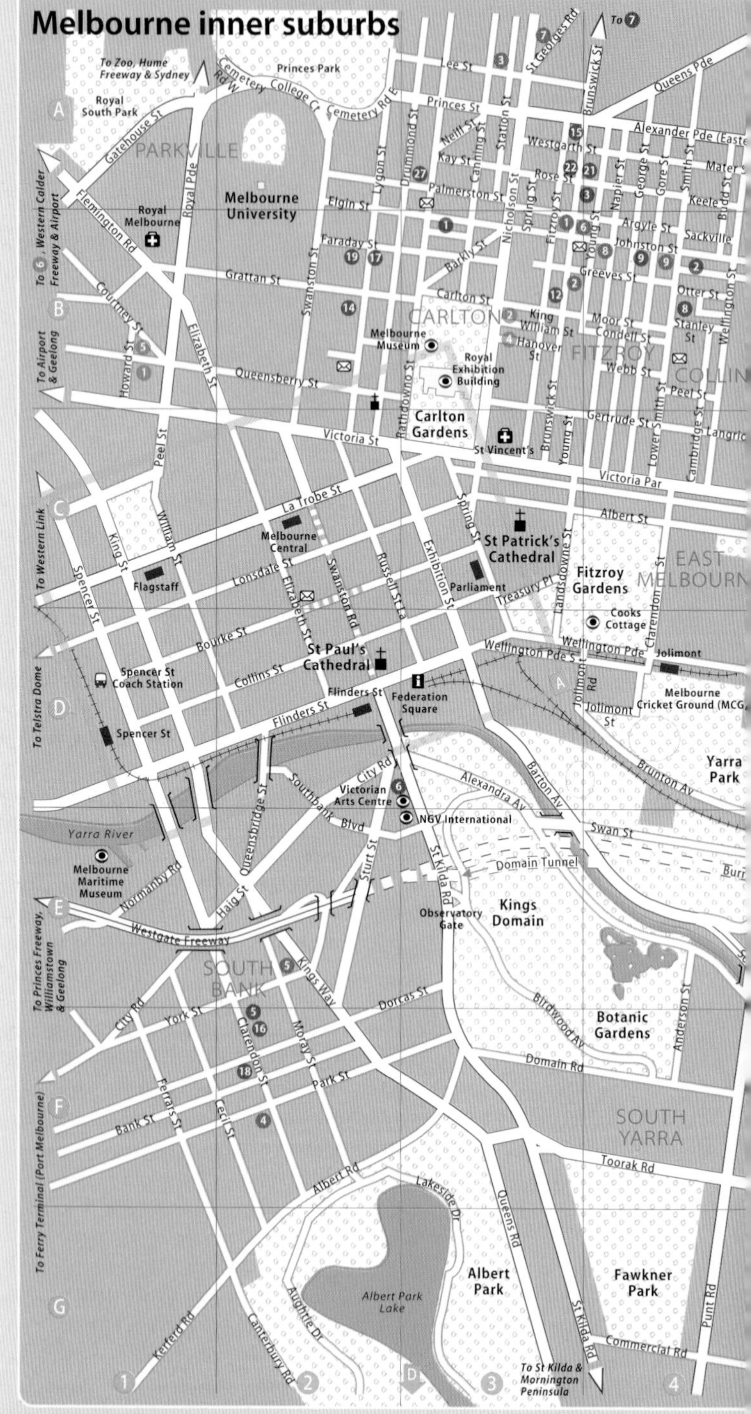

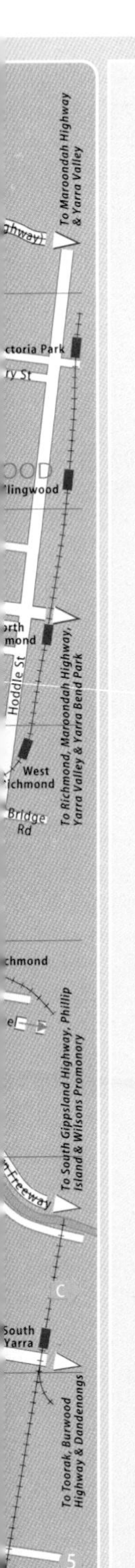

N

500 metres
500 yards

Sleeping

Chapman Gardens YHA **6** *B1*
City Scene **1** *B1*
King **2** *B3*
Melbourne Metro YHA **5** *B1*
Nunnery Accommodations **4** *B3*

Eating

Abla's **1** *B3*
Aussie Indian Trendy Cuisine **2** *B4*
Babka **3** *A4*
Clare Castle **27** *A3*
Clarendon Fish & Chippers **5** *F2*
EQ **6** *D2*
Gluttony It's a Sin **8** *B4*
Guru da Dhaba **9** *B4*
Kazen **12** *B3*
Moroccan Soup Bar **7** *A4*
Notturno **14** *B2*
Retro **15** *A3*
Sakura Teppanyaki **16** *F2*
Shakahari **17** *B2*
Spring **18** *F2*
Thresherman's Bakehouse **19** *B2*
Vegie Bar **21** *A4*
Viet Rose **22** *A3*

Bars & clubs

Bar Open **1** *B3*
Black Cat **2** *B3*
Brandon **3** *A3*
Limerick Arms **4** *F2*
Maori Chief **5** *E2*
Night Cat **6** *B4*
North Fitzroy Star **7** *A3*
Purple Turtle **8** *B4*
Tote **9** *B4*

local Koorie people, an extensive reference library and a small shop selling some original and reproduction art.

Parliament House

ⓘ *Spring St, T9651 8568, www.parliament.vic.gov.au, tours Mon-Fri when Parliament is not sitting, 40 mins, free. Call for sitting details.*
Due south of Carlton Gardens stands the extravagant colonnaded Parliament House, at the head of a group of government buildings and the manicured parkland of the Treasury and Fitzroy Gardens (see below). It was built at the height of the gold rush in 1856 and this is reflected in its grandeur and interiors lavished with gold. Victoria's Parliament House was also the first home of the Australian Parliament after Federation in 1901. When parliament is sitting visitors can watch from the Public Gallery.

Fitzroy and Treasury Gardens

Some Melbournians consider these gardens the best in the city for their small scale, symmetry and avenues of European Elm trees. Nearby is **Cook's Cottage** ⓘ *T9414 4677, 0900-1700, $3.70, children $1.80, concessions $2.35*, a tiny stone house that used to belong to Captain James Cook's family and was transported from England in 1934 to commemorate the centenary of the state of Victoria. After sunset many possums come out of the trees in Treasury Gardens and are often fed by visitors.

Melbourne Cricket Ground

ⓘ *Jolimont St, T9657 8864, www.mcg.org.au, 0930-1630, $8, children and concessions $5, tours run from 1000-1500 on days without events.*
For some sports fans the MCG, as the ground is universally known, approaches the status of a temple. Built in 1853 the ground became the home of the Melbourne Cricket Club and has hosted countless historic cricket matches and Aussie Rules (Australian football) games as well as the 1956 Olympics, rock concerts and lectures. Tours of the MCG are one of Melbourne's most popular attractions and include walking into a players changing

room, stepping on to the 'hallowed turf' and visiting the members' swanky Long Room. The tour also includes entry to the Australian Gallery of Sport, the Olympic Museum, the Australian Cricket Hall of Fame, and exhibitions on Aussie Rules and extreme sports. The interesting highlights include Don Bradman's cricket bat, Ian Thorpe's swimming costume, Cathy Freeman's running outfit, lots of Olympic medals and memorabilia, and the original handwritten rules, drafted in 1859, of the Aussie Rules game.

Southbank

Melbourne's Southbank is the heart of the cultural and entertainment precinct. At the western end the vast, shiny **Crown Entertainment Complex**, more commonly known just as 'the casino', includes an enormous casino, hotel, cinema, over 35 restaurants, around 20 bars and nightclubs, and boutiques. To the west, beyond the Spencer Street Bridge, is the **Melbourne Exhibition Centre**, and the *Polly Woodside*, an 1885 Belfast-built iron barque sitting in a rare wooden-walled dry dock and the star attraction of the **Melbourne Maritime Museum** ⓘ *T9699 9760, www.nattrust.com.au, 1000-1600, $11, children $6.50, concessions $8.*

At the eastern end of Southbank, by Princes Bridge, is the **Victorian Arts Centre** ⓘ *T9281 8000, www.vicartscentre.com.au, Mon-Fri 0700-late, Sat 0900-late, Sun 1000-last show*, comprising the circular Concert Hall and the Theatres Building crowned by a steel net and spire. The arts centre also has free galleries, a café, quality arts shop and it is possible to tour the complex. The city's best art and craft market is held here on Sundays. One of the most pleasant ways to see Southbank and the impressive border of the CBD is from the river. There are many operators offering river cruises in front of Southgate, the cruises depart regularly and generally last about an hour, costing about $17.

Botanic Gardens

ⓘ *Birdwood Av, South Yarra, T9252 2300, www.rbg.vic.gov.au. Apr-Oct daily 0730-1800; Nov-Mar 0730-2030. Free; Visitor Centre Mon-Sat 0900-1700, Sat-Sun 0930-1700. Discovery tour Sun-Fri 1100, 1400, $4.50; Aboriginal heritage tours Thu 1100 and alternate Suns at 1030 (bookings essential, T9252 2429), $15.50, children $6.60.*

The gardens are a large oasis just to the south of the CBD. Bordered by very busy roads with the city's skyscrapers looming above it's not easy to forget that you are in a city, but the emerald lawns, ornamental lakes and wide curving paths provide a soothing respite from crowds and concrete. The main entrance is at Observatory Gate, where there's a visitor centre and the **Observatory Café**. There is also a quieter and rather more upmarket tearoom, **The Terrace**, by the lake. Check at the Visitor Centre for daily events, there are often theatre and cinema shows outdoors in summer. There are several walking tours, including one looking at the highlights and history of these gardens. Another explores the heritage of the local Aboriginal people and examines the traditional uses for plants with an Aboriginal guide.

Inner suburbs » pp75-91.

The city centre has traditionally been thought of by visitors as the area enclosed by the circle tram, but it is far better to think of Melbourne city as a collection of inner-city villages. Just to the north are Carlton, Fitzroy and Collingwood. Their proximity to the city meant that these were among the first areas to be developed as the city expanded rapidly during the gold rush. **Carlton** is best known for being an area where Italian immigrants settled. It's now a middle-class area where yuppies enjoy the Italian food and cafes of Lygon Street. Neighbouring **Fitzroy** also has some fine boom-time domestic architecture but had become a slum by the 1930s. Cheap rents attracted immigrants, students and artists and the area gradually gained a reputation for bohemianism. Brunswick Street is still lively and alternative

Sunset over the Yarra River

although increasingly gentrified. The alternative set now claim Smith Street in **Collingwood**, just a few blocks to the east, as their own. Johnston Street, crossing Brunswick, is the centre of Melbourne's Spanish community. These areas are the liveliest of Melbourne villages and have some of the city's best cheap eating, edgy shopping, colourful street art and raw live music venues.

Just to the west of the CBD is a vast area known as **Docklands**, as big as the CBD itself. This was the city's major port until the 1960s when containers began to be used in world shipping and acres of holding sheds were no longer needed. The area is to continue to undergo massive redevelopment over the next 10 years to turn it into a waterfront precinct

Great Ocean Road

The three great natural attractions of Australia are often said to be 'the road, the rock and the reef'. The 'road' is the Great Ocean Road, which runs west from Anglesea, round the treacherous Cape Otway, to Warrnamboo. It is, truly, one of the great coastal routes of the world and has everything, from stylish villages such as Lorne and Apollo Bay, backed by a lush hinterland of forests and waterfalls inhabited by glow worms and platypuses, to Port Campbell National Park, whose famous golden rock stacks are seared into the minds of most travellers long before they ever see them for real.

Getting around The road is very congested all year round, but particularly in summer, when it becomes a procession of slow coaches. If you can, plan a route from west to east to avoid it all. Most traffic and tours travel west from Melbourne along the Great Ocean Road, then return eastwards to the city along the faster inland route, the Princes Highway. There are V~Line bus services along the Great Ocean Road to Apollo Bay from Geelong which stop regularly along the way. A connecting service to Warrnambool operates on Friday only (plus Monday, December to January). Backpacker buses from Melbourne also have a Great Ocean Road service (see page 89) and there are daily V~Line direct train services from Geelong to Warrnambool (two hours 20 minutes).

Tourist information The VIC on the M1 north of Geelong, T1800 620888, www.greatoceanrd.org.au, 0900-1700, is for the whole region – from Geelong to Port Fairy. There are also VICs in Port Campbell, Morris St, T5598 6089, portcampbellvisitor@corangamite.vic.gov.au, and Apollo Bay, T5237 6529, 0900-1700.

Start off at Lorne, a glamorous coastal town of classy boutiques and fine restaurants surrounded by the thick forest, rivers and waterfalls of Angahook-Lorne State Park. Next up is Apollo Bay, a relaxed and friendly town and a good base from which to explore the Otway National Park, just to the west. Amongst the highlights of Otway National Park is Maits Rest Rainforest Walk. The towering mountain ash surrounding the upper edges of the gully are also impressive. Koala, swamp wallabies and yellow-bellied gliders live in the park and the very rare spot-tailed quoll.

West of the cape the sheer limestone cliffs have been eroded into a series of huge rock stacks, sculpted by the elements themselves into a series of arches, caves and tapering sails. The most famous group of stacks, the Twelve Apostles, were dramatically reduced to 11, when one of the stacks collapsed into the sea in June 2005, an event witnessed by a group of tourists (minus video camera, unfortunately). The most fascinating area of this stretch of the road is beautiful Loch Ard Gorge, named after the ship that was wrecked on Mutton Bird Island in 1878, killing 52 people on board. There is a walk from a lookout over the wreck site to the gorge and beach and then to the cemetery.

Beyond Port Campbell are more rock features, The Arch, London Bridge and The Grotto. The latter is probably the most interesting but London Bridge is famous for losing the arch connecting it to the mainland in 1990 and leaving some astonished tourists stranded on the far side. Adjoining Port Campbell, beyond the tiny settlement of Peterborough, is the Bay of Islands Coastal Park, an area of countless striking rock stacks. At Warrnambool the Great Ocean Road meets the Princes Highway. Only a stone's throw from here is the long, curving Lady Bay, with some of the coast's best swimming and boogie-boarding beaches, and the rugged low headlands and tiny bays that stretch away from the breakwater at its western end. The Thunder Point Coastal Walk runs along the top of these cliffs and at low tide offers the opportunity to wade out to Middle Island, with its rocky outcrops, caves and small fairy-penguin rookery. Just to the east of the town, across Hopkins River, there is a very good opportunity for seeing southern right whales from the free viewing platforms at Logans Beach (between mid-July and mid-September).

Sleeping

Accommodation is very expensive in the high season but Apollo Bay has a couple of real gems.

C-D **Angela's Guesthouse**, 7 Campbell Court, T5237 7085, www.angelas.tourvic.com.au. Spacious rooms with cheerful linen, spotless bathrooms and balconies. Angela provides the warmest hospitality imaginable and the rooms are unbelievably good value.

B-C **Cape Otway Lighthouse**, in the old keeper's cottage. For something a bit different check out this large residence has 4 comfortable bedrooms, and lounges with sofas and open fire, as well as the incredible position. Also 2 studio rooms for couples.

for inner city apartments, offices, restaurants, shops and entertainment. The already complete flagship of the development is the Telstra Dome, the major new venue for Aussie Rules football matches and rugby league games.

Southeast of the centre, **Richmond** is the place to come for Vietnamese cuisine and offers the inner city's best range of factory outlet shopping on Bridge Road and Swan Street. Greeks populated the suburb before the Vietnamese and the community is still represented in the restaurants of Swan Street. South of the river, **Toorak** and **South Yarra** have long been the most exclusive residential suburbs, and this is mirrored in the quality of the shops and cafés at the northern end of Chapel Street. The southern end becomes funkier and less posh as it hits **Prahan**, where Greville Street is full of second-hand clothes shops, bookshops and cafés, and Commercial Street is the centre of the city's gay community. These suburbs are among the most fashionable and stylish, and unsurprisingly Chapel Street is a wonderful destination for clothes shopping.

Down by the bay **St Kilda** has a charm all of its own. An early seaside resort that became seedy and run down, it's now a cosmopolitan and lively suburb but still has an edge. Only the well-heeled can afford to buy here now and though some of them aren't too keen on living next to the junkies and prostitutes still seen on Grey Street, the picturesque foreshore makes this the most relaxed of the inner suburbs and a great place to base oneself for a few days. Here also is **Luna Park** ⓘ *Cavell St, T9534 5764, www.lunapark.com.au, open 23 Apr-16 Sep Sat-Sun 1100-1800 and 17 Sep-23 Apr Fri 1900-2300, Sat 1100-2300, Sun 1100-1800, from $33.95, child, $23.95 and family $100*, a fairground with some impressive rides and an unmistakeable front door.

The rural area northeast of Melbourne is promoted as a Valley of the Arts for its past and present links with artists' communities. A path winds along the Yarra River from the city centre to **Eltham** (25 km) so hiring a bicycle is a good way to explore these leafy and tranquil areas beyond the city. An important stop along the way is the **Heide Museum of Modern Art** ⓘ *7 Templestowe Rd, Bulleen, signposted from Eastern Freeway, T9850 1500, www.heide.com.au, Tue-Fri 0900-1700, Sat-Sun 1200-1700, $8, children free, concessions $5-7*, the former home of art patrons John and Sunday Reed during the 1930s and 1940s. The museum is set in beautiful bushland by the river and includes a sculpture garden with works by Anish Kapoor and Anthony Caro. The gallery has an exceptional collection of modern Australian art and hosts temporary exhibitions of contemporary art.

Around Melbourne » *pp75-91.*

There is great variety of scenery and many activities around Melbourne so even if you are short of time you can still see something of the state's attractions within a day. The Yarra Valley is a beautiful wine region with some of the most sophisticated cellar doors and accompanying restaurants in Australia. Nearby, Healesville has a wonderful wildlife sanctuary and just beyond there is a very scenic winding drive through forest and ferns on the way to Marysville. Heading south, the Dandenongs is a fine area in which to walk or drive through towering Mountain Ash forests, and if you're lucky you might just see an elusive lyrebird. The Mornington Peninsula, often just called 'the bay', has some great beaches as well as diving or swimming with dolphin trips, and the penguins of Phillip Island are among the region's most popular attractions.

Ins and outs

Mornington Peninsula VIC ⓘ *Point Nepean Rd, at the base of Arthur's Seat, Dromana, T5987 3078, 0900-1700, www.visitmorningtonpeninsula.org.* **Phillip Island VIC** ⓘ *1 km past the bridge on Phillip Island Tourist Rd, T5956 7447, 0900-1700*, has a great range of local information. **Phillip Island Nature Park** ⓘ *T1300-366422, www.penguins.org.au*, manage most of the

Background

Going for gold

Melbourne boomed during the goldrushes of 1850s. The population exploded and the money fuelled unbelievably fast growth. By 1861 the town had founded a university, built splendid municipal buildings including a public library and Museum of Art, had installed street lighting, clean water and gas supplies. It couldn't last though and at the turn of the decade banks collapsed like cards, building ground to a halt and unemployment soared. Nearly a quarter of all Melbournians were forced to leave the city between 1891 and 1900.

The resurgence came in 1956 when the city hosted the Olympic games, the task that finally caused it to emerge from over half a century of relative inactivity. The next couple of decades were ones of consolidation rather than flair, while by contrast its northern rival was building its famous opera house. In the 1980s Melbourne realised it was rich once more, both in finances and its diverse multicultural bedrock. The vibrant culture of today began to take shape and the city experienced ambition not seen for a century. As well as attaining the title of Australia's cultural capital, aggressive state governments set out to cement its reputation as the country's sporting centre, despite Sydney landing the 2000 Olympics.

wildlife attractions. Saver tickets (the Nature Park Pass) can be bought at the VIC. **Dandenongs VIC** ⓘ *Burwood Highway, Upper Fern Tree Gully, T9758 7522, www.yarrarangestourism.com, 0900-1700.* They sell the Parks Victoria walking map for $2.

Mornington Peninsula

This is Melbourne's beach playground, where you can swim with dolphins, dive and sail, or take a trip to French and Phillip Islands. The peninsula's popularity and its proximity to Melbourne has resulted in a suburban sprawl creeping down as far as Rye, but beyond this things improve dramatically. The pristine south coast is protected by the Mornington Peninsula National Park; and the beaches and cafés of Sorrento and Portsea can make for a memorable stay.

Just east of the coastal suburb of Dromana, is **Arthur's Seat**, a 300-m-high hill in Arthur's Seat State Park with striking views over Port Phillip Bay. At the top there are some pleasant, easy walks in the state park, as well as the Seawinds Botanic Gardens and a maze. The scenic **chairlift** ⓘ *1000-1700, $8.50, children $6*, is a great way to ascend from the highway, even if you have your own transport.

Near the tip of Mornington's curving arm is **Sorrento**, its shore lined with jetties, boats and brightly coloured bathing boxes. The town has been popular for seaside holidays since the 1880s and consequently has many fine old limestone buildings along the main street, Ocean Beach Road. A few kilometres further on is **Portsea**, a small suburb frequented by wealthy Melbournians and boasting the stunning Portsea Back Beach. Both Sorrento and Portsea are full of stylish cafés, pubs and shops. **Point Nepean** is the long, thin tip of the Mornington peninsula, where it's possible to explore the gun emplacements, tunnels and bunkers of **Fort Nepean** ⓘ *0900-1700, $7.20, children $3.60.* From the Visitor Centre there is a short drive to Gunners car park; from here you can walk to the fort, about 3½ km, with magnificent views over Bass Strait and the Bay, or you can take the visitors' bus ($13, children $8).

Colourful beach huts at Brighton Beach, Port Phillip Bay

This long, straight strip of **Mornington Peninsula National Park** stretches from Portsea down to Cape Schank, protecting the last bit of coastal tea-tree on the peninsula and the spectacular sea cliffs from the golden limestone at Portsea to the brooding black basalt around Cape Schank. There are picnic areas and a lighthouse at the cape and some good walks. There are also regular tours of the light station and the lighthouse keepers' cottages have been renovated for holiday letting. There is a short walk with excellent views from the Cape Schank car park out to the end of the cape. For a longer walk, **Bushrangers Bay Track** is a great coastal route along the cliffs to Bushranger Bay, ending at Main Creek (45 minutes one-way).

Phillip Island

Phillip Island is one of Victoria's biggest attractions, with 3½ mn visitors a year. Connected to the mainland by a bridge, the island is 26-km long and 9-km wide. It certainly has its natural attractions, such as the rocky coves and headlands in the south and sunny north-facing beaches around Cowes, but the island has long since been tamed. Some wildlife continues to thrive, however, and this has been the lynchpin of the island's tourism success, particularly the rather overrated Penguin Parade. Other visitors come for the superb surfing breaks along the dangerous south coast, and the safe swimming beaches on the sandy northern shores. There are some pleasant walking tracks throughout the island, particularly on **Cape Woolamai**. **Newhaven**, by the bridge, and **Cowes** are the main towns, while **Rhyll** has a quiet charm away from the crowds. **San Remo** is the 'gateway' town, with accommodation a shade cheaper than on the island itself. The **Australian Motorcycle Grand Prix** is held here. ❂ ›› *p87.*

At the far end of the island are the **Nobbies**, a series of rocky islands joined to the coast at low tide, and beyond them **Seal Rocks**, home to Australia's largest fur seal colony. A series of boardwalks weave their way down past the now defunct Seal Rocks visitor centre through penguin habitats to the rock shelf below. The seals can only be seen with powerful binoculars, but fairy penguins and gulls can often be seen sheltering under the boardwalks. The road out there is closed at dusk, when the **Penguin Parade** ⓘ *visitor centre from 1000, parade from dusk, $17, children $8.50, concessions $11.20*, gets into gear. Fairy penguins

A busy weekend at the Williamstown Sailing Club

burrow in their thousands in the dunes along this stretch of coast, coming ashore in the darkness after a hard day at sea. Huge grandstands and powerful lights have been erected to allow thousands of visitors to watch the tired birds struggle out of the water and up the beach. Koalas are best seen at the **Koala Conservation Centre** ⓘ *Phillip Island Rd, 1000-1700, $9, children $4.50, concessions $6*, via an excellent series of elevated boardwalks through stands of gum trees. Other spots include **Swan Lake**, the island's only freshwater lake near Penguin Parade, **Cape Woolamai**, with its popular and pleasant walking tracks, and **Rhyll Inlet**, a wetland habitat favoured by migratory wading birds. Swan Lake and Rhyll both have boardwalks and bird hides.

Dandenong Ranges

Also referred to as the 'Dandenongs' or simply 'the mountain', these ranges comprise a hilly forested massif just to the east of Melbourne. They are a very popular destination for day-trippers, and some parts are swamped with them at weekends and school holidays. Several loosely connected chunks have been designated the **Dandenong Ranges National Park** and are criss-crossed with some wonderful walking tracks. Great views can be had from several points, the best over Melbourne being from the summit ⓘ *$2.20 per car, entry before 1600*, of Mount Dandenong itself. At the base of the mountain are the service towns of Fern Tree Gully and Belgrave. At the latter is the station for **Puffing Billy** ⓘ *T9754 6800, www.puffingbilly.com.au, from 1030, from $28.50, children $14*, the popular picturesque steam train that winds its way through scenic hilly country east to Gembrook, 24 km away. On the mountain itself **Sassafras** is the largest and most popular town, with a good range of facilities.

There are hundreds of interconnecting walking trails, and it is possible to organize circular walks from 10 minutes to three days in length, though longer walks may require short stretches on vehicular roads, and there is no camping on the mountain. Grants Picnic Grounds, just south of Kallista, is the start of several good loop tracks which pass through spectacular Mountain Ash forests and fern gullies. Lyrebirds live in these forests but are shy and difficult to spot. For an excellent circular walk through their territory, park at Cook's Corner and head down the Lyrebird Walk (7 km, two hours).

The Yarra Valley is one of Victoria's best known and most visited wine districts, but not content with creating great wine some of the wineries here have restaurants of the highest standard...

Yarra Valley and around

The Yarra Valley is one of Victoria's best known and most visited wine districts, but not content with creating great wine some of the wineries here have restaurants of the highest standard, and dining rooms and terraces that rank amongst the most striking and scenic in the country. In summer the valley gets very busy, particularly at weekends Just east of the valley is another excellent reason to visit – Healesville Sanctuary, the best native wildlife park of its kind in Australia.

There are some 30 plus wineries in the valley, most of which offer food. This is just a sample. **Eyton** ⓘ *Maroondah Highway, T5962 2119, wines $20-50, cellar door daily 1000-1700, lunches 1200-1500*, is striking for its modern architecture and has a fine dining room overlooking a lake. The excellent Merlot and the expensive modern Australian cuisine is regarded by many as the best in the valley. In summer, outdoor classical concerts add to the experience. At **Yering Station** ⓘ *Melba Highway, T9730 1107, wines $15-50, cellar door 1000-1700, lunches daily*, tastings and Yarra Valley produce are held in an old farm building, but don't miss a stroll around the new restaurant and cellars. This graceful sweep of stone and glass has the feel of a Bond movie, and the massive terrace has huge views. **McWilliam's Lilydale** ⓘ *Davross Court, T5964 2016, wines $20-25, cellar door daily 1100-1700, flexible lunch hours*, is a small and very friendly winery with an octagonal conservatory dining room and vine-hung garden gazebo, both looking out over vines and gum woods. There are simple cheap platters and cook-it-yourself BBQ meals. The salad bar is balanced by the scrumptious puddings. **Domaine Chandon** ⓘ *Maroondah Highway, T9739 1110, wines $25-50, cellar door daily 1030-1630*, is part of the Möet group. Stylish but relaxed tasting room with a high arched window looking out over the valley. A small savoury platter is served with each $5-10 glass of bubbly. A couple are good for a snack lunch. There are no free tastings. Finally, **Long Gully** ⓘ *Long Gully Rd, T9510 5798, wines $15-30, cellar door daily 1100-1700*, is a small easy-going winery with a very picturesque setting in its own mini-valley. Excellent and good value wines. Picnickers are welcome on the cellar door balcony.

Healesville Sanctuary ⓘ *T5957 2800, www.zoo.org.au, 0900-1700, $21, children $10.50, concessions $15.80. A few buses daily from corner of Green St and Maroondah Highway, Healesville, Mon-Fri from 0925, Sat 0858, Sun 1133.*, 4 km from the little town of Healesville, on Badger Creek Road, is the best native wildlife park of its kind in Australia. It is devoted to the conservation, breeding and research of Australian wildlife. The appeal of this place is seeing animals being so well cared for, including species that are almost impossible to see in the wild, including Tasmanian devils, platypus, the endangered orange-bellied parrot, the lyrebird and leadbeater's possum. The sanctuary has 30 ha of bushland with Badger Creek running through its centre. Visitors walk along a wide circular path (1½ km), taking side loops to see the creatures that interest them. Highlights are the Animal Close-Up sessions, held several times a day, when visitors can get as close as is legally allowed to wombats and koalas. The star exhibit is the World of the Platypus, a nocturnal tunnel with glass windows where you can watch the little fellas swimming and hunting.

Budget busters

Melbourne sleeping

LL-L **The Prince**, 2 Acland St, St Kilda, T9536 1111, www.theprince.com.au. Sleek boutique hotel, the height of hushed minimalist luxury. The 40 en suite rooms are seriously stylish and the pool and deck one of Melbourne's finest posing spots. The smart fine dining restaurant, Circa, offers a business lunch for $25. The basement Mink bar plays the tune to an Eastern bloc theme with deep leather couches and more varieties of vodka than a Russian distiller on speed. Recommended. **Aurora**, part of the Prince of Wales, 2 Acland St, St Kilda, T9536 1130, is one of the largest and most decadent spa and treatment centres in the country.

Melbourne dining

Flower Drum, 17 Market Lane, T9662 3655. Mon-Sat 1200-1500, 1800-2300, Sun 1800-2230. Considered by many to be the best Chinese restaurant in Australia and well worth the painful hit to the wallet. The finest Cantonese cuisine in a light, elegant dining room, impeccable service and an excellent wine list. The Peking Duck must be tried. Expect to spend about $130 for 2 without wine. Recommended.

Walter's Wine Bar, Upper level South- gate, T9690 9211, www.walterswinebar.com.au. Daily 1200-late. One of the most treasured places on Southbank, both hip and relaxed. Also fantastic views of the river, the 'best wine list in the land', and wicked deserts.

Sleeping

Melbourne has a huge range of accommodation. The centre is first choice for most visitors, put off by the term 'suburbs', but the suburbs are only a 10-min walk away, boast an equally buzzing café society and nightlife as the centre and also offer better value and, in peak times, more choice. Most places are priced at a year-round rate, though some hostels will be cheaper in winter. St Kilda is something of a backpacking stronghold, though be aware that the quality of accommodation varies considerably. Almost everyone will hike their prices up for the big events: the Melbourne Cup, Australian Open, Grand Prix and AFL Grand Final.

City centre *p59, map p60*

A-B **Hotel Y**, 489 Elizabeth St, T8327 2777, www.hotely.com.au. Very slick. Singles, doubles and some self-contained apartments.

B **Explorers Inn**, 16 Spencer St, T9621 3333, www.explorersinn.com.au. Second in a new chain, boasting the 'cheapest 3-star hotel' in Melbourne. Being relatively new helps it feel very comfortable as well as being good value.

C **Hotel Enterprize**, 44 Spencer St, T9629 6991, entrpriz@ozemail.com.au. A modest contemporary chain hotel with good value en suite doubles, but sadly, no Captain Kirk, Scotty or energizing from foyer to room.

C-D **Toad Hall**, 441 Elizabeth St, T9600 9010, www.toadhall-hotel.com.au.

140-bed hotel with very comfortable doubles, some en suite. Backpacker dorms, some all-female en suite. Excellent communal facilities, parking $6. Not the cheapest hostel beds, and not really party central, but worth every extra cent.

D **Greenhouse**, 228 Flinders Lane, T1800-249207, greenhouse@friendlygroup.com.au; and

D-E **Elephant**, 250 Flinders St, T9654 2616. Each has around 200 beds and a distinctly corporate feel, these backpacker hostels are not home-from-home, but both are modern, clean with good facilities and lots of organized events. Some doubles. Linen, pick-ups, internet included at Greenhouse, while the Elephant is cheaper.

D-E **Melbourne Connection**, 205 King St, T9642 4464, www.melbourneconnection.com. One of the smaller city centre hostels with around 80 beds, including 5 simple but pleasant doubles, stripped wood floors and comfortable communal facilities (though the kitchen could be bigger). Friendly and helpful owners give the place a good atmosphere. Off-street parking $5 a day.

North of the centre *p66, map p64*

A-B **King**, 122 Nicholson St, T9417 1113, www.kingaccomm.com.au. Contemporarily furnished B&B in an 1867 end-of-terrace home. This place is truly exquisite, light and white with stripped wood floors and balconies overlooking Carlton Gardens. The largest of the 3 rooms is one of the most desirable in the city. Cooked breakfast, licensed. Rates do not vary. Recommended.

B-E **Nunnery Accommodations** , 116 Nicholson St, T9419 8637, www.bakpak.com. Friendly, funky backpacker hostel in a rambling Victorian terraced house with a seriously comfortable front lounge. Free linen, breakfast, and lots of laid-on activities. Range of doubles, twins and 3-bed to the cheaper 12-bed dorms. There is also boutique accommodation available in newly refurbished premises in Fitzroy.

C-E **Melbourne Metro YHA**, 78 Howard St, T9329 8427, melbmetro@yhavic.org.au. Massive purpose-built, 350-bed hostel with mostly 4-bed dorms, doubles and twins, some en suite. All the usual YHA facilities include free use of bikes and car parking.

D-E **Chapman Gardens YHA**, 76 Chapman St, T9328 3595, chapman@yhavic.org.au. Smaller and more homely, this backpackers has 120 beds, but again all in 4-bed dorms or smaller, and good value doubles. Modern and comfortable with a lovely gazebo and garden, free bike hire and car parking.

D-E **City Scene**, 361 Queensberry St, T9348 9525, www.cityscene.com.au. Small friendly hostel, within easy walking distance of the Queen Victoria Market and city centre.

Southeast of the centre

p70, maps p60 and p64

B-E **Claremont Hotel**, 189 Toorak Rd, Toorak, T9826 8000, www.hotelclaremont.com. Bottom end of the category, it has 77 clean, bright but sparse rooms of good value and also 12 serviced apartments nearby. Mostly singles, doubles and twins. Linen, substantial continental breakfast, use of small kitchenette.

C-D **Olembia**, 96 Barkly St, St Kilda, T9537 1412, www.olembia.com.au. Comparable with Toad Hall, a very comfortable hostel that a lot of thought has gone into. 50 beds, including a dozen doubles and twins with shared bathroom facilities. Very competent, friendly and knowledgeable management. Bike hire, free off-street parking and secure bike shed.

C-F **Base Backpackers**, 17 Carlisle St, St Kilda, T8598 6200, www.basebackpackers.com. Hip and modern and part of the expanding Australasian chain. Chicks can stay on a girls only floor and benefit from hair straigheners, make up boxes etc! Red laminate floors, futon-style beds, in-house bar, fast internet.

Budget busters

Around Melbourne sleeping

L **Glen Harrow**, Old Monbulk Rd, Belgrave, Dandenong Ranges, T9754 3232, www.glenharrow.com.au. Oozing character, it has 4 exquisite old gardeners' cottages, set in 20 acres of wild, bushy gardens. Completely self-contained and furnished mostly with antiques.

L **Queenscliff Hotel**, 16 Gellibrand St, Queenscliff, T5258 1066, www.queenscliff hotel.com.au. At the southeasterly tip of the Bellarine Peninsula, southeast from Geelong, is the graceful, genteel Edwardian seaside resort of Queenscliff. One of the grandest hotels in town, and a real window into Edwardian decadence, is this beautifully restored place. Not only is it a most sumptuous place to stay but the high standards are also reflected in what comes out of the kitchens. Lunches in the shop café, also bar meals, bistro and a separate dining room.

D-E **Chapel St Backpackers**, 22 Chapel St, Prahan, T9533 6855, www.csbackpackers.com.au. Right at the bottom of this street is this friendly, family-run hostel with 48 beds. Mostly doubles, twins and 4-bed dorms, some all-female. Almost all are en suite with a/c, modest facilities. Linen and breakfast included.

D-E **Jacksons Manor**, 53 Jackson St, St Kilda, T9534 1877, www.jacksons manor.com.au. Large, rambling 1845 building with 80 beds. Doubles to 8-bed dorms. Car parking, cable TV.

Mornington Peninsula *p71*

C **Lighthouse keepers' cottages**, Cape Schank, T5988 6184, capeschank@ austpac inns.com.au. These have been renovated for holiday letting and can be booked by the room or as a whole.

C **Oceanic Whitehall**, 231 Ocean Beach Rd, Sorrento, T5984 4166. A grand old limestone guesthouse, traditional rooms with shared facilities, also some motel rooms with en suite, spa, open fire.

C-D **Bayplay Adventure Lodge**, 46 Canterbury Jetty Rd, Blairgowrie, T5988 0188, www.bayplay.com.au. Good hostel run by dive operators (see Activities and tours p88), with rooms, dorms, pool and café. Also offer transfers to and from Melbourne.

D **Sorrento Beach House YHA**, 3 Miranda St, Sorrento, T5984 4323, sorrento@yhavic.org.au. Small, clean and very friendly hostel, owners will help with arranging work (Apr-Jul) in local wineries, and with tours and transport.

Phillip Island *p72*

Most of the accommodation for casual visitors is in Cowes, though there are a few options elsewhere on the island. There are dozens of motels and cheaper caravan parks. Most get booked out for long weekends and school holidays. Reserve a bed early.

C **Glen Isla**, 234 Church St, 2 km from central Cowes, T/F5952 2822. This motel has basic but comfortable self-contained units, spa and sauna.

C-D **Beach Park**, 2 McKenzie Rd, T5952 2113. Has a wide range of sites, cabins and units, camp kitchen.

D **Corrigan's**, 8 Beach Rd, Rhyll, T5956 9263. 2 self-contained units with sunrise views over the bay.

D-E **Amaroo Park YHA**, 97 Church St, T5952 2548, phillipisland@yhavic.org.au. Of the two very good and friendly backpacker hostels, this is by far the larger, with more facilities, very cheap breakfasts and dinners (available to non-residents), a bar and pool. They also operate the Duck Truck and offer free transportation from Melbourne.

E Jock's Place, 33 Chapel St, Cowes, T5952 3600, jocksplace@waterfront.net.au. The second backpackers, this is a much smaller, cosier and quieter place to stay.

Dandenong Ranges *p73*

There are over 100 B&Bs on the mountain itself, but no hostels or caravan parks and no camping facilities, though there are a couple of cheaper motels along Burwood Highway.

A Winter Rose Cottage, 213 Mount Dandenong Tourist Rd, Ferny Creek, T9755 1269, www.winterrosecottage.com. Small but charming self-contained 1890s cottage. Most places have cheaper week-day rates though none better value than their 4-day special at $99 per night (**C**).

Yarra Valley and around *p74*

The valley is awash with boutique hotel and B&B accommodation, but budget options are very thin on the ground, though there are a couple in Healesville. Although Marysville is a small town there are over 30 accommodation options of all types.

B Art at Linden Gate, 899 Healesville Yarra Glen Rd, T9730 1861, erfrics@netstra.com.au. Single self-contained B&B apartment, with limited kitchen facilities, in the mud-brick house of a local sculptor. Isolated grounds encompass a hobby vineyard and a tiny wine cellar. The upstairs gallery has a range of contemporary work.

B Brentwood, 506 Myers Creek Rd, T5962 5028, www.brentwoodbandb.com.au. Another secluded hosted B&B (vegetarian) in its own wooded clearing adjacent to the state forest. Lots of wildlife and walking tracks from the back door. Very friendly, 3 en suite rooms in this 100-year-old home. .

C Keppels, Murchison St, Marysville, T5963 3207, www. keppels.net. Modern, colourful pub with pleasant lounge areas, mid-range meals daily and a range of hotel and motel rooms.

C Nanda Binya, 29 Woods Point Rd, Marysville, T5963 3433, nandabinya@virtual. net.au. Built as a ski lodge this modern building has 6 spacious, simple en suite rooms, some sleeping up to 5. Optional cooked breakfasts and dinners. Continental breakfast included, bikes for guest use, piano, sauna and outdoor jacuzzi.

C-D Healesville Hotel, 256 Maroondah Highway, Healesville, T5962 4002, www.healesvillehotel.com.au. This pub has 7 funky, spacious and brightly coloured rooms upstairs with shared facilities and a good bistro with great country cooking (mid-range). Meals 1200-1430 Thu-Mon, 1800-2030 daily. Book ahead for rooms at weekends.

Eating

Melbourne is foodie heaven. It boasts an incredible variety at inexpensive prices. In fact, the choice of restaurants can be overwhelming. A quarter of all Melbournians were born outside Australia and there are roughly 110 ethnic groups living in the city who have enriched Melbourne cuisine. The best option is to head for an 'eat street' or area known for a particular cuisine, such as Brunswick St in Fitzroy or the Vietnamese restaurants of Richmond, and stroll up and down to see what appeals. During the day look out for the Mon-Fri business lunches at some of the fancier restaurants – starter, main and glass of wine for $20-30. Despite the vast number of seats, try to book in summer and at weekends.

City centre *p59, map p60*

City centre eating tends to be lunch-based. For greater choice in the evening most people head for the inner suburbs although Chinatown (Little Bourke St) and the Southbank remain busy dinner spots. There are cheaper options on Russell St. Hardware Lane, to the west of Elizabeth St, has a strip of restaurants and cafés that buzz at lunchtimes. Centre Lane, off Collins St, at first glance looks like a grimy dark alley but is one of the best places in the city centre for a cheap lunch.

🍴🍴 **EQ**, Victorian Arts Centre (Riverside Terr, 100 St Kilda Rd), T9645 0644. Mon-Sat 1100-late. A little further south of the centre, for good casual Mediterranean food in a combined bar and café. Noisy but lively contemporary space.

🍴🍴 **Rosati**, 95 Flinders La, T9654 7772. Mon-Fri 0730-2200, Sat 1800-2200. Large, light Italian café-bar in an old glass-ceilinged warehouse which the owners have succeeded in giving a welcoming, classical feel.

🍴🍴 **Sakura Teppanyaki**, 331 Clarendon St, South Bank, T9699 4150. Mon-Fri 1100-1500, daily 1700-2300, later Fri-Sat. Leaving the centre southwards, the chefs throw all their lively personality into their cooking, and things can get pretty boisterous here. Good fun.

🍴 **Blue Train Café**, mid-level Southgate, T9696 0440, www.bluetrain.com.au. Daily 0700-2400. Fashionable and casual spot for drinks, snacks, pasta or wood-fired pizza. Also a popular spot for breakfast and Sunday brunch. Good value.

🍴 **Café All Angolo**, corner of Hardware Lane and Little Bourke St, T9670 1411. Ideal for a fast and reliable bowl of pasta in simple and unpretentious surrounds, very popular with nearby office workers. Good value breakfasts.

🍴 **Caffeine**, Swanston St, north of La Trobe. Mon-Fri 0700-1930. This dark and groovy café is next to the RMIT so it is full of students and has good quality baguettes, sushi, cakes and muffins at low prices.

🍴 **Clarendon Fish and Chippers**, 293 Clarendon St. Daily by 1130, until at least 2100. Healthy fast food, one of the very best in Melbourne, with fresh fish and great chips. A bit south of the centre.

🍴 **Laurent**, 306 Little Collins St, T9654 1011. Mon-Fri 0700-1900, Sat 0800-1800, Sun 0900-1700. An elegant Parisian-style patisserie that is begging for haute couture, but instead serves baguettes, coffee and exquisite pastries. Licensed.

🍴 **Nudel Bar**, 76 Bourke St, T9662 9100. Small and spartan, serving excellent noodle dishes and some pasta. Good vegetarian selection.

🍴 **Nyonya**, 14 Market Lane, T9663 2611. Daily 1200-1415, 1730-2200. Small, friendly Malaysian restaurant with a wide-ranging menu including several good value set meals.

🍴 **Pellegrinis**, 66 Bourke St, T9662 1885. Mon-Sat 0800-2330, Sun 1200-2000. Melbourne's original Italian café (it opened in 1954), it hasn't really changed much since then and still remains as a vibrant, crowded small space serving wonderful coffee and cheap pasta dishes.

🍴 **Spencer**, 475 Spencer St, T9329 5111. Food served Mon-Fri 1200-1500 and 1830-2100 (Sat 1830-2100). Victorian pub, now with a seriously smart, highly-regarded and usually lively restaurant in the lounge area. The quality rubs off on the cheap counter meals, which are well worth the stroll out from the city. Budget accommodation upstairs (**D-E**).

🍴 **Spring**, 316 Clarendon St. Mon-Fri 0800-2000, Sat 1030-1600. A healthy fast-food joint serving 98% fat-free breakfasts, burgers and curries as well as salads and smoothies. A healthy stroll south of the centre!

North of the centre *p66, map p64*

Carlton's Lygon St is sometime s called 'Little Italy' for its string of Italian restaurants. Brunswick St in Fitzroy is probably the most diverse eating street in Melbourne.

🍴🍴 **Abla's**, 109 Elgin St, T9347 0006. Mon-Wed and Sat 1800-2300, Thu-Fri 1200-1500. This small olive-green formal dining room consistently serves the best Lebanese food in town. Multi-course banquets.

ⲮⲮ **Gluttony It's a Sin**, 278 Smith St, 9416 0336. Tue-Sat 0830-2300, Sun 1000-2100. Rich food in a café atmosphere. Everything is oversized and over-indulgent, but exceptional quality is always maintained.

ⲮⲮ **Shakahari**, 201 Farady St, T9347 3848. Long-standing vegetarian restaurant with a warm, earthy but stylish interior. The limited but very fine menu will not disappoint.

Ⲯ **Aussie Indian Trendy Cuisine**, 25 Johnston St, T9419 2118. Daily 1730-2330. Good food at laughingly cheap prices, BYO and friendly service. The banquet for 2 is $25. Also takeaway.

Ⲯ **Babka**, 358 Brunswick St, Fitzroy, T9416 0091. Tue-Sun 0700-1900. Closed most of Jan. Friendly, unassuming and unpretentious bakery is simply perfection in everything it does.

Ⲯ **Clare Castle**, 421 Rathdowne St, T9347 8171. Mon-Sat 1200-1500, Tue-Sat 1830-2130. Has an unremarkable public bar but a deep blue dining room serving up some of the best Italian home cooking in the area.

Ⲯ **Guru da Dhaba**, 240 Johnston St, T9486 9155. Very cheap but filling northern Indian dishes in a warm and noisy dining room with terracotta walls and simple black tables. BYO.

Ⲯ **Kazen**, 201 Brunswick St, T9417 3270. Tue-Sun 1200-1500, 1800-2230 (Sun 1800-2300 only). Small, Italian-influenced Japanese with dark, blue-stone walls but a much lighter atmosphere. Excellent and interesting food, licensed but cheap corkage for BYO.

Ⲯ **Moroccan Soup Bar**, 183 St Georges Rd, North Fitzroy, T9482 4240. Huge and superbly authentic Moroccan, vegetarian meals.

Ⲯ **Notturno**, at No 179, T9347 8286. Daily 0600-0200. Of the many Italian cafés and restaurants in Lygon St, this large one is one of the least expensive. Good breakfasts, pasta, pizzas, cakes and coffee.

Ⲯ **Retro**, 413 Brunswick St, Fitzroy, T9419 9103. Daily 0700-2400. Cavernous bare-brick café with distressed wood floor and lots of formica tables. This is a grazer's paradise with loads of nibbles, plates and dips on the extensive cheap menu. Also good all-day breakfast and veggie options, licensed.

Ⲯ **Thresherman's Bakehouse**, 221 Faraday St, Carlton. Daily 0630-2400. Spacious, relaxed café in an old car-repair shop. Great juices, soups and cafeteria meals as well as cakes and sandwiches.

Ⲯ **Vegie Bar**, 380 Brunswick St, T9417 6935. Daily 1100-2200. A relaxed, friendly vegetarian café-bar in a large old bare-brick warehouse. Great menu includes wood-fired pizzas, wraps, burgers and salads.

Ⲯ **Viet Rose**, 363 Brunswick St, T9417 7415. Generous quantities of laksa, vegetarian rolls and rice will defeat your stomach before your wallet.

Southeast of the centre

p66, maps p60 and p64

Richmond is one of the most international of the foodie suburbs. Most eateries are on Bridge Rd, but just to the north is Melbourne's 'Little Saigon', Victoria St, where around 50 Vietnamese restaurants jostle for attention. Greek food can be found on Swan St. In Prahan and Toorak there is no particular foodie area, the cafés and restaurants here dotted amongst the shops on Chapel St and Toorak Rd, but the choice is phenomenal. The eating in St Kilda has been traditionally clustered along Acland St and Fitzroy St, though since the on-going renovation of St Kilda Baths, the choice on the foreshore has tripled. Italian predominates.

ⲮⲮⲮ-ⲮⲮ **Richmond Hill Café and Larder**, 48 Bridge Rd, East Melbourne, T9421 2808, thecafe@rhcl.com.au. Daily 0830-1700. Hugely indulgent café and restaurant with wonderful cheese shop attached. Lunch includes the cheese platter and dinners are a culinary event.

ƗƗ **Borsch, Vodka & Tears**, 173 Chapel St, Prahan, T9530 2694. Daily 1000-2130. Vibrant, friendly eastern European restaurant specializing in Polish broth and vodka… and tears (of laughter!). Live, gypsy-style music Mon, Wed, Sun. Evening bookings essential on music nights and weekends.

ƗƗ **Flavours of India**, 68 Commercial Rd, Prahan, T9529 8711. Small, smart curry bar, popular with locals for food of exceptional quality. Also takeaway.

ƗƗ **Kanzaman**, 488 Bridge Rd, Richmond, T9429 3402. Daily 1200-1500, 1800-2400. Excellent Lebanese with an exotic, richly decorated interior.

ƗƗ **Mexicali Rose**, 103 Swan St, Richmond, T9429 5550, www.mexicalirose.com.au. Fri 1130-1430, daily 1800-2100. Friendly, earthy Mexican with generous servings of all the classics, plus a few interesting variations.

ƗƗ **Minh Tan 2**, 192 Victoria St, Richmond, T9427 7131. Daily 1000-2230. One of the busiest and most respected Vietnamese restaurants, with a huge menu including fantastic mud crabs.

ƗƗ **Stokehouse**, 30 Jacka Bvd, St Kilda, T9525 5555. Bar: Mon-Fri 1200-2200, Sat 1100-2400, Sun 1000-2200. Dining room: daily 1200-1500, 1900-2200. With the best spot on the foreshore this award-winning bar-bistro is packed out year round. Simple ground floor bar and beach-facing terrace. Bookings not taken so arrive early for a good spot. Upstairs is an expensive, airy formal dining room, focusing on modern Australian seafood, which has the best balcony tables in Melbourne (bookings taken).

Ɨ **E Lounge**, 409 Victoria St, Richmond, T9429 6060, elounge@tpg.com.au. Not an internet café, but some of the best thin and crispy wood-fired pizzas in the city. Very friendly, very orange. Also takeaway.

Ɨ **Greasy Joe's**, 70 Acland St, St Kilda, T9525 3755. Daily 0700-2400. American retro bar and grill with excellent burgers, breakfasts and lots of pavement tables.

Ɨ **Il Fornaio**, 2 Acland St, St Kilda, T9534 2922. 0700-2200. Small, but warehousey with lots of cheap eats and pavement tables, great for breakfast. French/Italian bakery.

Ɨ **Momotaro Rahmen**, 392 Bridge Rd, Richmond, T9421 1661. Tue-Sat 1130-1430, Tue-Sun 1800-2100. Small restaurant much loved for its homemade, fresh rahmen noodles and uncompromising flavours.

Ɨ **Pier Pavilion**, perched right at the end of St Kilda pier, St Kilda. 1000-sunset, 1000-2300 peak summer. Great spot for breakfast or simply one of the excellent coffees with a substantial slice of cake. Also cheap lunches.

Ɨ **Salona**, 260 Swan St, Richmond, T9429 1460. Mon-Fri 1100-2200, Sat-Sun till 2300. The best of a small cluster of traditional Greek restaurants.

Ɨ **Torch**, 178 Swan St, Richmond, T9428 7378. Daily 0830-1800. Small and welcoming, this is one of a few excellent cafés on this street. Busy but relaxed with cheap light lunches and all-day breakfasts. Good value.

Ɨ **Veg Out Time**, 63 Fitzroy, St Kilda, T9534 0077. Tiny vegetarian using very healthy cooking methods to produce a great variety of dishes, including curries and stir-fries. Also takeaway.

Mornington Peninsula *p71*

ƗƗ **The Baths**, on Sorrento foreshore overlooking a long skinny jetty, T5984 1500. Daily 0800-2100. For expensive but relaxed dining. Also a fish & chip kiosk.

ƗƗ **Continental**, 1-21 Ocean Beach Rd, Sorrento, T5984 2201. A funky choice. Meals, including breakfast, are served in a large room hung with modern art. A nightclub operates upstairs on Sat.

Ɨ **Coppins**, 250 Ocean Beach Rd, T5984 5551, Daily 1000-1630. Sits above Sorrento Back Beach and is a wonderful place for a casual lunch or tea and scones on a sunny afternoon.

Ɏ **Just Fine Food**, 23 Ocean Beach Rd, Sorrento, T5984 4666. Gourmet deli and café with busy pavement tables.

Phillip Island *p72*

Ɏ **Euphoria**, 13 Thompson Ave, Cowes. A nice casual place for lunch.

Ɏ **Foreshore Bar Café**, 11 Beach Rd, Rhyll, T5956 9520. Thu-Mon 1000-2000. Facing the sea, is the locals' favourite spot for fish and chips. It also has a funky bar serving platters and nibbles.

Ɏ **Island Food Store**, 75 Chapel St, Cowes. For high-quality cake and coffee or a salad, set back from Chapel St past the supermarket.

Ɏ **Jetty**, on the Esplanade, Cowes, T5952 2060. Also faces the water and is a large, lively and cheap place, particularly good for seafood. Attracts busloads of tour groups in summer.

Ɏ **Terrazzo**, 5 Thompson Ave, Cowes, T5952 3773. Wed-Sun 1700-2030. Good cheap place for Italian.

Dandenong Ranges *p73*

As you would expect there are dozens of restaurants, cafés and bistros on the mountain. A couple of the best are almost opposite each other on the main road through Olinda, which is a good place to pick up picnic ingredients. A visit to **Ripe**, on the main street, is a must for any visitor.

ɎɎ-Ɏ **Ranges**, Olinda, T9751 2133. All day from 0900. Bright, large, cheerful and popular place for good value breakfasts, light lunches and, from Tue-Sat, mid-range Asian influenced dinners.

Ɏ **Cook's Corner Café**, Kallista-Emerald Rd. Daily. Off the beaten track, with a cosy, relaxed interior and a few tables in the pleasant ramshackle gardens.

Ɏ **Rendezvous Bakery and Café**, Mt Dandenong Tourist Road (at the other end of the mountain). Daily 0700-1900. Wonderful views and divine breakfasts, baguettes, cakes and coffee.

Yarra Valley and around *p74*

ɎɎ **Yarra Valley Dairy**, just south of Yarra Glen on McMeikans Rd, T9739 0023, www. yarravalleydairy.com.au . As an alternative to a winery lunch (see page 74) try this place. It is a licensed, full working dairy with a lively and relaxed café and views over cow-filled fields. Mid-range platters and light lunches, book ahead at weekends. Cheese tastings daily 1030-1700, café closes a little before.

ɎɎ-Ɏ **Pasta Shop**, next door to **Bodhi Tree**. Tue-Fri 0900-1730, Sat-Sun 0830-1700, restricted hours in winter. Cheery 2-room cottage café that does Healesville's best breakfast, tasty lunches and sells fresh handmade pasta and gourmet foods.

Ɏ **Bodhi Tree**, 317 Maroondah Highway, Healesville, T5962 4407. Wed 1200-1700, Thu-Sun 1200-2100, daily in summer. Rustic, laid-back café with wholesome food and an assortment of tables in the large outdoor area, live acoustic music Fri nights.

Bars and clubs

The city is bursting with watering holes from the sleekest cocktail bar to the grungiest of Victorian-era pubs with sticky carpets. The city centre bars tend to be the most sophisticated with many wine bars and cocktail bars crossing the line into club territory and a sprinkling of traditional pubs frequented by office workers during the week. The large student population to the north of the city means that Carlton, Fitzroy and Collingwood have the heaviest concentration of live band venues and alternative pubs and bars. The inner suburbs south of the Yarra have some of the most fashionable bars and respected live music venues. Many pubs and bars also serve good food at reasonable prices and liberal licensing laws mean it is possible to get a drink well into the small hours. Many club nights move regularly and the clubs themselves open and close frequently. Entry is usually about $12-15.

King St has a lot of clubs but is known for being slightly seedy. Most of the clubs listed are city based but Chapel St in South Yarra is also a hot-spot.

Free newspapers, mostly catering for the clubbing and music scenes, come and go but currently include *Beat* and *Inpress*. *Bnews* and *MCV* cover the gay and lesbian scene. All are widely available in cafés and music shops. There are general listings and entertainment guides in the Thu *Herald* Sun and Fri *Age* newspapers.

City centre *p59, map p60*

Bridie O'Reilly's, 62 Little Collins St. Out-of-the-way Irish theme bar with 20-odd beers on tap. Pub grub 1200-1430, 1800-2100 and mainly Irish acoustic live music Tue-Thu, cover bands Fri-Sat.

Hairy Canary, 212 Little Collins St. Mon-Fri 0730-0300, Sat 1000-0300, Sun 1000-0100. A smart, trendy bar and café, serving food all day. Rocks into the early hours.

The Limerick Arms, corner of Clarendon St and Park St, South Bank. Cheap meals daily 1200-1430, 1800-2100. Had a revamp a few years ago to more reflect its name and cash-in on the rise of Irish theme bars. This isn't too forced, however, and the result is a pleasant, traditional Aussie drinking bar with an Irish flavour. DJs Fri-Sat.

The Maori Chief, corner of Moray and York sts, South Bank, T9696 5363. Meals 1200-1400 Mon-Fri, 1800-2130 Mon-Sat. Combines a groovily shabby bar, dimly lit and furnished with retro couches, with good cheap casual food.

The Mitre, 5 Bank Place. A traditional British-style pub, now hemmed in by the high-rises, which has been quietly pulling pints since the 1860s.

Stork, 504 Elizabeth St, T9663 6237. Welcoming, relaxed front bar with pool table and open fire. Independent bands daily with a wide mix of styles. Seriously cheap, good quality bar food and cheap, surprisingly sophisticated bistro. Also pleasant, good value double and twin rooms with kitchen and lounge facilities (**D**).

North of the centre *p66, map p64*

Bar Open, 317 Brunswick St, Carlton. Small, grungy bar with an open fire, armchairs and live music Wed-Sun.

Black Cat, 252 Brunswick St. Wed 1800-2300, Thu-Fri 1800-0100, Sat-Sun 1400-0100. Slick, seductive cabaret bar with live blues and jazz Thu-Sun.

The Brandon, corner of Station St and Lee St. Goes out of its way to source real ales, both keg and bottled. Simple friendly front bar and large retro lounge. Equally simple pub grub, but with interesting touches.

Night Cat, 141 Johnston St, Fitzroy, T9417 0090. Lush, stylish bar with roomy couches and swing and salsa bands Thu-Sun.

North Fitzroy Star, 32 St Georges Rd, Fitzroy, T9482 6484. Food daily 1100-2300. Contemporary, often exuberant styling in this traditional Victorian pub. Welcoming, with lots of nooks and crannies and open fires, the food is also well worth the trip. Cheap, inventive light lunches and bar nibbles, and a set mid-range menu later on.

Purple Turtle, 166 Johnston St, Fitzroy, T9416 5055. Food daily 1200-2200, 1200-1600 Mon-Wed in winter. Chic, contemporary bar- restaurant in an old Victorian pub with live blues, funk and jazz Fri-Sat and Sun afternoons. The cheap interesting menu still gives a nod to a few pub favourites, and can be served in the formal dining room with its open fire.

The Tote, 71 Johnston St, Fitzroy, isn't a gambling den, but is dark and smoky all the same with a crowd of students, crusties and band types here for the alternative live music Tue-Sat. Features 'tight-arse Tuesdays' when pots are under $2 and there's cheap entry to 3 bands.

Southeast of the centre

p66, maps p60 and p64

Candy Bar, 162 Greville St, Prahan. Food daily 1200-2400, late licence Fri-Sat. Groovy, laidback and friendly bar and café with sculpted fireplaces of antiqued

Hebel blocks and retro furniture. DJs Thu-Sun play progressive house and there's celebrity bingo on Mon.

Dizzy's Jazz Bar, 92 Swan St, Richmond. Hosts live jazz Thu-Sat, check the playlist on www.dizzys.com.au

The Elephant and Wheelbarrow, Fitzroy St, St Kilda. London-style pub with over 20 beers on tap, most British or Irish. Live music Wed-Sun and a 'meet-the-Neighbours' session (really) on Mon. Cheap, feelgood meals, including breakfast, daily 1100-1430, 1700-2100.

The Esplanade, Esplanade, St Kilda. Something of a Melbourne institution for live music, cheap food and a raucous atmosphere.

Frost Bites, corner of Chapel St and Simmons St, Prahan, www.frostbites.com.au. The bar to be seen at. The cool warehouse look is complemented by industrial quantities of slush cocktails waiting on tap. Very cheap café meals, and live music Wed-Thu and Sun. Late license most nights.

George, corner of Fitzroy St and Grey St, St Kilda. Slick wine bar, in sharp contrast to the lively and grungy **gpb** beneath. The latter serves cheap pub grub daily 1200-0100, and there's interesting live music 1600-1900 Sat and 1800-2100 Sun.

Greyhound, 1 Brighton Rd, St Kilda, T9534 4189, www.atthegreyhound.com. Relaxed comfortable pub and a good live venue for everything from roots to rock and Sun night karaoke.

The Pint on Punt, 42 Punt St, St Kilda, 9510 4273, www.pintonpunt.com.au. One of Melbourne's best drinking holes. A simple, warm country-Irish-style pub with open brick fires and bare wood floors. They also have good hostel accommodation upstairs (**D-E**).

Prince of Wales, 29 Fitzroy St, St Kilda. A magnet for all types from the divine to the desperate and consequently has an unpredictable energy. Lots of pool tables, cheap pots on Mon and a busy live venue next door.

Vineyard, 71 Acland St, St Kilda, T9534 1942. Daily 1000-0300. The seriously laidback and cool frequent this joint. A long, casual space that can be opened onto the side street on a sunny day. Also great café food.

Entertainment

Melbourne *p58, map p60*

For details of events visit the VIC and pick up a free copy of the *Official Visitor's Guide*, a useful rundown of highlights, and Melbourne Events, an excellent monthly publication that has details of every event and attraction in the city. See also Bars and clubs for live music venues in pubs/bars. The main agencies are **Ticketek**, T132849, www.ticketek.com, and **Ticketmaster**, T136100, www.ticketmaster7.com. There is a half-price ticket booth in Bourke St Mall, opposite Myer, for same-day performances only. No telephone number – you have to go in person. Open 1000-1400 Mon, Sat, 1100-1800 Tue-Thu, 1100-1830 Fri.

Cinema

Astor, 1 Chapel St, border of Prahan and St Kilda, T9510 1414. A different contemporary or classic movie every day, with lots of double bills.

George, 135 Fitzroy St, St Kilda, T9534 6922. Mainstream movies, cheap tickets for guests at some local hostels, including Olembia.

Village cinema, at the Jam Factory, 500 Chapel St, Prahan, T1300 555 400, www.villagecinemas.com.au, and others at 206 Bourke St, T9667 6565, and the Crown complex, T9278 6666.

Live music

Major acts play at the **Rod Laver Arena**, the **Melbourne Concert Hall** and the **MCG** and tickets for these type of events are usually sold through ticketing agencies. **Melbourne Concert Hall**, part of Victorian Arts Centre, is home of Melbourne Symphony Orchestra.

Festivals and events

Melbourne *p58, map p60*

Melbourne puts on an extraordinary spread of festivals throughout the year. Many of these attract the best talent in the country and bring over prestigious international artists. To see what's on and how to buy tickets pick up a copy of the free monthly *Melbourne Events* from the VIC. For forward planning see www.thatsmelbourne.com.au. All of the festivals listed below are annual. Sports fans should also watch out for the Australian Open in January, F1 Grand Prix in March and the Australian Football League Grand Final in September.

Jan Midsumma, T9415 9819, www.midsumma.org.au, is a gay and lesbian celebration of pride, presence and profile. Running for 3 weeks it involves street parties, events and the Midsumma Carnival.

Mar Melbourne Food and Wine Festival, T9823 6100, is a prestigious gastronomic celebration that showcases talent and the produce of the city and region. Events include master classes, food writers' forum, tasting tours and the 'world's longest lunch'. It's held over the Labour Day weekend.

Apr Melbourne International Comedy Festival, www.comedyfestival.com.au, held over 3 weeks, is one of the world's largest laugh-fests. A month of comedy in every guise, from more than a thousand Australian and international performers.

Jul Melbourne International Film Festival, T9417 2011, www.melbournefilmfestival.com.au, showcases about 350 of the best films from Australia and around the world. The 2-week festival includes features, documentaries, shorts and discussion sessions with film makers in 4 main theatre venues.

Sep and **Oct** Melbourne Fringe Festival, T8412 8788, www.melbournefringe.com.au, lasts for 10 days. It is an off-shoot of the main Melbourne Festival with a more anarchic spirit. Showcases new and innovative art in all fields and has lots of free events, parties and a legendary parade down Brunswick St, Fitzroy.

Melbourne Festival, T9662 4242, www.melbournefestival.com.au, takes place over 3 weeks. It is the city's major arts festival showing the cream of local and overseas talent in theatre, dance, opera, music and the visual arts in indoor and outdoor venues all over Melbourne.

Oct Spring Racing Carnival, www.racingvictoria.net.au, is the horse-racing festival linked to several major races. The highlight is 'the race the nation stops for', the Melbourne Cup (a public holiday in Melbourne) held at Flemington Racecourse. Traditionally celebrated with champagne, fancy frocks, oversized hats and a bet. It is held the first Tue in Nov. Entry about $30 from Ticketmaster7, T136122, or at the turnstiles on the day.

Shopping

Melbourne *p58, map p60*

Art and crafts

There are some fine Aboriginal art galleries at the eastern end of Flinders Lane. There are a couple of upmarket shops on Bourke St, such as **Aboriginal Creations**, at No 50, but there are also other options. **Koorie Heritage Trust** (see page 63) is one. Another is the **Aboriginal Handicrafts Shop**, the mezzanine part of the Uniting Church Shop at 130 Little Collins St. It may be small, but they have an excellent range of affordable pieces, from bark and paper art to didge- ridoo, carved wood and woven baskets. All profits go directly back to the originating communities. Open Mon-Fri 1000-1630.

Bookshops

Booktalk, 91 Swan St, Richmond. Mon-Sat 0830-1730, Sun 0900-1600. Also a café with good value breakfasts.

Brunswick Street Bookstore, 305 Brunswick, Fitzroy. Daily 1000-2300. Large independent with a well-chosen range.

Grub Street, 379 Brunswick St, Fitzroy. Great collection, covering a wide range of contemporary issues, non-fiction and fiction.

Hill of Content, 86 Bourke St. Small classy shop with a discerning collection of general fiction and non-fiction.

Map Land, 372 Little Bourke St, T9670 4383, www.mapland.com.au. Has an excellent range of maps and guides, and offers good general advice. Mail order available.

Readings, 309 Lygon St, Carlton. One of the largest independents with an excellent range, including music CDs, and knowledgeable staff.

Clothes

Melbourne is famous for its wonderful clothes shopping. People fly from all over Australia just to have a shopping weekend in Melbourne. **Crown casino complex** has some of the city's most exclusive boutiques, such as Armani and Versace. Equally swanky shopping can be found on Collins St, Toorak Rd and the city end of Chapel St, which is lined with designer label shops and chain stores, becoming steadily cheaper as you head south. In the city centre the eastern end of Collins St has expensive designer boutiques. More funky independent designers populate Little Collins St and Flinders Lane such as the fascinating and colourful **Christine**, 181 Flinders Lane, and **Alice Euphemia**, Shop 6/ 37 Swanston St, supporting Australasian design talent.

Brunswick St, Fitzroy, is still a good spot for finding choice second-hand articles, and it gets positively bargain-basement over in neighbouring Smith St. South of Commercial Rd on Chapel St, Prahan, and on the side-road Greville St, are a couple of dozen small and chic shops, including the wildly exuberant **Shag**, 130 Chapel, which is difficult to leave without having been tempted into buying something that'll turn heads. Open daily 1200-1800.

There are a couple of interesting shops on Barkly St, St Kilda, near the junction with Acland St, and on Acland by the junction with Albert St.

Markets

Gleadell St Market, Richmond. Sat 0700-1300. A cheap, old-fashioned street market where few stallholders speak much English. Fruit, veggies, bread, flowers and fish.

Prahan Market, Commercial Rd. Dawn-1700 Tue, Sat, dawn-1800 Thu-Fri. Fabulous and fancy fresh-food market.

Queen Victoria Market 513 Elizabeth St. Tue, Thu 0600-1400, Fri 0600-1800, Sat 0600-1500, Sun 0900-1600. The market has expanded and evolved since the 1870s, and now consists of a substantial brick building housing the meat and dairy sections and a vast area of open-air sheds, selling fruit and vegetables, clothing and souvenirs. The meat hall has fresh meat, fish and seafood and the dairy hall includes nearly 40 delicatessen stalls selling bread, cheese, sliced meats, pickles, dips and sauces. The sheds can be a good place to find cheap leather goods but generally hold a lot of low-quality, mass-market junk but the food sections are well worth a wander for the friendly banter of the stall holders and extremely tempting sights and smells. There is a food court and there are places in the dairy hall to grab a bite and sit down. Visit the market as part of the Heritage Tour, Tue, Thu-Sat 1030, $16.50 including morning tea. There are also entertaining tours focusing on either history or tastes, such as the Foodies Dream Tour, Tue, Thu-Sat 1000, $25 including samples along the way. Bookings essential, T9320 5835.

St Kilda Market takes place every Sun along the curve of the Esplanade. The string of stalls offer mostly craft and gifts with a few clothes stalls.

Victorian Arts Centre Market, Southbank has high-quality art and craft stalls, Sun 1000-1800.

Budget busters

Aerial tours

Melbourne Seaplanes, Williamstown's Gem Pier, T9547 4454, www.seaplane.com.au. Specializes in 4 main flights: a short 15-min loop around the city from $85, to a 55-min loop around Port Phillip Bay for $195, which, at an extra cost, can be broken by a stop in Sorrento for lunch. Minimum 2 people.

Balloon Sunrise, T9427 7596, www.ballonsunrise.com.au. Strange as it may seem it is possible to balloon more or less right over the Melbourne skyline. Very experienced, departures from Richmond, $310-375.

Activities and tours

Melbourne *p58, map p60*

City tours

Melbourne Explorer, T9650 7000, is a conventional tour operator. This jump-on, jump-off London bus drives around 2½-hr circuits designed to take in a good many of the city's major attractions, with about 30 stops along the way. The bus can be boarded at any point and stops include the Town Hall, the Aquarium, Flinders St Station, St Patrick's Cathedral, Melbourne Museum, Melbourne Zoo, and Bourke St Mall (Swanston St end). The Southbank and Parliament ('downtown') circuit leaves the Town Hall on the hr 1000-1200 and 1400. The longer Museum, Zoo and Swanston St ('uptown') circuit leaves the Town Hall on the ½ hr 0930-1430. Operates daily except major event days and public holidays (1 day $33, children $16.50, concessions $28; 2 days $55, children $30, concessions $50).

Cricket

The annual highlight is the Melbourne Boxing Day Test Match. International test matches are played regularly in summer at the MCG, T136122, www.mcg.org.au. Tickets from **Ticketmaster7**.

Cycling

A great way to see some of the sights and parks of the city and inner suburbs is to cycle around them.

City Cycle Tours, T9585 5343, provide the bike, refreshments and a guide for a variety of tours. Price around $10 per hr. Departure from the Treasury Gardens.

There are plenty of hire outlets. Bike hire costs round $10 for 2 hrs, $20 per day.

Borsari Cycles, 193 Lygon St, Carlton, T9347 4100. **Freedom Machine**, 401 Chapel St, Prahan, T9827 5014.

Hire A Bicycle, Southbank by Princes Bridge, T04-1261 6633. **St Kilda Cycles**, 11 Carlisle St, T9534 3074.

Horse racing

The Spring Carnival's **Melbourne Cup** is one of the country's major events, held on the first Tue in Nov at Flemington Racecourse. Grandstand tickets aren't cheap but ground entry is more reasonable (from $40). Tickets from **Ticketmaster7**. For more information T1800-352229, www.racingvictoria.net.au.

Motor racing

The first Grand Prix of the F1 season is held at Albert Park in early Mar. Tickets cost about $100 for day entry, $160 for 4-day entry and from $350 for a 4-day reserved grandstand ticket. Note the Grand Prix is very much geared around the corporates so public access and views are limited. If you do not have a corporate ticket be prepared to be disappointed in what you see and where you can go. More details at www.grandprix.com. au. Tickets from **Ticketmaster7**.

Neighbours tours

There are various tours and pub nights, solely aimed at British backpackers. **Backpacker King**, T9534 4755, has the neighbourhood covered. Tours to 'Ramsay Street' run Mon-Fri (3 hrs, $30) and include lots of soap gossip, photo stops in front of the houses, Erinsborough High School and the possibility of seeing some filming on set. 'Ramsay' Street is an ordinary residential street in the outer suburbs of Melbourne so only the outdoor filming is done here. Even more exciting for the soapoholic is the chance the press some Neighbours flesh at 'Meet the Neighbours'. Several cast members come along to the **Elephant and Wheelbarrow** (see Bars and clubs, page 84), every Monday night for a raucous trivia night ($30). Bookings essential for tours and trivia night.

Penguin spotting

Penguin Waters, T9386 8488, www.penguinwaters.com.au, have sunset Fairy Penguin-watching tours departing from Southgate (berth 1, 2 hrs, $55). BBQ and refreshments included.

Sightseeing

Autopia Tours, T1800-000507, www.autopiatours.com.au, has day-trips to Phillip Island, Great Ocean Road, and the Grampians all around $90), plus 3-day trip options.
Go West, T1300 736 551, www.gowest. com.au, (around $70), is one of the best day tours along the Great Ocean Rd. They pick up from about a dozen Melbourne backpacker hostels between 0715 and 0820 every day, returning about 2130.
Wild-Life Tours, T9741 6333, www.wildlifetours.com.au, has similar options with a day-tour of the Great Ocean Rd from $80, plus a trip to Ballarat, and another to the Dandenongs. Both companies offer a 2-day tour of the Great Ocean Rd plus the Grampians for around $150, and have backpacker bus routes to Adelaide and Sydney. Larger coach companies (with larger coaches and slightly larger fares) such as **APT**, T1300-655965, www.aptours.com.au, **AAT Kings**, T1800-334009, www.aatkings. com.au, and **Gray Line**, T1300-858687, www.grayline.com, offer a wider range of day tours as far as Ballarat, Echuca, Mt Buller and the Yarra Valley.

Walking

For details of Melbourne's excellent free guided walks courtesy of the Greeter Service, see page 58. The VIC has free brochures and maps for a variety of self-guided walks such as art walks along Swanston St and the Yarra River and heritage walks. The Golden Mile walk is a 4-km route through the city past the most significant architectural and historical features. It can be done as a self-guided walk ($4) or guided ($20, 2 hrs) on Wed, Fri, Sat at 1030 and 1330. Bookings essential, T1300 135757.

Mornington Peninsula *p71*

Diving

The diving is superb with shipwrecks and j-class submarines, sheer-wall and fast-drift dives, leafy sea dragons and stingrays. Operators include **Dive Victoria**, 3752 Point Nepean Rd, Portsea, T5984 3155, www.divevictoria.com.au; and **Bayplay Adventure Lodge**, 46 Canterbury Jetty Rd, Blairgowrie, T5988 0188, www.bayplay.com.au.

Dolphin tours

Bottlenose dolphins live in Port Phillip Bay and swimming with them is becoming increasingly popular (from Oct-Apr). **Polperro**, T5988 8437, www.polperro.

com.au, take care to protect the dolphins and take small groups. Departing from Sorrento Pier 0830, 1330, $99 ($44 observers), bookings essential.

Surfing

Surfing lessons are available with **Sorrento Surf School**, T5988 6143.

Phillip Island *p72*

Seal spotting

The only way to get close to the seals is to take one of a range of excellent boat trips with **Bay Connections**, T5678 5642, www. bayconnections.com.au, who operate out of Cowes ($55, 2 hrs). They also run cruises out to French Island (see page 71), Wilson's Promontory (see page 93), and **whale watching** in winter.

Sightseeing tours

Afternoon or evening tours from Melbourne are offered by all the major operators. One of the best, and best value is run by **Autopia**, T9326 5536, www.autopiatours.com.au.

Duck Truck, T5952 2548, www.amaroopark.com/ducktruck. Offers a variety of very good value tours from Cowes or Melbourne, around the island and out to Wilson's Promontory. Their 3-night package from Melbourne includes some meals, transfers, some entry fees and accommodation.

Surefoot Explorations, T5952 1533. Has a wide range of guided walks, provides transport, packed lunches and equipment.

Surfing

Out There, T5956 6450, or **Island**, T5952 3443. Would-be surfers can take a lesson with these outfits. Island also has 3 shops around the island and hire out equipment and wetsuits.

Yarra Valley and around *p74*

Several companies run day-trips from Melbourne. **Tasting Tours Backpacker Winery Tours**, T9419 4444, www.backpackerwinerytours.com.au, takes medium-sized groups out to 4 wineries including Domaine Chandon. From $85, includes lunch, wine and afternoon tea. Pick-ups from Melbourne (Flinders St Station, Queensbury Hill and St Kilda). If you fancy seeing the wineries from a hot air balloon rather than the bottom of a wine glass, check out **Global**, T1800 627661, or **Go Wild**, T9890 0339, www. gowildballooning.com.au.

Transport

Melbourne *p58, map p60*

Most of the major sights can be reached on foot and using the free City Circle tram, which travels along Flinders St, up Springs St, along La Trobe St and around Telstra Dome down Harbour Esplanade.

Air

Flight information is available at www.melair.com.au or by ringing the relevant airline. See also p58. **Qantas Virgin Blue** and **Jetstar**are the principal suppliers of interstate flights with direct daily services to all state capitals.

Bus

Local There is a bus for almost anywhere you could wish to go within Greater Melbourne, but the further out they travel the less frequently they go. City Saver, 2-hr and daily tickets can be bought on board and notes are accepted.

Long distance Greyhound has a service to **Sydney** and **V~Line** have a daily bus/train service to **Canberra** from Spencer St Station and also operate most state services to Victorian country towns with a few Gippsland services from Flinders St Station.

Backpacker Autopia, T1800-000507, www.autopiatours.com.au, run trips to **Sydney** (3½ days, $195, non-inclusive).

Car

The city has 3 arterial CityLink road tollways which electronically read 'e-tags' in vehicles: great for residents, a real pain for visitors (www.citylink.com.au). Passes can be purchased, in advance or until midnight the day after you travel (the fine for travelling without a pass is about $100), from post offices and the CityLink Customer Centre, 67 Lorimer St, just off the Westgate Freeway. With a credit card passes can be bought (single use up to $3.60, 24 hr or weekend $10.20) over the phone, 0800-2000, T132629, or via the website. Motorcyclists get to use the CityLinks for free. To avoid the tolls when entering the city from the Westgate Freeway (Geelong, Highway 1) take the Kings Way exit for Richmond, Prahan and St Kilda, and the Power St exit for the city, Carlton and Fitzroy. From the South Eastern Freeway (the east, Highway 1) take the Toorak Rd exit and turn left for the city centre and suburbs. From the Calder/Tullamarine Freeways (the northwest and the airport) take the first exit after the junction of the two freeways. This drops onto Bulla Rd which eventually becomes Elizabeth St. Beware of metered parking in the city centre, it extends as late as 2400.

Car hire A cheap option is Rent-a-Bomb, T131553, www.rentabomb.com.au, who hire out cars for $164 per week for use within 50 km of the city centre.

Ferry

Spirit of Tasmania, T1800 634906, www.spiritoftasmania.com.au, operate nightly overnight ferries from Port Melbourne to Devonport in Tasmania (13 hrs, prices vary from $99 per passenger and from $59 per car).

Taxi

Arrow, T132211, Black Cabs, T132227, Silver Top, T131008.

Train

Local Used mostly to service to the outer suburbs. Various networks extend regular services to destinations including **Belgrave** (the Dandenongs), **Frankston** (connections to the Mornington Peninsula), **Lilydale** (connections to the Yarra Valley and beyond), **Stony Point** (ferry connections to French and Phillip Islands), **Werribee** and **Williamstown**. Tickets must be bought at departure stations.

Tram

Trams are the main way to get about the city centre and inner suburbs. They operate more like a bus than a train so you'll need to hail one if you want to get on, and push the buzzer to indicate to the driver that you want to get off. The network of trams mostly radiate out from the city centre to the inner suburbs but some routes travel from suburb to suburb through the centre. City Saver and 2-hr tickets can be bought on board, but the dispensers take coins only. Daily tickets must be purchased in advance from a newsagent displaying the Metcard logo.

Mornington Peninsula *p71*

Bus

From **Frankston** the Portsea Passenger Bus Service, T5986 5666, operates services down the Port Phillip Bay coast, with stops including **Dromana**, **Sorrento** (stop 18, corner of Melbourne Rd and Ocean Beach Rd) and **Portsea** (stop 1, National Park entrance). Full-run 1½ hrs. Mon-Fri services every 1-2 hrs, 0700-1900 (plus 2040 Fri); every 2 hrs from 0800-2000 weekends. Last buses back from Portsea at 1915 Mon-Fri, 1800 Sat and 1735 Sun. Backpacker bus through Bayplay Adventure Lodge, T5988 0188, bookings@ bayplay.com.au, offers transfers from **Melbourne** daily.

Ferry

Passenger-only and car ferries operate from **Sorrento** to **Queenscliff** on the Bellarine Peninsula. Ferries from 1030-1700 (50 mins, $9, children and concessions $8). The larger, vehicle ferry, crosses daily, year-round, on the hour 0700-1800. Same pedestrian prices, cars under 5½ m $45 plus passengers. T5258 3244, www.searoad.com.au.

Dandenong Ranges *p73*

Bus/train

There are metropolitan train services daily between **Melbourne** City Circle stations, **Upper Fern Tree Gully** (1 hr) and **Belgrave**, running every 20-30 mins. **US Bus Lines**, T9754 8111, www.usbus.com.au, runs services between **Belgrave** station and **Olinda** (the 694), stopping at **Sherbrook** and **Sassafras**. Services at 0620, 0700 and 5 past the hr from 1000-1500 Mon-Fri, and every 1-2 hrs 0820-1620 Sat. They also have a service between **Upper Fern Tree Gully** and Olinda (the 698), following the commuter hrs of 0730 and 0830, and 1610-1940 Mon-Fri only. Metropolitan fares apply, so get a day ticket in Melbourne. There are no local bus services on Sun.

Yarra Valley and around *p74*

There are metropolitan train services daily between Melbourne City Circle stations and Lilydale (40 mins), running every 20-30 mins. **McKenzie**, T5962 5088, www.mckenzies. com.au, runs less frequent daily bus services between **Lilydale**, **Yarra Glen**, **Healesville** and **Marysville**. Call for times.

Directory

Melbourne *p58, map p60*

Banks ATMs are on all the major shopping and eating streets. **American Express**, 233 Collins St. Mon-Fri 0900-1700, Sat 0900-1200. **Thomas Cook**, 257 Collins St. Mon-Fri 0900-1700, Sat 1000-1400. Also 261 Bourke St, near Swanston St. Mon-Sat 0900-1700, Sun 1100-1500. **Travelex**, 231 Collins St. Mon-Fri 0800-1830, Sat 0800-1730, Sun 1000-1630.
Health centres Travellers Medical and Vaccination Centre, Level 3, 393 Little Bourke St, T9602 5788. **City Health Care**, 255 Bourke St, T9650 1711. Mon-Fri 0900-1800, Sat 1000-1700, and **Acland St Medical Centre**, 171 Acland St, St Kilda, T9534 0635. Mon-Thu 0900-1900, Fri 0900-1800, Sat 0900-1200, are both visitor-friendly and bulk bill. Medicare at Centre Point Mall, corner of Bourke St and Swanston St. Mon-Fri 0900-1645.
Hospitals Royal Melbourne, Grattan St, Parkville, T9342 7000; **St Vincent's**, 41 Victoria Pde, Fitzroy, T9288 2211.
Internet Global Gossip, 440 Elizabeth St, city centre. Daily 0900-2400. **Net City**, 65 Fitzroy St, St Kilda. Daily 0930-2300.
Pharmacy Hunter Naughton, 470 Collins St, T9629 1147. Daily 0700-1900. Sally Lew, 41 Fitzroy St, St Kilda, T9534 8085. Daily 0900-2100. Cheap film processing. **Post** Main Post Office, Elizabeth St, Mon-Fri 0815-1730, Sat 0900-1600. Poste Restante (take photo ID to collect mail) Mon-Fri 0900-1730, Sat 0900-1200. **Useful numbers** Police, 637 Flinders St, T9247 5347.

Phillip Island *p72*

Banks Most major banks have ATMs on Thompson St, Cowes.
Internet Library, Thompson Av, T5952 2842, or Waterfront Computers, 130 Thompson Ave (next to Mobil), T5952 3312. Mon-Fri 0900-1700, Sat 1000-1300. **Post** 73 Thompson Ave.

Southeast Victoria

Lying east of Melbourne and extending from the mountains to the coast, Gippsland is the rural heartland of Victoria, a rich landscape of rolling green dairy pasture. In the far south is the main attraction, Wilson's Promontory, a low range of forest-covered granite mountains, edged with isolated sandy bays and golden river inlets and marked only by the occasional walking track. Carefully maintained as a wilderness, the 'Prom' offers intimate encounters with wildlife and is a stunning place to walk, swim, camp or simply laze about. In the centre of the region, the Gippsland Lakes system forms the largest inland waterway in Australia, where every small town has jetties festooned with yachts and fishing boats. Heading inland, the landscape rises to the limestone caves of Buchan and the rugged forest and gorges of the Snowy River National Park. Further east on the coast, is Croajingolong National Park, a wilderness of dense bush and river inlets, the largest of which is overlooked by one of Victoria's loveliest small towns, Mallacoota, an isolated and peaceful haven.

Getting there Interstate bus network.
Getting around Limited local bus networks, hire car/campervan.
Time required 2 days.
Weather Generally warm,dry and settled in summer and cool and unsettled in winter.
Sleeping Smattering of hostels, traditional budget hotels and motor parks. National park campsites recommended.
Eating Few quality restaurants, try traditional hotel 'pub-grub'.
Activities and tours Fishing, boating and walking.
★ **Don't miss** Croajingolong National Park. ▸▸ p95

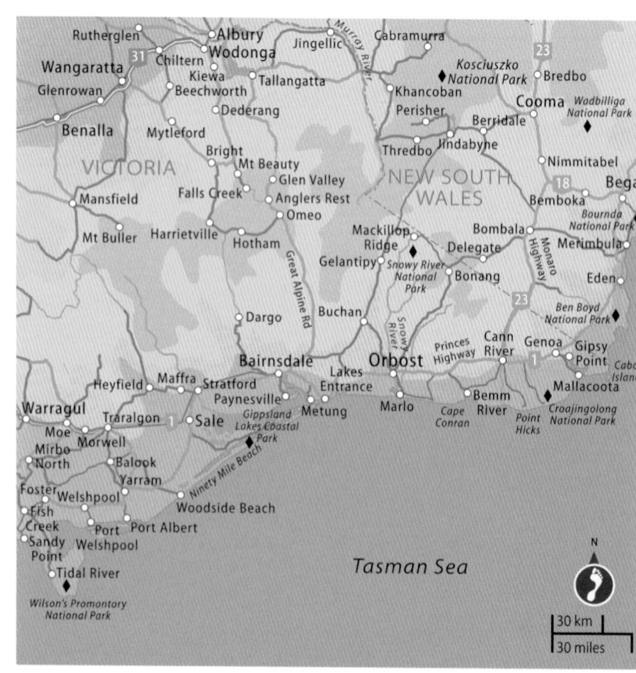

Ins and outs

Getting there and around

The main V~Line train line heads out from Melbourne through Dandenong and Warragul to Sale. From Dandenong there are connecting bus services to Bass then Newhaven and Cowes on Phillip Island; to Wonthaggi and Inverloch; and to Yarram via Leongatha, Fish Creek, and Foster. From Sale change to buses for Bairnsdale, Lakes Entrance and other stops to the NSW border. There are also ferries to Cowes from Stony Point on the Mornington Peninsula. A V~Line railway line heads out from Melbourne to Sale. From here buses take over. The route heads east via Bairnsdale, Lakes Entrance, Orbost, Cann River and Genoa to the NSW border. From Cann River there is a set-down-only service to Canberra and another up the coast to Batemans Bay. » *p101.*

Tourist information

If heading east out of Melbourne along the Princes Highway you can stock up on information from the main Melbourne VIC. Within the region itself the main accredited VICs are east in Sale, the **Central Gippsland Information Centre** ⓘ *8 Forster St, T1800-677520, www.gippslandinfo.com.au*, or, if travelling south, out of Melbourne towards Wilson's Promontory along the South Gippsland Highway, the **Prom Country Information Centre** ⓘ *on the highway in Korumbarra, T5655 2233, infocentre@sgsc.vic.gov.au, 0900-1700*. The general tourism website is www.gippslandtourism.com.au.

Wilson's Promontory National Park » *pp97-101.*

'The Prom', as it is known by Victorians, is one of the state's top attractions, with granite-capped mountains covered in forest sloping down to the purest of white sand beaches and tannin-stained rivers meandering down to the sea. The northeastern region is a wilderness area only accessible to bushwalkers and boats. The park's most accessible beaches and bushwalks are on the western coast near Tidal River, the only 'settlement', where parrots, wombats and kangaroos roam (and fly) around freely. 2005 saw two notable events on 'The Prom', first in summer when wildfires decimated the region, and then, ironically, the first snowfalls in years in August.

Ins and outs

There are two main routes down to the 'Prom'. The more direct route heads through the heart of dairy country, taking in Koonwarra and Fish Creek. The longer route heads south to the coast via the 'Big Worm' and Wonthaggi. Tiny **Koonwarra**, 140 km Melbourne and 80 km from Wilson's Promontory, is a worthy distraction thanks to the **Koonwarra Store** (daily 0800-1700) a café/restaurant serving country breakfasts, lunches and dinners of the highest quality, and a takeaway. Fish Creek is another tiny and charming settlement. **Foster**, 30 km from Koonwara, is the closest major town to Wilson's Promontory and is well supplied with supermarkets and bakeries to fuel camping expeditions.

The **Parks office** ⓘ *Tidal River, T5680 9555, www.parkweb.vic.gov.au, 0900-1700*, issues permits, has detailed notes on day and overnight walks and can offer advice on activities in the park. Park entry at the gate $9.50 car per day.

Around the park

The park offers dozens of trail options. **Squeaky Beach**, **Picnic Bay** and **Whisky Bay** can be reached by very short walks from car parks but the best walk is to all of these beaches from

 Tidal River along the coast and return (9 km return). The best views of the Prom are from the top of **Mount Oberon**. The walk up from Telegraph Saddle car park, 3½ km from Tidal River, is wide and easy with a few rock-cut steps at the top (7 km, two hours return). Sunrise is the best time for photographs of Norman Bay below. A good spot for sunset is Whisky Bay. A very popular day walk from the same car park is the track to **Sealers' Cove** (9½ km, 2½ hours one-way) passing through thick rainforest to the eastern side of the Prom. The cove has a long arc of golden sand, tightly fringed by bush. There is a basic campsite at Sealers Creek. The cove is beautiful but the walk has little variety and the return leg can feel like a bit of a slog. A more interesting day-walk is the **Oberon Bay** loop that also starts from Telegraph Saddle (19km, six hours). There is also an extended walk (38 km, two to three days) to the lighthouse that sits on a great dome of granite on the southern tip of the promontory. The **Lighthouse Trek** can be done independently or from October to May with a ranger guide ($300-450 including accommodation and meals). Accommodation is in cottages at the lighthouse that are equipped with bunks, kitchen and bathroom. The cottages can be booked by the bed or exclusively for groups (**C-D**).

Gippsland Lakes » *pp97-101.*

The break between central and eastern Gippsland is marked by a series of connected lakes, separated from the sea only by the long thin dune system of the eastern end of Ninety Mile Beach. This strip of sand, designated the Gippsland Lakes Coastal Park, is accessible only by boat and is relatively unspoiled, even in peak season. The main service town in the area is Bairnsdale, but there are some pretty settlements dotted around the margins of the lakes, and Metung is particularly picturesque. Soon after Yarram is the turning to Woodside Beach, which marks the start of Ninety Mile Beach, the long golden stretch of sand that curves all the way to Lakes Entrance.

Sale, the administration centre for Gippsland, has all the usual services but few attractions for visitors. The **VIC** ⓘ *T5144 1108, www.gippslandinfo.com.au, 0900-1700* is on Princes Highway, just west of the town centre. **Bairnsdale** is the largest town in the Lakes area, though it isn't actually on a lake shore itself. It is worth stopping here to see the Aboriginal **Krowathunkalong Keeping Place** ⓘ *Dalmahoy St, T5152 1891, Mon Fri 0900-1200, 1300-1700, $3.50, children $2.50, concessions $1.50*, which features chillingly frank descriptions of the brutal Gunnai massacres that took place in Gippsland during the 1830s-50s. For a deeper insight into the local Gunnai people, contact **Boran Glaat Cultural Tours** (T/F5152 2585). The excellent **VIC** ⓘ *240 Main St, T5152 3444, bairnsdalevic@egipps.vic.gov.au, 0900-1700*, will help with information and bookings for the whole Lakes region as well as Bairnsdale itself.

Bigger than Metung, but less tacky than Lakes Entrance, **Paynesville** hugs a stretch of lake shore facing **Raymond Island**, a small haven for wildlife, especially koalas, with one of the country's most concentrated wild populations. It's not a park, however, and the Paynesville township effectively extends across the car ferry (every half an hour, $4 return, pedestrians free) to claim a portion of the island as a suburb. Further offshore, **Rotamah Island** is home to a Bird Observatory ⓘ *T5146 0278, rotamah@i-o.net.au*. A wonderful retreat, this homestead has five rooms sleeping 19 people on a fully catered basis (around $75 a night). Own linen required. The island is teeming with wildlife, not just birds, and the owners can arrange boat transport from Paynesville.

Metung is on a small spit only a few hundred metres wide, giving it the feel of a village surrounded by water. Most of the homes spreading up the low wooded hill to the rear overlook Bancroft Bay, lined with yachts and jetties. The well-heeled visitor is well catered for here, with a couple of good restaurants, wonderful day and sailing options and some luxurious accommodation.

Standing at the only break in the long stretch of dunes that separate the Gippsland Lakes from the sea is **Lakes Entrance**. Once a small fishing village, this town is dominated by dozens of motels and caravan parks strung out in two long rows along the lake side, 2 km from end to end. Over the footbridge is the **Entrance Walking Track**, a leisurely and rewarding two-hour return stroll through dunes and bush to **Ninety Mile Beach** and **Flagstaff Lookout**. **Wyanga Park Winery**, see Eating page 99, runs popular day and evening cruises from the town's Club Jetty on their launch, the Corque. The **VIC** ⓘ *T5155 1966, lakes@lakesandwilderness.com.au, 0900-1700*, is at the very western end of town, on the highway.

East to Mallacoota ›› *pp97-101.*

Orbost

The Yalmy Road continues down to Orbost, sitting at the point at which the Snowy River meets the Princes Highway. Though well placed to capitalize on the considerable tourist traffic, the small town offers little to the traveller except the cheapest petrol and last decent supermarkets until well into NSW, and a helpful **VIC** ⓘ *13 Lochiel St, T5154 2424, orbost@lakesandwilderness.com.au, 0900-1700.*

Marlo and Cape Conran

The tiny fishing community of Marlo at the mouth of the Snowy River is a popular long-weekend destination for Victorians, and there is a variety of caravan and cabin accommodation available. There are few facilities, however, aside from a couple of small grocery shops, one doing takeaways, and the an impressive pub with guesthouse facilities. There are several good marked walking trails around **Cape Conran**, where there are two beautiful sandy beaches which are generally fine for swimming. There is also camping, see Sleeping.

Croajingolong National Park

This wonderful park, a narrow strip south of the Princes Highway that runs for 100 km west of the state border, is best known for its long stretch of wild coastline but also encompasses eucalypt forests, rainforests, granite peaks, estuaries and heathland. The remoteness of much of the park has led to diverse flora and fauna, with over 1,000 native plants and more than 300 bird species and it has been recognized as a World Biosphere Reserve.

Point Hicks was the first land in Australia to be sighted by the crew of Captain's Cook's *Endeavour* in 1770 and mainland Australia's tallest lighthouse was built here in 1890. The track to Point Hicks (2¼ km) starts at the end of the road past Thurra River campsite, and passes Honeymoon Bay. There are fantastic views from the top of the **lighthouse** ⓘ *tours 1300 Fri-Mon, $5, children $3*, and southern right whales are often seen just off shore in winter. For details of staying in the lighthouse or campsite see page 97. It is possible to walk the coast from **Bemm River** right over the NSW border into the **Nadgee Nature Reserve**. Trekking on the wild beaches makes up the bulk of the experience, but walkers will also encounter a range of spectacular coastal scenery. There are a number of campsites with facilities along the route, though water can get scarce and walkers need to carry a couple of days' supply. Numbers are restricted on all stretches of the trek, and permits are required. Contact the Cann River or Mallacoota Parks Victoria office, see below.

Mallacoota

Perched on the edge of the Mallacoota Inlet and the sea, Mallacoota is a beguiling and peaceful place. Surrounded by the Croajingolong National Park and a long way from any large cities, it's a haven for wildlife, particularly birdlife. The quiet meandering waters of the inlet are surrounded

The iconic and often audible Kookaburra

by densely forested hills. To the south are several beautiful coastal beaches, like **Betka Beach**, a popular local swimming beach. Spectacular layered and folded rocks can be seen at **Bastion Point** and **Quarry Beach**. There are almost unlimited opportunities for coastal walks, bushwalking, fishing and boating. Once a year in April there is an explosion of creativity at the **Carnival in Coota** – a week-long festival of theatre, visual arts, music and literature.

The **Mallacoota Walking Track** is a 7-km loop, signposted from the main roundabout, that goes through Casuarina forest and heathland, along the beach to Bastion Point and back towards town past the entrance. To explore the inlet by water there are several options. Motor boats, canoes and kayaks can be hired from the caravan near the wharf. Several cruising boats are also based at the wharf, visit their kiosks for bookings. For details, see Tours and activities page 100. There are magnificent views of the area from **Genoa Peak**, the access road is signposted from the Princes Highway, 2 km west of Genoa. From the picnic and parking area there is a 1½-km walking track to the summit, steep for the last 100 m. Further afield is tiny **Gabo Island**, home to one of the largest fairy penguin colonies in the country, plus one of the highest lighthouses. ▸▸ *p100.*

Buchan and around ▸▸ *pp97-101.*

Tiny Buchan is best known for its limestone caves but it is also just south of the Snowy River National Park. Consequently it is a good area for walking, canoeing and rafting as well as caving. There are over 300 caves in the region, the best of which are contained in the **Buchan Caves Reserve** ⓘ *entrance is just north of town, before the bridge, T5155 9264, Oct-Mar 1000, 1115, 1415, 1530, Apr-Sep 1100, 1300, 1500. $12.50, children $6.50, concessions $10*, which has two well-lit show caves with spectacular golden cave decorations. **Fairy Cave** and **Royal Cave** are famous for their pillars, stalactites, stalagmites, flowstone and calcite pools. There are 'adventure' caving tours available during Easter and Christmas holidays or when numbers permit, and some good short walks in the reserve. The 3-km **Spring Creek Walk** is a loop that heads uphill to Spring Creek Falls and passes through remnant rainforest, mossy rocks and ferns. Lyrebirds, kookaburras and parrots may be seen (or heard) on this track. Detailed walking notes and bookings for cave tours are available from the Parks Victoria office in the reserve. Limited information is available from the post office or general store in Buchan.

Sleeping

Wilson's Promontory National Park *p93*

The Prom is so popular that accommodation is allocated by ballot for Dec-Jan (including campsites). Even at other times, weekends may have to be booked a year in advance. Also, check out www.promaccom.com.au.

B **Tingara View Tea House and Cottages**, 10 Tingara Close, Yanakie, T/F5687 1488, www.promcountry.com.au/ tingaraview. Three pretty, colonial-style one-room cottages with lovely views, cooked breakfast served in main house, dinner and afternoon tea also offered.

B-D **Park cabin/campsite**, T5680 9555, wprom@parks.vic.gov.au. The best place to stay is undoubtedly within the park itself. There is a good range of accommodation in cabins, units and huts. **Camping** in the park is fantastic. There is an (unbookable) international campers area available for 1-2 nights.

Gippsland Lakes *p94*

In Bairnsdale there are a couple of caravan parks, and several motels and B&Bs. Accommodation may be plentiful in Lakes Entrance, but there's not a room or patch of earth to be had in the summer school holidays as hordes descend from Melbourne. Squeezed in among the motels and caravan parks are a handful of options offering something a bit different, listed below. The villages of Paynesville and Metung are particularly lovely.

L-B **Deja Vu**, just to the north of Lakes Entrance over the lake on Clara St, T5155 4330, www.dejavu.com.au. This modern, glass-filled, hosted B&B, set in 7 acres of wild lakeside country, has rooms with private lake-view balconies and the first-class service is friendly and attentive, with some unexpected and unusual flourishes. Also a couple of suitably alluring self-contained properties fronting the lake. Book well in advance. Lovely.

A-B **BelleVue**, 201 Esplanade, Lakes Entrance, T5155 3055, www.bellevuelakes.com. A cracking little day-time café and decent mid-range seafood restaurant help make this very comfortably furnished, family-run motel stand out from the crowd.

B **Anchorage**, The Anchorage, Metung, T5156 2569, www.anchoragebedandbreakfast.com.au. Comfortable B&B with particularly wonderful wooden breakfast atrium.

C **Arendell cabins**, Metung, T/F5156 2507, www.arendellmetung.com.au. There are various self-contained options, including this spacious and well-furnished lot set in lawned gardens.

C **Bellbrae**, 4 km out on Ostlers Rd, Lakes Entrance, T5155 2319, www.lakes-entrance.com/bellbrae. Very similar cabins, but cheaper and better spaced out in a forest setting.

C **Espas**, Raymond Island, near Paynesville, T/F5156 7275, www.espas.com.au. Very simple but stylish en suite cabins, one with full disabled access, homely shared kitchen and living area. Also excellent modern food in the striking café (🍴 Fri-Sat 1000-2030, Sun 1000-1700) with an outdoor deck facing Paynesville across the water.

C **Lazy Acre**, 35 Roadknight St, Lakes Entrance, T5155 1323, lazyacre@net-tech.com.au. Several well-maintained and self-contained log cabins, one specifically designed for the disabled, each sleeping up to 6.

D **Old Hotel**, Esplanade, Paynesville, T5156 6442. Five pub rooms, unusually all en suite, freshly decorated and furnished, continental breakfast, pleasant verandah. Bistro with a cheap menu, superb salad and veggie bar.

E **Riviera Backpackers**, 669 Esplanade, Lakes Entrance, T5155 2444, lakesentrance@yhavic.org.au. Very well run and equipped YHA hostel with a good range of rooms, including several doubles (some ensuite), all at a good value per-head price. Cheap bike hire, pool. Friendly and knowledgeable owners.

East to Mallacoota *p95*

If using Orbost as a base for exploring the local national parks, the most interesting place to stay is out on the Buchan Road. Most of the accommodation in Mallacoota is self-contained holiday flats or caravan parks . Book ahead for Dec-Jan and during Carnival.

L **Point Hicks Lighthouse Keepers' Cottages**, T5158 4268, www.pointhicks.com.au. In Croajingolong National Park, with verandahs overlooking the sea, sleeps 8. Very comfortable and consequently heavily booked at peak times. If free the managers will offer a 'rock-up rate' of $100 double or offer accommodation to backpackers in a simple bungalow. Call in advance to arrange an unlocked gate.

B **Gypsy Point Lodge**, signposted on the road to Mallacoota, T5158 8205, www.gipsy point.com. A friendly, homely guesthouse with great views of the Genoa River. Particularly popular with birdwatchers. Price includes dinner. Also 3 self-contained cottages (C), and a restaurant for guests, dinner from $55.

B-C **Karbeethong Lodge**, Schnapper Point Dr, Mallacoota, T5158 0411, www.karbeethonglodge.com.au. Comfortable old guesthouse, 4 km north of the town centre, with wide verandas overlooking the inlet, 12 rooms, some with en suite, communal kitchen facility. Not suitable for kids.

B-C **Marlo**, 17 Argyle Pde, Marlo, T5154 8201, an impressive pub and guesthouse with 3 en-suites.

An 11,000-ha, relatively undisturbed park extends from **Cape Conran** up to the Croajingolong.

C **Kuna Kuna**, 8 km from Orbost, T5154 1825. Working dairy farm and B&B with a real family atmosphere. Two twin rooms and a hearty breakfast.

C-D **Adobe Mudbrick Flats**, 14 Karbeethong Hill Av, just north of the Lodge, Mallacoota, T5158 0329, www.adobeholidayflats.com.au. Ten original and delightful hand-built self-contained flats with superb views of the inlet. This 70-acre property is shared by countless birds, possums, and even koalas. The very welcoming, knowledgeable hosts help make a stay here a real experience.

C-F **Parks Victoria**, T5154 8438, www.parks vic.gov.au. Manages cabins at the **Cape Conran**, sleeping up to 6 people, and a camping ground with fire places, toilets and bush showers. At peak times cabins are allocated by lottery, and campsites are booked months in advance.

D-E **Mallacoota**, 51 Maurice Av, Mallacoota, T5158 0455. Lively pub, particularly on a Fri, serves cheap light lunches and mid-range dinners, including a good range of vegetarian options. They have 20 motel rooms and also a few shared rooms designated for backpackers with a small but clean kitchen. Food daily 1200-1345, 1800-2000.

Camping Campsites in Croajingolong National Park must be booked at the parks office. Book well in advance for Dec-Jan and Easter. The main camping areas are all situated where rivers and creeks meet the coast, **Thurra River** (46 sites) and **Wingan Inlet** (24 sites) both have stunning locations but the sites are close together and do get very busy in peak summer and holiday periods. Still sleepy in comparison to the Prom though!

Buchan and around *p96*

B **Snowy River Wildernest**, T5154 1923, www. Snowyriverwildernest.com. An isolated 150-ha deer farm, 30 km towards Orbost, snuggled in a wooded valley on a beautiful stretch of the Snowy River, with 2 spacious but basic self-contained houses, sleeping 11 and 10. The cheap restaurant is in a rustic terrace by the main homestead which is friendly and cosy.

C **Buchan Valley Log Cabins**, Gelantipy Rd, just over the bridge, Buchan, T/F5155 9494, www.buchanlogcabins.com.au. Self-contained, 2-bedroom cabins, set on a hillside overlooking the valley. Serviceable furnishings, large deck.
E **Buchan Lodge**, Saleyard Rd, heading north, take first left after the bridge, Buchan, T5155 9421, www.buchanlodge.com.au. Excellent pine-log backpackers' hostel with warm, homely open kitchen and dining hall. Peaceful, rural location.
Camping D-F There is a camping ground in the Buchan Caves Reserve with cabins, bookings at the Parks Office, T5155 9264.

Eating

Wilson's Promontory National Park *p93*

Fishy Pub, on the highway, Fish Creek. Daily 1200-1400, 1800-2000. Has a reputation for excellent food, also live music most weekends.

Koonwarra Store, Koonwarra, T5664 2285. Daily 0800-1700, wine bar and diner Fri-Sat 1830-2130. Café/restaurant serving country breakfasts, lunches and dinners of the highest quality, and a takeaway. Book for meals at weekends.

Flying Cow, Fish Creek, T5683 2338. Wed-Sun 1000-1700. Warm and friendly place for wholesome lunches (mostly vegetarian), cakes and decent coffee. Also casual country dinners on Sat nights Jan-Apr.

Rhythm, 3 Bridge St, Foster, T5682 1612. Thu-Tue 0900-1700, daily 1800-2100 in peak summer. There aren't many places to eat but this café is excellent. Scrumptious breakfasts, casual lunches and cakes in a small, bright jazzy room.

Places to eat in the park are limited to lacklustre fast food from the café at Tidal River or **Yanakie's Roadhouse**, the closest decent food is in Fish Creek or Foster. There is also a shop at Tidal River stocking a limited range of groceries and petrol.

Gippsland Lakes *p94*

Miriam's, 3 Bulmer St, Lakes Entrance, T5155 3999. 1800-2130. First-floor, funky restaurant, great balcony tables in summer, abundant candles and candelabras in the darker months. Good seafood.

Fisherman's Wharf Pavilion, Paynesville, T5156 0366, is right on the water and a wonderful spot either summer or winter. A café by day with breakfasts and interesting light lunches, mid-range restaurant Thu-Sat to 2000.

Little Mariner's, 57 Metung Rd, Metung, T5156 2077. Tue 1800-2030, Wed-Thu 1200-2030, Fri-Sat 0830-2030, Sun 0830-1700. Also has great seafood, but a slightly more casual feel in 2 stylish rooms. Lots of fish and variety from a long specials menu. Breakfasts at weekends.

Wyanga Park Winery, 10 km north of Lakes Entrance on Baades Rd, has tastings and a colourful, characterful café open daily 1000-1700, doubling as a restaurant, Thu-Sat 1800-2000.

Central, Lakes Entrance, is a pub with a large bistro area. Surprisingly good meals, with a self-serve salad and veggie bar. Daily 1200-1400, 1800-2000.

Other than that you will find plenty of the traditional cafes and fish and chippies along the Esplanade.

East to Mallacoota *p95*

See also Sleeping above.
Despite its size and isolation Mallacoota has a few excellent places to eat.

The Tide, at the end of Maurice Av, Mallacoota, T5158 0100. Daily 1130-1345, 1700-2100. The smartest restaurant, with a lovely wooden deck facing the water. Mid-range seafood, fish and steak dishes, also good casual lunches.

Buchan and around *p96*

Willow Café, Buchan, T5155 9387. No fixed hours but generally open daily for breakfast, lunch and dinner. A decent place to eat.

Activities and tours

Wilson's Promontory National Park *p93*
Bay Connections, T1300 763739, www.bay connections.com.au, runs occasional day cruises from Port Welshpool that include stops at Waterloo Bay, Refuge Cove and cruising around the lighthouse, skull rock and a seal colony (Pt Welshpool $145, 7 hrs).
Bunyip Tours, T9531 0840, www.bunyip tours.com, is an eco-friendly outfit who take small groups out to Wilson's Promontory. It offers 2 and 4-day guided treks, camping along the way (2 days $195, 4 days around $425). Equipment, bar sleeping bags and a backpack, and food included.
Prom Coast Backpackers YHA, T5682 2171, runs a minibus to Tidal River from Foster on demand for a minimum of 2, ($30pp return, 50 mins).
Guided walks Surefoot Explorations, Cowes, T5952 1533, offers a day-trip with short walks (suitable for disabled) and can provide transport, packed lunches and equipment such as binoculars.

Gippsland Lakes *p94*
Virtually all activity revolves around the water, with several ways of getting out onto the 100s of square kilometres of lakes.
Lakes Entrance Paddle Boats, over the footbridge in Lakeside to the spit, T0419 552753. Can provide anything from a body board to a small catamaran, hourly/daily hire.
Victor Hire Boats, Marine Parade, T5155 3988. Motor boats can be hired from here.
Riviera Nautic, Metung, T5156 2243, www. rivnautic.com.au, is one of the most highly regarded tourist operators in Australia, offering superb service. They have various overnight motor-cruisers and sailboats for hire, from around $450 a day (minimum 2 days), which is the best way to experience the lakes.
The Spray, T0428 516055, is a 14-m-long historic ketch sailing out of Metung when there are sufficient numbers.
Clint's Ski School, Paynesville, T5156 6518, offers good value private lessons ($30 for 40 mins), multiple runs for the more experienced and ski-tube runs. Equipment supplied.

East to Mallacoota *p95*
Natural Adventures Mallacoota, T5158 0166, Unit 3, 57/59 Bastion Point Rd, Mallacoota, offers a good range of tours ($100 a day) in the national park. River and sea kayak tours get close to birds, water lizards or seals, or there are 4WD and mountain bike tours. Also bike and kayak hire (bike $25 day, kayak $45 day).
Tony Gray's Backpacker's Shuttle, T5158 1472, runs drop-off and pick-up services for walkers at Croajingolong National Park.
To explore the inlet at Mallacoota:
MV Lochard, Mallacoota, T0438 580667, is an old ferryboat taking larger groups on 2- to 3-hr cruises around the inlet while the *The Porkie Bess*, Mallacoota, T5158 0109, is a smaller wooden affair built in 1947 skippered by a knowledgeable local.
Wilderness Coast Ocean Charters, Mallacoota, T5158 0701, for trips further afield, including Gabo Island.

Buchan and around *p96*
Adventurama, T9819 1300, www.adventur ama.com.au, offers abseiling, caving and rafting. Their half to full day rafting options start from $75 to a 5-day 'self-sufficient' rafting trip down the Snowy River for around $1,000.
Victorian Canoe Association, T9459 4251, www. Canoevic.org.au, for information on canoeing trips and hire.

Top tips

State phone codes and time difference

There are no area phone codes. Use a state code if calling outside the state you are in. These are: 02 for ACT/NSW (08 for Broken Hill), 03 for VIC and 07 for QLD. Note that NSW operates daylight saving, which means that clocks go forward one hour from October and March.

Transport

Wilson's Promontory *p93*
From Fish Creek, **V~Line** buses leave from the BP service station for Dandenong and Melbourne (3 hrs) at 0800 Mon-Sat and 1537 Sun. Services east to Foster leave at 1927 Mon-Fri, 2132 Fri, 2130 Sat and 2040 Sun. From Forster, **V~Line** buses leave from Pulham's Store, Main St, for Fish Creek, Dandenong and Melbourne (3 hrs) at 0749 Mon-Sat and 1525 Sun.

Gippsland Lakes *p94*
For bus service timetables and fares throughout the Gippsland region contact **V~Line**, T136196, www.vlinepassenger.com.au. From **Bairnsdale**, buses run to **Sale** and **Melbourne** from the railway station at 0600, 1225, 1535 Mon-Fri, 1250 Sat and 1401 Sun. Buses leave from the corner of Main St and Bailey St for **Lakes Entrance** 4-5 times a day Mon-Fri, 1246 Sat, and from the railway station at 1345 Sun. **Canberra** buses leave the station at 1145 Mon, Thu and 1240 Sat, also stopping at Orbost and Cann River.

From **Lakes Entrance**, there are V~Line bus services to **Bairnsdale** and **Melbourne** (4-5 hrs) from the Post Office at 0515, 1140, 1455 Mon-Fri, 1205 Sat and 1320 Sun. An additional Bairnsdale-only service departs 1830 Mon-Fri. Buses leave for **Orbost**, **Cann River**, **Genoa** and NSW stops to **Narooma** or **Batemans Bay** at 1216 Mon-Fri, 1311 Sat and 1415 Sun. The **Canberra** buses leave at 1215 Mon, Thu and 1310 Sat, also stopping at Orbost and Cann River.

East to Mallacoota *p95*
From **Orbost**, V~Line bus services to **Lakes Entrance**, **Bairnsdale** and **Melbourne** (6-7 hrs) from the Post Office at 1100 Mon-Fri, 1120 Sat and 1225 Sun. Buses leave for **Cann River**, **Genoa** and NSW stops to **Narooma** or **Batemans Bay** at 1300 Mon-Fri, 1355 Sat and 1500 Sun. **Canberra** buses leave at 1300 Mon, Thu and 1355 Sat, also stopping at Cann River. From **Mallacoota**, **V~Line** bus services to **Orbost**, **Lakes Entrance** and **Melbourne** (8-9 hrs) from the Genoa general store, at 0900 Mon-Fri, 0920 Sat and 1025 Sun.

Buchan and around *p96*
Wild-Life Tours buses leave from Buchan Lodge, 1000 Thu, Sun for **Melbourne**, via **Lakes Entrance**, **Bairnsdale**, **Phillip Island** ($65, 5 hrs). Contact the Lodge, see Sleeping.

Sydney & South Coast NSW

The unmistakeable 'sails' of the Sydney Opera House

Don't miss...

1. Soaking up the atmosphere around **Circular Quay** ▸▸ *p109.*
2. People watching on **Bondi Beach** ▸▸ *p123.*
3. The viewpoints of the **Blue Mountains National Park** ▸▸ *p158.*
4. Making friends with the tame kangaroos at **Murramarang National Park** ▸▸ *p175.*
5. Winter snow or spring flowers at altitude in the **Kosciuszko National Park** ▸▸ *p179.*

Introduction

Sydney has come a long way since January 1788, when Captain Arthur Phillip, commander of the 'First Fleet', weighed anchor in Port Jackson and declared the entire continent a British penal colony. Where once was a collection of sorry-looking shacks and lock-ups full of desperate, hopeless convicts, stands a forest of glistening modern highrises. In their shadow, hordes of free-spirited, cosmopolitan city workers have every reason to be proud of their beautiful city, one that, in their eyes, is the 'real' capital of Australia.

One of the best about things Australia's largest city is that you are never too far away from water. To the south, are the little-known coastal towns of Jervis Bay, Batemans Bay and Narooma, all of which act as gateway to the greatest concentration of parks in the state. Less than two hours from Sydney is the Greater Blue Mountains region. Named after the visual effects of sunlight on eucalyptus oil released by the cloak of gum trees that liberally swathe the valleys and plateaus, the 'Blueys' now attract over one million visitors a year, that flock to delight in the stunning vistas, walk its numerous tracks or simply relax in its many quaint and characterful hotels and B&Bs.

Ratings

Landscape
★★★★

Relaxation
★★★★

Activities
★★★★

Wildlife
★★★★

Costs
$$$$

Sydney

Many adjectives and superlatives have been used to describe Sydney but the feeling stirred on seeing the city for the first time go beyond mere words. Seasoned travellers often complain that the world's great cities can seem a trifle disappointing; their icons somehow seeming smaller in reality than the imagination. But not so Sydney. That first sighting of its majestic harbour from Circular Quay, with the grand Opera House on one side and the mighty Harbour Bridge on the other, is one that always exceeds expectations. Aussie writer and TV personality Clive James aptly described it as looking 'like crushed diamonds'. The 2000 Olympics only added to the city's reputation. Vast sums were spent on inner-city rejuvenation, transportation and state-of-the-art sports venues, all of which provided the infrastructure and the stage for what many agree were the best games yet. Afterwards things just went back to normal in a city whose inhabitants know that their lifestyle is one of the best in the world. Sydney also has a whole lot to offer tourists, from its fascinating museums and galleries to world-class restaurants and beaches to its renowned 24-hour entertainment.

Getting there International and interstate flights; interstate and regional bus and rail networks.
Getting around Bus, train, harbour ferries and on foot.
Time required 3 days minimum.
Weather Warm and dry in summer, mild in winter.
Sleeping Full range of options.
Eating Huge range of global cuisines, from expensive to cheap and cheerful.
Activities and tours Harbour Bridge Climb, surfing lessons and sailing on the harbour.
★ Don't miss Soaking up the atmosphere around Circular Quay ›› *p109*.

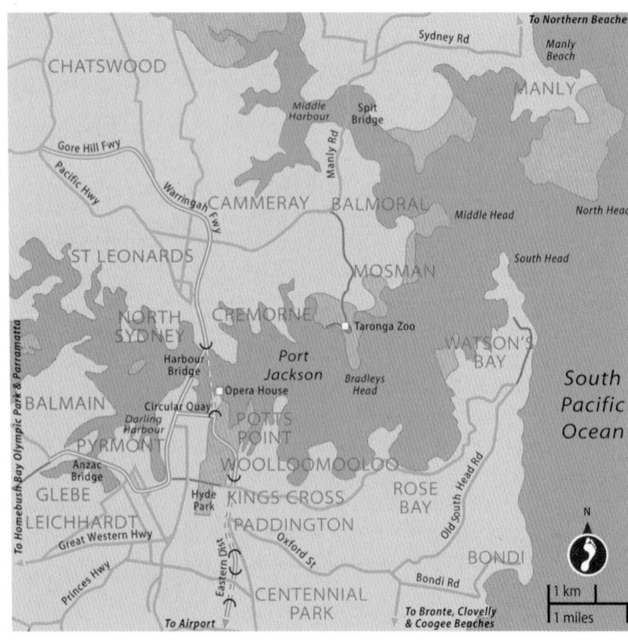

The Sydney Harbour Bridge and Opera House during the City Lights Festival 2004

Ins and outs

Getting there

Sydney's **Kingsford Smith Airport**, www.sydneyairport.com, is 9 km south of the city centre. Following its major overhaul for the Olympics, its negotiation is straightforward and the facilities are excellent. There is a **Tourism New South Wales** (T9667 6050) information desk in the main arrivals concourse where help is at hand to organize transport and accommodation bookings, flight arrival information and airport facilities. There are ATMs, a Thomas Cook and Travelex Foreign Exchange, car hire, a post office and medical centre (open 0400-2300). The Domestic Terminal is a short distance west of the International Terminal.

Public transport to the city centre is available within a short walk of the terminal building. **Airport Express**, T131500, daily 0500-2300, run services the city centre including the Central Railway Station, Circular Quay and Wynyard bus and rail stations (#300, $8, child $4, return $14, tickets from the driver) with connecting services to Kings Cross, Bondi, Coogee (No 350) and Darling Harbour, Glebe (No 352). There is a ticket booth in the main bus area. Taxis are available outside the terminal (south). A trip to the centre takes 30 minutes, $30. Various independent shuttle operators and courtesy accommodation shuttles also operate door-to-door from outside the terminal building, including **Kingsford Smith Transport**, T9666 9988, which runs every 20-30 minutes anywhere in the city (one-way $9 for adults and $14 return, $5 for children, four-12 years). There is also a rail link every 10-15 minutes to the city ($12).

All interstate and NSW state destination trains arrive and depart from Sydney's **Central Railway Station**, Eddy Avenue. **Countrylink** (T132232, www.countrylink.info), is the main interstate operator with a combination of coach and rail to all the main interstate and NSW destinations. They have a Travel Centre at Central Station (open 0630-2200), while Town Hall Station, Wynyard Station, Circular Quay and Bondi Junction all have on-the-spot **CityRail** information booths.The main **coach station** is in the Central Railway Station (T9212 3433, daily 0600-2230). Left-luggage and showers are available. » *p152*.

A couple find a quiet spot near Observatory Hill overlooking the Sydney Harbour Bridge

Getting around

Public transport in Sydney is generally efficient and convenient. The great hub of public transportation in the city centre revolves around Circular Quay at the base of the CBD. It is from there that most ferry (**Sydney Ferries**), and many suburban rail (**CityRail**) and bus (**Sydney Buses**) services operate. State Transit (STA) own and operate the principal suburban ferry and bus services. Other principal terminals are Wynyard on York Street for northbound bus and rail services, Town Hall on George Street, and the Central Railway Station. For information about all public transport, T131500 (0600-2200). For discount passes see box on page 153. Once in the city, ferry and rail route maps are available from information centres. The free leaflet *CBD Access Map Sydney*, available from the VICs or information booths, is a very useful map and guide for the disabled. » *p152.*

Tourist information

Beyond the Visitor Information booth at the airport international arrivals terminal, the first stop for any visitor should be the **Sydney Visitors Centre** ⓘ *106 George St, The Rocks, T9240 8788, www.sydneyvisitorcentre.com, 0900-1800.* The centre provides information, brochures, maps and reservations for hotels, tours, cruises, restaurants and other city-based activities. There is another principal VIC ⓘ *Darling Harbour, 33 Wheat Rd, T9240 8788, www.darlingharbour.com.* It offers much the same in services as the Rocks centre but has an emphasis on sights and activities within Darling Harbour itself. Neither centre issues public transport tickets. Manly, Parramatta, Homebush Bay and Bondi also have local information centres while small manned information booths are located on the corner of Pitt Street and Alfred Street, Circular Quay; opposite St Andrew's Cathedral near the Town Hall on George Street and on Martin Place, near Elizabeth Street.

The main daily newspaper in Sydney is the excellent *Sydney Morning Herald* which has comprehensive entertainment listings daily (see the pull-out Metro section on Friday) and regular city features. There are some excellent, free tourist brochures including the *Sydney Official Guide*, the *This Week in Sydney*, *Where Magazine*, the very interesting suburb-oriented *Sydney Monthly* and for the backpacker *TNT* (NSW Edition). For entertainment look out for *The Revolver* and *3-D World*. All these and others are available from the principal VICs, city centre information booths or from some cafés, newsagents and bookshops.

The wharf at Darling Harbour, Sydney

Circular Quay and the Rocks » pp127-155.

Sydney is without doubt one of the most beautiful cities in the world and the main reasons for this are its harbour, Opera House and Harbour Bridge. The first thing you must do on arrival, even before you throw your bags on a bed and sleep off the jet lag, is get yourself down to Circular Quay, day or night. Circular Quay also provides the main walkway from the historic and commercial Rocks area to the Opera House and the Botanical Gardens beyond. It is a great place to linger, take photographs or pause to enjoy the many bizarre street performers that come and go with the tides.

Sydney Opera House

ⓘ *T9250 7777, www.sydneyoperahouse.com, lines open Mon-Sat 0900-2030, for the latest schedules, and for tours, see below.*

Even the fiercest critics of modern architecture cannot fail to be impressed by the magnificent Sydney Opera House. Built in 1973, it is the result of the Danish architect, Jorn Utzon's revolutionary design, and every day, since this bizarre edifice was created, people have flocked to admire it. At times the steps and concourse seem more like the nave of some futuristic cathedral than the outside of an arts venue, with hordes of worshippers gazing in reverential awe. The Opera House is best viewed not only intimately from close up, but also from afar. Some of the best spots are from Mrs Macquarie's Point (end of the Domain on the western edge of farm Cove) especially at dawn, and from the Park Hyatt Hotel on the eastern edge of Circular Quay. Also any ferry trip east bound from Circular Quay will reveal the structure in many of its multi-faceted forms.

The Opera House has five performance venues ranging from the main, 2,690-capacity Concert Hall to the small Playhouse Theatre. Combined, they host about 2,500 performances annually – everything from Bach to Billy Connolly. The Opera House is also the principal performance venue for Opera Australia, The Australian Ballet and Contemporary Dance Companies, the Sydney Symphony Orchestra and the Sydney Theatre Company. There are two tours and three performance packages available. The Tour of the House provides an insider's view of selected theatres and foyers (every 30 minutes, daily 0900-1700, $23, children and concessions $16). The Backstage Tour, as the name suggests, takes you behind

Background

Sydney Harbour's wildlife

Amidst all the human activity on Sydney Harbour you may be surprised to learn that it is not unusual to see a penguin dodging the wakes of boats in the inner harbour. Incredible as it may seem, little blue penguins live and breed in Sydney Harbour, and at the harbour mouth, in late winter and spring, migrating humpback whales are also regularly seen. Also, around The Rocks at dusk and after dark, keep your eye open for huge flying foxes (fruit bats). These stray from the large colony resident in the Botanical Gardens.

the scenes and includes breakfast in the staff restaurant (two hours, daily 0700, $140), T9250 7250. The Performance Packages combine a range of performance, dining and tour options.

From the Opera House to the Rocks

At the eastern edge of the quay the new **Opera Quays** façade provides many tempting, if expensive, cafés and restaurants as well as an art gallery and a cinema. Look out for the '**Writers Walk**' which is a series of plaques on the main concourse with quotes from famous Australian writers.

Justice and Police Museum ⓘ *T9252 1144, www.hht.nsw.gov.au, Sat-Sun 1000-1700, Sat-Thu in Jan, $7, children $3*, housed in the former 1856 Water Police Court, features a magistrates court and former police cells, as well as a gallery, and historical displays, showcasing the antics and fate of some of Sydney's most notorious criminals. Nearby, facing the quay, is the former 1840 **Customs House** which now houses several exhibition spaces, café-bars and popular **Café Sydney**, see page 133. The **Object Galleries** (third floor) feature craft and design, while on the fourth floor, the **City Exhibition Space** showcases historical and contemporary aspects of the city with a 1:500 model of the CBD being its main attraction.

At the southwestern corner of Circular Quay it is hard to miss the rather grand art deco **Museum Of Contemporary Art** ⓘ *T9245 2400, www.mca.com.au, 1000-1700, free with a small charge for some visiting exhibitions, tours available Mon-Fri 1100 and 1400, Sat-Sun 1200 and 1330.* Opened in 1991, it maintains a collection of some of Australia's best contemporary works, together with works by renowned international artists like Warhol and Hockney. The museum also hosts regular national and international exhibitions.

A little further towards the Harbour Bridge is the rather incongruous **Cadman's Cottage**, overlooking the futuristic Overseas Passenger Terminal. Built in 1816, it is the oldest surviving residence in Sydney and was originally the former base for Governor Macquarie's boat crew. The cottage is named after the coxswain of the boat crew, John Cadman, who was sent to Australia for stealing a horse. The cottage is now the base for the **Sydney Harbour National Park Information Centre** ⓘ *110 George St, T9247 5033, www.nationalparks.nsw.gov.au, Mon-Fri 0900- 1630, Sat-Sun 1000-1630, free*, which is the main booking office and departure point for a number of harbour and island tours, see page 146.

The Rocks

Below the Bradfield Highway, which now carries a constant flow of traffic across the Harbour Bridge, is the historic Rocks village. It was the first site settled by European convicts and troops as early as 1788 and, despite being given a major facelift in recent decades (and losing its erstwhile reputation as the haunt of prostitutes, drunks and criminals), still retains much of its original architectural charm. Old and new is married in an eclectic array of shops, galleries, arcades, cafés and some mighty fine pubs and restaurants.

By far the best way to see the Rocks properly is to join the official **Rocks Walking Tour**, which is an entertaining and informative insight into the past and present, see page 146. **Rocks Market**, held every weekend, is perhaps the most popular in Sydney. It features a fine array of authentic arts, crafts, bric-a-brac and souvenirs. For live entertainment head for the **Rocks Square** where you'll find jazz, classical or contemporary music every day from midday for two hours. **Rocks Toy Museum** ⓘ *2-6 Kendall Lane, T9181 2311, Sat-Sun 1030-1700, free*, is housed in a former 1854 coachhouse and boasts over 3,000 toys spanning two centuries. Also in Kendall Lane is the **Puppet Theatre** with free shows at 1100, 1230 and 1400 weekends (daily during school holidays). To escape the crowds, head up Argyle Street, and the steps to Cumberland Street, taking a quick peek at the historic row of cottages at **Susannah Place**, 58-64 Gloucester Street, west side, below the popular Australian hotel and pub, before walking through the pedestrian walkway to **Observatory Park**, which offers some fine views of the bridge and is home to the **Sydney Observatory** ⓘ *T9241 3767, www.sydneyobservatory.com.au, exhibition daily 1000-1700, free, space theatre daily 1100, 1200, 1400 and 1530, $6, children $4, evening tour $15, children $10, concessions $12*, Australia's oldest. There is an interesting exhibition here covering early aboriginal and European astronomy, as well as 3D space theatre and telescope tours during the day, and evening tours offering a chance to view the heavens. From Observatory Park it is a short walk further along Argyle Street to enjoy a small libation and a bite to eat at the **Lord Nelson**, Sydney's oldest pub, see page 137, before walking north down Lower Fort Street to **Dawes Point Park** with its dramatic bridge perspectives. At 43 Lower Fort Street, you may like to dip into **Clydebank** ⓘ *T9241 4776, $8*, a restored mansion with its period furnishings and collection of former Rocks memorabilia.

The Harbour Bridge

From near or far, above or below, day or night, the Harbour Bridge is impressive and imposing. The 'Coat hanger', as it is often called, was opened in 1932, taking nine years to build, and it remains one of the longest single span bridges in the world. The deck supports eight lanes of traffic – accommodating around 150,000 vehicles a day – a railway line and a pedestrian walkway, which forms a crucial artery to the North Shore and beyond. For over six decades the best views from the bridge were accessed by foot from its 59-m high deck, but now the **'Bridge Climb'** experience, which ascends the 134-m high, 502-m long span, has become one of the city's 'must-do' activities, see page 146. Not as thrilling, but far cheaper, are the views on offer from the top of the **Southeastern Pylon Lookout**, which can be accessed from the eastern walkway and Cumberland Street, the Rocks. The pylon also houses the **Harbour Bridge Exhibition** ⓘ *T9240 1100, www.pylonlookout.com.au, 1000-1700, $8.50, children $3.*

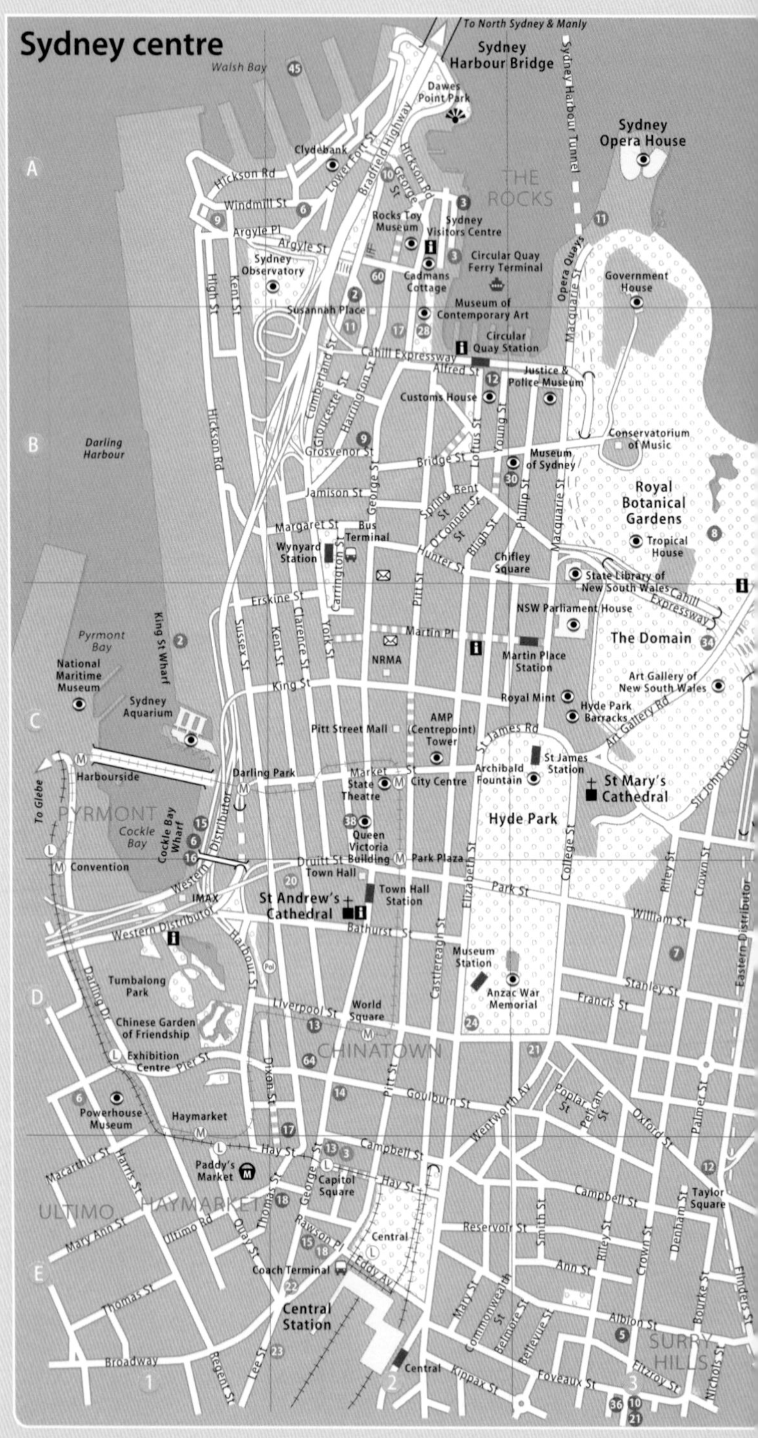

Sydney centre
To North Sydney & Manly
Sydney Harbour Bridge
Sydney Opera House
Walsh Bay
Dawes Point Park
THE ROCKS
Sydney Harbour Tunnel
Clydebank
Hickson Rd
Windmill St
Argyle Pl
Argyle St
Sydney Observatory
Rocks Toy Museum
Sydney Visitors Centre
Circular Quay Ferry Terminal
Cadmans Cottage
Museum of Contemporary Art
Government House
Susannah Place
Circular Quay Station
Cahill Expressway
Alfred St
Justice & Police Museum
Customs House
Conservatorium of Music
Darling Harbour
Grosvenor St
Bridge St
Museum of Sydney
Royal Botanical Gardens
Jamison St
Tropical House
Margaret St
Bus Terminal
Wynyard Station
Chifley Square
State Library of New South Wales
Erskine St
NSW Parliament House
Martin Pl
The Domain
Pyrmont Bay
King St Wharf
National Maritime Museum
NRMA
Martin Place Station
Art Gallery of New South Wales
King St
Royal Mint
Hyde Park Barracks
Sydney Aquarium
AMP (Centrepoint) Tower
Pitt Street Mall
St James Rd
St James Station
Harbourside
Darling Park
Market St
State Theatre
City Centre
Archibald Fountain
St Mary's Cathedral
To Glebe
PYRMONT
Cockle Bay
Cockle Bay Wharf
Western Distributor
Queen Victoria Building
Park Plaza
Hyde Park
Convention
Druitt St
Town Hall
IMAX
St Andrew's Cathedral
Town Hall Station
Park St
William St
Bathurst St
Museum Station
Tumbalong Park
Anzac War Memorial
Stanley St
Francis St
Liverpool St
World Square
Chinese Garden of Friendship
CHINATOWN
Exhibition Centre
Pier St
Goulburn St
Powerhouse Museum
Haymarket
Wentworth Av
Poplar St
Pelican St
Oxford St
Hay St
Campbell St
Paddy's Market
Capitol Square
Taylor Square
ULTIMO
HAYMARKET
Reservoir St
Mary Ann St
Ultimo Rd
Rawson Pl
Central
Coach Terminal
Eddy Av
Ann St
Thomas St
Central Station
Albion St
SURRY HILLS
Broadway
Kippax St
Foveaux St
Fitzroy St
Eastern Distributor
Sir John Young Cr

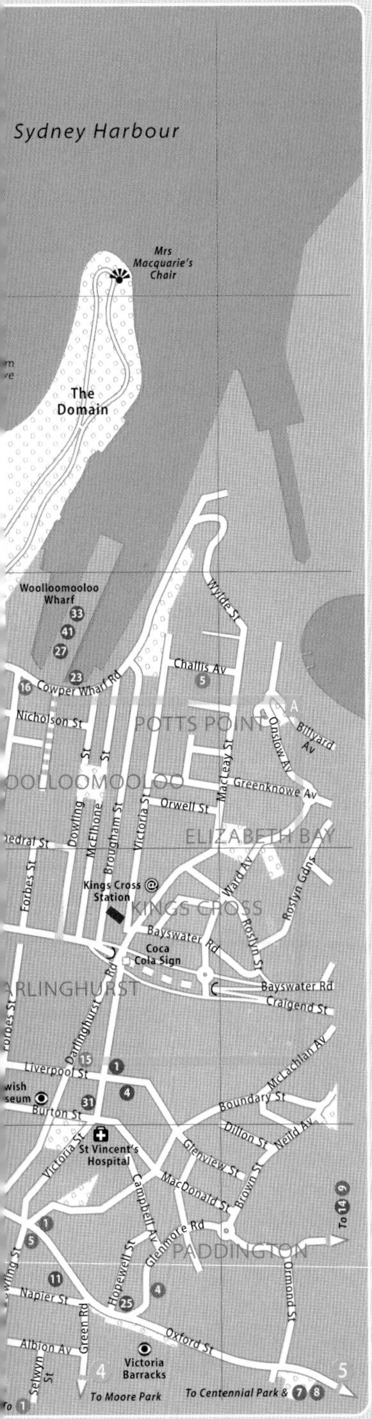

Sleeping

B&B Sydney Harbour **11** *B2*
Base Backpackers **20** *D2*
Capitol Square **3** *E2*
Challis Lodge **5** *C4*
Glasgow Arms **6** *D1*
Kangaroo Bakpak **1** *E4*
Lord Nelson **9** *A1*
Railway Square YHA **23** *E2*
Royal Sovereign **15** *D4*
Russell **17** *B2*
Sydney Central YHA **18** *E2*
Wake Up **22** *E2*
Y on the Park (YWCA) **21** *D3*

Eating

Australian Hotel **2** *A2*
BBQ King **64** *D2*
Bill's **4** *D4*
Bill's 2 **5** *E3*
Blackbird Café **6** *C1*
Botanical Gardens Café **8** *B3*
Brooklyn Hotel **9** *B2*
Café Centaur **11** *E4*
Café Sydney **12** *B2*
Casa Asturiana **13** *D2*
Chinta Ria – The Temple of Love **15** *C1*
Coast **16** *C1*
Dickson House Food Court **17** *D2*
Emperor's Garden Seafood **18** *E2*
Fuel **21** *E3*
Harry's Café de Wheels **23** *C4*
Hot Gossip **7** *E5*
Hyde Park Café **24** *D2*
Indian Home Diner **25** *E4*
La Renaissance **60** *A2*
Manta Ray **27** *C4*
MCA Café **28** *B2*
MG Garage **10** *E3*
MOS Café **30** *B3*
Oh! Calcutta! **31** *D4*
Otto **33** *C4*
Pavilion on the Park **34** *C3*
Prasit's Thai Takeaway **36** *E3*
Quay **3** *A2*
Royal Hotel **14** *E5*
Shimbashi Soba on the Sea **41** *C4*
The Tearoom **38** *D2*
Una's **1** *D4*
Wharf **45** *A2*

Bars & clubs

Albury Hotel **1** *E4*
Cargo **2** *C1*
Cruise **3** *A2*
Durty Nelly's **4** *E4*
Grand Pacific Blue Room **5** *E4*
Harbour View Hotel **6** *A2*
Hard Rock Café **7** *D3*
Hero of Waterloo **6** *A2*
Kitty O'Sheas **8** *E5*
Lord Dudley **9** *E5*
Mercantile **10** *A2*
Opera Bar **11** *A3*
Oxford Hotel **12** *E3*
Paddy McGuires **13** *E2*
Scruffy Murphys **14** *D2*
Scubar **15** *E2*
Woolloomooloo Bay Hotel **16** *C4*

LightRail Station Ⓛ
MonoRail Station Ⓜ

 From below, the best views of the bridge can be enjoyed from Hickson Road and Dawes Point (south side) and Milson's Point (north side).

Harbour Islands

Sydney harbour is scattered with a number of interesting islands, most of which hold some historical significance. **Fort Denison**, just east of the Opera House, is the smallest, and by far the most notorious. Its proper name is Pinchgut Island – so called because it was originally used as an open-air jail and a place where inmates were abandoned for a week and supplied with nothing except bread and water. In 1796, the Governor of NSW left a sobering warning to the new penal colony by displaying the body of executed murderer, Francis Morgan, from a gibbet on the island's highest point. The island was later converted to a fort in the 1850s (for fear of a Russian invasion during the Crimean war). There is a café and tours are available through the NPWS, from $22, T9247 5033. A little further east, off Darling Harbour, is **Clark Island**, a popular picnic retreat for those with their own transport (landing fee $5, must be pre-booked and paid). East again, off Rose Bay, is **Shark Island**, so called because of its shape. It served as a former animal quarantine centre and public reserve, before becoming part of the Sydney Harbour National Park in 1975. Access is via Matilda ferry leaving Circular Quay at the weekends (1030, 1145, 1345 and 1530) and costs $16 return, children $13.50. Picnic hampers can be bought for $20, T9247 5033. West of the bridge is the largest of the harbour's islands, **Goat Island**, site of a former gunpowder station and barracks. ▸▸ *p146.*

City centre ▸▸ *pp127-155.*

Many visitors find the city centre a chaotic place. It is cooler, owing to the highrises, but much noisier, disturbed by the collective din of corporate Sydney. Despite this, it is worth taking the plunge and joining the purposeful flood of humanity through its gargantuan corridors to discover some hidden gems.

Museum of Sydney

ⓘ *37 Philip St, T9251 5988, www.hht.nsw.gov.au, 0930-1700, $7 (2 for the price of 1 vouchers are available in the café), children $3, family $17.*

Museum of Sydney (MOS) was opened in 1995 and is a clever and imaginative mix of old and new. Built on the original site of Governor Phillip's former 1788 residence and incorporating some of the original archaeological remains, it contains uncluttered and well presented displays that explore the history and stories surrounding the creation and development of the city, from the first indigenous settlers, through the European invasion and up to the modern day. Art is an important aspect of this museum and as well as dynamic and temporary exhibitions incorporating a city theme there are some permanent pieces, the most prominent being the intriguing 'Edge of the Trees', a sculptural installation. Shop and café on site.

Macquarie Street

Macquarie Street forms the eastern fringe of the CBD and is Sydney's most historic street and the site of many important and impressive buildings. Heading north to south, near the Opera House, in its own expansive grounds, is **Government House** ⓘ *T9931 5222, Fri-Sun 1030-1500, guided tours only every ½ hr from 1030, free*, a Gothic revival building completed in 1837. The interior contains many period furnishings and features giving an insight into the lifestyle of the former NSW Governors and their families. Further up Macquarie Street, facing the Botanical Gardens, is the **State Library of New South Wales** ⓘ *T9273 1414, www.sl.nsw.gov.au, Mon-Fri 0900-2200, Sat 1100-1700*. Its architecture speaks for itself, but housed within its walls are some very significant historical documents, including most of the

(Left) The Sydney Harbour Bridge and Opera House from Milsons Point, North Shore; (Right) A corridor of high-rises in Sydney's CBD.

diaries of the First Fleet. Also worth a look is the foyer floor of the **Mitchell Library** entrance, one of three Melocco Brothers' mosaic floor decorations in the city. The library also hosts visiting exhibitions that are almost always worth visiting and offers an on-going programme of films, workshops and seminars. Shop and café on site.

Next door, the original north wing of the 1816 **Sydney Hospital**, formerly known as the Rum Hospital, is now the **NSW Parliament House**. Free tours are offered when Parliament is not in session, and when it is, you can visit the public gallery. The south wing of the hospital gave way to the **Royal Mint** ⓘ *small museum display open Mon-Fri 0900-1700, free*, in 1854 during the gold rush. The **Hyde Park Barracks**, on the northern edge of Hyde Park, were commissioned in 1816 by Governor Macquarie to house male convicts. It was later utilized as an orphanage and an asylum. The renovated buildings now house a modern museum displaying the history of the Barracks and work of the architect Francis Greenway. Tours are available, with the unusual option of staying overnight in convict hammocks.

Central Business District

Sydneysiders are very fond of the **AMP ('Centrepoint' or 'Sydney') Tower** ⓘ *100 Market St, T9223 1341, restaurant T8223 3800, observation deck Sun-Fri 0900-2230, Sat 0900-2330, $22, children $13.20, family $55*. This slightly dated landmark, built in 1981, has a distinctive 2,239 tonne golden turret. The view from one of Australia's highest buildings is mighty impressive. As well as enjoying the stunning vistas from the tower's **Observation Deck**, you can also experience a virtual 'Great Australian Expedition' tour, or dine in one of two revolving restaurants. Given the high price of entry to the Observation Deck alone, it goes without saying that you should keep an eye on the weather forecast and pick a clear day.

While you are on Market Street it is worth taking a peek at the impressive interior of the 1929 **State Theatre** ⓘ *49 Market St, T9373 6861, www.statetheatre.com.au*. Much of its charm is instantly on view in the entrance foyer, but the 20,000-piece glass chandelier and Wurlitzer organ housed in the auditorium steal the show. Just around the corner from the State Theatre, on George Street, taking up an entire city block, is the grand **Queen Victoria Building**

(Left) Hopefully not a case of 'been there, done that' near Manly, Sydney; (Right) Ornate stairwells and stained glass windows are a major feature of Sydney's Queen Victoria Building (QVB)

ⓘ *T9264 9209, www.qvb.com. au, Mon-Wed, Fri-Sat 0900-1800, Thu 0900-2100, Sun 1100-1700, tours available Mon-Sat 1130 and 1430, Sun 1200 and 1430.* Built in 1898 to celebrate Queen Victoria's Golden Jubilee and to replace the original Sydney Markets, the QVB (as it is known) is a prime shopping venue, containing three floors of boutique outlets, but the spectacular interior is well worth a look in itself. At the northern end is the four-tonne **Great Australian Clock**, the world's largest hanging animated turret clock. It is a stunning creation that took four years to build at a cost of $1.5 mn. Once activated with a $4 donation (which goes to charity) the clock comes alive with moving picture scenes and figurines. At the southern end is the equally impressive **Royal Clock**, which includes the execution of King Charles I. There are also galleries, historical displays, restaurants and cafés.

Across the street from the QVB is the **Town Hall** ⓘ *corner of George St and Druitt St, T9265 9007, 0900-1700, free*, built in 1888. It also has an impressive interior, the highlight of which is the 8,000-pipe organ, reputed to be the largest in the world. Self-guided tour brochure available in the foyer. Next door to the Town Hall is the newly renovated **St Andrew's Cathedral** ⓘ *T9265 1661, free, built between 1819 and 1868*, with regular choir performances.

Hyde Park and around

Hyde Park is a great place to escape the mania of the city and includes the historic grandeur of the 1932 Archibald Fountain and 1934 **Anzac War Memorial**. It's also great for people-watching. At the north-eastern edge of the park, on College Street, is **Saint Mary's Cathedral** ⓘ *crypt 1000-1600, free tours on Sun afternoons*, which is well worth a look inside. It has an impressive and wonderfully peaceful interior, with the highlight being the Melocco Brothers' mosaic floor in the crypt. Further south along College Street is the **Australian Museum** ⓘ *T9320 6000, www.austmus.gov.au, 0930-1700, $10, children $5, family $17.50 (exhibitions extra), Explorer Bus route, stop 7*, established in 1827, but doing a fine job of keeping pace with the cutting edge of technology, especially the modern Biodiversity and Indigenous Australians Displays. Try to coincide your visit to the Indigenous Australians section with the live didgeridoo playing and very informative lectures. Kids will love the Search and Discover section.

Royal Botanical Gardens and Macquarie Point

The 30-ha Botanical Gardens ⓘ *0700-sunset, free*, offers a wonderful sanctuary of peace and greenery only a short stroll east of the city centre. It boasts a fine array of mainly native plants and trees, an intriguing pyramid shaped **Tropical House** ($5), roses and succulent gardens, rare and threatened species and decorative ponds, as well as a resident colony of wild flying foxes (fruit bats). There is a visitors centre and shop located in the southeastern corner of the park. There you can pick up a self-guided tour leaflet or join a free organized tour at 1030 daily. A specialist Aboriginal tour, exploring the significance of the site to the Cadigal (the original Aboriginal inhabitants) and the first European settlers' desperate attempts to cultivate the site, is available on request. **Gardens Café and Restaurant** is one of the best places to observe the bats. You'll see lots of tropical ibis birds around the gardens – the descendants of a tiny group that escaped from Taronga Zoo.

From the Botanical Gardens it is a short stroll to Macquarie Point, which offers one of the best views of the Opera House and Harbour Bridge. Mrs Macquarie's chair is the spot where the first Governor's wife came to reflect upon the new settlement. One can only imagine what her reaction would be now.

The Domain and the Art Gallery of New South Wales

ⓘ *Art Gallery Rd, The Domain, T9225 1744, www.art gallery.nsw.gov.au, 1000-1700 and Wed 1700-2100, free (small charge for some visiting exhibitions).*

Inside its grand façade, Australia's largest gallery houses the permanent works of many of the country's most revered contemporary artists as well as a collection of more familiar international names like Monet and Picasso. The Yiribana Gallery, in stark contrast, showcases a fine collection of Aboriginal and Torres Strait Islander works and is a major highlight. The new Asian Gallery is also well worth a look. The main gallery also features a dynamic programme of major visiting exhibitions, and there is a great bookshop and café. Be sure not to miss the quirky and monumental matchsticks installation by the late Brett Whiteley, the city's most celebrated artists, behind the main building. More of his work can be seen at the Brett Whiteley Museum in Surry Hills, see page 122. The Gallery is on the Sydney Explorer Bus route, stop 6. The Domain, the pleasant open park sitting between the Art Gallery and Macquarie Place, was declared a public space in 1810. It is used as a free concert venue especially over Christmas and during the **Sydney Festival**.

Darling Harbour and Chinatown » pp 127-155.

Created to celebrate Sydney's Bicentennial in 1988, revitalized Darling Harbour was delivered with much aplomb and has proved such a success that even the waves seem to show their appreciation. Day and night, ferries and jetcats bring hordes of visitors to marvel at its modern architecture and aquatic attractions, or to revel in its casino and trendy waterside bars and restaurants. Framed against the backdrop of the CBD, it is intricately colourful, urban and angular. In contrast, the Chinese Garden of Friendship towards the southwestern fringe provides a little serenity before giving way to the old and chaotic enclave of Chinatown, the epicentre of Sydney's Asian community and the city's most notable living monument to its cosmopolitan populace.

Sydney Aquarium

ⓘ *Aquarium Pier, T8251 7800, www.sydneyaquarium.com.au, 0900-2200, $26, children $13.50, concessions $14-16, Explorer bus stop 23.*

This modern, well-presented aquarium, has over 650 species, but it's not all about fish. On show is an imaginative array of habitats housing saltwater crocodiles, frogs, seals, penguins

Outdoor art installations dominate the walkways of Darling Harbour

and platypuses. The highlight of the aquarium is the Great Barrier Reef Oceanarium: a huge tank that gives you an incredible insight into the world's largest living thing. Of course, many visit the aquarium to come face-to-face with some of Australia's deadliest sea creatures, without getting their feet, or indeed their underwear, wet. There is no doubt that such beauty and diversity has its dark side, as the notorious box-jellyfish, cone shell, or rockfish will reveal.

National Maritime Museum

ⓘ *2 Murray St, T9298 3777, www.anmm.gov.au, 0930-1700, free except Warship & submarine $18, children and concessions $8; heritage galleries and James Craig $10, children and concessions $6; combination ticket $30, children and concessions $16.*

The museum, designed to look like the sails of a ship, offers a fine mix of old and new. For many, its biggest attractions are without doubt the warship *MHS Vampire* and submarine *HMAS Onslow*, the centrepiece of a fleet of old vessels sitting outside on the harbour. Both can be thoroughly explored with the help of volunteer guides. The interior contains a range of displays exploring Australia's close links with all things nautical, from the early navigators and the *First Fleet*, to the ocean liners that brought many waves of immigrants. Other attractions include a café, sailing lessons and a range of short cruises on historical vessels. Don't miss the beautifully restored, 1874 square rigger, *The James Craig*, which is moored to the north of the museum at Wharf 7, when not out on pleasure sails. It is easily reached by foot across the Pyrmont Bridge, or by Monorail, LightRail or the Sydney Explorer bus, stop No 20.

Sydney Fish Market

ⓘ *T9004 1143, www.sydneyfishmarket.com.au, tours operate Mon-Fri from 0700.*

For anyone interested in sea creatures, the spectacle of the Sydney Fish Market is recommended. Every morning from 0530, nearly 3,000 crates of seafood are auctioned to a lively bunch of 200 buyers using a computerized clock system. The best way to see the action, and more importantly the incredible diversity of species, is to join a tour group, which will give you access to the auction floor. Normally the general public are confined to the viewing deck high above the floor. Also within the market complex are cafés, some excellent seafood eateries and a superb array of open markets where seafood can be bought at competitive prices. Sydney Light Rail runs by, or catch bus routes 443 from Circular Quay and 501 from Town Hall.

Powerhouse Museum

ⓘ *500 Harris St, Ultimo, T9217 0111, www.powerhousemuseum.com, 1000-1700, $10, children $4, concessions $5.*
With nearly 400,000 items collected over 120 years, the Powerhouse is Australia's largest museum and half a day is barely enough to cover its floors. Housed in the former Ultimo Power Station, there is an impressive range of memorabilia, from aircraft to musical instruments, mainly with an emphasis on Australian innovation and achievement, and covering a wide range of general topics from science and technology to transportation, social history, fashion and design. Shop and café on site. Access by Monorail, LightRail or Sydney Explorer bus, stop No 17.

Chinatown

The Chinese have been an integral part of Sydney culture since the Gold Rush of the mid-1800s, though today Chinatown is also the focus of many other Asian cultures, including Vietnamese, Thai, Korean and Japanese. The district offers a lively diversion, with its heart being the Dixon Street pedestrian precinct, between the two pagoda gates facing Goulburn Street and Hay Street. Here, and in the surrounding streets, you will find a wealth of Asian shops and restaurants. At the northwestern corner of Chinatown is the **Chinese Garden of Friendship** ⓘ *0930-dusk. $6, children $3, families $15*, which was gifted to NSW by her sister Chinese province, Guangdong, to celebrate the Australian Bicentenary in 1988. It contains all the usual beautiful craftsmanship, landscaping and aesthetics.

In stark contrast is **Paddy's Market**, on the corner of Hay Street and Thomas Street, one of Sydney's largest, oldest and liveliest markets, though somewhat tacky. The best time to arrive is about 0600. Things start to wind up by about 1000.

City West » pp 127-155.

Glebe

To the southwest of Darling Harbour, beyond Ultimo, and separated by the campus of **Sydney University** (Australia's oldest), are Glebe and Newtown. Glebe prides itself on having a New Age village atmosphere, where a cosmopolitan, mainly student crowd sits in the laid-back cafés, browses old-style bookshops or bohemian fashion outlets, or seeks the latest therapies in alternative health shops. **The Saturday market** ⓘ *Glebe Public School, Glebe Point Rd, T9660 2370, Sat 0800-1600*, provides an outlet for local crafts people to sell their work as well as bric-a-brac, clothes etc. Glebe can be reached by bus from George Street in the city (431 or 434).

Newtown

South beyond the university is **King Street**, the hub of Newtown's idiosyncratic range of shops, cafés and restaurants. Here you can purchase anything from a black leather cod-piece to an industrial size brass Buddah, dribble over the menus of a vast range of interesting eateries, or simply idle over a latte and watch a more alternative world go by. A few hour's exploration, Sunday brunch or an evening meal in Newtown's King Street is recommended. Don't miss **Gould's Secondhand Bookshop** at 32 King Street, which is an experience in itself. Newtown can be reached by bus from Loftus Street on Circular Quay, or George Street (422, 423, 426-428). The Newtown Railway Station is on the Inner West/Bankstown (to Liverpool) lines.

Leichhardt

Although receiving less attention than the eccentricities of Glebe and Newtown, Leichhardt is a pleasant suburb, famous for its Italian connections and subsequently its eateries and cafés. There are numerous places on Norton Street to enjoy a fine expresso, gelato or the full lasagne. Try Leichhardt institution **Bar Italia** at No 169. Catch bus 400 or 445 from the QVB in the city to get here.

Balmain

Straddling Johnstons Bay and connecting Darling Harbour and Pyrmont with the peninsula suburb of Balmain is Sydney's second landmark bridge, the **Anzac Bridge**, opened in 1995. It is a modern and strangely attractive edifice, which makes an admirable attempt to compete with the mighty Harbour Bridge. The former working-class suburb of Balmain has undergone a quiet metamorphosis to become an area with some of the most sought after real estate in Sydney. The main drag of **Darling Street** now boasts a eclectic range of gift shops, modern cafés, restaurants and pubs, which provide a pleasant half-day escape from the city centre. Try the cosy **Sir William Wallace Hotel**, 31 Cameron Street, or the more traditional and historic 1857 **Dry Dock Hotel**, corner of Cameron and College streets. There's a popular Saturday market in the grounds of St Andrew's Church. Arrive by bus from the QVB, numbers 441-444, or ferry from Circular Quay, Wharf 5.

Homebush Bay Olympic Park

ⓘ *Centre, 1 Herb Elliot Ave, near Olympic Park Railway Station, T9714 7545, www.sydneyolympicpark.com.au, 0800-1800.*

Although the vast swathes of Sydney's Western Suburbs remain off the radar for the vast majority of tourists, there are a few major and minor sights worth a mention. Topping the list is of course the multi-million dollar Homebush Bay Olympic Park with its mighty stadium, the centrepiece of a vast array of architecturally stunning sports venues and public amenities. Tours are available of the venues, see the visitor centre on Herb Avenue for details. The Park lies about 14 km west of the centre and is best reached by train or RiverCat from Circular Quay (Wharf 5) to Homebush Bay Wharf. Olympic Explorer Bus leaves every 15 minutes between 0920-1700 daily from the VIC on Herb Elliot Avenue (T131500).

Telstra Stadium (formerly Stadium Australia) was the main focus of the games, being the venue for the opening and closing ceremonies, as well as track and field and soccer events. Although the Olympic flame has long been extinguished, it remains an important national venue for international and national rugby union, rugby league, Aussie rules football and soccer matches. Olympic Park will also be the main venue for Catholic World Youth Day and associated visit of Pope Benedict XVI in 2008. The opening ceremony is expected to attract well over 100,000 worshipers.

Next door is the state-of-the-art **Sydney Superdome** which hosted basketball and gymnastics during the games and now offers a huge indoor arena for a range of public events from music concerts to Australia's largest agricultural show, the Royal Easter Show. Perhaps the most celebrated venue during the games was the **Sydney International Aquatic Centre** where the triumphant Aussie swimming team took on the world and won with the help of such stars as Thorpe and Klim. The complex still holds international swimming and diving events and is open to the public. The Olympic Park has many other state-of-the-art sports facilities and is surrounded by superb parkland. **Bicentennial Park** ⓘ *T9763 1844*, is a 100-ha mix of dry land and conservation wetland and a popular spot for walking, jogging, birdwatching or simply feeding the ducks.

The Sydney Harbour Bridge and Opera House during the City Lights Festival 2004

Parramatta and around

About 6 km further west from Homebush is Parramatta, often dubbed the city within the city, a culturally diverse centre which boasts some of the nation's most historic sites. When the First Fleeters failed in their desperate attempts to grow crops in what is now the city centre, they penetrated the upper reaches of the Parramatta River and established a farming settlement, first known as Rose Hill, before reverting to its original Aboriginal name. The oldest European site is **Elizabeth Farm** ⓘ *70 Alice St, Rosehill, T9635 9488, 1000-1700, $7, children $3, family $17*, a 1793 colonial homestead built for John and Elizabeth Macarthur, pioneers in the Australian wool industry. The homestead contains a number of interesting displays and is surrounded by a recreated 1830s garden. Also of interest is the 1799 **Old Government House** ⓘ *T9635 8149, Mon-Fri 1000-1600, Sat-Sun 1100-1600, $12*, in Parramatta Park. It is Australia's oldest public building and houses a fine collection of Colonial furniture. **Experiment Farm Cottage** ⓘ *9 Ruse St, T9635 5655, Tue-Fri 1030-1530, Sat-Sun 1130-1530, $5.50*, is the site of the colonial government's first land grant to former convict James Ruse in 1791. The cottage itself dates from 1834. The **Parramatta River** which quietly glides past the city is without doubt its most attractive natural attraction and it features in a number of heritage walking trails. These and many other historical details are displayed at the **Parramatta Heritage and VIC** ⓘ *346a Church St, T8839 3311, www.parracity.nsw.gov.au, daily 0900-1700.*

City East » *pp 127-155.*

Kings Cross

Even before arriving in Sydney you will have probably heard of Kings Cross, the notorious hub of Sydney nightlife and the long-established focus of sex, drugs and rock and roll. Situated near the navy's Woolloomooloo docks 'The Cross' (as it's often called) has been a favourite haunt of visiting sailors for years. The main drag, **Darlinghurst Road**, is the focus of the action, while Victoria Road is home to a rash of Backpacker hostels. At the intersection of both, and the top of William Street, which connects The Cross with the city, is the huge Coca Cola sign, a popular meeting point. The best time to visit The Cross is in the early hours when the bars, the clubs and ladies of the night are all in full swing. It is enormously popular with backpackers and Sydneysiders alike and can provide a great (and often memorable) night out. It is also a great place to meet people, make contacts, find work and even buy a car. Amidst all the mania there are a number of notable and more sedate sights in and around Kings Cross. **Elizabeth Bay House** ⓘ *7 Onslow Av, Elizabeth Bay, T9356 3022, www.hht.nsw.gov.au, Tue-Sun 1000-1630, $7, children $3, family $17*, is a revival style estate that was built by popular architect John Verge for Colonial secretary Alexander Macleay in 1845. The interior is restored and faithfully furnished in accordance with the times and the house has a great outlook across the harbour. By bus Sydney Explorer stop No 9 or regular bus services Nos 311, 323-325, 327, 333.

Woolloomooloo

To the northwest of Kings Cross, through the quieter and more upmarket sanctuary of Potts Point, is the delightfully named suburb of Woolloomooloo. 'Woo' is the main east coast base for the Australian Navy and visiting sailors also weigh anchor here, heading straight for the Kings Cross souvenir shops. Other than the warships and a scattering of lively pubs, it is the **Woolloomooloo Wharf** and a pie cart that are the major attractions. The new wharf has a rash of fine restaurants which are a popular dining alternative to the busy city centre. If the wharf restaurants are beyond your budget, nearby is one of Sydney's best cheap eateries. **Harry's Café de Wheels**, near the wharf entrance (see page 136), is an institution, selling its own $3 range of meat, mash, pea and gravy pies 24 hours a day (well, almost).

Darlinghurst and Surry Hills

The lively suburb of Darlinghurst fringes the city to the west, Kings Cross to the north and Surry Hills to the south. Both Darlinghurst and Surry Hills offer some great restaurants and cafés with Darlinghurst Road and Victoria Street, just south of Kings Cross, being the main focus. Here you will find some of Sydney's most popular eateries. **Jewish Museum** ⓘ *148 Darlinghurst Rd, T9360 7999, www.sydneyjewishmuseum.com.au Sun-Thu 1000-1600, Fri 1000-1400, $10, children $6*, has displays featuring the holocaust and history of Judaism in Australia.

Surry Hills is a mainly residential district and does not have quite the pizzaz of Darlinghurst, but it is well known for its very traditional Aussie pubs that seem to dominate every street corner. One thing not to miss is the **Brett Whiteley Museum and Gallery** ⓘ *2 Raper St, T9225 1881, Sat-Sun 1000-1600, $7, children and concessions $5*. The museum is the former studio and home of the late Whiteley, one of Sydney's most popular contemporary artists. Both places can be reached by foot from the city via William Street, Liverpool Street or Oxford Street or by bus Nos 311-399.

Paddington

The big attraction in Paddington is **Oxford Street**, which stretches east from the city and southwest corner of Hyde Park to the northwest corner of Centennial Park and Bondi Junction. The city end Oxford Street, surrounding Taylor Square, is one of the most happening areas of the city with a string of cheap eateries, cafés, restaurants, clubs and bars. It is also a major focus for the city's gay community. Then as Oxford Street heads west into Paddington proper it becomes lined with boutique clothes shops, art and book shops, cafés and a number of good pubs. Many people coincide a visit to Oxford Street with the colourful **Paddington Market** ⓘ *395 Oxford St, T9331 2923*, held every Saturday from 1000. Behind Oxford Street, heading north, are leafy suburbs lined with Victorian terrace houses, interspersed with commercial art galleries and old pubs, all of which are hallmarks of Paddington.

South of Oxford Street is the **Victoria Barracks,** a base for British and Australian Army battalions since 1848. It remains fully functional and visitors can see a flag-raising ceremony, a marching band and join a guided tour on Thursdays at 1000.

Just to the south of the Barracks, in **Moore Park**, is the famous **Sydney Cricket Ground (SCG)** and, next door, the **Sydney Football Stadium (SFS)**. The hallowed arena of the SCG is a veritable cathedral of cricket, considered by many as Australia's national sport. In winter the SCG is taken over by the Sydney Swans Australian Rules Football team. The Sydney Football Stadium was, for many years, the focus of major national and international, rugby union, league and soccer matches but it now plays second fiddle to the mighty (and far less atmospheric) Telstra Stadium in Homebush. Tours of both stadiums are available to the public, T9380 0383.

Fringing the two stadiums and Fox Studios Complex is **Centennial Park**, the city's largest green space. It provides a vast area for walking, cycling, horse riding, roller blading and birdwatching. The Parklands Sports Centre also provides tennis, roller-hockey and basketball. In late summer there is a nightly outdoor **Moonlight Cinema** programme, which often showcases old classics (T9339 6699).

Paddington can be reached by foot from the southeast corner of Hyde Park via Oxford Street. By bus 378-382, or the Bondi and Bay Explorer (stop No 14).

Watson's Bay

Watson's Bay, on the leeward side of **South Head**, guarding the mouth of Sydney Harbour, provides an ideal city escape and is best reached by ferry from Circular Quay. As well as being home to one of Sydney's oldest and most famous seafood restaurants – **Doyles** – it offers some quiet coves, attractive swimming beaches and peninsula walks. The best beaches are to be found at **Camp Cove** about 10 minutes walk north of the ferry terminal. A little further north is **Lady Bay Beach**, which is very secluded and a popular naturist beach. The best walk in the area is the one- to two-hour jaunt to the 1858 **Hornby Lighthouse** and South Head itself, then south to the **HMAS Watson Naval Chapel** and the area known as **The Gap**. The area also boasts some interesting historical sites. Camp Cove was used by Governor Phillip as an overnight stop before reaching Port Jackson in the Inner Harbour. **Vaucluse House** ⓘ *Wentworth Rd, T9388 7922, Tue-Sun 1000-1630, \$7, children \$3, family \$17*, was built in 1827 and is a fine example of an early colonial estate. Many people spend a morning exploring Watson's Bay before enjoying a leisurely lunch at **Doyles**, which sits just above the beach and ferry terminal on Marine Parade, or next door at the **Watsons Bay Hotel**, a more casual affair offering equally good views of the city skyline and a superb outdoor BBQ area (see Eating, page 137). Take the ferry from Circular Quay Wharves 2 and 4, or take bus 342 or 325.

Bondi, Bronte and Coogee beaches

Bondi Beach is by far the most famous of Sydney's many ocean beaches. Its hugely inviting stretch of sand is a prime venue for surfing, swimming and sunbathing. Behind the beach, Bondi's bustling waterfront and village offers a tourist trap of cafés, restaurants, bars, surf and souvenir shops. For years Bondi has been a popular suburb for alternative lifestylers and visiting backpackers keen to avoid the central city. It is also the place to see or be seen by all self-respecting beautiful people. If you intend swimming at Bondi note that, like every Australian beach, it is subject to dangerous rips so always swim between the yellow and red flags, clearly marked on the beach. Watchful lifeguards, also clad in yellow and red, are on hand. Bondi Beach is the focus of wild celebrations on Christmas Day with one huge beach party, usually culminating in a mass naked dash into the sea.

To the south of Bondi Beach and best reached by a popular coastal walkway, is the small oceanside suburb of **Bronte**. This little enclave offers a smaller, quieter and equally attractive beach with a number of very popular cafés frequented especially at the weekend for brunch.

Bondi Beach, the most famous stretch of sand in Australia

A little further south is **Clovelly**, which has another sheltered beach especially good for kids and snorkelling. Many people finish their walk at **Coogee**, which has a fine beach and bustling waterfront. Although playing second fiddle to Bondi, it is also a popular haunt for those keen to stay near the beach and outside the centre. Bondi can be reached by car from the city, via Oxford Street, by the Bondi and Bay Explorer, or buses 321, 322, 365, 366, 380. By rail get to Bondi Junction (Illawara Line) then take the bus (as above). For Coogee buses 372-374 and 314-315.

City North » *pp 127-155.*

North Sydney and surrounds

On the northern side of the Harbour Bridge a small stand of highrise buildings with neon signs heralds the mainly commercial suburb of North Sydney. There is little here for the tourist to justify a special visit, but nearby, the suburb of **McMahons Point**, and more especially **Blues Point Reserve**, on the shores of Lavender Bay, offers fine city views. Another good vantage point is right below the bridge at **Milsons Point**. **Kirribilli** is a serene little suburb lying directly to the east of the bridge. Admiralty House and **Kirribilli House**, the Sydney residences of the Governor General and the Prime Minister, sit overlooking the Opera House on Kirribilli Point. Both are closed to the public and are best seen from the water.

Mosman

Mosman has a very pleasant village feel and its well-heeled residents are rightly proud. Situated so close to the city centre, it has developed into one of the most exclusive and expensive areas of real estate in the city. However, don't let this put you off. Mosman, in unison with its equally comfy, neighbouring, beachside suburb of **Balmoral**, are both great escapes by ferry from the city centre and offer some fine eateries, designer clothes shops, walks and beaches, plus one of Sydney's 'must-see' attractions, **Taronga Zoo**. Mosman is best reached by ferry from Circular Quay (Wharf 4) to the Mosman Bay where a bus awaits to take you up the hill to the commercial centre.

The beach at Manly, North Shore, Sydney

Taronga Zoo

ⓘ *T1900 920218, www.zoo.nsw.gov.au, 0900-1700. $30, child $16.50, concessions $21. A Zoo Pass combo ticket (including ferry transfers and zoo), $36, child $18. Best reached by ferry from Circular Quay (Wharf 2), every half hour Mon-Fri from 0715-1845, Sat 0845-1845 and Sun 0845-1730.*

First opened in 1881 in the grounds of Moore Park, south of Centennial Park, before being relocated to Bradley's Head, Mosman in 1916, Taronga contains all the usual suspects of the zoological world. It also has the huge added attraction of perhaps the best location and views of any city zoo in the world. You will almost certainly need a full day to explore the various exhibits on offer and there are plenty of events staged throughout the day to keep both adults and children entertained. The best of these is the Kodak Bird Show which is staged twice daily in an open-air arena overlooking the city. If you are especially interested in wildlife it pays to check out the dynamic programme of specialist public tours on offer. The 'Night Zoo' tour after hours is especially popular. Taronga is built on a hill and the general recommendation is to go up to the main entrance then work your way back down to the lower gate. Alternatively for a small additional charge on entry you can take a scenic gondola ride to the main gate.

Balmoral, Middle Head and Bradley's Head

Balmoral Beach is one of the most popular and sheltered in the harbour. Here, more than anywhere else in the city, you can observe Sydneysiders enjoying something that is quintessentially Australian – the early morning, pre-work dip. Balmoral Beach overlooks **Middle Harbour**, whose waters infiltrate far into the suburbs of the North Shore. On **Middle Head**, which juts out into the harbour beyond Mosman, you will find one of Sydney's best and most secluded naturist beaches – **Cobblers Beach**. The atmosphere is friendly and the crowd truly cosmopolitan, though the less extrovert among you should probably avoid the peninsula on the eastern edge of the beach. Access is via a little known track behind the softball pitch near the end of Military Road. You can also walk to the tip of Middle Head, where old wartime fortifications look out across North Head and the harbour entrance, or enjoy the walk to the tip of **Bradleys Head**, below the zoo, with its wonderful views of the city.

Manly

Manly is by far the most visited suburb on the North Shore and is practically a self-contained holiday resort, offering an oceanside sanctuary away from the manic city centre. The heart of the community sits on the neck of the **North Head** peninsula, which guards the entrance of Sydney Harbour. **Manly Beach** is very much the main attraction. At its southern end, an attractive oceanside walkway connects Manly Beach with two smaller, quieter alternatives, **Fairy Bower Beach** and **Shelly Beach**. As you might expect, Manly comes with all the tourist trappings, including an attractive, tree-lined waterfront, fringed with cafés, restaurants, souvenir and surf shops and a wealth of accommodation options.

Connecting Manly Beach with the ferry terminal and **Manly Cove** (on the western or harbour side) is the **Corso**, a fairly tacky pedestrian precinct lined with cheap eateries, bars and souvenir shops. Its only saving grace being the market held at its eastern end every weekend. **Oceanworld** ⓘ *T8251 7877, www.oceanworld.com.au, 1000-1730, $18, children $13, concessions $10, regular tours available, 'Swim with the sharks' $235, sharks fed on Mon, Wed and Fri at 1100*, a long-established aquarium, although looking tired, is still worth a visit if you have kids or fancy a swim with the star attractions on the aquarium's unusual 'Swim with the sharks' tour. **Manly Art Gallery and Museum** ⓘ *T9949 1776, Tue-Sun 1000-1700, $3.50*, showcases an interesting array of permanent historical items with the obvious emphasis on all things 'beach', while the gallery offers both permanent and temporary shows of contemporary art and photography. The 10 km **Manly Scenic Walkway** from Manly to Spit Bridge is an excellent scenic harbour walk, arguably the city's best. Meandering through bush and along beaches while gazing over the harbour it is hard to believe that you are in the middle of the Australia's biggest city. The walk starts from the end of West Esplanade, takes from three to four hours and is clearly signposted the whole way. Walk on a weekday if possible: Sundays can be very busy. The best way to reach Manly is by ferry from Circular Quay (wharves 2 and 3), $6, children $3, 30 minutes or the JetCat for $7.90 taking 15 minutes. Both leave on a regular basis daily.

North Head

The tip of North Head, to the south of Manly is well worth a look, if only to soak up the views across the harbour and out to sea. The cityscape is especially stunning at dawn. Just follow Scenic Drive to the very end. The **Quarantine Station** ⓘ *T9247 5033, tours Thu and Sun, 2-hrs, from $11, Ghost Tours Wed and Fri-Sun, at 1930, 3-hr, from $27.50 includes a light supper, kids' version Fri at 1800, 2-hr, from 1320, bookings recommended, bus 135 from Manly wharf*, taking up a large portion of the peninsula, was used from 1832 to harbour ships known to be carrying diseases like smallpox, bubonic plague, cholera and Spanish influenza and to protect the new colony from the spread of such nasties. The station closed in 1984 and is now administered by the NSW Parks and Wildlife Service.

Northern beaches

The coast north of Manly is indented by numerous bays and fine beaches that stretch 10 km to **Barrenjoey Head** at Broken Bay and the entrance to the Hawkesbury River harbour. Perhaps the most popular of these are **Narrabeen**, **Avalon** and **Whale Beach**, but there are many to choose from. Narrabeen has the added attraction of a large lake, used for sailing, canoeing and windsurfing, while Avalon and Whale Beach, further north, are smaller, quite picturesque and more sheltered. A day trip to the very tip and Barrenjoey Head is recommended and the area is complemented by **Palm Beach**, a popular weekend getaway with some fine restaurants. There are many water activities on offer in the area focused mainly on **Pittwater**, a large bay on the sheltered western side of the peninsula. Whether just for a day trip or a weekend stay get hold of the free *Northern Beaches Visitors Guide* from the Sydney VIC. The L90 bus from Wynyard in goes via all the main northern beaches suburbs to Palm Beach, every 30 minutes.

Sleeping

Sydney has all types of accommodation to suit all budgets. Most of the major luxury hotels are located around Circular Quay, Darling Harbour and the northern CBD. Other more moderately priced hotels, motels and small boutique hotels are scattered around the southern city centre and inner suburbs. It is worth considering this option as many in the suburbs provide an attractive alternative to the busy city centre. There are trillions of backpacker hostels scattered throughout the city with most centred around Kings Cross. The CBD is best for convenience, Kings Cross is best for social activities, or beachside resorts such as Manly or Bondi for the classic Sydney lifestyle. A less obvious option are serviced apartments in the CBD. **Medina**, T9360 1699, www.medina apartments.com.au, has several establishments throughout the city. At anytime in the peak season (Oct-Apr) and especially over Christmas, the New Year and during major sporting or cultural events, prebooking is advised for all types of accommodation. If you have not pre-booked the Rocks VIC is a good place to start.

Circular Quay and the Rocks

p109, map p112

LL-B **B&B Sydney Harbour**, 140 Cumberland St, T9247 1130, www.bbsydneyharbour.com.au. Friendly B&B with 12 rooms that capture something of the building's century-plus of history without sacrificing those little luxuries. Shared and en suite. Breakfast is out in the tucked-away courtyard.

L-A **Russell Hotel**, 143A George St, T9241 3543, www.therussell.com.au. Set right in the heart of the Rocks with views of the harbour, retaining a historic ambience and offering a good range of singles, en suites, standard rooms and suites. Also has an appealing rooftop garden.

A-B **Lord Nelson Pub and Hotel**, corner of Kent St and Argyle St, The Rocks, T9251 4044, www.lordnelson.com.au. This historic hotel has some very pleasant, new and affordable, en suites above the pub. The added attraction here is the home-brewed beer, food and general ambience. The pub closes fairly early at night, so noise is generally not a factor.

City Centre *p114, map p112*

At the northern edge of the CBD, fringing Circular Quay, there are reliable chain hotels that still offer a peek across the harbour. Around Haymarket the hotels become cheaper and begin to be replaced by hostels.

L **Capitol Square**, corner of Campbell St and George St, T9211 8633, www.capitolsquare. com.au. Right next door to the Capitol Theatre is this friendly boutique hotel. It has cosy en suite rooms, a good restaurant and is one of the best affordable 3-4-star hotels in the city centre.

A-E **Alfred Park Budget Accommodation**, 207 Cleveland St, Redfern, T9319 4031, hotels@g-day.aust.com. A good 10-min walk south of Central Station, down Chalmers St and across Prince Alfred Park is this cross between a budget hotel and a backpackers, offering peace and quiet. It is well kept and very clean, offering tidy dorms, and spacious singles, doubles and twins. Modern facilities and free guest parking.

A-E **Wake Up**, 509 Pitt St, T9288 7888, www.wakeup.com.au. Opposite Central railway station with 24 hour check-in, this is huge, but convenient, safe, clean and well-run. It has nicely appointed doubles/twins, some with en suite, and a range of dorms, plus kitchen facilities, a newly established café, bar, travel desk and employment information.

B-D **Railway Square YHA**, 8-10 Lee St, T9281 9666, railway@yhansw.org.au. An excellent new 280-bed YHA hostel in the station area itself, with accommodation, including some en suite doubles, and facilities in railway carriages.

Budget busters

Sydney sleeping

LL **Doyle's Palace Hotel**, Watson's Bay, T9337 5444, www.doyles.com.au. From the same people who brought you the legendary seafood restaurant (see box on page 135), comes this fabulous boutique hotel with 32 suites, each with its own breathtaking view from the balcony. Easily reached by ferry.

LL **L'Otel**, 114 Darlinghurst Rd, Darlinghurst, T9360 6868, www.lotel.com.au. Very classy yet given its minimalist decor perhaps not everyone's cup of tea. Very hip and very much a place for the modern couple. Excellent personable service and a fine restaurant attached.

LL-L **Trickett's Luxury B&B**, 270 Glebe Point Rd, T9552 1141, www.tricketts.com.au. A beautifully restored Victorian mansion, decorated with antiques and Persian rugs and offering spacious, nicely appointed en suites.

B-D **Base Backpackers**, 477 Kent St, T9267 7718, www.basebackpackers.com. Modern backpackers right in the heart of the city. Large, spacious and well-facilitated, it has fine doubles, twins and dorms.

B-E **Y on the Park (YWCA)**, 5-11 Wentworth Av, T9264 2451, www.ywca-sydney.com.au. Pitched somewhere between a budget hotel and a hostel it welcomes both male and female clients, has a good range of clean, modern, spacious and quiet rooms and boasts all the usual facilities. It is also well placed between the city centre and social hub of Oxford St.

C-D **Sydney Central YHA**, corner of Pitt St and Rawson Pl, T9218 9000, www.yha.com.au. Vast and very popular, next to Central Station and the main interstate bus depot, this huge heritage building has over 500 beds split into a range of dorms, doubles and twins, with some en suite. Naturally, it also offers all mod cons including, pool, sauna, café, bar, internet, mini-mart, TV rooms and employment and travel desks.

Darling Harbour and Chinatown

p117, map p112

L-A **Glasgow Arms Hotel**, 527 Harris St, Ultimo, T9211 2354. Good value, friendly, located just on the edge of Darling Harbour the hotel offers basic yet cosy rooms, entertaining bar and an affordable pub restaurant with a courtyard downstairs.

City West *p119*

Glebe

Glebe is especially popular as an alternative backpackers venue offering a village-type atmosphere with interesting cafés, shops and pubs all within easy walking distance.

B-D **Alishan International Guesthouse**, 100 Glebe Point Rd, T9566 4048, www.alishan.com.au. Halfway between a small hotel and a quality hostel, is this spacious, renovated Victorian mansion with spotless doubles, twins and family en suites, all with TV and fridge. Shared accommodation is also available and overall the facilities are excellent. A great value budget option, especially for couples looking for a place away from the city centre. Limited off street parking.

C-E Wattle House, 44 Hereford St, T9552 4997, www.wattlehouse.com.au. Another great option is this lovingly restored Victorian house, with a very cosy, homely feel and friendly owners. It also has great double rooms and is especially popular for those looking for a quieter more intimate place to stay. Book well in advance.

D-E Glebe Point YHA, 262 Glebe Point Rd, T9692 8418, www.yha.com.au. A popular place with a nice atmosphere, offering fairly small twin and 4-share dorms and modern facilities throughout. BBQs on the roof are a speciality. Regular shuttle to the city and transport departure points.

D-E Glebe Village Backpackers, 256 Glebe Point Rd, T9660 8878, www.glebevillage.com. A large, working backpacker's favourite. It offers a range of dorms and a few doubles (some en suite) and is friendly, laid-back and of course prides itself on finding work for guests. In-house café, pick-ups and regular day tours to beaches and other locations.

City East *p121, map p112*

There is no shortage of accommodation in Kings Cross and its surrounding suburbs, with everything from the deluxe 5-star hotels to the basic and affordable hostel. Most backpackers are located along Victoria St, Orwell St or on the main drag, Darlinghurst Rd. Others are scattered in quieter locations around the main hub, especially towards Potts Point.

Kings Cross *map p130*

B The Barclay, 17 Bayswater Rd, T9358 6133, barclayhotel@bigpond.com. Modern and good value, with a touch of class.

D-E Backpackers Headquarters, 79 Bayswater Rd, T9331 6180, www.backpackershqhostel.com.au. Immaculately kept and well run, the layout is a little odd but otherwise it is a fine choice in a quiet location, yet close to the action.

D-E Funk House, 23 Darlinghurst Rd, T9358 6455, www.funkhouse.com.au. Set right on Darlinghurst Rd, this is definitely one for the younger party set. Zany artworks don the walls and doors. 3-4 bed dorms and double/twins all with fridge, TV and fan. Lots of freebies. Their legendary rooftop BBQs are a great place to meet others. Good job search assistance.

D-E Jolly Swagman, 27 Orwell St, T9358 6400, www.jollyswagman.com.au. Another buzzing hostel set in the heart of the action. Very professionally managed with all the usual facilities. TV, fridge and fan in most rooms. Excellent travel desk and job search assistance. Social atmosphere. 24-hr check in, fast internet and free beer on arrival.

D-E The Original Backpackers Lodge, 160-162 Victoria St, T9356 3232, www.originalbackpackers.com.au. Possibly the best hostel in Kings Cross if not the city and certainly one of the best facilitated and managed. The historic house is large and homely, nicely appointed and comfortable, offering a great range of double, twin, single, triple and dorm rooms all with TV, fridge and fans (heated in winter). There is a great open courtyard in which to socialize or enjoy a BBQ. Cable TV. The staff are always on hand to help with onward travel, job seeking or things to see and do. Book ahead.

D-E The Pink House, 6-8 Barncleuth Square, T/F9358 1689, www.pinkhouse.com.au. An historic mansion offering a homely feel that is lacking in many of the other Kings Cross hostels, deservingly popular, especially for those tired of the party scene. Lots of quiet corners and a shady courtyard in which to find peace of mind. Large dorms and some good doubles, Cable TV and free internet.

D-E The Virgin (V) Backpackers, 144 Victoria St, T9357 4733, www.vbackpackers.com. Quite modern and chic the 'V' offers good facilities, a nice balance between the lively and quiet. Tidy doubles and twins with TV and fridge and dorms. Well-travelled, helpful managers internet café with good cheap meals.

LL-A Victoria Court, 122 Victoria St, T9357 3200, www.VictoriaCourt.com.au. This is a delightful and historic boutique hotel in a quiet location. It comes complete with period antiques, well appointed en suites, fireplaces and 4-poster beds. The courtyard

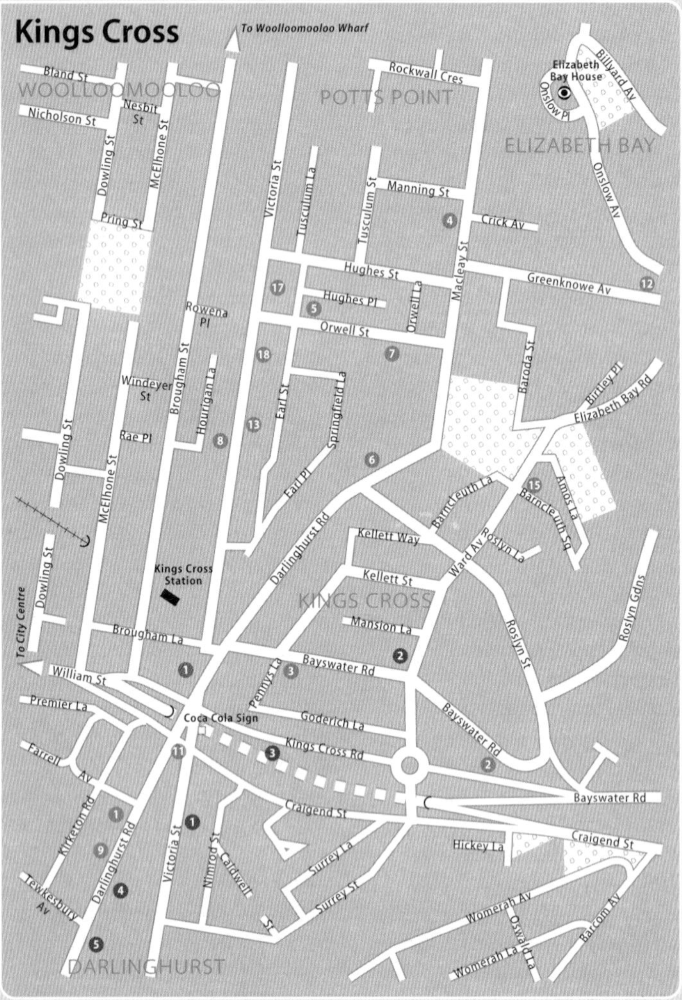

Kings Cross

To Woolloomooloo Wharf

To City Centre

Sleeping
Altamont **1**
Backpackers Headquarters **2**
Barclay **3**
Blue Parrot **4**
Eva's **5**
Funk House **6**
Jolly Swagman **7**
Kanga House **8**
Kirketon **9**
L'Otel **11**
Manhattan Park Inn **12**
Original Backpackers Lodge **13**
Pink House **15**
Victoria Court **17**
Virgin (V) Backpackers **18**

Eating
Bar Coluzzi **1**
Bayswater Brassserie **2**
Café Hernandez **3**
Govinda's **4**
Le Petit Creme **5**

Bars & clubs
Kings Cross Hotel **1**

conservatory is excellent.

A Manhattan Park Inn, 8 Greenknowe Av, T9358 1288, www.parkplaza.com.au. North, away from the mania of Kings Cross proper, this is one of the cheapest standard hotels.

D-E Blue Parrot, 87 Mcleay St, T9356 4888, www. blueparrot.com.au. Located towards Potts Point. Modern and clean with an attractive courtyard garden to escape the hype of the Cross.

C-E Challis Lodge, 21-23 Challis Av, T9358 5422, challislodge@wheretostay.com.au. An historic mansion, cheaper than **Victoria Court**, and therefore less salubrious, yet with a good range of singles, twins and doubles, some with en suites.

D-E Kanga House, 141 Victoria St, T9357 7897, www.kangahouse.com.au. Offers a warm welcome and if you are lucky you may be able to secure a room with a view of the Opera House.

D-E Eva's, 6-8 Orwell St, T9358 2185, www.evasbackpackers.com.au. This is another clean and well managed hostel that offers a distinctly homely feel. Arty rooms with some en suites. Rooftop space used for social BBQs and offering great views across the city.

Darlinghurst and Surry Hills

Separated only by a river of traffic Darlinghurst offers a fine alternative to Kings Cross. Surry Hills has few options.

L-B Hotel Altamont, 207 Darlinghurst Rd, Darlinghurst, T9360 6000, www.altamont.com.au. Classy, traditional hotel with beautiful spacious deluxe rooms with wooden floors and fittings. Some are fantastic value.

L-B Kirketon, 229 Darlinghurst Rd, Darlinghurst, T9332 2011, www.kirketon.com.au. Modern, chic and minimalist with a bar and restaurant to match.

A Royal Sovereign Hotel, corner of Liverpool St and Darlinghurst Rd, Darlinghurst, T9331 3672, www.darlobar.com.au. For something more traditional look no further than here. The newly refurbished range of rooms above the popular 'Darlo' bar are spotless and great value. Shared bathroom facilities.

C-E Kangaroo Bakpak, 665 South Dowling St, Surry Hills, T9319 5915, www.kangaroo bakpak.com.au. A quiet backpacker option.

Bondi and Coogee

The older, well-established beachfront hotels in Bondi look a little garish but their interiors will not disappoint, and they are only yards from the world famous beach. There are around a dozen backpackers. Coogee is steadily growing in popularity as a viable and often cheaper alternative to Bondi Beach.

LL-A Coogee Bay Hotel, 9 Vicar St, Coogee, T9665 0000, www.coogeebay hotel.com.au. Very pleasant, newly refurbished, boutique style rooms in addition to good, traditional pub-style options. Well appointed, en suite, ocean views and are good value. The hotel itself is also a main social focus in Coogee both day and night.

LL-B Ravesi's, corner of Campell Parade and Hall St, Bondi, T9365 4422, www.ravesis.com.au. Stylish and intimate with pleasant, good value 3-star standard rooms, standard suites and luxury split level suites, most with balconies overlooking all the action. The balcony restaurant is one of the best in the area.

A-B Hotel Bondi, 178 Campell Pde, Bondi, T9130 3271, www.hotelbondi.com.au. Traditional, with a popular public bar downstairs, a good café and a nightclub/performance space, 'Zinc' with live bands, DJ's and pool competitions most nights.

B Bondi Beachside Inn, 152 Campbell Pde, Bondi, T9130 5311, www.bondiinn.com.au. Another beachfront option, pitched somewhere between a hotel and motel, offering tidy rooms and suites with kitchen- ettes and ocean views to match the more expensive hotels. Good for families or couples.

B-D Beachouse Private Hotel, 171 Arden St, Coogee, T9665 1162.

A quiet, personable option. Lone travellers, especially girls, are well looked after. Free breakfast.

B-E Coogee Beachside Backpackers, 178/172, Coogee Bay Rd, Coogee, T9315 8511, www.sydneybeachside.com.au. Just as good as **Surfside** but smaller and with more character. There are two houses (Wizard of Oz and Beachside). The rooms, especially the doubles, are excellent. Good facilities, friendly staff with good work contacts. A 5-min walk to the beach. Ask about flat shares if you intend to stay long-term.

C-E Surfside Backpackers, 186 Arden St, Coogee, T9315 7888, www.surfsidebackpackers.com.au. The largest of the several backpackers and renovated in 2003, this is beachside and very social with a solid reputation and modern facilities. Two-bedroom flats available for small groups with balcony and ocean view.

D-E Noah's Bondi Beach Backpackers, 2 Campbell Parade, Bondi, T9365 7100, www.noahs bondibeach.com.au. Perched on the hill, overlooking the beach as you descend to Bondi proper is this large place, popular due to its position and price. As such it is certainly not the quietest. Former hotel rooms converted to dorms, twins and doubles (some with ocean view). Rooftop BBQ area offers great views.

D-E Lamrock Lodge Backpackers, 19 Lamrock Av, Bondi, T9130 5063, www.lamrocklodge.com. Offers new, modern facilities and all rooms, dorm, single, twin and double have cable TV, fridge, kitchenette and microwave. Good value.

City North *p124*

North Sydney and surrounds

The quiet yet central suburb of Kirribilli, across the water from the Opera House, is an excellent place to base yourself, with a short, and spectacular ferry trip to the CBD. There is very little in the way of accommodation but that is part of its charm.

B-D Glenferrie Lodge, 12A Carabella St, T9955 1685, www.glenferrielodge.com. A vast, 70-room Victorian mansion with quality budget accommodation. The range of shared, single, twin or doubles are superb with some having their own balconies. Cheap dinners are on offer nightly. Very friendly.

Manly

Being a well-established resort within the city there is no shortage of accommodation in Manly. The VIC on the Forecourt beside the ferry wharf has detailed listings, maps and can help arrange bookings, T9977 1088, www.manly.nsw.gov.au.

L-B Manly Lodge Boutique Hotel, 22 Victoria Pde, T9977 8655, www.manlylodge.com.au. A homely option, popular and good value.

L-E Manly Beach Resort, 6 Carlton St, T9977 4188, www.manlyview.com.au. For a motel option try this 3-star resort, all rooms are en suite and breakfast is included. Backpacker style accommodation also available. Pool and spa.

C-E Wharf Backpackers, 48 East Esplanade (right opposite the ferry terminal), T9977 2800. Cheap and arty, this is also popular.

D Steyne Hotel, corner of Ocean Beach and The Corso, T9977 4977, www.steynehotel.com.au. Older, cheaper and traditional pub style hotel with standard, deluxe and backpacker rooms, including breakfast.

D Manly Bungalow, T9977 5494, www.manlybungalow.com. Bright and sunny budget accommodation with value double and family rooms with kitchenettes.

D-E Manly Backpackers Beachside, 28 Raglan St, T9977 3411, www.manlybackpackers.com.au. Well-rated and busy with some en suite doubles and small dorms.

Northern beaches

C-D Collaroy YHA (Sydney Beachhouse), 4 Collaroy St, Collaroy Beach, T9981 1177, www.sydneybeachouse.com.au. The Hilton of Sydney backpackers offers tidy dorms, twins, doubles and family rooms (some en suite) and great over all facilities, including a heated pool, spacious kitchen, dining areas, TV rooms, free equipment hire and organized day trips. Even free didgeridoo lessons. It deserves its reputation as one of the best backpackers in the city. Book ahead Catch the L90 or L88 bus from Central, Wynyard or QVB.

D-E **YHA Pittwater**, via Halls Wharf, Morning Bay, via Church Pt, T9999 5748, www.yha. com.au. A real getaway located in the Ku-ring-gai National Park and accessible only by ferry. It has dorms and a few doubles. Plenty of walking and water-based activities or simple peace and quiet. Phone for details, take all your supplies and book ahead.

Eating

When it comes to quality and choice there is no doubt that Sydney is on a par with any major city in the world and with over 3,000 restaurants to choose from you have to wonder where on earth to start. As a general rule you will find the best of the fine dining establishments specializing in Modern Australian cuisine in and around Circular Quay, The Rocks, the CBD and Darling Harbour, though pockets of international speciality abound, from chow mein in Chinatown to pasta in Paddington. Sydney's thriving café culture is generally centred around the suburbs of Darlinghurst, Glebe, Newtown and the eastern beaches of Bondi and Bronte.

Circular Quay and the Rocks

p109, map p112

On the eastern side of the Quay you will find mid-range and expensive options with lots of atmosphere and memorable views under the concourse of the Opera House and within 'The Toaster'.

TT **Australian Hotel**, 100 Cumberland St, T9247 2229. Daily for lunch and dinner. Come here for a taste of Aussie pub life. It has a wonderful atmosphere and all the classic Australian beers. Good value, good al fresco and menu, which includes pizza, croc, emu and roo steaks.

TT **Café Sydney**, Level 5, 31 Alfred St, T9251 8683. Daily for lunch, Mon-Sat for dinner. Set high above Circular Quay at the top of Customs House, this place offers superb views and al fresco dining. The food is traditional Modern Australian with a nice atmosphere and occasional live jazz.

TT **The Wharf**, Pier 4, Hickson Rd, Walsh Bay, T9250 1761. Lunch and dinner Mon-Sat. Off the beaten track and a firm local favourite is this option located at the end of one of the historic Walsh Bay piers. It has a great atmosphere and wonderful views of the busy harbour. Modern Australian.

TT-T **MCA Cafe**, 140 George St, T9241 4253. Lunch Mon-Fri and breakfast and lunch Sat-Sun. At the Museum of Contemporary Art, this café is ideally located next to all the action on Circular Quay. It is a bit expensive but worth it and the seafood is excellent. **The Rocks café** is a cheaper option around the back of the MCA and also good (daily 0800-2130).

T **La Renaissance**, 47 Argyle St, The Rocks. Head to this patisserie for a simple lunch. Authentic French baguettes and pastries in a quiet leafy courtyard or to takeaway.

City Centre *p114, map p112*

The sheer chaos and noise that surrounds you in the CBD is enough to put anyone off eating. A retreat to the Botanical Gardens or Hyde Park is recommended.

TT **Brooklyn Hotel**, corner of George St and Grosvenor St, T9247 6744. Lunch Mon-Fri. Well known for its meat dishes, especially steak and has plenty of inner city pub atmosphere.

TT **Pavilion on the Park**, 1 Art Gallery Rd, The Domain, T9232 1322, sits opposite the Art Gallery and is the perfect escape from the city centre, offering al fresco dining with an eclectic Modern Australian menu. Perfect for lunch after a tour of the gallery.

Botanical Gardens Cafe, Mrs Macquarie Rd, T9241 2419. Daily 0830-1800. For sublime tranquillity amidst the Botanical Gardens, the bat colony might not be everybody's cup of tea but for environmentalists and botanists it's really hard to beat.

Casa Asturiana, 77 Liverpool St, T9264 1010. Daily for lunch and dinner. In Sydney's Spanish quarter and well known for its Spanish cuisine, tapas in particular. Lots of atmosphere and regular live music.

Hyde Park Cafe, corner of Elizabeth and Liverpool sts, T9264 8751. Daily from 0700-1630. A great spot for escaping the crowds, breakfast, light lunches, coffee and people-watching.

MOS Cafe, corner of Bridge and Phillip sts, T9241 3636. Mon-Fri from 0700-2100 and Sat-Sun 0830-1700. Below the Museum of Sydney is this congenial café offering imaginative and value Modern Australian for lunch.

The Tearoom, on the top floor of the QVB, George St. Sun-Fri 1100-1700, Sat 1100-1500. If the shopping all gets too much escape to this gracious room where you can sink into a large comfy chair and have an enormous afternoon tea.

Darling Harbour and Chinatown

p117, map p112

Coast, Roof Terrace, Cockle Bay Wharf, Darling Park, 201 Sussex St, T9267 6700. Lunch Mon-Fri and Sun, daily for dinner. Offers a fine range of Modern Australian dishes and has a formal, yet relaxed atmosphere and great views across Darling Harbour.

BBQ King, 18 Goulburn St, T9267 2586. Daily 1130-0200. This Sydney institution is the first place to head for if you fancy Chinese. There's nothing special about the decor or service but the food is always excellent and good value.

Blackbird Cafe, Mid Level, Cockle Bay Wharf, T9283 7385. Deservedly popular, congenial, laid back and good value with a huge selection from pasta to steak.

Dickson House Food Court, corner of Little Hay St and Dixon St. Daily 1030-2030. Has a wealth of cheap Asian takeaways with generous meals for under $6.

Chinta Ria – The Temple of Love, Roof Terrace, Cockle Bay Wharf, 201 Sussex St, T9264 3211, www.chintaria.com. Daily for lunch and dinner. With a name like that who can resist? Great aesthetics, buzzing atmosphere with quality Malaysian cuisine.

Emperor's Garden Seafood, 96 Hay St, T9211 2135. Daily 0800-0100. Moving into Haymarket is one of the most reliable of the Chinatown restaurants, always bustling, offering great service and value for money.

City West *p119*

Glebe

Boathouse on Blackwattle Bay, Ferry Rd, T9518 9011, www.boathouse.net.au. Lunch and dinner Tue-Sun. A quality upmarket (yet informal) seafood restaurant offering refreshingly different harbour views than those sought at Circular Quay and Darling Harbour. Here you can watch the lights of Anzac Bridge or the comings and goings of Sydney's fishing fleet while tucking in to the freshest seafood.

Badde Manors, 37 Glebe Point Rd, T9660 3797. Daily from 0730 till late. Something of institution in Glebe for many years this favourite student hangout can always be relied on for atmosphere and character, which is more than can be said for the service.

Flavour of India, 142A Glebe Point Rd, T9692 0662. Quite simply Glebe's best Indian restaurant with lots of character, great service and value for money.

Iku, 25A Glebe Point Rd, T9692 8720. Mon-Fri 1130-2100, Sat-Sun 1130-2100. The first of what is now a chain of fine vegetarian and macrobiotic vegan cafes under the 'Iku' banner, offering a delicious array of options.

Toxteth Hotel, 345 Glebe Point Rd, T9660 2370. Daily 1100. Modern, traditional Australian pub serving

Budget busters

Sydney eating

Doyle's on the Beach, 11 Marine Parade, T9337 2007. Daily for lunch and dinner. Sydney's best known restaurant for years. It has been in the same family for generations and has an unfaltering reputation for superb seafood, atmosphere and harbour/city views that all combine to make it a one of the best dining experiences in the city, if not Australia. If you can, book well ahead and ask for a balcony seat. Sunday afternoons are especially popular and you could combine the trip with a walk around the heads. Book ahead.

Quay, Upper Level, Overseas Passenger Terminal, Circular Quay West, T9251 5600. Lunch Mon-Fri and dinner daily. Close to the water and offering great views of the bridge and the Opera House is this Euro- influenced restaurant. Expensive, but one to remember.

MG Garage, 490 Crown St, Surry Hills, T9383 9383. Lunch Mon-Fri and dinner Mon-Sat. Classic cars meet costly cuisine in this unique place with expensive autos surrounding the tables. Book ahead.

mountainous plates of good pub grub at very cheap prices.

Well Connected, 35 Glebe Point Rd, T9566 2655. 0700-2400. One of the city's 1st internet cafés. Laid-back with a whole floor upstairs full of sofas dedicated to surfing the web. Not a bad cup of coffee either.

Newtown

Cinque, 261 King St, Newtown, T9519 3077. Daily 0730-late. Another popular café located next to the Dendy Cinema and a small bookshop. Great all day breakfasts, coffee.

Old Fish Shop Cafe, 239 King St, T9519 4295. Daily from 0730-2300. A charming little café and one of Newtown's best and most popular haunts, especially for breakfast and good coffee.

Thai Pothong, 294 King St, T9550 6277. Lunch Tue-Sun, daily for dinner. On a street with more Thai restaurants than you can shake a chopstick at, this one stands head and shoulders above the rest. Good value, good choice and good service.

Thanh Binh, 111 King St, T9557 1175. Lunch Thu-Sun, daily for dinner. Good value Vietnamese offering delicious dishes from simple noodles to venison in curry sauce.

Kings Cross *map p130*

As you'd expect there are a million and one fast food outlets here and other budget eateries catering for the cash-strapped backpacker and night owls.

Bayswater Brasserie, 32 Bayswater Rd, Kings Cross, T9357 2177. Mon-Thu 1700-2300, Fri 1200-2300, Sat 1700-2300. A reliable choice and immensely popular for its laid-back, yet classy atmosphere and imaginative Modern Australian cuisine. At the top end of this price range.

Café Hernandez, 60 Kings Cross Rd, Kings Cross, T9331 2343. Great, eccentric 24-hr café serving Spanish fare, great coffee and with lots of character.

Govinda's, 112 Darlinghurst Rd, Kings Cross, T9380 5155. Restaurant and cinema combo offering great value 'all-you-can-eat' vegetarian buffet plus the movie ticket.

Woolloomooloo

The wharf has a growing reputation as one of the best places for fine dining in the city.

Otto, 8 The Wharf, Cowper Wharf Rd, T9368 7488. Very trendy, quality Italian with all the necessary trimmings including extrovert waiters.

Manta Ray, 9 The Wharf, 6 Cowper Wharf Rd, T9332 3822, Lunch Mon-Fri and dinner daily. Classy seafood restaurant. Some say one of the best in the city.

Harry's Café de Wheels, Cowper Wharf. Sun-Thu 0700-0200, Fri-Sat till 0300. Harry's is something of a Sydney institution, offering the famously yummy pies with pea toppings and gravy. One is surely never enough, as the photos of satisfied customers will testify. However, rumour has it that Russell Crowe, who has a luxury apartment on the wharf, did not agree, abusing the staff and walking off in disgust.

Shimbashi Soba on the Sea, 6 The Wharf, Cowper Wharf Rd, T9357 7763. Daily 1100-2200. A fine Japanese restaurant that just adds to the sheer choice and quality to be found on the Wharf strip in 'Woolie'. Good mix of pure Japanese cuisine with more familiar meat and poultry dishes. Good value.

Darlinghurst and Surry Hills

Bar Coluzzi, 322 Victoria St, Darlinghurst, T9380 5420. Daily from 0500-1900. A well-established café that consistently gets the vote as one of Sydney's best. The character, the truly cosmopolitan clientele and the coffee are the biggest draw as opposed to the food.

Bill's, 433 Liverpool St, Darlinghurst, T9360 9631. Breakfast and lunch daily from 0730-1500. One of the city's top breakfast cafés with legendary scrambled eggs. Small and at times overcrowded but that's part of the experience. Also **Bill's 2**, at 359 Crown St, Surry Hills.

Fuel, 488 Crown St, Surry Hills, T9383 9388. Daily from 0800 for breakfast, lunch and dinner. Part of a car dealership – complete with vehicles! Affordable bistro-style cuisine, especially popular for weekend brunch.

Le Petit Creme, 118 Darlinghurst Rd, Darlinghurst, T9361 4738. Daily from 0800. Superb little French number with all the classics, from baguettes to cavernous bowls of café au lait. Great omelettes for breakfast or lunch.

Oh! Calcutta!, 251 Victoria St, Darlinghurst, T9360 3650. Lunch Fri and dinner Mon-Sat. An award winning Indian restaurant and by far the best in the inner east. Book ahead.

Prasit's Thai Takeaway, 395 Crown St, Surry Hills, T9332 1792. Lunch and dinner Tue-Sun. Great value Thai restaurant and take away and the locally recommended cheap option here. Don't automatically expect to get a seat however. Plenty of vegetarian options.

Una's, 340 Victoria St, Darlinghurst, T9360 6885. Daily from 0730-late. Local favourite offering generous hangover cure breakfasts and Euro influenced lunches, including schnitzel and mouth watering strudel.

Paddington

Royal Hotel, 237 Glenmore Rd, T9331 2604. Lunch and dinner from 1200. One of the best choices at the increasingly popular Five Ways crossroads in Paddington. A grand old pub with gracious yet modern feel. Excellent Modern Australian cuisine is served upstairs in the main restaurant or on the prized verandah. Perfect for a lazy afternoon.

Indian Home Diner, 86 Oxford St, T9331 4183. You really can't go wrong here with the usual great value (if mild), Indian combo dishes and on this occasion, a small courtyard out back.

Café Centaur, 19 Oxford St, T9560 3200. Daily 1000-2330. Pleasant quiet little café in a great bookshop that will delay your touristical wanderings for hours. Light fare, delectable sweets and good coffee.

Hot Gossip, 438 Oxford St, T9332 4358. Daily 0730-late. A well-established 'Paddo' café with retro 50s furnishings and an interesting clientele. Good food, healthy smoothies and a great cake selection.

Watson's Bay Hotel, 1 Military Rd, T9337 4299. Located right next door to the famous **Doyle's**, **Watson's** offers some stiff competition in the form of quality, value seafood al fresco, with lots of choice. You can even cook your own. Great for a whole afternoon, especially at the weekend.

Bondi, Bronte and Coogee

Hugo's, 70 Campbell Parade, Bondi Beach, T9300 0900. Daily for dinner, Sat-Sun for breakfast and lunch. A well-established favourite in Bondi, offering a combination of classy atmosphere, quality Modern Australian cuisine and fine views of the iconic beach.
Icebergs Dining Room & Bar, 1 Notts Av, Bondi Beach, T9365 9000. Tue-Sun 1200-1500, 1830-2200. Trendiest new dining space in the city, hanging over the beach and attracting a glamour crowd to its modern Italian cuisine and sharp design.
Jenny's, 485 Bronte Rd, T9389 7498. Daily 0700-1830. Has competition on both sides, but is consistently the café of choice on the 'Bronte strip'. Favourite breakfast spot at weekends and a great start (or finish) to the cliff-top walk between Bronte and Bondi.
Coogee Bay Hotel, corner of Coogee Bay Rd and Arden St, T966 5000. The most popular spot in Coogee day or night with multiple bars, huge open air eating, value pub-grub and live entertainment.

City North *p124*

Manly

Manly is blessed with numerous restaurants and cafés and a wide range of choice.
Le Kiosk, Shelly Beach, T9977 4122. Daily for lunch and dinner. Simple beach house ambience in a beautiful setting right on the beach. Reliable modern Australian cuisine.
Manly Wharf Hotel, T9977 1266. This fabulous redeveloped pub on the wharf is the hottest spot in Manly over summer. Classy food in a bustling, open space.
Bower Restaurant, 7 Marine Parade, T9977 5451. Daily for breakfast and lunch, Thu and some weekends for dinner. Located right at the end of Marine Parade with memorable views back towards Manly Beach. Great spot for breakfast.
Out of Africa, 43 East Esplanade, Manly, T9977 0055. Daily for dinner, Thu-Sun for lunch. Good value, authentic African cuisine with all the expected furnishings. Seems oddly out of place in Manly, but remains refreshingly different.

Bars and clubs

Sydney has pubs to suit most tastes both in the city centre and suburbs. Most are the traditional, street corner Australian hotels, but there are lots of modern, trendy establishments, pseudo Irish pubs and truly historic alehouses on offer. Many pubs, especially those along Oxford St and in Kings Cross, attract a distinctly metrosexual clientele. See also Entertainment p140 for gay nights. For the latest in club information and special events get hold of the free *3-D World* magazine, available in many backpackers, cafés or the clubs, www.threedworld.com.au.

Circular Quay and the Rocks

p109, map p112

Bars

The best single drinking venue in Sydney is undoubtedly The Rocks, where history, aesthetics, atmosphere and most importantly darn good beer combine to guarantee a great night out.
Australian Hotel, 100 Cumberland St, T9247 2229. From the **Orient** negotiate the steady climb up to Cumberland St (the steps are located on the right, before the bridge behind the Argyle Stores) and reward yourself with an obligatory Australian beer. You may also like to sample a kangaroo, emu or crocodile steak for dinner. This hotel is also makes for a good B&B sleeping option (**B**) with 10 comfortable doubles (share bathrooms) and a small rooftop terrace.

Cruise, by the Passenger Terminal on the Rocks side, and **Harbour View Hotel**, 18 Lower Fort St, are both good choices with fine views.

Hero of Waterloo, 18 Lower Fort St, T9252455. Just around the corner from the **Nelson** is this smaller and characterful pub which can be a bit of a squeeze but is always entertaining.

Lord Nelson, corner of Argyle St and Kent St (top end), T9251 4044. Past Observatory Park and down to Argyle St is Sydney's oldest pub. Within its hallowed, nautically-themed walls, it brews its own ales and also offers some fine pub grub and accommodation.

Mercantile, 25 George St, T9247 3570. A chaotic Irish pub, it is often busy but offers a fairly decent pint of Guinness as well as great live traditional music until late.

Opera Bar, nestled in the lower concourse just short of the Opera House, is outdoor s and serves great bar food, has regular live music and offers stunning views.

Clubs

Basement, 29 Reiby Pl, T9251 2797, www.thebasement.com.au, is ever-popular, and **Jacksons on George**, 176 George St, T9247 2727, is a huge club spread over 4 floors with 5 bars, dining, dancing, live bands and pool, open 24 hrs.

City Centre *p114, map p112*

Bars

Paddy McGuires, on the corner of George and Hay, T9212 2111. Pretty authentic Irish pub which has just been refurbished and offers pleasant surroundings in which you can actually have a decent conversation or sample a fine range of beers. Live music.

Scruffy Murphys, on the corner of Goulburn St and George St, T9211 2002. Popular, well-established Irish pub that always draws the crowds. It's a great place to meet people and the live bands and beers are good, but there really is very little Irish about it. Open well into the early hours.

Scubar, corner of Rawson Pl and Rawson Lane, T9212 4244, www.scubar.com.au. Popular backpacker oriented pub that offers cheap beer, pizzas, pool, big TV screens and popular music until late.

Clubs

Chinese Laundry, 111 Sussex St, T9299 1700, has a solid reputation, $10-15.

Civic Hotel, 388 Pitt St, corner of Goulburn St, T8267 3181. Though essentially a pub, cocktail bar and restaurant, this is a traditional weekend haunt for a cosmopolitan crowd who repeatedly come to enjoy old anthems and classics. Under $10.

Gas, 477 Pitt St, Haymarket, T9211 3088, is one of the best venues for dance music in the city with excellent, clued-up DJs revving up the crowds to a range of soul, funk, hip-hop, house and R&B, especially on Fri-Sat. Open 2200-0400, $15-25.

The Globe, corner of Park and Elizabeth sts, T9264 4844. Open daily 1100-2200, Fri/Sat 1100-0600, Fri $10, Sat $15, is the place to go to get the funk out of yer face.

Orbit Bar, Level 47, Australia Square, 264 George St, T9247 9777. Upping the tone – and altitude – considerably is this retro revolving bar (and expensive restaurant). Definitely a place to impress, and be impressed. Faultless, friendly service, great bar snacks and wonderful views.

Slip Inn, 111 Sussex St, T9299 4777, is a trendy night spot with 3 rooms and a courtyard that fills with the young and beautiful, who let rip to a mix of house and rave. Good Vibrations on a Sat is especially popular, and with a name like that, so it should be. Free entry before 2200.

Darling Harbour and Chinatown

p117, map p112

Bars

Cargo Bar, 52-60 The Promanade, Darling Harbour, T9262 1777. One of a few hip bars on Kings St Wharf with outdoor seating.

Clubs

Cave Nightclub, in the Star City Complex, 80 Pyrmont Rd, T9566 4755. Highly trendy, it offers good dance and R&B combo, and far more girls than guys.
Home, Cockle Bay Wharf, T9266 0600, is one of the country's largest, state of the art nightclubs. Here, on 4 levels, you can get on down to house and trance. Every Sat there is a kinkidisco. Open 2200-0600, $15.

City West *p119*

Friend In Hand Pub, 58 Cowper St, Glebe, T9660 2326. 'World Famous', it looks more like a venue for an international garage sale, but oozes character and also offers a bar café and Italian restaurant. Look out – the Cockatoo does bite!
Toxteth Hotel, 345 Glebe Point Rd, Glebe, T9660 2370, is a far more modern, traditionally Australian affair. It is always pretty lively, has pool competitions and serves mountainous plates of good pub grub.
Kuleto's Cocktail Bar, 157 King St, Newtown, T9519 6369. **Kuleto's** offers something completely different.
The Bank on King St, just south of the railway station, Newtown, is always busy thanks to its dark and rambling succession of rooms and bars. It also has a great Thai restaurant in the beer garden.

City East *p121, map p112*

Bars

Kings Cross is perhaps a little overrated when it come to pubs but Paddington has quite a few old traditional pubs (see below). If these are not to your taste you might like to try the more cutting-edge establishments where the music and atmosphere that the cosmopolitan and mixed gay and straight (but always trendy) clientele hold dear. Some great examples are:
Grand Pacific Blue Room, corner of Oxford St and South Dowling St, T9331 7108; **The Oxford Hotel**, 134 Oxford St, T9331 3467, and; **Albury Hotel**, 6 Oxford St, T9361 6555.
Coogee Bay Hotel, 9 Vicar St, Coogee, T9665 0000. Has multiple bars and live music at this beachside hotel.
Durty Nelly's, 9 Glenmore Rd, Paddington, T9360 4467, is the smallest, the best and most intimate Irish pub in the city, offering, nice surroundings and a grand congenial jam session on Sun evenings (last orders 2330).
Hard Rock Café, 121 Crown St, T9331 1116. Between the city and Kings Cross, just off William St, is this old favourite with suspended automobiles, electric guitars and band memorabilia that have now been the trademark of the global outlets for 30 years. Roll in for their 'two-for-one-drinks', Mon-Fri from 1700-1900.
Hotel Bondi, 178 Campell Parade, Bondi, T9130 3271, has a lively bar with live bands and a nightclub attached.
Kings Cross Hotel, 248 William St, Kings Cross, T9358 3377. In the shadow of the huge Coca Cola sign is the bizarre interior of this rowdy backpacker favourite open well into the early hours.
Kitty O'Sheas, 384 Oxford St, Paddington, T9360 9668. Another Irish offering, it is a large place and very popular especially at weekends when live bands play. If you need to escape the mêlée, try the bar upstairs.
Lord Dudley, 236 Jersey Rd, T9327 5399, www.lorddudley.com.au. Deep in the Paddington suburbs is this grand historic rabbit warren. There is also some great, if expensive, pub grub on offer.
Royal Hotel, Glenmore Rd, crossroads with Goodhope St and Heeley St, Paddington, T9331 2604, has a large atmospheric public bar downstairs and a fine restaurant on the 2nd floor.
Tilbury, Nicholson St, corner of Forbes St, Woolloomooloo. Attracts a good looking crowd to its slick, open spaces. Noisy thanks to the acres of shiny chrome and pale timber but it's always humming.

Water Bar, just inside the Wharf at Woolloomooloo. Gorgeous, dark and groovy.

Woolloomooloo Bay Hotel, 2 Bourke St, Woolloomooloo, T9357 1177, has karaoke nights and regular DJs. When you can no longer pronounce their name is definitely time to go home!

Clubs

Paddington Oxford St, is, of course, a major focus for nightlife and the main haunt for the gay and lesbian community. Kings Cross is the main focus for travellers, particularly backpackers, but is not necessarily the best venue in town.

Arq, 16 Flinders St, Paddington, T9380 8700. It has 2 large dance floors, plenty of space and a good balcony from which to watch a friendly crowd of both straight and gay.

Goodbar, 11A Oxford St, Paddington, T9360 6759, is a well-established club and an old favourite amongst Sydnesiders, from the sexy young things to the sexually confused and the odd forgot-how-to-be-sexy fossils. Mixed music and good value, $6.

Sapphire Suite, 2 Kellet St, Kings Cross, T9331 0058, modern and trendy offering a fine range of expensive cocktails, acid jazz, house and rave. Open 2200-500, From $5-15.

World, 24 Bayswater Rd, Kings Cross, T9357 7700. Newly refurbished, this is a laid-back club set in grand surrounds and offering mainly UK house music, Fri-Sat cover charge after 2200.

Lepanic, 22 Bayswater Rd, Kings Cross, T9368 0763, is another intimate new club come cocktail bar with a must-see eclectic décor. Again it concentrates on progressive house music. Open Thurs-Sun from 1900. Fri nights are especially good.

Entertainment

There is always a wealth of things to entertain in Sydney. For the latest information and reviews check the *Metro* section in the Fri *Sydney Morning Herald*. *The Beat* and *Sydney City Hub* are free weeklies that are readily available in restaurants, cafés, bars and bookshops in and around the city centre. On the net consult the websites already listed on page 108, or try www.whats-on-in-sydney.com.au.

The usual ticket agent is **Ticketek**, Sydney Entertainment Centre, Harbour St, Haymarket, T9266 4800, www.ticketek.com.au. They produce their own monthly events magazine *The Ticket*. **Ticketmaster**, T136100, also deals with theatre tickets.

Cinema

For listings see the *Sydney Morning Herald*. A movie ticket will cost from $13, children $10. Cheap tickets are often offered on Tue nights.

In the city centre most of the major conventional cinema complexes are to be found along George St between Town Hall and Chinatown. On Oxford St is **Chauvel**, corner of Oxford St and Oatley Rd, T9361 5398, which showcases more retro, foreign or fringe films.

Hayden Orpheum Cinema, 180 Military Rd, Cremorne, T9908 4344, on the North Shore, is a wonderful art deco cinema offering a fine alternative to the modern city cinemas.

Moonlight Cinema, Centennial Park, T1300 551 908, www.moonlight.com.au, (23 Nov-23 Feb). Old classics, take a picnic and cushions.

Open Air Cinema, Royal Botanical Gard- ens near Mrs Macquarie's Chair (summer only), new releases and smart deli food.

IMAX Theatre, Darling Harbour, T9281 3300, www.imax.com.au, is a huge 8-storey high affair showcasing 3D movies from 1000, from $16, child $11.

Contemporary music

Australian

You will almost certainly hear the bizarre and extraordinary tones of the didgeridoo some- where during your explorations be it the buskers on Circular Quay or in the many souvenir shops in the city. For live perform- ances of traditional Aussie instruments try the **Australia's Northern Territory and Outback Centre**, 28 Darling Walk, Darling Harbour, Tue-Sun 1300, 1500 and 1700, or **Reds Australian Restaurant**, 12 Argyle St, The Rocks, T9247 1011, daily 1745 and 1930.

Folk

All the Irish pubs offer folk jam nights early in the week and live bands from Wed to Sun. For some of the best try the **Merchantile Hotel**, 25 George St, The Rocks, **Scruffy Murphys**, corner of Goulburn St and George St, T9211 2002, **Kitty O'Shea's**, 384 Oxford St, T9360 9668, and **O'Malley's Hotel**, 228 William St Kings Cross, T9357 2211. Two excellent quieter options are **Paddy McGuires**, on the corner of George and Hay, T9212 2111, and **Durty Nelly's** (the best), on Glenmore Rd off Oxford St, which is a more intimate Irish pub offering low key jam sessions on Sun afternoons.

Jazz and blues

Soup Plus, 383 George St, T9299 7728, **The Basement**, 29 Reiby Pl, Circular Quay, T9251 2797, www.thebasement.com.au, and the **Harbourside Brasserie**, Pier One, The Rocks, T9252 3000, are the major local jazz venues. **Zambezi Blues Room**, 481 Kent St, behind Town Hall Sq, T9266 0200, is a fine venue and free. For daily details of jazz gigs tune into the Jazz Gig Guide at 0800 on Jazz Jam, 89.7FM Eastside Radio, Mon-Fri. For **Sydney Jazz Club** call T9798 7294.

Rock

The three main rock concert venues are: the massive **Sydney SuperDome**, Homebush Bay Olympic Park, T8765 4321, www.superdome.com.au; the 12,000-seat **Sydney Entertainment Centre**, 35 Harbour St, City, T9320 4200; and **Metro**, 624 George St, T9287 2000. Tickets for a big international band will cost anything from $60-150.

Comedy

National or international comedy acts are generally hosted by the smaller theatres, like the **Lyric** and the **Belvoir** (see Performing arts below). **Club Luna**, at the Basement, 29 Reiby St, T9251 2797, is excellent on Sun nights, from $13. A number of inner city hotels have comedy nights once a week including the **Exchange Hotel**, corner of Beattie St and Mullins St, Balmain, T9810 6099 (Wed,); and the **Marlborough Hotel**, 145 King St, Newtown, T9519 1222 (Tue), both of which are good. Another long-established venue is the **Unicorn Hotel**, 106 Oxford St, Paddington, T9360 3554, (Mon). Other venues with more regular acts are the **Comedy Store**, Bent St, Fox Studios, T9357 1419 (Tue-Sat, from $10-27), the **Laugh Garage**, 1st floor, **Macquarie Hotel**, corner of Goulburn St and Wentworth Av, T9560 1961, Thu-Sat, from $11-22, and the **Comedy Cellar**, 1 Bay St, Ultimo, T9212 3237.

Gambling

You will find that almost every traditional Australian hotel and pub in Sydney has the omnipresent rows of hyperactive pokies (slot machines), which to the uninitiated, need a PhD in bankruptcy and visual literacy skills to play (whatever happened to a row of lemons or cherries?). The main focus for trying your luck in Sydney is the **Star City Casino**, 80 Pyrmont St, a coins roll from Darling Harbour, T9777 9000, www.starcity.com.au. This vast arena has 200 gaming tables, 1,500 pokies and lots of anxious faces. Open 24 hrs. Smart casual dress mandatory.

Gay and lesbian

Sydney has a thriving gay and lesbian community that has reached legendary status through the **Mardi Gras Festival** held every Feb, which culminates in the hugely popular parade through the city on the first Sat of Mar, www.mardigras.org.au.

The main focus for social activity is Oxford St, especially at the western end between Taylor Sq and Hyde Park, while Newtown, in the inner west, is home to Sydney's lesbian scene. There are many clubs and cafés that attract a casual mix of both straight and gay. Some of the more gay-oriented bars are **Albury Hotel**, **Beauchamp Hotel** and **Oxford Hotel** on Oxford St, and the **Newtown Hotel**, 174 King St, Newtown. Some popular nightclubs for men are **Midnight Shift**, 85 Oxford St, and **The Barracks**, 1 Flinders St. **DCM**, 33 Oxford St, T9267 7380, and the **Taxi Club**, 40 Flinders St, Darlinghurst, attract a mixed crowd. For more info and venues look out for the free gay papers *Capital Q* (weekly) and *Sydney Star Observer* available at most gay friendly restaurants, cafés and bookshops, especially on Oxford St. **The Bookshop**, 207 Oxford St, T9331 1103, is a good source.

Performing arts

Naturally the focus for the performing arts in Sydney is the **Sydney Opera House**. It offers five venues, the **Concert Hall**, the **Opera Theatre**, the **Drama Theatre**, the **Playhouse** and the **Studio**. The Concert Hall is the largest venue and home to the Sydney Symphony Orchestra. The Opera House is the home of Opera Australia, the Australian Ballet and the Sydney Dance Company. The Drama Theatre is a performing venue for the Sydney Theatre Company while the Playhouse is used for small cast plays, more low-key performances, lectures and seminars. The Studio is used for contemporary music and performance. Prices and seats range from about $35-200. For details call the box office, T9250 7777, or www.soh.nsw.gov.au.

The beautiful and historic **State Theatre**, 49 Market St, T9022 6258, www.statetheatre.com.au, offers a dynamic range of specialist and mainstream performances and cinema. Similarly the lovingly restored **Capitol**, 13 Campbell St, T9320 5000, offers a diverse range of performances, while the **Theatre Royal**, MLC Centre, 108 King St, T136166, is noted for its musicals and plays. The **Lyric Theatre** and the **Showroom**, at the Star City complex, 80 Pyrmont St, T9777 9000, offer theatre, concerts, comedy, dance and musicals. From around $40-80 for a major performance.

The **Wharf Theatre**, Pier 4, Hickson Rd, The Rocks, is the home of the Sydney Theatre Company, T9250 1777, www.sydneytheatre .com.au. Bangarra are a contemporary Aboriginal dance group and are based at Wharf 4, Walsh Bay, The Rocks, T9251 5333, www.bangarra.com.au. The **Wharf Restaurant** next door is a superb for pre-performance dining and 'Behind the Scenes Tours' are available, T9250 1777, $5.

The **Belvoir Theatre**, 25 Belvoir St, Surry Hills, T9699 3444, www.belvoir.com.au, is another less well known venue offering a good range of performances. The **City Recital Hall**, Angel Pl, City, T9231 9000, www.cityrecitalhall.com.au, offers a programme of regular classical music performances from around $50. The newly refurbished **Sydney Conservatorium of Music**, near the Botanical Gardens, off Macquarie St, T9351 1222, www.music.usyd.edu.au, also hosts occasional live performances.

The **Sydney Entertainment Centre**, 35 Harbour St, City, T9320 4200, www.sydentcent.com.au is one of the city's largest and most modern performance venues, hosting a wide range of acts, shows, fairs and sporting events.

❂ Festivals and events

Jan New Year kicks in with spectacular fireworks and celebrations that centre around The Rocks and the Harbour Bridge. Other good vantage points include Milsons Point, The Opera House and Cremorne Point.

Sydney Festival and Fringe Festival takes place through most of the month. It is a celebration of the arts including the best of Australian theatre, dance, music

and visual arts and is held at many venues throughout the city. For many the highlights are the free open air concerts in the Domain, including Opera in the Park and Symphony under the Stars, check www.sydneyfestival.org.au.
The 26th sees the annual **Australia Day** celebrations with the focus being a flotilla of vessels flying the flag on the harbour, www.australiaday.com.au.
Feb Without doubt the most famous Sydney event is the legendary **Gay and Lesbian Mardi Gras Festival and Parade** held throughout the month. It is an opportunity for the gay community to celebrate, entertain and shock. The highlight is a good shake of the pants and cod pieces (or very lack of them) during the spectacular parade from Liverpool St to Anzac Parade (held at the end of the festival), T9557 4332, www.mardigras.org.au.
Mar The **Royal Agricultural Easter Show** is held every **Easter** and now uses the state of the art facilities at Olympic Park as a venue.
Apr The 25th sees the annual **Anzac Day** service at the Martin Place Cenotaph and a parade down George St.
May The annual **Sydney Morning Herald Half Marathon** is a great attraction, especially when it involves crossing the Harbour Bridge. **Australian Fashion Week** celebrations showcase some of the country's top designers. (There is also another fashion week in Nov to preview the best of the winter collections).
Jun **Sydney Film Festival**, a 2-week fest for film buffs featuring over 150 features from 40 countries, T9660 3844, www.sydney filmfestival.org.
Aug **Sun-Herald City to Surf**, a 14-km race from Bondi Beach to the City Centre, T9282 2747.
Sep **Festival of The Winds** at Bondi Beach is a colourful festival of kites and kite flying, while the avid sports fans fight over tickets and take several days drinking leave for the Rugby League and Rugby Union **Grand Finals**.
Oct The weekend **Manly Jazz Festival** is a gathering of Australia's best along with some fine foreign imports. Stages located in several public arenas including the beachfront and the Corso, as well as hotels, restaurants and bars, T9977 1088.
Nov **Sydney to the Gong** (Wollongong – 80 km) cycle race.
For details contact Bicycle NSW, T9283 5200, www.bicyclensw.org.au.
Dec **Carols by Candlelight** is the main festive public celebration of song in the Domain, while the wild and wicked grab a beer glass and a patch of sand at the **Bondi Beach Christmas Party**, which usually ends up as a mass streak into the waves. Far more serious is the **Sydney to Hobart** sailing race, which departs from the inner harbour, winds allowing, every **Boxing Day**.

O Shopping

Sydney can offer a superb, world-class shopping experience. The most popular shopping venues are to be found in the city centre, but many of the suburban high streets also support a wide range of interesting outlets and colourful weekend markets. In the city most of the large department stores, arcades, malls and specialist boutiques are to be found along **George St** and in the area around **Pitt St Mall, Castlereagh St** and **King St**. The suburbs of **Newtown** (King St) and Glebe (Glebe Point Rd) have some fascinating shops selling everything from cod pieces to second-hand surfboards. **Double Bay**, **Mosman** and **Paddington** (Oxford St) are renowned for their stylish boutique clothes shops and **The Rocks** is definitely the place to go for a didgeridoo or cuddly koala.

Art

For authentic Aboriginal art look out for the National Indigenous Arts Advocacy Association Label of Authenticity. For the best in authentic and original examples try: **Authentic Aboriginal Art Centre**, 45 Argyle St, The Rocks, T9251 4474, open daily 1000-1700; **Aboriginal Dreamtime Fine Art Gallery**Shop 8/ 199 George St, T9241 2953;**The Coo-ee Emporium and Aboriginal Art Gallery**, Bondi, T9300 92300, www.cooeeart.com.au, (by appointment); the **Hogarth Galleries**, 7 Walker La, T9360 6839. Further afield try the **Boomalli Aboriginal Artists Co-operative**, 55 -59 Flood St Leichhardt, T9560 2541, and **OZbiz Aboriginal Art and Craft**, 36 The Corso, Manly, T9977 3677.

There are many art galleries showcasing some of the best Australian contemporary artists with most being in **The Rocks** or **Paddington**. Try to get hold of *Art Find* brochure from one of the galleries or the Sydney VIC. **Ken Done** is one of the most famous Sydney-based artists. He has a colourful style which you will either love or hate. His main outlet is at 123 George St, The Rocks, T9247 2740, www.done.com.au.

Bookshops

Dymocks are the major player with outlets throughout the city. The largest (and appar- ently the largest bookshop in Australasia) is at 424 George St, T1800 688 319, www.dy mocks.com.au, Mon-Wed and Fri 0900-1800, Thu 0900-2100, Sat-Sun 0900-1700.

Travel Bookshop, 175 Liverpool St (southern edge of Hyde Park), T9261 8200, Mon-Fri 0900-1800, Sat 1000-1700, is a good source of travel information, books and maps.

Goulds Book Arcade, 32 King St, Newtown, is the largest and most bizarre second-hand bookshop in the city, it's a 'lost world'.

Clothes

You will find all the major labels in the major central city shopping streets, arcades and department stores (see section below). **Oxford St** in Paddington and also the suburbs of **Double Bay** and to a lesser extent **Chatswood**, are renowned for their boutique clothes stores and Australian designer labels. Names and labels to look for include **Helen Kaminski, Collette Dinnigan, Morrissey, Bare, Isogawa** and **Bettina Liano**. For designer bargains try the **Market City** above Paddy's Markets in Haymarket. Finally, if you are looking for something different then head for **King St** in Newtown.

You'll also find all the Aussie classics such as Akubra hats, RM Williams boots and Driza-Bone oilskin coats. These are all beautifully made and well worth the money. A pair of RM's boots for example will, provided you look after them, last a lifetime. **RM Williams clothing outlets** can be found at 389 George St and Shop 1-2 Chiefly Plaza, corner of Hunter St and Phillip St, www.rmwilliams.com.au.

Goodwood Saddlery, 237-239 Broadway, T9660 6788, Mon-Fri 0900-1730, Thu until 2000, Sat 0900-1700, Sun 1000-1600, or **Strand Hatters** in the Strand Arcade, 412 George St, T9231 6884, for Akubra Hats and Driza-Bones.

Department stores/arcades

Queen Victoria Building, T9264 9209, www. qvb.com.au, is not to be missed. This vast and historic edifice has levels of retail therapy that are legendary, see also p115. On Market St there are great Sydney institutions, the characterful department stores of: **Grace Bros**, T9238 9111, www. gracebros.com.au; **David Jones**, T9266 5544, www.david jones.com.au; and **Gowings**, T9287 6394, www.gowings.com.au.

Food and wine

If you are a novice or even a seasoned wine buff, before purchasing any Australian labels you might benefit from a trip to the **Australian Wine Centre**, 1 Alfred St, Circular Quay, T9247 2755, www.australianwine centre.com. The staff are very knowledgeable and are backed by a great collection of over 1,000 wines. They

(Left) The Strand Arcade off George Street, originally built in 1892; (Right) A typical retail outlet in Chinatown

also offer a world-wide delivery service. Open daily. For a taste of Australian foods take a look at the food hall in the elegant **David Jones** department store, Market St, T9266 5544. Even if you don't like seafood a trip to the **Sydney Fish Markets**, Pyrmont, is fascinating with the stalls setting up their displays of Australia's best from about 0800 (see page 118).

Handicrafts

Craft Australia Boutique, David Jones department store, Market St, 4th floor, T9266 6276. For unique Australian crafts. **Object**, 415 Bourke St, Surry Hills, T9361 4555, www.object.com.au, showcases the best in authentic Australian crafts. **The Rocks and the weekend Rocks Market** sell a good range of souvenir-based products. **Australia's Northern Territory and Outback Centre**, 28 Darling Walk, Darling Harbour, T9283 7477, www.outbackcentre. com.au, sell a good range of Australiana. **Didj Beat Didgeridoo Shop**, Clocktower Square Mall, The Rocks, T9251 4289, www.didjbeat.com. Although didgeridoos and boomerangs are sold all over the city, this place is perhaps the best outlet. It has over 2,000 'didjies' on show. A free 1-hr workshop is offered with your purchase (from $55-1,500) and they also stock a good selection of original Aboriginal art. Open 1000-1830 daily. The website is also highly entertaining.

Jewellery

Given the fact Australia produces over 90% of the world's opals it is not surprising to find a wealth of specialist dealers. To ensure authenticity and good workmanship only purchase opals from retailers who are members of the Australian Opal and Gem Industry Association Ltd (AOGIA) or the Jewellers Association of Australia. Some of the best retailers include: **Flame Opals**, 119 George St, T9247 3446, www.flameopals.com.au, Mon-Fri 0900-1845, Sat 1000-1700, Sun 1130-1700; **Opal Minded**, 36-64 George St, T9247 9885, 1000-1800; and **Australian Opal Cutters**, Suite 10, 3rd floor, 295 Pitt St, T9261 2442. Pearls from the great Australian 'pinctada maxima' oyster, from gold to snow white, are also big business in Sydney and for some of the best and biggest look no further than

 Bunda, Shop 42, Ground Floor, QVB, George St, T9261 2210.

Markets

There are plenty of weekend markets held in the inner city that offer a range of new and second-hand clothes, arts, crafts and foods. **The Rocks Market** held every Sat-Sun at the top end of George St, is the most popular market and is supplemented on Sun with an uncluttered open-air market on the Opera House concourse, which concentrates mainly on arts, crafts and souvenirs. **Paddy's Markets**, Haymarket, Thu-Sun, is the biggest in the city centre is the fairly tacky and mildly amusing. Good inner suburbs markets include: **Paddington Market** held every Sat in the grounds of the church at 395 Oxford St; **Balmain Market** at St Andrew's Church, corner of Darling St and Curtis St, also on Sat; **Glebe Market**, in the grounds of Glebe Public Schools, Glebe Point Rd every Sun; and **Bondi Markets**, Campbell Parade, every Sun.

Outdoor

Kent St is the place to start looking for camping and outdoor equipment. **Paddy Pallin**, 507, T9264 2685, www.paddypallin.com.au; **Mountain Equipment**, 491, T9264 5888, www.mountainequipment. com; and **Patagonia**, 497, T9264 2500, are all near to each other.

Activities and tours

Sydney is the venue for some of the most important major national and international sporting events in Australia. The huge success of the 2000 Olympic Games has left the city legacy of some superb sporting venues. Most are to be found at the Homebush Bay Olympic Park, see page 120. Test Rugby, Aussie Rules and Test Cricket match tickets are often very hard to come by and any attempt must be made well in advance. A ticket will cost from $40-100 for a cricket test match and $40-150, for a rugby Grand Final. The usual ticket agent is Ticketek, T9266 4800, www.ticketek.com. au. If you cannot secure tickets or don't rate your chances securing a spare ticket outside the venue (often possible), joining the throngs of Sydneysiders in the city pubs can be just as enjoyable and atmospheric.

Aerial tours/activities

Scenic flights

There are a number of fixed-wing and helicopter scenic flight companies including **Sydney Heli-Aust**, T9317 3402, www.heli aust.com.au, is based at the airport but offers pick-ups from the city. **Palm Beach Seaplanes**, based in Rose Bay (eastern harbour suburbs) and Palm Beach (Pittwater), T1300 656 787, www.sydneyby seaplane.com.au, offers an interesting alternative. A 15-minute flight around the harbour will cost you from $95, children $50, while a 90-min trip taking in the harbour, beaches and Blue Mountains costs from $620, children $310. If you want to see the northern beaches from the air and to arrive in Palm Beach by style the one-way trip will cost you a hefty $435.

There are a number of scenic flight companies based at Bankstown Airport, T9796 2300.However the adventurous should contact **Red Baron Scenic Flights** run by the Sydney Aerobatic School, T9791 0643. They offer unforgettable scenic harbour flights from an open cockpit Pitts Special from $400 and might even throw in a loop or two. **Seaplanes over Sydney**, T1300 780 284, www. southerncrossseaplanes.com.au also offer a range of luxury flights from and above the harbour, from $145.

Sky diving

You can also try your courage at sky diving in and around Sydney. Companies include **Simply Skydive**, CM12, Mezzanine, Centre- point, T9223 8444, www.simply skydive.com.au, and **Sydney Skydiving**

Detail of the Sydney Harbour Bridge at sunset

Centre based out at Bankstown Airport, T9791 9155, www.sydneyskydivers.com.au. Jumps start from about $325.

Ballooning

Cloud 9, T1300 555 711, www.cloud9balloonflights.com and **Balloon Aloft**, T1800 028 568, www.balloonaloft.com, offer early morning flights over the outer suburbs or in the Hunter Valley from $285, children $170.

Cruises

There are numerous good value Harbour Cruises on offer with most being based at Circular Quay. Trips vary from a sedate cruise on a replica of the Bounty to paddle steamers and fast catamarans. In recent years whales have occasionally appeared in the inner harbour which is believed to be a sign of improving water quality. For whale-watching cruises from Sydney Harbour check out www.whalewatchingsydney.net. Thanks to the increase of whale numbers, they can guarantee sightings on their daily cruises which departing from Darling Harbour and Circular Quay from late May to early Nov. Vessels include the new luxury flagship *Ocean Dreaming*, a 34-m catamaran.

Land-based activities

Walking

The VIC has a number of free walking brochures including the detailed *Go Walkabout* produced by Sydney Ferries, Sydney Harbour Foreshore Walks, Historical Sydney, Sydney Sculpture Walk and the Manly Scenic Walkway. **Aboriginal Discoveries** is an aboriginal owned and operated outfit that offers day, half-day and 1½-hour guided tours and cruises covering some of Sydney's most significant Aboriginal sites, T9568 6880. There are many bushwalks in the city suburbs.

Sightseeing tours

Rocks Walking Tour

This is the best, most entertaining and informative way to get to know this area. Bookings (advised) can be made at the Sydney VIC, 106 George St, or at the Walks Office, 23 Playfair St, T9247 6678, www.rockswalkingtours.com.au. Tours take 90 mins, departing at 1030, 1230 and 1430 weekdays and 1130 and 1400 weekends. From $20, children $10.50, family $50.

Harbour Islands Tours

For all island access, tour information and bookings contact the Sydney

Outback New South Wales

Some 1160 km west of Sydney, Broken Hill, or 'Silver City' as it is dubbed, is the most famous mining town in Australia, its gracious, dusty streets looking like something out of an Aussie version of Hollywood's 'Wild West'. As well as all the obvious historical and mine based attractions Broken Hill is also home to a thriving arts community and numerous colourful galleries. There are also tour operators to escort you to the surreal settlement of Silverton, as well as offering true outback adventures to some superb regional national parks and lake systems. **Broken Hill VIC** ⓘ *corner of Blende St and Bromide St, T8088 9700, www.visitbrokenhill.com.au, 0830-1700*, have city and regional maps as well as a detailed, self-guided heritage walk and trail leaflet and organize two-hour guided tours.

First off, pay a visit to the **Line of Lode Visitors Centre and Miners' Memorial** ⓘ *T8087 1345, www.lineoflode brokenhill.org.au, 0900-2200, access to memorial $2.50*, which tells the town's history. It stands atop the mullock heaps immediately to the east of the town centre. Their on-site MacGregor's Café, is the best place to eat in town. Perched on the mullock heap just below the Line of Lode is **Delprats Mine** ⓘ *T8088 1604, which offers 2-hour underground tours 200 m below the surface. Mon-Fri 1030, Sat 1400, $40, child $30. Book ahead at the VIC or at the mine, 15 mins prior to tour time*. In contrast the **Daydream Mine** ⓘ *20 km west of Broken Hill, signposted off the Silverton Rd, T2788 5682, www.day dreammine.com.au, tours on the hour from 1000-1530, $15*, is an 1882 original with a walk-in mine, once, believe it or not, mined by children as well as adults.

Broken Hill has a thriving arts community creating very diverse works inspired by the landscapes, colours, light and perspectives of the surrounding outback. **Broken Hill Regional Art Gallery** ⓘ *T8088 5491, Argent St, Mon-Fri 1000-1700, Sat/Sun 1300-1700, $3*, is the oldest regional gallery in NSW and has a fine mix of local and national works. The **Living Desert and Sculpture Symposium** is a collection of sandstone sculptures commissioned in 1993 and located on the summit of a hill, 12 km northwest of the town. Sunset is the most popular time to visit but a far quieter time to visit is at dawn. There are also numerous tours on offer from Broken Hill, from scenic flights and 4WD to local mine tours and even camel rides. The VIC has full details.

The tiny former mining town of **Silverton**, just a short journey from Broken Hill, is pure 'outback', with wide, red, dusty roads and some mighty eccentric residents. The village and the surrounding landscape is so typical it has featured in numerous magazine advertisements, television commercials and as the backdrop to some well known films, including '*Mad Max II*'. Right in its heart is the famous Silverton Hotel, which featured in the film '*A Town Like Alice*', which does a good lunch, has a fine atmosphere (ask if you can 'take the test') and has accommodation. Don't be surprised if you see the odd camel around Silverton. They belong to the Silverton Camel Farm where treks and safaris are offered from $15 (15 minutes), $50 (sunset safari), T8088 5316, www.silvertoncamels.com. There is no public transport to Silverton but it is on the agenda of most Broken Hill tour operators. There is also no fuel on sale here.

Sleeping

LL **Imperial Hotel**, 88 Oxide St, T8087 7444, imperial@pcpro.net.au. Beautifully renovated with excellent en suites or rooms with shared facilities all with a very pleasant historic feel.

C-F **YHA Tourist Lodge**, 100 Argent St, T8088 2086, mcrae@pcpro.net.au. Deservingly popular for both budget style motel accommodation and backpackers is this friendly, family run lodge. It offers dorms, doubles/twins with spacious facilities, pool and bike hire. The owners are very active in the community and local gurus when it comes to town and regional sights and activities advice.

D-E **Silverton Hotel**, T8088 5313. To this day, the hotel - which featured in the film 'A Town Like Alice' - still plays host to Max fanatics. Good lunches, a fine atmosphere (ask if you can 'take the test'), hotel rooms and self-contained accommodation.

Transport

Broken Hill Airport is 4 km southwest of the town via Bonanza St, T8087 4128. A taxi, T8088 1144, to/from the airport to the city centre costs about $14. **Regional Express**, T131713, www.rex.com.au, and **Qantas** both offer regular services to Sydney and Adelaide. Long-distance coaches stop at the coach terminal, T8087 2735, beside the VIC. **Greyhound**, T132030, offers 3 weekly services onthe Dubbo (Sydney) to Adelaide route. **Countrylink**, T132232, provides regular coach/rail services to Sydney via Dubbo. Buses stop outside the VIC on Anson St. The train station is on Crystal St, T8087 1400. **Countrylink** and **Great Southern Railways**, T132147, offers India-Pacific or Ghan services between Sydney and Perth (via Adelaide) twice weekly.

Harbour National Park Information Centre, Cadman's Cottage, 110 George St, The Rocks, T9247 5033, www.nationalparks.nsw.gov.au Mon-Fri 0900-1630, Sat-Sun 1000-1630.

Bridge Climb

The most high-profile activity in the city is the award-winning **Bridge Climb**, 5 Cumberland St, The Rocks, T8274 7777, www.bridgeclimb.com, 0700-1900, which involves the ascent of the 134-m Harbour Bridge span. The 3-hr climb can be done day or night and in most weather conditions besides electrical storms. As well as the stunning views from the top the climb is most memorable. Although it is fairly easy-going and is regularly done by the elderly, the sight and noise of the traffic below adds a special edge. You cannot take your own camera on the trip – for safety reasons. Climbs during the week cost from $165, children $100, weekends $185, children $125. Twilight climbs cost from $245, children $185.

Watersports

Diving

Although diving is best at the Barrier Reef, if you are heading north to Queensland, NSW and Sydney has some good diving. The southern beaches, La Perouse and the Botany Bay National Park offer the best spots. There are dive shops in the city and companies offering tuition and trips. These include the popular **Dive Centre** bases at both Manly (10 Belgrave St, T9977 4355) and Bondi (192 Bondi Rd, T9369 3855), www.dive sydney.com. They offer shore and boat dives from $50 (own gear), $90 (hire) and Open Water Certificates from $350.

Pro Dive, 478 George St, T9264 6177, www.prodive.com.au, offers local trips and training and stock a good range of equipment.

Fishing

The VIC has listings of other charters based in Sydney, many of which also offer whale-watching trips from Jun-Oct. Despite all the harbour activity, both the fishing and the water quality in Sydney Harbour is said to be pretty good. There are a number of fishing charters available including: **Charter One**, T04-0133 2355, www.charterone.com .au, based in Manly. Trips range from a 3-hr jaunt from $95 to full-day $135, including tackle hire; **Quayside Charters**, T9341 8226, www.quaysidecharters.com.au at Circular Quay.

Surfing

The famous surf spots are of course Bondi and Manly but some of the lesser-known Sydney beaches offer better surf. Try some of the northern beaches, such as Curl Curl (home to Layne Beachley), or see what the surf report recommends.

Manly Surf School, at the North Steyne Surf Club, Manly Beach, T9977 6977, www.manlysurfschool. com, offers good value daily classes from 1100-1300, from $50 for one lesson to 5-day lessons from $170.

Dripping Wet Surf Company, Shop 2, 93-95 North Steyne, Manly, T9977 3549, www.drippingwetsurf.com, offers boards, body boards, flippers and wetsuits for hire. Board hire costs from $13 per hr.

Aussie Surf Adventures, T1800 113 044, www.surfadventures.com.au, is another company that offers multi-day surf trips and intensive lessons from Sydney to Byron Bay, 5 days from $575.

Sailing

Sydney Harbour offers some of the best sailing in the world. On Boxing Day every year, at the start of the **Sydney to Hobart race**, the inner harbour becomes a patchwork of colourful spinnakers raised to the mercy of the winds.

Sydney Mainsail, T9979 3681, www.sydneymainsail.com.au, offers 3-hr trips 3 times daily with highly experienced skippers.

Australian Spirit Sailing Company, T9878 0300, www.austspiritsailingco.com.au, offers similar trips.

The replica 'Bounty' crossing the line during Australia Day's traditional Tall Ships Race on Sydney Harbour

Sydney by Sail, at National Maritime Museum , T9280 1110, www.sydneybysail.com runs social day trips and introductory lessons from $75.
The office is based below the lighthouse.

Swimming

Swimming is of course a popular pastime. South of the Heads, the beaches at Bondi, Bronte, Clovelly and Coogee are hugely popular while to the north, Manly, Collaroy, Narra- been, Avalon, Ocean Beach and Palm Beach are also good spots. Lifeguards patrol most beaches in summer and you are strongly advised to swim between the yellow and red flags. These are clearly staked out along the beach and placed according to conditions. Most of the city beaches also have safe, open-air, salt-water swimming pools to provide added safety, especially for children. **Bondi Icebergs pool** is a Sydney landmark but there are also quiet neighbourhood pools such the charming **McCallum Pool**, a small outdoor pool on Cremorne Point (off Milson's Road) with great views across the harbour.

Sea kayaking

Sea kayaking is a great way to explore the backwaters and bays of the suburbs. The Middle Harbour, which branches off between Middle Head and Clontarf, snakes over 10 km into the lesser-known North Shore suburbs and is especially good. It offers a quiet environment and more wildlife. It is not entirely unusual to see the odd sea eagle or fairy penguin. Kayaks can be hired from the **Sydney Kayak Centre**, Spit Rd, Spit Bridge, T9969 4590. **Sydney Harbour Kayaks**, 3/235 The Spit Rd, Mosman, T9960 4389, www.sydneyharbourkayaks.com.au, offers guided trips.

Transport

Air

For information and flight arrivals/ departures, T9667 6065, www.sydney airport.com.au. See also p21 and p107.

Bus

Local

The STA (Sydney Buses) are the principal operators with the standard buses being blue and white, the Airport Express a very Aussie green and yellow, the **Sydney Explorer** red and the **Bondi Explorer** blue. Standard bus fares are between $1.60-5.20 depending on distance and subsequent zone. If you intend to travel regularly by bus a Travel Ten ticket is recommended ($13-44) while further savings can be also be made with the TravelPass and Sydney Pass system (see box, p). The Explorer buses cost $36 for the full return trip ($62 2-days). There is an on-board commentary and you can hop on and off at will. Both leave at regular intervals from Circular Quay. For all of the above bus fares children travel half-price and there are also family concessions. Note most Explorer buses operate between 0840 and1722 only.

There are also local (green) **Olympic Explorer** offering trips around the Homebush Bay site and links with ferry services from Circular Quay ($20 with ferry, $10 without), while the weekend (blue and yellow) **Parramatta Explorer** leaves every 20 mins from the RiverCat ferry terminal in Parramatta, $10 (ex RiverCat).

For information about suburban buses in Sydney, T131500, www.131500.com.au. Drivers do not automatically stop at bus stops. If you are alone you must signal the driver, or at night gesticulate wildly.

Long distance

Sydney Coach Terminal is in the Central Railway Station, Shop 4-7, Eddy Av, T9212 3433, daily 0600-2230. Interstate services from Sydney include: **Brisbane**, Greyhound, 5 daily, 20 hrs, $107; **Byron Bay**, Greyhound, 4 daily,18 hrs, $98. **Cairns**, Greyhound, 5 daily, 46 hrs, $322. **Canberra**, Greyhound, 10 daily, 5 hrs, $37. **Melbourne**, Greyhound, 5 daily, 14 hrs 20 mins, $68. Premier Motor Services also offer similar services throughout the East Coast.

Car/campervan

Travelling by car around Sydney is a nightmare with numerous tolls, expensive parking and omnipresent parking wardens. There really is no need to see the sights by car but if you must take lots of change. Note that as of December 2004 only vehicles with the city auto-toll E-Tag system will be able to use the harbour tunnel. The toll for the harbour bridge ($3 south-bound, free north-bound) will remain payable by cash or E-Tag. NRMA are located at 74-76 King St, CBD, T132132.

Top tips

Ticket to ride

There are numerous, popular travel pass systems in operation through the STA. The DayTripper Pass gives all-day access to Sydney's trains, bus and ferries within the suburban area from $15, child $7.50. Tickets can be purchased at any rail, bus or ferry sales or information outlet or on the buses themselves. TravelPass allows unlimited, weekly, quarterly or yearly combined travel throughout designated zones or sections. A 7-day pass for example, covering the inner (orange) zone, costs $36, child $18.50. For the tourist staying only a few days, however, the best bet is the The Sydney Pass which offers unlimited travel on ferry and standard buses as well as the Sydney and Bondi Explorer routes and the four STA Harbour Cruises. They are sold as a 3-day ($100, child $50), 5-day ($130, child $65) or 7-day ($150, child $75) package. Return Airport Express transfers are also included and family concessions apply. Note that discount, ten-trip 'TravelTen' (bus) and 'FerryTen' passes are also available and recommended, from $12.70.

Car hire offices at the airport (Arrivals south) include **Avis**, T136333, **Hertz** T133039, **Thrifty** T136139, **Budget** T132727, **National**, T131390, and **Red Spot**, T1300 668 810. In the city try **Avis**, **Budget** and **Ascot** centred on or around William St, Darlinghurst. Cheaper options often include **Dollar**, Domain Car Park, Sir John Young Crs , T9223 1444, and **Bayswater Rentals**, 180 William St, Kings Cross, T9360 3622. Rates can get as low as $30 per day. Campervan hire from **Maui**, T1300-363800, www.maui-rentals.com; **Britz**, free call T9667 0402 www.britz.com.au.

Second-hand car and campervan dealers include **Travellers Auto Barn**, 177 William St, Kings Cross, T1800-674374, www.travellers-autobarn.com.au, **Kings Cross Car Market**, Ward St Car Park, Kings Cross, T1800-808188, www.carmarket.com.au (good buy and sell).

Cycling

The pace of cycling is perfect for sightseeing. Unfortunately the rest of the road users don't agree. Travel by bike within the city centre can be hairy to say the least. Several companies offer bike hire from about $30 per day or $170 per week, including **Inner City Cycles**, 151 Glebe Point Rd, Glebe, T9660 6605; **Woolly's Wheels**, 82 Oxford St, T9331 2671, and the **Manly Cycle Centre**, 36 Pittwater Rd, Manly, T9977 1189. For general advice contact **Bicycle NSW**, Level 5, 822 George St, T9281 4099, www.bicyclensw. org.au. For *Sydney Cycle Ways* maps and information contact the **RTA**, T9218 6816.

Ferry

A trip on one of Sydney's harbour ferries is a wonderful experience and an ideal way to see the city, as well as reach many of the major attractions and suburbs. The principal operator is **Sydney Ferries** who operate the 'green and golds' and also the fast **JetCats** to Manly and **RiverCat** to Homebush Bay/Parramatta. Several independent companies also operate out of Circular Quay offering cruises as well as suburban trans- portation and water taxis. See Cruises page147.

Like the buses, ferry fares are priced according to zone and start at a single trip for $4.80. If you intend to travel regularly by ferry a FerryTen ticket (from $30.30) is recommended, while further savings can also be made with the TravelPass and Sydney Pass system, see box p153. Various travel/entry combo tickets are offered to the major harbourside sights including Taronga Zoo (Zoo Pass $37, child $20) and Sydney Aquarium (Aquarium Pass $29.10, child $14.50). Children travel half-price and there are also family concessions on most fares. For ferry information T131500, www.sydneytransport.com.au. The main Sydney Ferries Information Centre can be found opposite Wharf 4, Circular Quay.

MonoRail and LightRail

MonoRail

MonoRail, www.metromonorail.com.au, runs in a loop around Darling Harbour and South Western CBD and provides a convenient way of getting from A to B. They run every 3-5 mins, Mon-Thu 0700-2200, Fri-Sat 0700- 2400, and Sun 0800-2200. The standard fare (1 loop) is $4, a Day Pass costs $9. Children under 5 years travel free and discounts are available to some major attractions.

LightRail

The new **LightRail** network is Sydney's newest transport system linking Central Station with Lilyfield, via a number of stops within the southwest CBD and Darling Harbour, as well as the Casino, Fish Market and Glebe. It is a 24-hr service with trains every 10-15 mins from 0600-2400 and every 30 mins from 2400-0600. There are 2 fare zones starting at a single journey at $2.90. A Day Pass with unlimited stops costs $8.40. Children travel at half price. For information, T8584 5288, www.metromonorail.com.au.

Taxi

Land based

Sydney's once rather dubious taxi service was given a major revamp for the 2000 Olympics and it is now much improved. Ranks are located near every railway station, at Circular Quay and numerous spots in the CBD, otherwise hail one as required. From 2200-0600 higher tariffs apply. On short journeys tipping is not expected. There are several companies including **Combined** T8332 8888, **ABC** T132522, **Premier** T131017, **Legion** T131451, and **RSL** T132211.

Water based

Water taxis operate all over the harbour with most being based on the western edge of Circular Quay. The main operators are **Water Taxis Combined** Circular Quay, T9555 8888, and **Yellow Water Taxis** T9299 0199.

Train

Local

Sydney's 24-hr double-decked train services are a convenient way to reach the city centre and outlying areas, or to link in with bus and ferry services. Fares start at $2.80 and savings of up to 40 per cent can be made with 'Off-Peak Tickets', which operate after 0900 on weekdays. Further savings can be made with the TravelPass and Sydney Pass (see box p153). There are coloured routes with the green/purple City Circle (Central, Town Hall, Wynyard, Circular Quay, St James and the Museum) and blue Eastern Suburbs Line (Central, Town Hall, Martin Place, Kings Cross, Edgecliff, Bondi Junction) being the most convenient. Tickets and information are available at all major stations. For information about suburban trains in Sydney, T131500, www.131500.com.au.

Long distance

All interstate and NSW State destination trains arrive and depart from the Central Railway Station on Eddy Av, just south of the city centre. There is an information booth and ticket offices on the main platform concourse. **Countrylink** are the main interstate operators operating with a combination of coach and rail to all the main interstate and NSW destinations, T132232 (daily 0630-2200), bookings@ countrylink. nsw.gov.au. **Countrylink Travel Centre**'s are at the railway station, T9955 4237; Town Hall Station, T9379 4076; Wynyard Station, T9224 4744; Circular Quay, T9224 3400; and Bondi Junction T9377 9377. First class and economy fares vary so you are advised to shop around and compare prices with the various coach operators. The railway station also houses the main interstate city coach terminal (**Greyhound**) and from there, or Pitt St and George St, you can pick up regular city and suburban buses. The Airport Express also stops outside the train station (coach terminal). For information T131500, www.sydney transport.net.au. **Countrylink** operates the 'XPT' (11 hrs, twice daily, 1 overnight) between Sydney-Melbourne and Sydney-Cairns.

Directory

Banks

The major banks have ATMs on all the major shopping and eating streets. Foreign Exchange is readily available on the arrivals concourse of Sydney Airport. In the city there are many outlets especially around Circular Quay and along George St.

Hospital

St Vincent's Hospital, Victoria St, Darlinghurst, T9339 1111; **Royal North Shore Hospital**, Pacific Highway, St Leonard's, T9926 7111; **Prince of Wales Hospital**, High St, Randwick, T9382 2222; **Sydney Children's Hospital**, T9382 1111.

Internet

Internet is widely available throughout the city with the southern end of George and Pitt sts (between Liverpool and Hay) and the western end of Oxford St (between Crown and College) having numerous outlets. Most backpackers offer their own internet facilities and outlets, especially in the outer suburbs.
Global Gossip have several Sydney outlets including 14 Wentworth Av, 790 George St in the CBD, and 37 Hall St, Bondi. Expect to pay from $4 to $10 per hr (be careful to confirm your start and finish time; 'rounding up' seems to be common).

Post

There are Post Shops dotted around the city marked with the prominent red and white circular logo. The main General Post Office is located at 1 Martin Pl, T131318, Mon-Fri 0815-1730, Sat 1000-1400.
Post Restante is based on the 3rd floor, 310 George St (across the road from the Wynyard Station entrance). Log your name into the computer to see if any mail awaits. The city centre post restante code is NSW 2001. Open Mon-Fri 0830-1700.

Useful contacts

For the police, emergency T000, general enquiries T9690 4960. **City of Sydney Police Station**, 192 Day St, T9265 6499.

Around Sydney

One of the wonderful things about Australia's largest city is that you are never too far away from water or parks and nature reserves. To the west, a mere 70 km delivers you to the fringes of some of the state's largest and most celebrated national parks, all within the Greater Blue Mountains region. Once a major barrier to the exploration of the interior, until the route west was finally opened up in the first half of the the 19th century, the 'Blues' now serve as a natural wonderland; a vast playground for over one million visitors a year who come to explore the eroded valleys, gorges, bluffs and amazing limestone caves. Even closer to home is the Ku-ring-gai Chase National Park to the north and the Royal National Park to the south, the latter tragically destoryed by the terrible bush fires that have ravaged huge swathes of the country in successive recent years. Between Ku-ring-gai and what's left of Royal National Park is the tiny Botany Bay National Park, site of Captain Cook's first landing in April 1770.

Getting there Regional rail and bus.
Getting around Local bus and rail networks, or hire car/campervan.
Time required 2-4 days.
Weather Warm and dry in summer with occasional storms, mild in winter.
Sleeping B&Bs and the YHA hostel recommended in the Blue Mountains. Good national park campsites.
Eating Plenty of choice in Katoomba.
Activities and tours Hiking, canyoning or abseiling in the Blue Mountains. Bush or coastal walks in the Ku-ring-gai Chase.
★ Don't miss The views and walks around Wentworth, Katoomba and Blackheath (Blue Mountains). » p158

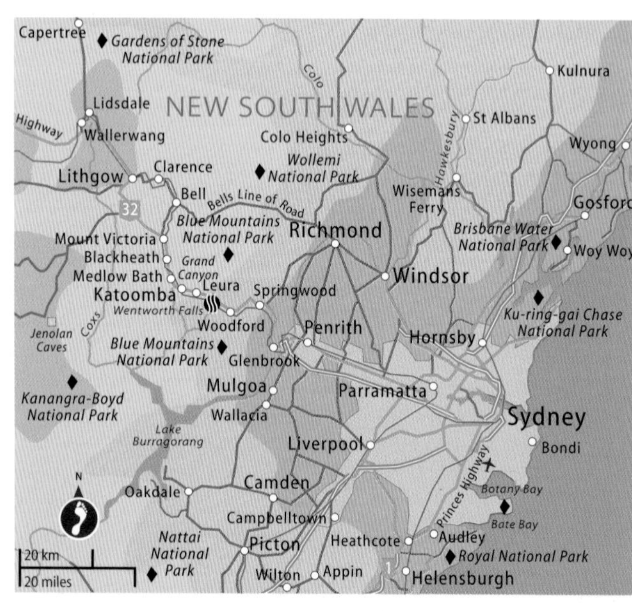

Botany Bay National Park pp168-170.

Botany Bay holds a very special place in Australian (European) history as the site of Captain Cook's first landing, in April 1770. The landing site is near what is now Kurnell on the southern shores of Botany Bay, which along with La Perouse on the northern shore, comes under the auspices of the 458-ha Botany Bay National Park. As well as possessing highly significant historical sites for both the European and Aboriginal cultures it presents plenty of walking opportunities and ocean views.

Within the small northern sector of the park, around **La Perouse** on the northern headland, you can take a tour of **Bare Island Fort** ⓘ *T9311 3379, guided tours Sat-Sun, $7.70, child $5.50*, built amidst wartime paranoia and the perceived threat of foreign invasion. Also located on the headland is the **La Perouse Museum and Visitors Centre** ⓘ *Cable Station, Anzac Parade, T9311 3379, Wed-Sun 1000-1600, $5.50, child $3.30*, on the actual site of the first landing of the First Fleet in 1788. The museum explores the great historical event and the fate of French explorer Captain La Perouse, as well as local Aboriginal and European heritage.

The southern sector is larger and and has the best walks including the short (1km) **Monument Track** and the more demanding **Coast Walk** to Bailey lighthouse. It also hosts the **NPWS Botany Bay National Park Discovery Centre**, a good source of park and walks information and an interesting display surrounding Cook's landing.

Royal National Park pp168-170.

The 15,080-ha Royal National Park was the first national park in Australia gazetted in 1879. As well as providing over 100 km of walking tracks, many taking in terrific ocean views, there are some beautiful beaches and other activities ranging from swimming to scuba diving. However, the park is subject to the constant threat of fire and more than once in the last decade the Royal has been almost completely (but temporarily) destroyed by bush fires. The main hub of human activity centres around historic **Audley** at the park's northern entrance, where you will find the NPWS Royal National Park Visitors Centre ⓘ *Farnell Av, T9542 0648, 0830-1630*. **Wattamolla**, **Garie** and **Burning Palms** are three beautiful beaches and the choice of walks ranges from the 500-m (wheelchair-accessible) **Bungoona Track** to the 26-km **Coast Track** (Bundeena to Otford) which guarantees some glorious coastal views and on occasion (from June to September) the odd whale sighting. You can hire rowboats and canoes at the Audley Boatshed, near the visitors centre for a paddle up Kangaroo Creek. Mountain bikes are also available for hire but trail routes are limited and there is good surfing at the patrolled **Garie Beach**. Several freshwater pools also provide swimming. By car from Sydney take the Princes Highway south and follow signs for Audley (left, at Loftus on Farnell Avenue and McKell Avenue). Vehicle entry costs $11 per day.

Ku-ring-gai Chase National Park pp168-170.

Though a few wealthy Sydney entrepreneurs might see Ku-ring-gai Chase as little more than 14,883-ha of wasted prime real estate, just 26 km north of Sydney. The rugged sandstone country that fringes the mighty Hawkesbury River, with its stunning views and rich array of native wild animals and plants, is thankfully safe from further suburban encroachment and has been since it was designated as a National Park in 1894. As well as the stunning views across Pittwater and Broken Bay, the park offers some lovely bush walks, secluded beaches and regionally significant Aboriginal rock art. It is also a great place to see that much celebrated state flower, the warratah, in bloom. Without doubt the highlight of the park is the **West Head Lookout**, high above the peninsula overlooking

Broken Bay and the mouth of the **Hawkesbury River**. To the north is the beginning of the central coast and Brisbane Water National Park, while to the west is the tip of the northern beaches and the historic Barrenjoey Lighthouse. West Head is criss-crossed with walking tracks that start from West Head Road. Aboriginal rock art can be seen along the **Basin Track** – which falls to the Basin Beach campsite and the arrival/departure point of the Palm Beach ferry – and the 3½-km **Red Hand Track** (Aboriginal Heritage Track). **Bobbin Head** at the western end of the park is a popular base for water-based activities. Here, too, is the VIC, which can supply details on walks. NPWS Bobbin Head Information Centre ⓘ *Bobbin Inn, Bobbin Head Road (western side of the park), T9472 8949, 1000-1600*, or the Kalkari Visitors Centre ⓘ *Chase Rd, between Mount Colah and Bobbin Head, T9457 9853, 0900-1700*, can supply walks, camping information and maps. By car access is via Bobbin Head Rd, via the Pacific Highway (from the south) or from Ku-ring-Gai Chase Road via F3 Freeway (from the north). Access to the eastern side (West Head Road and West Head Lookout) is from Mona Vale Road, Northern Beaches. Vehicle entry costs $10 per day.

Blue Mountains » *pp168-170.*

The 'Blues', as they are affectionately known, form part of the Great Dividing Range, 70 km, or two hours, west of Sydney and contain no less than five national parks covering a total area of 10,000 sq km. They are not really mountains at all, but a network of eroded river valleys, gorges, and bluffs, that have formed over millions of years. The result is a huge wonderland of natural features, from precipitous cliffs, to dramatic waterfalls and canyons, not to mention the most dramatic limestone caves on the continent. Once the home of the Daruk Aboriginals, the Blue Mountains were seen by the first Europeans merely as a highly inconvenient barrier to the interior and for almost a quarter of a century they remained that way, before finally being traversed in 1813 by explorers Blaxland, Wentworth and Lawson. To this day the impenetrable geography still limits transportation and essentially the same two convict-built roads and railway line completed over a century ago reach west through a string of settlements from Glenbrook to Lithgow on the other side. For decades the 'Blues' have been a favourite weekend or retirement destination for modern-day Sydney escapees, who welcome the distinctly cooler temperatures and the colourful seasons that the extra elevation creates. But superb scenery and climate aside, there are some excellent walking opportunities, as well as abseiling, canyoning and rock climbing. Given the region's popularity there are also a glut of good restaurants and a wide range of places to stay from showpiece backpackers to romantic hideaways.

Ins and outs

Getting there Although public transport to and around the Blue Mountains is good you are advised to take your own vehicle or hire one, allowing you to make the most of the numerous viewpoints and sights within the region. Trains are the best way to arrive independently leaving Sydney's Central Station (Countrylink and CityLink platforms) on the hour daily, stopping at all major towns through the Blue Mountains, T132232. The journey to Katoomba takes about two hours and costs around $22 day-return. Numerous coach companies and hostels offer day sightseeing tours from Sydney. Some may allow overnight stops. The accredited VIC in Sydney can assist with the extensive choice and bookings. Most of the buses leave from Circular Quay.

Getting around The route through the Blue Mountains is easily negotiable. From the west (Sydney) you take the M4 (toll), eventually crossing the Neapean River, before it forms the Great Western Highway at Glenbrook (65 km). Then, you pass through Blaxland, Springwood, Faulconbridge and Woodford, before arriving at Wentworth Falls. Here you essentially reach the top of the main plateau at an average height of just above 1,000 m. From

Wentworth Falls the road then continues west through the northern edges of Leura and Katoomba, then north, through the heart of Blackheath and Mount Victoria. From Mount Victoria you then begin the descent to Lithgow (154 km). The rather peculiarly named Bells Line of Road provides another access point across the mountains from Windsor on the east to Mount Victoria on the Great Western Highway (77 km). Katoomba is the largest of the towns and has the best amenities. ▸▸ *See under the relevant destinations for further details.*

Tourist information The main accredited VICs are in **Glenbrook**, **Katoomba** (Echo Point, T1300-653408, www.bluemountainstourism.org.au, daily 0900-1700), **Lithgow** (1 Cooerwull Rd, at the western end of town, T6353 1859, www.tourism.lithgow.com, 0900-1700), and **Oberon** (west, near the Jenolan Caves). The main NPWS office is at the Heritage Centre, near Govetts Leap, Blackheath. These are listed under the relevant section. If approaching from the east, stop at the Glenbrook VIC to begin with and stock up with the free visitors guide and maps. All regional centres also offer a free accommodation bookings service. The NPWS stock a wide range of books covering the numerous walks within the national parks, as well as topographical maps.

The national parks

The Blue Mountains region contains five national parks which cover an area of 10,000 sq-km, with half of that being considered 'wilderness area'. The largest, at an expansive 4,876 sq km (and the second largest in the state after Kosciuszko National Park) is **Wollemi National Park**, to the north of the Bells Line of Road. It incorporates the state's most extensive officially recognized wilderness area and is very rugged and inaccessible. As well as its complex geology, topography, Aboriginal art sites and botanical features it is also home to a rich variety of birds. Of all the parks in the region it is the one for the well-prepared modern-day explorer. There are basic NPWS campsites at Wheeny Creek, Colo Meroo, Dun's Swamp and Newnes. Main access is from Putty Road, 100 km northwest of Sydney or via Rylstone.

The most famous and accessible park is the 2,470-sq-km **Blue Mountains National Park**, straddling the Great Western Highway and a string of mountain villages and towns, from Glenbrook in the east to Lithgow in the west. Only recently expanded in the 1980s, it contains natural features that range from deep canyons and forested valleys to pinnacles and waterfalls, as well as an abundance of flora and fauna. Although now receiving over one million visitors a year, much of the park remains extremely inaccessible, with over 500 sq km considered official wilderness area. Sadly, the Blue Mountains, like so many national parks in NSW, has suffered in recent years from the temporary impact of widespread bush fires. There are basic NPWS campsites at Euroka Clearing near Glenbrook, Ingar near Wentworth Falls and Perry's Lookdown near Blackheath. You can also camp anywhere within 500 m from roads and facilities. Access is from many points east and west off the Great Western Highway, or from the Bells Line of Road 70 km west of Sydney.

Next up is the beautiful 680-sq-km **Kanangra-Boyd National Park**, to the southwest of Katoomba. Fringed by the Blue Mountains National Park on all but one side it contains a similar geology and topography but is particularly famous for two natural features, the Jenolan limestone caves and the Kanangra Walls (a series of outstanding bluffs). Both are well worth visiting, with the latter considered one of the great walks in the region. There is a basic NPWS campsite at Boyd River. Access is via Mount Victoria and the Jenolan Caves 180 km west of Sydney.

To the southeast of Kanangra-Boyd and the Blue Mountains National Parks is the 860-sq-km **Nattai National Park**. It touches the region's largest body of water, Lake Burragorang, and contains the region's largest populations of eastern grey kangaroos as well as many rare plants and animals. NPWS camping near the lake. Access is 110 km south of Sydney between Warragamba Dam and Wombeyan Caves Road.

The smallest national park in the group is the 12,000-ha **Gardens of Stone National Park** north of Lithgow. Adjoining Wollemi it is most noted for its prominent and shapely limestone outcrops and sandstone escarpments. Birdlife is once again prolific. There are no campsites. Access is 30 km north of Lithgow via Mudgee Road.

Glenbrook to Wentworth Falls

Proud of its European roots and its railway heritage, the pretty village of Glenbrook, just beyond the Nepean River, acts as the unofficial gateway to the Blue Mountains. Along with Katoomba this is the main tourism administration and information centre for the Blue Mountains. **NPWS Conservation Hut** ⓘ *Fletcher St (off Falls Rd), T4757 3827*, can provide walks information and has a small shop and café. **Glenbrook VIC** ⓘ *off the Great Western Highway, T1300 653408, www.bluemountainstourism.org.au, daily 0900-1700.*

Fringing the village, south of the highway, is the southern section of the Blue Mountains National Park and access to numerous attractions, including the **Red Hands Cave**, a fine example of Aboriginal rock art. The distinctive hand stencils made on the cave wall are thought to be over 1,600 years old. You can reach the caves either by road or by foot (8 km return) from the Glenbrook Creek causeway, just beyond the park entrance. There are also shorter walks to the **Jellybean Pool** and the **Euroka Clearing**, a basic NPWS campsite and the ideal spot to see grey kangaroos, especially early or late in the day. To reach the park gate ($6 per day, walkers free), take Ross Road behind the VIC onto Burfitt Parade and then follow Bruce Road. The lookouts at **The Bluff**, at the end of Brook Road (slightly further east off Burfitt, then Grey), are also worth a look. North of the highway in Glenbrook you can also follow signs to the **Lennox Bridge** the oldest in Australia, built by convicts in 1833.

Beyond Blaxland and Springwood is the small settlement of **Faulconbridge**, home to the **Norman Lindsay Gallery and Museum**. Lindsay (1879-1969) is just one of many noted artists who found the Blue Mountains conducive to their creativity and his studio remains very much the way he left it. For most, it is the stunning lookouts across **Wentworth Falls** and the **Jamieson Valley** that offer the first memorable introduction to the dramatic scenery of the Blue Mountains – assuming the weather is clear, of course. The car park is the starting point for some superb walking tracks, best of which is the four-hour **Wentworth Pass Walk** which crosses the top of the falls, and then descends precariously down to the valley floor. Then, if that were not enough, the track skirts the cliff base, through rainforest, before climbing back up via the dramatic **Valley of the Waters** gorge to the **Conservation Hut** (see above). From there it's an easy walk back to the car park. Another excellent walk is the five-hour **National Pass Walk** which follows a cutting halfway up the cliff, carved out in the 1890s. Both walks involve steep sections around cliff edges and laddered sections, but if you have a head for heights either one is highly recommended. Give yourself plenty of time and make sure you get maps from the Conservation Hut before setting out.

For something less demanding, try the **Den Fenella Track**, which will take you to some good lookouts, then you can return or preferably keep going (west) to the Conservation Hut along the **Overcliff Track**. Better still, is the magical **Undercliff Track** to **Princes Rock Lookout**.

Leura

Although the pretty village of Leura plays second fiddle to Katoomba, the two essentially merge into one. Possessing a distinct air of elegance, the residents of Leura are proud of their village and in particular their gardens. **Everglades Gardens** ⓘ *37 Everglades Ave, T4784 1938, 1000-1700, $6, concessions $4, children $2*, provide the best horticultural showpiece and has done since the early 1930s. **Leuralla and NSW Toy and Railway Museum** ⓘ *Olympian Parade, T4784 1169, 1000-1700, $10, child $2*, is well worth a look, for kids and parents alike. There are several walks and lookouts around the cliff fringes in Leura with the best being the

The sheer sandstone cliffs of the Blue Mountains, near Sydney

short 500-m walk to the aptly named **Sublime Lookout**, offering arguably the best view of the Jamieson Valley and Mount Solitary. Follow signs from Gladstone Road, west of the Mall.

Katoomba

Considered the capital of the Blue Mountains, the erstwhile mining town of Katoomba offers an interesting mix of old and new and a truly cosmopolitan ambience. As well as the wealth of amenities and activities based in the town, many come here simply to see the classic picture-postcard view of the Blue Mountains from the famous **Three Sisters lookout**. The steady stream of tourist traffic flows down Katoomba's main drag towards **Echo Point** to enjoy this view. It is little wonder the place is so popular. Built precariously

Katoomba

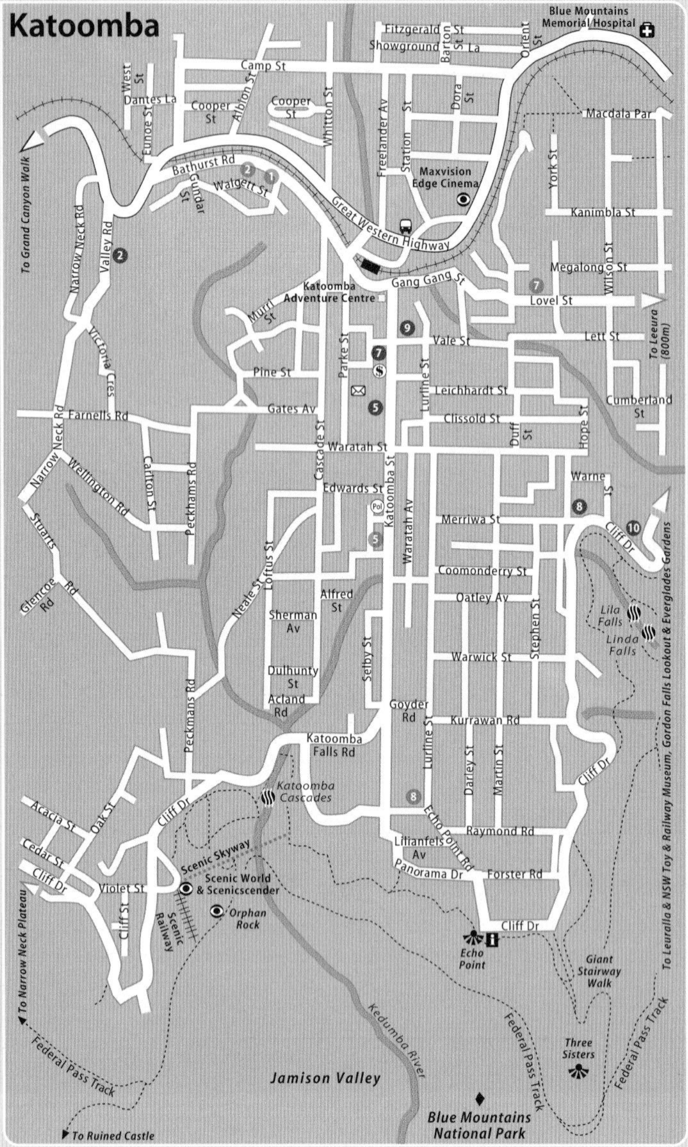

Sleeping
Balmoral Guesthouse 1
Flying Fox Backpackers 2
Katoomba Blue Mountains YHA 5
No14 Budget Accommodation 7
Three Explorers Motel 8

Eating
Arjuna 2
Elephant Bean 5
Paragon 7
Rooster 8
Savoy 9
Solitary 10

170 m above the valley floor, the lookout seems to defy gravity. Dawn and sunset are the best times to visit. From the lookout it is possible to walk around to the stacks and descend the taxing **Giant Stairway Walk** (30 minutes) to the valley floor. From there you join the **Federal Pass Track**, back through the forest below the cliffs to the **Katoomba Cascades** and **Orphan Rock** (a lone pillar that became separated from the nearby cliff over many centuries of erosion). From Orphan Rock it is a short walk to a choice of exits: the hard option, on foot, up the 1,000-step Furbers Steps, or for the less adventurous, the Scenic Railway, see below. Give yourself three hours.

Katoomba presents many other excellent walking options, including the **Narrow Neck Plateau** (variable times) and the **Ruined Castle** (12 km, seven hours). The latter starts from the base of the Scenic Railway and can be made as part of an extended overnight trip to the summit of Mount Solitary. Recommended, but go prepared. The **Grand Canyon** walk (5 km, four hours) from Neates Glen, Evans Lookout Road, Blackheath, is also a cracker.

West of Echo Point the junction of Cliff Drive and Violet Street will deliver you to the highly commercial **Scenic World** ⓘ *T4782 2699, www.scenicworld.com.au, 0900-1700, Railway and Scenicsender $16 (one way $8), Skyway $16,,* with its various unusual scenic transportations. The **Scenic Railway** option takes you on an exhilarating descent to the valley floor; on what is reputed to be the world's steepest 'inclined funicular railway'. At the bottom you can then take a boardwalk through the forest to see an old coal mine with an audio-visual display and bronze sculpture. In contrast, the new **Scenic Skyway** provides a more sedate bird's-eye view of the valley floor and the surrounding cliffs. The last, and most recent, of the trio, is the **Scenicscender**. If you survive that there is also a cinema showing a Blue Mountains documentary on demand and a revolving restaurant, which no doubt is their last gasp effort to see you on your way with an empty stomach.

Maxvision Edge Cinema ⓘ *225 Great Western Highway, T4782 8900, from 1020, from $14.50,* with its six-storey, 18-m high, 24-m wide screen, is worth visiting for its precipitous film of the Blue Mountains, 'The Edge'.

Medlow Bath, Blackheath and Megalong Valley

From Katoomba the Great Western Highway heads north through the pretty villages of Medlow Bath, Blackheath and Mount Victoria. Although, not as commercial as their bustling neighbour all provide excellent accommodation, restaurants and are fringed both north and south by equally stunning views and excellent walks. To the east is the easily accessible **Megalong Valley**, particularly well known for its horse trekking, with **Grose Valley** to the west. **Evans and Govetts Leap Lookouts**, east of Blackheath, provide the best easily accessible viewpoints, but there are also some lesser-known spots well worth a visit.

In **Medlow Bath** is the historic **Hydro Majestic Hotel**, built in 1903 and the longest building in Australia at the time. Though a hotel in its own right, its original function was as a sanatorium, offering all manner of health therapies, from the sublime – mud baths and spas – to the ridiculous – strict abstinence from alcohol. At the time the rarefied air in the Blue Mountains was hailed as a cure-all for city ills and people flocked to the Hydro. Today, although the mud baths (and thankfully the prohibition) have gone, the hotel still provides fine accommodation and a great spot for afternoon tea.

Blackheath is a sleepy little village with a lovely atmosphere, enhanced in autumn when the trees take on their golden hues. There are two lookouts well worth visiting. The first, **Evans Lookout**, is accessed east along Evans Lookout Road and provides the first of many viewpoints across the huge and dramatic expanse of the Grose Valley. One of the best walks in the region, the **Grand Canyon Trail**, departs from Neates Glen, off Evans Lookout Road (5 km, five hours). From there you descend through the rainforest and follow Greaves Creek through moss-covered rock tunnels and overhangs, before climbing back up to Evans

Canberra; Australia's capital city

Derived from the Aboriginal word 'Kamberra' meaning 'meeting place', Australia's capital is, sadly, one of the most underrated cities in he world. It lacks a certain intimacy and is too modern to have developed a real sense of history, but, if you can ignore the negative publicity, it's actually a very nice place and offers a great deal to see and do. A sightseeing bus tour is a good way of experiencing the sights, particularly if you are short of time. Cycling is also a great way to get around the city, with numerous purpose-built cycleways. An efficient bus service runs throughout the city and to the airport. The **VIC** ⓘ *330 Northbourne Av, 3 km north of the city centre, T6205 0044, www.canberratourism.com.au, Mon-Fri 0900-1730, Sat-Sun 0900- 1600*, can supply more detail and maps.

If you are short of time don't miss the National Museum, the New Parliament Building and the National Capital Exhibition, all of which are neatly contained within the National Triangle, or Parliamentary Triangle. Although the temptation is to head straight for the Triangle's crowning glory, the New Parliament Building, start your tour instead at the **National Capital Exhibition** ⓘ *Regatta Point, Commonwealth Park, T6257 1068, www.nationalcapital.gov.au, 0900-1700, free*, which imaginatively outlines the fascinating history of the nation's capital from its indigenous links to the intriguing landscaped metropolis we see today. The views across Lake Burley Griffin are memorable.

Completed in 1988, **New Parliament House** ⓘ *T6277 5399, www.aph.gov.au, 0900-1700, guided tours every half hour from 0900* is, without doubt, the architectural showpiece of Canberra and surely right up there along with the other great Australian man-made wonders, like Sydney's Opera House and Harbour Bridge. Where else in the world is there a building that has its lawn on the roof? Once you have trampled all over it and taken in the angles, perspectives and views you can then turn to matters of the interior. As well as more fascinating architecture the interior's publicly accessible areas host precious Australian art and craft, including Arthur Boyd's impressive Shoalhaven Tapestry. When Parliament is sitting, access is allowed to 'Question Time' in the House of Representatives and begins at 1400. Tickets are free and bookings can be made through the 'Seargent of Arms' office.

Facing Lake Burley Griffin, in the heart of the National Triangle, is the **Old Parliament House** completed in 1927, hub of the nation's political life until the New Parliament House took over in 1988. Immediately outside is the Aboriginal Tent Embassy which serves as a pertinent reminder that the Aboriginal people of Australia were living here for tens of thousands of years before the first acre of land was ever purchased, or brick of any parliament house was ever laid. Sitting proudly and defiantly on the shores of Lake Burley Griffin, the **National Museum of Australia** ⓘ *T6208 5000/1800-026132, www.nma.gov.au, 0900-1700, free (admission charge to some specialist displays)*, is quite superb. It presents a range of exciting displays and themed galleries that convey all things 'Aussie' and can answer just about every conceivable question you may have wanted to ask about the country, all beautifully designed and presented.

Sleeping

The VIC has listings and offer a bookings service, T1800100660, www.canberra tourism.com.au/getaways.

LL **Hotel Kurrajong**, 8 National Circuit, Barton, T6234 4444, www.hotelkurrajong.com.au. Considered one of the capital's best boutique hotels. It is well positioned between the lively suburb of Manuka and the National Triangle in Kingston and also offers a good range of rooms as well as dinner, bed and breakfast packages.

A-D **Canberra City Accommodation**, 7 Akuna St, City centre, T6257 3999, www.canberracityaccommodation.com.au. This is probably the best budget option. It charges more than you're average hostel but it is certainly worth it. Plenty of rooms, from dorm to en suite doubles, as well as kitchen, bar, pool and spa.

Transport

Canberra's international airport, T6209 3336, www.canberraairport.com.au, is about 8 km east of the city centre via Morshead Drive. **QantasLink**, **Virgin Blue** and **Regional Express** fly to/from Sydney, Brisbane and Melbourne.

Long-distance coaches stop at the Jolimont Tourist Centre, 65 Northbourne Ave, Civic T02-6249 6006. **Greyhound** and **Premier Motor Services** have services to Sydney, Brisbane and Melbourne. Canberra train station is in the suburb of Kingston, 6 km south of the city centre, off Cunningham St, T6257 1576. **Countrylink**, T132232, runs regular daily services to/from Sydney and Melbourne (train/coach).

 Lookout. Recommended. The other lookout, **Govetts Leap**, is a stunner and has the added attraction of the **Bridal Veil Falls**, the highest (but not necessarily the most dramatic), in the Blue Mountains. Just before the lookout car park is the **NPWS Heritage Centre** ⓘ *0900-1630. T4787 8877, www.npws.nsw.gov.au*, which is worth a visit providing walks information, maps, guide and gifts. **Fairfax Heritage Track**, built to accommodate wheelchairs, links the centre with the lookout. From Govetts Leap you can walk either north to reach Pulpit Rock or south to Evans Lookout via the falls.

Although Govetts and Evans are both stunning, three other superb lookouts await your viewing pleasure and can be accessed from Blackheath. These are often missed, but no less spectacular. The first, **Pulpit Rock**, can be reached by foot from Govetts (1½ hours, 2½ km) or better still, by 2WD via (unsealed) Hat Hill Road. The lookout, which sits on the summit of a rock pinnacle, is accessed from the car park by a short 500-m walk. From the same car park then continue north to **Anvil Rock**, being sure not to miss the other short track to the bizarre geology of the wind-eroded cave. Perry Lookdown is 1 km before Anvil Rock and a path from there descends into the valley to connect with some demanding walking trails. Also well worth a visit is the aptly-named **Hanging Rock**, which will, on first sight, take your breath away. Watch your footing and do not attempt to climb to the point, as tempting as it may be. It is also a favourite abseiling spot. Like all the other lookouts on the southern fringe of the Grose Valley, sunrise is by far the best time to visit. The rock can be reached along a rough, unsealed track (Ridgewell Road), on the right, just beyond Blackheath heading north. It is best suited to 4WD but if you don't have your own transport most local 4WD tours go there.

Megalong Valley, accessed on Megalong Valley Road, west of Blackheath town centre, provides a pleasant scenic drive and is one of the most accessible and most developed of the wilderness Blue Mountains valleys. **Megalong Australian Heritage Centre** ⓘ *T4787 8188, www.megalong.cc, 0800-1730*, offers a whole range of activities from horse trekking and 4WD adventures, to livestock shows.

Lithgow

Lithgow marks the western boundary of the Blue Mountains and was founded in 1827 by explorer Hamilton Hume. An industrial town and Australia's first producer of steel, its main tourist attraction is the remarkable Zig Zag Railway (see page 167), 10 km east in Clarence, as well as a scattering of historical buildings. The town also acts as the gateway to the Jenolan Caves and Kanangra-Boyd National Park to the south and the wilderness Wollemi National Park, to the north. Wollemi is one of the largest and the most inaccessible wilderness areas in NSW, a fact that was highlighted in no uncertain terms in 1994 with the discovery of the Wollemi Pine, a species that once flourished over sixty million years ago. The exact location of the small stand of trees is kept secret.

There are two fairly low-key museums in the town. **State Mine and Heritage Park and Railway** and **Lithgow Small Arms Museum**. **Eskbank House Museum** is a Georgian homestead built in 1842, complete with period furnishings and Lithgow pottery. The VIC can supply town maps and accommodation listings. Of far more natural and historic appeal are the derelict villages of **Newnes** and **Glen Davis**, to the north of Lithgow, between the scenic Gardens of Stone National Park and the western fringe of the Wollemi National Park. Both were once thriving villages supporting a population of thousands that worked in the two large oil-shale refineries during the early 1900s. South of Newnes an added attraction is the old 400-m rail tunnel that was once part of a busy line that connected the shale plants with Clarence Station. Now left dark and forbidding, the tunnel is the silent home of glow worms (gnat larvae), which light up its walls like a galaxy of stars. All along the unsealed roads to both Newnes and Glen Davis look out for the prolific birdlife.

In **Clarence**, 10 km east of Lithgow, you will find the **Zig Zag Railway** ⓘ *T6353 1795, $20, concessions $16, child $10*, a masterpiece of engineering originally built between 1866 and 1869. Operated commercially up until 1910 as a supply route to Sydney it now serves as a tourist attraction with lovingly restored steam trains making the nostalgic 8-km (1½ hours) journey from Clarence to Bottom Points (near CityRail's Zig Zag Station). They leave Clarence on Wednesdays and at the weekend at 1100, 1300 and 1500. On other weekdays the less exciting motorized trains take over and leave at the same time. Request drop off if you are arriving by CityRail from Sydney/Katoomba at the Zig Zag Station.

Jenolan Caves

ⓘ *T6359 3911, www.jenolancaves.org.au, the main caves can only be visited by guided tour, daily from 1000-2000, '1 hr' caves $16, child $10, '1½ hr' caves $23, child $15. Cave combo tickets from $24-$40.*

The Jenolan Caves, on the northern fringe of the Kanangra-Boyd National Park, south of Lithgow, comprise nine major (and 300 in total) limestone caves considered to be amongst the most spectacular in the southern hemisphere. After over 160 years of exploration and development – since their discovery in 1838 by pastoralist James Whalan – the main caves are now well geared up for your viewing pleasure with a network of paths and electric lighting to guide the way and to highlight the bizarre subterranean features. As well as guided cave tours, some other caves have been set aside for adventure caving, and above ground, there is a network of pleasant bush trails. If you are short of time the **Lucas Cave** and **Temple of Baal Cave** are generally recommended. The **Chiefly Cave** is the most historic and along with the **Imperial Cave** it has partial wheelchair access. The **River Cave** is said to be one of the most demanding. On your arrival at the caves you immediately encounter the **Grand Arch** a 60-m wide, 24-m high cavern that was once used for camping and even live entertainment to the flicker of firelight. Nearby the historic and congenial **Caves House** has been welcoming visitors since 1898 (see Sleeping, page 168).

Bells Line of Road

Bells Line of Road is named after Archibald Bell, who discovered the 'second' route through the Blue Mountains to Lithgow from Sydney, in 1823, at the age of 19. Starting just west of Richmond in the east, then climbing the plateau to fringe the northern rim of the Grose Valley, it provides a quieter, more sedate, scenic trip across the Great Divide. Just beyond the village of Bilpin, west of Richmond, the huge basalt outcrop of Mount Tomah (1,000 m) begins to dominate the scene and supports the 28-ha cool-climate annexe of the **Sydney Botanical Gardens** ⓘ *T4567 2154, 1000-1600, $4.40, children $2.20*. Opened in 1987, the garden's rich volcanic soils nurture over 10,000 species, including a huge quantity of tree ferns and rhododendrons. Although the gardens are well worth visiting in their own right, it is the views, the short walks and the restaurant that make it extra special. Just beyond Mount Tomah (right) is the **Walls Lookout**, with its expansive views across the Grose Valley. It requires a one-hour return walk from the Pierces Pass Track car park but the effort is well worth it. Back on the Bells Line of Road and just a few kilometres further west is the junction (north, 8 km) to the pretty village of **Mount Wilson** which is famous for its English-style open gardens. These include **Linfield Park** and **Nooroo**. Also of interest is the '**Cathedral of Ferns**' at the northern end of the village. The **Wynnes** and **Du Faurs Lookouts** can also be reached from Mount Wilson and are signposted, east and west of the village centre.

Sleeping

Ku-ring-gai Chase National Park *p157*
C-E **Pittwater YHA**, T9999 5748, pittwater@yhansw.org.au. Take the ferry from Church Point to this great place.

Blue Mountains *p158, map p162*
Leura has many excellent historic B&Bs and self-contained cottages and Katoomba has plenty of choice and Wentworth also has plenty of good B&Bs. If you prefer something quieter, the villages north of Katoomba – Medlow Bath, Blackheath and Mount Victoria – all provide excellent accommodation. There is plenty of accommodation in and around Jenolan. Prices are higher at weekends and you are advised to book ahead at any time of year, especially winter.

LL-D **Jenolan Caves Resort**, Jenolan Caves, T6359 3322, www.jenolan caves.com. Grand and multi-facilitated, this resort has the reowned Caves House. it offers a range of rooms and suites, plus self-contained cottages with a restaurant, bistro, bar and a host of activities.

L-A **Jemby-Rinjah Eco Lodge**, 336 Evans Lookout Rd, Medlow Bath, T4787 7622, www.jembyrinjah lodge.com.au. Has 1- or 2-bedroom, self-contained, modern cabins (one with a Japanese hot tub), log fires, all in a beautiful bush setting close to the lookout and walks. Dinner, bed and breakfast packages are also available.

L-B **Glenella Guesthouse**, 56 Govetts Leap Rd, Medlow Bath, T4787 8352. Well known and surprisingly affordable, historic guesthouse, with a reputable restaurant attached, plus all the comforts including sauna, open fires and cable TV.

B-E **Imperial Hotel**, 1 Station St, Mount Victoria, T4787 1878, www.bluemts.com.au/hotelimperial. Reputedly the oldest tourist hotel in Australia. Beautifully restored it is a fine place to soak up the history and offers a wide range of well-appointed rooms from the traditional to the 4-poster with double spa. Breakfast included, good restaurant, bar and live entertainment at the weekends.

B **Balmoral Guesthouse**, 196 Bathurst Rd, Katoomba, T4782 2264, www.bluemts.com.au/balmoral. One of the many fine historic B&Bs, lodges and self-contained cottages in and around Katoomba. This one is long- established, large with plenty of old world charm, period decor, en suites with spa, log fires, bar and is close to all amenities.

A-B **Three Explorers Motel**, 197 Lurline St, Katoomba, T4782 1733, www.3explorers.com.au. For a motel option try this locally recommended and unconventional option. They also offer a nice fully self-contained 2-bedroom cottage.

A-C **Jenolan Cabins**, Porcupine Hill, 42 Edith Rd, Jenolan Caves, T6335 6239, www.blue mts.com.au/JenolanCabins. Self-contained cabins sleep 6 with one queen size and bunks. The owners also operate local tours.

A-E **Blackheath Caravan Park**, Prince Edward St, Blackheath, T4787 8101. In a quiet suburban bush setting within walking distance of the village. On-site vans, powered and non-powered sites, BBQ and kiosk, but no camp kitchen.

B-E **Katoomba Blue Mountains YHA**, 207 Katoomba St, Katoomba, T4782 1416, bluemountains@yhansw.org.au. Beautifully renovated art deco building it is something of a showpiece hostel for the YHA and fast developing a reputation as one of its best. Its modern, spacious, well facilitated and friendly. Trips arranged, also bike hire and internet.

C-E **The Flying Fox Backpackers**, 190 Bathurst St, Katoomba, T1800-624226, www.theflyingfox.com.au. Long-established and sociable, owners also run the Katoomba Adventure Centre. Campers and campervans welcome.

D-E **No14 Budget Accommodation**, 14 Lovel St, Katomba, T4782 7104, www.blue mts.com.au/no14, is another alternative, providing a peaceful, relaxed atmosphere in a old former guesthouse with double/twin, single and family rooms.

Eating

Blue Mountains *p158, map p162*
Katoomba and the Blue Mountains generally pride themselves in offering some classy restaurants and fine cuisine. Book ahead for the expensive places. See also Sleeping.

YYY **Silk's Brasserie**, 128 The Mall, Leura, T4784 2534. Daily for lunch and dinner (book ahead). One of the many fine restaurants and cafés in Leura, this one offers fine modern Australian cuisine.

YYY **Solitary**, 90 Cliff Dr, Katoomba, T4782 1164. Lunch Sat-Sun and public/school holidays and dinner Tue-Sat. A very classy award winner with a fine reputation offering imaginative modern Australian cuisine and fine views across the Jamieson Valley.

YY **Arjuna**, 16 Valley Rd, Katoomba, T4782 4662. Thu-Mon at 1800 (book ahead). The best Indian restaurant in the region and the views are almost as hot as the curry.

YY **The Rooster Restaurant**, Jamieson Guesthouse, 48 Merriwa St, Katoomba, T4782 1206. Daily for dinner and for lunch Sat-Sun. An old favourite that serves good value French-influenced cuisine, with fine views to boot. Also very good accommodation.

YY **The Savoy**, 26 Katoomba St, Katoomba, T4782 5050. 1100-2000. Good value, especially for its conventional and kangaroo steak dishes.

YY **Vulcans**, 33 Govetts Leap Rd, Blackheath, T4787 6899. Fri-Sun for lunch and dinner. Another well-known Blackheath institution; only drawback is the limited opening.

Y **Elephant Bean**, 159 Katoomba St, Katoomba, T4782 4620. Wed-Mon 0800-1500. A fine café especially for lunch.

Y **Paragon**, 65 Katoomba St, T4782 2928. Daily 0800-1700. If you have a sweet tooth you just cannot afford to miss out on this art deco Katoomba institution.

Activities and tours

Blue Mountains *p158, map p162*
All the below are based in Katoomba unless stated. See the VIC for full listings.

Australian School of Mountaineering, 166 Katoomba St, T4782 2014, www.asmguides.com. Hard-core professional rock climbing and bush craft trips, plus others.

Blue Mountains Adventure Company, 84a Bathurst Rd, T4782 1271, www.bmac.com.au. A reputable outfit.

Blue Mountain Horse Riding Adventures, T4787 8188, www.megalong.cc. Based in the Megalong Valley west of Katoomba, offer hour/half/full and multi day horse rides from $45.

Getabout 4WD Adventures, T1300 305 660, www.getabout.com.au. Professional 4WD tours with a tag-along option allowing you to take your own vehicle.

High 'N' Wild, 3/5 Katoomba St, T4782 6224, www.high-n-wild.com.au. Good mountain biking trips.

Katoomba Adventure Centre, 1 Katoomba St, T1800-824 009, www.kacadventures.com. Very clued-up and eco-friendly, offer great advice on independent walking as well as numerous adventure options, including full-day abseiling from $129, canyoning (repelling) from $139, rock climbing from $139 and adventure walks from $75.

Blue Mountains Explorer Double-Decker Bus, T4782 4807, www.explorerbus.com.au. A local service with 27 stops around Katoomba and Leura, hourly between 0930 and 1730. An unlimited jump-on/off day pass costs $25, concessions $22, child $12.50.

Mountainlink, 285 Main St, T4751 1077/1800-801577. Runs a 29-stop trolley bus tour around the main sights of Katoomba and Leura, with an all day unlimited stop travel pass, daily from 1015-1615, for $12.

Transport

Botany Bay National Park *p157*
Access to the northern sector is via Anzac Parade. **Sydney Buses**, T131500, offers regular daily bus services from Railway Sq (No 393) or Circular Quay (No 394) in Sydney's CBD. To get to the southern sector by car, follow the Princes Highway south, take a left on to The Boulevarde, and then follow Captain Cook Dr. Vehicle entry to the park costs $7. By train from Sydney's Central Station, take **CityRail**, T131500, to Cronulla (Illawarra line), then **Kurnell Bus**, T9523 4047, No 987 to the park gates.

Royal National Park *p157*
By **train** take **CityRail** (Illawarra line) from Central Station to Loftus (4 km from Audley), Engadine, Heathcote, Waterfall or Otford. You can also alight at Cronulla and take the short crossing by ferry to Bundeena at the park's northeastern corner, T9523 2990, from $3.

Ku-ring-gai Chase National Park *p157*
The nearest public transport (western side) by train is with **CityRail**, T131500 (Northern Line), from Central Station to Berowa, Mt Ku-ring-gai and Mount Colah, then walk to Bobbin Head (3-6 km). A better alternative is to catch a bus (No L90) to Palm Beach (eastern side) then catch the ferry to Basin Beach. Ferry cruises also run to Bobbin Head (see page 126).

Blue Mountains *p158, map p162*
Katoomba train station is off Main St, at the northern end of Katoomba St. Trains leave Sydney's Central Station on a regular basis. **Countrylink**, T132232, offers daily services to/from Sydney hourly. **CityRail**, T131500, with **Fantastic Aussie Tours**, T1300-300915, also offer a number of rail/coach tour options with Blue MountainsLink, operating Mon-Fri and Blue Mountains ExplorerLink, operating daily. Prices include return transport and a tour on arrival in **Katoomba**. Greyhound has coaches on the westbound run from Sydney to Dubbo, stopping behind the train station near the **Gearin Hotel**, Great Western Highway.
Blue Mountains Bus Co, T4782 4213, offers a standard Hail 'n' Ride service around Katoomba, Leura and Wentworth Falls. Mon-Fri from 0745-2025, Sat 0800-1530, Sun 0915-1530, from $2. **Katoomba Radio Cabs**, Katoomba, T4782 1311, operates a 24-hr taxi service between Mount Victoria and Wentworth Falls.

Medlow Bath, **Blackheath** and **Mount Victoria** are all on the main local bus/train routes to/from Katoomba. The train station is in the centre of town off the Great Western Highway and on Station St, off the Great Western Highway in Mount Victoria.

Lithgow is on the main local and westbound bus/train route to/from Katoomba and Sydney. See above for details of tours and services. The train station is on Main St, **Countrylink** and **CityRail**, both offer regular daily services east and west.

There is no public transport to the **Jenolan Caves**, but tour operators in Katoomba and Sydney run tours. A basic day tour to the caves will cost about $85 exclusive of caves tour, $100 with one cave inspection and $155 with one cave inspection and a spot of adventure caving. The VICs in Katoomba or Sydney have full details. See also Activities and tours, p169.

Directory

Katoomba *p158, map p162*
Banks Most bank branches with ATMs are located along Katoomba St.
Hospital Blue Mountains Memorial Hospital, Great Western Highway (1 km east of the town centre), T4784 6500.
Internet Available at **Katoomba Adventure Centre**, 1 Katoomba St, T1800-624226. **Post** Behind Katoomba St, at 14 Pioneer Pl. Mon-Fri 0900-1700.

South Coast NSW

Few visitors have any idea that this little corner of NSW is just as beautiful as anywhere else in the state. Overshadowed by Sydney and the north coast, it has pretty much been left alone. But the south coast has over 35 national parks and nature reserves, more than any other region in the state and most are above the waterline. The south coast also has its fair share of beautiful unspoiled beaches and stunning coastal scenery. South of Wollongong and Kiama the coast is split into three quite distinct regions: the Shoalhaven Coast which extends from Nowra to Batemans Bay; the Eurobodalla Coast which stretches from Batemans Bay to Narooma; and the Sapphire Coast which idles its way to the Victorian border.

Getting there Regular buses run up and down the coast. Rail terminates at Kiama.

Getting around Limited local bus networks. Hire car/campervan recommended.

Time required 5 days minimum.

Weather Warm and dry in summer, mild in winter.

Sleeping Good hostels and motor camps in all main towns. National park campsites recommended.

Eating Fish and chips recommended, especially in Batemans Bay.

Activities and tours Fishing, wildlife watching.

★ Don't miss Murramarang National Park » p175.

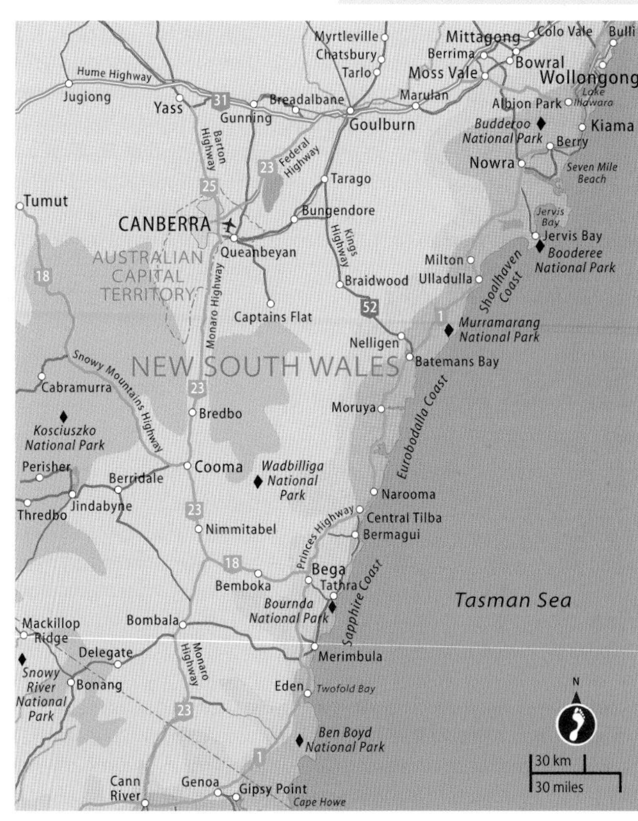

Wollongong and around

pp178-183.

Wollongong is a very attractive place, despite the stark industrial landscapes of Port Kembla to the south, and without doubt its greatest assets are its beaches, its harbour (with its historic lighthouse) and behind that, **Flagstaff Point** headland and the **Wollongong Foreshore Park**. Either side of Flagstaff Point over 17 patrolled beaches stretch from the Royal National Park in the north to Bass Point in the south, all providing excellent opportunities for sunbathers, swimmers and surfies. In the heart of the city the **Wollongong City Gallery** ⓘ *corner of Kembla St and Burelli St, T4228 7500, www.wollongongcitygallery.com, Tue-Fri 1000-1700, Sat-Sun 1200-1600, free*, is definitely worth a visit. Considered one of the best and one of the largest regional galleries in NSW, it offers a wide range of media and an exciting programme of local, regional and interstate exhibitions. For train enthusiasts the **Cockatoo Run** ⓘ *T1300-653801, www.3801 limited.com.au, Wed and Sun 1055, from $40, child $30, lunch an extra $25, bookings required*, is a scenic mountain railway that climbs through the Illawarra Ranges from Wollongong to Robertson in the Southern Highlands. Extended tours throughout the state are also on offer. South of the city centre, in the suburb of Berkeley, is Wollongong's most unique attraction – the **Nan Tien Buddhist Temple** ⓘ *Berkeley Rd, T42720600, www.nantien.org.au Tue-Sun 0900-1700, $3.30, vegetarian lunch $8 per person*, the Southern Hemisphere's largest Buddhist temple which is open to visitors and offers a varied programme of weekend workshops and accommodation, see Sleeping, page 178. Public transport to the Temple is with Premier Illawarra Bus Company (route 34) from Marine Drive. Wollongong offers some excellent surfing with the best breaks on **North Beach**, just north of Flagstaff Point, and **Bulli Beach**, 12 km north of the centre. There are plenty of places to hire equipment (see Activities and tours, page 182). **VIC** ⓘ *93 Crown St, T4227 5545, www.tourismwollongong.com.au, Mon-Fri 0900- 1700, Sat 0900-1600, Sun 1000- 1600.*

The **Illawarra Ranges**, flanking Wollongong inland, have some excellent viewpoints that are well worth seeing, such as the **Mount Keira Lookout** in the Illawarra Escarpment State Recreation Area (left on Clive Bissell Road), and **The Bulli Lookout** (right), both off Highway 1 (Ousley Road), just north of the city. There are numerous fine beaches north of the city. **Bulli Beach** is perhaps the best, but it is literally a case of taking your pick, all the way from the city centre to **Otford** at the southern edge of the **Royal National Park**. Another great local attraction just to the south of the city, and beyond Port Kembla, is **Lake Illawarra**. Essentially a saltwater harbour, sheltered from the ocean by a narrow strip of land, it provides a haven for a wide range of watersports, from sailing to kayaking.

Kiama and Berry

pp178-183.

Just to the south of Lake Illawarra, the pretty coastal town of Kiama is the first of many that are encountered on the journey between Wollongong and the Victorian border. The centre of activity revolves around **Blowhole Point**, crowned by its 1887 lighthouse. During a good southeasterly the surging waves can plough into the blowhole with awesome power, creating a thunderous roar and spout of mist, as if issued from some angry subterranean dragon. To the north of Blowhole Point is **Pheasant Point**, with its rock pool and north again **Bombo Beach**, a favourite amongst the local surf set. **VIC** ⓘ *Blowhole Point, T4232 3322, www.kiama.com.au, 0900-1700.*

South, beyond the Mount Pleasant Lookout on the Princes Highway, is **Werri Beach**, a good one for surfing, then via Crooked River Drive, the headland villages of **Gerringong** and **Gerroa**. At Gerroa, the **Crooked River Winery** ⓘ *11 Willow Vale Rd, 9 km south of Kiama, T4234 0975*, can provide a congenial stop with the added bonus of a fine café and coastal views. From the **Kingsford Smith Lookout** in Gerroa – which pays tribute to Australia's most

Heavy seas find landfall at Kiama NSW south coast

famous aviator – it is hard to resist the temptation to explore the vast swathe of **Seven Mile Beach**, which beckons from below the rooftops. Inland, via the little village of **Jamberoo**, 10 km away, is the **Minnamurra Rainforest**, which forms part of the **Budderoo National Park**. The popular **NPWS Minnamurra Rainforest Centre** ⓘ *T4236 0469, www.nationalparks.nsw.gov.au, 0900- 1700, $11 vehicle entry, café and shop*, signposted off Jamberoo Mountain Road, heading west, acts as a base for explorations of the forest and the Minnamurra Falls.

Roughly halfway between Kiama and Nowra is the delightful little village of **Berry**, which is well worth a stretch of the legs to take a closer look. Almost impossible to miss is the bizarre façade and interior of the **Great Southern Hotel Motel**, on 95 Queen Street. Not only is there a small fleet of rowboats on the roof and a signpost laden with markers to all conceivable destinations, there's also, next door, a bottle shop completely decked in shiny hubcaps. But it doesn't end there. Inside, the bar is decked with a wide array of objects including a centrepiece First World War torpedo set proudly above the pool table. During the great Pacific nuclear testing controversy in the mid-1990s, said torpedo was actually rammed at admirable speed into the gates of the French Embassy in Canberra atop a VW beetle. There are plenty of nice cafés and restaurants along Berry's main drag.

The Shoalhaven coast » *pp178-183.*

Beyond Berry you reach the Shoalhaven River and the twin towns of **Bomaderry** and **Nowra**. From here you are entering the south coast proper and an area known as Shoalhaven, which extends from Nowra to **Batemans Bay**. Although the town of Nowra is a fairly unremarkable introduction to the south coast, just to the east and especially around Jervis Bay and beyond, its true magic begins to be revealed, with some of the best beaches and national parks in the state. Nowra is home to the **Shoalhaven VIC** ⓘ *corner of Princes Hwy and Pleasant Way, T4421 0778, www.shoalhaven.nsw.gov.au, 0900-1630*, as well as the **NPWS office** ⓘ *104 Flat Rock Rd, West Nowra, T4428 6300.*

Paringa and Nowra Park, to the west of Nowra, fringes the riverbank and offers a riverside walk that takes in the 46-m **Hanging Rock Lookout** and a number of unadvertised climbing sites. There are also river cruises, see page 182. Some 8 km south, **Australia's Museum of Flight** ⓘ *T4424 1920, www.museum-of-flight.org.au, 1000-1600, $10, child $5*, is

Tame kangaroos invite themselves to tea at Murramarang National Park

the country's largest aviation museum covering the nation's considerable contribution since before the Wright Brothers first powered flight in 1903.

Jervis Bay and around

Jervis Bay is a deep, sheltered bay that sits neatly in the embrace of the Beecroft Peninsula to the north and the exquisite Booderee National Park to the south. It is blessed with stunning coastal scenery, beautiful white beaches, a marine park with world-class dive sites and even a resident pod of over 60 playful dolphins, all of which combine to earn it the quiet reputation as the jewel of the NSW South Coast. Local information is available from **Huskisson Trading Post** ⓘ *3 Tomerong Rd, Huskisson, T4441 5241, www.jervisbaytourism.com.au, 0900-1700.*

The old ship building town of **Huskisson** (known as 'Husky') and its neighbour **Vincentia** are the two main settlements on Jervis Bay and together form the gateway to the bay's water-based activities. The diving in the **Jervis Bay Marine Park** in particular is said to be second only to the Great Barrier Reef and is well known for its marine variety and water clarity. A couple of companies here offer whale- and dolphin-watching, kayaking, diving trips and so on, see Activities and tours, page 182.

Booderee National Park – formerly known as the Jervis Bay National Park – takes up almost the entire southern headland of Jervis Bay and is, without doubt, one of the most attractive coastal national parks in NSW. Owned and administered by a collaboration of Parks Australia and the Wreck Bay Aboriginal Community, it offers a wealth of fine, secluded beaches, bush walks, stunning coastal scenery and a rich array of wildlife. Not to be missed are **Green Patch Beach**, the further flung **Cave Beach**, a good surf spot, and **Summercloud Bay**. The walking track to **Steamers Beach** (2.3 km) is also recommended although there are many fine options to choose from. Another unique attraction in the park is the 80-ha **Booderee Botanic Gardens** ⓘ *Mon-Fri 0800-1600, Sat-Sun 1000-1700, free with park entry fee*, created in 1952 as an annex of the Australian National Botanic Gardens in Canberra. There are over 1,600 species centred around the small freshwater Lake McKenzie, with most being coastal plants more suited to the local climate. There are a number of short walks and nature trails. The **VIC** ⓘ *Village Rd, T4443 0977, www.booderee.np.gov.au, 0900-1600*, at the park entrance, can supply detailed information about the park, its attractions, walks, amenities and its scattering of great campsites. Note the day fee (including and per car) costs $10 and

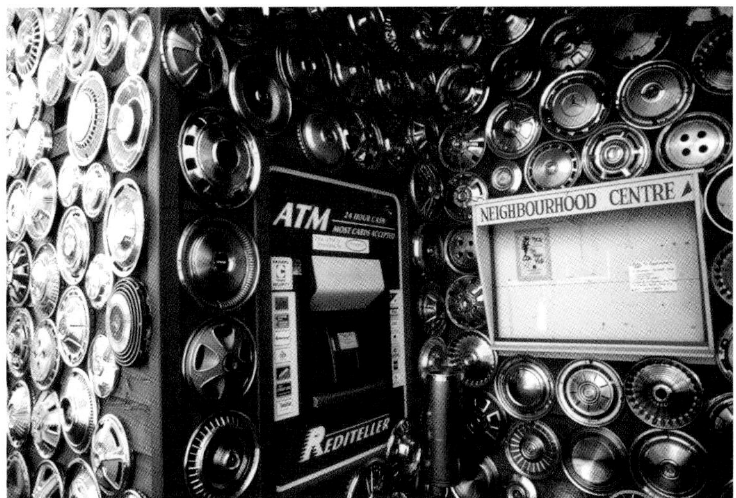

Hub caps adorn the walls of a building on Berry's main street

camping fees (from $12-$27) must be paid on top of that. Provisions can be bought at the general store in Jervis Bay Village, off Jervis Bay Road, which is within the park boundary (open 0700-2100, or 1900 outside school holidays).

Murramarang National Park

The 11,978-ha Murramarang National Park is most famous for its tame and extremely laid-back population of Eastern grey kangaroos. Here they not only frequent the campsites, and the foreshore, but on occasion are even said to cool off in the surf. The park is a superb mix of forest and coastal habitat that offers a host of activities from swimming, surfing and walking to simple socializing with the resident marsupials. Of the beaches and campsites, **Pebbly Beach** and **Depot beach** are the most popular spots, but **Durras North**, south of Depot Beach and Pretty Beach to the north, is also great. There is a network of coast and forest walks available including the popular 'Discovery Trail' off North Durras Road, which skirts the edge of **Durras Lake**. There is also a fine coastal track connecting Pretty Beach with Pebbly Beach. Access to Pebbly Beach is via Mount Agony Road (unsealed) right of the Princes Highway 10 km north of Batemans Bay. Depot Beach and Durras North are accessed via North Durras Road off Mount Agony Road. Pretty Beach and the Murramarang Aboriginal Area are accessed via Bawley Point and Kioloa on Murramarang Road (sealed) off the Princes Highway 16 km south of Ulladulla. Day-use vehicle entry costs $6, pedestrians free.

The Eurobodalla Coast » *pp178-183.*

The Eurobodalla coastal region stretches from Batemans Bay in the north to Narooma in the south. The bustling seaside resort of **Batemans Bay** provides an ideal stopover along the coastal Princes Highway. Most of the Bay's beaches are located southeast of the town centre and if you have time it is worth heading that way. Tomakin and Broulee offer the best surf and fishing sites and jet skis can be hired on Coriggan's Beach. On the river you can take a leisurely three-hour cruise upstream to the historic riverside village of Nelligen. The area offers some excellent sea kayaking. There are numerous excellent dive sites around the Bay. See Activities and tours, page 182, for details. Just off the Princes Highway near the town centre is the very helpful VIC ⓘ *T4472 6900, www.naturecoast-tour ism.com.au, 1900-1700.*

Nestled on a headland in the glistening embrace of the Wagonga River Inlet and surrounded by rocky beaches, national parks and the odd accessible island, **Narooma** has all the beauty and potential activities for which the south coast is famous. The biggest attraction is **Montague Island**, about 8 km offshore. Officially declared a nature reserve and administered by the National Parks and Wildlife Service, Montague has an interesting Aboriginal and European history and is crowned by a historic lighthouse built in 1881. But perhaps its greatest appeal are the colonies of fur seals and seabirds – including about 10,000 pairs of fairy penguins – that make the island home. Between October and December humpback whales can also be seen on their annual migration. There are tours of the island, see page 182.

Back on the mainland the immediate coastline offers a number of interesting features including **Australia Rock**, which as the name suggests, looks like the outline of Australia. It is however not the rock that plays with the imagination but a hole in its middle. Access is via Bar Rock Road beyond the golf course, right at the river mouth on Wagonga Head. Further south **Glasshouse Rocks** is another interesting geological formation. On the western side of town the Wagonga Inlet presents opportunities for fishing and river cruises (see page 182). The VIC ⓘ *T4476 2881, www.naturecoast-tourism.com.au, 0900-1700*, is off the Princes Highway at the northern end of town.

The Sapphire Coast » *pp178-183.*

From Narooma to the Victorian border is a region known as the Sapphire Coast. Just south of Narooma, in the shadow of Gulaga Mountain, are the quaint and historic villages of **Central Tilba** and **Tilba Tilba** with a population of around 100. Now classified by the National Trust, they boast many historic cottages and also offer some of the South Coast's best cafés and arts and crafts outlets. Ask for a self-guided heritage leaflet from the VIC in Narooma. They can also provide listings for numerous cosy B&Bs in and around the two villages. **Tilba Valley Wines Vineyard** ⓘ *off the Princes Highway, 5 km north of Tilba Tilba, T4473 7308, www.tilbavalleywines.com, open from 1000*, was established in 1978 and produces Shiraz, Semillon and Chardonnay. It offers tastings and has a small tavern-like restaurant.

Next up are the villages of **Bega** and **Tathra**. Bega's biggest tourist draw is its famous **cheese factory** ⓘ *Lagoon St, T6491 7777, www.begacheese.com.au, 0900-1700, free*. To the north and west of Bega is the 79,459 ha **Wadbilliga National Park**, a wilderness region of rugged escarpment and wild rivers. Along the road to the **Brogo River Dam** you can stay at **Fernmark Inn**, a perfect base from which to explore the park's rivers, which is perhaps best done by canoe (see page 182). From Bega you can then head straight for **Merimbula** or take a diversion to the coastal village of **Tathra**, where you can laze on the beach or explore the many pleasant features in the **Bournda National Park**. The 10-km Kangarutha Track from Tathra South to Wallagoot Lake is recommended. The VIC ⓘ *off the Princes Highway, 91 Gipps St, T6492 2045, begatic@acr.net.au*, in Bega has information and listings.

Merimbula serves as the capital of the Sapphire Coast and receives most of its tourist traffic. Surrounded by fine beaches and bisected by Merimbula Lake (which is actually a saltwater inlet), it offers plenty to see and do, with **Main Beach**, south of the lake, being the most popular for swimming and bodyboarding. The lake itself is a great venue for boating, windsurfing and fishing. The surrounding coast also offers some good diving and is the happy home of a resident pod of dolphins. From September to December migrating whales join the party making cruising the town's speciality. On the northern bank of Merimbula Lake is the VIC ⓘ *Beach St, T6497 4901, www.sapphirecoast.com.au, 0900-1700*, which has full details of diving, horse trekking and scenic flights, see also page 182. The NPWS ⓘ *on the corner of Sapphire Coast and Merimbula Drive, T6495 5000, 0830-1630*, has a great Discovery Centre, offering parks and regional walks information, natural history displays, maps and gifts.

The surreal and colourful 'Pinnacles' of the Ben Boyd National Park

Ben Boyd National Park » pp178-183.

Sheer wilderness, beautiful coastal scenery, sublime walks, strange, colourful geological features, great campsites and even a remote lighthouse all combine to make the Ben Boyd National Park one of the best coastal parks in NSW. The 9,490-ha park straddles Twofold Bay and the fishing village of Eden.

Ins and outs

Access to the park is off Princes Highway (signposted). Roads within the park are both sealed and unsealed. Unsealed sections are badly rutted, but negotiable by 2WD when dry. Day-use vehicle entry to the park costs $6. NPWS office in Merimbula (see above), can provide detailed information on the park, its walks and its campsites.

Around the park

In the northern section of the park, the main feature are '**The Pinnacles**', a conglomerate of white and orange, sand and clay that has eroded into strange pinnacle formations over many thousands of years. They can be reached on a short 500-m-circuit walk from the car park off the 2 km Haycock Road, which is partly sealed and signposted off the Princes Highway. To the north, at the end of Edrom Road (16 km, signposted off the Princes Highway), is **Boyd's Tower**, which though very grand, never served its intended purpose as a lighthouse. Below the tower a clearing looks down to clear azure waters and the strange volcanic convolutions of the red coastal rocks. Another diversion off Edrom Road, to the west, takes you to the remains of the **Davidson Whaling Station**, created in 1818 and the longest-running shore-based station in Australia, ceasing operations in 1930. Further south off Edrom Road an unsealed, badly rutted road leads to the delightful and wildlife rich **Bittangabee campsite** (15 km, then 5 km on the left).

Back on the main track the Disaster Bay Lookout is worth a look before it terminates at the 'must-see' Green Cape Light Station (21 km). Surrounding by strange, rust-coloured rocks, pounded by surf and home to laid-back kangaroos, it is a wonderful place to find some solitude. **City Rock**, accessed down a short badly rutted track, off the lighthouse road, is signposted also well worth seeing. The wave action against the rock platform is dramatic and a favourite haunt for sea eagles. The superb but demanding (30 km) **'Light to Light' Walking Track** connects the Green Cape light station with Boyd's Tower, passing the Bittangaee and **Saltwater Creek** campsites along the way. It is one of the best and most remote coastal walks in NSW.

Sleeping

Wollongong and around *p172*

C Pilgrim Lodge, at the Nan Tien Buddhist Temple, Berkeley Rd, Berkeley, T4272 0500, www.nantien.org.au For something completely different, this offers comfortable, modern en suite doubles, triples and family rooms, with meals if required. Specialist meditation weekend packages.

C-E Keiraview Wollongong YHA , 73-75 Kembla St, T4229 1132, bookings@keiraviewaccommodation.com.au. The city's best backpackers with modern facilities, dorms, doubles and singles, most ensuite, parking and internet.

Kiama and Berry *p172*

L-D East's Van Park, Ocean St, East's Beach, Kiama, T4232 2124. For a well-facilitated motor park look no further than this option.

B-E Great Southern Hotel Motel, 95 Queen St, Berry, T4464 1009. Well-established and full of character with tidy motel units and a famous pub attached.

C-D Berry Hotel (Pub-stay), 120 Queen St, Berry, T4464 1011, www.berryhotel.com.au. Good rooms and an award-winning restaurant.

C-E Nestor House YHA, Fern St, Gerringong, T4232 1249. Head a little further south for this YHA. It is fairly basic offering 3 small dorms and 2 family rooms, but is well located a short stroll from Seven Mile Beach.

Shoalhaven Coast *p173*

L-F Rest Point Garden Village, Browns Rd (5 km south of Shoalhaven), T4421 6856. The most modern motor park in the area offering the full range of accommodation including powered and non-powered sites.

Jervis Bay

LL-L Paperbark Lodge and Camp, 605 Woollamia Rd, T44416066, info@paperbark camp.com.au. An excellent eco-tourist set up in a quiet bush setting with luxury en suite tent units, outdoor camp fire, good on-site restaurant (see Eating below), tours and activities. Book ahead. There's also a scattering of upmarket B&Bs, motels, pub-hotels, budget and motor park options in and around Huskisson, including **A Bayside Motor Inn**, corner of Hawke St and Bowen St, Huskisson, T4441 5500. Also the well-located **C Husky Pub**, Owen St, T4441 5001, which offers traditional rooms.

Booderee National Park

There are good campsites with hot showers at **Green Patch**, while the similarly facilitated **Bristol Point** is designed for groups. Camping with cold showers is available at **Cave Beach** but there is a 250 m walk to the site from the car park. All the campsites have groups of tame kangaroos and rosellas. Campsites of various sizes range in price from \$11-17.30 for 5, to \$27 for groups of 10. Note the camping fee does not include

Going further

Kosciuszko National Park

At over 600,000 ha, the Kosciuszko National Park is the largest in New South Wales and certainly one of the most beautiful. Home to the continent's highest peak, the 2,228-m Mount Kosciuszko, the famous Snowy River and the country's best skiing and snowboarding resorts, the park also offers a plethora of year-round mountain activities, such as hiking, mountain biking, white-water rafting, horse trekking and fishing. And with much of the park being wilderness, it also offers sanctuary to many rare native plants and animals. Jindabyne, at the eastern fringe of the park, is the main satellite town for the skiing and snowboarding resorts and has a huge range of accommodation and restaurants. It is also hosts the NPWS Snowy Region Visitors Centre, just off Kosciuszko Road ⓘ *T6450 5600, www.nationalparks.nsw.gov.au, 0830-1700.*

The best of the skiing and snowboarding resorts is Thredbo, set in a beautiful river valley, overlooked by the Crackenback Mountain Range. For a full list of the many accommodation and acitivity options, visit the excellent VIC ⓘ *6 Friday Drive, T6459 4294, www.thredbo.com.au, winter 0800-1800, summer 0900-1600.* Things don't grind to a halt after the snow disappears. In summer Thredbo becomes an alpine walking centre and the Valley Chairlift stays open, offering walkers the shortest route to the summit of Mount Kosciuszko.

Transport Countrylink has daily coach services to Jindabyne from Sydney, while V-Line has services from Melbourne. To get to the ski fields, the 8-km long Skitube at Bullock's Flat, 20 km east of Jindabyne (Alpine Way), connects the Thredbo Valley with the Perisher Blue Resort and the summit of Blue Cow Mountain. It operates daily in winter on the hour from 0900-1500. A shuttle bus service runs between Jindabyne and Thredbo.

vehicle entry so that does add extra costs, but it is well worth it! For bookings, T4443 0977, www.deh.gov.au/parks/booderee. Book well ahead during public holidays.

Murramarang National Park

LL-E Murramarang Resort, Banyandah St, South Durras, T1300 767255, www.murramu rangresort.com.au. A top spot and although not in the park itself it has its own tame kangaroos and some sublime coastal scenery. There are a choice of luxury cabins, ensuite/standard powered and non-powered sites, pool, bar/restaurant, camp kitchen, organized activities and canoe/bike hire.

Others include: **L-F Depot Beach**, T4478 6582, with cabins, powered and non-powered sites with modern facilities; and **C-F Pretty Beach**, T4457 2019, which offers powered and non-powered sites with similar facilities. There's a **F NPWS campsite**, at Pebbly Beach, T4478 6023, www.nationalparks.nsw.gov.au, which has just been renovated and is therefore well facilitated, with hot showers and fire sites. A warden collects fees daily. It's often busy so book ahead.

Eurobodalla Coast *p175*

The VIC in Bateman's Bay has full accommodation listings. There are several other motorparks located beachside along Beach Rd southeast of the centre as well as the one mentioned below. In Narooma there are plenty of standard motels for which the VIC has full listings. There also a couple of options out of town that are worth the trip.

Bateman's Bay

LL-A Bridge Motel, 29 Clyde St (200 m west of the bridge), T4472 6344. For tidy motel accommodation.

A Bay Waters Inn, on the corner of Princes Highway and Canberra Rd (just north of the bridge), T4472 6333. Another decent motel.

A-E Shady Willows Holiday Park, Old Princes Highway, corner of South St, T4472 4972, www.shadywillows.com.au. Backpackers and those in camper vans should head here. It incorporates a YHA with dorm or on-site caravans for couples, fully equipped kitchen, pool, internet, bike hire.

F The best place for camping are the NPWS sites in the kangaroo infested Murramarang National Park.

Narooma

L-E Island View Beach Resort, Princes Highway (5 km south of the town centre), T4476 2600, www.islandview.com.au. Convenient position with full motor park facilities including a camp kitchen and internet

A-B Priory at Bingie, Priory Lane, Bingie, 26 km north, T4473 8881, www.bingie.com. This delightful B&B is in a stylish modern home, offering 3 nice doubles, plenty of peace and quiet, an art gallery/workshop and great ocean views.

A Mystery Bay Cottages, 121 Mystery Ray Rd, Mystery Bay, 3 km off the Princes Highway, 10 km south of Narooma, T4473 7431, www.mysterybaycottages.com. A good self-contained option in a rural setting and close to the beach.

Sapphire Coast *p176*

There are plenty of motels and self-contained apartments in Merimbula. The VIC has full details.

L-E Merimbula Beach Holiday Park, Short Point Beach, east on Short Point, Merimbula, T1300 787837, www.holiday park .com.au. One of the best placed motor parks for peace and quiet, facilities and beach access. Camp kitchen.

A Fernmark Inn, 610 Warrigal Range Rd, Brogo, T6492 7136, www.fernmark.com.au. Worldly themed ensuites, health treatments and fine cuisine, this place makes a good base to explore the surrounding area.

C-E Wandarrah Lodge YHA, 8 Marine Parade, Merimbula, T6495 3503, wanlodge@asitis.com. au. Excellent and purpose-built, providing modern en suite dorms, double and family rooms, a well equipped kitchen, 2 lounges, internet, free breakfast.

NPWS camping, T6495 4130, is available at Hobart Beach, off Sapphire Coast Drive, south of Tathra.

Ben Boyd National Park *p177*

A-D **Wonboyn Lake Resort** 1 Oyster La, 19 km off Princes Highway, T6496 9162, www.wonboynlakeresort.com.au. Self-contained ensuite cabins, shop, spa and restaurant.

A-E **Wonboyn Cabins and Caravan Park**, Wonboyn Rd, (33 km south of Eden), T6496 9131, www.wonboyncabins.com.au. On-site vans, powered and non-powered sites.

F **Saltwater Creek** and **Bittangabee Bay**, T6495 5000. Basic (but delightful) camping is available here. Self-registration, fees apply. Book well ahead.

There is also modern, self-contained accommodation available in the lighthouse, T6495 5000, eden.district@npws.nsw.gov.au.

Eating

Wollongong and around *p172*

YYY **Beach House**, 16 Cliff Rd, T4228 5410. Lunch and dinner daily from 1200. A well-established and locally recommended seafood restaurant.

YYY **Silver Boat Bar and Restaurant**, Cliff Rd, almost next door to **The Beach House**, T4229 9991. From 1200 daily for lunch and dinner. Another fine seafood and modern Australian option with a classy, ambience and wide ranging menu clearly giving its neighbour some stiff competition.

YY **Stingray Café**, Shop 5, 1-5 Bourke St, T4225 7701. Mon-Fri from 1000, Sat-Sun from 0800. Just around the corner from the last two, is this chic, local favourite with modern Australian and al fresco dining.

Keira St is good for cheap eats, including Y **The Food World Gourmet Café**, 148 Keira St, T4225 9655, a great value Chinese.

Kiama and Berry *p172*

There are plenty of pleasant cafés and affordable eateries in Kiama with most located along Terralong St and Collins St or beside the harbour.

YYY**Cargo's Restaurant** , on the Wharf, T4233 2771. Daily for lunch and dinner.

YY **Chachi's Italian**, T4233 1144, 5/32 Collins St. Closed on Tue.

YY **Mango Moon Thai Restaurant**, 68 Manning St, T4233 1668. Open for dinner Tue-Sun. Excellent, very popular, but also quite small, so book ahead.

YY **Ritzy Gritz New Mexican Grill**, Collins St, T4232 1853. Open daily. A more affordable option, locally popular and colourful.

There are plenty of nice cafés and restaurants along Berry's main drag, and if the pub food in the **Southern Hotel** is not sufficient, then try the more formal surrounds of the award winning **Coach House Restaurant** in the Berry Hotel. See Sleeping for details.

Shoalhaven Coast *p173*

In the centre of Nowra, Kinghorne St is the main drag and best place to cruise menus.

YYY **Boatshed Restaurant**, 10 Wharf Rd, south bank below the bridge, T4421 2419. Open Tue-Sat from 1800. For fine dining it's hard to beat.

Jervis Bay

YYY **Gunyah Restaurant**, at the Paperbark Camp (see above, open daily for dinner). For fine dining (out of town). Recommended. Also Y **Husky Pub**, Owen St, for no-nonsense, value pub food.

Eurobodalla Coast *p175*

Batemans Bay

YYY **On the Pier**, Old Punt Rd, just north and west of the bridge, T4472 6405. Lunch and dinner, closed Mon. This one can always be relied on for excellent seafood as well as classy modern Australian.

Y **The Boatshed**, Clyde St. For fresh fish and chips with the seagulls on the waterfront.

Sapphire Coast *p176*

Market St and Beach St in Merimbula have numerous affordable cafés and restaurants. The **Wharf Restaurant**, overlooking the inlet at Merimbula Aquarium, Lake St, T6495 4446, open daily for lunch and Wed-Sat for dinner, is locally recommended

Activities and tours

Wollongong and around *p172*

The Boat Shed, Windang, near the harbour entrance, T4296 2015, rents boats, canoes and kayaks for Lake Illawarra. **Adrenaline Sports Skydiving**, T4225 8444, www.sportskydiving.com.au, from $275 (cheaper for groups). **Sydney Hang Gliding Centre**, T4294 4294, www.hanggliding.com.au, has trips around Stanwell Park and the Illawarra Ranges north of Wollongong. It is also the base for Australian champion Tony Armstrong, T04-1793 9200, www.hangglideoz.com.au, who will take you up tandem, from $195.

Shoalhaven Coast *p173*

In Jervis Bay, Huskisson has 3 companies offering whale (Jun-Nov) and dolphin watching (year round) as well as standard bay cruises of 2-4 hrs from $20-$40: **Dolphin Watch**, 50 Owen St (main drag), T4441 6311, www.dolphinwatch.com.au; **Dolphin Explorer**, 62 Owen St, T4441 5455; and **Seaspray**, 47 Owen St, T4441 5012.

Jervis Bay Kayak Co, T4441 7157, www.jervisbaykayaks.com, offers excellent half/full/weekend and multi day sea kayaking trips in Jervis Bay or further afield from $90. Independent hire also available. **Pro Dive**, 64 Owen St, T4441 5255, www.divejervisbay.com.au. This is a very knowledgeable, professional operation offering a range of diving options and courses. Bike hire also available.

Eurobodalla Coast *p175*

Bateman's Bay

You can take a leisurely 3-hr cruise to the historic riverside village of Nelligen (30 mins stop over) on the locally built *Clyde Princess*, at 1100, from $24, child $12 (lunch options available), T4478 1005. **Bay and Beyond Sea Kayaks**, T4478 7777, www.naturecoast-tourism.com.au/bayandbeyond, is a offers good half or full day and river and lake tours, from $55-110. **National Diving Academy**, 5/33 Orient St, T4472 9930, access, trips and gear hire.

Narooma

Island Charters, T4476 1047, www.islandchartersnarooma.com offers independent sightseeing, fishing or dive charters, from $55, Montague Island from $60, child $45. **NPWS** conducts a 4-hr guided tour of Montague Island at 0930 and a 3½-hr evening tour at dusk. All tours are weather permitting and numbers are limited, from $79, child $59. Tours depart from the town wharf on Blue Water Drive. One to two night island accommodation packages are also available. Book at the VIC.

The knowledgeable crew aboard the 90-year-old *Wagonga Princess*, T4476 2665, offer 3-hr cruises up the river with an emphasis on wildlife and history. Departs 1300 daily in summer and Sun, Wed and Fri off season, from $30.

Sapphire Coast *p176*

Brogo Wilderness Canoes, T6492 7328, www.acr.net.au/~brogocanoes, offers trips (including overnight camping), from $15 (full day from $30). **Cycle 'N' Surf**, 1B Marine Parade, Merimbula, T6495 2171, hires bikes, surf/body boards and fishing tackle. **Merimbula Marina**, T6495 1686, has a 2-hr Dolphin Cruise. It costs around $40-80. Book at the VIC. **Sinbad Cruises**, Merimbula, T6495 2037, offers cruises on the Pambula River and Pambula Lake from $27, child $18 (lunch $38/$22).

Transport

Wollongong and around *p172*

Murray's, T132251, www.murrays.com.au offers a daily service to **Canberra** and **Narooma** via **Batemans Bay** from $24. Long-distance coaches stop at the Wollongong City Coach Terminal, corner of Keira St and Campbell Sts, T4226 1022. Open Mon-Fri 0745-1730, Sat 0745-1415. **Greyhound**, T132030, and **Premier Motor Services**, T133410, offer daily services to **Sydney** (Brisbane) and **Canberra** (Melbourne) via the **Princes Highway**. Taxi from **Wollongong Radio Cabs**, T4229 9311.

The train station is west of the city centre at the end of Burrelli St and Station St. **CityRail** offers regular daily services to/from **Sydney** to **Bomaderry** where the line ends.

Kiama and Berry *p172*

Kiama Coachlines, T4232 3466, offers services from the Bong Bong Rd train station to the **Minnamurra Rainforest**, daily at 1005. Long-distance coaches stop in the centre of town on Terralong St, or at the Bombo Railway Station 1½ km north. **Premier** and **Greyhound** offer daily services between **Canberra** (Melbourne) and **Sydney** (Brisbane).

Bike hire is available with **Kiama Cycles and Sports**, 27 Collins St, T4232 3005. Taxi from T4237 7505. The train station is off Bong Bong Rd in the centre of town. **CityRail**, T131500, offers regular daily services from **Sydney**.

Shoalhaven Coast *p173*

In **Nowra** numerous long-distance coach and local bus companies base their operations from the bus terminal on Stewart Pl. **Premier** and **Greyhound** offer daily services between **Canberra** (Melbourne) and **Sydney** (Brisbane). Taxi from T4421 0333. **Bomaderry** train station sees the termination of the line from Sydney. **CityRail**, T131500, offers daily services via **Kiama** and **Wollongong**.

Nowra Coaches, T4423 5244, operates regular daily bus services between **Nowra**, **Huskisson**, **Vincentia** and **Wreck Bay**. For bike hire contact **Pro Dive**, see Activities and tours, p182.

Access to **Booderee National Park** is via Jervis Bay Rd off the Princes Highway and south of Huskisson and Vincentia. By bus/taxi $3.

Eurobodalla Coast *p175*

Batemans Bay

Long-distance coaches stop outside the Promenade Plaza on Orient St or Post Office on Clyde St. **Premier**, **Greyhound** and **Priors**, T44724040, offer daily services between **Canberra** (Melbourne) and **Sydney** (Brisbane). **Murray's**, T132251, also offers services to **Canberra**, north to **Nowra** and south to **Narooma**. **Travelscene**, Shop 6, 8 Orient St, T4472 5086, can assist with bookings.

Narooma

Long-distance coaches stop in the town centre on Princes Highway, with services between **Canberra** (Melbourne) and **Sydney** (Brisbane). **Murray's** also offers services to **Canberra** and north to **Nowra**.

Sapphire Coast *p176*

From Merimbula **Deanes Buses**, T6496 1422, offers local daily services to **Bega**, **Eden** and **Pambula**. Long-distance coaches stop at the Ampol Service Station in the town centre. **Premier** and **Greyhound**, offer daily services between **Melbourne** and **Sydney** (Brisbane). **V-Line**, T136196, and **Sapphire Coast Express**, T1800-812135 (Tue and Fri), both offer additional services to **Melbourne**.

DHD

Central & North Coast NSW

Surfers eye the waves and queue up to enter the fray at the surfing mecca of Coolangatta

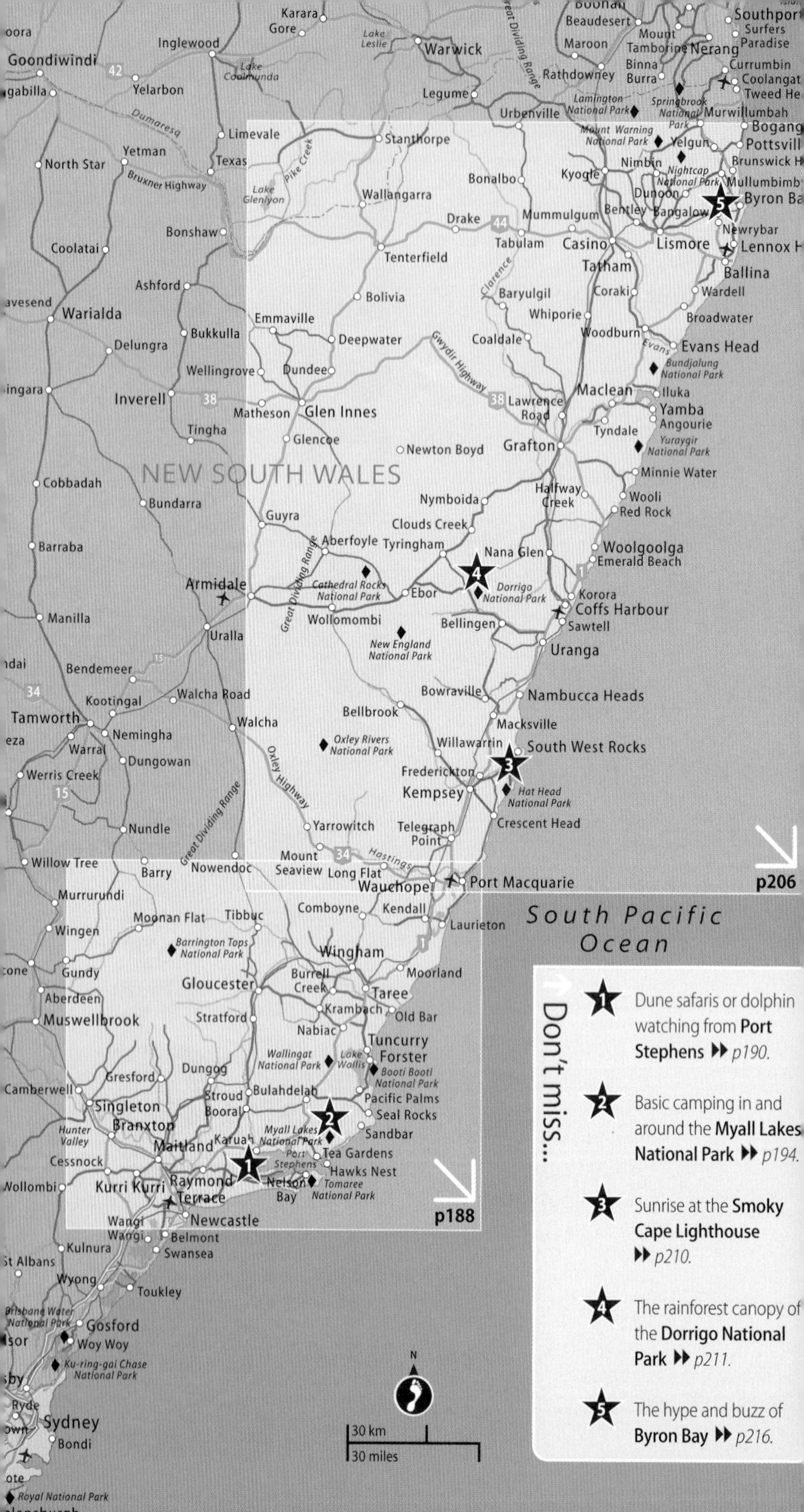

NEW SOUTH WALES
South Pacific Ocean
Goondiwindi
Karara
Gore
Inglewood
Lake Leslie
Warwick
Lake Coolmunda
Yelarbon
Legume
Beaudesert
Maroon
Mount Tamborine
Nerang
Binna Burra
Rathdowney
Lamington National Park
Springbrook National Park
Southport
Surfers Paradise
Currumbin
Coolangatta
Tweed Heads
Murwillumbah
Urbenville
Mount Warning National Park
Yelgun
Bogangar
Pottsville
Brunswick Heads
Mullumbimby
Nimbin
Nightcap National Park
Dunoon
Bentley
Bangalow
Byron Bay
Newrybar
Lennox Head
Lismore
Kyogle
Bonalbo
Drake
Mummulgum
Tabulam
Casino
Tatham
Ballina
Wardell
Coraki
Broadwater
Woodburn
Evans Head
Bundjalung National Park
Iluka
Yamba
Angourie
Maclean
Yuraygir National Park
Tyndale
Lawrence Road
Grafton
Minnie Water
Wooli
Red Rock
Halfway Creek
Woolgoolga
Emerald Beach
Korora
Coffs Harbour
Sawtell
Uranga
Nambucca Heads
Macksville
South West Rocks
Hat Head National Park
Crescent Head
Kempsey
Frederickton
Willawarrin
Bowraville
Bellingen
Dorrigo National Park
Nana Glen
Nymboida
Clouds Creek
Tyringham
Ebor
Aberfoyle
Cathedral Rocks National Park
New England National Park
Wollomombi
Armidale
Uralla
Guyra
Glencoe
Glen Innes
Matheson
Newton Boyd
Emmaville
Deepwater
Dundee
Wellingrove
Bolivia
Tenterfield
Wallangarra
Stanthorpe
Lake Glenlyon
Limevale
Texas
Yetman
North Star
Bruxner Highway
Gwydir Highway
Bonshaw
Coolatai
Ashford
Warialda
Bukkulla
Delungra
Inverell
Tingha
Bundarra
Cobbadah
Barraba
Manilla
Bendemeer
Walcha Road
Walcha
Kootingal
Tamworth
Nemingha
Warral
Dungowan
Werris Creek
Nundle
Oxley Rivers National Park
Oxley Highway
Great Dividing Range
Yarrowitch
Telegraph Point
Mount Seaview
Long Flat
Wauchope
Port Macquarie
Hastings
Laurieton
Kendall
Comboyne
Willow Tree
Barry
Nowendoc
Murrurundi
Moonan Flat
Tibbuc
Barrington Tops National Park
Wingen
Gundy
Aberdeen
Muswellbrook
Gloucester
Wingham
Burrell Creek
Moorland
Taree
Krambach
Old Bar
Stratford
Nabiac
Tuncurry
Forster
Wallingat National Park
Lake Wallis
Booti Booti National Park
Pacific Palms
Seal Rocks
Sandbar
Bulahdelah
Stroud
Booral
Dungog
Gresford
Camberwell
Singleton
Branxton
Hunter Valley
Maitland
Karuah
Myall Lakes National Park
Port Stephens
Tea Gardens
Hawks Nest
Nelson Bay
Tomaree National Park
Raymond Terrace
Kurri Kurri
Cessnock
Wollombi
Newcastle
Wangi Wangi
Belmont
Swansea
Kulnura
Wyong
Toukley
Brisbane Water National Park
Gosford
Woy Woy
Ku-ring-gai Chase National Park
Ryde
Sydney
Bondi
Royal National Park
p206
p188
30 km
30 miles
Don't miss...
1 Dune safaris or dolphin watching from Port Stephens ▸▸ p190.
2 Basic camping in and around the Myall Lakes National Park ▸▸ p194.
3 Sunrise at the Smoky Cape Lighthouse ▸▸ p210.
4 The rainforest canopy of the Dorrigo National Park ▸▸ p211.
5 The hype and buzz of Byron Bay ▸▸ p216.

Introduction

The north coast of New South Wales stretches almost 900 km from Sydney to Tweed Heads, a seemingly endless string of beautiful beaches, bays and headlands, crystal clear waters and national parks. There are so many stunning natural features that, after a while, they all seem to merge into one golden memory of sun-drenched sands and crystal clear waters with the constant soundtrack of rolling surf. Such appeal, however, has its downside, and the weak-willed traveller may suffer from severe option paralysis, especially with so many acitvities to choose from: surfing, sea kayaking, diving, sailing, fishing, kiteboarding and koala-spotting are all here in abundance. As a general guide, from north to south, extended stops in Nelson Bay (Port Stephens), Myall Lakes National park, Port Macquarie, South West Rocks, Coffs Harbour, Bundjalung National Park, and of course, Byron Bay, are all recommended. Also, try to break up the journey with the odd trip inland, especially to Bellingen, the Dorrigo and New England national parks and the numerous other superb national parks in the Rainbow Region, inland from Byron Bay.

Ratings

Landscape
★★★★★

Relaxation
★★

Activities
★★★★

Wildlife
★★★★

Costs
$$$

Sydney to Port Macquarie

With the lure of Byron Bay to the north, few take the time to explore the coast and national parks between Sydney and Port Macquarie. But to do so is to miss out on some of the best coastal scenery in the state. Myall Lakes National Park offers a superb diversion and a couple of days exploring the beaches and lakes is highly recommended. Just inland are the vineyards of Hunter Valley, a name synonymous with fine waines and world-class vineyards – a little piece of Australia that conjures up images of mist-covered valleys and rolling hills, networked by patchworks of grape-laden vines. Although not necessarily producing the best wines in Australia, this is one of the best venues in the country to learn something of the process or sample that classic vineyard ambience and enjoy the congenial conviviality of fine wine, fine food and fine accommodation. To the north, are the high and secluded river valleys of the Barrington Tops National Park, an area renowned for its unpredictable climate and diverse wildlife, while back on the coast is Nelson Bay, an ideal stopover on the route north and gateway to the beautiful Tomaree Peninsula.

Getting there Interstate bus network. Rail less convenient.

Getting around Local bus network or hire car/campervan.

Time required 5-6 days.

Weather Warm and dry in summer, mild in winter.

Sleeping Good hostels and motor camps in all main centres. National park campsites recommended.

Eating Few quality restaurants outside the Hunter Valley.

Activities and tours Off-road sand dune tours or dolphin/whale watching from Nelson Bay. Hunter Valley winery tours.

★ **Don't miss** Myall Lakes National Park (especially Seal Rocks) and the climb to the summit of Tomaree Head, Port Stephens. ▸▸ *p191 and 194.*

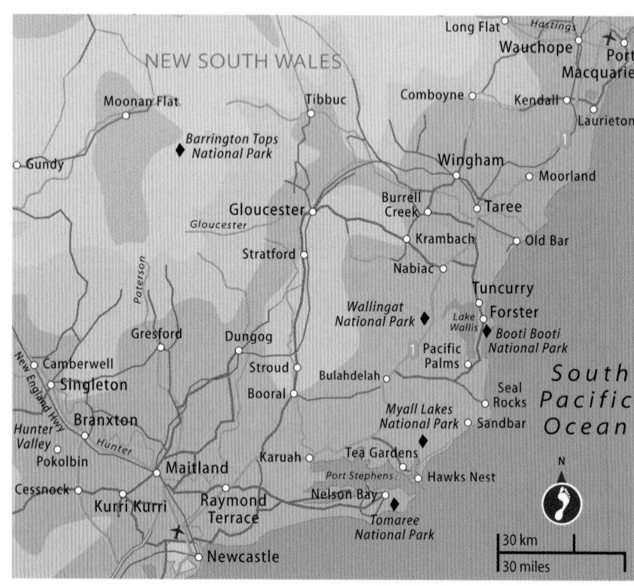

Newcastle and the Hunter Valley » pp198-205.

As one of the most industrialized cities in Australia – with a main drag and a city centre mall as inspiring as a bowl of week-old porridge – Newcastle has limited tourist appeal. It is mostly used as a base from which to visit the Lower Hunter Valley, home to dozens of wineries, which provide one of the finest 'winery' experiences in the world. From Newcastle, the Hunter River becomes more and more scenic, with rolling hills draped in vineyards backed by wilderness forest, given over to the vast Wollemi National Park.

Ins and outs

Getting there and around The nearest main airport to Hunter Valley is at Newcastle. Shuttles ferry people to and from the airport to the Valley. There are plenty of coaches and tours from Sydney, Newcastle and Port Stephens and trains arrive at Maitland and Scone. From Newcastle there are regular coach and train connections with the main surrounding cities and tourist centres, with frequent daily services from Sydney and Port Stephens. » *p 203.*

Tourist information Hunter Valley (Wine Country Tourism) VIC ⓘ *455 Wine Country Drive (4 km north of the town centre), T4990 4477, www.winecountry.com.au, Mon-Thu 0900-1730, Fri 1800, Sat 1700, Sun 1600*, is the principal centre, well set up with a café and winemaking display. They provide detailed and objective vineyard information as well as accommodation and tour bookings. You are strongly advised to pick up the free detailed maps from the VIC. Newcastle VIC ⓘ *361 Hunter St, opposite the Civic Rail Station, T4974 2999, www.visitnewcastle.com.au, Mon-Fri 0900-1700, Sat-Sun 1000-1630.*

Newcastle

Newcastle grew from its humble beginnings as a penal colony to become one of the largest coal ports in the world, shipping vast amounts of the black stuff from the productive Hunter Valley fields. Major steel production followed, until its rapid decline at the end of the 20th century. To add insult to injury, the city suffered Australia's worst earthquake in modern times, in 1989. Despite this, the city still boasts some very fine and gracious historical buildings, including the 1892 **Christ Church Cathedral**, the 1890 **Courthouse** and several classics on and around Hunter and Watt streets such as the **post office** (1903), the **railway station** (1878) and **Customs House** (1877). There are a number of good galleries and museums in the city with the **Regional Museum** and the **Newcastle Regional Art Gallery** (closed Mondays, free entry) both being worthy of investigation. The beaches on the eastern fringe of the city are superb and well known for their excellent surfing, swimming (patrolled in summer) and fishing.

Hunter Valley

The Hunter Valley is really two distinct regions, the Lower Hunter Valley and Upper Hunter Valley, with the vast majority of the vineyards (over 80) in the lower region. Both are bisected by the Hunter River and the New England Highway. The Lower Hunter Valley encompasses the area from Newcastle through Maitland to Singleton, with Cessnock to the south considered the 'capital' of the Lower Hunter Valley's vineyards which are concentrated in a few square kilometres to the northwest. Though the region's true heritage lies below the ground, in the form of coal, it is vineyards that dominate the economy these days, producing mainly shiraz, semillons and chardonays. They range from large-scale producers and internationally recognized labels to low-key boutiques. Despite the sheer number, the emphasis in the Hunter Valley is defintely on quality rather than quantity. Though the vineyards are all comprehensively signposted around Cessnock, you are strongly advised to pick up the free detailed maps from the VIC.

Top tips

A vine romance

With so many vineyards, choosing which to visit can be tough. There are many tours on offer, which avoids a severe bout of option paralysis, but for those with little prior knowledge, it is advised to mix some of the large, long-established wineries and labels with the smaller boutique affairs. Although many of the 'big guns' are well worth a visit, you will find a more, relaxed and personalized service at the smaller establishments. Also be aware that almost every vineyard has received some award or another and this is not necessarily a sign that they are any better than the next. The following wineries are recommended and often considered the 'must-sees' but it is by no means is it a comprehensive list. Of the large long-established vineyards (over a century) **Tyrells**, **Draytons** and **Tullochs** (all in Pokolbin) are recommended, providing fine wine and insight into the actual wine-making process. Tyrells also has especially nice aesthetics. **Lindemans** and **McGuigans** (again in Pokolbin) and **Wyndhams** (Branxton), are three of the largest and most well known labels in the region, offering fine vintages and a broad range of facilities. McGuigans and Wyndhams also offer guided tours. Of the smaller boutique wineries **Oakvale**, **Tempus Two**, **Tamburlaine** and **Pepper Tree** – with its class restaurant and former convent guesthouse an added attraction – are also recommended. All are located in Pokolbin. Then, for a fine view as well as vintage, head for the **Audrey Wilkinson Vineyard**, DeBeyers Road, Pokolbin, or **De Luliis**, Lot 21, Broke Road with its lookout tower. The VICs have full details.

Given the fact that copious wine tasting and responsible driving do not mix, organized tours are by far the best way to tour the vineyards. All-day, jump-on-jump-off services are also available around the main vineyards. Another fine alternative is to visit the various vineyards by bike. For details of the various tours on offer, see page 201.

For many, their first introduction to the great wine growing region is the decidedly drab and disappointing former mining town of **Cessnock**. Head north and west, however, and disappointment very quickly turns to satisfaction as you reach the vineyard communities of **Pokolbin**, **Broke** and **Rothbury**.

Nelson Bay and around » *pp198-205.*

Nelson Bay is the recognized capital of an area known as Port Stephens, a name loosely used to describe both the large natural harbour (Port Stephens) and the string of foreshore communities that fringe its southern arm. Nelson Bay is fast developing into a prime New South Wales coastal holiday destination and provides an ideal first base or stopover from Sydney. Other than the stunningly beautiful views from Tomaree National Park and from

The Hunter Valley boasts some mighty vine labels

Tomaree Heads across the harbour to Tea Gardens and Hawks Nest, there are an ever-increasing number of activities on offer, from dolphin watching to camel rides.

Ins and outs

Getting there The nearest airport is at Newcastle (Williamstown), 30 km away, with regular connections to main centres. Coaches serve Nelson Bay from Sydney direct or connect with interstate services in Newcastle. ▸▸ *p203.*

Getting around Nelson Bay is small enough to navigate on foot. Local regional buses connect the town with surrounding attractions of Port Stephens.

Tourist information Port Stephens VIC ⓘ *Victoria Parade, T4980 6900, www.portstephens.org.au, 0900-1700*, has a free Port Stephens Guide. **NPWS** ⓘ *12B Teramby Rd (Marina Complex), T4984 8200, hunter@npws.nsw.gov.au*, has national parks and camping information.

Sights

Even if you do nothing else around the Nelson Bay area except laze about on its pretty beaches, do climb to the summit of **Tomaree Head**, at the far west end of Shoal Bay, which is particularly spectacular at sunrise or sunset. The views that reward the 30-minute, strenuous ascent are truly memorable.

The best beaches in the area are to be found fringing the national park, east and south of Nelson Bay. To the east, **Shoal Bay** is closest to all amenities while farther east still, within the national park boundary, **Zenith Beach**, **Wreck Beach** and **Box Beach** all provide, great surfing, solitude and scenery. Two kilometres south of Shoal Bay the glorious beach that fringes **Fingal Bay** connects Point Stephens with the mainland. You can access the headland and its fine walking tracks at low tide. South of Fingal Bay, though not connected to it by road, **One Mile Beach** is a regional gem while **Samurai Beach**, just north of that, is the local naturist beach. West of One Mile Beach **Boat Harbour** gives way to **Anna Bay** which forms the northern terminus of **Stockton Beach**, stretching for over 30 km all the way down to Newcastle. It's well worth a visit simply to see the endless sweep of dunes. If you have 4WD you can 'let rip' but a permit must be obtained from the Council (or the VIC). See also Tours and activities page 201.

There is a healthy suburban population of **koalas** in the region and the best places to see them are the fringes of Tomaree National Park or wooded areas of the Tilligerry Peninsula (via Lemon Tree Passage Road, off Nelson Bay Road, 30 km south of Nelson Bay). There are guided walks, see Tours and activities page 201. While you are in the area you may also be tempted to visit **Tanilba House** ⓘ *Caswell Corner, Tanilba, T4982 4866, Wed/Sat/Sun 1030-1630, from $8, child $2*, one of the oldest homesteads in Australia, built by convicts in 1831. Closer to Nelson Bay is the **Nelson Head Inner Lighthouse**, *T4984 9758, 1000-1600*, set just above Little Bay, 1.5 km east of the town centre, with guided tours, great views and a small café. Little Bay is also a great place to see pelicans as they wait patiently for fishermen's' handouts late on in the day.

Barrington Tops National Park

ⓘ *$7.50 per day. NPWS office, 59 Church St, Gloucester, T6538 5300, Gloucester@npws.nsw.gov.au, Mon-Fri 0830-1700, is the nearest to the park. There is also an office in Nelson Bay.*

The 40,453-ha Barrington Tops National Park encompasses a 25-km long plateau extending between a series of extinct volcanic peaks in the Mount Royal Ranges, north of the Hunter Valley. Rising to a height of 1,577 m at Polblue Mountain, the plateau forms one of the highest points on the Great Dividing Range and contains a diverse range of habitats from rainforest to alpine meadows with many waterfalls and glorious views. The high elevation also results in unpredictable weather year-round and an annual rainfall of over 2 m, with sub-zero temperatures and snow in winter. Given its geographical position, the park hosts a diverse range of species including lyrebirds, bandicoots and spotted tailed quolls. At the very

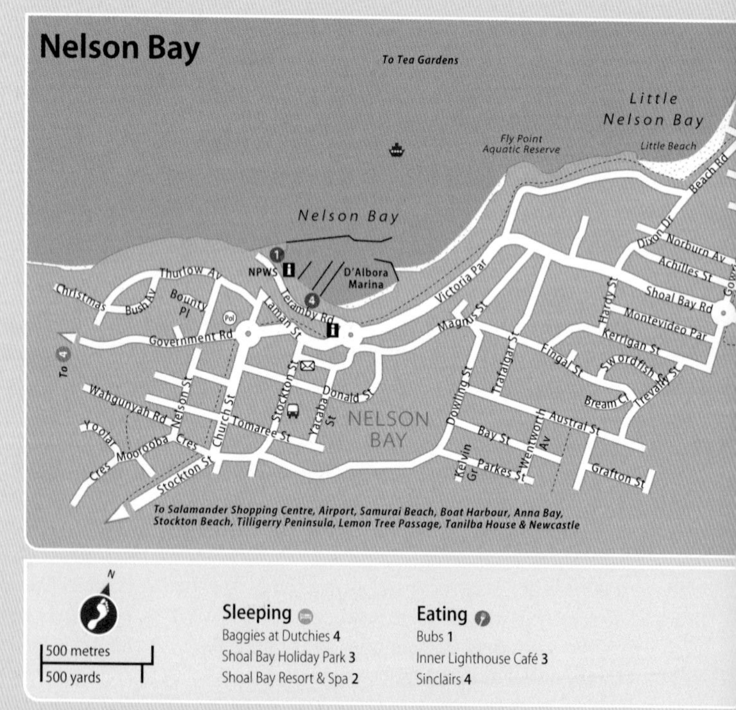

least you are almost certain to encounter kangaroos as well as small squadrons of elegant and very vocal black cockatoos.

The scenery and wildlife alone make a day-trip well worthwhile, but given the many excellent B&Bs, campsites, walks and activities available you may well be tempted to extend your stay. The Great Lakes VIC in Forster (see below) handles Barrington Tops information. Look out for the free brochure, Barrington Tops World Heritage Area, and also visit www.barringtons.com.au. If you have your own transport there are various routes. From the south and east, the park and the two main fringing communities of Dungog and Gloucester are best reached from Bucketts Way Road (Highway 2) which heads northwest off the Pacific Highway 33 km north of Newcastle. Alternatively, the northern sector of the park (and Gloucester) can be accessed west off the Pacific Highway at Nabiac, 160 km north of Newcastle. If you have 2WD and are limited for time, the drive up the Gloucester River Valley to Gloucester Tops is recommended. Take the Gloucester Tops Road off Bucketts Way Road, 10 km south of Gloucester. The climb to the plateau begins at the Gloucester River Camping Area (see Sleeping, page 199). The northern sector of the park offers a more extensive 78-km scenic drive (mostly unsealed) from Gloucester to Scone via Scone Road and then Barrington Tops Road, west of Gloucester. Sadly, the best views from Carey's Peak and its surrounding campsites can only be reached by 4WD south off Forest Road, just west of the Devils Hole Camping Area. The southern sector of the park is accessed 40 km northwest of Dungog, via Salisbury and the Williams River Valley Road.

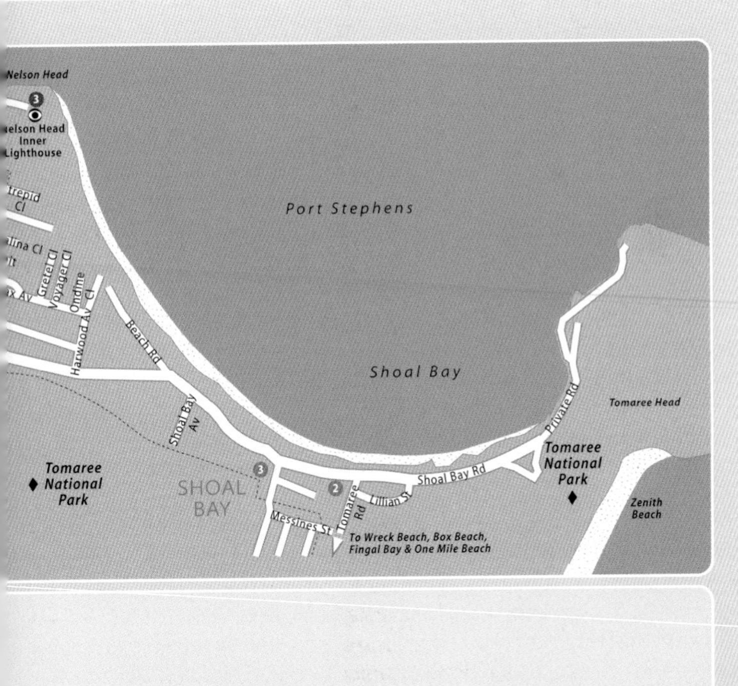

Myall Lakes National Park » pp198-205.

Myall Lakes National Park, or Great Lakes as they are known, combine beautiful coastal scenery with a patchwork of inland lakes, waterways and forest to create one of the best-loved eco-playgrounds in NSW. Only four hours north of Sydney, the only drawback is its inevitable popularity during holidays and weekends. However, given the sheer scale of the area (21,367 ha), of which half is water, there is always somewhere to escape the crowds. The main settlements fringing the national park are Tea Gardens and Hawks Nest, on the northeastern shores of Port Stephens, Bulahdelah on the Pacific Highway to the northwest and the popular surf spots of Bluey's Beach and Pacific Palms to the north. If you have at least two days, the route below, from Tea Gardens in the south to Pacific Palms in north, or vice versa, is recommended.

Ins and outs

Getting there Myall is best explored by car though there are regional bus services between Taree and Sydney. » p203.

Getting around For navigation, whether on foot, by car or paddle, the Great Lakes District Map ($8) is not only recommended but essential. Copies can be bought in the VIC. There are daily local bus services around the area, paddle boat hire and houseboat for hire.

Tourist information Great Lakes VIC in Forster serves as the region's principal centre. Local VICs are in Tea Gardens ⓘ *Myall St, T4997 0111, 1000-1600*; Bulahdelah ⓘ *corner of Pacific Highway and Crawford St, T4997 4981, 0900-1600*, and Pacific Palms ⓘ *Boomerang Dr, Bluey's Beach, T6554 0123, 1000-1600*. All can provide NPWS information – the nearest NPWS office is in Nelson Bay. Also visit www.greatlakes.org.au.

Tea Gardens and Hawks Nest

The little known but fast developing coastal settlements of Tea Gardens and Hawks Nest, on the northeastern shores of Port Stephens, serve not only as excellent holiday destinations in themselves but as the main southern gateway to the Myall Lakes National Park. Straddling the Myall River and host to beautiful beaches, headlands, coastal wetlands and forest, these twin towns offer a wealth of activities from surfing to koala spotting, though most come here simply to escape the crowds, relax and enjoy the beautiful scenery and laid-back atmosphere.

The place to be is **Bennetts** (Ocean Beach) at the southeastern end of Hawks Nest. From there you can access the **Yaccaba Walk** (3 km return) to the summit of the Yaccaba Headland affording some memorable views across the mouth of Port Stephens and the numerous offshore islands. To reach Bennetts Beach, cross the bridge from Tea Gardens on Kingfisher Avenue, turn right on Mungo Brush Road, then left to the end of Booner Street. The bridge connecting the two towns is often called 'The Singing Bridge' because of its tendency to 'sing' in strong winds.

Another excellent but far more demanding walk is the **Mungo Track** that follows the Myall River through coastal forest to the **Mungo Brush Campsite** (15 km one-way). It starts on the left, off Mungo Brush Road, 600 m past the national park boundary. The detailed booklet, *Walkers Guide to The Mungo Track*, breaks the entire walk into sections with additional alternatives and is available from the VIC Tea Gardens, NPWS or Hawks Nest Real Estate on Tuloa Avenue. Look out for koalas along the way, especially late in the day. Dolphin-watching cruises, diving, golf, fishing charters, boat, sea kayak, canoe and surf ski hire are all readily available in the twin towns. Tea Gardens VIC has full listings.

The heights of Barrington Tops are home to a diverse range of habitats and wildlife

Hawks Nest to Bulahdelah

From Hawks Nest, Mungo Brush Road heads north, parallel with the Myall River, to meet the southern boundary of the Myall National Park (4.5 km). From there the road remains sealed and cuts through the littoral rainforest and coastal heath for 15 km to the Mungo Brush Campsite beside the Bombah Broadwater, the second largest of the Great Lakes.

Before reaching Mungo Brush consider stopping and walking the short distance east to the long swathe of deserted beach. **Dark Point**, about 5 km north of the southern boundary at Robinson's Crossing, is an interesting rocky outcrop and the only significant feature along this 44 km of beach between Hawks Nest and Seal Rocks. It is an interesting spot and the site of a midden (ancient refuse tip) used by the Worimi Aboriginal peoples for centuries before they were displaced by invading European cedar cutters. This particular example is thought to be at least 2,000 years old. Lying tantalisingly offshore lies **Broughton Island**, accessed by day trip from Nelson Bay.

From Mungo Brush the road skirts the northern shores of **Bombah Broadwater**, turning inland past increasingly thick stands of paperbark trees to reach the Bombah Point ferry crossing which runs daily every half an hour from 0800 to 1800 and costs $3. **Bombah Point** is dominated by the large, yet unobtrusive, **Myall Shores Ecotourism Resort**. Ten kilometers from Bulahdelah, on the same road, are the new **Bombah Point Eco Cottages**. See page 198 for details.

Bulahdelah, Seal Rocks and Sanbar

From Bombah Point 16 km of partly sealed roads takes you to the small community of **Bulahdelah** and the Pacific Highway. Bulahdelah has a helpful VIC and is the main venue for houseboat hire for the region. Four kilometres north of Bulahdelah, the Lakes Way – the main sealed access road through the Great Lakes region – heads east, eventually skirting Myall Lake, the largest of the lakes. Before reaching the lake, however, you may consider the short diversion 5 km north along **Stoney Creek Road**. Some 38 km into the southern fringe of the

Bluey's Beach, Myall Lakes National Park

Bulahdelah State Forest, along Wang Wauk Forest Drive, is '**The Grandis**', a towering 76-m flooded gum reputed to be the highest tree in NSW.

Back on the Lakes Way, between Myall Lake and Smiths Lake, Seal Rocks Road (unsealed) heads 11 km southeast to reach the coast and the pretty beachside settlement of **Seal Rocks**. The residents of this sublime little piece of wilderness know all to well that it is the jewel in the Myall and do not really want to advertise the fact. There is a superb beach and short rainforest and headland walks – the 2-km stroll to the **Sugarloaf Point Lighthouse** past the **Seal Rocks Blow Hole** is well worth it. The views from the lighthouse (no public access to the interior) are excellent and Lighthouse Beach to the south is more than inviting. Seal Rocks lie just offshore and serve as a favourite regional dive site (they are home to numerous grey nurse sharks). Since 1875 there have been 20 shipwrecks with the *S.S Catterthun* being one of the nation's worst with the loss of 55 lives.

Back on the Lake Way, just before **Smiths Lake** look out for signs to the **Wallingat National Park**. If it is a fine day, an exploration (4WD and map required) of the forest is recommended, with the steep climb to **Whoota Whoota Lookout** providing fine views north over the lakes and coast.

Sandbar, 1 km past the turn off to Smiths Lake village, is also a sight for sore eyes. Here you'll find some excellent, quiet beaches (500-m walk), good birdwatching along the sandbar that holds the lake back from the sea and many lakeside activities based at the delightful caravan park.

Pacific Palms and Bluey's Beach

Four kilometres north of Smiths Lake is the small community of **Pacific Palms** fringing the southern shores of Lake Wallis. Two kilometres east are the delightful little communities of **Bluey's Beach**, **Boomerang Beach** and **Elizabeth Beach**. While Pacific Palms boasts its lakeside charms and activities, Bluey's and its associates are something of a local surfing Mecca. Bluey's Beach itself is idyllic and further north, beyond Boomerang Point, Boomerang Beach only marginally less attractive. Further north the rather unfortunately named Pimply Rock and Charlotte Head give way to **Elizabeth Beach**, which is an absolute stunner.

The beach at Forster

Forster-Tuncurry and around » pp198-205.

The twin coastal towns of Forster-Tuncurry, which straddle Wallis Lake and the Cape Hawke Harbour, are a favourite domestic holiday destination forming the northern fringe of the park and providing the northern gateway to the superb Great Lakes Region. Although the towns themselves have some fine beaches and numerous water-based activities, it is the lakes, beaches and forests of the Booti Booti and Myall Lakes National Parks to the south that keep visitors coming back. As one of the most appealing coastal regions between Sydney and Byron Bay, a few days here is highly recommended. For all the necessary amenities Forster is the place to stay but there are some superb alternatives in the national park and coastal villages to the south (see Myall Lakes National Park above).

Ins and outs

Great Lakes VIC ⓘ *beside the river on Little St, Forster, T6554 8799, www.greatlakes.org.au, 0900-1700*, serves Forster-Tuncurry and the Great Lakes (Myall) Region as far south as Tea Gardens and Hawks Nest. To find your way around the twin towns and region ask for the free *Cartoscope Great Lakes Region Map*. The Great Lakes District Map ($8) is recommended if you intend to explore the Myall Lakes and National Park fully. The VIC also supplies NPWS camping and national parks information. » p203.

Sights

Many short-term visitors find ample satisfaction on Forster Beach, which sits at the mouth of the Hawke Harbour Inlet, just north of Forster's main drag, Head Street, but better beaches await your attention further east. **Pebbly Beach**, only a short walk along the coast from Forster Beach (or alternatively accessed by car, just beyond the junction of Head Street and MacIntosh Street), is a great spot for families and despite the name does possess some sand. At the western end of town, **One Mile Beach** is the town's true favourite offering great views and good surfing at its northern end. It is best accessed via Boundary Street, south off Head Street/Bennetts Head Road, then east down Strand Street. **Bennetts Head**, at the terminus of Bennetts Head Road, also provides good views south along the One Mile Beach, north to Halliday's Point and straight down into almost unbelievably clear waters.

If you can drag yourself away from the town beaches, the **Booti Booti National Park**, straddling the Lakes Way and the distinctly svelte strip of terra firma between Lake Wallis and the ocean, is well worthy of investigation. At the park's northern fringe, head east along Minor Road (just south of Forster, off the Lakes Way) and climb to the top of **Cape Hawke** where there is a lookout tower (40 minutes return). **McBride's Beach** sits in almost perfect isolation below and is one of those beaches that instantly has you mesmerized. It is as good as it looks and the ideal place to escape for the day, provided you are up for the 20-minute walk from the parking area just west of the lookout car park. To the south **Seven Mile Beach** stretches to **Booti Hill**, **The Ruins** and **Charlotte Head**. The Ruins has a good NPWS campsite and the southern edge of the park offers some excellent walks, with the 7-km track from The Ruins to Elizabeth Beach being recommended. **Elizabeth Beach** is another regional gem that has the habit of detaining all who visit – sometimes for days! On the western side of Lakes Way, **Wallis Lake** provides saltwater swimming, fishing, boating and numerous picnic sites.

Sleeping

Newcastle and Hunter Valley *p189*

There are dozens of B&Bs, guesthouses, self-contained cottages and restaurants set amongst the vineyards of Hunter Valley, mainly around Pokolbin and Rothbury. If you are on a budget or searching for a bargain, aim to stay midweek, when accommodation is cheaper. In and around Cessnock you will find operators have to offer lower rates due to the huge competition in and around the vineyards.

L-B Four Horizons Eco-Lodges, in the Watagan Forest, 20 mins from the vineyards, T49986257, www.fourhorizons.com.au. For plenty of peace and quiet and interesting modern design try these self-contained eco-lodges. Two nights minimum stay.

B-D Moffat Falls Cottage, T6775 9166, Point Lookout Rd, www.moffatfalls.com.au. Comfortable, self-contained option in New England National Park with a wood fire and 2 bedrooms. There is also a self-contained room in the lodge and cheaper, value cabins on the property.

B-E Newcastle Beach YHA, 30 Pacific St, Newcastle, T4925 3544. Housed in a gracious heritage building, complete with chandeliers, ballroom, large open fireplaces and leather armchairs. Deservingly popular, it offers numerous spacious dorms and doubles and the odd family and single room. Also on offer is internet, free use of surf/boogie boards. An added attraction are the weekly all-you-can-eat BBQs and $5 pizza nights. Parking can be a problem during the day (metered).

C-D Wentworth Hotel, 36 Vincent St, Cessnock, T49901364, www.wentworthhotelcessnock.com.au. Tidy and recently renovated, this option has a wide range of tastefully decorated rooms and also has a small Irish pub and restaurant attached.

Nelson Bay and around *p190, map p192*

There is plenty of choice in and around Nelson Bay, from resorts and modern self-contained apartment blocks to tidy B&Bs and koala infested hostels.

L-A Shoal Bay Resort and Spa, Shoal Bay Rd, T4981 1555, www.shoalbayresort.com.au. Enjoying a recent upgrade, this resort has apartments, suites, family and standard rooms (all en suite) with B&B or half board, pool, à la carte, casual dining and of course some very inviting spas. Located overlooking the bay and near to all amenities.

L-E Shoal Bay Holiday Park, Shoal Bay Rd, T4981 1427, shoalbay@beachsideholidays.com.au. For a good motor park, look no further than the excellent beachside, modern and friendly option. It is close to all amenities and offering the full range of accommodation options, including camping. Great camp kitchen.

A-E Samurai Beach Bungalows, corner of Frost Rd and Robert Connell Close, approach from Nelson Bay Rd, Anna Bay,

Budget busters

Hunter Valley sleeping and eating

LL **Casuarina Restaurant and Country Inn**, Hermitage Rd, Pokolbin, T4998 7888, www.casuarina-group.com.au. One of several world-class establishments combining fine accommodation with fine dining. It offers 9 exquisite, beautifully appointed, themed suites from the 'French Bordello' to the 'British Empire'.

LL **Peppers Convent**, Halls Rd, Pokolbin, T4998 7764, www.peppers.com.au. As the name suggests, this is a renovated convent with 17 rooms all beautifully appointed and with a tariff to match. It has all the usual extras, including pool, spa and the obligatory open fires. Widely believed to have one of the best restaurants in the area.

LL-L **Hunter Country Lodge**, 220 Cessnock-Branxton Rd, North Rothbury, T4938 1744, www.huntercountrylodge.com.au. A quirky motel/restaurant combo with log-cabin-style rooms. Their restaurant is equally quirky and adds to the attraction.

T4982 1921, samurai@nelsonbay.com. This eco-friendly YHA affiliate is recommended. Although on the bus route, it is some distance from Nelson Bay (5 km) but its position amidst bush at the edge of the Tomaree National Park gives it a more relaxed atmosphere. Accommodation options range from dorm to en suite double bungalows (with TV and mini kitchen). The general facilities are also excellent. Free sand, surf and boogie board hire, bike hire (free with 3-night stay) and pick ups.
B **Baggies at Dutchies**, 9 Burbong St, Nelson Bay, T49843632, www.dutchies.com.au. A very tidy self-contained option with both standard units and a deluxe unit with good deck views across the harbour and a spa.

Barrington Tops National Park *p192*
The local VICs have full accommodation listings including the numerous quaint B&Bs that surround the park. The NPWS can also supply details of the many campsites.
L-B **Barringtons Country Retreat**, Chichester Dam Rd, 23 km north of Dungog, T4995 9269, www.thebarringtons.com.au. A popular bush resort offering comfortable lodges, à la carte (BYO) restaurant, pool, spa and organized activities including horse riding.
L-B **Salisbury Lodges** T02-49953285, www.salisburylodges.com.au. On the southern slopes of the national park about 40 km northwest of Dungog this establishment gets consistently good reviews. Peaceful, well facilitated with spas and log fires in 3 lodges, a deluxe spa room and very cute cabin. Also offers an in-house restaurant. Recommended for couples.
F **Gloucester River Camping Area**, Gloucester Tops Rd, T6538 5300. Fine riverside spot at the park boundary and comes complete with tame kangaroos but no showers. No bookings required.

Myall Lakes National Park *p194*
L-A **Bombah Point Eco Cottages**, 10 km from Bulahdelah on the same road as **Myall Shores Ecotourism Resort**, Bombah Point, T02-49974401, www.bushandbeach.com.au. Consists of 6 very classy, self-contained, modern

eco-friendly cottages in a peacefully setting. Very popular, so book ahead.

L-E Sandbar Caravan Park, 3434 The Lakes Way, in Sandbar, T6554 4095, sandbar@paspaley.com.au. This lakeside park offers self-contained cabins, powered and non-powered sites, BBQ, kiosk, fuel, canoe and bike hire and a 9-hole golf course.

LL-F Myall Shores Ecotourism Resort, Bombah Point, T4997 4495, www.myallshores.com.au. Provides a range of accommodation from luxury waterfront villas, en suite cabins and budget bungalows to shady powered and non-powered sites. There is also a small licensed restaurant, a café/bar, fuel, a small store, boat and canoe hire.

B Moby's Beachside Retreat, Redgum Rd (off Boomerang Dr), Pacific Palms, T65910000, www.mobys.com.au. Recently upgraded and now offers boutique style, one to three bedroom villas, with a smart restaurant, pool and spa. Also convenient for surf beaches.

A-C Bluey's by the Beach, 184 Boomerang Dr, Pacific Palms, T6554 0665, blueys@midcoast.com.au, is a good motel option with 9 tidy units an outdoor pool and spa, all within a short stroll from the beach.

A-E Seal Rocks Camping Reserve, Kinka Rd, Seal Rocks, T4997 6164. This is the best facilitated of the 3 campsites in and around Seal Rocks. It overlooks the main beach and offers a handful of self-contained cabins, powered and non-powered sites.

Forster-Tuncurry and around *p197*

L-E Forster Beach Caravan Park, Reserve Rd, T6554 6269 / 1800 240 632. Centrally placed park is right beside the Harbour Inlet and Forster Beach, within walking distance of Forster town centre. It has a good range of cabins and BBQs but lacks privacy.

A Tokelau guesthouse, 2 Manning St, T65575157, www.tokelau.com.au. Opposite the bridge on the north bank (Tuncurry). Historic and beautifully renovated heritage home offering 2 cosy en suites one with spa, or a traditional clawfoot bath.

C-E Dolphin Lodge YHA, 43 Head St, T6555 8155, dolphin_lodge@hotmail.com. This YHA is quiet, friendly and offers tidy motel-style double/twin/single rooms and dorms, well-equipped kitchen, free use of boogie boards, bike hire and internet. Some 500 m from the beaches, VIC and long-distance bus terminal.

NPWS Ruins campsite, beneath Booti Hill at what is known as the 'Green Cathedral' about 20 km south, T6591 0300. This is the best bet if you do not wish to be in town. It is in a great position, beach or lakeside, with good coastal and forest walks. Self-registration, hot showers, but no fires allowed.

Eating

Newcastle and Hunter Valley *p189*

The main venues for fine dining in Newcastle are Queens Wharf and The Promenade beside the river, while Beaumont St in the suburb of Hamilton, has the widest selection of lively and affordable cafés and pubs. In the Lower Hunter Valley the best restaurants are mostly found in the hotels of the vineyards. You can expect to pay more for a meal here (most often with a main between $25-35), but the quality almost always makes up for it. Book well in advance.

YYY Scratchley's, 200 Wharf Rd, on the Promenade, Newcastle, T4929 1111, www.scratchleys.com.au. Daily for lunch, Mon-Sat for dinner. Something of a regional institution over the last decade combining excellent cuisine – comprising mainly seafood and steak – with great views across the river. Book ahead.

YY The Cellar Restaurant, Broke Rd, Pokolbin, T4998 7584, www.the-cellar-restaurant. com.au. Daily for lunch, Mon-Sat for dinner. Highly regarded.

YY Shakey Tables Restaurant, Hunter Country Lodge, 220 Cessnock-Branxton Rd, North Rothbury, T4938 1744, www.shakey tables.com.au.

Daily for dinner and Sun from 1230. An unusual and colourfully decorated place for a tasty meal.

¥¥-¥ **Kent Hotel**, 59 Beaumont St, Newcastle, T4961 3303. One of many traditional and often historic pubs in the city which can provide quality, quantity and good value. This hotel also hosts jazz on weekend afternoons.

Nelson Bay and around *p190, map p192*

Most of Nelson Bay's eateries are to be found in the D'Albora Marina Complex on Victoria Parade.

¥¥¥ **Sinclair's**, D'Albora Marina Complex, T4984 4444. This is a fine dining, award-winning option. It's fully licensed, has a varied traditional Australian menu and comes recommended, especially for seafood. Daily 1000-late.

¥ **Bubs**, T4984 3917, daily from 1100-1800. A short stroll further west, for good fish and chips.

¥ **Inner Lighthouse Café**, Nelson Head, above Little Beach, T4984 9758. A decent café with great harbour views. Daily 1000-1600.

For something different consider the dinner cruise options with **Moonshadow**, see Activities and tours opposite.

Myall Lakes National Park *p194*

¥¥ **Oyster Hut**, Marine Parade, Tea Gardens, T4997 0579. This is the place to sample local fare selling fresh, locally harvested oysters.

Forster-Tuncurry and around *p197*

¥¥¥ **Poets Corner**, Memorial Dr, T65575577. For fine dining, this intimate place enjoys a loyal local following.

¥¥ **Divino**, Shop 4, Centre Arcade, Wharf St, T6557 5033. Congenial and good value Italian. Daily lunch 1100-1500, dinner from 1800.

¥ Other than the fish and chip shops, **Lobby's** and **Beach St Seafoods**, you will find more value seafood and pub grub at the popular, **Lakes and Ocean Hotel**, corner of Little and Lake Sts, T6555 4117. Across the bridge, the **Fisherman's Co-Operative** on the riverbank (right, heading north) is also a good bet.

Festivals and events

Newcastle and Hunter Valley *p189*

The highlight of the busy events calendar is the wonderfully hedonistic and convivial **Lovedale Long Lunch**, held over a weekend every **May** where several top wineries and chefs combine with music and art, www.lovedalelonglunch.com.au. Other top events include the **Jazz in the Vines Festival**, www.jazzinthevines.com.au, and **Opera in the Vines**, both held in **Oct**.

Activities and tours

Newcastle and Hunter Valley *p189*

Harbour cruises

Moonshadow, T4984 9388, www.moonshadow.com.au. Modern catamaran company offering a 1½-hr harbour cruise, with refreshments, from $19, child $10.50.

Hot air balloon tours

Balloon Aloft, Rothbury, T4938 1955, www.ballona loft.com. From around $280. If you find this too dull, you can always try a tandem skydive.

Wine tours

If you have the time, the best way to experience the area's delights, is to splash out on 3 days of relaxation, vineyard tours, fine dining and one of its many cosy B&Bs. However, for most a day tour taking in about 5 wineries with numerous tastings and the purchase of 1 or 2 bottles of their favourite vintage will have to suffice. There are numerous tour operators offering a whole host of options and modes of transport, from the conventional coaches and mini-vans to horse-drawn carriages and bikes. Most of the smaller operators will pick you up from your hotel and many can supply lunch or dining options.

Vineyard Shuttle Service, T4991 3655, www.vineyardshuttle.com.au. Local mini-van firm offering both flexibility and good value, from $38.

Hunter Valley Limousines, T4961 6111. Offers a more upmarket approach.

Pokolbin Vintage Tours, T4358 3298. Tours in period costume and an ancient bus.

Shadow's, T4990 7002. Great value, on board a fleet of old buses, including a double-decker bus (from Newcastle), from $50.

Pokolbin Horse Coaches, T4998 7305. More horse, less power, from $35.

Grapemobile, T0500 804 039, www.grapemobile.com.au. For traditional pedal power, from $30.

Nelson Bay and around *p190, map p192*

The VIC opposite has a comprehensive list of daily tours and excursions and can assist with bookings. Tour schedules are reduced across the board in winter.

Amphibious tours

Duck Dive, T4981 5472, www.duckdive.nelsonbay.com. Tours in an amphibious vehicle. A novel way to see the sights as well as providing a range of additional activities including diving, snorkelling, boom netting and boogie boarding. From $60, child $20.

Bus tours

Hunter and District Excursions, T4981 0100, and **Baydreamer**, T49820700 (good value), offer more conventional road tours to local and regional sights including the Hunter Valley vineyards (from $50), Newcastle ($50) and the Barrington Tops National Park ($85)

Diving

Pro Dive, D'Albora Marina, Teramby Rd, T4981 4331, www.prodivenelsonbay.com, and **DiveOne**, T4984 2092, www.diveone.com.au, both offer local dive and snorkelling trips in the Fly Point Aquatic Reserve, 1 km east of the town centre.

Dolphin and whale watching

Dolphin watching (year round) and whale watching (Jun-Nov) are top of the agenda with numerous vessels operating.

Imagine, T4984 9000, www.imaginecruises.com.au. Comfortable and less crowded cruises of 11/2-4 hours on board a sail catamaran, from $20-50. Recommended.

Moonshadow, Shop 3/35 Stockton St, T4984 9388, www.moonshadow.com.au. The biggest operator with the largest, fastest and most comfortable vessels (Supercats). They offer daily cruises from 11/2 to 4 hrs in search of sea mammals (1030/1330/1530 from $19-45), 7 hr trips to Broughton Island off the Myall Coast (Tue/Thu/Sun 1000 from $59) and also twilight dinner and entertainment trips around the Port, from 1900, $55.

4WD and ATV and horse trekking tours

Stockton Beach, south of Nelson Bay, with its incredible dune habitat and wrecks, provide a major playground for 4WD and ATV (4 or 8WD motorbikes) tours, as well as horse trekking.

Port Stephens Dune Adventures, T0500 550066, www.bushmobile.com.au. Offer a 6X6, yellow monstrosity with the 1½-hr, standard Dune Adventure (all weather) 1100/1230 with sand boarding thrown in, $20, child $15, while their extended 2½-hr trip taking in 'Tin City' (a hidden ramshackle settlement, threatened by the encroaching sand) costs from $35, child $25.

Sand Safari Active Adventure Tours, T49650215, www.sandsafaris.com.au. Recommended. 2½-hr, 3-hr, 20/30-km trip on ATVs, with sand boarding included, from $115, child $54.

Sahara Trails, T4981 9077, www.saharatrails. com.au, from $35, **Rambling Sands**, Janet Parade, off Nelson Bay Rd, Salt Ash, T4982 6391, and **Beach and Bush Riding Adventures**, 2630 Nelson Bay Rd, T4965 1877, horseparadise@bigpond.com, all offer horse trekking. The latter are located closest to the dunes at Stockton beach and offer trips of 1-3 hrs, from $35.

Sea kayaking

Blue Water Sea Kayaking, T4981 5177, www.seakayaking.com.au. Guided day or sunset trips suitable for beginners, and for the more experienced, excursions further afield around Broughton Island and up the Myall River. Tours start from 1 hr, $30 and they offer pick-ups. Recommended.

Surfing

Surfing lessons and surf gear hire are available with Anna Bay Surf School, T49819919, www.surfschool.portstephensnsw.com.au, from $40, kids welcome, hire from $33, 2 hrs. If it is a fast 'bottom breaking' jet boat ride with full 360-degree spins you seek then contact **X-Jet**, T4984 1262, from $40, child $20.

Walking tours

Tilligerry Habitat, T49824441. 2-hr guided koala walks around Tilligerry Peninsula at 1030 and 1400, from $15, child $10.

Myall Lakes National Park *p194*

Watersports

Pacific Palms Windsurfing (Tiona Park), T6554 0309. Windsurfing lessons from $40 per hr.

Pacific Palms Kayaking Tours, T6554 0079, www.ppkayaktours.com.au. Explore the local coast by sea kayak and get to places otherwise inaccessible on half-, full-day or overnight trips from $45.

Forster-Tuncurry and around *p197*

Boat tours

All manner of watercraft, from BBQ boats to canoes, can be hired along the waterfront. **Tikki Boatshed**, 15 Little St, T6554 6321, opposite the VIC. Offer all manner of watercraft, from BBQ boats to canoes.

Dolphin Watch Cruises, Fisherman's Wharf, T6554 7478. The only local operators permitted to put people in the water with dolphins, from $55 (swim) $35 (spectators), child $25.

Diving

There are several excellent dive sites in the region including Seal Rocks, *The SS Satara* wreck dive, Bennetts Head and the Pinnacles which are all well known for their grey nurse sharks. There are several local dive operators including **Forster Dive Centre**, 11-13 Little St, T65554477, and **Action Divers**, Shop 4/1-5 Manning St, Tuncurry, T6555 4053, www.actiondivers.com.au.

Transport

Newcastle and Hunter Valley *p189*

Air

Newcastle Airport, T49289800, www.newcastleairport.com.au, is 24 km north of the city centre. **Qantas**, T131313, newcastle@Qantas.com.au; **Jet Star**, T131538, www.jetstar.com.au; **Virgin Blue**, T136789, www.virginblue.com.au; and **Regional Express**, T131713, www.rex.com. au, offer regional services from Sydney and elsewhere.

Port Stephens Coaches, T49822940, www.pscoaches.com.au stop off at the Williamstown (Newcastle) Airport ($5.50) while **Happy Cabby**, T49763991, www.happycabby.com offers transfers to and from Newcastle and Sydney from $35. Newcastle-based **Vineyard Shuttle Service**, T49913655, offer shuttle services from the airport to Hunter Valley accommodation.

Bus and ferry

Local Newcastle Bus and Ferry, T131500, provide local bus and ferry services. Fares start at $2.70 and allow an hours unlimited travel with an all-day pass costing $8.10. Bus/ ferry and train/bus/ferry passes are available.

Ferry Services, T131500, link central Newcastle (Queens Wharf) with Stockton 0515-2400 Mon-Sat, 0830-2200 Sun, $2, child $1 one-way, tickets on board. **Rover Coaches**, 231 Vincent St, Cessnock, T4990 1699, www.rovercoaches.com.au, runs services between **Newcastle** and **Cessnock** as well as an all-day jump on jump off service around the vineyards from $35.

Coach companies **Greyhound** , T131499, and **Keans Travel**, T65431322, stop at all major towns along the **New England Highway**, with daily services from **Sydney**. **Long distance** Coaches stop next to the train station in Newcastle. **Greyhound**, T131499, have daily **Sydney** and north/southbound services. They stop at all major towns along the **New England Highway**. **Countrylink Travel Centre** acts as booking agents. **Port Stephens Coaches**, T4982 2940, www.pscoaches.com, also provides daily services to **Sydney** and **Port Stephens**, while **Rover Coaches**, T49901699, www.rovercoaches.com.au, covers the Hunter Valley. If you intend to pass through the Great Lakes Region and Myall National Park, **Busways**, T1300 555 611, offers a daily regional bus service (152) between **Taree** and **Sydney**, via **Forster-Tuncurry**, **Bluey's Beach**, **Hawks Nest** and **Newcastle**.

Taxi

If you want to avoid driving between your accommodation and restaurant **Vineyard Shuttle Service**, T4991 3655, based in Cessnock, offers local transfers or call a conventional taxi, T4990 1111.

Train

The main train station is located at the far end of Hunter St. **Cityrail**, T131500, has regular daily services to Sydney. **Countrylink**, T4962 9438, has a travel centre at the station (daily 0900-1700) and luggage storage. Note state-wide service connections are from Broadmeadow, 5 mins west. The nearest train station for Hunter Valley is Maitland which links with **Newcastle** and **Sydney**'s **Cityrail**, T131500. **Countrylink**, T132232, offers state-wide services to **Queensland** via **Scone**.

Nelson Bay and around *p190, map p192*

Air

The nearest airport is near Newcastle (Williamstown), 30 km south (see page 191).

Bus

Baydreamer, T4982 0700, runs shuttles, while **Port Stephen's Coaches**, T4982 2940, www.pscoaches.com, has regular bus services between the airport and Port Stephens, local bus services and a daily Sydney service. **Long-distance** coaches stop on Stockton St in Nelson Bay. **Port Stephens Coaches**, T4982 2940, www.pscoaches.com.au, serves Nelson Bay from Sydney direct. Another alternative is to use the more frequent Newcastle bound services (see page 204), then catch the regular daily service from Newcastle to Nelson Bay.

If you intend to pass through the **Great Lakes Region** and **Myall National Park**, **Busways**, T4983 1560, www.busways.com. au, has daily services between **Taree** and Sydney via **Tuncurry-Forster**, **Bluey's Beach**, **Hawks Nest** and **Newcastle**.

Car

Car hire from **Nelson Bay Rent-A-Car**, 28 Stockton St, Nelson Bay, T4984 2244, or **Avis**, Newcastle Airport, T4965 1612.

Ferry

Ferry services, T4126 2117, link **Nelson Bay** with **Tea Gardens**, 4 times daily from Nelson Bay, $17, child $9 return.

Train

Train services to Newcastle with onward bus connections.

Barrington Tops National Park *p192*

Bus

The only way to access the park by public transport is with the **Forster Bus Service** (#308), T6554 6431, which accesses Gloucester, Mon-Fri, from Forster-Tuncurry.

Myall Lakes National Park *p194*

Bus

Busways, T49831560, and **Forster Bus Service**, T6554 6431, offers daily local bus services around **Tea Gardens** and **Hawks Nest** and south as far as **Pacific Palms**, **Bluey's Beach** and **Smith Lake** (weekdays). **Busways**, T49831560, also offers regional bus services between **Taree** and **Sydney** via **Forster-Tuncurry**, **Bluey's Beach**, **Hawks Nest** and **Newcastle**.

Ferry

Passenger Ferry Services, T0412682117/ 41262117, link **Nelson Bay** with **Tea Gardens**, daily (from Nelson Bay 0830/1200/ 1530/1630, $17, child $9 return. Boat hire is available in **Tea Gardens** and **Hawks Nest**.

Forster-Tuncurry and around *p197*

Bus

Forster Bus Service, T6554 6431, offers daily local bus services around the twin towns. (weekdays). Long-distance buses stop outside the VIC on Little St. VIC also acts as booking agents. Greyhound, T131499, services from Sydney or Port Macquarie. Busways, T4983 1560, www.busways.com.au, also offers services between Taree and Sydney via Tuncurry Forster, Bluey's Beach, Hawks Nest and Newcastle.

Train

The nearest train station is at Taree. Countrylink, T132232, offers daily services north and south. Busways (above), or Eggins Coaches, Taree, T65522700, provide links between the train station and Forster.

Directory

Newcastle and Hunter Valley *p189*

Banks Most of the major banks with ATMs can be found along the Hunter St Mall in Newcastle. **Internet** VIC Hunter St. Also, free with a purchase at the Regional Museum Café, 787 Hunter St (see above) or at the Regional Library, Laman St, T4974 5300, Mon-Fri 0930-1700, Tue 0930-200, Sat 0930-1700. Book ahead. Battleground, Shop 2, 169-173 King St, has the fastest terminals. **Post office** Ground Floor, 1 Market St, Mon-Fri 0830-1700. **Useful numbers** Police, corner of Church and Watt sts, T4929 0999.

Nelson Bay and around *p190, map p192*

Banks Most of the major branches with ATMs are to be found along Stockton or Magnus St, Nelson Bay. **Internet** AACF, Shop 2, 106 Magnus St, T4984 3057, till 2100. Terrace Cafe, opposite the VIC in the mall, 0800-1500. Tomaree Library, Salamander Shopping Centre, T4982 0670, Mon, Wed, Fri 1000-1800, Tue, Thu 1000-2000, Sat 0930-1400. **Police** Government Rd, Nelson Bay, T4981 1244. **Post office** 97 Magnus St. Mon-Fri 0900-1700.

Myall Lakes National Park *p194*

The main amenities such as **post offices**, **service stations** and **supermarkets** can be found on Marine Drive in Tea Gardens, Mungo Brush Rd and Booner St in Hawks Nest and Boomerang Drive in Bluey's Beach.

Forster-Tuncurry and around *p197*

Internet Available at the library on Breeze Pde, T6591 7256 (Tue-Sat), or the YHA, 43 Head St, T6555 8155.

Port Macquarie to Byron Bay

There are some great stops on this route. Port Macquarie itself is often unfairly overlooked. The fast developing coastal town of South West Rocks near Smoky Cape and the sublime coastal Hat Head National Park are relaxing places to explore. For many the main destination on the north NSW coast is laid-back Byron Bay, usually the last port of call before crossing the state border. It's well worth diverting inland, however, especially to the arty village of Bellingen, a pleasant stop on the way to the Dorrigo and New England National Parks, both of which offer some superb views and bush walks.

Getting there Interstate bus network. Rail less convenient.

Getting around Local bus network or hire car/campervan.

Time required 7 days.

Weather Warm and dry in summer, mild in winter.

Sleeping Good hostels and motor camps in all main centres.

Eating Fresh seafood in Port Macquarie or Coffs Harbour.

Activities and tours Diving, surfing and hinterland tours from Byron Bay.

★ **Don't miss** Sunrise from the summit of Mount Warning. ▸▸ *p221.*

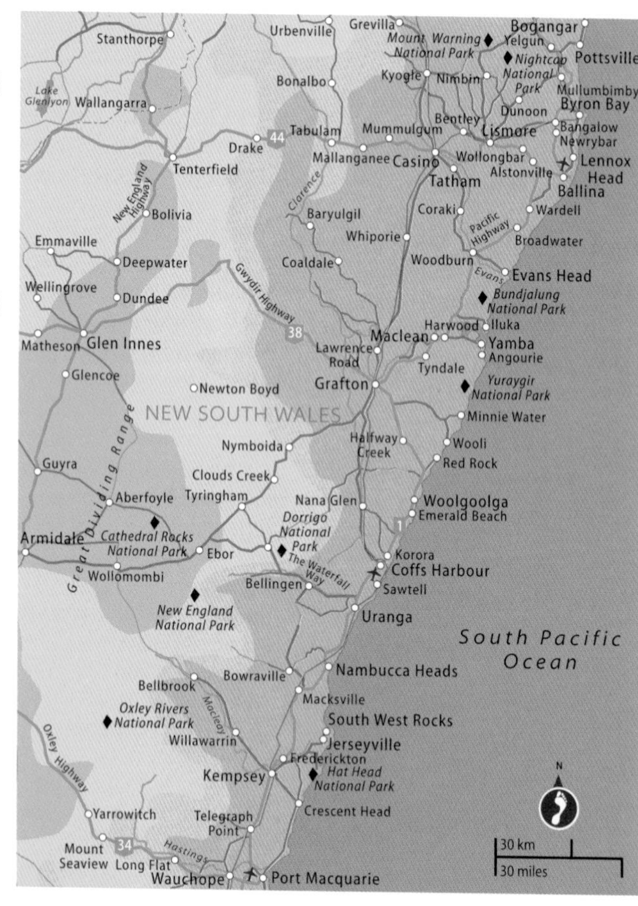

Port Macquarie » pp222-235.

Officially declared as possessing the best year-round climate in Australia, and blessed with a glut of superb beaches, engaging historical sights, wildlife rich suburban nature reserves and water-based activities, the former penal colony of Port Macquarie is rightfully recognized as one of the best holiday destinations to be found anywhere in NSW. Due perhaps to more domestically oriented advertising, or simply the 6 km of road between the town and the Pacific Highway, it seems the vast majority of international travellers miss Port Macquarie completely as they charge northwards towards more high-profile destinations such as Byron Bay. But if you make the effort and the short detour, you will not be disappointed.

Ins and outs

Getting there Port Macquarie is 10 km east of the Pacific Highway along the Oxley Highway. The airport is 3 km away. Long-distance buses serve the town and there is a train station 18 km away with connecting buses to the town centre. » p233.

Tourist information The **VIC** is located right in the heart of town ⓘ *on the corner of Clarence St and Hay St, T1300 303155/65818000, www.portmacquarieinfo.com.au, Mon-Fri 0830-1700, Sat/Sun 0900-1600*. **NPWS** ⓘ *152 Horton St, T6586 8300, port@npws.nsw. gov.au, Mon-Fri 0830-1700.*

Sights

Allman Hill on Stewart Street is home to the settlement's first cemetery (where the gravestones will reveal the obvious hardships and life expectancies). Nearby is **Gaol Point Lookout**, site of the first gaol, now offering pleasant views across the harbour and Town Beach. If you would like to quietly search the heavens, the **Observatory** in Rotary Park on William Street has viewing nights ⓘ *Wed and Sun in summer from 1930, $5, child $4*. On the eastern side of Rotary Park is **Town Beach**, the most convenient for swimming with good surfing at the northern end. South of here, the **Maritime Museum** ⓘ *6 William St, Mon-Sat 1100-1500. $4, child $2*, is worth a look for a delve into the coast's turbulent history.

The 1869 **Courthouse** ⓘ *T6584 1818, Mon-Sat 1000-1600, $2*, at the corner of Clarence Street and Hay Street, served the community for over 117 years and has been refurbished faithfully. Across the road is the **Historical Museum** ⓘ *$5*, housed in a former convict-built store (1835) and containing 14 rooms of historical artefacts.

St Thomas's Church ⓘ *T6584 1033, Mon-Fri 0930-1200/1400-1600, donation*, on the corner of Hay Street and William Street, is the fifth oldest Anglican Church still in use in Australia, built by convict labour in the late 1820s. Its most interesting feature actually lies buried beneath one of the pews, in the form of one Captain Rolland – the port's former gaol supervisor - who died from sunstroke. He was buried inside to avoid his body being dug up by vengeful convicts.

A healthy suburban population of koalas lives in the area's nature reserves and parks and numerous roadside signs are testament to this. In town one of the best places to spot a wild koala is in Sea Acres Nature Reserve (see below), but if you have no joy there is always the **Koala Hospital** ⓘ *T6584 1522, daily, donation*, in the Macquarie Nature Reserve, on Lord Street. Although you cannot see any of the sick marsupials, some of the pre-release critters are usually on display. Feeding takes place daily, 0800 and 1500. There's also the **Billabong Koala Breeding Centre** ⓘ *61 Billabong Dr, 10 km from the town centre, T6585 1060, 0900-1700. $9.50, child $6*, which not only provides copious koala-patting but also the usual array of Australian natives such as wallabies, wombats and rainbow lorikeets in six acres of landscaped gardens. Café, BBQ and picnic areas.

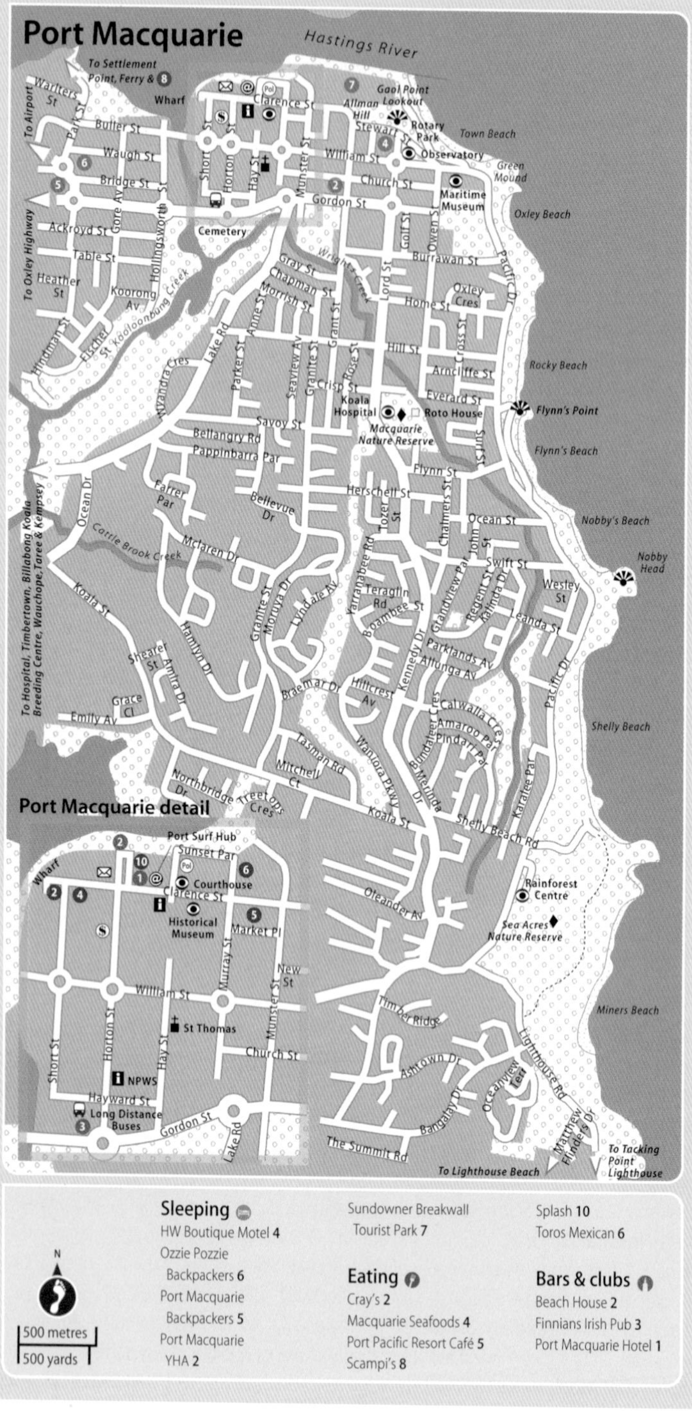

Port Macquarie

Port Macquarie detail

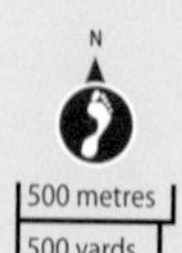

Sleeping
HW Boutique Motel 4
Ozzie Pozzie Backpackers 6
Port Macquarie Backpackers 5
Port Macquarie YHA 2
Sundowner Breakwall Tourist Park 7

Eating
Cray's 2
Macquarie Seafoods 4
Port Pacific Resort Café 5
Scampi's 8
Splash 10
Toros Mexican 6

Bars & clubs
Beach House 2
Finnians Irish Pub 3
Port Macquarie Hotel 1

The beaches that fringe the western suburbs of the town from the Hastings River mouth, south to Tacking Point and beyond, are simply superb offering excellent swimming, fishing, surfing, walks and views. Even north of the town the great swathe of **North Beach**, stretching 15 km to Point Plomer, fringed by the diverse coastal habitats of **Limeburners Creek Nature Reserve**, provides almost total solitude. South, beyond Green Mound, **Oxley Beach** and **Rocky Beach** are less accessible. Beyond those, **Flynn's Beach** and **Nobby's Beach** are two other favourite spots with good swimming as well as fossicking and snorkelling on the extensive rock platforms. Flynn's Point and Nobby Head also provide great views. South of Nobby Head the coastal fringe gives way to **Shelly Beach** and the 72-ha coastal **Sea Acres Nature Reserve** ⓘ *T6582 3355, 0900-1630, $10, children under 7 free, family $27*, one of the best places in town to spot wild koalas (particularly in the late afternoon). This sublime piece of rainforest is preserved with a 1.3-km boardwalk providing the ideal viewpoint. The boardwalk starts and finishes at the Rainforest Centre which itself houses an interesting range of displays, a café and shop. Guided tours are available and recommended. Then it's on to **Miners Beach**, reached by a coastal path from the same car park. This is a favourite spot for naturists. At the terminus of Lighthouse Road is Tacking Point, named by Matthew Flinders in 1802, and the pocket-sized Tacking Point Lighthouse built in 1879. From there you are afforded great views south, along Lighthouse Beach towards Bonny Hills and North Brother Hill.

South West Rocks and Hat Head » *pp222-235.*

South West Rocks is the best-kept secret on the NSW north coast. It has everything that Byron Bay has, except the footprints. Long swathes of golden sand, great fishing and swimming, a cliff-top lighthouse, stunning views and a superb local national park – Hat Head – combine to make South West Rocks the ideal place to get away from it all for a few days. Here, you can watch dolphins surfing rather than people. South West Rocks is best reached and explored using your own transport.

Ins and outs

South West Rocks Visitors Centre ⓘ *Ocean Dr, end of Gregory St, T6566 6621, www.kempsey.midcoast.com.au, 1000-1600*, is housed in one of the two historic 'Rocks' Boatman's Cottages. **Kempsey VIC** ⓘ *South Kempsey Park, off Pacific Highway, Kempsey, T6563 1555, www.kempsey.midcoast.com.au, daily*, is a good source of information. They have NPWS national parks information. » *p234.*

Sights

South West Rocks sits at the southern bank of the Mcleay River mouth and western end of Trail Bay, where the colourful, wave-eroded rocks that earned the village its name form the perfect playground for swimmers and snorkellers. At the eastern end of Trial Bay the charming settlement of **Arakoon** fringes the Arakoon State Recreation Area and Laggers Point, site of the pink granite monolith of **Trial Bay Gaol** ⓘ *T6566 6168, 0900-1700, $4*, built in 1886 and now housing a small museum that offers an insight into the torrid existence of its former inmates. Trial Bay was named after *The Trial*, a vessel that was stolen by former convicts and wrecked in the Bay in 1816. Several other vessels with more conventional crews were wrecked in Trial Bay in the 1970s. A few rusting remnants still reach out from their sandy graves. At the terminus of Wilson Street, at the western end of Arakoon, is **Little Bay**, with its sublime, people-free beach. The car park also provides access to the **Graves Monument walking track** (2 km return) which provides memorable views back across Trial Bay and the Trail Bay Gaol. **Gap Beach**, accessed a little further south, is another fine spot, especially for the more adventurous surfer. South of Arakoon (3 km), Lighthouse Road provides access to the northern fringe of the **Hat Head**

 National Park, **Smoky Beach** and the **Smoky Cape Lighthouse**. The 1891 lighthouse is one of the tallest and oldest in NSW and provides stunning views south to Crescent Head and north down to the beckoning solitude of North Smoky Beach.

South of South West Rocks, accessed via Hat Head Village Road and Kinchela, the small village and headland of **Hat Head** sits in the heart of the national park separating the long swathes of Smoky Beach north and Killick Beach to the south. The village has a caravan park, limited amenities and walking access to Hat Hill, Korogoro Point, Connor's Beach and the Hungry Hill Rest Area.

Bellingen and Dorrigo National Park » *pp222-235.*

Away from the coast, sitting neatly on the banks of the Bellinger River in the heart of the Bellinger Valley, is the pleasant country village of Bellingen, renowned for its artistic and alternative community, its markets, music festivals and laid-back ambience. Simple relaxation or country walks are the name of the game for travellers here, before they continue further inland to explore the superb national parks of Dorrigo (see below), and Oxley and New England (see page 212), or resume the relentless journey northwards up the coast. The village has its own nickname used affectionately by the locals – Bello.

Ins and outs

Getting there There aren't any long-distance connections to Belligen – you must travel to Nambucca Heads or Urunga and then get a connection. For transport details for Dorrigo National Park, see page 233.

Tourist information Bellingen VIC ⓘ *T66555711, www.bellingen.com, Mon-Sat 0900-1700, Sun 1000-1400*, is beside the Pacific Highway, in Urunga, just south of the Bellingen turn-off. Ask for a free street map of the town. **Dorrigo VIC** ⓘ *Hickory St, T66572486, www.dorrigo.com.au, 1000-1600*, offers local listings. Ask for a free street map. **NPWS Dorrigo National Park Rainforest Visitors Centre** ⓘ *Dome Rd, T6657 2309, www.nationalparks.nsw.gov.au*, supplies national parks, walks and some local information.

Bellingen

Bellingen's peaceful tree-lined streets are lined with some obvious heritage buildings many of which are protected by the National Trust. The small **Bellingen Museum** ⓘ *Civic Sq, Hyde St, T6655 0289, Mon and Wed-Fri 1000-1200*, contains a low-key collection of photos and artefacts from the mid-1800s. The **Old Butter Factory** ⓘ *Doepel Lane, 0930 to 1700*, on the western approach to the village, and the unmistakable **Yellow Shed** ⓘ *2 Hyde St, 0930 to 1700*, are the two main arts and crafts outlets in the village selling everything from opals to wind-chimes. The Old Butter Factory also has a café and offers a range of relaxation and healing therapies including iridology, massage and a float tank. The colourful **Bellingen craft and produce market** is considered one of the best in the region and is held in the local park on the third Saturday of the month. The village also hosts a top quality **Jazz Festival, www.bellingenjazzfestival.com.au** in mid-August, and the equally popular **Global Carnival**, which is an entertaining celebration of world music held in the first week in October.

Nature lovers should take a look at the large (and smelly) flying fox (fruit bat) colony on **Bellingen Island** (which is now no longer an island) beside the river, within easy walking distance of the village. The best place to see the bats is from the Bellingen Caravan Park on Dowle Street (cross the Bridge off Hyde, on to Hammond then turn right in to Dowle), while the best time is around dusk when they depart to find food. But even during the day it is an impressive sight indeed as they hang like a thousand grotesque Christmas decorations from almost every tree.

Dorrigo National Park is a wonderland of rainforest walks and exotic wildlife

Dorrigo and Dorrigo National Park

Provided the weather is kind and the clouds do not blind you, you are in for a scenic treat here. Even the **Dorrigo National Park Rainforest Visitors Centre** ⓘ *T6657 2309, 0900-1700*, has amazing views. Sitting right at the edge of the escarpment, the view across the forested slopes and across the Bellinger Valley towards the coast is even better from the slightly shaky 100-m **Skywalk** that sits like a jetty out across the rainforest canopy. From its edge you can survey the glorious scene and listen to the strange and distant calls of elusive rainforest birds. You may also see the odd python curled up in a branch or right next to the handrail. The visitors centre itself has some good interpretative displays and a small café. The main office and shop can provide the necessary detail on the excellent rainforest walks (ranging from 400 m to 5 km) that begin from the centre and descend in to the very different world beneath the forest canopy.

From the Rainforest Centre it is then a short, scenic 10-km drive along the edge of the escarpment to the **Never Never Picnic Area**, which is a fine network of rainforest walks, including the 5.5-km **Rosewood Creek Track to Cedar Falls**, the 4.8-km **Casuarina Falls Track** and the 6.4-km **Blackbutt (escarpment edge) Track**. Before heading into Dorrigo township itself, it is worth taking the short 2-km drive to **Griffith's Lookout** for its memorable views across the Bellinger Valley. The road to the lookout is signposted about 1 km south of Dome Road off the Waterfall Way. Just north of Dorrigo (1.5 km), the **Dangar Falls** may prove a disappointment after long dry periods but after rain can become a thunderous torrent of floodwaters.

Coffs Harbour » *pp222-235.*

Roughly halfway between Sydney and Brisbane and the only spot on the NSW coast where the Great Dividing Range meets the sea, Coffs Harbour is a favourite domestic holiday resort and the main commercial centre for the northern NSW coast. Surrounded by rolling hills draped in lush banana plantations and pretty beaches, it's a fine spot to kick back for a couple of days. The main activities in town are centred around the attractive marina where regular fishing, whale

Going further

New England and Cathedral Rocks national parks

The 71,207 ha New England National Park is breathtaking. What makes it so special is not only its sense of wilderness and rich biodiversity, but its stunning vistas, Point Lookout being the most popular and accessible, and truly memorable. Do not venture here automatically expecting to see those views however. What adds a very atmospheric and unpredictable edge to this viewpoint is its height, which, at over 1,564 m often results in a shroud of mist or worse still, sheets of rain. It really can be a glorious day in Armidale and along the coast and yet Point Lookout is like Edinburgh Castle in mid-winter. Still, if you can afford a couple of days the camping, the views and the varied walks around Point Lookout (2.5 km to full day) are well worthwhile.

Just north of Point Lookout Road, Round Mountain Road (8 km) ventures into the heart of Cathedral Rock National Park. The main feature here is the magnificent granite tors – Cathedral Rocks – and in spring, vivid displays of wildflowers. The 6-km Cathedral Rock Track from the Barokee Rest Area provides a circuit track with a 200-m diversion to the 'Rocks'.

The VIC and NPWS office in Armidale and the **Dorrigo Rainforest Centre** ⓘ *T66572309, www.npws.nsw.gov.au*, both stock the relevant leaflets and information surrounding the park, its walks, camping and self-contained accommodations. For the New England and Cathedral Rocks national parks, Point lookout Rd is unsealed and accessed (signposted) off the Waterfall Way, 5 km south of the Waterfall Way/Guyra Rd Junction (3 km west of Ebor). It is then 11 km to the park boundary and a further 3 km to Point Lookout.

and dolphin watching cruises are on offer, together with highly popular diving and snorkelling trips to the outlying Solitary Islands. The island group and surrounding coast is gazetted as a marine park and considered to have one of the most diverse marine bio-diversities in NSW. Other principal attractions include Muttonbird Island, guarding the entrance to the harbour and offering sanctuary to thousands of burrowing seabirds and, in complete contrast, the kitschy Big Banana complex on the northern edge of the town. Often overlooked is the fast developing, but still pleasant, beachside community of Sawtell which is worth the trip.

Information

VIC ⓘ *corner of Elizabeth St and Maclean St, T6652 1522, www.coffscoast.com.au, 0900-1700.* Ask for the free Coffs Coast Visitors Guide.

Sights

The rather unsightly and uninspiring main drag, **Grafton Street**, has seen something of an improvement in recently, with the creation of the Palms Centre Arcade, and redevelopment of the Mall and Park Avenue, which, combined, form the hub of the town centre. From the end of the Mall, **High Street** heads 3 km southeast to the **harbour**, which is hemmed in by the town's three main beaches: **Park Beach**, which straddles Coffs Creek to the north, **Jetty Beach**, beside the harbour and **Boambee Beach** to the south. Park Beach is the most popular and is regularly patrolled in summer. Jetty Beach is considered the safest. The view from **Beacon Hill Lookout**, at the end of Camperdown Street, off High Street, offers fine 360-degree views across the harbour, the coast, and the green rolling hills of the Great Dividing Range to the west. There are also numerous other, excellent beaches, stretching 20 km north all the way to Woolgoolga.

Linked to the mainland by the marina's 500-m sea wall is **Muttonbird Island Nature Reserve**, which offers more than just a pleasant walk and some memorable views back towards the town. From October to April Muttonbird Island and others in the Solitary Island group are home to thousands of breeding wedge-tailed shearwaters (muttonbirds) that nest in a warren of burrows across the entire island. The birds are best viewed just after dusk, when they return in number to feed their mates or chicks hiding deep within the burrows. Although the birds were once easily harvested for food, they are now, thankfully, fully protected and for obvious reasons, do not stray from the main pathway. Also keep a lookout for humpback whales which are often spotted just offshore from June to September.

Solitary Islands offer some fine dive sites with such evocative names as 'Grey Nurse Gutters' and 'Manta Arch', a wealth of marine life (90 species of coral and 280 species of fish) and the densest colonies of anemones and anemone fish (clown fish) in the world. For detailed information contact the NPWS, see above. Coffs Harbour is one of the cheapest places to get certified on the NSW coast. For details of diving and snorkelling trips, see page 231.

It's incredible that by building an oversize banana next to the main highway, you attract people like bees to honey. Coff's famous icon and monument of marketing genius, the **Big Banana** ⓘ *T6652 4355, www.bigbanana.com.au, 0900- 1600, free, rides from $5 and tours from $12, child $7.50*, located just north of the town on the Pacific Highway, fronts a banana plantation that hosts a number of activities from a train plantation tour to a lookout, toboggan rides, 'snow-tubing', ice skating and lots of souvenir kitsch. It is however, perhaps entertainment enough, to sit in the café and watch people posing for photos in front of the main attraction.

Also north of town is the **Legends Surf Museum** ⓘ *T66536536, Gauldrons Rd, left off the Pacific Highway, 1000-1600, $5, child $2*, run by enthusiastic and enigmatic Scott Dillon, ex-master of the waves. There are over 120 classic boards on display as well as the odd canoe, photos and other such enlightening memorabilia.

Sawtell, a seaside village 6 km south of Coffs Harbour, is blessed with some fine beaches and a pleasant laid-back atmosphere that has quietly attracted domestic holidaymakers for years. Now the secret is well and truly out, like most of the east coast's beachside communities the influx of city 'sea changers' may well prove its very demise. Other than the obvious attractions of the beach, the **Cooinda Aboriginal Art Gallery** ⓘ *Shop 1/4 First Ave, T66587901, www.cooinda-gallery.com.au*, recently relocated from Coffs Harbour is well worth a look. It showcases some excellent examples of the unique and spiritually loaded 'dot-style'.

Coffs Harbour to Byron Bay » *pp222-235.*

Ins and outs

Lower Clarence Visitor Centre ⓘ *Ferry Park, just south of the turn-off for Yamba, and 2 km south of MacLean, T6645 4121, www.clarencetourism.com, 0900-1700*, has full accommodation, events and activities listings for the region.

Yamba, Angourie and Yuraygir National Park (North)

The coastal fishing town of **Yamba**, 13 km east of the Pacific Highway (exit just before the Clarence River bridge) and on the southern bank of the Clarence River mouth, is famed for its prawn industry and its fine surf beaches. Serving mainly as a domestic holiday destination, it offers the opportunity to spent two or three days away from the mainstream tourist resorts further north. **Main Beach**, below Flinders Park, is the most popular of Yamba's many golden strands but **Turners Beach**, between the main breakwater and lighthouse, **Covent Beach**, between Lovers Point and Main Beach, and **Pippie Beach**, the most southerly, are all equally as good. **Clarence River Delta** and **Lake Wooloweyah**, 4 km south, all provide boating, fishing and cruising opportunities. The Yamba-Iluka ferry shuttles back and forth daily (see below), providing access to some sublime beaches and bluffs, a stunning rainforest reserve and the wilderness of Bundjalung National Park (see below).

Iluka and Bundjalung National Park

If you can give yourself at least two to three days to explore the Iluka area, you won't regret it. Other than the superb coastline contained within the southern sector of the Bundjalung National Park and one of the best campsites on the northern NSW coast at **Woody Head**, the

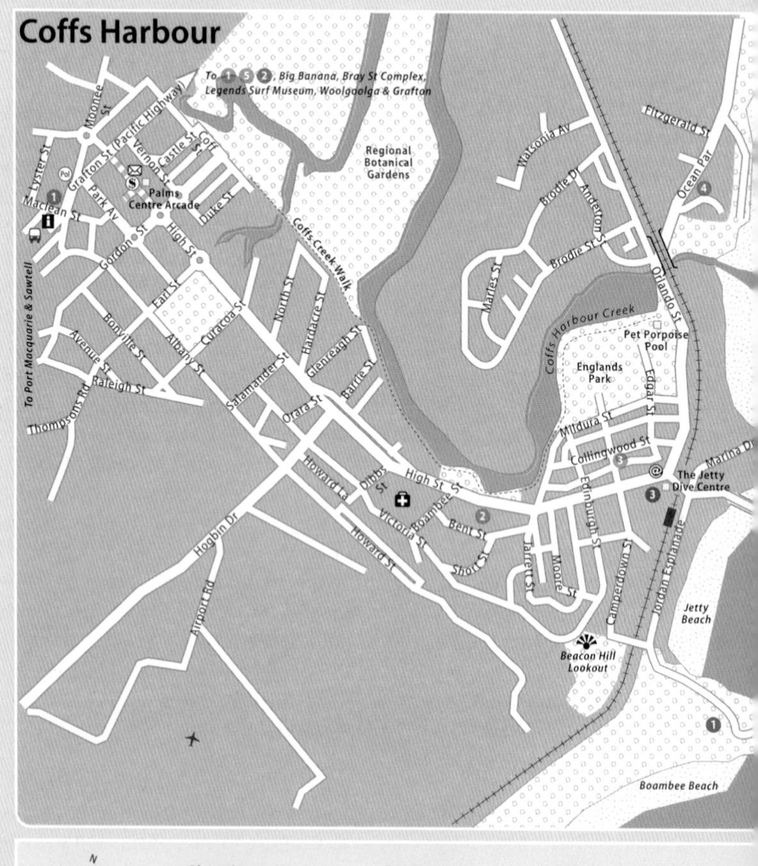

N

200 metres
200 yards

Sleeping
Aussitel Backpackers **2**
Coffs Harbour YHA **3**
Country Comfort Motel **1**
Emerald Beach Holiday Park **5**
Park Beach Caravan Park **4**

Eating
Fisherman's Co-op **2**
Foreshore Café **3**
Ocean Front Brasserie **1**
Tide & Pilot Brasserie **6**

big attraction at the sleepy fishing village of **Iluka** is the World Heritage Rainforest Walk through the **Iluka Nature Reserve**. The 136-ha reserve contains the largest remaining stand of littoral rainforest in NSW – a rich forest habitat unique to the coastal environment and supporting a huge number of species such as the charmingly-named lily pilly tree and noisy pitta bird. The 2.5-km rainforest walk can be tackled either from the north at the Iluka Bluff Car Park (off the main Iluka Road opposite the golf club) or from the caravan park at western edge of the village (Crown Street).

Iluka Beach is another fine quiet spot reached via Beach Road (head west from the end of Iluka Road). Further north, just beyond Iluka Bluff, **Bluff Beach** and **Frazer's Reef** are popular for swimming and fishing. The Whale Viewing Platform on Beach Road can guarantee panoramic views of the area and the possibility, in season (June to November), of seeing mainly humpback whales migrating up and down the coast.

Two kilometres north of Iluka and Woody Head, the 18,000 ha wilderness of **Bundjalung National Park** with its 38 km of beaches, littoral rainforest, heathlands, unusual rock formations, lagoons, creeks and swamps is an eco-explorer's paradise. Sadly, access from the south is by 4WD only ($16 permit), or on foot. There is better access from the north along the 21-km unsealed road. Go up to Gap Road, off the Pacific Highway, 5 km south of Woodburn, to the Black Rocks campsite. Accommodation and park information, maps and internet are available at the Lower Clarence Visitor Centre (see page 213 for details).

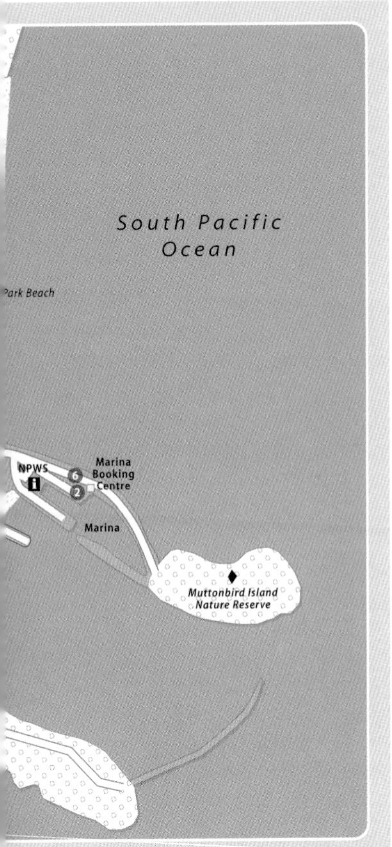

Bars & clubs
Fitzroy Hotel **1**
Greenhouse Tavern **2**

Lennox Head

The small, beachside settlement of Lennox Head is world famous for the long surf breaks that form at the terminus of Seven Mile Beach and Lennox Point. For information on surfing lessons, page 229. Even without a board, the village offers a quieter, alternative destination in which to spend a relaxing couple of days, away from the clamour of Byron Bay. Just south of the village the eponymous heads offers excellent views north to Cape Byron and are considered a prime spot for hang-gliding and dolphin/whale spotting. The **Lennox Reef**, below the heads, known as 'The Moat', is also good for snorkelling. At the northern end of the village **Lake Ainsworth** is a fine venue for freshwater swimming, canoeing and windsurfing. **Lennox Head Sailing School**, beside the lake on Pacific Parade, hires watersports equipment and offers lessons. The lake edge also serves as the venue for the coastal markets that are held on the second and fifth Sundays of the month.

“” Anything goes in Byron Bay. This town would love to have its own passport control to prevent entry to anyone who is remotely conservative or thinks surfing is something you do in front of a computer...

Byron Bay » pp222-235.

Anything goes in Byron Bay. This town would love to have its own passport control to prevent entry to anyone who is remotely conservative or thinks surfing is something you do in front of a computer. Only three decades ago 'Byron' was little more than a sleepy, attractive coastal enclave. Few strayed off the main highway heading north except a few alternative lifestylers who found it an ideal escape and the land prices wonderfully cheap. But news spread and its popularity exploded. It lacks the glitz of the Gold Coast and the conformity of many other coastal resorts, but there is little doubt it is perilously close to the level of popularity that can turn to 'a love it or hate it' experience. Despite all this, however, it remains a beautiful place (no high-rise hotels here) and boasts a wonderfully cosmopolitan mix of humanity. Few people leave disappointed.

Ins and outs

Getting there The two nearest airports are Coolangatta (north) and Ballina (south) with good daily services and shuttle buses to town. There are plenty of long-distance buses and trains from Sydney, Cairns, Brisbane, etc. Both the train station and bus station are in the centre of town.

Getting around You can enjoy all the offerings of Byron Bay on foot, or, to cover more ground, hire a bike. There are local bus services for getting around town and also to sights around Byron Bay such as Ballina and Lennox Head. » p234.

Tourist information Byron Bay VIC ⓘ *80 Jonston St, T6680 8558, www.visitbyronbay.com.au, 0900-1700.* See also page 232, for tour operators.

Sights

The main attraction in Byron, beyond its hugely popular social and creative scene, are of course the surrounding beaches and the stunning Cape Byron Headland Reserve. There are over 37 km of beaches, including seven world-class surf beaches stretching from Belongil Beach in the west to Broken Head in the south. Byron also hosts an extensive array of organized activities to lure you from your beach based relaxation. Surfing is, of course, the most popular pastime. For details see page 233.

Only metres from the town centre **Main Beach** is the main focus of activity. It is patrolled and safest for families or surfing beginners. West of Main Beach, **Belongil Beach** stretches about 1 km to the mouth of Belongil Creek. About 500 m beyond that (accessed via Bayshore Drive), there is a designated naturist beach. East of the town centre, Main Beach merges with **Clark's Beach**, which is no less appealing and generally much quieter. Beyond Clark's Beach and the headland called **The Pass** - a favourite surf spot - **Watego's**

Youth surf competition, Byron Bay

and **Little Watego's beaches** fringe the northern side of Cape Byron, providing more surf breaks and some dramatic coastal scenery. South of Cape Byron, **Tallow Beach** stretches about 9 km to Broken Head and is a great spot to escape the crowds (but note that it is unpatrolled). Several walks also access other more remote headland beaches within the very pretty **Broken Head Nature Reserve**. In the heart of Byron Bay itself, 2.5 km from the shore, is the small and clearly visible rocky outcrop known as **Julian Rocks Marine Reserve**. It is listed in Australia' s 'top ten' dive sites, with over 400 species of fish including sharks and manta ray, with turtles and dolphins often joining the party. If you are not a certified diver, a snorkelling trip to the rocks is recommended.

Crowning the **Cape Byron Headland** is the **Byron Bay Lighthouse** ⓘ *0800-1930 (1730 in winter), 30 mins walk from the town, tours 40 mins, daily except Wed and Fri*, that was built in 1901. It sits only metres away from Australia's easternmost point. As well as the dramatic coastal views east over Byron Bay and south down Tallow Beach to Broken Head, the headland provides some excellent walking opportunities, with the track down from the lighthouse to Little Watego's Beach being the most popular. Humpback whales can often been seen offshore during their annual migrations in mid-winter and early summer, while dolphins and the occasional manta ray can be spotted in the clear waters below the cliffs year round.

The town has a number of galleries worth seeing including the **Colin Heaney Glass Blowing Studio**, at 6 Acacia Street, and the superb works of local photographer John Derrey, at **Byron Images**, on the corner of Lawson Street and Jonson Street (see www.johnderrey.com.au). The VIC has full gallery listings, and a tour to meet local artists and see their work and studios is offered by **Studio Arts Tours**, details from the VIC. Byron also hosts an arts and crafts market on the first Sunday of the month on Butler Street.

The Rainbow Region *pp222-235.*

Inland from Byron Bay, lies the so-called Rainbow Region, a collection of bohemian, arty villages famous for their alternative lifestyle. This very pleasant, scenic area, often called the Northern Rivers, stretches from Murwillumbah in the north to Kyogle in the west, Lismore and Ballina in the south and Byron Bay on the coast to the east.

Geologically the region is dominated by the Mount Warning shield volcano and its vast caldera (crater), the largest of its type in the southern hemisphere. The huge volcano, which erupted about 23 mn years ago, produced a flat shield-shaped landform with its highest point rising almost twice that of Mount Warning (1,157 m), which is all that remains today of the original magma chamber and central vent. If viewed from the air the huge eroded bowl of the caldera can be seen stretching almost 60 km inland from the coast, with the dramatic peak of Mount Warning in its middle. The original lava flows reached as far as Canungra in the north, Kyogle to the west, Lismore and Ballina in the south and almost 100 km out to sea. Today, after millions of years of wind and water erosion, the region is rich in dramatic geological features. Around the rim of the caldera and fringing plateaux lush rainforest covered landscapes have risen form the ashes, while the floor of the caldera acts as a vast watershed for the Tweed River which debouches at the border of New South Wales and Queensland. There are no fewer than nine national parks in the area, offering magnificent scenery and walking opportunities.

Ins and outs

Nimbin VIC ⓘ *northern end of Cullen St, (81), T6689 11383, nimbin@nsw.net.au, Mon-Fri 1000-1700, Sat 0900-1700, Sun 1000-1600*, offers transport and accommodation bookings, internet access and maps.

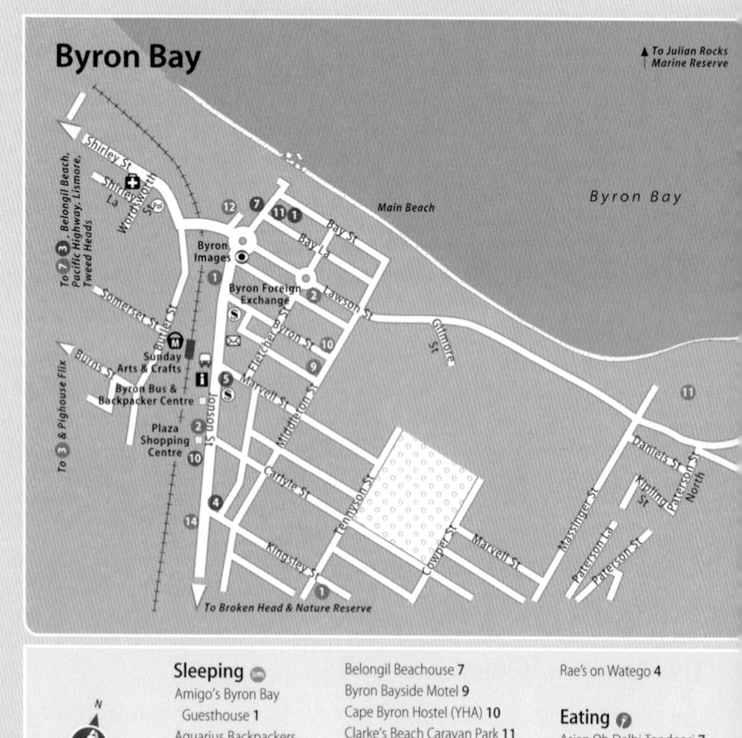

Mullumbimby

Northwest from Byron, the little village of Mullumbimby is about as charming as its name suggests and offers a fine stop or diversion on the way to Nimbin and the Nightcap National Park. There is a scattering of historic buildings along Dalley and Stuart streets, including the 1908 **Cedar House**, that now serves as an antique gallery and the old 1907 post office which houses a small museum. **Crystal Castle** ⓘ *T6684 3111, 1000-1730, free*, south of Mullumbimby on Monet Drive, has a fine display of natural crystals, gardens and a café. You might also be tempted to checkout your psychedelic colours as seen through the 'aura camera' or try some crystal healing, a tarot card reading or massage.

Nimbin

Up until the 1970s, the sleepy dairy village of Nimbin had changed little since its inception by the first European settlers over a century before. Then, in 1973 the Australian Union of Students (AUS) chose the Nimbin Valley as the venue for the 'experimental and alternative' **Aquarius Festival**. The concept was to create 'a total cultural experience, through the lifestyle of participation' for Australian creatives, students and alternative lifestylers. Of course, with many of that generation eager to maintain the ideologies and practices of the sixties, the very concept became like a red rag to the proverbial, 'alternative' bull and when the time arrived it all inevitably went in to orbit. In many ways Nimbin never got over the invasion, the

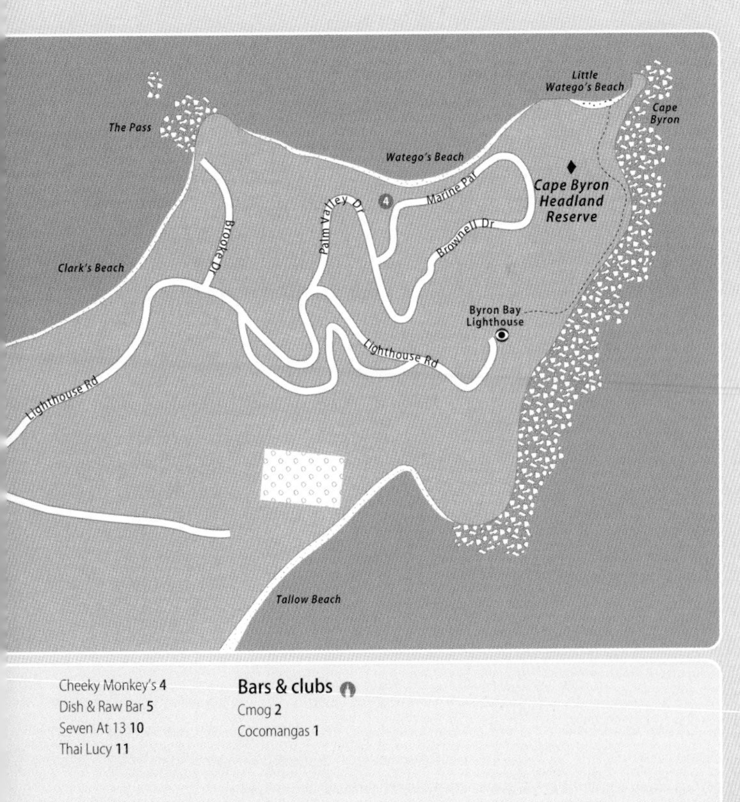

Cheeky Monkey's **4**
Dish & Raw Bar **5**
Seven At 13 **10**
Thai Lucy **11**

Bars & clubs
Cmog **2**
Cocomangas **1**

excitement or indeed the hangover and its more enlightened long-term residents have been joined by a veritable army of society's drop-outs, man.

In many ways the colourful main street of Nimbin, **Cullen Street**, is the single collective 'sight' in the village and one that speaks very much for itself. Amidst a rash of laid-back cafés, alternative health and arts and craft shops, is **Nimbin Museum** ⓘ *62 Cullen St, T6689 1123, 0900-1700, $2*. Entirely true to the unconventional and the alternative ideology, it goes deliberately beyond any conventional concepts. It is perhaps simply unique in its creative, historical and often humorous interpretations and expressions of the village, its inhabitants and Australia as a whole.

On the other side of Cullen Street, the loudly advertised **Hemp Embassy** (free) is also worth a look but, as you can imagine, has little to do with gardening or fashion wear. As well as supporting the multifarious and controversial uses of hemp, the Nimbin Valley is also well known for fruit growing and permaculture. For the visitor the **Djanbung Gardens Permaculture Centre** ⓘ *74 Cecil St, T6689 1755, 1000-1200, Tue-Fri 1000-1500, other days 1000-1200, tours Tue/Thu 1030, Sat 1100*, offers garden tours, herbal crafts, environmental workshops and an organic café.

The most obvious volcanic feature around Nimbin are the **Nimbin Rocks**, which are estimated to be over 20 mn years old. There is a lookout on **Lodge Road**, 3 km south of the village. If you fancy a further investigation try a bicycle tour, see page 232 for details.

Nightcap National Park and Whian Whian State Forest

The World Heritage 8,145-ha Nightcap National Park is located on the southern rim of the Mount Warning caldera and adjacent is the Whian Whian State Forest Park. Combined, they offer a wealth of volcanic features including massifs, pinnacles and cliffs eroded by spectacular waterfalls and draped in lush rainforest. Some unique wildlife also resides in the park including the red-legged pademelon (a kind of wallaby), the Fleay's barred frog and the appealingly named wompoo fruit-dove.

The main physical features of the park are **Mount Nardi** (800 m), 12 km east of Nimbin; **Terania Creek** and the **Protestors Falls**, 14 km north of The Channon; and **Whian Whian State Forest** and 100-m **Minyon Falls**, 23 km southwest of Mullumbimby. The 30-km Whian Whian Scenic Drive (unsealed), which can be accessed beyond the Minyon Falls, traverses the forest park and takes visitors through varied rainforest vegetation and scenery including the memorable **Peates Mountain Lookout**. Nightcap National Park also holds the rather dubious accolade of receiving the highest mean rainfall in the State.

Popular long walking tracks include the moderate-to-hard 7.5-km **Minyon Loop**, which starts from the Minyon Falls Picnic Area and takes in the base of the falls and the escarpment edge, and the moderate-to-hard 16-km **Historic Nightcap Track**, which follows the former pioneer trails that once connected Lismore and Mullumbimby. Other, shorter and easier possibilities are the 3-km **Mount Matheson Loop** and 4-km **Pholis Gap walks**, which both start from Mount Nardi, and the 1.5-km **Big Scrub Loop** which starts from the Gibbergunyah Range Road in Whian Whian State Forest. It is said to contain some of the best remnant rainforest in the region. Protestors Falls, which were named after a successful six-week protest to prevent logging in the late1970s, are reached on a 1.5-km return track from the Terania Creek Picnic Area.

The Mount Nardi section of the park is accessed via Newton Drive, which is off Tuntable Falls Road west out of Nimbin. The Terania Creek and Protestors Falls are reached via Terania Creek Road north out of The Channon and the Minyon Falls and Whian Whian State Forest is reached via Dunoon or Goonengerry southwest of Mullumbimby.

Mount Warning, scene of a daily pilgrimage to catch the first rays of sunlight to touch the Australian mainland

Murwillumbah

The pleasant, sugar cane town of Murwillumbah sits on the banks of the Tweed River, at the eastern edge of the Mount Warning caldera, and serves as a major gateway to the Rainbow Region. Most people who visit the town gather what information they need from the World Heritage Rainforest Centre (see below) and then 'head for the hills', however, if you can spare an hour or so the small **Tweed Regional Art Gallery** ⓘ *Mistral Rd, T6670 2790, Wed-Sun 1000-1700*, is worth a look. As well as its permanent collection of Australian and international art, it features some fine works by local artists and also hosts the very lucrative Doug Moran National Portrait Prize. Murwillumbah VIC shares its office with the NPWS and the **World Heritage Rainforest Centre** ⓘ *corner of Tweed Valley Way and Alma St, T6672 1340, www.tweedcoolangatta.com.au, open till 1600*. Combined they offer insight and information surrounding the region and the parks.

Mount Warning National Park

The 1157-m peak of Mount Warning is all that remains of the magma chamber and vent that formed the vast caldera that shaped much of the Northern Rivers region. Other than its stunning scenery and rich flora and fauna, the great appeal of Mount Warning is the pilgrimage to the summit to see the first rays of sunlight to hit the Australian mainland. The moderate to hard 4.4-km ascent starts from the Breakfast Creek Picnic Area, 17 km southwest of Murwillumbah at the terminus of Mount Warning Road. To ensure you reach the summit for sunrise you are advised to set off about 2½ hours beforehand. Murwillumbah, see above, serves as an overnight stop for those undertaking the dawn ascent. For the less energetic,

 Lyrebird Track crosses Breakfast Creek before winding 200 m through palm forest to a rainforest platform. To learn more about the Aboriginal mythology surrounding the mountain and its diverse wildlife, you might like to join either the sunrise or daytime summit walking tours on offer from Byron Bay (see page 232). Access to Mount Warning is via Mount Warning Road, 11 km south of Murwillumbah on the main Kyogle Road.

Sleeping

Port Macquarie *p207, map p208*
There are plenty of accommodation options in and around Port Macquarie, from basic NPWS campsites to luxury resorts. During holiday periods and in the high season you are advised to book ahead.

LL-L **HW Boutique Motel**, 1 Stewart St, T6583 1200, www.hwmotorinn.com.au. For a really chic motel in the ideal position, look no further than this. The rooms are well appointed with most offering views across the rivermouth and Town Beach.

L-E **Sundowner Breakwall Tourist Park**, beside the river mouth, 1 Munster St, T6583 2755, www.sundowner.net.au. Of the many motor parks in the area this one is hard to beat for position. Vast, well facilitated with a pool and camp kitchen.

B-E **Port Macquarie YHA**, 40 Church St, T6583 5512. Newly renovated and the closest hostel to the beaches, offering tidy dorms, twins and family rooms, spacious facilities, free bikes, internet, pick-ups from the bus station.

C-E **Port Macquarie Backpackers**, 2 Hastings River Dr, T6583 1719, lindel@midcoast.com.au. A friendly, family-run historic house with lots of character, dorms, twins and doubles, pool, 24-hr kitchen and TV room, free use of boogie boards, fishing gear, bikes, pool table, internet and pick-ups.

C-E **Ozzie Pozzie Backpackers**, 36 Waugh St, T6583 8133, www.nomadsworld.com. More modern, activity oriented backpackers well in tune with travellers needs, good facilities, dorms, doubles/twins, internet, pick-ups, free use of boogie boards, bikes and fishing gear.

Remote NPWS camping is available at Big Hill and Point Plomer in the Limeburners Creek Nature Reserve, T6586 8300.

South West Rocks and Hat Head*p209*
L-A **Rockpool Motel**, 45 McIntyre St, T6566 7755, www.rockpoolmotorinn.com.au. Modern motel complex 1 km east of the town centre.

A-B **Bay Motel**, Prince of Wales Ave, T6566 6909. Another motel only older and cheaper, right on the main shopping street.

A-E **Horseshoe Bay Beach Park**, Livingstone St, T6566 6370. Overlooks the river, ocean and the sheltered Horseshoe Bay Beach and is within yards of the town centre. Busy and beautifully placed this motor park offers cabins, on-site vans and powered sites (some en suite). Hugely popular with locals so book well in advance.

D **Arakoon State Recreation Area**, T6566 6168, Laggers Point, beside the Trail Bay Gaol. Equally fine aesthetics and more seclusion can be secured here. It's a great spot and the best for camping.

F **Hungry Rest Area**, south of Hat Head village. A good basic NPWS campsite with pit toilets, no water and fires are permitted. Self-registration including day-use fees apply, T6584 2203. Contact for both sites.

F **Smoky Rest Area**, near the lighthouse, excellent for wildlife, is this good basic NPWS campsite.

Bellingen *p210*
There are plenty of good B&Bs and self-contained cottages in verdant country settings.

L **Fernridge Farm Cottage**, 1673 Waterfall Way (4 km west), T6655 2142, www.bellingenaccommodation.com.au. Peaceful, cosy, self-contained accommodation in a 19th-century 'Queenslander' cottage on an 120 ha alpaca farm.

L **Monticello Countryhouse**, 11 Sunset Ridge Drive, (2 km), T6655 1559, www.monticello.com.au. Popular B&B, with classy, good value double, twin and singles, within easy reach of the village.

A **Promised land Cottages**, 934 Promised Land Rd, T6655 9578, www.promisedland cottages.com.au. Good value quality self-contained options 15 mins outside of the village.

B **Rivendell guesthouse**, 12 Hyde St, T6655 0060, www.rivendellguesthouse.com.au. A historic guesthouse with 3 queen rooms situated right in the heart of the village.

B-F **Bellingen YHA Backpackers**, 2 Short St, T6655 1116, backpack@bellingenyha.com.au. Consistently receives rave reviews and deservedly so. Housed in a beautifully maintained 2-storey historic homestead in the heart of the village, with large decks overlooking the river valley, it oozes character and has a great social, laid-back atmosphere. It has a range of dorms, double/twins, family rooms and camping facilities, internet, musical instruments, hammocks and entertaining trips to Dorrigo National Park. Lining the hallways are tasteful photographs of over 200 guests willing to get buck naked in the name of art.

Dorrigo and Dorrigo National Park

p210

A **Fernbrook Lodge**, 470 Waterfall Way, 6 km west, T6657 2573, fernbrooklodge@midcoast.com.au. Offers great views and is recommended.

B-C **Historic Dorrigo Hotel**, corner of Hickory St and Cudgery St, T6657 2016, www.hotelmoteldorrigo.com.au. Traditional pub rooms at affordable prices in the centre of town.

C-D **Gracemere Grange**, 325 Dome Rd, 2 km from the Rainforest Centre, T6657 2630, gracemere@dorrigo.com. Comfortable B&B accommodation.

C-F **Dorrigo Mountain Resort**, on the southern edge of the town, Waterfall Way, T6657 2564. Standard self-contained cabins, powered and non-powered sites, BBQs, but no camp kitchen.

Coffs Harbour *p211, map p214*

There is a rash of motels and resorts located along the Pacific Highway on the north and south approaches and along the waterfront on Ocean Parade. There are plenty of motor parks in the area with the best-located north or south of the town. The hostels are lively places – very activity and party oriented.

L-A **Country Comfort Motel**, 353 Pacific Highway, T6652 8222, www.countrycomfort.com.au. Next to the Big Banana, this modern, convenient and good value motel is a good choice if you are merely passing through. Pool, sauna and spa.

L-F **Park Beach Caravan Park**, Ocean Pde, T6648 4888. If you must stay in the town itself this is the best facilitated motor park beachside.

A-E **Emerald Beach Holiday Park**, Fishermans Dr, Emerald Beach, T6656 1521. 18 km north of Coffs, this motor park has luxury villas, standard cabins, on-site vans, powered and shaded non-powered sites in bush setting with shop, café and pool. The beach is only yards away and is simply superb with headland walks nearby. Recommended.

A-E **Sawtell Beach Caravan Park**, Lyons Rd, Sawtell (6 km), T6653 1379. South of town is this motor park close to the surf beach and local amenities with camp kitchen.

C-E **Coffs Harbour YHA**, 51 Collingwood St, T6652 6462. Friendly, spotless and well managed. Recently relocated to a spacious modern facility in a suburban setting close to the beach, offering dorms, doubles/twins and family rooms (with en suite), pool, internet, cable TV and free bikes, surf/body boards and pick-ups. Recommended.

C-F **Aussitel Backpackers**, T6651 1871/1800 330 335, www.aussitel.com.

Budget busters

Port Macquarie to Byron Bay sleeping

L **Smoky Cape Lighthouse**, T6566 6301, www.smokycapelighthouse.com.au. The most unusual accommodation in the area has to be these former keepers quarters. Totally refurbished in the interior it provides self-contained or B&B options, modern facilities, a '4-poster' and stunning views south across the national park. Book well in advance.

L **Friday Creek Retreat**, 267 Friday Creek Rd, Upper Orara, 17 km west of town, T6653 8221, www.fridaycreek.com.au. Sheer luxury, as well as complete peace and quiet in a country setting is offered here. There are 9 superb fully self-contained cottages with spas, open fires, hammocks and great views, free bike hire, complimentary breakfast and dinner by arrangement.

Also near the beach on Harbour Drive (312) this a highly social place with emphasis on discounted activities and its own attractive dive packages being a specialty. Dorms, twins and doubles, large kitchen, common area, internet, pool, bikes, surf/body boards, wetsuits etc.

Coffs Harbour to Byron Bay *p213*

Most of Yamba's amenities can be found along its main drag, Wooli St, or Yamba St off Wooli St, which terminates at Pippie Beach.

LL-A **Surf Motel**, 2 Queen St, Yamba, T6646 2200. Modern, well-appointed motel option right next to Main Beach.

LL-E **Blue Dolphin Holiday Resort**, Yamba Rd, Yamba, T6646 2194. This 5-starresort offers luxury/standard self-contained cabins, en suite/standard powered and non-powered sites, café, pool and camp kitchen.

B-E **Lake Ainsworth Caravan Park**, Pacific Parade, Lennox Head, T6687 7249. For campers and campervans this option is ideally located next to the lake and offers en suite/standard cabins, powered and non-powered sites but no camp kitchen. Activities include windsurfing, sailing and canoeing.

C-E **Lennox Head Beachouse YHA**, 3 Ross St, T6687 7636, lennoxbacpac@hotmail.com.au. Purpose-built hostel with a great laid-back, friendly atmosphere, near the beach and Lake Ainsworth. Dorms and small doubles and free use of surf/boogie boards, bikes and fishing gear. Free sailing and windsurfing lessons can also be arranged and there is a natural therapies (massage) clinic on-site, as well as their legendary chocolate cake.

D-F **Woody Head Campsite**, beside the beach off Iluka Rd, 14 km west of the Pacific Highway, 4 km north of Iluka, T6646 6134, www.nationalparks.nsw.gov.au. This NPSW campsite is simply superb. Non-powered sites, toilets, water, hot showers, boat ramp and fires permitted, plus 3 cabins with cooking facilities. Book well ahead.

Byron Bay *p216, map p218*

There is certainly plenty of choice in Byron with the emphasis on backpacker hostels and upmarket boutique hotels, B&Bs and guesthouses. There are over a dozen very competitive backpackers in town all having to maintain good standards. Mostly the choice comes down to availability – book well ahead for all accommodation but particularly the backpackers. If the options below don't suffice the VIC has a very good accommodation booking service.

See www.byron-bay.com and www.byronbayaccom.net.

L-D **Belongil Beachouse**, Childe St (Kendal St, off Shirley St), T6685 7868, www.belongilbeachouse.com.au. Also east of the town centre and in contrast to the Arts Factory this option offers a wide range of modern, well-appointed options from dorms and private double/twins with shared facilities, to luxury motel-style rooms with spas, or two-bedroom self-contained cottages. Quiet setting across the road from the beach. Balinese style café and float/massage therapy centre on site. Internet, bike, body/surf board hire and courtesy bus.

L-E **Broken Head Caravan Park**, Beach Rd, Broken Head (8 km), T6685 3245. Further afield and much quieter, the appeal of this motor park is its friendly atmosphere, beachside position and proximity to the Broken Head Nature Reserve. It has cabins, powered and non-powered sites, small shop, BBQ but no camp kitchen.

L-E **Clarke's Beach Caravan Park**, off Lighthouse Rd, T6685 6496. Further west, with prettier surroundings and right beside Clark's Beach, this motor park offers self-contained and standard cabins, powered and shady non-powered sites, no camp kitchen just BBQs.

L-E **First Sun Holiday Park**, Lawson St (200 m east of the Main Beach Car Park), T6685 6544, www.bshp.com.au/first. The most convenient to the town centre and Main Beach, it offers a range of self-contained/standard cabins, powered and non-powered sites, camp kitchen.

A **Byron Bayside Motel**, 14 Middleton St, T6685 6004, www.byronbaysidemotel.com.au. This 3-star motel is well placed in the heart of town, modern and good value.

A-B **Amigo's Byron Bay Guesthouse**, corner of Kingsley St and Tennyson St, T6680 8662, www.amigosbb.com. Doubles (one en suite one with shared bathroom), bike and body board hire and massage.

A-E **Aquarius Backpackers Motel**, 16 Lawson St, T6685 7663,

Smoky Cape Lighthouse

www.aquarius-back pack.com.au. Large and lively complex offering dorms, doubles and spa suites (all en suite, with 'proper beds'), pool, good-value licensed café/bistro, internet, free boogie boards, bikes, pool tables and courtesy bus.

A-E **Cape Byron Hostel** (YHA), T6685 8788, www.yha.com.au. Offers modern, clean dorms, double and twins (some en suite/a/c) centred around a large courtyard with pool. Well managed and friendly. Good kitchen facilities, café, free BBQ nights, large games room, internet and tours desk. Dive shop next door.

A-E **Holiday Village Backpackers**, 116 Jonson St, south of town centre, T6685 8888. Offers modern dorms, doubles and motel-style apartments (some en suite with TV), large courtyard with pool, spa, well equipped kitchen, all-you-can-eat BBQs, internet, free surf/body boards, scuba lessons, bike hire.

A-F **Arts Factory**, Skinners Shoot Rd (via Burns St, off Shirley St), T6685 7709, www.artsfactory.com.au. For the quintessential 'alternative' Byron experience this place takes some beating. It offers a

Budget busters

Byron Bay and around sleeping

LL **Rae's on Watego**, overlooking Watego's Beach, T6685 5366, www.raes.com.au. This sits firmly at the top of this price category and is the most luxurious hotel in Byron. It was voted in Conde Naste Traveller Magazine (and others) as being in the top 50 worldwide. Although location has a lot to do with that accolade, the place itself is superb and cannot be faulted. It has an in-house restaurant that is also excellent and open to non-guests.

LL **Crystal Creek Rainforest Retreat**, Brookers Rd, Murwillumbah, T6679 1591, www.crystalcreekrainforestretreat.com.au. This award-winning retreat is located on the edge of the Numinbah Nature Reserve, about 23 km west of Murwillumbah, with modern design, 7 well-appointed self-contained bungalows, spa baths, excellent cuisine, local forest walks and even the odd hammock across the creek. Transfers from Murwillumbah by arrangement.

wide range of 'funky' accommodation, from the 'Love Shack' and 'Island Retreats', to 'The Gypsy Bus', tepees and campsites. Excellent amenities, pool, sauna, internet, café (plus vegetarian restaurant nearby)', bike hire, tours desk and unusual arts, relaxation or music based activities including didgeridoo making, drumming and yoga. The Pighouse Flix Cinema is also next door. It may not be everybody's cup of herbal tea, but for an experience it is recommended.
C-E **Cape Byron Lodge**, 78 Bangalow Rd, (1 km from town centre), T6685 6445, www.capebyronlodge.com. People come here for the free pancakes, all the usual facilities and a nice atmosphere. Also free shuttle in to town.

Rainbow Region *p217*
L **Ecoasis** near the village of Uki, Mt Warning, T6679 5959, www.ecoasis.com.au. These couple-oriented bush villas are an excellent choice.
B-E **Mount Warning Caravan Park**, about 3 km up Mount Warning Rd, T6679 5120. Camping is available at this privately run caravan park. It has cabins, on-site vans, powered and non-powered sites and a camp kitchen.
B-F **Midginbil Hill Country Resort**, near Murwillumbah, also has a full range of accommodation from B&B to camping with the added attraction of in-house canoe trips, archery and horse riding.
C-E **Mount Warning/Murwillumbah YHA**, 1 Tumbulgum Rd, Murwillumbah (first right across the bridge, 200 m, across the river from the VIC), T6672 3763, mbahyha@norex.com.au. This is the best budget option. Located right next to the river and with a deck overlooking Mt Warning, it is a friendly and homely place, run by a caring and dedicated manager. Dorms and double/ twins, free use of canoes and transport to Mt Warning if you stay 2 nights.
C-F **Nimbin Rox YHA**, 74 Thorburn St, Nimbin, T6689 0022, www.nimbinroxhostel.com. Relatively new and deservingly popular, this YHA is set in an elevated position just west of the village, offering great views across Nimbin Rocks (hence the name). Offers the full range of rooms and modern facilities, including the obligatory tepee for that essential Nimbinesque ambience. Internet, pool and bike hire. Camping sites also available.

C-F Rainbow Retreat Backpackers, 75 Thorburn St, Nimbin, T6689 1262. You are invited to 'Live the Nimbin Dream' at this unusual, good value and suitably laid-back backpackers. Not surprisingly, it provides a range of highly unconventional accommodation options from Malay-style huts to VW Kombis, dorms and secluded campsites, all set in a quiet 18-acre site near the edge of the village. Both the facilities and atmosphere are excellent with regular musical jam sessions, visiting chefs preparing $5 meals, alternative practitioners and performers, not to mention the odd platypus in the creek or harmless python up a tree. Over all, it provides the ideal way to experience the true spirit of Nimbin. Recommended. Peterpan in Byron (T1800 252 459) provide free transport.

D-E Nimbin Caravan and Tourist Park, 29 Sibley St, Nimbin, T6689 1402. Has basic, facilities, on-site vans, powered and non-powered sites, within easy walking distance of the village.

Eating

Port Macquarie *p207, map p208*

Seafood rules in Port Macquarie from the full plate of oysters to humble fish and chips. The main outlets can be found at the Wharf end of Clarence St. The vineyards are also worth considering, especially for lunch.

TTT **Cray's**, beside the wharf at 74 Clarence St, T6583 7885. Daily for lunch and dinner. Fantastic seafood and good steak is served in this fine restaurant.

TTT **Scampi's**, Port Marina, Park St, T6583 7200. Daily from 1800. Along with **Cray's**, the best venue for quality à la carte seafood in congenial surroundings.

TT **Ca Marche**, 764 Fernbank Creek Rd (corner of Pacific Highway), T6582 8320. Daily 1030-1600. Out of town a little but worth the journey is this small, award-winning French/Mediterranean restaurant at the Cassegrain Winery, with a congenial atmosphere and nice views across the vines.

TT **Splash Restaurant**, 3/2 Horton St, T6584 4027. Daily lunch and dinner. Overlooking the green, this restaurant offers imaginative seafood amidst its modern Australian menu and would do the kiwis proud with their steamed green lipped mussels.

TT **Toros Mexican**, 20 Murray St, T6583 4340. Long-established and good value venue that does a wicked fajita.

T **Macquarie Seafoods**, corner of Clarence St and Short St, T6583 8476. Daily 1100-2100. For great fish and chips look no further than here.

T **Port Pacific Resort Café**, 14 Clarence St, T6583 8099. All-you-can-eat breakfasts for around $10.

South West Rocks and Hat Head *p209*

TT **Geppy's**, corner of Livingstone St and Memorial Ave, South West Rocks, T6566 6196. Well known for good seafood, Italian and modern Australian cuisine. Live jazz and blues on Wed.

TT **Pizza on the Rocks**, Prince of Wales Ave, South West Rocks, T6566 6626. Locally recommended.

TT **Trial Bay Kiosk**, Arakoon, overlooking the Trail Bay Goal and beach, T6566 7100. Daily for breakfast and lunch 0800-1600 and Thu, Fri and Sat for dinner. Superb location, al fresco dining and quality, though fairly pricey, fare. Good breakfasts and coffee.

Bellingen *p210*

TTT **No 2 Oak St**, T6655 9000. Tue-Sat, from 1800. This place is recommended for fine dining. Housed in a 1910 heritage cottage it offers an excellent and innovative menu. Book ahead.

TT **Café Bare Nature**, 111 Hyde St, T6655 1551. Daily from 1700. For gourmet pizza.

TT **Lodge 241**, 121 Hyde St, T6655 2470. Daily 0800-1700. Overlooking the river valley is this café and gallery combined, offering fine local cuisine and good coffee.

Ψ **Cool Creek Café**, Church St. Thu-Mon. Nice atmosphere, good value and offers live music.

Dorrigo and Dorrigo National Park *p210*

ΨΨΨ **Misty's**, 33 Hickory St, T6657 2855. Wed-Sat from 1800 and Sun from 0730 for brunch. For fine dining.
ΨΨ **Historic Dorrigo Hotel**, corner of Hickory St and Cudgery St, T6657 2016. For classic pub grub.
Ψ **Art Place Gallery**, 20 Cudgery St, T6657 2622. Daily 1000-1630. For coffee and light snacks.

Coffs Harbour *p211, map p214*

ΨΨΨ **Olive Oyls**, 21 First Ave, T6653 1951. One of the best venues in Sawtell (6 km south of town), earning a good reputation for its innovative Asian cuisine and pasta dishes.
ΨΨΨ **Tide and Pilot Brasserie**, Jordan Esplanade, T6651 6964. Daily for breakfast, lunch and dinner from 0700. A pre-dinner walk to Muttonbird Island can be followed by quality al fresco dining at this award-winning and congenial restaurant.
ΨΨ **Ocean Front Brasserie**, Coffs Harbour Deep Sea Fishing Club, Jordan Esplanade, T6651 2819. Daily 1200-1430 and 1800-2030. Good value and offers great views across the harbour.
Ψ **Fisherman's Co-op**, 69 Marina Dr, T6652 2811. Daily until 1800. *The* place for fish and chips.
Ψ **Foreshore Café**, Jetty Strip, 394 High St, T665 23127. Daily, for a good breakfast, coffee and lunch locals swear by this place.

Coffs Harbour to Byron Bay *p213*

In Yamba: ΨΨ **Pacific Hotel**, 18 Pilot St, T6646 2491, overlooking the ocean, is an old favourite for value bistro meals daily and also offers budget accommodation, while ΨΨ **Restaurant Castalia**, 1/15 Clarence St, Yamba, T6646 1155. Wed-Sat for lunch and dinner. Offers good modern Australian fare.
In Iluka: ΨΨ **Golf Club**, Iluka Rd, Iluka, T6646 5043, Tue-Sun, is the best of a poor selection, while ΨΨ **Sedger's Reef Bistro**, 5 Queens St, Iluka, T6646 6119, is one of very few open daily.
In Lennox Head: ΨΨ **Lennox Head Pizza and Pasta** 56 Ballina St, T6687 7080, is a good option.

Byron Bay *p216, map p218*

Although Jonson St and the various arcades host some good restaurants and cafés most folk gravitate towards Bay Lane where you will find plenty of atmosphere.
ΨΨΨ **Dish Restaurant**, corner of Jonson St and Marvel St, T6685 7320. An award winning, very chic place with fine innovative international and Australian cuisine. Also run the the **Raw Bar**.
ΨΨ **Asian Oh Delhi Tandoori**, 4 Bay Lane T6680 8800. Daily 1200-2200. Tasty scran, great value and very satisfying.
ΨΨ **Beach Hotel Bistro**, Bay Lane. Lunch and dinner from 1200-2100. Never fails to attract the crowds and wins hands down for atmosphere.
ΨΨ **Thai Lucy**, Bay Lane, T6680 8083. Daily 1200-1500 and 1730-2200. Offers excellent dishes, good value and lots of atmosphere, but book ahead.
Ψ **Arts Factory Backpackers (Supernatural Restaurant)**, 1 Skinners Shoot Rd. Daily from 1800. Good value vegetarian dishes. Also does meal/movie deals with the Buddah Bar next door.
Ψ **Belongil Beach Café**, just above Belongil Beach Café on Childe St, T6685 7144. Daily 0800-2200. If a beach stroll is in order you will find a good coffee and generous breakfasts at this very congenial café.
Ψ **Cheeky Monkey's**, 115 Jonson St, T6685 5886. Mon-Sat, 1900-0300. Backpacker specials (as little as $6) are regularly on offer in order to tempt you to stay late at the bar and nightclub.
Ψ **Seven At 13**, in the Woolies Plaza, Jonson St, T6685 7478. Daily for breakfast, lunch and dinner. Pure, modern organic cuisine in a pleasant al fresco setting.

Rainbow Region *p217*
In Nimbin: ¥¥-¥ **Bush Theatre**, northern end of Cullen St, T6685 1111, Fri-Sat 1930, Sun 1830, is a popular venue, combining a cinema and a café and offering the occasional good value movie/ meal deal; ¥¥-¥ **Rainbow Café** is the oldest of the alternative eateries in Nimbin.
In Murwillumbah: ¥¥ **The Imperial Hotel**, 115 Main St, T6672 2777, offers pub rooms as well as value pub lunches and dinners.

Bars and clubs

Port Macquarie *p207, map p208*
For up to date listings pick up the free, weekly *Hastings Happenings* at the VIC.
Beach House, on the Green, 1 Horton St, T6584 5692. Nightly, free entry until 2300. Modern and popular night-club with occasional jazz on Sun afternoons.
Finnians Irish Pub, 97 Gordon St. For a quieter night out try this friendly pub which stages live bands at weekends.
Port Macquarie Hotel, corner of Clarence St and Horton St, T65807888. This newly renovated venue is the most popular pub in town.

Coffs Harbour *p211, map p214*
Ex-serviceman's Club, Vernon St, T6652 3888. A popular haunt for cheap food and drinks, especially on Fri night, but ID is required for entry.
Fitzroy Hotels, Grafton St. Cheap drinks, pool and regular live entertainment staying open well into the wee small hours.
Greenhouse Tavern, corner of Bray St, opposite the Bray St Complex. A more modern pub with live music and a good atmosphere at the weekend.

Byron Bay *p216, map p218*
Beach Hotel, facing the beach off Bay St, T6685 6402. Huge and the place too see and be seen, popular both day and night, with the lively atmosphere often spilling out on to beer garden. Live bands Thu-Sun.
Cocomangas, 32 Jonson St. Open 2100-0300, free entry before 2330. Retro 80s on Wed and Disco Funk and House on Sat.
Cmoog,in the northwest corner of the Plaza, off Jonson St, T6685 6170. Open until 0300. Smaller nightclub.

Festivals and events

Byron Bay *p216, map p218*
Blues and Roots Festival, held every Easter weekend, www.bluesfest.com.au. The most lauded annual festival in Byron is a popular affair attracting its fair share of international stars, wannabes or has-beens.

Shopping

Byron Bay *p216, map p218*
Byron offers a wealth of 'alternative' and arts & crafts shops selling everything from futons to $300 hand-painted toilets seats. With so many image conscious backpackers around the town is also becoming saturated with lingerie shops.
Byron Images, corner Lawson St and Jonson St, T6685 8909, www.johnderry.com.au. For a lasting image of Byron, look no further than John Derrey's photography work.
Byron Bay Camping and Disposals, Plaza, Jonson St, T6685 8085. Can oblige should you need camping gear and supplies.

Activities and tours

Port Macquarie *p207, map p208*
Boat trips and cruises
Hastings River Boat Hire, T6583 8811, and **Jordan's Boat Hire**, in the Caravan Park on Settlement Point Rd (North Shore), T6583 1005 (and at Settlement Point itself) offer independent boat and canoe hire starting at about $20 per hr.
Port Macquarie River Cruise (Port Venture), Clarence St, T6583 3058, www.portventure. com.au. Over 200

Background

Market forces

One of the great tourist attractions in the Rainbow Region are its colourful weekend markets. These operate in a circuit throughout the region, mostly on Sundays. Byron Bay Market is held in the Butler Street Reserve on the first Sunday of the month, while Lismore hosts a regional Organic Produce Market at the Lismore Showgrounds every Tuesday between 0700-1000, as well as the Lismore Showground Markets every second Sunday. The excellent Channon Craft Market, kicks off in Coronation Park on the second Sunday, while the Aquarius Fair Markets, in Nimbin are on the third and fifth Sunday and Bangalow holds their market in the local show grounds on the fourth Sunday.

passengers can be carried onboard the *MV Venture* for a scenic 2-hr River Cruise, 1000/1400, most days, from $25, child $12; 5-hr BBQ Cruise 1000 Wed, from $60, child $20, and a 3.5-hr BBQ Cruise, from $40, child $20.

Skydiving and paragliding

Coastal Skydivers, T6584 3655, www.coastal skydivers.com.au, offers 10,000-ft tandem skydives for a reasonable $300.

High Adventure Air Park, Pacific Highway, Johns River, T1800 063 648, www.highadven ture.com.au, offers an exciting range of activities including tandem paragliding (30 mins from $130) and 30min microlight flights from $150.

Horse and camel riding

Bellrowan Valley Horse Riding, 35 mins from Port Macquarie. Professional outfit offering rides of 1 or 2 hrs. The $50/75 includes refreshments and pick-ups from Wauchope (transfer from the Port $10). A half-day ride with BBQ lunch costs $125, T6587 5227, www.bellrowanvalley.com.au.

Camel Safaris, Lighthouse Beach, T6583 7650. Rides are from 20 mins to 1 hr, from $35.

Watersports

C-Spray, northern end of the Wharf, Short St, T0428-656933. Jet ski hire from $50 for 15 mins.

Dawn Light Surf School, T6584 1477 and **Port Macquarie Surf School**, T6585 5453, www.portmacquariesurf school.com.au, both offer lessons from $40 per hour.

Stoney Park, Telegraph Point, T6585 0080, www.stoneypark.com.au. Specialist water-ski and wakeboarding complex offering single lessons (from $40) or day packages (from $130). Recommended. Accommodation also available.

South West Rocks and Hat Head *p209*

The area is renowned for its excellent dive sites including the 120-m Fish Rock Cave. The entrance to the Macleay River offers good snorkelling at peak tide.

South West Rocks Dive Centre, 5/98 Gregory St, T6566 6474, www.southwestrocks dive.com.au. Offers both trips and rooms with dives to see grey nurse sharks and the Fish Rock Cave.

Bellingen *p210*

Bellingen offers a fine base from which to explore the numerous excellent rainforest walks of the Dorrigo National Park. The river also offers some exciting

A street vendor silhouetted against his colourful light-shades, Byron Bay

opportunities; either by canoe or on a river cruise.

Bellingen Canoe Adventures, T6655 9955, www.bellingen.com/canoe. Half-day guided trips from $44, full-day trips from $88, a sunset tour from $66 and independent hire from $11 per hr.

Hinterland Tours, T6655 2957, www.hinterlandtour.com.au. Informative half- and full or multi-day eco-walks/tours of the Dorrigo Plateau and national park, from $75.

Coffs Harbour *p211, map p214*

The VIC has full activity listings and can offer non-biased advice. For general activity information visit www.coffscentral.com.au. **Marina Booking Centre** based at the marina also act as booking agents for most regional activities and cruises, T6651 4612.

Diving

Jetty Dive Centre, 398 High St, T6651 1611, www.jettydive.com.au. Small group PADI certification from $215, day-long introductory dives from $145 and snorkelling trips from $50.

Dolphin, whale-watching and fishing

Blue Wing (Jetty Dive), T6651 1611. Good value whale-watching trips in season twice daily at 0830 and 1330, from $44.

Bluefin II, T04 2866 8072, *Adriatic III*, T6651 1277, and the classy *Cougar Cat 12*, T6651 6715, all offer entertaining fishing trips from around $88 for a half-day and big game fishing. Whale-watching trips in season cost $44.

Pacific Explorer, T6652 7225, www.pacificexplorer.com.au. Sedate half-day island/dolphin and whale watching cruise on board their sailing catamaran with snorkelling and boom netting departing 0900 and 1330, from $49.

Spirit of Coffs Harbour Cruises, Shop 5, Marina, T6650 0155, www.spiritofcoffs.com.au. Has a range of cruise options including a 3-hr Solitary Island trips/dolphin spotting, departing 0930 Mon, Wed, Fri, Sat and Sun, whale-watching (mid May- mid Nov) and a Luncheon/ Waterslide Cruise, departing 0930 Tue and Thu, from $45.

Horse trekking

Valery Trails, T6653 4301, www.valerytrails.com.au. Award winning outfit suited to advanced and beginners, 13 km south of Coffs. It offers 1-2-hr breakfast; BBQ, moonlight and camp ride outs from $45. Backpacker accommodation available.

Skydiving

Coffs City Skydivers, T6651 1167, www.coffsskydivers.com.au, offers tandem skydiving, 10,000 ft, from $304.

Watersports

Liquid Assets, T6658 0850, liquidassets1@yahoo.com.au. An exhilarating range of aquatic adventures, including half- or full-day whitewater rafting on the Goolang River (grade III) and the Nymbodia River which is a scenic grade III-V, from $80/$125. Sea kayaking, half day from $40. Surf rafting, half-day from $40 and flat water kayaking in Bongil Bongil National Park, half day from $40. Big Day Out sea kayak, surf rafting and white water rafting combo costs from $135.

East Coast Surf School, T6651 5515, www.eastcoastsurfschool.com.au. Lessons at Diggers Beach (near the Big Banana) 1030-1230, private lessons, from $60 per hr, group from $50 per person and weekend camp/surf from $330.

Coffs Harbour to Byron Bay *p213*

Iluka Naturally Tours, T6646 6134, offer informative ecotours in the local rainforest and national park.

Yamba Kayak Tours, Yamba, T6646 1137, www.yambakayak.com.au. 3-hr guided trips from $40 and half-day or full-day tours on demand.

Byron Bay *p216, map p218*

As well as all the activity options on offer, Byron Bay also supports a large number of massage, yoga practitioners and health therapists. Look out for the free *Body and Soul* brochure at the VIC for full listings and prices.

Rockhoppers, Shop1/87 Jonson St, T0500 881 881, www.rockhoppers.com.au, are one of the largest operators, offering an attractive range of single or combination activity packages, from mountain biking to wake boarding. they run the **Grasshoppers Nimbin Eco-Explorer Tour**, which is recommended if you want to see some of the hinterland's best sights, from $35. Transport to the Nimbin backpackers is also an additional option. They also offer day-long 'triple challenge' waterfall abseiling, rappelling and canyoning in the hinterland rainforest, $119, as well as guided sunrise treks on Tue/Thu/Sun, with breakfast or day treks to the summit of Mount Warning from $55.

Jim's Alternative Tours, T6685 7720, www.jimsalternativetours.com, offers an wide array of entertaining options from simple lighthouse or market trips to dolphin watching and national park ecotours. Day tour departs Mon-Sat at 0900, from $35.

Diving

Sundive, opposite the Court House on Middleton St, T6685 7755, www.sundive.com.au, offers courses, half-day introductory dives (from $150) and snorkelling from $50.

Byron Bay Dive Centre, 9 Marvel St, T6685 8333 , www.byronbaydive centre.com.au, offers a range of trips from full to half-day.

Health and spa therapies

There are now numerous alternative and conventional health therapies available: **Samadhi's**, 107 Jonson St, T6685 6905; and **Aroma Spa**, T6684 7630 (which also offers courses and accommodation) are just two. **Byron Bay Yoga**, T6687 2622, www.byronbayyoga.com, for yoga classes.

Kiteboarding

Byron Bay Kiteboarding, T1300-888938, www.byronbaykiteboarding.com. Half-, 2- or 3-day packages to master the new and increasingly popular art of kite boarding, full day from $250.

Mountain biking

Mountainbike Tours, T1800 122504, ride@mountainbiketours.com.au. Great range of informative eco-based biking adventures in the hinterland national parks.

Sea kayaking

Dolphin, T6685 8044, www.dolphinkayaking.com.au. Good trips around the headlands with chance encounters with dolphins, departing at 0900 and 1400 daily from $40.

Skydiving and gliding

Byron Bay Skydiving Centre, T1800 800840, www.skydivebyronbay.com, based near Brunswick Heads. Owned by Australian World representative and 'skysurfer' Ray Palmer. The team offer a range of professional services including tandems. The views from the jump zone across Byron Bay to the headland and beyond are stunning. Jumps are pretty cheap and range from $239 (8000-ft) to $344 (12,000-ft).
Skydive Cape Byron, 2/84 Jonson St, T6685 5990, www.skydive-cape-byron.com.au. Another reputable outfit, offering tandems from 8,000 ft (from $239) to 12,000 ft (from $344). Video and digital images extra.
Byron Soaring Centre, Tyagarah, T6684 7572, www.byron-bay.com/soaringadventures. Entertaining trips in a 'motorglider'-a sort of glider and microlight cross, of 20/35/60 mins from $90.

Surfing

With so many superb surf breaks around Byron there is no shortage of surfing opportunities for pros and grommets alike. Most operators operators offer surf hire with short boards starting at about $5 per hr, $12 for 4 hrs and around $20 or 24 hrs.
Byron Bay Surf School, T1800 707 274, www.byronbaysurfschool.com. 1-, 3- and 5-day packages, from $60 (3-day $150, 5-day $200, private 2-hr lesson from $120).
Style Surfing, T6685 5634, www.byron-bay.com/byronbaystylesurfing. Offers a 3½-hr beginners package or advanced courses daily at 0900, 1100 and 1300, from $60, or private lessons from $180 for 2 hrs.
Surfaris, T1800 634 951, www.surfaris.com.au. This operation is for real enthusiasts or serious learners. It offers a week-long Sydney-Byron trip (from $499) or a 4-day/ 3-night Byron-Noosa-Hervey Bay trip, from $365.

Rainbow Region *p217*

Midginbil Hill Country Resort, 30 km west of Murwillumbah, T66797158, www.midginbilhill.com.au. Offers 2-hr eco-based canoe trips from $23 as well as horse riding from $45.
Mountainbike Tours, Nimbin, T1800 122 504, ride@mountainbiketours.com.au. Informative eco-based biking adventures in the hinterland national parks, from $80.

Transport

Port Macquarie *p207, map p208*

Bus

To access the eastern beaches jump on the #334, #332 or #324. Long-distance buses stop at the bus terminal on Hayward St. **Premier Motor Service** have a booking office at the terminal, T6583 1488. Mon-Fri 0830-1700, Sat 0830-1200. **Greyhound**, T131499, also offer daily state-wide services. Keans Coaches, T1800 043 339, run a service from Port Macquarie to Scone (via the **Waterfall Way**, **Dorrigo**, **Bellingen**, **Armidale** and **Tamworth**) on Tue, Thu and Sun. **Busways**, 6 Denham St, T1300 555611 www.busways.com.au, offers both local and regional bus services between **Sydney** and **Yamba**.

Cycling

Bike hire available from **Shaws Cycle De Sport**, 4/A-2 Murray St, T6584 4177.

Train

The nearest train station is at Wauchope, 19 km west of the city, T132232. The connecting bus to Port Macquarie is included in the fare.

South West Rocks and Hat Head *p209*
Busways, T1300 555 611, run a **Kempsey** (Belgrave St) to **South West Rocks** (Livingstone St) bus #350, Mon-Sat. Rocks Travel, Shop 1/3 Livingstone St, T6566 6770, www.rockstravel.com.au, can assist with onwards travel.

Bellingen *p210*
Busways, T1300 555 611, runs between **Nambucca Heads**, **Urunga**, **Coffs Harbour** and **Bellingen** several times daily, Mon-Fri, from $5.80. See above for Keans Coaches service from **Scone** to **Port Macquarie** and **Coffs Harbour**. Long-distance buses do not make the detour to Bellingen. The nearest stop is Nambucca Heads or Urunga.

The nearest train station is in Urunga. Countrylink, T132232, offers state and interstate services.

Dorrigo and Dorrigo National Park *p210*
See above for Keans Coaches service from **Scone** to **Port Macquarie**. From local towns you can catch local services to the national parks.

Coffs Harbour *p211, map p214*
Bus Busways, T1300 555 611, www.busways. com.au, is the local suburban bus company with daily, half-hourly services from 0715-1730. To get from Park Ave in the town centre to the jetty, take #365E. Ryan's Buses, T6652 3201, offers local services Mon-Sat to Woolgoolga and Grafton. Sawtell Coaches, T66533344, offers daily local services to Sawtell #364.

Long-distance buses stop beside the VIC on Elizabeth St. Greyhound, T131499 and Premier, T133410, offers daily interstate services. See under Port Macquarie for Keans Coaches service to **Scone**.
Cycle/scooter Hire from Bob Wallis Bicycle Centre, corner of Collingwood and Orlando sts, T6652 5102, from $25 per 24 hr ($50 deposit).
Train The station is at the end of Angus McLeod St (right off High St and Camperdown St), near the harbour jetty. Countrylink, T132232, offers daily services to **Sydney** and **Brisbane**.

Coffs Harbour to Byron Bay *p213*
Busways, T66458941, provides daily services for **Grafton-Yamba-Maclean-Iluka**. The **Iluka-Yamba** ferry, T0408 664 556, departs 4 times daily from the River St Wharf, Yamba, from $5.

Byron Bay *p216, map p218*

Air

The closest airports to Byron Bay are Coolangatta to the north (90 km, Gold Coast), see page 289, and Ballina to the south (31 km), see page 216. Both are served by QantasLink, T131313; Regional Express, T131713, www.rex.com.au, and Virgin Blue, T136789, www.virginblue.com.au. Airporter Shuttle, T04 1460 8660, and Byron Bay International, T6685 7447, serve Coolangatta from about $30 one-way. Airlink Byron Bay, T6681 3232, also serve Ballina, from $25 one-way.

Bus

Local Blanch's Buses, T6686 2144, runs local services within **Byron Bay** (#637) and also south to **Ballina** via **Lennox Head** (#640) and north to **Mullumbimby** (#640).
Long distance The long-distance bus stop is located right in the heart of town on Jonson St. Greyhound, T131499, and Premier Motor Services, T133410, run daily inter-state services north/south. Kirklands, T6622 1499, run services to **Brisbane**, **Ballina**, **Lismore** and **Coolangatta**. Byron Bay Bus and Backpacker Centre, 84 Jonson St, T6685 5517, acts as the local booking agents. Also of note is Brisbane Express, T0733-423564, www.brisbane2byron.com, which offers 2-hr transfers to the city centre for $30.

Car/motorcycle

Byron Car Hire, T6685 6345, from $40 per day. **Byron Bus**, Transit Centre, T6685 5517, and **Hertz**, 5 Marvel St, T66807925. **Byron Odyssey**, T1800 771 244. Car servicing at **Bayside Mechanical**, 12 Banksia Drive, T6685 8455. Hire of motorcycles and scooters from **Ride On**, 105 Jonson St, T6685 6304 from $105 per-day.

Cycling

Byron Bay Bicycles, Shop 8, The Plaza, T6685 6067, **Byron Bay Bike Hire**, (free delivery), T0500 856 985, or **Rockhoppers** (see Activities and tours).

Train

The station is also located in the heart of town, just off Jonson St. **Countrylink**, T132232, runs daily services south to **Sydney** and beyond, and north (with bus link) with **Queensland Rail**, T132232, to **Brisbane**.

Rainbow Region *p217*

Bus

For **Murwillumbah**, regional **Kirklands**, T1300 367077, and interstate **Greyhound**, T132030, stop outside **Tweed Valley Travel**, on the corner of Main St and Queen St. Northbound buses and trains both stop in Murwillumbah. **Nimbin-Byron Shuttle Bus**, T6680 9189, operates daily, departing from Jonson St, Byron Bay at 1000, returning at 1730, from $30 return.

Train

Murwillumbah station is opposite the VIC and is served by **Countrylink**, T132232.

Directory

Port Macquarie *p207, map p208*

Banks All major branches with ATMs can be found along Clarence St and Horton St. **Internet** Port Surf Hub Internet Lounge, 57 Clarence St, T6584 4744. Daily until around 1900. **Medical services** Port Macquarie Base Hospital, Wright Rd, T6581 2000. **Post office** Shop 2, Palm Court Centre, 14-16 William St. Mon-Fri 0900-1700. **Useful numbers** Police, 2 Hay St, T6583 0199.

Bellingen *p210*

Internet Available next door to the Golly Gosh Café, Church St. Mon-Fri 0900-1700 or round the corner at the YHA, Short St. **Travel agents** Bellingen World Travel, 42 Hyde St, Bellingen, T6655 2158, offers local information and can assist with travel bookings and enquiries.

Coffs Harbour *p211, map p214*

Banks Major branches with ATMs can be found on the Mall or along Grafton St and Park Ave. **Internet** The Internet Room, Shop 21, Jetty Village Shopping Centre, T6651 9155. Mon-Fri 0900-1800, Sat-Sun 1000- 1600, or Jetty Dive Centre, 398 High St, T66511611. **Post office** Palms Centre Arcade, Vernon St. Mon-Fri 0830-1700, Sat 0900-1300. Postcode 2450. **Medical services** Hospital, T66567000. **Useful numbers** Police, Moonee St, T6652 0299.

Byron Bay *p216, map p218*

Banks Most major branches with ATMs are represented along Jonson or Lawsons St. Currency exchange is readily available including Byron Foreign Exchange, Shop 4 Central Arcade, T66857787. 0900-1800. **Internet**Omnipresent, including Wicked Travel, 29 Jonson St, T1800-555-339, 0800-2400. **Post office** 61 Jonston St. Mon-Fri 0900-1700, Sat 0900-1300. Postcode 2481. **Medical services** Byron Bay Hospital, Shirley St, T6685 6200, and Byron Bay Medical Clinic, T6685 6206. **Travel agents** Backpackers World, Shop 6 Byron St, T6685 8858. Backpackers Travel Centre, Cavanbah Arcade, Jonson St, T6685 7085. **Useful numbers** Police, corner of Shirley St and Butler St, T6685 9499.

Brisbane & South Coast QLD

Stephen's Cathedral set amidst the high-rises of Brisbane's CBD

p292
p252
p240
30 km
30 miles
South Pacific Ocea
QUEENSLAND
Marlborough
Byfield
Byfield National Park
Mt Etna Caves National Park
Capricorn Caves
Yaamba
Yeppoon
Rosslyn Bay
Great Keppel Island
Emu Park
Keppel Sands
Parkhurst
Kabra
Rockhampton
Stanwell
Gavial
Westwood
Broadmount
Gogango
Bouldercombe
Mount Morgan
Bajool
Port Alma
Marmor
Curtis Island
Heron Island
Burnett Highway
Raglan
Ambrose
Mount Larcom
Wowan
Dululu
Dixalea
Gladstone
Yarwun
Lady Musgrave Island
Cooneel
Rannes
Boyne Island
Tannum Sands
Calliope
Jambin
Baralaba
Benaraby
Lake Awoonga
Eurimbula National Park
Lady Elliot Island
Banana
Town of 1770
Agnes Water
Biloela
Thangool
Bororen
Miriam Vale
Nagoorin
Deepwater National Park
Many Peaks
Bruce Highway
Lowmead
Kalpower
Berajondo
Rosedale
Theodore
Monto
Avondale
Lake Monduran
Burnett Heads
Mon Repos Turtle Rookery
Mulgildie
Bucca
Bargara
Cracow
Lake Wuruma
Boolboonda
Gin Gin
Bullyard
Bundaberg
Elliot Heads
Sandy Cape
Wolca
Wallaville
Orchid Beach
Mt Perry
Cordalba
Woodgate
Waddy Point
Booyal
Burnett
Great Sandy National Park
Eidsvold
Childers
Buxton
Hervey Bay
Toogoom
Binjour
Dallarnil
Howard
Moon Point
Hervey Bay
Fraser Island
Mundubbera
Biggenden
Torbanlea
Urangan
Coalstone Lakes
Gayndah
Maryborough
River Head
Kingfisher Bay
Lake McKenzie
Ban Ban
Brooweena
Central Station
Eurong
Tuan
Dilli Village
Tiaro
Bauple
Gundiah
Hook Point
Tin Can Bay
Lake Boondooma
Windera
Tansey
Rainbow Beach
Cloyna
Kilkivan
Proston
Gunalda
Cooloola Coast
Murgon
Goomeri
Durong
Upper Widgee
Gympie
Great Sandy National Park
Cherbourg
Wondai
Glastonbury
Tingoora
Lake Cootharaba
Sunshine Coast
Kingaroy
Brisbane Range
Tewantin
Noosa Heads
Eumundi
Noosa National Park
Nambour
Coolum Beach
Nanango
Jimma Range
Mapleton
Maroochydore
Montville
Mooloolaba
Yarraman
Conondale
Palmview
Wondai
Caloundra
Blackbutt
Harlin
Kilcoy
Landsborough
Woodford
Glass House Mountains National Park
Toogoolawah
Wamuran
Bribie Island
Crows Nest
Caboolture
Woorim
Esk
Lake Wivenhoe
Deception Bay
Hampton
Mount Nebo
Margate
Moreton Island National Park
Moreton Bay
Helidon
Lowood
Brisbane
Gatton
Walloon
Ipswich
Redland Bay
Blue Lakes National Park
Rosewood
Peak Crossing
Hirstglen
Beenleigh
North Stradbroke Island
Mistake Mountains
Kalbar
Jimboomba
South Stradbroke Island
Great Dividing Range
Oxenford
Boonah
Mount Tamborine
Southport
Surfers Paradise
Gold Coast
Maroon
Nerang
Currumbin
Binna Burra
Coolangatta
Tweed Heads
Springbrook National Park
Legume
Lamington National Park
Yelgun
Bogangar
Pottsville
Urbenville
Stanthorpe
Limevale
Pike Creek
Texas
Yetman
Nimbin
Bonalbo
Kyogle
Brunswick Heads
Mullumbimby
Tara
Don't miss...
1 Possum spotting in the Lamington National Park ▸▸ p246.
2 A cool dip in the South Bank Lagoon, Brisbane ▸▸ p253.
3 A drive through the Blackall Range ▸▸ p271.
4 A swim at idyllic Lake McKenzie on Fraser Island ▸▸ p278.
5 Laying or hatching time at the Mon Repos turtle rookery, near Bundaberg ▸▸ p294.

Introduction

Heading north from New South Wales, you pass the forest of high-rises strung along the infamous Gold Coast, before emerging in the relaxing embrace of the state capital, Brisbane. Shrugging off its non-progressive reputation, Brisbane has enjoyed phenomenal growth, especially since hosting the Commonwealth Games in 1982, Expo 88 and most recently, the 2001 Goodwill Games.

What the Gold Coast is to glitz and theme parks and Far North Queensland to the barrier reef and rainforests, the Sunshine and Fraser coasts are to sand, surf and sunshine. North of Noosa the coastal strip succumbs to the vast expanses of the Great Sandy Region, with its ancient coloured sands, sand blows, freshwater lakes and unusual wildlife. The mainland (Cooloola) section is well worthy of investigation but offers only a taste of something even better: Fraser Island, the largest coastal sand island in the world. Fraser is without doubt, the biggest tourist attraction in Southern Queensland. With its unique range of habitats, natural features and rich biodiversity, all of which can only be fully explored by 4WD, Fraser presents the opportunity for a truly memorable eco-experience.

Ratings

Landscape
★★★★★

Relaxation
★★★★

Activities
★★★★

Wildlife
★★★★

Costs
$$$

Gold Coast

With almost five million visitors a year the 'Coast With the Most' is Australia's most popular domestic holiday destination and for some inexplicable reason is seen by some native Australians as the perfect piece of real estate. Like any place that is bold and brash, the Gold Coast's reputation precedes it and no doubt those who have never been will already have formed a strong opinion. Sure it's a concrete jungle and a womb of artificiality, but for lovers of the laid-back beach lifestyle, socialites seeking a hectic nightlife, theme park and thrill ride junkies and shopaholics, it can promise more than just a 'surfers' paradise'. For those of you just itching to scratch the mighty Gold Coast from your travelling agenda at the mere prospect of such a place, think again. Even for the greatest cynic, the worst (or the best) of the Gold Coast can prove utterly infectious and lead to a thoroughly enjoyable experience. Turning your back on the coast, only an hour away, is one of the Gold Coast's greatest assets and the 'Green behind the Gold' in the form of the Springbrook and Lamington national parks, two of Queensland's best; perfect retreats from all the chaos.

Getting there International and interstate flights; interstate bus networks, rail from Sydney or Brisbane.
Getting around Local bus network or hire car/campervan.
Time required 3-5 days.
Weather Warm, dry and sometimes humid in summer, mild in winter.
Sleeping Numerous options.
Eating Good range of quality eateries and cheap takeaways.
Activities and tours Shopping and theme parks.
★ **Don't miss** Lamington National Park. ▸▸ *p245*.

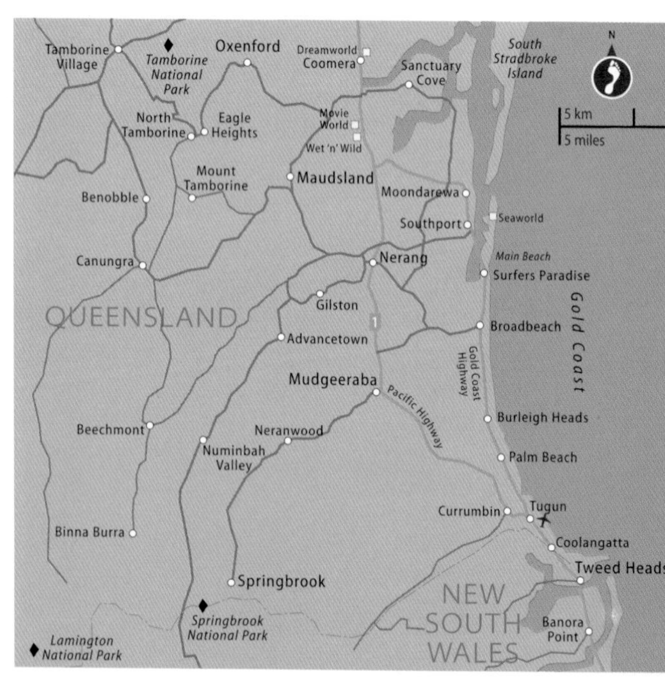

Currumbin to Surfers Paradise

Just off the Gold Coast Highway is **Currumbin Wildlife Sanctuary** ⓘ *T5534 1266, www.currumbin-sanctuary.org.au, 0800-1700, $25, child $17*, one of the most popular parks in the area. A small train takes you into the heart of the park where you can investigate the various animal enclosures housing everything from Tasmanian devils to tree kangaroos. One of the most recent inmates is a saltwater crocodile captured in Far North Queensland after posing a threat to humans (and also 4WD vehicles!). But without doubt the highlight of the day is the rainbow lorikeet feeding. To either partake or spectate at this highly colourful and entertaining 'avian-human interaction spectacular' is truly memorable and thoroughly recommended. Just before feeding time the air fills with the excited screeching of the birds and the trees are painted in their radiant hues, while below the human participants are all given a small bowl of liquid feed. Given that 80% of Australia's native wildlife is nocturnal, the 'Wildnight' tour programme is also well worth considering (from 1920-2145). It includes an Aboriginal dance display.

Burleigh Heads, an ancient volcano, forms one of the few breaks in the seemingly endless swathe of golden sand and offers fine views back towards Surfers. There are also world-class surf breaks and several good walking tracks through the Burleigh Heads National Park. West of Burleigh Heads, **David Fleay Wildlife Park** ⓘ *signposted 3 km west of Gold Coast Highway on Burleigh Heads Rd, T5576 2411, 0900-1700, $13, child $6.50*, is home to all the usual suspects (koalas, crocs, kangaroos and cassowaries), and some less well known species, like bilbies, brolgas and dunnarts. Overall it offers a fine introduction to Australia's native species. The park is especially well known for its nocturnal platypus displays, breeding successes and care of sick and injured wildlife.

Surfers Paradise » *pp247-251.*

From its humble beginnings as a single hotel four decades ago, Surfers Paradise has mushroomed and now epitomises all the worst aspects of the Gold Coast. An endless line of high-rise apartment blocks tower over shopping malls and exclusive real estate properties and a thousand and one tourist attractions, many of them planted firmly and unashamedly at the kitsch end of the market, provide round-the-clock entertainment.

Ins and outs

Getting there and around As the transport hub of the Gold Coast, there are frequent links with all major towns and cities. The airport is at Coolangatta, 22 km south, with regular shuttles to Surfers, which is a small place with most of the action centering in and around the Cavill Avenue Mall and adjacent nightclub strip, Orchid Avenue. » *p250.*

Tourist information VIC ⓘ *Cavill Ave Mall, T5538 4419, www.goldcoasttourism.com.au, Mon-Fri 0830-1730, Sat 0830-1700, Sun 0900-1600*, is an incredibly small affair. Try to get a copy of the official *Gold Coast Holiday Guide*. The nearest QPWS office ⓘ *Kabool Rd, West Burleigh, T5520 9600, www.epa.qld.gov.au*, stocks detailed information on the national parks of the Gold Coast Hinterland.

Sights

Surfers Paradise Beach is, of course, the big draw. If you can, take a stroll at sunrise along the 500-m sand-pumping jetty at the end of The Spit, north of Sea World. It opens at 0600 and for $1 you can walk out to the end and take in the memorable view of the entire beach and the glistening high-rises disappearing into the haze, all the way to Tweed Heads.

Gold Coast
To Sea World, The Spit & Sand Pumping Jetty
To Sanctuary Cove
Marina Mirage Complex
Mariners Cove
The Broadwater
SOUTHPORT
500 metres
500 yards
Sleeping
Backpackers in Paradise 1
Main Beach Tourist Park 5
Sleeping in Surfers 7
Surfers Paradise Backpackers Resort 8
Trekkers 9
Eating
Bellissimo Italian 1
Charlie's 2
Clock Hotel 3
Donto Sapporo 4
Grumpy's 7
Lansdowne Irish Pub 9
Lemongrass on Tedder 6
Restaurant B 11
Southport SLC 12
To Gold Coast Hospital
To Nerang Train Station
To Robina Train Station
MAIN BEACH
Nerang River
SURFERS PARADISE
Surfers Paradise Beach
South Pacific Ocean
Arts Centre
BROADBEACH
Conrad Jupiter's Casino
To Burleigh Heads, Palm Beach, Airport, Tweed Heads
Surfers Paradise
Chevron Renaissance Mall
1hr Photo Shop
Wharf
Transit Centre
Paradise Centre

(Left) A surfer checking wave conditions, Surfers Paradise; (Right) A wall of apartments, Surfers Paradise

Gold Coast City Art Centre ⓘ *135 Bundall Rd, 3 km west of Surfers, T5581 6500, www.gcac.com.au, Mon-Fri 1000-1700, Sat-Sun 1100-1700, free*, presents a dynamic programme of local contemporary work as well as a more wide-ranging historical collection. It is also home to one of Australia's longest running art prizes, now titled the Conrad Jupiters Art Prize, which has provided an exciting overview of contemporary Australian Art since 1968. The outdoor sculpture walk is also worth looking at.

Between Surfers Paradise and The Spit, **Main Beach** fringes the southern shores of Broadwater Bay and the Nerang River Inlet. The Marina Mirage shopping complex contains some of the best restaurants in the region, most of which offer al fresco dining overlooking Mariners Cove, the departure point for most scenic cruises and helicopter flights.

The Gold Coast is often labelled as Australia's **Theme Park** capital, with millions visiting annually. The stalwarts are Sea World, Dreamworld and Movie World, with other less high-profile parks like Wet'n'Wild providing back up. Entry for each is expensive, from $38-60, but that usually includes all the rides and attractions. The VIC can help you secure the latest discounts. **Sea World** ⓘ *Main Beach (1 km), T5588 2205, www.seaworld.com.au, 1000-1700, $60, child $38*, has been successfully developing its sea-based attractions for over 30 years, picking up numerous awards along the way and earning the reputation as one of the world's best theme parks. The main attractions are the dolphin and seal shows, thrill rides and water-ski stunts, resident polar bears (!) and multi-million dollar 'Shark Bay', which guarantees to get you up close and personal.

Movie World ⓘ *Pacific Highway, T5573 8485, www.movieworld.com.au, 1000-1730, $58, child $37*, is perhaps the most popular of all the theme parks. Even if you are not a great fan of Scooby Do and Co, cartoons or science fiction generally, a peek at the sets, props and costumes from the latest big release will certainly impress. Aside from the special effects of the main exhibits, thrill seekers can hit the water on the Wild West Adventure Ride, or even risk the Lethal Weapon rollercoaster.

Background

Making waves

Between Snapper Rocks and Kirra Point is the so-called **'Superbank'**, a man-made phenomenon that has created one of the world's greatest point breaks and most incredible surfing experiences. In the early nineties a scheme was proposed to remove sand from the mouth of the Tweed and relocate it to the northerly points. This was completed in 2001 and sand is now pumped from the mouth of the river, underground to spots at Froggies Beach – just to the south of Snapper – Rainbow Bay and Kirra. However no one expected the scheme to produce such an amazing sandbank or to have such a profound effect on the surf. On a perfect day, machine-like waves roll along the shallow sandbank in one unending steam-train. The 'Superbank' is capable of producing rides of 2 km in length and multiple ten-second barrel rides, making it one of the most popular breaks on the entire Australian east coast.

Coolangatta and Tweed Heads pp247-251.

What Surfers Paradise is to rollercoasters and shopping malls, Coolangatta is to sand and surf. Its greatest attraction is undoubtedly its beaches and the mighty surf that breaks upon them. The coast around Coolangatta and Tweed Heads is not only renowned as one of the world's premier surf spots, it has also produced many world class surfers such as the legendary Michael Peterson (MP), ex-world champions Peter Townend (PT) and Wayne 'Rabbit' Bartholomew. Such popularity has led to something of a population boom in the Coolangatta region, and this coupled with an increase in the popularity of surfing, has caused a massive increase in the numbers of surfers in the water on any good day.

Ins and outs

Getting there and around The airport is 2 km from Coolangatta. Major bus companies have services to the town, which is small enough to navigate on foot, with local bus services to surrounding sights. p250.

Tourist information Gold Coast (Coolangatta) VIC *Shop 14B, Coolangatta Pl, corner of Griffith St and Warner St, T5536 7765, www.goldcoasttourism.com.au, Mon-Fri 0800-1700, Sat 0800-1600, Sun 0900-1300.* **Tweed Heads VIC** *Tweed Mall, Wharf St, T5536 6151, www.tweedcoolangatta.com.au, Mon-Fri 0900-1700, Sat 0900-1200.* There is a town map in the useful, free brochure *Tweed-Coolangatta Visitors Guide.*

Sights

Coolangatta is fringed with superb beaches that surround the small peninsula known as Tweed Heads. The tip of the peninsula, named **Point Danger** by Captain Cook in 1770, provides a fine starting point from which to survey the scene. Below and to the right is **Duranbah Beach** which flanks the sea wall at the mouth of the Tweed River. Like all the beaches around the heads it is a popular surf spot and Point Danger provides a good vantage point from which to spectate.

Surfers riding the waves with Gold Coast high-rises in the background

To the left is **Snapper Rocks**, one of the most popular surf spots on the southern Gold Coast. It's a great place to watch the surfers as you can literally sit on the rocks beside the 'launch zone' only metres away from all the action. Just to the west of Snapper Rocks is the pretty little beach called **Rainbow Bay**, which is the first of the beaches that combines both good surfing with safe swimming. Continuing west, Rainbow Bay is then separated from **Greenmount Beach** by a small headland that offers fine views from **Pat Fagan Park**. Greenmount Beach then merges with Coolangatta Beach, both of which are idyllic, excellent for swimming and enormously popular with families. At the western end of Coolangatta Beach, **Kirra Point** also provides great views back down Greenmount and Coolangatta beaches and north, beyond **North Kirra Beach**, to Surfers Paradise.

Gold Coast Hinterland » *pp247-251.*

Less than an hour's drive from the Gold Coast are its greatest inland attractions – the national parks of Lamington, Springbrook and Mount Tamborine. Labelled 'the Green Behind the Gold', they provide their own natural wonderland of pristine subtropical rainforest, waterfalls, walking tracks and stunning views. The weather here can also be dramatically different with much more rain and the coolest temperatures in the State.

Ins and outs

Tourist information The main QPWS offices are located within the parks ⓘ *Springbrook, T5533 5147, and Lamington, T5544 0634*, www.epa.qld.gov.au. Walking track guides with maps and details are available from each office. There is also an office on the coast, Kabool Road, West Burleigh (T5520 9600, www.epa.qld.gov.au). For vineyard information visit www.goldcoastwinecountry.com.au. » *p250.*

Springbrook National Park

Springbrook National Park (2,954 ha), 29 km south from Mudgeeraba on the Pacific Highway, is the most accessible for the coast and sits on the northern rim of what was once a huge volcano centred on Mount Warning (see also page 221). The park is split into three sections: **Springbrook Plateau**, **Natural Bridge** and the **Cougals**. The Natural Bridge section of the park is accessed from the Nerang to Murwillumbah Road (see tour operators on page 246 if you don't have your own transport).

Like Lamington, Springbrook offers a rich subtropical rainforest habitat of ancient trees and gorges, interspersed with creeks, waterfalls and an extensive system of walking tracks. In addition, the park is well known for its many spectacular views including **Canyon**, **Wunburra**, **Goomoolahara** and the aptly named **Best of All**. Other attractions include the **Natural Arch** (1-km walk) – a cavernous rock archway that spans **Cave Creek** and the 190-m **Purling Brook Falls** (4-km walk). Natural Arch also plays host to a colony of glow-worms. See Tour operators (page 246) if you don't have your own transport.

Mount Tamborine

Mount Tamborine is a name used loosely to describe the 17-section **Tamborine National Park** and the picturesque settlements of **Mount Tamborine**, **Tamborine Village** and **Eagle Heights**. Combined, they offer an attractive escape from the coast with fine coastal views, walking tracks, vineyards, B&Bs, teahouses and arts and craft galleries. One of the most popular sections is the **Witches Falls**, first designated a national park in 1908, making it Queensland's oldest. Other popular spots include **Cedar Creek** section, with its pleasant 3-km walk to some pretty waterfalls, or the **Joalah** section, where, if you are lucky, you may see – or more probably hear – one of its best-known residents, the mimicking lyrebird.

Mount Tamborine is accessed via the Oxenford-Tamborine Road (Oxenford turn-off) or the Nerang-Tamborine Road (Nerang turn-off) both on the Pacific Highway. There is no public transport to Mount Tamborine but various tours are available. The VICs can supply information, while the QPWS at West Burleigh (see Ins and outs on previous page) or the **Doughty Park Information Centre** ⓘ *off Main Western Rd, North Tamborine, T5545 3200, www.tamborine tourism.com.au*, stocks walks and parks information. There are no QPWS campsites.

Lamington National Park

The 20,500-ha Lamington National Park sits on the border of Queensland and New South Wales and comprises densely forested valleys and peaks straddling the **McPherson Range** and an ancient volcanic area known as the **Scenic Rim**, about 60 km inland from the Gold Coast. The park is essentially split into two sections: the **Binna Burra** to the east and the **Green Mountains** (O'Reilly's) to the west. Combined, they offer a wealth of superb natural features and a rich biodiversity that can be experienced on over 100 km of walking tracks. Green Mountains were first settled in 1911 by the O'Reilly family, who established a number of small dairy farms before consolidating their assets in 1915 with the opening of their, now internationally famous, guesthouse (see Budget Busters box on next page). Other than the sense of escape and surrounding beauty, its most popular draw is the treetop canopy walkway which is an ideal way to see the rainforest habitat. There are also some excellent walking tracks offering spectacular views and numerous waterfalls. Guided tours are available, along with a broad range of places to stay. The Green Mountains (O'Reilly's) section is accessed from Canungra.

The most accessible section is Binna Burra, 35 km south west of Nerang on the Pacific Highway. From Brisbane you can travel south via Nerang or via Mount Tamborine and Canungra. If you don't have your own transport, there are numerous tour operators, see page 250. Like the Green Mountains, Binna Burra offers a wealth of excellent rainforest walking opportunities and plays host to another historic guesthouse (see Budget Busters box on next page). Guided tours are available from the lodge and there is a QPWS centre and campsite.

Budget busters

Gold Coast hinterland sleeping

LL-L **O'Reilly's Rainforest Guesthouse**, Lamington National Park Rd (via Canungra), Lamington National Park, T5544 0644, www.oreillys.com.au. Has a range of room options from luxury suites to standard, pool, sauna, spa and restaurant. Package includes meals and some tours.

LL **Binna Burra Mountain Lodge**, Binna Burra Rd, Beechmont (via Nerang), Lamington National Park, T5533 3758, www.binnaburralodge.com.au. Offers well-appointed en suite cabins with fireplace (some with spa), activities, meals included.

Sleeping

Surfers Paradise *p241, map p242*
The Gold Coast has accommodation of all types to suit all budgets. But even with the 55,000 beds currently available you are advised to book in advance. Prices fluctuate wildly between peak and off-peak seasons. Stand-by deals and packages are always on offer so you are advised to shop around and research thoroughly. Booking at least 7 days in advance will usually work out cheaper.

Here we list a small selection. For a much greater choice pick up the free Qantas and Sunlover Gold Coast brochures available from travel agents. Accommodation agents include the **Gold Coast Accommodation Service**, Shop 1, 1 Beach Rd, Surfers, T5592 0067, www.goldcoastaccommodation service.com.au. The Gold Coast City Council operates a number of excellent facilities up and down the coast. Look out for their free *Gold Coast City Council Holiday Parks* brochure or visit www.gctp.com.au.

A-E **Main Beach Tourist Park**, Main Beach Parade, T5581 7722, www.gctp.com.au. This park offers cabins, en suite/standard powered and non-powered sites, with good facilities and camp kitchens, all nestled quietly amongst the high-rises and across the road from the main beach.

C-E **Sleeping in Surfers**, 26 Peninsular Dr, T5592 4455, www.sleepinginn.com.au. Newly relocated backpackers with modern facilities but a wider choice of room options than most; from dorms and singles to doubles, twins and self-contained units with TV and living room. It can also throw a good party.

C-E **Backpackers in Paradise**, 40 Whelan St, just west of the Transit Centre, T1800-268621, www.backpackersin-paradise.com. Lively, colourful, friendly and well-equipped. Dorms and 3 spacious doubles (en suite), café, bar, pool, broadband internet, tours desk and a comfy TV lounge with a huge screen.

C-E **Surfers Paradise Backpackers Resort**, 2837 Gold Coast Highway, T5592 4677, www.surfersparadisebackpackers.com.au. Lively and popular purpose-built place on the border of Surfers and Broadbeach. It offers tidy en suite dorms, units (some self-contained with TV) and good facilities, including well-equipped kitchen, bar, free laundry, pool, sauna, gym, volleyball pitch, TV/games room, internet, party and activity tours, pick-ups and off-street parking.

C-E **Trekkers**, 22 White St, in Southport 2 km north of Surfers, T5591 5616, www.trekkers backpackers.com.au.

The best backpackers in the region. Small traditional suburban Queenslander, offering cosy, well appointed rooms including en suite doubles with TV, nice pool and garden. Great atmosphere, friendly, family-run business with the emphasis on looking after each guest rather than the turnover.

Coolangatta and Tweed Heads *p244*

A-E **Kirra Beach Tourist Park**, Charlotte St, off Coolangatta Rd, T5581 7744, www.gctp.com.au. Spacious and well facilitated, offering powered/non-powered sites, cabins, camp kitchen and salt water pool.

B-D **Sunset Strip Budget Resort**, 199-203 Boundary St, T5599 5517, www.sunsetstrip.com.au. Much closer to the beach and the town centre, this is an old, spacious hotel with unit style singles, doubles, twins, quads and family rooms with shared bathrooms, excellent kitchen facilities, large pool and within yards of the beach. Basic but spacious, good value. Fully self-contained 1 and 2 bedroom holiday flats are also available.

C-E **Coolangatta/Kirra Beach YHA**, 230 Coolangatta Rd, T5536 7644, booking@coolangattayha.com. Near the airport and facing the busy Pacific Highway, offers tidy dorms, doubles/twins, pool, bike and surfboard hire, internet. **Coachtrans** service goes direct to the hostel (T3238 4700).

Gold Coast Hinterland *p245*

D-E **Springbrook Mountain Lodge YHA**, 317 Repeater Station Rd, Springbrook (near the Best of All Lookout), T5533 5366, springbrooklodge@ion.com.au. This small lodge offers a fine retreat and has 1 dorm and 4 double/twins with private bathroom.

QPWS campsites for Lamington National Park at both Binna Burra, T5533 3584, and Green Mountains (200 m from O'Reilly's) with water, hot showers and toilets. Fees apply, book ahead through the ranger/information centres at each location. Also at Purling Brook Falls, Springbook National Park, T5533 5147.

Eating

Surfers Paradise *p241, map p242*

There are too many good restaurants to list here; best to browse the menus at your leisure. The Marina Mirage in Main Beach is also a favourite haunt, but don't expect a cheap deal. Further north, Sanctuary Cove is a fine spot for lunch but is also expensive. To the south, Burleigh Heads provides excellent views, while the many surf lifesaving clubs offer great value as do the many dinner cruise options.

TTT **Lemongrass on Tedder**, 6/26 Tedder Ave, T5528 0289. Of the many Thai options this one stands out for quality and value for money, but book ahead.

TT **Bellissimo Italian Restaurant**, Broadbeach, directly opposite Jupiter's Casino, T5570 3388. Has a fine reputation and live music Fri-Sat.

TT **Clock Hotel**, Chevron Renaissance Mall, T5539 0344. At the northern entrance, this place enjoys a good reputation as a top lunch venue.

TT **Donto Sapporo**, 2763 Gold Coast Highway, T5539 9933. Considered one of the best Japanese restaurants in the city.

TT **Grumpy's Restaurant**, at the river end of Cavill Mall (Tiki Village), T5531 6177. Well known for its affordable seafood, casual atmosphere and pleasant views.

TT **Landsdowne Irish Pub**, Chevron Renaissance Mall, T5531 5599. Offers traditional wholesome pub food at reasonable prices.

TT **Restaurant B**, Shop 8, 20 Tedder Ave, T5564 0900, Good value al fresco restaurant offering an imaginative and wide ranging menu, good service and chic, contemporary decor.

T **Charlie's Restaurant**, Cavill Ave Mall, T5538 5285. Offers decent meals 24 hrs a day and a good breakfast.

T **Southport SLC**, McArthur Parade, Main Beach, T5591 5083, and the **Palm Beach SLC**, 7th Ave and Jefferson Lane, Palm

Beach, T5534 2180, are a couple of the many surf lifesaving clubs (SLCs) along the coast, offering great value meals.

Coolangatta and Tweed Heads *p244*

The Fisherman's Cove Seafood Taverna, at **Oaks Calypso Resort**, Griffith St, T5536 1646. Many come here for the affordable and fine fishy fare.

Little Malaysia, Shop 14, Beach House Complex Marine Parade, T5536 2690. For great value Asian cuisine.

Four Leaf Clover Café, 1/40 Griffith St, T5536 5636. For healthy snacks and sandwiches.

Uno Café, 82 Marine Parade, T5599 5116. Mon-Fri 1000-late, Sat-Sun 0800-late. Best value for breakfast.

Bars and clubs

Surfers Paradise *p241, map p242*

If you are staying at any of the hostels you will be well looked after by the staff and will only need to 'go with the flow'. If not, **Orchid Ave**, off the Cavill Ave Mall, is the main focus for clubbing with most staying open until about 0300. Dress is smart casual, carry ID and be prepared to kiss your money goodbye. Entry ranges from $10-15, which is manageable, but the drinks are expensive. For a more sophisticated night out try **Lansdowne Irish Pub** T5531 5599 (live music every Fri-Sat), or the **Clock Hotel** T5539 0344 (live music most nights), both at the Chevron Renaissance Mall.

Entertainment

Surfers Paradise *p241, map p242*

Conrad Jupiter's Casino, off Hooker Blvd, off Gold Coast Highway, Broadbeach, T5592 8100, www.conrad.com.au. 2 floors of gaming tables and pokies. Open 24 hrs.

There is a cinema and theatre at the **Arts Centre**, 135 Blundall Rd, T5588 4008, and other mainstream cinemas in the malls.

Festivals and events

Surfers Paradise *p241, map p242*

The Gold Coast hosts a number of exciting annual events most of which involve lots of money, fireworks and parties, festivals, races and sporting spectaculars. Although listed under Surfers, many of these events are spread out along the coast. For a detailed calendar of events visit www.goldcoasttourism.com.au.

Jan kicks off with **Conrad Jupiter's Magic Millions**, a 10-day horseracing event with a very popular fashion event. In **Mar** the beach becomes the main focus with the **Australian Surf Life Saving Championships**, which is arguably the Gold Coast's most famous event. It attracts over 7,000 national and international competitors, all trying to out swim, run and row each other, for the prestigious Iron Man or Iron Woman trophy. **Jul** also sees the **Gold Coast Marathon** – considered Australia's premier long-distance running event. In **mid-winter** it's green for go with the ever-popular **Honda Indy 300**, when the streets of Surfers are alive to the sound of racing cars and, in the the evenings, to the heady beat of parties, parades and the mardi gras. Numerous food festivals are also held throughout the year, including the **Gold Coast Food Festival** in **Sep**, the **Broadbeach Festival** in **Oct** and the **Gold Coast Signature Dish Competition** in **Dec**.

Shopping

Surfers Paradise *p241, map p242*

The Gold Coast offers a healthy dose of retail therapy with some 3,500 shops, all of which contribute to over $3 bn of visitor spending per annum.

Paradise Centre, Cavill Ave, is a focus for mainly tourist based products and more bikinis than an episode of Baywatch.

Marina Mirage, Main Beach and Sanctuary Cove, is more upmarket but lacks atmosphere.

Activities and tours

Surfers Paradise *p241, map p242*
Other than the beach, shopping and the theme parks, Surfers presents a mind-blowing array of additional activities which goes way beyond the scope of this guide. Visit the VIC for the full list. If anything is to be recommended, it has to be a rainforest tour to the stunning Lamington and Springbrook National Parks (see below), an hour's drive inland. The resorts on South Stradbroke Island also offer a suitable coastal escape (see Moreton Bay page 255).

Rainforest tours

Bushwacker Ecotours, T5520 7238, www.bushwacker-ecotours.com.au. Day walk/tours and night spotting to Springbrook, from $59.

Watersports

For anything water-based, including self-hire, shop around at the Cruise Terminal, at Mariners Cove (Main Beach) or the wharf at the western end of Cavill Ave. **Beach Club House**, 189 Paradise Centre, Cavill Ave, T5526 7077. For surfboard hire, from $40 per day. For surfing lessons try **Cheyne Horan**, T1800-227873, www.cheynehoran.com.au.

Gold Coast Hinterland *p245*
Several tour operators offer day trips to Springbrook from both Brisbane and the Gold Coast including **Scenic Hinterland Tours**, Tue, Thu and Sun, T5531 5536, and **Bushwackers Ecotours** (day and night tours), T5520 7238. **Mountain Trek Adventures**, T5524 1090, sherpa@bigvolcano.com.au, are one of many operators who run tours to Lamington National Park daily. The VIC has full listings.

Transport

Getting around the Gold Coast is generally very easy, with 24-hr local bus transport, numerous companies offering theme park/airport transfers and car, moped, and bike hire. **Surfside Buslines**, T5574 5111, www.gcshuttle.com.au, is the principal local operator and offer a 'Freedom Pass' of 3-14 days from $47/child $24. Surfside also offer airport (Coolangatta) transfers from $15. **Airtrain**, T131230, also offer suburban services, theme park and airport transfers ($15) between 0830-2245 (main trunk services from Coolangatta to Southport 24 hrs).

Surfers Paradise *p241, map p242*

Bus

Con-X-ion, T5556 9888, **Coachtrans**, T3238 4700, www.coachtrans.com.au, **Murray's**, T132259, and **Active Tours**, T5597 0344, all offer regular shuttles between **Brisbane City** and/or Airport to the **Gold Coast**, from about $35, child $18. For theme park transfers contact **Con-X-ion**, T5556 9888, www.con-x-ion.com.au, **Active Tours**, T5597 0344, or **Coachtrans**, T3238 4700.

The long-distance terminal is on the corner of Beach Rd and Remembrance Dr. Most of the major coach companies have offices within the complex (open 0600-2200). **Premier Motor Services**, T133410, and **Greyhound**, T131499, offer daily inter-state services. **Coachtrans**, T3238 4700, www.coachtrans.com.au, are recommended for Brisbane City/Airport transfers. **Kirklands**, T1300-367077, www.kirklands.com.au, and **Suncoast Pacific**, T5531 6000, offer regular services to Byron Bay and the NSW coast.

Cycling

Bike hire is available from **Red Rocket Rent-A-Car**, Shop 9,The Mark, Orchid Ave, T5538 9074.

Mopeds/jeeps

Yahoo, 88 Ferny Ave, T5592 0227, from $30 ($150 deposit), for mopeds. **Rent-A-Jeep**, corner Palm and Ferny Ave, T1800-228085, for small jeeps and microscopic Smart Cars from about $75 per day to hire.

Train

Both Robina and Nerang train stations (15 km/10 km southwest/west of Surfers respectively) are served by **Airtrain**, T3216 3308, from **Brisbane** (with connections to Brisbane airport), from $40, child $20. **Airtrain Connect**, T5574 5111, and **Surfside Buslines** (Nos 2 and 11) then offer road transport to the coast.

Coolangatta and Tweed Heads *p244*

Air

Gold Coast Airport is near Coolangatta, 22 km south of Surfers, T5589 1100, www.GoldCoastAirport.com.au. **Qantas**, T131313, www.qantas.com.au, **Virgin Blue**, T136789, www.virginblue.com.au, **Freedom Air**, T1800-122000, www.freedomair.co.nz, and **Jet Star**, T131538, www.jetstar. com.au, all offer domestic services (and/or international connections). **Con-X-ion**, T5556 9888, and **Surfside Buses**, T5589 1100, offer local transfers, from $12, child $6.

Bus

Premier Motor Services, T133410, and **Greyhound**, T5531 6677, offer daily inter-State services, while **Coachtrans**, T3238 4700, www.coach trans.com.au, offer regular shuttles up and down the coast, to **Brisbane** and to/from the airport. **Kirklands**, T1300-367077, www.kirklands.com.au, and **Suncoast Pacific**, T5531 6000, have regular services to **Byron Bay** and the **NSW coast**. For other Byron Bay based operators refer to the relevant text.

All long-distance buses stop outside the main booking agent, **Golden Gateway Travel**, 29 Bay St, T5536 1700. **Surfside Buslines**, T131230, www.gcshuttle.com.au, is the main suburban bus company with regular links north to **Surfers**.

Taxi

For a taxi, T5536 1144.

Gold Coast Hinterland *p245*

O'Reilly's Mountain Coach Company, T5524 4249, and **Mountain Way Transfers**, T5545 2380, offer transportation to and from the Gold Coast (via Mount Tamborine) to Tamborine Mountain and O'Reilly's Resort in the Lamington National Park.

O'Reilly's Mountain Coach Company (Green Mountains section), T5524 4249, offers transportation to and from the Gold Coast to O'Reilly's Resort, daily from $45, child $22 return. **Binna Burra Mountain Lodge** also has their own bus service, (Binna Burra section), T5533 3758, from both the Gold Coast and Brisbane, from $44, child $22 return.

Directory

Surfers Paradise *p241, map p242*

Banks All major branches with ATMs and currency exchange are around the Cavill Mall-Gold Coast Highway intersection. **Hospitals** **Gold Coast Hospital**, 108 Nerang St, Southport, T5571 8211. **Paradise Medical Centre**, Paradise Centre, T5592 3999 (24-hr). **Internet** **1 hour Photo Shop**, 3189 Gold Coast Highway, T5538 4973. Open 0900-2100. **Email Centre**, next door to **Shooters**, Orchid Ave, T5538 7500. Open 0830-2400. **Post** Cavill Ave Paradise Mall, T5538 4144. Postcode 4217. Open Mon-Fri 0830-1730, Sat 0900-1200. **Pharmacy** **Day and Night**, Piazza On Boulevard (ANA Hotel), 3221 Gold Coast Highway, Surfers, T5592 2299, open 0700-2200. **Useful numbers** **Police**, 68 Ferny Ave, **Surfers**, T5570 7888. **RACQ**, T5532 0311.

Brisbane and Moreton Bay

Brisbane has come an awfully long way since its days as a penal settlement. A lot of money was pumped into the city for its Expo 88 and Brizzie has never looked back. South Bank, especially, represents the very essence of modern-day Brisbane with numerous cultural attractions and even its own beach. Australia's only true tropical city also enjoys a near perfect climate. Wherever you go, al fresco restaurants, cafés and outdoor activities dominate. Nearby, the sand islands of Moreton Bay offer a wonderful opportunity to enjoy some peace and quiet.

Getting there International and interstate flights; interstate bus and rail networks.
Getting around Bus, train, river or island ferries and on foot.
Time required 3-5 days.
Weather Hot and humid in summer; mild to warm in winter.
Sleeping Full range of options in the city. A few budget options and campsites on the islands.
Eating Seafood a speciality.
Activities and tours River or island cruises, wildlife park tours.
★ Don't miss South Bank lagoon. » *p253.*

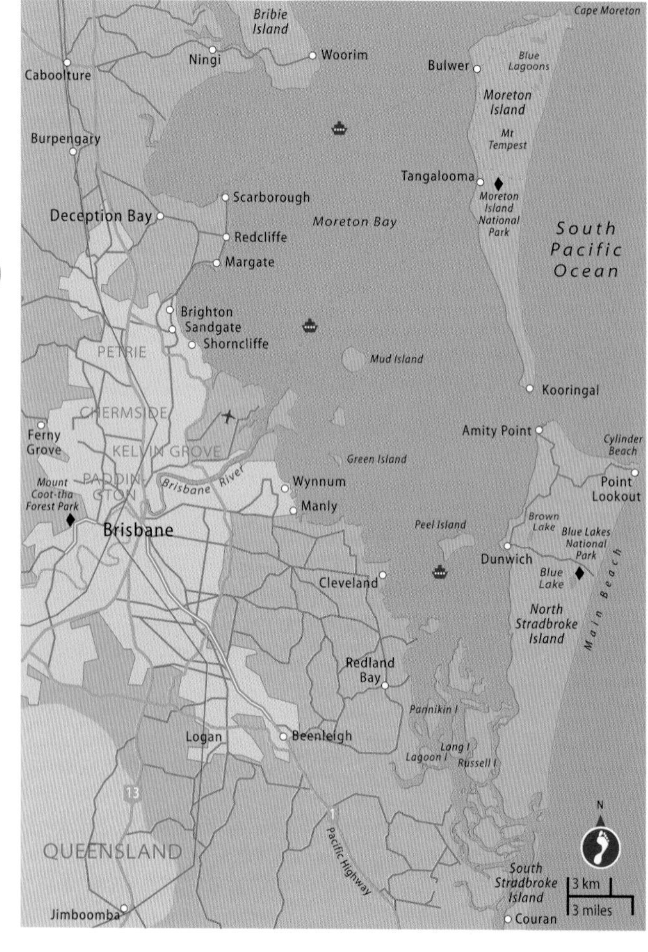

Ins and outs

Getting there Trains and buses connect the CBD with both airport terminals: **Airtrain**, T3216 3308, www.airtrain.com.au, departs from Central (top end of Edward Street), Roma (Transit Centre) and Brunswick Street (Fortitude Valley) four times per hour from $11, child $5.50. **Coachtrans** (SkyTrans service), T3238 4700, www.coachtrans.com.au, departs from the Roma Street Transit Centre every 30 minutes (0500-2100) from $9. Accommodation pick-ups cost about $2 extra. A taxi to the airport will cost about $35. There are frequent long-distance buses and trains to the city from major centres and cities. ▸▸ *p266.*

Getting around There is an efficient transport system with the river playing a large part in navigating the city. The main centre is within walking distance. The city tours, see page 264, are a great way to get around and see the sights, especially if short of time.

Tourist information Queen Street Mall VIC ⓘ *corner of Albert St and Queen St, T3006 6290, www.brisbanetourism.com.au, Mon-Thu, 0900- 1730, Fri 0900-1900, Sat 0900-1700, Sun 0930-1630*, offers free city maps and can assist with accommodation bookings. The free *This Week in Brisbane* booklet is also useful. QPWS main office ⓘ *160 Ann St, T3227 7111, Mon-Fri 0830-1700.*

Sights ▸▸ *pp260-268.*

Central Brisbane

There are a number of historical buildings that stand out amidst the glistening high-rises. At the top end of Albert Street is **City Hall** ⓘ *T3403 8888, 0800-1700, free, guided tours available, lift $2, Mon-Fri 1000-1500, Sat 1000-1400*, with its 92-m Italian renaissance clock tower. Built in 1930, it became known as the 'Million Pound Town Hall' due to its huge and controversial construction cost. The ride in the old lift to the top for the views is a highlight but the interior of the building is also worth a look. The **Museum of Brisbane** showcases the various aspects of contemporary social history and culture with a heavy emphasis on local writers and artists. Around the corner on George Street and the riverbank is the grand 19th-century façade of the former **Treasury Building, now a casino.**

To the east beside the Botanical Gardens is the 1868 French Renaissance-style **Parliament House** ⓘ *T3406 7562, www.parliament.qld.gov.au, Mon-Fri 0900-1700, Sat-Sun 1000-1400, free*, which was commissioned when Queensland was declared a separate colony in 1859. Visitors can join tours conducted by Parliamentary Attendants. Nearby is the **Old Government House** ⓘ *2 George St, T3864 8005, www.ogh.qut.edu.au, 1000-1600, free*, built in 1862 as the official residence of the state's governors and now housing the HQ of the National Trust. It is also open to the public by prior arrangement.

Further north, beyond the modern architecture and chic restaurants of Waterfront Place, Eagle Street Pier and the Riverside Centre, is **Customs House** ⓘ *399 Queens St, T3365 8999, www.customshouse.com.au, daily 1000-1600, tours Sun*. Built in 1889, it resembles a miniature version of St Paul's cathedral in London. Directly opposite the Customs House is the city's best-known and most-photographed sight – the **Story Bridge**. It was built between 1935 and 1940 and due to the lack of bedrock has some of the deepest (42 m) foundations of any bridge in the world.

Overlooking the high-rises on the southern bank of the Brisbane River is the remarkable 17-ha 'oasis in the city' known as **South Bank**. Built primarily as the showpiece for Expo 88, the 1-km stretch of parkland remains as a fascinating and functional recreational space and includes riverside walks, shops, restaurants, open-air markets and a swimming lagoon with

Australia Day, South Bank, Brisbane

its very own beach. This area is also the venue for the colourful **South markets** held every Friday night, Saturday and Sunday and the **Al Fresco Cinema** in February and March, Wednesday to Saturday.

At the northwestern end of the park, straddling Melbourne Street, is the **Queensland Cultural Centre**, encompassing the State Library, Queensland Museum, Queensland Art Gallery and Queensland Performing Arts Complex. **Queensland Art Gallery** ⓘ *T3840 7303, www.qag.qld.gov.au, Mon-Fri 1000-1700, Sat-Sun 0900-1700, free, tours at 1100, 1300 and 1400*, is Brisbane's premier cultural attraction, featuring a huge and diverse collection of Aboriginal, European, Asian and contemporary Australian art. Early works include paintings by John Russell and Rupert Bunny, two of the nation's most noted expat artists, as well as more familiar international names such as Rubens, Degas, Picasso and Van Dyck. Kurilpa Point on the South Bank will form a second site to the existing gallery and house the **Queensland Gallery of Modern Art**, making the combination the second largest public art museum in Australia. Public opening is scheduled for the end of 2006.

Next to the art gallery is the **Queensland Museum** ⓘ *T3840 7555, www.Qmuseum.qld.gov.au, 0930-1700, free*, which is noted for its prehistoric and natural history displays. The museum also hosts an entertaining and educational range of interactive exhibits that will keep little Einsteins amused for hours. On the opposite side of Melbourne Street is the **Queensland Performing Arts Complex** which houses several theatres and concert venues. At the southeastern end of the South Bank is the **Queensland Maritime Museum** ⓘ *T3844 5361, www.qmma.ecn.net.au, 0930-1630, $6, child $3*, which houses all the usual relics from anchors to lifebuoys. Most of the larger vessels, which include the Second World War warship *The Diamantina*, sit forlornly in the adjacent dry dock. All this is best viewed from the futuristic **Goodwill Bridge**, built in celebration of the 2001 Goodwill Games.

Brisbane suburbs

West of the city, reached via Milton Road, is the **Botanical Gardens-Mount-Coot-tha** ⓘ *T3403 2535, 0830-1730, free, tours Mon-Sat 1100 and 1300 or pick up a free self-guided leaflet*, considered Queensland's finest, featuring over 20,000 specimens of 5,000 species. Within the grounds is also a **Planetarium** and **Lakeside Restaurant** (0900-1700).

A wall of high-rises flank the Brisbane River

Set high above the gardens is the **Mount Coot-tha Lookout**, which offers superb views across the city and out across Moreton Bay to Moreton, North Stradbroke and Bribie Islands. **Summit Restaurant** and **Kuta Café**, see page 262, provide an ideal place for lunch, dinner or just a glass of vino while soaking up the sun and the city vistas. Backing onto the lookout complex is the **Mount Coot-tha Forest Park** which consists of 1500 ha of open eucalyptus forest, networked with walking tracks and containing over 350 weird and wonderful native species. Catch bus #471 from Adelaide Street or alternatively, join the City Sights or City Nights Tours. ▸▸ *p264.*

Moreton Bay and Islands ▸▸ *pp260-268.*

Although much smaller than Fraser and less dramatic, the Moreton Bay islands are easily accessible and remarkably unspoilt. Of the 300 odd islands scattered around the bay, the two largest and most popular are Moreton Island and North Stradbroke Island. Moreton, which lies 37 km northeast of the Brisbane River mouth, is almost uninhabited and famous for its 4WD opportunities, its shipwrecks and its pod of friendly dolphins. Further south, North Stradbroke (or 'Straddie') is the largest of the islands, a laid-back place with world-class surf beaches, awesome coastal scenery and the chance to watch breaching whales and dolphins and manta rays glide past beneath the waves. ▸▸ *p268.*

North Stradbroke Island

ⓘ *Stradbroke VICs 300 m from the ferry wharf on Junner St, Dunwich, T3409 9555, www.stradbroketourism.com, Mon-Fri 0830-1700, Sat-Sun 0830-1500. They stock island maps and can assist with general information.*

Wedge-shaped North Stradbroke, or 'Straddie' as it is affectionately known, is the largest, most inhabited and most accessible of the Moreton Bay Islands. Some 30 km southeast of Brisbane, it is 36 km long and 11 km at its widest point. Separated from its southerly neighbour, South Stradbroke, by a fierce cyclone in 1896, it has become a magical tourist attraction often overlooked due to its proximity to the competing attractions of Brisbane and the Gold Coast. In many ways it is similar to Fraser Island, offering diverse and unspoilt coastal scenery and a rich biodiversity that is so typical of 'sand islands'. The three picturesque villages

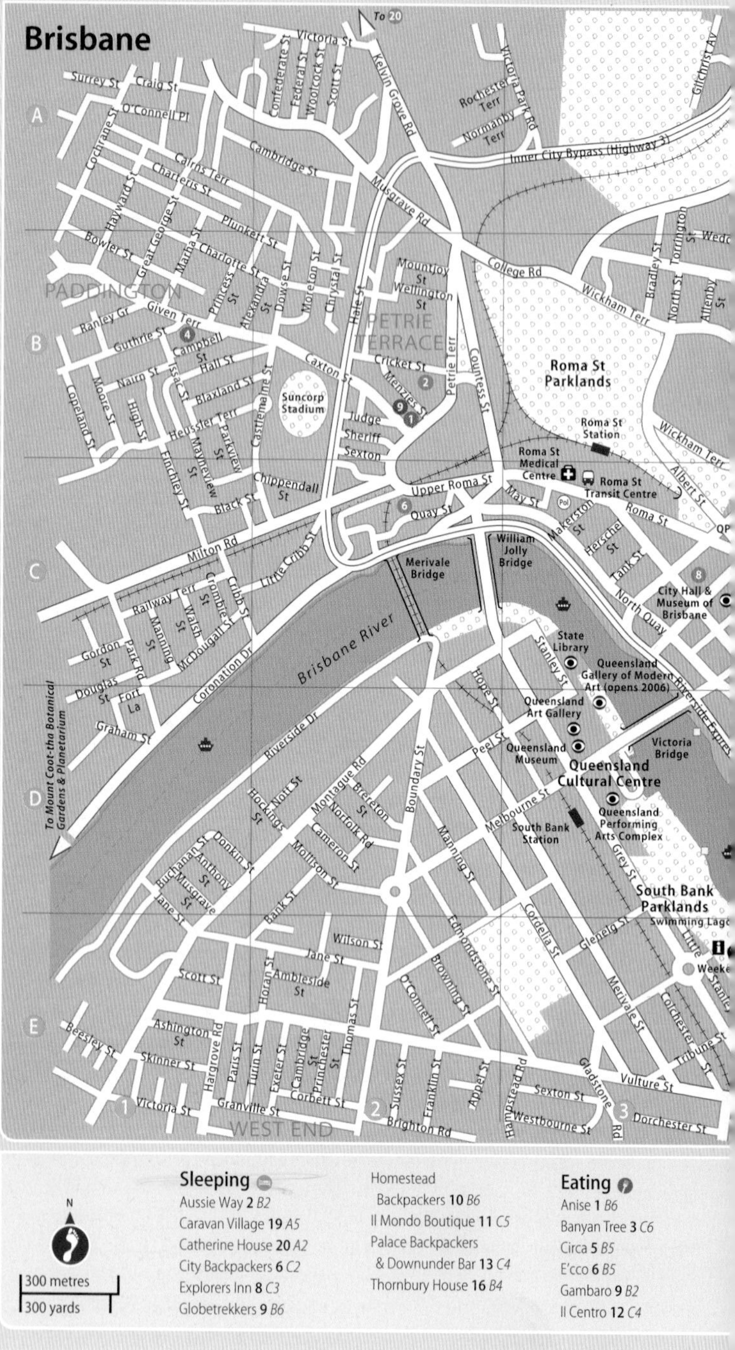

Brisbane

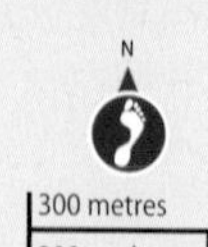

Sleeping

Aussie Way **2** *B2*
Caravan Village **19** *A5*
Catherine House **20** *A2*
City Backpackers **6** *C2*
Explorers Inn **8** *C3*
Globetrekkers **9** *B6*
Homestead Backpackers **10** *B6*
Il Mondo Boutique **11** *C5*
Palace Backpackers & Downunder Bar **13** *C4*
Thornbury House **16** *B4*

Eating

Anise **1** *B6*
Banyan Tree **3** *C6*
Circa **5** *B5*
E'cco **6** *B5*
Gambaro **9** *B2*
Il Centro **12** *C4*

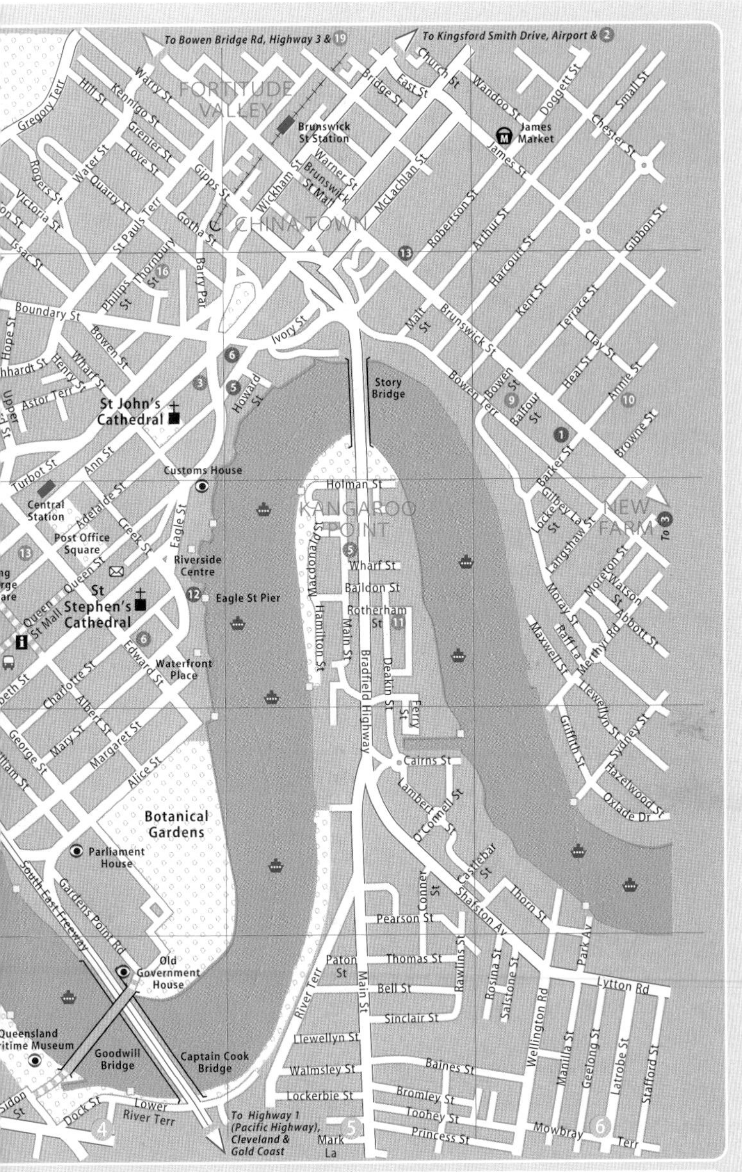

Isis Brasserie **13** *B5*
Pier Nine **12** *C4*

Orient Hotel **3** *B4*
Paddo Tavern **4** *B1*
Storey Bridge Hotel **5** *C5*
Victory **6** *C4*

Bars & clubs

Breakfast Creek Hotel **2** *A6*
Hotel LA **1** *B2*

Keep an eye open for the street art in Fortitude Valley, Brisbane

of Dunwich, Amity Point and Point Lookout offer a broad range of accommodation, excellent beaches and plenty of water-based activities. Surfing is the obvious speciality.

Dunwich, a former penal colony and quarantine station, is on the west mid-section of the island and the main arrival point. The small museum (open Wednesdays and Saturdays), on Welsby Street explores the island's rich aboriginal and early settler history. **Amity Point**, first settled in 1825, sits on the northwest corner, 17 km from Dunwich, while **Point Lookout**, the main focus for today's tourist accommodation, sights and activities, is 21 km away on the northeast corner. If you only have one or two days on the island the place to be is Point Lookout, with its golden surf beaches and dramatic headland. At the terminus of East Coast Road is the start of the **North Gorge Headlands Walk** (1 km one way). Before you set off take

Travellers' tales

Anyone for dolphins?

On our road trip up and down the East coast we fancied exploring a couple of the islands off the coast of Brisbane. We decided on Moreton Island as our guidebook [not this one obviously! – Ed] said you could feed and swim with the dolphins. This was one of my dreams so we booked our ferry ticket and off we set. Imagine our disappointment when we arrived to be told that unless we were residents of the one and only faded seventies resort on the island (complete with its own derelict whaling station and purposely sunk rusty wrecks) then we weren't allowed to take part. Well, we didn't cry for too long. As we stayed to watch, we witnessed hordes of people having to make several orderly queues on the beach, wait their turn for half an hour and then get called to go in one at a time to knee level, throw one fish, told not to touch the dolphins under any circumstances, and then ushered back by the staff. In contrast, we had a great time on South Stradbroke Island, also off the coast near Brissie, in a quiet resort, a great air conditioned thatched hut, beautiful beaches and lots of activities. These were fun, despite the fact that the list of participants usually comprised the two of us and the organiser. When it came to tennis doubles, some hapless guy had to be dragged away from the bar to make up the teams. I'm no Venus Williams, and my slim chances of winning began to look positively anorexic as I watched my partner staggering around in the heat, stubby in one hand, racquet in the other, swiping at thin air. Needless to say, we didn't need a third set!

Sophie TJ, Wilts, UK

a look at **Frenchman's Bay** below, which gives you a flavour of the dramatic scenery to come. Follow the track, through wind-lashed stands of pandanus palms to **The Gorge**, a narrow cleft in the rock that is pounded endlessly by huge ocean breakers. Further on, **Whale Rock** provides an ideal viewpoint from which to spot migrating humpback whales between June and October. Manta rays, turtles and dolphins are also a familiar sight all year round. At the far end of the walk the vast swathe of **Main Beach** hoves into view, stretching 34 km down the entire length of the island's east coast. It offers some excellent 4WD action, fishing, surfing and a few mosquito-infested campsites. **Cylinder Beach**, back along East Coast Road, provides the best recreational spot with great surf breaks and safe swimming. If you do swim always stick to patrolled areas between the flags.

Other attractions on the island include **Blue Lakes National Park**, which is reached via Trans Island Road, from Dunwich. The lake itself, a 2.5-km walk from the car park, is freshwater and fringed with melalucas and eucalypts, providing the perfect spot for a cool swim. To reach Main Beach from there requires 4WD. **Brown Lake**, which is bigger and only 2 km outside Dunwich, is a less popular spot.

Moreton Island

Moreton Island, which lies to the north of the Stradbroke Islands, is often considered the jewel of the Moreton group by virtue of its lack of inhabitants and unspoilt beauty. It is another 'sand mass'; almost 20,000 ha of long, empty beaches, dunes, forest, lagoons and heathlands with abundant wildlife. Other than the beauty and solitude, the greatest attractions are its 4WD opportunities, fishing, camping, wreck-snorkelling/diving and the pod of 'wild' Tangalooma bottlenose dolphins that put in a nightly appearance at the island's **Tangalooma Wild Dolphin Resort** (see Traveller's tales box above). Other attractions include the Tangalooma Desert, a large sand blow near the resort, and the Blue Lagoons, a group of 15 deliberately sunken shipwrecks which provide excellent snorkelling. If you do have the freedom of the island with a 4WD, Cape Moreton at the northeastern tip of the island is worth a visit to see the 1857 lighthouse – the oldest in Queensland. Mount Tempest (285 m) dominates the heart of the island and is reputed to be the highest coastal sand dune in the world (a strenuous 5-km walk). For details, see Activities and tours page 266.

Sleeping

Central Brisbane *p253, map p256*

Brisbane boasts more than 12,000 beds from large 5-star hotels and modern apartment blocks to numerous backpacker and budget options plus a good selection of B&Bs, some of which present an ideal opportunity to experience a traditional 'Queenslander' house. The only thing lacking is a selection of good motor parks within easy reach of the city centre. Although there are plenty of hostels you are still advised to book a budget bed at least 2 days in advance. There are good options on Upper Roma St just 500 m southwest of the transit centre and around Fortitude Valley.

LL-C **Il Mondo Boutique Hotel**, 25 Rotherham St, T3392 0111, www.ilmondo.com.au. Across the river on Kangaroo Point, this modern, chic hotel offers 1-3 bedroom self-contained apartments, al-fresco restaurant, a lap pool and relative peace from the centre. It is also within walking distance of all the action via a typical Brizzie ferry ride from the Holman St Wharf.

A **Explorers Inn**, 63 Turbot St, T3211 3488, www.powerup.com.au/~explorer. One of the best value (and certainly the best placed) of the budget hotel options. Friendly, it offers tidy (if small) doubles/twins/family rooms and singles and has a cheap but cheerful restaurant/bar. It is only 500 m from the transit centre and Queens St.

B-C **Thornbury House**, 1 Thornbury St, 10-min walk from CBD, T3832 5985, www.babs.com.au/thornbury. Another traditional Queenslander with good-value king, twin, triple and attic suites, all traditionally furnished with private bathrooms.

C-E **Aussie Way**, 34 Cricket St, T3369 0711, aussieway15@hotmail.com. West of the CBD, this hostel is handy for Caxton St nightlife and Paddington. A tidy 1872 colonial house, it offers small but comfortable dorms, singles and doubles, pool, quiet verandahs, free pick-ups and internet.

C-E **City Backpackers**, 380 Upper Roma St, 500 m southwest of the transit centre, T3211 3221, www.citybackpackers.com. Deservedly popular and well managed, it offers spotless en suite doubles and dorms, modern kitchen, excellent security, roof decks, pool, internet and a great bar. It's a very social place that can throw a great party at the weekend.

C-E **Palace Backpackers**, corner of Ann St and Edward St, T3211 2433, www.palacebackpackers.com.au. Right in the heart of the CBD, this large elegant and historic landmark building has been fully revamped offering large dorms, doubles and small singles with all amenities including a/c, cable TV, café and the rowdy **Down Under Bar and Grill.**

24-hr reception so a good place to stay if you plan nights out on the town.

D-E **Globetrekkers**, 35 Balfour St, New Farm, T3358 1251, www.globetrekkers.net. A small, ageing, yet characterful, 2-storey house with caring owners, cosy and homely, with dorms, doubles (some en suite), internet, free pick-ups and off-street parking.

C-E **Homestead Backpackers**, 57 Annie St, New Farm, T3258 3538. One of the Valley's liveliest offering tidy 3/4/7 dorms, doubles (some en suite), internet, pool, off-street parking and a whole list of 'freebies' from pick-ups, bike hire, fun-filled day trips to Mount Coot-tha and organized socials with other backpackers.

Brisbane suburbs *p254, map p256*

L-E **Caravan Village**, 763 Zillmere Rd (off Gympie Rd), on the northern approach, 12 km from the CBD, T3263 4040, www.caravanvillage.com.au. This is the best motor park, offering a wide range of options from luxury cabins, en suite/standard powered and non-powered sites, pool, store, internet and an excellent camp kitchen.

B-C **Catherine House**, 151 Kelvin Grove Rd, Kelvin Grove (2 km northwest), T3839 6988, www.babs.com.au/catherine. Large Victorian colonial home with 3 beautifully appointed rooms and 2 self-contained boutique apartments, pool and spacious gardens all within walking distance of the CBD.

North Stradbroke Island *p255*

There is a broad range of accommodation available on Straddie, with the vast majority being based in Point Lookout. Nevertheless, pre-booking is recommended in the summer, and on public/school holidays.

B-C **Sunsets at Point**, Lookout, 6 Billa St, T3409 8823, www.babs.com.au/sunsets. A B&B in a spacious, modern house with 3 en suites overlooking Home Beach.

B-F **Stradbroke Tourist Park**, Dickson Way, T3409 8127. This is the best-facilitated motor park/campsite. Located in Point Lookout it offers deluxe villas (with spa), en suite/standard cabins, powered and non-powered sites, salt-water pool, BBQ and camp kitchen.

C-E **Stradbroke Island Backpackers YHA** (above and part of the Dive Shop), 1 East Coast Rd, T3409 8888, www.stradbrokeislandscuba.com.au. Friendly and near the beach, with focus on dive trips. Pick-ups from Brisbane.

Moreton Island *p260*

LL-D **Tangalooma Wild Dolphin Resort**, T3268 6333, www.tangalooma.com.au. A fine resort offering a wide range of beachside accommodation, from luxury self-contained apartments and standard rooms/units to new backpacker/budget beds, a restaurant, bistro/bar café, pools and an environmental centre.

QPWS campsites, T3408 2710, www.epa.qld.gov.au. Available at The Wrecks, Ben-Ewa and Comboyuro Point on the west coast and Blue Lagoon and Eagers Creek on the east. The Wrecks campsite is about a 2-km walk from the resort. Each has toilets and limited supplies of water, cold showers. Fees apply ($4 per night).

Eating

Brizzie offers a vast choice. Outside the city centre and the Riverside (Eagle St) areas the suburbs of Fortitude Valley, New Farm (east), South Bank, the West End (south of the river) and Paddington (west) are well worth looking at. The main focus for Brisbane's café scene are Brunswick St Mall in Fortitude Valley, South Bank parklands, West End (Boundary St) and Petrie Terr/Paddington (Caxton and Given Terr). Worth checking out are the stunning views from The Summit Restaurant at Mount Coot-tha (see page 262); or a leisurely lunch or dinner cruise on a paddle steamer (see page 264). And for something uniquely Brisbane try the famed Moreton Bay Bugs (a delicious and very weird looking crab).

Central Brisbane *p253, map p256*

Circa, 483 Adelaide St, T3832 4722. Tue-Fri for lunch, Mon-Sat for dinner. Regular award winner offering a classy and European influenced menu.

E'cco, 100 Boundary St, T3831 8344. Tue-Fri for lunch, Tue-Sat for dinner. Home of internationally-acclaimed chef, Philip Johnson. Other than the food itself another great attraction is the unpretentious nature of the place, the bustling atmosphere and the staff.

Il Centro, Eagle St Pier, T3221 6090. Sun-Fri for lunch, Thu-Sun for dinner. Large Italian restaurant well renowned for its riverside location and stunning sand crab lasagne.

Pier Nine, Eagle St Pier, T32262100. Daily from 1200. Another riverside, Brisbane institution renowned for quality seafood.

Brisbane suburbs *p254, map p256*

Anise, 697 Brunswick St, New Farm, T3358 1558. Tue-Sun for lunch, daily for dinner. Small and congenial wine bar/ restaurant with a French influenced menu, lengthy wine listand great foie gras.

Banyan Tree, 148 Merthyr Rd, New Farm, T3358 1202. Tue-Sun from 1800. Considered by many as the best Indian in town. It caters well for vegetarians.

Gambaro, 33 Caxton St, Petrie Terr, T3369 9500. Sun-Fri for lunch, Mon-Sat for dinner. An old favourite offering good seafood.

Indus, Shop 3, 147 Latrobe Terr, Paddington, T3369 9599. Mon-Sat. A friendly, good value, no-nonsense, curry house.

Isis Brasserie, 446 Brunswick St, south towards New Farm, T3852 1155. Tue-Fri for lunch, Tue-Sun for dinner. Causing something of a stir winning awards and maintaining a loyal following who swear by the class and quality of both environment and cuisine consistently created by its youthful owners.

The Summit Restaurant, Mount Coot-tha, T3369 9922. Daily for lunch/ dinner and on Sun for brunch. Further afield and well worth the trip is this Brisbane classic with its superb views across the city and Moreton Bay.

North Stradbroke Island *p255*

La Focaccia Italian, Meegera Pl, off Mooloomba/East Coast Rd, T3409 8778. Open from 0900. For congenial, al fresco dining.

Straddie Beach Hotel, overlooking Cylinder Beach, T3409 8188, www.stradbrokeislandbeachhotel.com.au. Daily for breakfast lunch and dinner from 0730. A popular spot for value pub meals and has a large outdoor deck space.

Entertainment

Brisbane *p252, map p256*

Fortitude Valley (alias 'The Valley') is the best place to check out the latest local rock bands, with its many pubs hosting bands from Thu-Sat. Although a far cry from the spectacle of Sydney's diverse and emancipated club scene, you can still have a mighty night out in Brizzie. Fortitude Valley, The Riverside Centre (Eagle St, City) and Petrie Terrace are the main club and dance venues. For up-to-date listings and entertainment news consult the *Courier Mail* on Wed and Sat or the free street press publications, *Rave*, *ShowBriz* www.showbriz.com.au, *Time Off* and *Scene*.

Bars

Breakfast Creek Hotel, 2 Kingsford Smith Dr, T3262 5988. Although a bit of a trek the 111-year-old enterprise is something of a Brisbane institution. It retains a distinct colonial/art deco feel, has a large Spanish beer garden and serves up the best steaks in town.

Downunder Bar, beneath **Palace Backpackers**, 308 Edward St, T3002 5740. Open nightly until 0300. Backpackers tend to focus (or start) here.

Hotel LA, on the corner of Petrie Terr and Caxton St, T3368 2560. Attracts the loud

Travellers' tales

Tree wishes

Queensland Art Gallery in Brisbane has created the novel idea of an interactive 'Wishing Tree': a large series of boughs on the wall, decorated with coloured leaves or pieces of paper on which visitors write their greatest wish. Clutching my unwritten 'leaf', I first read the various offerings. It makes fascinating reading. All human traits are described, both good and bad – humility, courage, sadness, greed, joy, shallowness and ignorance, but above all our indestructible sense of hope. Examples include: Johnny Depp; gravy on my chips; a sister; a Barbie scooter; to go on a holiday and never come back; a pet penguin; several puppies; a sister; to fly; a good night's sleep; my dad to come back from overseas; and lots of partners (!).

There are the usual wishes for peace, love and understanding, many depressingly selfish requests for new Gameboys, mobile phones and laptops, a tragic roll call of lonely souls looking for love and desperate pleas from those grieving lost loved ones. Finally, to remind us all that of one of our most important human virtues is a sense of humour, are the funny ones. From one child there's 'a new brother', from another 'that mummy would not shout at me in the mooseum' and from one character 'a pair of wholesome breasts'. Perhaps best of all, though, is the disconcertingly straightforward 'I wish Sophie would think about me for once'. So, suppressing a giggle, I quietly ponder my own offering. I decide to keep it realistic: that England retain the Ashes down under!

M Jones, Bath, UK.

and pretentious and if you can get past the over ambitious 'fashion police' on the door, it will accommodate you well into the wee small hours.

Orient Hotel, corner of Queen St and Ann St, T38394625. Thu-Sat nightly until 0300. For a traditional street corner Australian try this place. It's well known for its live rock music.

Paddo Tavern, 186 Given Terr, Paddington, T3369 0044. Vast place and firm suburban favourite, with a fine beer garden and a comedy club.

Pig 'n' Whistle, 123 Eagle St, T3832 9099. This spacious and trendy English-style bar cost $3 mn and nestles comfortably and proudly amidst the expensive Pier side restaurants.

Storey Bridge Hotel, 200 Main St, Kangaroo Point, T3391 2266, www.storeybridgehotel.com.au. In the shadow of its namesake edifice, this is a firm favourite at any time, but most famous for hosting the annual Australia Day 'cockroach races' and the Australian Festival of Beers in Sep.

The Victory, corner of Edward St and Charlotte St, T3221 0444. Also an old Brisbane favourite with local (free) live bands Thu-Sun and a good beer garden.

Live music

Brisbane Jazz Club, 1 Annie St, Kangaroo Point, T3391 2006. Has a loyal following with regulars playing on Sat-Sun, from 2030 (cover around $12).

The **Jazz and Blues Bar** on the Ground Floor of the Centra on Roma St, T3238 2222, and **Jazzy Cat**, 56 Mollison St, West End, Kangaroo Point, T3846 2544, www.jazzycat.com.au, are two other good venues.

Festivals and events

Brisbane *p252, map p256*

The year begins with a bang with the New Year celebrations and fireworks display over the river beside the South Bank parklands. This is repeated with even more zeal on **26 Jan**, **Australia Day**, with other hugely popular and bizarre events including the annual cockroach races and even a little 'frozen chicken bowling'. In late **March 2006** the South Bank hosts the **Festival of Ideas**, four days of lectures, various events and exhibitions based around the concepts of innovation and invention. Over **Easter** the **Brisbane to Gladstone Yacht Race** leaves Shorncliffe, while later in the month the **Valley Jazz Festival** will no doubt build on the success of 2005. **May** sees the **Queensland Racing Festival** and **Jun** the annual **Queensland Day** celebrations. Fortitude Valley's Chinatown and Brunswick St becomes the focus for the lively **Valley Festival** in **Jul**, with the **Brisbane International Film Festival** at the end of month. The beginning of **Sep** sees the start of the 2-week **River Festival** which celebrates the 'city's lifeblood' with food, fire and festivities, which is echoed in **Sep** with the **National Festival of Beers** (Australia's biggest) held at the Storey Bridge Hotel. **Livid Festival** in **Oct** is Brisbane's biggest live music event with numerous city venues hosting the best of local talent and visiting bands. An up-to-date events listing is available at www.brisbanetourism.com.au.

Shopping

Brisbane *p252, map p256*

Brisbane is without doubt the Queensland Capital for retail therapy with over 1,500 stores and 650 shops in and around Queens St alone. Three department stores, 5 shopping centres and a rash of malls and arcades all combine to provide a vast array of choice from fashion to furnishings. The city also hosts a few good markets including the **South Bank markets** on Fri night, Sat and Sun, the **Riverside and Eagle St Pier markets** on Sun and the 'Valley' markets (Brunswick St) on Sat. The new **James Market** in New Farm is excellent for fresh produce and deli products and is surrounded by good cafés.

Activities and tours

Brisbane *p252, map p256*

Bus tours

Numerous bus companies offer a wide range of day tours around the city and region from the Gold and Sunshine coasts to Fraser Island and the Southern Queensland national parks.

Mr Day Tours, T3269 3913, www.mrdaytours.com.au. Wide range of destinations and options but concentrating on smaller groups and a far more personalized service. Half to full-day from $79.

City tours

CitySights lasts 1½ hrs, from $20, child $15, T131230, and takes in a total of 19 stops in the inner city. Tours leave every 45 mins from Post Office Square, from 0900-1545. A great way to see the inner city and the views from Mount Coot-tha, with the added bonus of free bus and CityCat travel. Also **CityNights** tours.

River cruises

Kookaburra River Queen paddle steamers, T3221 1300, www.kookaburrariverqueens.com. A familiar sight on the river offering a range of sightseeing/dining options: 2-hr lunch daily, from $42; 3-hr dinner Mon-Sat 1900, Sun 1830, from $60.

Background

Roach runners

Twenty years ago (or so the story goes) two Brisbanites were sitting in a bar arguing about whose suburb had the biggest, fastest cockroaches. Unable to reach a settlement, the following day they captured their very best and raced them. And with that the annual 'Cockroach Races' were born (and who said Queenslanders are not as mad as cut snakes!). Now, every Australia Day (26 January), the Storey Bridge Hotel in Kangaroo Point hosts the infamous and truly unique cocky races. Of course, the races, along with many other events and live entertainment (much of it involving the removal of girls' blouses), is merely an excuse to get utterly inebriated. Picture the scene for a second... small grandstands surround a central ring, bursting with rowdy punters, many with faces painted in national colours and wearing flags (often as the only item of clothing). The race is called and from deep within the crowd comes the sound of badly played bagpipes, heralding the arrival of the loveable little competitors. The sea of spectators parts and the scene is set. On the count of three, the plastic container, which covers the eager cockies in the middle of the ring, is lifted and off they run – in all directions. The crowd goes wild. The more squeamish onlookers scream as the insects run under bags, shoes and into sandwiches. As soon as the winner is declared (if, indeed, it can ever be found) it's drinks all round – and again – and again, until no one can remember who won. To say it is an experience is an understatement and not to missed if your visit coincides with the event. Just don't plan on doing anything the following day, except that is maybe checking the contents of your shoes. Check out details at www.storeybridgehotel.com.au.

River City Cruises, T0428-278473, www.rivercitycruises.com. A 1½-hr cruise on board the *MV Neptune* daily at 1030, 1230, 1800, from $20. Departs from River Lookout Terminal, South Bank Jetty A.

Mirimar Boat Cruises, departs daily from North Quay at 1000, T3221 0300, from $45, child $15.50 (including admission, returns at 1445). Combines a cruise upriver with a visit to the Lone Pine Koala Sanctuary.

North Stradbroke Island *p255*

VIC has all details of activities and operators and can book on your behalf. **Beach Island Tours**, T3409 8098, and **Kingfisher Tours**, T3409 9502, www.straddiekingfishertours.com.au, both offer excellent and informative 4WD tours.

Stradbroke Island Scuba Centre (Backpackers), 1 East Coast Rd, Point Lookout, T3409 8888, www.stradbroke island scuba.com.au. Daily boat dives to try to track down manta ray, turtle and dolphin, from $95, snorkelling from $60 and a 4-dive 2-night accommodation package from $211.

Straddie Adventures, T3409 8414, www.straddieadventures.com.au. Offers an exciting range of backpacker based tours and activities, including sand boarding from $28, sea kayaking, surf lessons and snorkelling from $35, full-day 4WD tours from $55.

Moreton Island *p260*

Tangalooma Wild Dolphin Resort, www.tangalooma.com.au, offers full-day tour options (from $40), with dolphin feeding/watching from $90 (see Sights p260), an excellent range of island excursions and activities from sand boarding, snorkelling and diving to scenic helicopter flights. Daily whale-watching cruises are also available Jun-Oct, from $98, child $60. Their website has all the details and is a fine introduction to both the resort and the dolphin programme.

Transport

Brisbane *p252, map p256*

For all public transport enquiries, T131230, www.transinfo.qld.gov.au.

Air

Brisbane's international and domestic airports are 16/18 km northeast of the city centre. **Qantas**, T131313, **Jet Star**, T131538, www.jetstar.com.au, and **Virgin Blue**, T136789, www.virginblue.com.au, all fly regularly to all main centres and some regional destinations.

Bus

Local Central Bus Station is downstairs in the Myer Centre, Queen St. **City Circle** 333 (blue and white) service the city centre circuit, **Citybus** (white and yellow) service the suburbs and **Cityexpress** (blue and yellow stripes) offers half hourly express services within Greater Brisbane area, T131230, www.transinfo.qld.gov.au. Fares work on a zone system from $2, child $1. Ten Trip Ticket from $16, child $10. For attractive saver passes in conjunction with the CityCat, ask at a ticket office.

Long distance All interstate and local buses stop at the multi-level Roma St Transit Centre, Roma Street. Open 0530-2030. Most of the major bus companies have internal offices on Level 3 (Coach Deck) and there are also lockers, internet and a visitors information desk, T3229 5918. Various food outlets and showers are available on Level 2. **Greyhound**, T131499, www.grey hound.com.au, **Premier Motor Services**, T133410, www.premierms.com.au, all offer north/southbound interstate services.

Coachtrans, T32361000, www.coachtrans.com.au, offers 4 daily services to the **Gold Coast** (including the airport) and 'Unlimited Travel Passes' for city sights, airport and Gold Coast. **Crisps Coaches**, T4661 8333, offers south and westbound services from Brisbane to

Toowoomba/Tenterfield. Sun Air, T5478 2811, www.sunair.com.au. Sunshine Coast Sunbus, T5450 7888, www.sunbus.com.au, and **Suncoast Pacific**, T5443 1011, www.suncoast pacific.com.au (latter recommended for Noosa), offer regular daily services to the **Sunshine Coast**. Brisbane Bus Lines, T3355 0034, also services the **Sunshine Coast** and **South Burnett Region**.

CityCat and ferry

Brisbane's famous, sleek blue and white **CityCats** glide up and down the river from Bretts Wharf (Hamilton) in the east, to the University of Queensland (St Lucia) in the west, stopping at selected wharfs on both sides of the river, daily from 0530-2230. The round trip takes about 2 hrs. Fares start at $2. A Day Rover Ticket costs $8.40, child $4.20. Ten Trip Saver and Off-Peak Saver tickets also apply in conjunction with city bus services, ask at the ticket office. **City Ferry** operates an inner city and cross-river service (every 15-20 mins) at various points along the river. Fares are determined by the number of sectors crossed and start at $2. Pick up a copy of the *Brisbane River Experience Guide*, which highlights the main attractions and specialist tours on offer. For general enquiries, T131230, www.transinfo.qld.gov.au.

Cycling

Brisbane is very well geared up for cyclists with over 350 km of city cycleways. Most of these have been established around the edge of the CBD along the riverbank, providing an excellent way to take in the sights and to get from A to B. VICs can supply the free and comprehensive *Brisbane Bicycle Maps* booklet. Hire from **Valet Cycle Hire and Tours**, T3630 2775, info@cyclebrisbane.com.

Taxi

Black and White Cabs, T131008, or **Yellow Cabs**, T131924.

Train

Queensland Rail Travel Centre is located on the Ground Floor, Roma St Transit Centre, T32351331, for general enquiries T132232 (0600-2000). **Citytrain**, T3606 5555, www.city train.com.au, services greater Brisbane with networks to the Gold Coast. The main city stations are Central (top end of Edward St), Roma (Transit Centre), South Bank (South Brisbane) and Brunswick St (Fortitude Valley). Fares are based on a zone system and start at $1.90-7.20, 'One-Day Unlimited Pass', from $8.60. **Airtrain**, services the airport and Gold Coast from the city centre stations from $11/$20 one-way, T3216 3308, www.airtrain.com.au. Northbound services include the *Tilt Train* (www.tilttrain.com.au) – the express service between **Brisbane-Rockhampton** (6½ hrs) – which is recommended for those travelling to Noosa via Nambour or Hervey Bay via Maryborough (free bus connection). It departs Sun-Fri 1100 and 1700 (Rockhampton $98/ Bundaberg $63 single). *Sunlander* (**Brisbane-Cairns**) departs 4 times weekly from Brisbane – Mon and Fri to Cairns (at 1825) Queenslander Class from $724, and Tue and Sat (at 0855) to Townsville without Queenslander Class, economy from $196. *The Spirit of the Outback* travels from Brisbane to Rockhampton where it heads west to Longreach. Departs Tue and Sat from $170 (Tue 1825, Sat 1310).

North Stradbroke Island *p255*

The ferry terminal is at Toondah Harbour, Cleveland. From Brisbane take the **Citytrain** from the Roma St Transit Centre, where a **National Bus** (T3245 3333) provides pick-ups to the ferry terminal, T131230. **Stradbroke Ferries**, T3286 2666, operates a passenger (water taxi) every hour Mon-Fri 0600-1915, Sat 0700-1815, Sun 0800-1800, from $15, child $11 return. **Sea Stradbroke** runs a vehicle and passenger service from the same harbour roughly every hour, from $88 return (passenger $11, child $5.50 return, bikes

$4). The crossing for both services takes 30 mins. **North Stradbroke Flyer** (Gold Cats), T3286 1964, www.flyer.com.au, also offers a fast passenger service (end of Middle St), daily every half hour from 0530-1830, from $14 return. Their bus meets the Cleveland train.

Once on the island, **North Stradbroke Bus Services**, T3409 7151, meet every scheduled ferry arrival or departure and operate between Dunwich, One Mile, Amity and Point Lookout daily 0700-1900. The return fare Dunwich to Point Lookout is about $10. For a taxi, T131924.

Moreton Island *p260*

Moreton Island Ferries (miCat), T3909 3333, www.moretonventure.com.au, runs a vehicle and passenger service from Howard Smith Drive, Brisbane (refer to website for detailed directions) to Tangalooma Wrecks (1 km from the resort). Depart Mon-Sun 0830, returning at 1530 with additional sailings Fri 1830, Sun 1430 (and on public holidays), from $135 return (with 4WD and 2 adults) and from $25 return for passengers, bikes $15.

The crossing takes 30 mins. The Vehicle/passenger barge **Combie Trader**, T3203 6399, www.moreton-island.com.au, sails to Moreton Island regularly from **Scarborough** (Redcliffe) to **Bulwer** on the island's northwest coast, from around $155 return (passenger $35 return).

There are no sealed roads on Moreton and independent access is by 4WD only ($33 fee for 1 month). **Moreton Island Ferries (miCat)** operate a minibus around the island as a day-trip package only, from $103, child $91. For those without a 4WD vehicle the best way to reach the island is through the **Tangalooma Resort**, which offers accommodation, day trips, tours and independent transfers, T1300-652250, www.tangalooma.com.au. Their launch leaves from the terminal on the northern bank of the Brisbane River, at the end of Holt St, and departs Sun-Fri 0930, from $40, child $25 (75 mins). A courtesy coach operates Roma St Transit Centre and most CBD hotels, at 0900, from $5, T1300-652250.

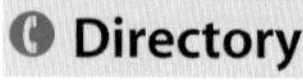

Directory

Brisbane *p252, map p256*

Banks All major bank branches with ATMs are found in the city centre, especially in the Queen St, Edward St and Eagle St malls. Foreign exchange also from **Travelex**, Bowman House, 276 Edward St, T32219422; Shop 149F Queen St Mall, T3210 6325. **American Express**, 344 Queen St, T3220 0878.
Hospital Mater Hospital (24 hr), Raymond Terrace, Woolloongabba, T3840 8111. **Roma St Medical Centre**, Transit Centre, T3236 2988. **Travellers Medical Service**, Level 5, 247 Adelaide St, T3221 9066.
Internet International Youth Service Centre, 2/69 Adelaide St, T3229 9985, daily 0800-2400; **Cyber Room**, Level 1, 25 Adelaide St, T3012 9331, or the **State Library**, South Bank, T3840 7666, 30-min free, book a day in advance, Mon-Thu 1000-2000, Fri-Sun 1000-1700.
Pharmacy Day and Night, 245 Albert St, T3221 8155. **Post** The central post office is at 261 Queen St, opposite Post Office Sq. Open Mon-Fri 0830-1730. Post Restante Mon-Fri 0900-1700.
Useful numbers **Police**, corner of Queen St and Albert St and opposite the Roma St Transit Centre, 200 Roma St, T3364 6464. **Emergency** T000. **RACQ**, 261 Queen St, T3872 8465.

North Stradbroke Island *p255*

Banks The post offices in Dunwich, Amity and Point Lookout all act as Commonwealth Bank agents. Eftpos is available in shops and resorts. There is an ATM at the **Stradbroke Island Beach Hotel**, Point Lookout. **Internet** Stradbroke Island Guesthouse, 1 East Coast Rd, Point Lookout, T3409 8888. **Post** Dunwich, Point Lookout (Megerra Pl). **Useful numbers** **Medical**, T3409 9059. **Police**, T3409 9020.

Sunshine and Fraser Coasts

Just an hour north of Brisbane, the spellbinding volcanic peaks known as the Glass House Mountains herald your arrival at the aptly named Sunshine Coast. For those who can drag themselves away from the coast, the hinterland promises a wealth of more unusual attractions, while north of Noosa the coastal strip gives way to the Great Sandy Region, the largest coastal sand mass in the world, with Fraser Island, the largest coastal sand island in the world.

Getting there Regional buses; ferries to Fraser Island.
Getting around Local bus network or hire car/campervan.
Time required 5-6 days
Weather Hot, often humid in summer; mild to warm in winter.
Sleeping Hostels, motor camps, campsites and resorts.
Eating Good range in Noosa.
Activities and tours 4WD safaris, whale watching.
★ **Don't miss** Swimming in Lake McKenzie. » *p278*.

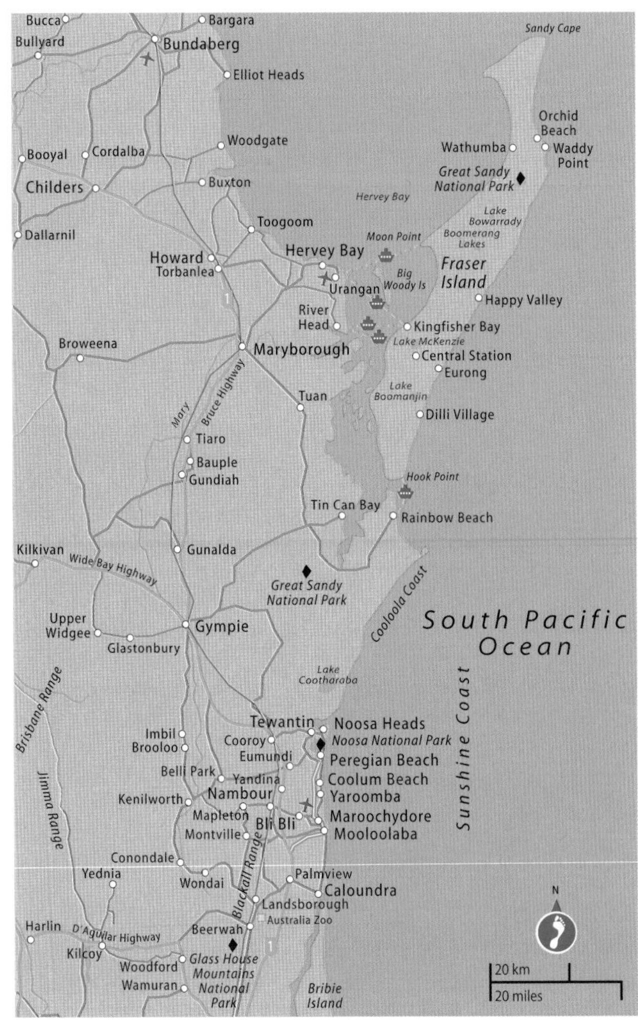

Noosa » pp279-291.

To some the former surfing backwater of Noosa is now little more than an upmarket suburb of Brisbane. However, it does have one of the finest surf beaches in Queensland, a climate that is 'beautiful one day perfect the next' and is fringed with two magnificent unspoilt national parks. In the last three decades, the string of coastal communities known loosely as 'Noosa' has rapidly metamorphosised into one of the most desirable holiday resorts and residential areas on the entire east coast with a corresponding population growth rate. If you can turn a blind eye to the pretentiousness of the place, it makes it a worthwhile stop on your way north.

Sights

Noosa Heads is the main focus of activity with the main surf beach at **Laguna Bay** and the chic tourist shops, accommodation and restaurants along Hastings Street. To the south is **Noosa Junction**, with Sunshine Beach Road providing the main commercial shopping area. From **Noosa VIC** ⓘ *Hastings St, Noosa Heads, T5447 4988, www.tourismnoosa.com.au, 0900-1700*, get hold of the free *Noosa Guide* with a detailed road and locality maps.

To the west of Noosa Heads is the pretty 454-ha **Noosa National Park** which offers an escape from all the sand and surf as well as some fine walks. The most popular of these is the 2.7-km **Coastal Track** which starts beside the information office at the end of Park Road (T5447 3243) and takes in a number of idyllic bays and headlands, before delivering you at **Alexandria Bay**. From there you can return the way you came, explore the interior of the park, continue south to the very plush northern suburbs of **Sunshine Beach**, or simply spend the day on the beach in relative isolation. Bear in mind that all the beaches that fringe the national park are unpatrolled and swimming is not recommended. The Noosa River runs both west and south from Noosa Heads in a tangled mass of tributaries to join **Lake Weyba** (south) and **Lakes Cooroibah and Cootharaba** (west and north). **Gympie Terrace**, in Noosaville, runs along the southern bank of the river and is the focus for most river and lake based activities.

(Left) The Big Pineapple, Nambour; (Right) Batik sarongs add colour to the Eumundi Markets, near Noosa

Sunshine Coast hinterland » pp279-291.

With a name like 'Sunshine Coast' it is hardly surprising that the vast majority of travellers head straight for the beach. But though the swathes of golden sand will not disappoint, if you allow some time to explore the hinterland you will find colourful markets, quaint villages, giant 'walk-in' fruits, and perhaps the greatest oddity of them all – television's infamous Crocodile Hunter. This area is best visited on a tour from Brisbane or Noosa (see pages 264 and 285) or in your own vehicle. The **Noosa VIC** (T5447 4988) can provide information on the major attractions, along with accommodation listings and location maps.

Eumundi

The historic 19th-century former timber town of Eumundi, 1 km off the Bruce Highway and 23 km west of Noosa, is pretty enough in its own right, but timing your visit to coincide with the town's famous markets is highly recommended. Every Saturday and, to a lesser extent, Wednesday morning, Eumundi becomes a creative extravaganza of over 300 fascinating arts, crafts and produce stalls, all offering excellent quality, as well as lots of atmosphere and colour. Everything, it seems, is on offer, from kites and bandanas to neck massages and boomerangs. The markets kick off at about 0700 and start winding up about 1500. The best time to go early is on Saturday early before the day heats up and the tourist buses arrive. It can get busy and a little stressful. There are plenty of small food outlets and established cafés on hand for coffee and breakfast or brunch.

Blackall Range Tourist Drive

Blackall Range Tourist Drive, which runs from **Nambour**, a busy agricultural service centre, to the Glass House Mountains, is highly recommended, offering everything from national parks with waterfalls and short rainforest walks to fine coastal views and cosy B&Bs. Pineapples are big business round here, and none more so than the **Big Pineapple Complex** ⓘ *T5442 1333, www.bigpineapple.com.au, 0900-1700, free*, 10 km south of Nambour, and 1 km west of the Bruce Highway. This 15-m high 'Big Pineapple', which, inexplicably, attracts visitors as nectar does bees, is just one of Australia's 33-strong inventory of 'big man-made monoliths' from koalas to bananas. As well as the obligatory photographs, you can take a tour of the pineapple plantation on a miniature train

Back on the Nambour-Mapleton Road, you begin the ascent up the Blackall Range to reach the pleasant little town of **Mapleton**. As well as its own great views and attractive B&Bs, Mapleton is the gateway to **Mapleton Falls National Park**. The heady views of the 120-m falls can be accessed 17 km west on Obi Obi Road. Nearby, the 1.3-km Wompoo Circuit walk winds through rainforest and eucalypts providing excellent views of the Obi Obi Valley. Obi Obi was a noted Aboriginal warrior and wompoo refers to a beautiful native pigeon.

From Mapleton the road heads south along the range through **Flaxton village** and the **Kondalilla National Park**. This 327-ha park is accessed and signposted 1 km south of Flaxton and offers views of the 90-m Kondalilla Falls, from the 2.1-km Picnic Creek trail and the 2.7-km Kondalilla Falls circuit, which winds its way down through rainforest to the base of the falls. Neither of the parks offers camping facilities.

First settled by fruit growers in 1887, historic **Montville**, 5 km south of Flaxton, is the main tourist hub along the Blackall Range. With its European-style historic buildings, chic cafés, galleries and souvenir shops, it provides a pleasant stop for lunch or a stroll. Nearby, Lake Baroon also offers a pleasant spot for a picnic. Although undoubtedly very touristy, Montville has not yet been spoiled and remains a delightfully quaint contrast to the coast. From Montville the road continues south taking in the **Gerrard** and **Balmoral Lookouts**. Both offer memorable coastal views from Noosa Heads in the north to Caloundra and Bribie Island in the south.

The distinctively shaped peaks of the Glasshouse Mountains

Turning inland you then arrive at the equally pretty town of **Maleny** which, like Montville, offers many interesting arts and crafts galleries, good B&Bs and a winery. At the far end of the town turn left down the narrow Maleny-Stanley Road to access Mountain View Road (left). Heading back towards the coast you are then almost immediately offered the first stunning views of the Glass House Mountains to the south from **McCarthy's Lookout**. A few kilometres further on is the 41-ha **Mary Cairncross Scenic Reserve**, named after the 19th-century environmentalist Mary Cairncross. Here you can admire the views, visit the environmental centre (T5499 9907), or take a stroll through the rainforest (1.7 km). From the Cairncross Reserve, the road descends towards **Landsborough**, which is the northern gateway to the Glass House Mountains.

Glass House Mountains National Park

The Glass House Mountains are indeed a wonderful sight but they do nothing for safe driving. These 13 volcanic peaks that dominate the skyline from all directions are utterly absorbing and will, if you are not careful, have you swerving off the road. Gradual weathering by wind and water over the last 20 million years created their distinctive shapes and earned them their unusual name from Captain Cook, who thought they resembled the glass furnaces in his native Yorkshire. The highest peak is **Mount Beerwah** (556 m), while everybody's favourite has to be the distinctly knobbly **Mount Coonowrin** (377 m). Although the best views are actually from Old Gympie Road – which runs north to south, just west of Landsborough, Beerwah and Glass House Mountains Village – there is an official lookout on the southern edge of the park, 3 km west off Old Gympie Road. When it comes to bush walking and summit climbing, **Mount Ngungun** (253 m) is the most accessible (Fullertons Road of Old Gympie or Coonowrin Roads) while **Mount Tibrogargan** (364 m) and Mount Beerwah also offer base viewpoints and two to three rough summit tracks. Sadly, pointy Mount Coonowrin is closed to public access due to the danger of rock falls. There is no camping allowed in the park, though several companies offer walking and climbing adventures (see Activities and tours on page 285).

Australia Zoo

ⓘ *Glass House Mountains Rd, Beerwah, T5436 2000, www.crocodilehunter.com.au, 0830-1600, $34, child $24.*

Of all Queensland's many wildlife attractions, it is the Australia Zoo that seems to arouse people's enthusiasm the most. The reason for this is the hype and exposure of the famous (or infamous) Crocodile Hunter (alias Steve Irwin), and his wife, Terri, to whom the zoo is official home-base. Founded by Steve's father, the collection is now – thanks to his son's antics – developing faster than a crocodile can clamp its jaws around a dead chicken. The zoo houses a wide array of well-maintained displays exhibiting over 550 native and non native species, ranging from mean-looking wedge-tailed eagles and insomniac wombats to enormous 20-ft pythons and senescent Galápagos tortoises. Of course, the biggest attractions are the numerous crocodiles, or more precisely, the croc feeding, enthusiastically demonstrated daily at 1330. Many visitors come to the zoo, despite the exorbitant entrance fees, to see Steve himself, in the hope of witnessing first hand his fearless (or downright reckless, depending on your viewpoint) style of feeding the mighty reptiles. However, Steve is rarely there and the job is most often left to his able staff. This is now particularly the case since the nasty 'baby in the enclosure incident' in 2004, when Steve took his infant son into the enclosure and, while holding him in one arm, fed a croc with the other. Not surprisingly, it caused international outrage and created a public relations nightmare that may haunt the couple for ever. Stupid antics aside, the park is magnificent and the animals are well looked after. What lets the place down is the sheer megalomania so apparent in the shop with its talking 'Steve' and 'Terri' dolls and personal clothing lines (which even include a special kids line after Bindi, their infant daughter). Truly nauseating. Free transportation is available daily from Noosa, Maroochy, Mooloolaba and Caloundra. Phone for details.

Cooloola Coast »» *pp279-291.*

With access limited to 4WD only from Noosa from the south and a 76-km diversion from Gympie on the Bruce Highway from the north, the mainland – Cooloola Coast – section of the Great Sandy National Park and its delightful, neighbouring coastal communities of Rainbow Beach and Tin Can Bay, are all too often missed by travellers in their eagerness to reach Hervey Bay and Fraser Island. As well as the numerous and varied attractions and activities on offer within the 56,000-ha park – including huge sand blows, ancient coloured sands and weathered wrecks – Tin Can Bay offers an opportunity to feed wild dolphins and Rainbow Beach is an ideal rest stop off the beaten track, as well as providing southerly access to Fraser Island.

Ins and outs

Cooloola VIC ⓘ *Bruce Highway, Kybong (15 km south of Gympie), T5483 5554, www.cooloola.org.au, 0900-1700.* Also in Tin Can Bay ⓘ *T5486 4855, www.tincanbaytourism.org.au.* QPWS ⓘ *Rainbow Beach Rd, T5486 3160, www.epa.qld.gov.au, 0700- 1600,* has detailed information on the Great Sandy National Park (including Fraser Island) and issue camping/RAM Fraser Island permits. »» *p290.*

Great Sandy National Park

Along with Fraser Island, Great Sandy National Park forms the largest sand mass in the world. For millennia, sediments washed out from the river courses of the NSW coast have been steadily carried north and deposited in vast quantities. Over time the virtual desert has been colonized by vegetation that now forms vast tracts of mangrove and rainforest, which in turn provides a varied habitat for a rich variety of wildlife.

The most notable feature of the park is the magnificent multi-coloured sands that extend from Rainbow Beach to Double Island Point. Over 200 m high in places and eroded into ramparts of pillars and groves, with a palette of over 40 colours, from blood red to brilliant white, they glow in the rays of the rising sun. Carbon dating of the sands has revealed some deposits to be over 40,000 years old. It is little wonder that they are steeped in Aboriginal legend. According to the Kabi tribe, who frequented the area long before the Europeans, the mighty sands were formed and coloured by the Rainbow Spirit who was killed in his efforts to save a beautiful maiden. Other features of the park include the Carlo Sand Blow, just south of Rainbow Beach, a favourite haunt for hang gliders, and the wreck of the cargo ship Cherry Venture which ran aground in 1973. The views from the lighthouse on Double Island – which is actually a headland, falsely named by Captain Cook in 1770 – will also prove memorable. All the features of the park can be explored by a network of 4WD and walking trails. At the southern end of the park (accessed from Noosa), the lakes Cootharaba and Cooroibah are popular for boating and canoeing.

Rainbow Beach and Tin Can Bay

Located at the northern edge of the park, the laid-back, yet fast developing, seaside village of Rainbow Beach provides an ideal base from which to explore the park and as a stepping-stone to Fraser Island. Inskip Point, 14 km north, serves as the southerly access point to the great island paradise. Tin Can Bay, west of Rainbow Beach on the banks of the Tin Can Bay Inlet, is a popular base for fishing and boating but by far its biggest attraction is the visiting wild dolphin called 'Mystique' who appears, religiously, for a free handout, usually early each morning around the Northern Point boat ramp.

Hervey Bay » *pp279-291.*

The sprawling seaside town of Hervey Bay, the main gateway to Fraser Island, may lack 'kerb appeal', but more than makes up for this in the huge numbers of visitors who flood in to experience two mighty big attractions – Fraser Island and the migrating whales that use the sheltered waters of the bay as a temporary stopover. Considered by many to be the whale-watching capital of the world, Hervey Bay tries hard to stand on its own as a coastal resort and retirement destination, but, despite its low-key attractions, activities and ubiquitous sweep of golden sand, it fails. The concerted attempts to keep people on the mainland for anything more than a day or a night seem futile and, as a result, it has become one of Queensland's most depressing tourist transit centres.

Ins and outs

For objective information (rare in these parts) visit the accredited **Maryborough Fraser Island VIC** ⓘ *BP South Tourist Complex, Bruce Highway, T4121 4111, www.maryborough.qld.gov.au, or www.frasercoast. org.au, Mon-Fri 0830-1700, Sat-Sun 1000-1600*. There is also an accredited centre 1 km before Hervey Bay (signposted) ⓘ *Maryborough/Hervey Bay Rd, T4125 9855, www.herveybaytourism.com.au.* » *p290.*

Sights

Hervey Bay is essentially a beachfront conglomerate of north facing suburbs, from Point Vernon in the east, through Urungan, Torquay, Scarness and Pialba in the west. Almost all major amenities are to be found along the Esplanade from the junction with Main Street in Pialba to Elizabeth Street, Urungan. The main Fraser Island ferry and whale-watching terminal is just south of Dayman Point in Urungan. The Esplanade has a footpath and cycle track, which offers a convenient way to soak up the seaside atmosphere.

In line with the area's obvious eco-theme is **Neptune's Reefworld** ⓘ *on the corner of Pulgul St and Kent St, Urungan, T4128 9828, from 0915, from $14, child $8 (shark feed 1400, swim with the sharks from $50, free pick ups*, where coral displays provide the decoration and turtles and reef sharks the interaction. The 1.5-km long **Urungan Pier** offers a pleasant breezy stroll and good fishing. Keep your eyes open for the aptly named soldier crabs on the beach at low tide. At the other end of the Esplanade (west) and still on the theme of sea creatures, it is well worth taking a look at the **Sea Shell Museum and gift shop** ⓘ *332 Esplanade, T4124 7229, www.seashellmuseum.com.au, 0900-1700, $4*. Even if you do not go into the museum itself, the range and beauty of the shells in the rather kitschy shop will have you fossicking on the seashore for hours.

Fraser Island » *pp279-291.*

Jutting out from the eastern Australian coast is the astounding 162,900-ha land mass known as Fraser Island – the biggest sand island in the world. Part of the Great Sandy National Park, which extends across to the mainland to the south, Fraser is now fully protected and was afforded World Heritage status in 1992. It is, without a doubt, a very special place; a dynamic 800,000-year-old quirk of nature blessed with stunning beauty and a rich biodiversity. For the vast majority of visitors, the island may come as something of a surprise. Beyond a few sand blows and long, seemingly endless, stretches of beach, this is no Sahara. Blanketed in thick rainforest, pockmarked with numerous freshwater lakes and veined by numerous small streams, it surely confounds the preconceived notions of even the most experienced environmentalist. As well as its stunning beauty, its sheer scale and rich wildlife, Fraser presents a great opportunity to try your hand at four-wheel driving and also plays host to one of the best resorts in the country. And despite the fact the island attracts over 300,000 visitors annually, it is still possible – only just – to find a little peace and solitude.

Ins and outs

Getting there Vehicular access is from Hervey Bay (Urungan) to Moon Point and Kingfisher Bay, River Head (20 minutes south of Hervey Bay) to Kingfisher Bay and Wanggoolba Creek and from Rainbow Beach to Hook Point which is the southernmost tip of the Island. » *p290.*

The cool, crystal-clear waters of Lake Mackenzie in the heart of Fraser Island

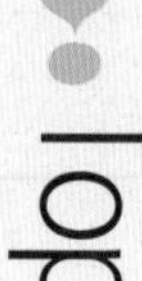

Top tips

Four-wheel driving on Fraser Island

Fraser Island has virtually no sealed roads and its single-lane tracks are 4WD only. This makes it one of the best 4WD venues in Australia. Although for the layman the tracks take some getting use to, and are rough and soft in some places, access around the island is generally good, if slow. On average it takes about 30 minutes to travel 10 km on inland roads where a 35 kmph speed limit is in force. Strict guidelines have been put in place for 4WD on the island and these should be adhered to at all times.

- East Beach is, essentially, a 90-km sand highway with a speed limit of 80 kmph but extreme care must be taken at all times, esecially at high tide, in soft sand and crossing creeks. Avoid the temptation to let rip as this has resulted in some nasty accidents. Also apply standard road rules when meeting on-coming traffic.
- Optimum driving conditions are 2 hrs either side of low tide. You are also advised to release some air from your tyres in soft sand conditions.
- All vehicles on the island require a RAM 4WD permit to be displayed on the windscreen. They can be obtained prior to arrival for $33 from the mainland QPWS offices, Hervey Bay City Council, 77 Tavistock St, T4125 0222, Hervey Bay Marina Kiosk, Boat Harbour, Urungan, T4128 9800, or River Heads Kiosk-Barge Car Park, Ariadne St, T4125 8473. On the island permits cost $42 and can be purchased from QPWS Eurong Office. An information pack containing a detailed colour guide, camping and walking track details is supplied with the permit.
- If you breakdown there are mechanical workshops at Eurong, T4127 9173, and Orchid Beach, T4127 9220. For tow truck, T4127 9167, and be prepared to wave the contents of your bank account bye bye.
- There are plenty of operators hiring 4WD, but generally hire does not include fuel, ferry, food or accommodation/camping permits, nor does it include the cost of camping gear, which is also an additional extra. The more professional companies will also give you a thorough briefing and maps. See Activities and tours, page 288, for companies offering tours.
- To hire a 4WD you must at least 21, hold a current drivers licence and provide a $500 bond or credit card imprint and a permit.

Getting around By far the best way to experience Fraser Island is to stay for at least three days and hire your own 4WD. Other than the freedom, this allows an ideal opportunity to get a feel of what an expensive 4WD is all about. Having said that, walking is hard to beat – to experience the sights, sounds and smells that would otherwise be missed. A vital piece of kit is the 1: 130,000 Fraser Island Tourist Map ($10) supplied by the resorts.

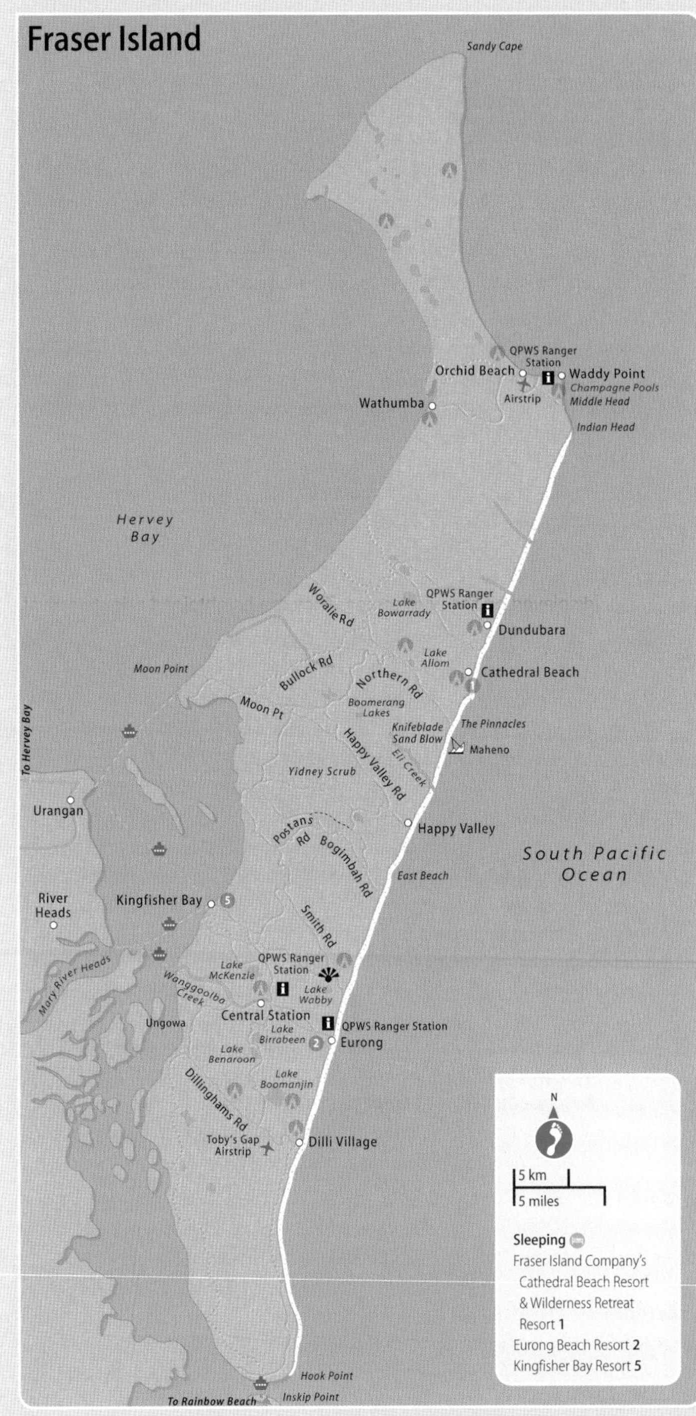
Fraser Island
Sandy Cape
QPWS Ranger Station
Orchid Beach
Waddy Point
Champagne Pools
Middle Head
Airstrip
Wathumba
Indian Head
Hervey Bay
Woralie Rd
Lake Bowarrady
QPWS Ranger Station
Dundubara
Lake Allom
Cathedral Beach
Moon Point
Bullock Rd
Northern Rd
Moon Pt
Boomerang Lakes
Knifeblade Sand Blow
The Pinnacles
Maheno
To Hervey Bay
Happy Valley Rd
Eli Creek
Yidney Scrub
Urangan
Postans Rd
Happy Valley
Bogimbah Rd
South Pacific Ocean
East Beach
River Heads
Kingfisher Bay
Smith Rd
Mary River Heads
Lake McKenzie
QPWS Ranger Station
Wanggoolba Creek
Lake Wabby
Central Station
Ungowa
QPWS Ranger Station
Lake Birrabeen
Eurong
Lake Benaroon
Lake Boomanjin
Dillinghams Rd
Toby's Gap Airstrip
Dilli Village
N
5 km
5 miles
Sleeping
Fraser Island Company's Cathedral Beach Resort & Wilderness Retreat Resort 1
Eurong Beach Resort 2
Kingfisher Bay Resort 5
Hook Point
To Rainbow Beach
Inskip Point

 Tourist information VICs and QPWS offices on the mainland can provide most of the necessary information. On the island there are QPWS ranger stations at Eurong (T4127 9128), Central Station (T4127 9191), Dundubara (T4127 9138) and Waddy Point (T4127 9190), all have variable opening times, call ahead. The resorts, especially Kingfisher Bay, are also a valuable source of information.

East Beach Highway (Eurong to Orchid Beach)

Fringed by pounding surf on one side and bush on the other, barrelling up and down the 92-km natural highway of East Beach is an exhilarating experience in itself. The main access point for those arriving on the west coast is Eurong, where you can fuel up and head north for as far as the eye can see. Of course you will not be alone and at times the beach looks like a 4WD version of a 'bikers meet' on their way to a rock'n'roll gig.

There are a number of sights as you head north, the first of which is **Lake Wabby** – 4 km north of Eurong. Reached, by foot – 4 km return on soft sand – Lake Wabby is one island lake that is at war with an encroaching sand blow creating a bizarre landscape and the potential for lots of fun partaking in sand surfing and swimming. For a really stunning elevated view of the scene you can head inland for 7 km, on Cornwells Road, 2 km north of the beach car park. This in itself will test your 4WD skills. A walking track (5-km return) connects the lookout car park with the lake.

Next stop is **Eli Creek** which offers a cool dip in crystal clear waters. Some 3 km beyond Eli Creek the rusting hulk of the *Maheno* – a trans-Tasman passenger liner that came to grief in 1935 – provides an interesting stop and a welcome landmark along the seemingly endless sandy highway. A further 2 km brings you to the unusual **Pinnacles** formation, an eroded bank of sand of varying gold and orange hues that look like some bizarre sci-fi film set. Just south of the Pinnacles, the 43-km Northern Road circuit ventures through ancient rainforest known as **Yidney Scrub** taking in views of the huge **Knifeblade Sand Blow**, the pretty, small **Lake Allom** and **Boomerang Lakes**, which, at 130 m above sea level, are the highest dune lakes in the world.

Back on East Beach, the colourful sandbanks continue to the **Cathedral Beach Resort** and the **Dundubara campsite** offering the fit and adventurous walker the chance to explore the turtle-infested **Lake Bowarrady** (16 km return). From Dundubara it is another 19 km to **Indian Head**. One of the very few genuine rocks on the island, the heads offers a fine vantage point from which to view the odd shark and manta ray in the azure waters below (demonstrating why swimming in the sea is ill advised around Fraser). Just beyond Indian Head, at the start of Middle Head, the track turns inland providing access to **Orchid Beach** and **Champagne Pools**. Named for their clarity and wave action, they provide a perfect saltwater pool for swimming amongst brightly coloured tropical fish. Beyond the settlement of Orchid Beach and Waddy Point, 4WD becomes more difficult with most hire companies banning further exploration north. But if you have your own vehicle, and enough experience, the northern peninsula can offer some welcome solitude and fine fishing spots all the way up to **Sandy Cape**, 31 km away.

The lakes

There are over 100 freshwater lakes on Fraser, forming part of a vast and complex natural water storage system. Surprisingly for a sand island, there is 20 times more water stored naturally here than is held back by the Wivenhoe Dam (which supplies the whole of Brisbane). The most popular and visually stunning lakes are scattered around the island's southern part. By far the most beautiful and frequented is **Lake McKenzie**, which can be accessed north of Central Station or via the Cornwells and Bennet roads from East Beach. With its white silica sands and crystal clear waters, it is quite simply foolish not to visit. Make sure to go either early in the day or late, to avoid the crowds. Also take sunglasses, sunscreen and insect repellent.

Further south, lakes **Birrabeen** and **Benaroon** offer fine swimming and are quieter than McKenzie but do not share quite the same beauty. Further south still is **Lake Boomanjin**, the largest 'perched' lake in the world, which means it ranks high on the humus podsol B Horizon with a large pH – it's very brown, in other words.

Central Station

For those arriving on the west coast, Central Station provides the first glimpse of just how wooded Fraser Island really is. Shaded by towering bunya pine, satinay and thick with umbrella-like palms, this green heart of Fraser has its own unique biodiversity. In the 50-m canopies many of the island's 240 recorded species of birds reside, from brightly coloured lorikeets and honeyeaters to tiny fairy wrens. On the ground echidna and dingoes roam and beneath it there are earthworms as long as your arm! One of the most pleasant features of Central Station are the crystal clear waters and white sandy bed of **Wanggoolba Creek** which is the main feature on the 450-m boardwalk. Central Station also serves as the departure point for some excellent walking tracks to Lake McKenzie and the Pile Valley where you will find yourself gazing heavenwards wondering if the trees could possibly grow any taller.

Sleeping

Noosa *p270, map p280*

Noosa is very much like a mini Gold Coast without the high-rises, yet with the same massive range of 4-star resort complexes, self-contained holiday apartments and backpacker options. Here we simply skim the surface. If you have a specific idea about what you want there are various agencies who can oblige including: Accommodation Noosa, T1800-072078, www.accomnoosa.com.au; Noosa Holidays, T5447 3811, www.noosare.com.au; and Peter Dowling, T5447 3566, www.peterdowlingnoosa.com.au. For something a little different, try out a houseboat, www.luxuryafloat noosa.com.au/.

A **Eumarella Shores**, 251 Eumarella Rd, T5449 1738, www.eumarella shores.com.au. Next to Lake Weyba. Offers something far removed from the resorts and tourist hype. Fully self-contained colonial and log cabin style cottages sleeping 2-6 in a bush setting overlooking the lake.

A-C **Colonial Resort Noosa**, 239-245 Gympie Terr, Noosaville, T5455 8100, www.colonial resortnoosa.com.au. In the heart of Noosaville and overlooking the river. Stylish fully self-contained rooms with decks, spa and all the usual facilities such as heated pool and secure parking.

D-E **Halse Lodge YHA**, Halse Lane, Noosa Heads, T5447 3377, www.halselodge.com.au. At the other end of the scale is this spacious lodge which is only a short walk from the long-distance bus stop. It is a historic 1880s Queenslander offering a good range of rooms from 6/4 dorms to doubles, twins and triple, all with shared bathrooms, bistro/bar, large quiet deck and social areas, good tour and activities desk, surf/body board hire.

C-E **Koala Beach Resort**, 44 Noosa Dr, just over the hill near Noosa Junction, Noosa Heads, T5447 3355, www.koalaresort.com.au. Offers fairly tired motel-style en suite dorms and doubles. It does however have its finger on the pulse and is considered the liveliest and most social of the backpackers, with a popular bar/bistro, pool and internet.

C-E **Noosa Backpackers Resort**, 9-13 William St, Noosaville, T5549 8151. This is the main backpacker option west of Noosa Heads. It offers tidy 4 bed dorms, en suite doubles, pool, cheap meals, cable TV and internet.

C-F **Gagaju**, Boreen Point, T5474 3522, www.travoholic.com/gagaju/. Characterful eco-backpackers-cum-bush camp, located between Lakes Cooroibah and Cootharaba, on the Noosa River. Everything is built from recycled timber with dorms, doubles and powered/non-powered, shaded campsites (campfires allowed), full kitchen facilities, TV lounge room and excellent in-house half, 1 and 3-day canoe trips on the river. Pick-ups are offered from Noosa Heads.

E-F Noosa River Caravan Park, Russell St, Noosaville, T5449 7050. This is the best motor park/camping option in the area. Hugely popular given its riverside location and views but sadly becoming the preserve of 4WD fashionistas, which reflects the rapid influx of wealth and snobbery in the area. Powered and non-powered sites, modern amenities and BBQ. Book at least 2 days in advance.

Sunshine Coast Hinterland *p271*

L-A Eyrie Escape B&B, 316 Brandenburg Rd, Bald Knob, Mooloolah, T5494 8242, www. eyrie-escape.com.au. A 'spa with a view' at this incredible and aptly named option.

C Montville Mountain Inn, Main St, Montville, T5442 9499, www.montvilleinn.com.au. Central and affordable option.

Cooloola Coast *p273*

B-E Rainbow Waters Holiday Park, Carlo Rd, Rainbow Beach, T5486 3200. A 3-star motor park set in 23 acres of parkland next to the water, with

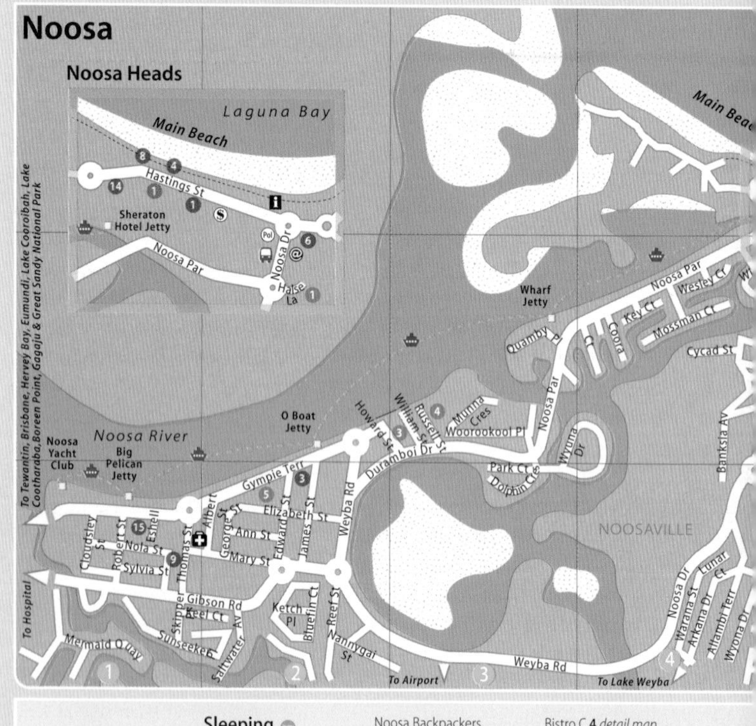

Sleeping
Colonial Resort Noosa **5** *C2*
Halse Lodge YHA **1** *detail map*
Koala Beach Resort **2** *B5*
Noosa Backpackers Resort **3** *B3*
Noosa River Caravan Park **4** *B3*

Eating
Aromas **1** *detail map*
Bistro C **4** *detail map*
Café Le Monde **6** *detail map*
Gusto Riverfront **3** *C2*
Lazuli Blue Café **7** *B5*
Lindoni's **8** *detail map*
Magic of India **9** *C1*

self-contained cabins, powered and non-powered sites, kiosk but no camp kitchen.

C-E **Dingo Backpackers**, Spectrum St, Rainbow Beach, T1800-111126, www.dingosatrainbow.com. The newest of the two backpackers in town is this modern, purpose-built option that offers en suite singles, doubles, dorms, bar/restaurant, pool and internet. Despite its location it is a busy place with an excited atmosphere (at the prospect of visiting Fraser). Book ahead.

E **Rainbow Beach YHA**, 18 Spectrum Ave, Rainbow Beach, T5486 8885, www.frasersonrainbow.com. Just down the road from Dingo Backpackers is the other backpackers, which is older but comfortable, with motel-style dorms,

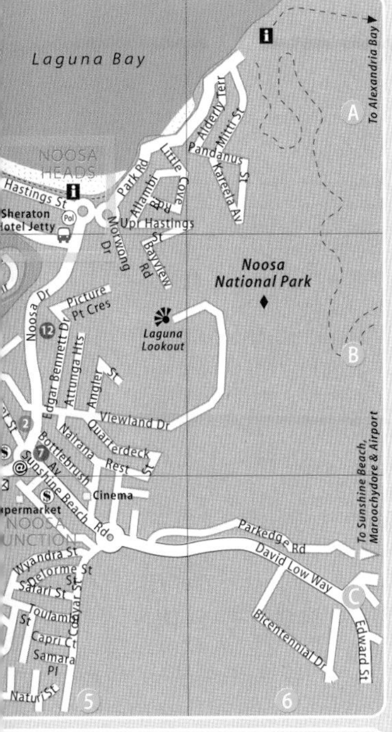

Noosa Reef Hotel **12** *B5*
Sierra Café **14** *detail map*
Thai Breakers **15** *C1*

Bars & clubs
Rolling Rock **1** *detail map*

doubles and twins, all with en suite. Facilities include internet, pool, a large well equipped kitchen and a bar. There are also budget meals on offer and plenty of assistance with organizing a trip to Fraser or onward travel via the Cooloola beaches to Noosa.

QPWS campsites can be found at Great Sandy National Park (Cooloola). There are 20 varied sites. The main one is the Freshwater camping area, 20 km southeast of Rainbow Beach. It provides water, showers and toilets, but fires are banned. Access is by 4WD only. Booking centre open Mon-Fri 1300-1500, T5486 3160, otherwise contact the QPWS office on Rainbow Beach Rd in Rainbow Beach.

Bush camping is available just north of Rainbow Beach at Inskip Peninsula. Sealed roads provide easy access to both bay or surf side campgrounds but the only facilities are composting toilets. Phone the QPWS for more details.

Hervey Bay *p274, map p284*

Hervey Bay offers plenty of accommodation options with a very heavy emphasis on backpackers and caravan parks. During the whale-watching season and public holidays book well ahead.

A-E **Colonial Backpackers Resort YHA**, corner of Pulgul St and Boat Harbour Dr (820), T4125 1844, www.coloniallog cabins. com. Closest to the harbour, this excellent backpackers offers a fine range of options from luxury villas and 1-2 bedroom cabins, to en suite doubles and dorms, a good bistro/ bar, pool, spa, internet, bike hire and tours desk.

A-E **Happy Wanderer Village**, 105 Truro St, Torquay, T4125 1103, www.hervey.com.au/hwanderer. For a motor park with an excellent range of options and facilities stay here. It offers good value fully self-contained duplex villas, studio/standard units, cabins, on-site vans (shared amenities), en suite/standard powered sites and non-powered sites, pool, camp kitchen. Backpacker cabins are also available.

Budget buster

Fraser Island sleeping

LL-L **Kingfisher Bay Resort**, T4125 5511, www.kingfisherbay.com.au. This multi award-winning resort is one of the best resorts in Australia. More an eco-village than a resort, it is highly successful in combining unique and harmonious architecture with superb facilities and a wide variety of accommodation options (fully self-contained holiday villas, lodges and luxury hotel rooms) centred around a spacious central lodge with landscaped pools and gardens. Within the main lodge are two excellent, if pricey, restaurant/bars, with a separate bistro/pizzeria and shopping complex nearby. The resort also offers a wide range of activities and tours and hires out 4WD vehicles. For those not visiting Fraser Island, the resort offers the excellent **Dinner Cruise** (🍴) which departs the Urungan Boat Harbour Sun-Thu, 1600-2000 and 1830-2330 (from $40, child $22) for a themed buffet and Fri and Sat, 1600-2200 and 1900-2330 ($50, child $30).

C-E **Friendly Hostel**, 182 Torquay Rd, T4124 4107, www.thefriendlyhostel.com. You are certain to get fine hospitality and some peace and quiet in this hostel. It is small and comfortable and more like a B&B, with tidy dorms (with single beds no bunks), doubles/twins with well-equipped kitchen facilities.

C-E **Woolshed**, 181 Torquay Rd, T4124 0677. In the heart of town, and a refreshing contrast to the party-hard establishments, is this characterful and friendly place. It has an exquisite range of nicely decorated (and very different) dorms and twin/double cabins and rooms with all the usual facilities and internet.

D-E **Billabong Beach House**, 335 Esplanade, Scarness, T4124 2877, www.billabongbeachhouses.com.au. A motel-cum-backpackers opposite the beach, it has some good value rooms for couples, small groups or families.

Fraser Island *p275, map p277*

LL-A **Eurong Beach Resort**, east coast, T4127 9122, www.eurong.com. Traditional resort offering the full range of options from tidy self-contained apartments, motel-style units and cabins to budget A-frame houses that can accommodate up to 8. Other budget units are also available. There is a spacious, yet fairly characterless, restaurant/bar, a pool and a range of organized tours and activities. Well-stocked shop, café and fuel on site. Comfortable and well situated for East Beach.

A-E **Fraser Island Company's Cathedral Beach Resort and Wilderness Retreat Resort**, 13 km further north, T4127 9177, www.fraserislandco.com.au. The only non-camping permit park on the island. It offers tidy cabins, on-site tents and vans all with fully equipped kitchens and non-powered sites with hot showers and a shop at Cathedral Beach and good value 1-bedroom or family self-contained timber lodges with pool, bistro and bar at Happy Valley south of Eli Creek.

QPWS campsites are at Central Station, Lake Boomanjin, Lake McKenzie, Lake Allom, Wathumba, Waddy Point and Dundubara. Facilities include toilets and cold showers. There are coin ($0.50) operated hot showers at Central Station, Waddy Point and Dundubara.

Beach camping is permitted all along the east coast and on a few selected sites on the west coast. A nightly fee of $4 ($16 per family) applies to all campsites

(Dundubara and Waddy Point must be pre-booked, all others cannot be pre-booked). QPWS fees do not apply to private resorts or campsites. **And don't feed the dingoes!**

Eating

Noosa *p270, map p280*

There are almost 150 restaurants in the Noosa area with 30 along Hastings St alone. Over the years many top national chefs have set up kitchen in the region, fed by their desire to escape the big cities and the stiff competition. Many foreign chefs have also followed suit, adding a distinctly cosmopolitan range of options. Other than the expensive offerings on Hastings St in Noosa Heads, the main culinary hot-spots are along Gympie Terr and Thomas St in Noosaville. The best budget options are to be found along lower Noosa Dr and Sunshine Beach Rd in Noosa Junction.

TTT **Café Le Monde**, 52 Hasting St, Noosa Heads, T5449 2366, www.cafelemonde.com. Daily 0630-late. One of the most popular socially with its large, covered, sidewalk courtyard and live entertainment 5 nights a week. It serves generous international and imaginative vegetarian dishes and is also popular for breakfast.

TTT **Lindoni's**, 13 Hastings St, Noosa Heads, T5447 5111. Daily 1800-2230. Of the Italian restaurants in Noosa, this place has the finest reputation, a nice atmosphere and entertaining, Italian-speaking staff.

TT **Bistro C**, 'On the Beachfront' Complex, Hastings St, Noosa Heads, T5447 2855, www.bistroc.com.au. Daily 0730-2130. This classy restaurant offers a good traditional Australian/seafood menu and a welcome escape from the main drag overlooking the beach. Excellent for breakfast.

TT **Gusto Riverfront Restaurant**, 2/257 Gympie Terr, Noosaville, T5449 7144, Mon-Sat from 1100-late, Sun from 0800. One of the most popular restaurants in the region, offering cuisine that locals describe as 'honest and fresh' and for which they keep coming back time and again. Seafood, meat and vegetarian all on offer. Book ahead.

TT **Jetty Restaurant**, Overlooking Lake Cootharaba at Boreen Point, T5485 3167. Offers a fine escape from the Noosa hype and is deservingly popular, especially for lunch. It has a mainly traditional menu.

TT **Thai Breakers**, 185 Gympie Terr, Noosaville, T5455 5500. Tue-Sun for lunch and daily for dinner from 1700. For excellent, healthy cuisine.

T **Aromas**, 32 Hastings St, Noosa Heads, T5474 9788. Daily 0700-late, Fri-Sat until 0100. Spacious and modern with a mainly Mediterranean influenced menu. They also serve excellent coffee and the streetside location is a great spot to watch the world go by.

T **Betty's Burgers**, Noosa Heads. An old favourite that can often be found trading from a caravan beside the beach at the end of Hastings St. The $2 burgers are legendary.

T **Lazuli Blue Café**, 9 Sunshine Beach Rd, towards Noosa Junction, T5448 0055. Good vegetarian dishes and breakfast for $5.

T **Magic of India**, across the road from **Thai Breakers**, Noosaville, T5449 7788. Reputed to be the best Indian takeaway in Noosa. Also open for sit-in meals Tue-Sun from 1730.

T **Noosa Reef Hotel**, towards Noosa Junction, on Noosa Dr, T5447 4477. Fine views, value for money and is especially good for families.

T **Sierra Cafe**, 10 Hastings St, Noosa Heads, T5447 4800. Very popular street side café with rather cramped seating, but a good laid-back atmosphere, good coffee and good value breakfasts. The seafood curry is recommended..

Sunshine Coast Hinterland *p271*

TTT **Yandina Station Homestead**, 684 Yandina Creek Rd, towards the coast via the Yandina-Coolum Rd, T5446 6000, www.yandinastation.com.au. Fri, Sat and Sun from 1200, Fri and Sat from 1800.

This historic 1853 homestead is one of the best restaurants in the region. Recommended. Book ahead.

¥¥ **King Ludwig's German Restaurant and Bar**, 401 Mountain View Rd, Maleny, T5499 9377. Open Wed-Sun. Overlooking the Glass House Mountains. Excellent food, good atmosphere.

¥¥ **Tree Tops Gallery Restaurant**, Kondalilla Falls Rd, near Flaxton, T1800-444350, www. treehouses.com.au. Also has equally excellent cabin-style accommodation.

Hervey Bay *p274, map p284*

Many of the upmarket resort complexes have restaurants offering fine dining. Cheaper eateries are to be found along the Esplanade in Torquay, Scarness and Pialba.

¥¥ **Beach House Hotel**, 344 Esplanade, Scarness, T4128 1233. Deservingly popular for both lunch and dinner, offers a good range of pub/café style options overlooking the beach. They also have live entertainment and pool tables.

¥¥ **The Black Dog Café**, corner of Esplanade and Denman Camp Rd, between Scarness and Torquay, T4124 3177. Wed-Mon 1030-1500, daily for dinner. A modern, classy restaurant with good value Japanese dishes.

¥¥ **Hoolihans Irish Pub**, 382 Esplanade, T4194 0099. Daily from 1100. Has a wide range of traditional offerings with an Irish flavour. Servings are generous and it's pricey, but then there is always the quality beer!

¥¥ **Le Café**, 325a Esplanade, Scarness, T4128 1793. Daily for breakfast, lunch and dinner, from 0645-2130. Offers classy surroundings, value for money and good coffee.

¥ **O'Reiley's**, 446 Esplanade, T4125 3100, Daily from 1700 and Sat-Sun from 0730. All-you-can-eat pizza and pancakes on Tue nights and reasonable value at other times. Good value breakfasts at weekend.

¥ **The RSL**, 11 Torquay Rd, Pialba, T4128 1133. Open daily. At the other end of town, this one can always be relied on for value for money and sedate entertainment.

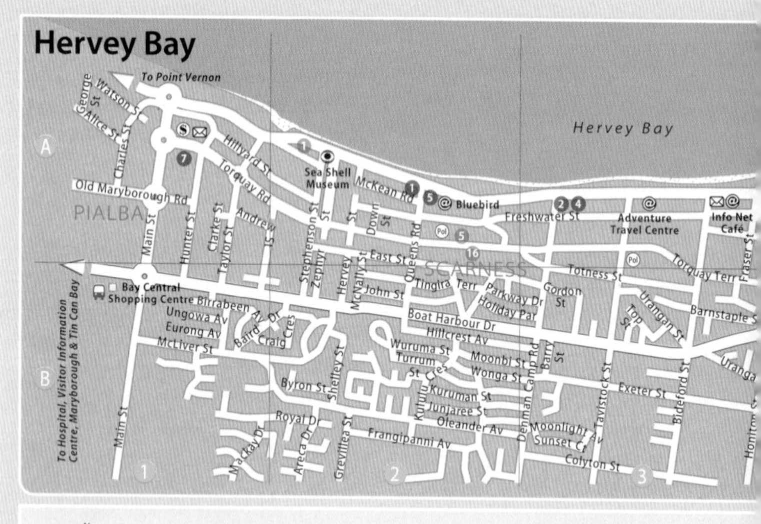

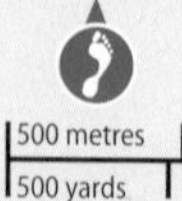

Sleeping
Billabong Beach House 1 A2
Colonial Backpackers Resort YHA 4 B6
Friendly Hostel 5 A2
Happy Wanderer Village 7 A4
Woolshed 16 A2

Eating
Beach House Hotel 1 A2
Black Dog Café 2 A3
Hoolihans Irish Pub 4 A3
Le Café 5 A2

Fraser Island *p275, map p277*
Resorts have restaurants/bistros and some campsites have fully-equipped kitchens. See Sleeping section above. Food on the island is expensive so if you are camping, you are advised to bring all your supplies from the mainland.

Bars and clubs

Noosa *p270, map p280*
Rolling Rock, on the upper level of the Bay Village Mall on Hastings St, T5447 2255. Daily 2100-0300. Fairly unremarkable and pretentious dance and live band venue. Smart/casual dress, $6 cover.
Koala Beach Resort, 44 Noosa Dr, T5447 3355. The in-house bar here is considered the liveliest under 30s haunt in town. Closes at 2400.
Reef Hotel's Reef Bar, further up the hill, towards Noosa Heads. Takes the overflow from **Koala Beach Resort** after it closes.

Activities and tours

Noosa *p270, map p280*
Aerial pursuits
Dimona Motor Glider Flights, based at the Sunshine Coast Airport, Maroochy, T0418-713903. Trips (15-30 mins) in something between a light aircraft and a glider, from $175.
Fly High Para flying, T0500-872123, offers short flights from Main Beach.
Noosa and Maroochy Flying Services, T5450 0516, www.noosaaviation.com.au. Range of scenic flights from coastal trips to Fraser Island and reef safaris, $50-450.
Sunshine Coast Skydivers, Caloundra Airport, T5492 6958, www.scskydivers.com. Large and reputable operator providing 12-15,000-ft tandems from $265.
Skydive Ramblers, T5446 1855, www.ramblers.com.au. Has a drop zone on Coolum Beach with 'photo specialist' tandems at around $350.

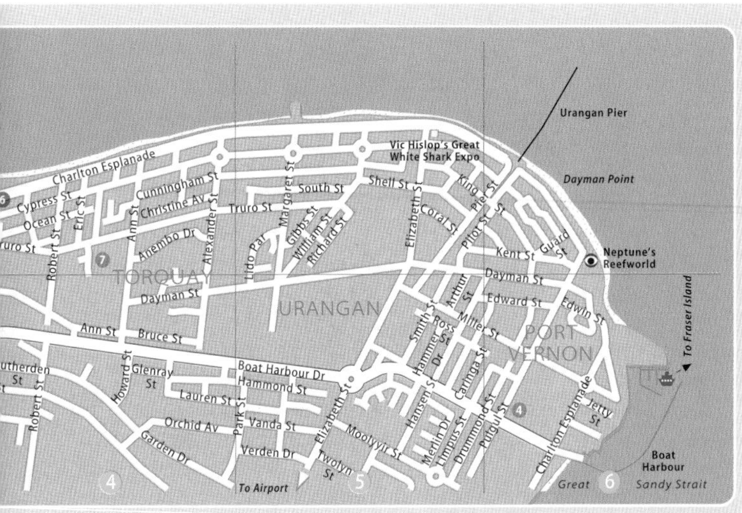

O'Reiley's **6** *A4*
RSL **7** *A1*

Camel safaris

Camel Safaris, based on Noosa North Shore, T5442 4402, www.camelcompany.com.au. Safaris of 1-2 hrs along Forty Mile Beach (Great Sandy National Park/ Cooloola) from $55, 6-day safari on Fraser Island from $1100. There is a weight restriction of 95 kg.

Cruises and boat hire

There are numerous operators along the riverbank from whom you can hire U-Drive Boats, BBQ Boats, speedboats, kayaks and jet skis at competitive prices. There are also plenty of operators offering sedate cruises up and down the Noosa River from Noosa Heads to Tewantin and beyond.

The main ferry terminals are (from west to east): **Harbour Marine Village** (Gympie Terr, Noosaville), **O Boat Jetty**, **Big Pelican**, **Noosa Yacht Club** and, at Noosa Heads, **Sheraton Hotel jetty**.

Beyond Noosa, T5449 9177, www.beyondnoosa.com.au. Cruise to Lake Cootharaba (lunch cruise from $74/ half-day from $59), with an additional 4WD combo that takes in the main sights of the Great Sandy National Park (Cooloola), from $139, child $90.

Noosa Ferry Cruise, T5449 8442, www.noosaferry.com. Runs regular services between all these stops, daily, from 0915-1800 (later at weekends), from $10.50, child $4, family $25 one-way. An 'All day pass' costs $14.50.

Noosa River Cruises, T5449 7362. 5-hr trip to Lake Cootharaba daily from $65.

Cycling/mountain biking

Bug Sports, T5455 3674, www.bug.com.au. Stylish outfit offering customized or scheduled guided trips according to your fitness and level of skill.

Mammoth Cycles, Shop 2, 23 Project Ave, Noosaville, T5474 0499. Hire from $20-35 per day.

Noosa Bike Tours and Hire, T5474 3322, www.noosabikehire.com. Delivery and pick-ups from around $35 per day.

Pedal & Paddle, T5485 4049, www.pedalandpaddle.com.au. Entertaining 4-hr mountain bike/kayak combo from $66.

Horse trekking

Clip Clop Horse Treks, 249 Eumarella Rd, Lake Weyba, T5449 1254, www.clipcloptreks.com.au. Wide range of options from 2-hr treks to 4-day adventures. Prices on application.

Kayaking and canoeing

Elanda Point Canoe Company, T5485 3165, www.elanda.com.au. Wide range of exciting adventures on the waterways of the Great Sandy National Park (Cooloola), from half-day (from $59), full-day backpacker special (from $110), to 5-day/4-night (from $980). Independent hire is also available.

Noosa Ocean Kayaking Tours, T0418-787577, www.learntosurf.com.au/kayaking. Sea kayaking around the Noosa National Park, from $50 (2 hrs) and river trips, from $45 (2 hrs). Independent hire is also available, from $40 per day.

Motorcycle tours

Aussie Biker Tours, 4/15 Venture Dr, Noosaville, T5474 1050, www.aussiebiker.com.au. Hire and guided day trips with a blast along the Cooloola Beach from $225.

Sightseeing tours

Noosa 4WD Eco Tours, T5471 1120, www.noosa4wdtours.com.au. Full and half-day tours throughout the week to the Great Sandy National Park (Cooloola) and beyond from $65-95.

Noosa Hinterland Tours, T5446 3111, www.noosahinterlandtours.com.au. Tours throughout the week to the Hinterland taking in a winery and the Glass House Mountains, from $54, child $20, the Eumundi Markets (Wed and Sat), from $15, child $10, and the Australia Zoo on demand from $36, child $18.

Spas

No doubt after a few hours on a camel or a horse your weathered cheeks and other bodily parts would greatly benefit from a spa or a massage. **Newland**, 28 Sunshine Beach Rd, T5474 8212, the **Noosa Spa** (South Pacific Resort), 167 Weyba Rd, T5447 1424, www.noosaspa.com.au and the 'mobile' **State of Health Company**, T0412-181396, can all oblige, from $70 per hr.

Surfing and kitesurfing

There are more 'Learn to Surf' operators on Main Beach than there are beach umbrellas. Generally they are all very professional and run by pros and/or experts. 2-hr session from about $50. **Wavesense**, T5474 9076, www.wavesense.com.au; **Learn to Surf**, with world champ Merrick Davies, T0418-787577; and for girls only, the **Girls Surf School**, T0418-787577, www.learntosurf.com.au. **Noosa Longboards**, Shop 4, 64 Hastings St, T5447 2828, hires long/short surfboards and body boards, from $25 per hr. **Kitesurf**, T5455 6677, www.kite-surf.com.au, and **Wind 'N' Sea**, T5455 6677, will introduce you to the the world of kite surfing, from $140 for 2 hrs.

Cooloola Coast *p273*

Horse trekking, diving, paragliding, canoeing and fishing all feature in the growing list of available activities and Cooloola VIC can provide detailed operator details. It is however 4WD tours that dominate with options both north to Fraser and south to the Cooloola Section of the Great Sandy National Park.

4WD tours

Aussie Adventure 4WD, T5486 3599. If you want to go it alone come here to hire 2-9 seat 4WD vehicles.
Sun Safari Tours, T5486 3154. Day or overnight trips to Fraser Island and the Great Sandy National Park (Cooloola), from $80.
Surf'n'Sand Safaris, T5486 3131. Half-day tour of the Cooloola Section Great Sandy National Park, taking in the expansive views from the lighthouse at Double Island Point and the Coloured Sand Cliffs near Rainbow Beach and local rainforest, from $55.

Dolphin-watching

Dolphin Ferry Cruise, T0428-838836. Departs Carlo Point daily for the dolphin feeding at Tin Can Bay, from $15. For Fraser Island ferry services, see Transport below.

Hervey Bay *p274, map p284*

Whale-watching

There are now more than 15 whale-watch cruise operators based at the Urungan Boat Harbour. There are various options and a variety of boats offering ½, ¾ and full-day tours, ranging in price from $85 upwards. The best way to choose is to head for the **Whale Watch Tourist Centre** (open daily 0600-1800) at the boat harbour, take a look at the various boats and compare their itineraries. With so many operators, other than cruise time, the differences really come down to minor details like the size of the group.
Tasman Venture II, T1800-620322, www.tasmanventure.com.au. Offers something different with a West Coast day tour which explorers the quiet and largely inaccessibly beaches of Fraser's west coast, with snorkelling and perhaps a bit of dolphin watching along the way, from $85.
Blue Dolphin, T4125 3727, offers a 'whales by sail', half-day and sunset cruise option, from $90.
Volante III and V are smaller launches that offer ¾ day and dawn trips from $80, child $50.
Mikat Whale Watch Safari (6 hrs from $80), T4125 2343, and **Whalesong**, T4125 6233, www.whalesong.com.au, both operate cruises on large catamarans. The latter do specialist year- round dolphin cruises, half-day from $85.

Background

A whale of a time

Every year from August to November, the waters around Hervey Bay echo to the haunting symphonies of whale song. These whales spend the warmer summer months in Antarctic waters feeding on krill before starting their annual migration north to the central and southern Great Barrier Reef where there calves are born in the warm waters. Finding temporary haven in the bay's calm waters, pods of humpback whales stop to socialize and play, often breaching the surface or slapping it with fins and tail, before moving on to the far more serious business of returning to their feeding grounds in Antarctica. Other marine animals, including dolphins, turtles and occasionally dugongs, also join the fray and can be seen all year round. See page 287 for tours.

Spirit of Hervey Bay, T1800-642544, www.spiritofherveybay.com, has the added luxury of a smooth glass bottom (½ day from $85).

Fraser Island *p275, map p277*
As you might expect, there are many tours on offer to Fraser from as far away as Brisbane and Noosa. To get the most from the island you really need at least 3 days, so a day tour should only be considered if you are hard pressed for time. If you want to explore the island in a short space of time try the excellent guided tours on offer through the resorts especially **Kingfisher Bay**, T1800-072555, www.king fisherbay.com.au. Their Wilderness Adventure Tours, of 3 day/ 2 night (from $312 quad share/364 twin) or 2 day/1 night (from $237 quad/$278 twin) are the most expensive, but for good reason, being very entertaining, professional and with an excellent standard of accommodation. Daily tours are also on offer from $$125, child $50.
Air Fraser Island, T4125 3600, is recommended if you're on your own or are a couple. They will fly you out to Eurong, where you are supplied with a small, economical 4WD (with camping gear if required, fuel not included) from around $125 per day. The only drawback is that the vehicles must stay on the island and be dropped off again at Eurong. This option does avoid the expensive vehicle ferry fees and is fine if you want fly back, but it can present problems if you wish to stay at the **Kingfisher Bay Resort** and/or get the ferry back on foot from the island's west coast.

In Noosa

Fraser Explorer Tours, T5447 3845, www. fraser-is.com. Their day tour has the added attraction of taking in the sights of the Cooloola section of the Great Sandy National Park on the way, from $110. A 2/3 day tour package costs from $180-350.
Fraser Island Adventure Tours, T5444 6957, www.fraserislandadventure tours.com.au. Exciting 4WD day trip to Fraser Island, taking in the main sights of the Great Sandy National Park (Cooloola) along the way, from $140, child $100.
Fraser Island Trailblazers Tours, T1800-626673, www.trailblazertours. com.au. Good value 'down-to-sand' 3-day Camping Safari, via the Great Sandy National Park (Cooloola section), from $295.

In Hervey Bay

Fraser Island Company, T4125 3933, www.fraserislandco.com.au. Offers a good range of 1-3 day safaris, from $109, child $65.
Fraser Venture, T1800-249122, day tours from $99, child $55 and multi-day packages with accommodation at the **Eurong Beach Resort**.
Koala, T1800-466444, www.koalaresort.com.au, and **Palace**, T1800-063168, are 2 backpackers offering their own vehicles, guides and budget packages (camping), from around $135.
Safari 4WD, 102 Boat Harbour Rd, T4124 4244, www.safari4wdhire.com.au. For those wishing to get a group together and go independently, this is one of the most professional. They offer a range of models from $140-200 a day, camping kits from $16 per day and hire/accommodation packages from $480.

Transport

Noosa *p270, map p280*

Air

The nearest airport is the Maroochydore (Sunshine Coast) Airport, www.sunshinecoastairport.com6 km north of Maroochy -dore. **Qantas**, T131313, www.qantas.com.au, **Virgin Blue**, T136789, www.virginblue.com.au, **Jet Star**, T131538, www.jetstar.com and **Sunshine Express**, T5450 6222, www.sunshineexpress.com.au, provide daily services from **Brisbane**. Local northbound bus services stop at the airport and a taxi to **Noosa Heads** will cost about $55. **Henry's**, 12 Noosa Dr, T5474 0199, www.henrys.com. au, offers express (non-stop) services between Brisbane Airport/Maroochydore Airport and Noosa Heads 7 times daily, from $20 each way. **Sunshine Shuttle**, T0412-507937, offers similar services.

Bus

Local Sunshine Coast Sunbus, T131230, www.transinfo.qld.gov.au, has services to Noosa Heads/Tewantin, (#10), north/southbound to the Sunshine Coast (#1), west to Eumundi/Cooroy/Nambour (#12). A free council run bus service every 15 mins between Tewantin and Noosa Fair is available and the information centre can provide times and routes.
Long distance The long-distance terminal is on the corner of Noosa Parade and Noosa Dr, Noosa Heads. **Greyhound**, T131499 and **Suncoast Pacific**, T54431011, offer daily north/southbound services and regular services to **Tin Can Bay**. **Harvey World Travel**, Shop 2 Lanyana Way, Noosa Heads, T5447 4077, and **Palm Tree Tours**, Bay Village, Hastings St, T5474 9166, act as local booking agents.

Car

Avis, corner of Hastings St and Noosa Dr, T5447 4933. **Budget**, Hastings St, Noosa Heads, T5447 4588. If you wish to explore the Great Sandy National Park there are several 4WD hire companies including **Henry's**, 12 Noosa Dr, T5474 0199, www.henrys.com.au; **Thrifty**, Noosa Dr, T136139; **Big Kahuna**, T5471 0047; and **Fraser Beach 4WD Hire**, 1 Beach Rd, Noosa Heads, T5474 5233. **Big Kahuna**, T5471 0047 hires 'mokes' and scooters from $55/$33 per day.

Ferry

The Tewantin car ferry crosses the Noosa River (end of Moorindil St) and provide access to the national park. It operates from Nov-Jan Sun-Thu 0430-2230, Fri-Sat 0430-0030 and Feb-Oct Mon-Thu 0600-2230, Fri 0600-0030, Sat 0500-0030, Sun 0500-2230, from $5.

Train

The nearest train station is at Cooroy, T132232. **Sunbus** offers services from there to Noosa Heads (route #12).

Cooloola Coast *p273*

Boat

Barges operating from Inskip Peninsula on the mainland to Hook point on Fraser Island run on demand every 10 mins or so. Pre-booking is not necessary but check tide times prior to departure, T5486 3227, from $70 return.

Bus

Polley's Coaches, T5482 2700, www.polleys.com.au offers twice daily (weekday) services from **Gympie** to **Tin Can Bay** and **Rainbow Beach**. Greyhound, T131499, and Suncoast Pacific, T5449 9966, offer daily coach services to **Tin Can Bay** and **Rainbow Beach**.

Car

Rainbow Beach is 76 km east of the Bruce Highway at Gympie and the road is sealed all the way. Alternative access is by 4WD only from Tewantin, 3 km east of Noosaville, Noosa River ferry 0600-2200, from $5.

Hervey Bay *p274, map p284*

Air

The airport is 2 km south of Urungan, off Elizabeth St/Booral Rd, at the eastern end of the city. Sunshine Express, T5450 6222, www.sunshineexpress.com.au, provides regular services from **Brisbane**. Taxis meet all scheduled flights.

Bus

Local Wide Bay Transit, T4123 1733, www.widebaytransit.com.au, runs local hail and ride bus services between Maryborough (including the railway station) and Hervey Bay (Route #5), taking in a circuit of the town along The Esplanade to Urungan and back via Boat Harbour Drive. Routes #16 and #18 also cover the main centres and the Urungan marina.

Long distance The long-distance bus terminal is in the Bay Central Shopping Centre, Boat Harbour Rd, Pialba, T4124 4000. Greyhound, T131499, Premier Motor Services, T133410, offer daily services north/south. Suncoast Pacific, T5443 1011, offers services to **Tin Can Bay** and Polley's Coaches, T5482 2700, offers onward transfers to Rainbow Beach.

Car

Car hire from Hervey Bay Economy Car Rentals, 83 Islander Rd, T4124 6240, from $50 per day, and Nifty Rent A Car, 463 Esplanade, T4125 6008. For 4WD hire, see Fraser Island section. Servicing/repair at Charlie's, 92 Boat Harbour Dr, T4124 1655.

Train

The nearest train station is in Maryborough, Lennox St, T4123 9264. Queensland Rail's, fast Tilt Train (**Brisbane** to **Rockhampton**) offers regular services north and south, T132232. Wide Bay Transit #5 service connects with every Tilt Train for transfers to and from **Hervey Bay**, T41231733. Hervey Bay Travel Centre, Bay Central Shopping Mall, T1800-815378, act as booking agents.

Fraser Island *p275, map p277*

Air

There are 2 small airfields on Fraser – Toby's Gap and Orchid Beach – but most light aircraft land on East Beach at Eurong or Happy Valley. **Air Fraser Island**, T4125 3600, offers daily services from $50 return. They also offer packages and scenic flights (see under Activities and tours above).

Boat

Rainbow Venture, Inskip Point, Rainbow Beach to Hook Point, departs mainland daily from 0630-1630 (15 mins), T5486 3227 (no bookings required), from $70 return, including driver, passenger-only, from $12. Fraser Venture, Mary River Heads (20 mins south of Hervey Bay), to Wanggoolba Creek, departs mainland Mon-Fri 0900, 1015, 1530, Sat 0700

Top tips

State phone codes and time difference

There are no area phone codes. Use a state code if calling outside the state you are in. These are: 02 for ACT/NSW (08 for Broken Hill), 03 for VIC and 07 for QLD. Note that NSW operates daylight saving, which means that clocks go forward one hour from October and March.

(30 mins), returning Mon-Fri 0930, 1430 and 1600, Sat 0730, T4125 4444 (pre book), price as above. Kingfisher Vehicular Ferry, Mary River Heads to Kingfisher Bay departs mainland daily 0715, 1100, 1430, returns 0830, 1330, 1600, T1800-072555 (pre book), price as above.

Ferry (passenger only)

Kingfisher Fast Cat, Urungan Boat Harbour, Hervey Bay to Kingfisher Bay Resort, departs mainland daily 0845, 1200, 1600, Sun-Thu also 1830, Fri-Sat also 1900, 2230, returns daily 0740, 1030, 1400, 1700, 2000, Sat-Sun extra at 2330, T4125 5511 (bookings preferable), from $48, child $24.

Directory

Noosa *p270, map p280*

Banks Most branches/ATMs are on Hastings St, Noosa Heads or Sunshine Beach Rd, Noosa Junction. Currency exchange at Harvey World Travel, Shop 2 Lanyana Way, Noosa Heads, T5447 4077. **Hospitals** Noosa Hospital, 111 Goodchap St, T5455 9200; Noosaville Medical Centre, corner of Thomas St and Mary St, T5442 4922, Mon-Thu 0800-2000, Fri-Sun 0800-1800. **Internet** Urban Mailbox, opposite the VIC on Noosa Dr, T5473 5151, has fast terminals, daily 0900-1900 (2200 high season). Travel Bugs, Shop 3/9, Sunshine Beach Rd, Noosa Junction, T5474 8530, but the terminals are very slow, daily 0800-2200. Koala Backpackers, 44 Noosa Dr, Noosa Junction. **Pharmacy** Chemist Night and Day, Hastings St, daily 0900-2100. **Post** 91 Noosa Dr, T5473 8591, Mon-Fri 0900-1730, Sat 0900-1230. Postcode 4567.

Hervey Bay *p274, map p284*

Banks Westpac and National are on the Esplanade Torquay, Commonwealth is on Bideford St, Torquay. **Hospital** Nissen St, T4120 6666. **Internet** Adventure Travel Centre, 410 Esplanade, T4128 9288, daily until late. **Pharmacy** 418 Esplanade, T4128 3899, 0830-2000. **Post** Office, 414 Esplanade, Torquay, Mon-Fri 0830-1700, Sat 0830-1200 and Shop 5/15 Central Ave Urraween, T131318. Postcode 4655. **Useful numbers** Police, 142 Torquay Rd, T4128 5333.

Fraser Island *p275, map p277*

Food, hardware, fuel and telephones are available at the Eurong Beach Resort, Fraser Island Retreat (Happy Valley), Kingfisher Bay Resort, Cathedral Beach Resort and Orchid Beach. Additional telephones are located at Ungowa, Central Station, Dundubara, Waddy Point and Indian Head. There are no banks or ATMs on the island but most major resorts accept EFTPOS. There are no medical services on the island. QPWS ranger stations and resorts all have basic first aid and can call in an air ambulance in an emergency, T000.

Capricorn Coast

Capricorn Coast begins north of Hervey Bay, where the great sand masses of the Fraser Coast give way to fields of sugar cane and, offshore, the start of the Great Barrier Reef. Near Bundaberg – or 'Bundy' – is Mon Repos, one of the world's most important and accessible mainland turtle rookeries. The once remote towns of 1770 and Agnes Water serve as gateway to the stunning southern reef island of Lady Musgrave, while even more beautiful Heron Island is accessed from the industrial port of Gladstone. East of Rockhampton, Queensland's 'beef capital', are the coastal resorts of Yeppoon and Emu Park, while just offshore Great Keppel Island offers many tourists their first taste of Queensland's many beautiful tropical island resorts.

Getting there Interstate flights (Rockhampton), rail and interstate bus networks.
Getting around Local bus network or hire car/campervan.
Time required 5 days.
Weather Hot or warm in summer and often humid with occasional storms. Mild to warm in winter.
Sleeping Good hostels and motor camps in all main centres. Try an outback farm-stay.
Eating Steak in Rockhampton.
Activities and tours Diving, reef island cruising and camping, farm-stays (from Rockhampton), crocodile farm and turtle rookery tours, caving adventures.
★ **Don't miss** Mon Repos Turtle Rookery. ▸▸ *p294.*

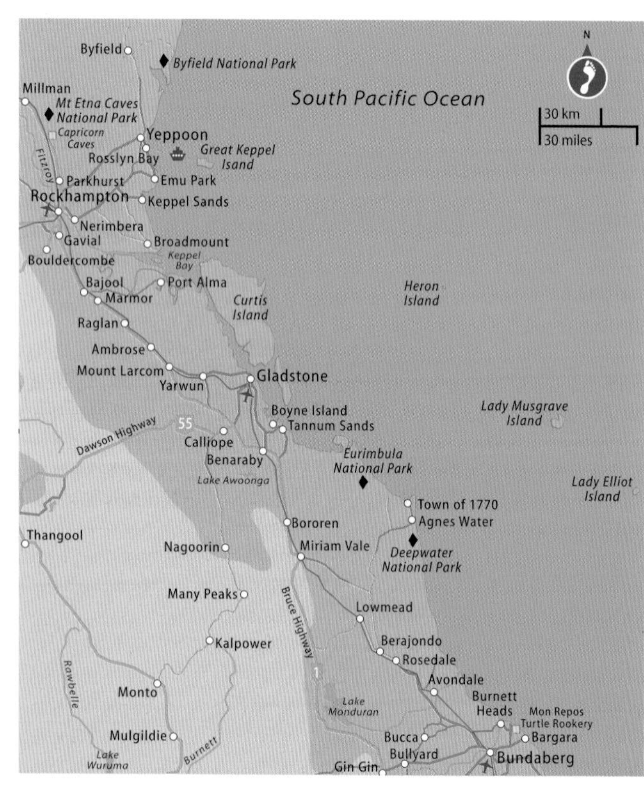

Bundaberg and Southern Reef Islands » pp301-307.

Little Bundaberg sits beside the Burnett River amidst a sea of sugar cane. The city relies far more on agriculture than tourism to sustain it and as a result is usually absent from most travel agendas. Many refer to the town as 'Bundy', though this affectionate nickname is most often used to describe its famous tipple, rum, which has been faithfully distilled in Bundaberg since 1883. Not surprisingly, the wonderfully sweet-smelling distillery is the biggest tourist attraction, while others nearby include the southern reef islands of Lady Musgrave and Elliot, both of which offer excellent diving, and the fascinating, seasonal action at the Mon Repos turtle rookery.

Ins and outs

Getting there and around Bundaberg's airport is 3 km from the city centre. All the main bus companies operate services to the city from the north and south. The Tilt train is the major train service from Brisbane. The reef ferries depart from the Bundaberg Port Marina, on the lower reaches of the Burnett River, about 19 km northeast of the centre. The coastal resorts of Bargara, Burnett Heads and the Mon Repos turtle rookery are 15 km east. Local coach operators run regular services. » *p306.*

Tourist information There are two **VICs**, with little difference between them. There's the accredited centre ⓘ *271 Bourbong St, T4153 8888, www.bundabergregion.org, 0900-1700*, and the City Council's own centre ⓘ *186 Bourbong St, T1800-308888, www.bundabergregion.info, Mon-Fri 0900-1700, Sat-Sun 0900-1200.*

Bundaberg

Before filling the nostrils with the sweet smell of molasses and titillating the taste buds with the dark nectar at the distillery, it is perhaps worth taking a quick, and sober, look at one or two of the historical buildings dominating the city centre. Most prominent is the 30-m clock tower of **Post Office building**, on the corner of Bourbong and Barolin streets, which has been in continuous operation since 1890. A few doors down is the 1891 **Old National Australia Bank**, with its distinctive colonnades and spacious verandahs embellished with cast iron balustrades.

An equally popular retreat is the city's **Botanical Gardens Complex** ⓘ *1 km north of the city centre, corner of Hinkler Ave and Gin Gin Rd, T4152 0222, 0730-1700, $3, child $1, museums 1000-1600*. Added to the obvious botanical attractions and landscaped ponds and gardens are the **Fairymead House Sugar Museum**, which documents the history of the region's most important industry, and the **Hinkler House Memorial Museum**, which celebrates the life and times of courageous local pioneer aviator, Bert Hinkler. Born in Bundaberg in 1892, Hinkler was the first person to fly solo from Australia to England, in 1928. Sadly, after going on to break numerous other records, he then died attempting to break the record for the return journey in 1933. There is also a working steam train that clatters round the gardens on Sundays.

Although a relatively small operation, the **Bundaberg Distillery** ⓘ *Avenue St (4 km east of the city centre, head for the chimney stack), T4131 2999, www.bundabergrum.com.au, tours daily on the hour Mon-Fri 1000-1500, Sat-Sun 1000-1400, from $10, child $4.40*, established in 1883, provides a fascinating insight into the distilling process. The one-hour tour begins with a short video celebrating the famous Bundy brand before you are taken to view the various aspects of the manufacturing process. First stop is a huge 5-million litre well of sweet smelling molasses which are gradually drawn through a maze of steel pipes, fermenters, condensers and distillers, before ending up in mighty vats within the maturing warehouses. With one vat alone being worth $5 million ($3 million of which goes to government tax) it is hardly surprising to hear the solid 'click' of lock and key and to be mildly aware of being counted on the way out! Then, with a discernably quickening pace, you are taken to an authentic bar to sample the various end products. Generous distillers they are too, allowing four 'shots', which is just enough to keep you below the legal driving limit.

Mon Repos Turtle Rookery

ⓘ *Grange Rd, off Bundaberg Port Rd, T4159 1652, www.epa.qld.gov.au. Turtle viewing Oct-May, 1900-0600 (subject to activity), information centre open daily 24 hrs Oct-May and 0600-1800 Jun-Sep, $6, child $4.*

Supporting the largest concentration of nesting marine turtles on the eastern Australian mainland and one of the largest loggerhead turtle rookeries in the world, the Coral Coast beach, known as Mon Repos (pronounced Mon Repo), is a place of ecological reverence. It can be found 12 km east of Bundaberg, near the coastal resort of Bargara. During the day Mon Repos looks just like any other idyllic Queensland beach and gives absolutely no indication of its conservation value. Yet at night, between mid-October and May, it takes on a very different aura. Hauling themselves from the waves, just beyond the tide line, with a determination only nature can display, the females (often quite elderly) dig a large pit in the sand and lay over a hundred eggs before deftly filling it in and disappearing beneath the waves, as if they had never been there at all. To watch this happen, all in the space of about 20 minutes, is a truly magical experience. And it doesn't end there. Towards the end of the season, from January to March, the tiny hatchlings emerge from the nest and make their way as fast as they can, like tiny clockwork toys, towards the relative safety of the water. Watching this spectacle is moving and, strangely, hilarious, despite the knowledge that only one in 1,000 of the hatchlings will survive to maturity and return to the same beach to breed. Of course, like any wildlife-watching attraction, there are no guarantees that turtles will show up on any given night, so you may need a lot of patience. While you wait at the Information Centre to be escorted in groups of about twenty to watch the turtles up close, you can view static displays, or better still, join in the staff's fascinating Q & A sessions, where you can learn all about the turtles' remarkable natural history, and sadly, the increasing threat that humans are placing upon them. Best viewing times for nesting turtles is subject to night tides between November and February. Turtle hatchlings are best viewed 1900-2400 from January-March.

Green turtles can be seen in the waters around Lady Musgrave Island

Southern Reef Islands

Lady Musgrave Island, 83 km northeast of Bundaberg, is part of the Capricornia Cays National Park and the southernmost island of the Bunker Group. With a relatively small 14 ha of coral cay in comparison to a huge 1192-ha surrounding reef, it is generally considered one of the most beautiful and abundant in wildlife, both above and below the water. The cay itself offers safe haven to thousands of breeding seabirds and also serves as an important green turtle rookery between November and March. Then, between August and October, humpback whales are also commonly seen. With such a large expanse of reef, the island offers some excellent snorkelling and diving as well as providing a pleasant escape from the mainland.

Budget busters

Coral sea islands

Lying 70 km east of the industrial town of Gladstone, just beyond the horizon, is one of the most beautiful of the picture-postcard Coral Sea Islands – Heron Island. As well as being a fairly accurate representation of most people's tropical fantasy, Heron is also considered one of the best dive sites on the reef. All this perfection comes at a price. Even getting there is an expensive business. Heron Island is 2 hours by launch or 30 minutes by helicopter. The resort launch leaves daily at 1100 from the Gladstone Marina on Bryan Jordan Drive in Gladstone and costs from $180 return. **Marine Helicopters**, T4978 1177, www.marineheli.com.au, fly daily from Gladstone Airport for around$500 return.
Accommodation is limited to the exclusive LL **P&O Heron Island Resort**, T132469, www.poresorts.com.au. Newly refurbished, the resort offers all the facilities you might expect for the location from luxury suites to beach houses, swimming pool, an à la carte restaurant, bar, dive shop and a host of other activities.

Lady Elliot Island, about 20 km south of Lady Musgrave, is one of the southernmost coral cays on the Barrier Reef. It's larger than Musgrave and though the surrounding reef is smaller, it is very similar in terms of scenery and marine diversity. The island is also a popular diving venue with numerous wrecks lying just offshore (about $30 a dive). ▸▸ *p304 and 306.*

Agnes Water, 1770 and around ▸▸ *pp301-307.*

With the dawning of the new millennium it was already obvious that both 1770 and Agnes would be changed from being fairly inaccessible, sleepy coastal neighbours into the next big thing on the southern Queensland coast. Sadly, this seems to have happened and they have fallen victim to the great East Coast property development phenomenon. As predicted, the money has moved in and the locals have moved out. Where wooded hillsides once created a soft green horizon, designer holiday homes owned by absentee landlords have appeared. Where once dunescapes created pockets of soporific seclusion, sterile and exclusive apartment resorts look set to dominate. Despite the decline, they are still extremely picturesque and

Lady Musgrave is one of the most beautiful of all Barrier Reef islands, both above and below the water

hemmed in by two fine national parks, Eurimbula and Deepwater. The Town of 1770 also acts as gateway to Lady Musgrave Island, an undeniable gem located 50 km offshore.

Ins and outs

Getting there and around Despite its increasing popularity the public transport services here are generally poor, but now that most roads are sealed, this situation will no doubt change. There are long-distance bus services and a train station at Miriam Vale, 55 km east. » *p306.*

Tourist information Miriam Vale VIC ⓘ *Bruce Highway in Miriam Vale, T4974 5428, www.gladstoneregion.org.au, Mon-Fri 0830-1700, Sat-Sun 0900-1700*, and **Discovery Centre** ⓘ *Captain Cook Dr, Agnes Water, T4902 1533, Mon-Sat 0830-1700*, are the two main sources of local information. **QPWS** ⓘ *Captain Cook Dr, Town of 1770, T4974 9350.*

Agnes Water and the Town of 1770

Agnes Water has a beautiful 5-km beach right on its doorstep, which offers good swimming and excellent surfing. More remote beaches offering more solitude and great walking opportunities can be accessed within the national parks. The small **museum** ⓘ *Springs Rd, Sat-Sun 1000-1200, Wed 1300-1500, $2,* touches on Aboriginal settlement, Cook's visit and the subsequent visitations by explorers Flinders and King, as well as more recent maritime and European settlement history.

The Town (village) of 1770 nestles on the leeward side of Round Hill Head and along the bank of the Round Hill Inlet, 6 km north of Agnes, and is a popular spot for fishing and boating. It also serves as the main departure point for local national park and reef island tours and cruises, see page 304.

Deepwater and Eurimbula national parks

Deepwater National Park, 8 km south of Agnes, presents a mosaic of coastal vegetation including paperbark, banksias and heath land fringed with dunes and a sweeping beach studded with small rocky headlands. As well as fishing and walking, there are fine opportunities for birdwatching and it is often used as a nesting site by green turtles between January and April. The roads within the park are unsealed so 4WD is recommended.

To the northwest of Agnes is Eurimbula National Park. Indented by the Round Hill Inlet and Eurimbula Creek, it is an area covered in thick mangrove and freshwater paperbark swamps. It is less accessible than Deepwater and best explored by boat. Other than the interesting flora and fauna, highlights include the panoramic views of the park and coastline from the Ganoonga Noonga Lookout, which can be reached by vehicle 3 km from the park entrance, 10 km west of Agnes Water. Again a 4WD is recommended, especially in the wet season.

Rockhampton and around » *pp301-307.*

Straddling both the Tropic of Capricorn and picturesque Fitzroy River, Rockhampton, or 'Rocky' as it is affectionately known, is the dubbed the 'beef capital' of Australia. First settled by Scots pioneer Charles Archer in 1855 (yet strangely bestowed the anglicised suffix 'Hampton', meaning 'a place near water'), the city enjoyed a brief gold rush in the late 1850s before the more sustainable bovine alternative finally sealed its economic fate. Although most visitors stay only very briefly, on their way to sample the coastal delights of Yeppoon and Great Keppel Island, 'Rocky' has a truly diverse range of tourist attractions, from the historical and cultural to the ecological and even subterranean. Then, of course, there is the town's legendary gastronomical delight, in the form of a steak the size of a small European country.

Ins and outs

Tourist information Capricorn Region VIC ⓘ *Gladstone Rd, T4927 2055, www.capricorntourism.com.au, daily 0900-1700*, is in the Capricorn Spire, which marks the point of the Tropic of Capricorn (23.5-degrees South) and caters for city and region. **Rockhampton VIC** ⓘ *208 Quay St, T4922 5339, www.rockhamptoninfo.com, Mon-Fri 0830-1630, Sat-Sun 0900-1600*, is housed in the grandiose 1902 Customs House. **QPWS office** ⓘ *corner of Yeppoon Rd and Norman Rd, T4936 0511.* » *p306.*

City centre

With its mineral and agricultural heritage, there are numerous historical buildings dominating the city centre. These include the 1902 **Customs House**, which now houses the VIC, the 1895 **Post Office**, on the corner of East Street Mall and Denham Street, the 1890 **Criterion Hotel**, on Quay Street, and the 1887 **Supreme Court**, on East Lane, which has been in continuous use now for over a century. As well as its numerous historical buildings, Rockhampton also boasts six bull statues, in celebration of its status as the beef capital of Australia.

Train enthusiasts will enjoy the **Archer Park Steam Tram Museum** ⓘ *Denison St, T4922 2774, www.steamtram.rockhampton.qld.gov.au, Sun-Fri 1000-1600, $5.50, child $2.20, tram operates Sun 1000-1300*. The town also has a number of art galleries. Best of the lot is the **Rockhampton Art Gallery** ⓘ *62 Victoria Parade, T4927 7149, Tue-Fri 1000-1600, Sat-Sun 1100-1600, free*, which displays a long-established collection of mainly 1940-70s Australian works and more recent contemporary acquisitions.

The small but tidy **Rockhampton Zoo** ⓘ *T4922 1654, 0800-1700, free*, on Spencer Street, has many natives on hand including koala and tame kangaroos and a charming pair of chimps called Cassie and Ockie (as in Dokie). Almost next door are the spacious **Botanical Gardens** ⓘ *0600-1800, free, guided walks are available Tue, Wed and Thu from 0930, $3.50*, first established in 1869. Amongst its leafy avenues of palms and cycads are a fernery, a Japanese garden and the peaceful garden tearooms. **Murray Lagoon** is also a fine place to stroll around.

Though not quite on a par with the Tjapukai Aboriginal Park near Cairns (see page 350) the **Dreamtime Centre** ⓘ *T4936 1655, www.dreamtimecentre.com.au. Mon-Fri 1000-1530, $12.75, child $6, guided tours start daily at 1030, dance performances on Mon,* is an entertaining introduction to Aboriginal and Torres Straight heritage using a wide range of displays and hands-on activities. Set in 30 acres of parkland just off the Bruce Highway, 6 km north of the city centre, a guided or self guided tour allows you to witness some masterful didgeridoo playing, before exploring the various displays outside in the Torres Straight Islander Village. These include traditional gunyahs (shelters) and the giant Dugong Complex, with artefacts and building materials. There is also a native plant garden where you can learn about their use as food and medicine. For many the highlight of their visit is the opportunity to throw a boomerang so it actually comes back.

Established over 20 years ago, **Koorana Crocodile Farm** ⓘ *Coowonga Rd, Emu Park, 33 km east of the city, T4934 4749, www.koorana.com.au, 1000-1500, $15, child $7, tours at 1030-1200 and 1300-1430, no public transport,* was the first private croc farm in Queensland and is home to some mighty large characters. Tours are available and there is an interesting video presentation that will avail you of many facts, the most memorable being that

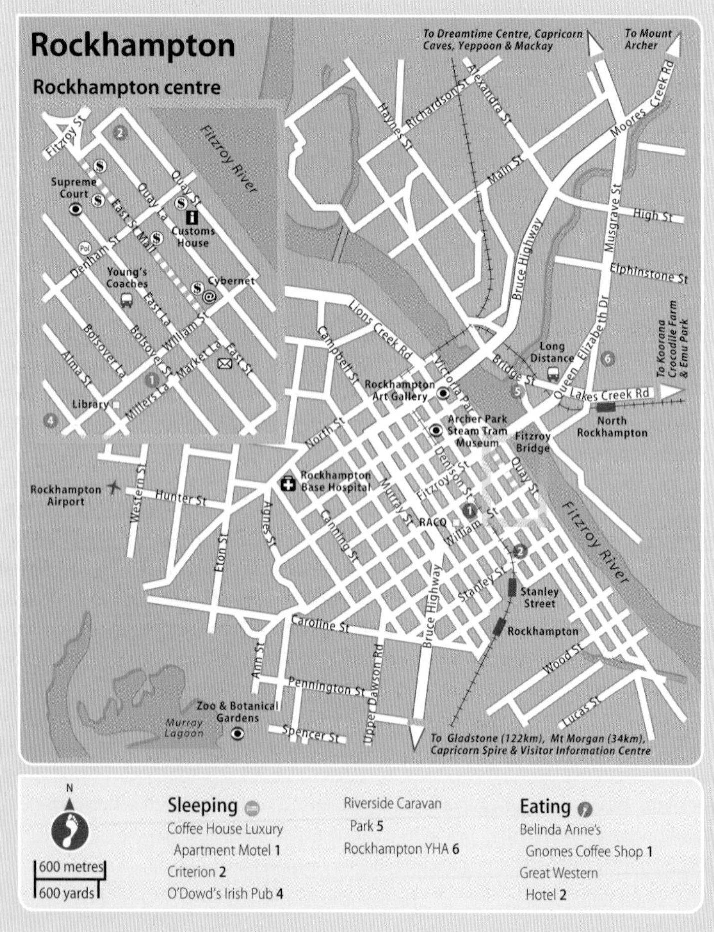

Murray Lagoon, near Rockhampton

crocodile dung was once used for contraception (though quite how, thankfully, remains an enigma). **Mount Morgan**, 38 km south of the city, has a steam railway and a small, but well-presented museum ⓘ *1000-1600, $5, child $1*, celebrating its highly productive gold and copper mining heritage. There is also a bat-infested cave nearby where dinosaur footprints were discovered in 1954. **Mount Archer** (604 m), which looms large above 'Rocky's' northeastern suburbs, has a fine summit walk and lookout. Access is from the end of Moores Creek Road, north of the Bruce Highway. Vehicular access to the summit is from Frenchville Road, off Norman, which is off Moores Creek Road.

Capricorn Caves

ⓘ *Olsen's Caves Rd, T4934 2883, www.capricorncaves.com.au, 0900-1600, standard tours $15, child $7.50, 3-hr caving with own transport from $60 (1300), also with transfers from Rockhampton available (Mon, Wed, Fri, Sat, Sun); half-day standard tour with transport daily from $33, full-day standard tour with transfers (Sun, Mon, Wed, Fri) from $64. Accommodation packages also available.*

This fascinating limestone cave system, 23 km north of Rockhampton, is well worth a visit. Privately owned and open to the public for over a century, the caves offer a memorable combination of subterranean sights and sounds and are home to an array of unusual wildlife. An entertaining guided tour takes you through numerous 'collapsed caverns', beautifully lit caves and narrow tunnels, to eventually reach a natural amphitheatre where stunning acoustics are demonstrated with classical music and then, utter silence. The venue is so special it is often used for weddings and Christmas carol concerts. During December and January, exiting visitors can witness a brilliant natural light spectacle created by the rays of the sun.

The cave system has been home to tens of thousands of bats and the odd harmless python for millennia, and although very few are seen, it adds that essential 'Indiana Jones' edge. The more adventurous can go on an exhilarating two- to four-hour caving tour and come face to face with the bats and pythons while squeezing through the infamous 'Fat Man's Misery'.

Yeppoon and around » pp301-307.

Blessed by a cooling breeze and a string of pretty beaches, the small seaside settlements of Yeppoon, Rosslyn Bay and Emu Park are the main focus of the Capricorn Coast and the region's principal coastal holiday resorts. Yeppoon – the largest – offers a wealth of affordable accommodation and safe swimming, while 7 km south, Rosslyn Bay provides the gateway to Great Keppel Island. One of the highlights of the area is the vast coastal wilderness of the **Byfield National Park** – a sanctuary to a rich variety of water birds and venue for some fine 4WD adventures.

Although most non-natives only stop briefly on their way to Great Keppel Island, the surrounding coastline offers plenty to see and do. There are beaches and headlands dotted all along the 16-km stretch of road between Yeppoon and Emu Park. South of Yeppoon the small national parks of **Double Head**, above Rosslyn Harbour, and **Bluff Point**, at the southern end of Kemp Beach, provide short walks and viewpoints across to Great Keppel Island. South of the Bluff, **Mulambin Beach** stretches south to **Pinnacle Point** and the entrance to **Causeway Lake**, a popular spot for fishing and boating. From there the road skirts **Shoal Bay** and **Kinka Beach**, considered by many as the best in the region, before arriving in Emu Park.

West of Yeppoon, just off the main highway, is the knobbly volcanic peak known as **Mount Jim Crow** (221 m). Who Mr Crow was exactly remains a mystery, but the peak was steeped in Aboriginal legend well before his arrival and can be climbed, with a bit of scrambling, from the old quarry.

To the north of Yeppoon, the seemingly boundless **Byfield Coastal Area** is one of the largest undeveloped regions on the east coast of Australia and, although the vast majority of it is taken up by the inaccessible Shoalwater Bay Military Training Area, the biodiversity of **Byfield National Park**, on its southern fringe, offers plenty of opportunity for camping, walking, boating, fishing, birdwatching and 4WD. The heart of the park is reached via the Byfield Road and Byfield State Forest, but you'll need 4WD, especially if you want to reach Nine Mile Beach. This is perhaps what makes the park so special. If such luxuries are beyond your budget then you can still get a feel for the place from the 'wetlands' west of the Rydges Capricorn Resort, or the Sandy Point Section of the park, to the north. Although the road is unsealed it is easily negotiable by 2WD and offers numerous access points to Farnborough Beach where you can have a stretch of pristine sand almost entirely to yourself. **Rydges Capricorn Resort** itself is also well worth a look, see Sleeping page 301.

Great Keppel Island » pp301-307.

Great Keppel Island (1,400 ha) is the largest of 18 islands in the Keppel group, which sits within easy reach of Rosslyn Bay. For many, Great Keppel provides the first real taste of Queensland's idyllic tropical islands. Although not quite on a par with Magnetic Island, it has a wealth of beautiful sandy beaches, walks and activities, with a good range of places to stay.

Despite having 17 beaches to choose from, few visitors venture beyond the main hub of activity at **Fisherman's Beach** which fronts the main resort and provides ferry access. You are far better to be more adventurous and seek out the quieter spots. A 20-minute walk to the south is **Long Beach**, which in turn provides access to **Monkey Beach**, 35 minutes away, across the headland to the west. North of the resort, beyond the spit, is **Putney Beach**, which offers pleasant views across to Middle Island. There are numerous walks around the island with the most popular being the 45-minute trek to **Mount Wyndam**, the highest point on the island. Longer excursions of around 1½ hours will take you to the realms of solitude and the island's northeastern beaches, including **Svendsen's**, **Sandhill** and **Wreck Beach**, or further still to the unremarkable light beacon on the island's southeast coast. Walking maps

Great Keppel Island offers the chance for some real get-away-from-it-all beach action

and descriptions are readily available from the ferries and resorts. With so many walks and beaches you will probably have very little time for anything else, but do check out the tame and beautiful rainbow lorikeets that frequent the resort's **Keppel Café**.

While Great Keppel Island is the main focus of activity, some of the other, smaller islands in the group offer more solitude, good snorkelling and camping. **Middle Island**, lying north of Great Keppel, is home to an underwater observatory that sits above a sunken Taiwanese wreck teeming with monster cod and other bizarre sea creatures. There is a QPWS campsite, but you will need to take your own water and gas stove. Other QPWS campsites are located at **Considine Beach**, **North Keppel Island**, and **Humpy Island**, renowned for its good snorkelling. Both sites have seasonal water supplies and toilets. For more details and permits contact QPWS office at the Rosslyn Bay Marina, T4933 6595. All the islands have a complete fire ban. **Pumpkin Island** (6 ha), just to the south of North Keppel, is privately owned but offers some accommodation.

Sleeping

Bundaberg and Southern Reef Islands *p293*

Beyond the usual rash of motels, Bundaberg has little choice. The town is short on quality backpackers with most catering for workers seeking cheap long-stays. If you have your own transport you are advised to head for the seaside resort of Bargara (12 km east) where you will find a number of pleasant low-key resorts and beachside motor parks.

L-C **Kacy's Bargara Beach Hotel and Motel**, corner of Bauer St and the Esplanade, Bargara, T4130 1100, www.bargaramotel.com.au. Has a good range of apartment and standard rooms and a good restaurant.

B **Inglebrae B&B**, 17 Branyan St, Bundaberg, T4154 4003, www.inglebrae.com. This traditional Queenslander style B&B is one of few in town and within walking distance of the town centre. It offers good-value, lovingly decorated en suites.

B-E **Cane Village Holiday Park**, Twyford St (2 km south of Bundaberg, off Takalvan St), T4155 1022. The best motor park in town, it has en suite/standard cabins, powered and non-powered sites and a camp kitchen.

B-E Turtle Sands Tourist Park, Mon Repos Beach, T4159 2340. This 3-star motor park is a good option if you are visiting the rookery as it's within walking distance of the information centre. It has beachside en suite/standard cabins, powered and non-powered sites, but no camp kitchen.
C-F Bargara Beach Caravan Park, The Esplanade, Bargara, T4159 2228. Spacious option near the amenities in Bargara, has good facilities and a camp kitchen.
D Bargara Gardens Motel and Villas, 13 See St, Bargara, T4159 2295. A good budget motel option with self-contained villas in a quiet tropical garden setting.
E Bundaberg Backpackers and Travellers Lodge, opposite the bus terminal on Targo St, Bundaberg, T4152 2080. An a/c dorms only hostel, friendly and popular with backpackers seeking work.
QPWS campsite, T4971 6500 (Gladstone), on Lady Musgrove Island. No water, and fires banned. Bookings essential and need to be arranged well in advance.

Agnes Water, 1770 and around *p295*
There is a good range of accommodation but both towns are getting increasingly busy, especially around Christmas and public holidays – book ahead.
L-A Beachshacks, 578 Captain Cook Dr, 1770, T4974 9463, beachshack@1770.net. Characterful, spacious, modern, fully self-contained bungalows complete with thatched roofs and decks overlooking the beach and next door to the local store and bottleshop.
A-F Captain Cook Holiday Village, 300 m further inland on Captain Cook Dr, 1770. Set in the bush and offers a good range of options from self-contained en suite cabins to campsites and a good bistro/bar. Fires are permitted and there is access to Agnes Water main beach.
B-F Agnes Beach Holiday Park, Jeffery Court, Agnes Water, T4974 9193. A 2 -star option handy for the beach and shops and offering self-contained units, cabins, powered and non-powered sites, but no camp kitchen.
C-E Cool Bananas 2 Springs Rd, Agnes Water, T1800-227660, www.coolbananas.net.au. Of the 2 backpackers in Agnes this is the newest and largest and has the most activity. It is a fine place, and very popular, with modern, purpose built facilities, fast internet, off-street parking and a wealth of organized activities, including surf lessons from $11. Excellent staff. Free pick-ups from Bundaberg on Mon, Wed and Fri.
C-E Backpackers 1770, Captain Cook Dr, Agnes Water, 1800-121770. This is the other backpackers in Agnes; smaller and quieter but no less impressive. Aesthetically unusual, it offers dorms and doubles with modern facilities.
E-F 1770 Camping Grounds, in 1770, T4974 9286. This is the most popular camping ground. It sits beachside on Captain Cook Drive and has powered and non-powered sites, a small camp kitchen and a shop. Fires are permitted.
QPWS campsites, at Wreck Rock, Deepwater National Park, 11 km south of Agnes, with toilets, rainwater supply and a cold shower, self-registration (fires are banned) and Bustard Beach, Eurimbula National Park, with bore water and toilets. Self- registration. Fires are banned. For more information on both parks contact the QPWS in Bundaberg, T4131 1770.

Rockhampton *p297, map p298*
There are plenty of good places in the centre of the city, and numerous motels and motor parks scattered around the outskirts and along the Bruce Highway.
L-B Coffee House Luxury Apartment Motel, corner of Williams St and Bolsover St, T4927 5722, www.coffeehouse.com.au. A tidy, modern establishment with well-appointed, fully self-contained apartments, executive and standard rooms. A fine café on site and internet.
B-D O'Dowd's Irish Pub, 100 William St, T4927 0344, www.odowds.com.au. Clean and good-value single, twin, double and family rooms.
B-E Rockhampton YHA, located across the river on MacFarlane St, T4927 5288,

Budget buster

Yeppoon and around sleeping

LL **Rydges Capricorn Resort**, Farnborough Rd, T49395111, www.capricornresort. com.au. This hugely popular resort is set in the perfect beachside spot on the fringe of the Byfield National Park. The focus of its popularity is not surprisingly its superb pool, golf courses and huge range of activities. It offers slightly aging apartments, suites and rooms with all the usual facilities, including 2 restaurants, a bistro and café. Although designed for extended package holidays they often offer very attractive short stay deals, especially on weekdays and in the low season. Bookings essential.

rockhampton@yhaqld.org. Rather plain but well maintained and well facilitated, it has standard doubles, some with en suite and dorms, new en suite cabins, a well-equipped kitchen, internet and tours desk. Onward trips to the coast and Great Keppel a speciality.

B-F **Capricorn Caves Eco-Lodge and Caravan Park**, Capricorn Caves, 23 km north of the city, T4934 2883, www.capricorncaves. com.au. Handy for visiting the caves.

C-D **Criterion Hotel**, Quay St, T4922 1225, www.thecriterion.com.au. Try this for a traditional, historical edge, overlooking the river, old fashioned and characterful rooms at good rates.

E **Riverside Caravan Park**, next to the river just across the Fitzroy Bridge, 2 Reaney St, T4922 3779. Basic, 3 star park. Convenient to the city centre, but only has powered and non-powered sites with limited facilities.

Yeppoon and around *p300*

L-F **Ferns Hideaway Resort**, located near Byfield, 50 km north of Yeppoon, T4935 1235, www.fernshideaway.com.au. Set deep in the rainforest, in near perfect isolation beside a creek, this colonial-style resort lodge offers log cabins with open fires and spa, basic budget rooms, campsites and a licensed bar and restaurant.

C-D **Sunlover Lodge**, 3 Camellia St, T4939 6727, www.sunlover.webcentral.com.au. Further afield in Kinka Beach is this excellent lodge offering a fine range of quiet, modern, fully self-contained cabins and villas, some with spa and all within a short stroll of the beach.

A-E **Capricorn Palms Holiday Village**, Wildin Way, Mulambin Beach (1 km south of Rosslyn Bay), T4933 6144, www.capricornpalms.com.au. This is the best motor park in the area with everything from deluxe villas to non-powered sites, a good camp kitchen and pool.

Great Keppel Island *p300*

The island is well known for offering a broad range of accommodation from luxury to budget. Before making a decision on island accommodation budget travellers should look into the numerous packages available, including those from Rockhampton/Yeppoon backpackers. This will save considerably on independent travelling costs.

A-E **Great Keppel Island Holiday Village** ('Geoff and Dianna's Place'), T4939 8655, wwwgkiholidayvillage.com.au. A laid-back place offering everything from a fully self-contained house to cabins, doubles/twins, dorms and custom built tents. Fully equipped kitchen, free snorkel gear and organized kayak trips.

A-E Self-contained cabins, on Pumpkin Island, T4939 4413. Each of the 5 cabins sleep 5 to 6 (from $155), there is a camping area with fresh water, toilet, shower and BBQ (from $10).

Eating

Bundaberg and Southern Reef Islands *p293*

ΨΨ **Bargara Beach Hotel and Motel**, corner of Bauer St and the Esplanade, Bargara, T4130 1100. Has a good bistro restaurant with Australian/Chinese, wood-fired pizza and is locally recommended.

ΨΨ **Numero Uno**, 167A Bourbong St, T4151-3666. Mon-Sat 1130-1400 and 1700-late, Sun from 1700. Licensed Italian restaurant offering value pastas and pizzas.

ΨΨ-Ψ **Grand Hotel**, corner of Targo St and Bourbong St, T4151 2441. Has a modern, licensed restaurant offering traditional pub grub, value breakfasts and good coffee.

Ψ **Ann's Kiosk**, in the Botanical Garden, Bundaberg, T4153 1477. Daily 1000-1600. Ideal for a light lunch in quiet surrounds.

Agnes Water, 1770 and around *p295*

ΨΨ-Ψ **Agnes Water Tavern**, 1 Tavern Rd, Agnes Water, T4974 9469. Daily for lunch and dinner. A popular haunt with long-term locals (now becoming an endangered species). Offers good value meals and has a pleasant garden bar.

ΨΨ-Ψ **Deck Restaurant**, Captain Cook Holiday Village, 1770 (see Sleeping above). Tue-Sat for lunch and dinner. Good value, local seafood, great views and a nice atmosphere.

Rockhampton *p297, map p298*

Unless you're a strict vegetarian, then you hardly need a menu in 'Rocky'. Big around here (literally) are the steaks.

ΨΨ **Criterion**, (Bush Inn), Quay St, T4922 1225 and the **Great Western**, 39 Stanley St, T4922 1862, are the best bets for steaks. Both are open daily from about 1100-late.

ΨΨ-Ψ **Belinda Anne's Gnomes Coffee Shop**, corner of Williams St and Denison Lane (mind the trains!), T4927 4713. Tue-Thu 1000-2200, Fri-Sat 1000-2300. With all the drooling carnivores around town it is not entirely surprising to find a fine vegetarian café. Full of character with an extensive blackboard menu.

Yeppoon and around *p300*

Ψ **Causeway Lake Kiosk**, beside the Causeway Bridge (between Rosslyn Bay and Kinka Beach). Daily until about 2000. The best fish and chips in the area.

Ψ **Keppel Bay Sailing Club**, above the beach on Anzac Parade, T4939 9500. Daily for lunch and dinner. Good value and a great view.

Ψ **Shorething Café**, 6 Normanby St, Yeppoon, T4939 1993. Has good breakfasts, coffee and internet.

Great Keppel Island *p300*

Other than the resort eateries (see Sleeping p301) there is **Keppel Island Pizza**, on the waterfront, T4939 4699, daily (except Mon) 1230-1400, 1800-2100. The resorts have limited groceries and they are pricey so you are advised to take your own food supplies.

Activities and tours

Bundaberg and Southern Reef Islands *p293*

Day-trips (by air) from Bundaberg to Lady Elliot Island cost from $239, child $119.

Footprints Adventures, T4152 3659, www.footprintsadventures.com.au. For local tours look no further than the dedicated team here. Turtle rookery night trips from $40.

Lady Musgrave Barrier Reef Cruises, at the Bundaberg Port Marina, 19 km northeast of Bundaberg, T4159 4519 www.imcruises.com.au. Day trips Mon, Thu, Sat, Sun (0800-1745), from $140, child $72. Certified diving is available, from $30, introductory dives from $70. Whale-watching trips operate between Aug-Oct. Camping transfers from$280. Day cruises are also available from the Town of 1770.

Salty's Dive Centre, 208 Bourbong St, T4124 9943, www.saltys.net. Offers a fine range of land and water based accommodation diving course packages (3-day from $510) which is good value for money compared with the high profile operators further north.

Agnes Water, 1770 and around *p295*

1770 Environmental Tours, 1770 Marina, T4974 9422, www.1770holidays.com. Offers an exciting and unique eco/history tour/cruise on board an amphibious vehicle (LARC), along the coast north of 1770 to Bustard Head and Pancake Creek. There are 2 tours on offer: Paradise Tour (Mon, Wed, Sat 0900-1600) which explores the beaches, Aboriginal middens and the stunning views from the Bustard Head Light Station and neighbouring cemetery, with a spot of sand boarding en route from $95, child $55. The second offering is Sunset Cruise (on demand, 1630) which is a 1-hr exploration of Round Hill Creek and Eurimbula National Park, from $25, child $12. Joyride is the same trip during daylight hours. Book ahead.
Reef Jet, T4974 7555, is another cruise operation offering exclusive day trips to Fitzroy Reef with snorkelling, sea mammal watching, reef surfing and scuba diving, from $130, child $70. Snorkelling trips to a 20-acre coral reef in Pancake Creek near Bustard Head are also available. A 2-day Reef and LARC combo costs from $195, child $110.
1770 Great Barrier Reef Cruises, based at the Marina, T4974 9077, www.1770reefcruises.com. Offers day trips and camping transfers to Lady Musgrave Island (51 km east of 1770), from $135, child $70 (plus $5 Reef tax). The cruise, dubbed the 'See More Sea Less' allows a whole 6 hrs on the reef, including a stop on a floating pontoon that acts as an ideal base for snorkelling, diving and coral viewing. Departs 0800 Tue-Sun. Lunch included and bookings essential. A shuttle bus is available from Bundaberg. Camping transfers to the island cost $270, child $140. For more information on Lady Musgrave Island see page 294.

Rockhampton *p297, map p298*

Farm stays

There are several renowned farm/station stays in the region, where you can go horse riding, on 4WD adventures and even learn how to milk a cow. These include **Kroombit Lochenbar Station**, 195 km away, T4992 2186, www.kroombit.com.au, a holistic outback nature experience with cattle drives, horse riding and 4WD tours (motor park on site), and **Myella Farmstay**, 125 km southwest of the city, T4998 1290, www.myella.com, 3 days, 2-night from $250 and day tours from $75.

Sightseeing tours

Beef-N-Reef Adventures, T1800-753786, offers an excellent, value range of full-day tours to numerous locations, including the Capricorn Caves or Croc Farm and then a taste of the outback, from $85.
Mt Etna Little Bent-Wing Bat Tours, T4936 0511, offers guided tours to see the comings and goings of tens of thousands of cave dwelling bats in the 'bat cleft' located in the Mount Etna Caves National Park. Dec-Jan only, 1730 on Mon, Wed, Fri, Sat, from $8, child $4. Own transport required.
Mount Morgan Experience, available from the city, with transport and lunch from $75. Contact the VIC or T4938 2312.

Yeppoon and around *p300*

Capricorn Coast Skydive, T4933 6688, www.skydivecapricorncoast.com.au. Jump out of a plane tandem, from $275/8000 ft- $355/12,000 ft.
Central Queensland Camel Treks, T4939 5248, camel rides from $10-50, and **Rydges Resort Horse Treks**, Farnborough Rd, T4939 5111.

Great Keppel Island *p300*

All the main accommodation establishments on Great Keppel offer their own range of activities and tours but day-trippers can access a huge variety of water-based activities and equipment from the beach hut directly opposite the ferry drop-off point. The island also offers some fine snorkelling and diving.

Freedom, T4933 6244, www.keppelbay marina.com.au. Range of cruise packages beyond their basic transfers to Great Keppel. These include a daily Coral Cruise in a glass bottom boat with fish feeding, from $56, child $30; a Boomnet Cruise from $60, child $35; a Snorkel Experience on the fringing reefs from $80, child $40 and a daily Lunch Cruise, from $65, child $35. Half-day/evening trips aimed at backpackers and including transfers to Rockhampton are also on offer weekly, from $40. Book ahead.

Great Keppel Island Holiday Village, T4939 8655. Excellent sea kayaking and snorkelling trips from $40.

Keppel Reef Scuba Adventures, Putney Beach, T4939 5022, www.keppeldive.com. Dive shop just beyond the Spit. Qualified dive from $77 including gear, introductory dive from $99, depart 0830 daily. They also offer island and beach drop-offs.

Transport

Bundaberg and Southern Reef Islands *p293*

Air Bundaberg airport is 3 km south of the city centre via the Isis Highway. Qantas, T131313, fly daily to **Brisbane**, **Rockhampton**, **Mackay** and **Townsville**.

For **Lady Elliot Island**, Whitaker Air, T4125 5344, www.ladyelliot. com.au, offers flight transfers from **Bundaberg** and **Hervey Bay** from $175, child $88. See also Activities and tours above (and for Lady Musgrave Island).

Bus Local services run by Duffy's Coaches, 28 Barolin St, T4151 4226, around the city, the Coral Coast, Rum Distillery, Bargara, Burnett Heads, Bundaberg Port Marina, several times daily. The long-distance bus terminal is at 66 Targo St, between Woondooma St and Crofton St. Greyhound, T131499, and Premier Motor Services, T133410, offer inter-State services north and south.

Train The station is right in the heart of city on the corner Bourbong St and McLean St. The *Tilt Train* is the preferred service between **Brisbane** and **Rockhampton** but other north/southbound services pass through daily, T132235. Stewart and Sons Travel, 66 Targo St, T4152 9700, act as booking agents for air, bus and train operators.

Agnes Water, 1770 and around *p295*

Bus Greyhound, T131499, offers part-transfers to Agnes (from the Bruce Highway) stopping at the Fingerboard Junction Service Station (about 30 km south of Agnes and 20 km east of Miriam Vale). There is a transfer bus from there. Bananas Backpackers offers their own pick-ups from Bundaberg.

Car/4WD The twin towns are best accessed from the Bruce Highway at Miriam Vale (55 km), or from the south via Bundaberg (120 km). All access roads are in the process of being sealed.

Street Beat, 8 Springs Rd, Agnes, T4974 7697, www.street-beat.com.au, from $65 per day for car and 4WD hire.

Train The nearest station is in Miriam Vale, T132232.

Rockhampton *p297, map p298*

Air Rockhampton Airport is 4 km west of the city centre. Qantas, T131313, and Jet Star, T131538, have regular schedules to main centres north, south and west. A taxi to town costs about $15.

Bus Capricorn Sunbus, T4936 2133, www.transinfo.qld.gov.au, is the local suburban bus company. Young's Coaches, 274 George St, T4922 3813, www.youngsbusservice.com.au, offers regular daily services to the train station, **Yeppoon** (Route 20); **Rosslyn Bay** (cruise boats); **Emu Park** and **Mount Morgan** (Route 22). The main local terminal is on Bolsover St. The Long-distance bus terminal, T4927 2844, is on the corner of Queen Elizabeth Dr and Bridge St, about

500 m north of the **Fitzroy Bridge**. Greyhound, T131499 and Premier Motor Services, T133410, offer north/southbound services.

Train The station is 1 km south of the city centre at the end of Murray St (off Bruce Highway). *Tilt Train* is the preferred daily service to **Brisbane**. Other slower services north/southbound are the budget *Sunlander* and luxury *Queenslander*. *Spirit of the Outback* heads west to **Longreach** Tue/Sat. There is a travel centre at the station, T132232.

Yeppoon and around *p300*

Bus Young's Coaches, 274 George St, T4922 3813, have regular daily services to Yeppoon (Route 20), Rosslyn Bay (cruise boats) and Emu Park.

Great Keppel Island *p300*

Air Great Keppel has its own airfield but services vary. For the latest details contact the VIC.

Bus Young's Coaches, T4922 3813, has regular daily services from Rockhampton to Rosslyn Bay (Route 20).

Ferry Both of the major ferry companies are based at Rosslyn Bay Harbour, 7 km south of Yeppoon. Freedom Fast Cats, T4933 6244, www.keppelbaymarina.com.au, are based at the new Keppel Bay Marina. They have a travel centre, shop, café and internet. Yacht charters are also available. The basic return fare to Great Keppel (30 mins) is $35, child $18. Ferries depart daily at 0900,1130 and 1530. See also Activities and tours above. Keppel Tourist Services, next door to the Keppel Bay Marina, T49336744, has a ferry terminal and offer a similar range of cruises and also provide transfers to Great Keppel. To reach the other islands, Rosslyn Bay ferry companies offer cruises daily to Middle Island. Other than Middle Island, all water transport must be arranged privately through the Keppel Bay Marina, T4933 6244, or water taxi, T4933 6133.

Directory

Bundaberg and Southern Reef Islands *p293*

Banks All the major branches have ATMs and can be found on Bourbong St. **Hospitals** Bundaberg Base Hospital, Bourbong St, T4152 1222. After Hours Medical Clinic, Mater Hospital, 313 Bourbong St, T4153 9500. Mon-Fri 1800-2300, Sat 1200-2300, Sun 0800-2300. **Internet** Cosy Corner, Barolin St (opposite the post office), T4153 5999, Mon-Fri 0700-1930, Sat 0700-1700, Sun 1100-1700. **Pharmacy** Amcal, 128 Bourbong St, T4151 5533. **Post** 157b Bourbong St, T131318. Postcode 4670. Mon-Fri 0900-1700, Sat 0830-1200. **Useful numbers** Police, 254 Bourbong St, T4153 9111.

Agnes Water, 1770 and around *p295*

Banks There is a Westpac Bank and ATM facilities in the Agnes Water's Shopping Complex. **Internet** Available at Bananas Backpackers, 2 Springs Rd.

Rockhampton *p297, map p298*

Banks All the main branches with ATMs are centred in and around the Mall on East St. Commonwealth Bank offer currency exchange services. **Hospital** Rockhampton Base Hospital, Canning St, T4920 6211. **Internet** Cybernet, 12 William St, T4927 3633. Mon-Fri 1000-1730, or the Library, corner of William St and Alma St, T4936 8265, Mon, Tue, Fri 0915-1730, Wed 1300-2000, Thu 0915-2000, Sat 0915-1630. Book in advance. **Post** 150 East St, Mon-Fri 0830-1730. Postcode 4700. **Useful numbers** Police, corner of Denham St and Bolsover St, T4932 1500.

Central & Far North QLD

Taking a cooling dip in the Mossman River

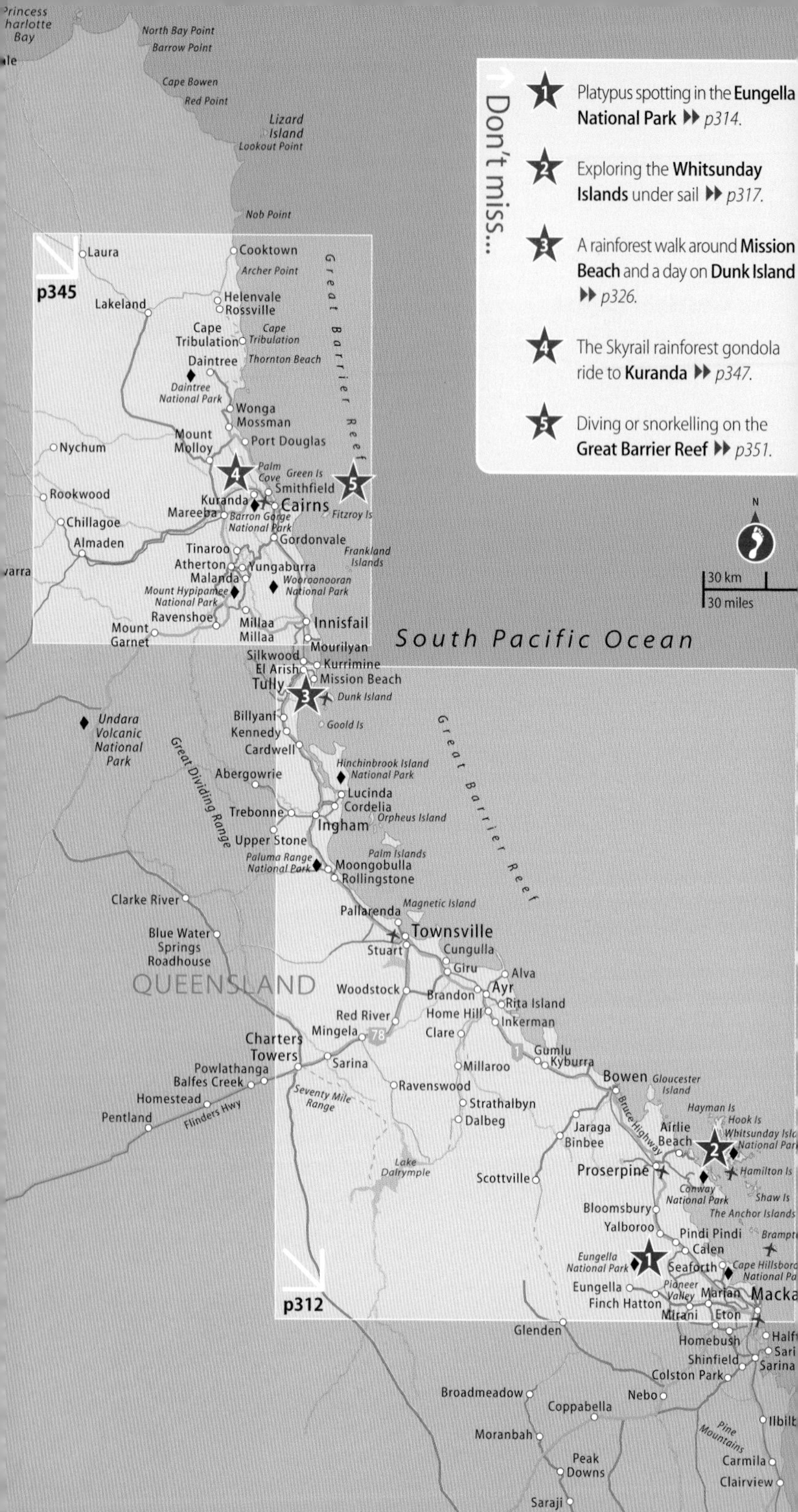

Don't miss...
1 Platypus spotting in the Eungella National Park ▶▶ p314.
2 Exploring the Whitsunday Islands under sail ▶▶ p317.
3 A rainforest walk around Mission Beach and a day on Dunk Island ▶▶ p326.
4 The Skyrail rainforest gondola ride to Kuranda ▶▶ p347.
5 Diving or snorkelling on the Great Barrier Reef ▶▶ p351.
30 km
30 miles
South Pacific Ocean
Great Barrier Reef
QUEENSLAND
p345
p312
Princess Charlotte Bay
North Bay Point
Barrow Point
Cape Bowen
Red Point
Lizard Island
Lookout Point
Nob Point
Laura
Cooktown
Archer Point
Lakeland
Helenvale
Rossville
Cape Tribulation
Daintree
Thornton Beach
Daintree National Park
Wonga
Mossman
Mount Molloy
Port Douglas
Nychum
Palm Cove
Green Is
Smithfield
Rookwood
Kuranda
Cairns
Mareeba
Barron Gorge National Park
Fitzroy Is
Chillagoe
Almaden
Gordonvale
Tinaroo
Frankland Islands
Atherton
Yungaburra
Malanda
Wooroonooran National Park
Mount Hypipamee National Park
Ravenshoe
Millaa Millaa
Innisfail
Mount Garnet
Mourilyan
Silkwood
Kurrimine
El Arish
Mission Beach
Tully
Dunk Island
Undara Volcanic National Park
Billyanı
Kennedy
Goold Is
Cardwell
Great Dividing Range
Hinchinbrook Island National Park
Abergowrie
Lucinda
Cordelia
Trebonne
Orpheus Island
Ingham
Upper Stone
Palm Islands
Paluma Range National Park
Moongobulla
Rollingstone
Clarke River
Magnetic Island
Pallarenda
Townsville
Blue Water Springs Roadhouse
Stuart
Cungulla
Giru
Alva
Woodstock
Ayr
Brandon
Rita Island
Home Hill
Red River
Inkerman
Mingela
Clare
Charters Towers
Gumlu
Kyburra
Sarina
Millaroo
Powlathanga
Bowen
Gloucester Island
Balfes Creek
Ravenswood
Seventy Mile Range
Homestead
Strathalbyn
Hayman Is
Hook Is
Pentland
Flinders Hwy
Dalbeg
Bruce Highway
Airlie Beach
Jaraga
Binbee
Lake Dalrymple
Proserpine
Hamilton Is
Scottville
Conway National Park
Shaw Is
Bloomsbury
The Anchor Islands
Yalboroo
Pindi Pindi
Calen
Eungella National Park
Seaforth
Eungella
Pioneer Valley
Marian
Finch Hatton
Mirani
Eton
Glenden
Homebush
Shinfield
Sarina
Colston Park
Broadmeadow
Nebo
Coppabella
Pine Mountains
Moranbah
Peak Downs
Carmila
Clairview
Saraji

Introduction

For many, the Central and North Coasts of Queensland are the raison d'être of an Australian holiday. Here are the sublime Whitsunday Islands, the effortlessly appealing Magnetic Island, heart-achingly beautiful Hinchinbrook and luscious Lizard Island. But it's not all about beaches, coral reef and tropical islands. Eungella National Park offers slopes draped in lush rainforest and cloaked in rain-baring clouds that in turn give rise to wonderful waterfalls and unusual wildlife, while, inland from Townsville, the historic gold-mining town of Charters Towers offers many their first taste of Queensland 'outback'.

Cairns is the region's tourist heart and gateway to the Great Barrier Reef and Wet Tropics Rainforest. Nowhere else on earth do two World Heritage listed eco-systems meet. North of Cairns is the small and sophisticated resort of Port Douglas, gateway to the wonderful Daintree National Park and the exhilarating route north to the wilds of Cape Tribulation. West of Cairns the lush, green plateau known as the Atherton Tablelands offers relief from the heat and humidity of the coast and a dramatic change in landscape.

Ratings

Landscape
★★★★★

Relaxation
★★★★

Activities
★★★★★

Wildlife
★★★★★

Costs
$$$

Central Coast

This is the home straight on the long trek north to Cairns and there's still an awful lot to pack in. The town of Mackay is the base from which to explore the reef island groups of Brampton, Newry and Carlisle. Inland, the lush slopes of Eungella National Park are home to wonderful waterfalls and unusual wildlife. Back on the coast the rush is on to reach the fast developing resort of Airlie Beach, gateway to the sublime Whitsunday Islands. Further north, Magnetic Island lives up to its name, attacting tourists with its beautiful beaches, while inland the historic gold-mining town of Charters Towers offers many their first taste of Queensland 'outback'. North again, is Mission Beach, like a mainland version of Magnetic Island, while, offshore, as always, are the tropical reef islands.

Getting there Interstate flights (Townsville); comprehensive interstate bus networks.
Getting around Local bus network or hire car/campervan.
Time required 7-8 days.
Weather Hot and humid in summer with occasional storms. Warm and dry in winter.
Sleeping Good hostels and motor camps in main centres; budget to luxury resorts on islands.
Eating Seafood recommended.
Activities and tours Sailing and island cruising, diving, white-water rafting, sky-diving, scenic flight-seeing, wildlife-watching – you name it, you can do it here!.
★ Don't miss Eungella National Park, the Whitsunday, Magnetic and Hinchinbrook Islands. » *p314, 317, 323 and 325.*

Mackay and around ▸▸ pp330-344.

Driving towards Mackay at night in early summer is a surreal experience. For miles around, sugar cane fields are awash with the orange glow of flames. Although the sugar cane industry is in crisis, and the burning of harvested cane fields in preparation for the next crop a less frequent sight, when it does happen it looks like the world is on fire. Ever since Scots pioneer John Mackay recognized the region's agricultural potential in 1862 it grew to become the largest sugar producing area in Australia and still hosts the biggest bulk processing facilities in the world. Although not tourist-oriented, Mackay provides a welcome stop halfway between Brisbane and Cairns and is also the gateway to several Barrier Reef and Whitsunday Islands and a fine base from which to explore the superb Eungella and Cape Hillsborough national parks.

Ins and outs

Mackay VIC ⓘ *320 Nebo Rd (Bruce Highway), T4944 5888, www.mackayregion.com, Mon-Fri 0830-1700, Sat-Sun 0900-1600*, housed in a former sugar mill, offers full booking services for local and island accommodation and tours. There is a smaller VIC in the Town Hall ⓘ *63 Sydney Rd, T4951 4803*. **QPWS office** ⓘ *corner of River St and Wood St, T4944 7800, www.epa.qld.gov.au, Mon-Fri 0830-1700*, offers information and permits for island and national park camping. ▸▸ p340.

Mackay

Although most of the Mackay's attractions are to be found beyond the city limits, the centre, with its palm-lined main street and pleasant river views, is worth a look. The heart of the city boasts some notable historical buildings, including the impressive façades of the **Commonwealth Bank** (1880), 63 Victoria Street, the former **Queensland National Bank** (1922), corner of Victoria Street and Wood Street, the Town Hall (1912) 63 Sydney Street

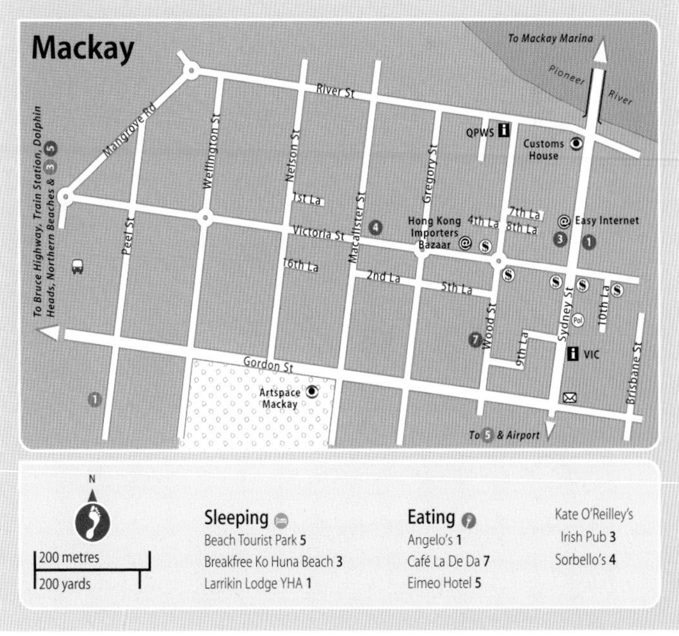

 (which houses the VIC and a small historical display) and the old **Customs House** (1902), corner of Sydney Street and River Street. The VIC stocks a free Heritage Walk leaflet.

The **Artspace Mackay** ⓘ *Gordon St Civic Centre Precinct, T4957 1775, www.artspacemackay.com.au, Tue-Sun 1000-1700, free*, is a welcome new architectural addition to the city. It houses an art gallery and museum showcasing the social and natural history of the region. Obviously the sugar industry features heavily but this is interspersed neatly with many contemporary displays including the school trophies of the city's most famous daughter, Olympic gold medal runner Cathy Freeman.

The beaches north of Mackay are well known for their tropical beauty and fine swimming and are a great place to recharge the travel batteries. The best spots are at **Black's Beach**, **Dolphin Heads** (Eimeo Beach) and **Bocasia Beach** and are best accessed from the Mackay-Bucasia Road off the Bruce Highway.

Aside from the lure of the beach, there is an opportunity to visit to one of the local sugar mills. **Fairleigh Sugar Mill** ⓘ *T4957 4727, Mon-Fri at 1300 Jun-Nov, access and tour $14, child $7.50*, in Fairleigh, northwest of Mackay, is open to the public during the crushing season. To the southwest **Polstone Sugar Cane Farm** ⓘ *Masottis Rd, Homebush, T4959 7298, Mon, Wed and Fri at 1330, Jun-Nov*, also offers tours.

Brampton and Carlisle islands

The islands of Brampton (464 ha) and Carlisle (518 ha) are part of the **Cumberland Islands National Park** which lies 32 km northeast of Mackay. Both are practically joined by a sandbank that can be walked at low tide and have a rich variety of island habitats, rising to a height of 389 m on Carlisle's Skiddaw Peak and 219 m on Brampton's namesake peak. The waters surrounding both islands are part of the Mackay/Capricorn Section of the Great Barrier Reef Marine Park, offering some excellent dive sites. There are 11 km of walking tracks on Brampton giving access to Brampton Peak as well as several secluded bays and coastal habitats. In contrast walking on Carlisle Island is rough with no well-formed paths. Instead you are better to explore the beaches or take to the water with a snorkel and mask, especially in the channel between the two islands. Day trips aren't available and the minimum stay is one night.

Newry Islands

The Newry group, also part of the Great Barrier Reef Marine Park, consists of six national park islands 50 km northeast of Mackay. Like the Cumberlands, they are hilly, diverse in coastal habitat types and rich in wildlife, including sea eagles, ospreys, echidna and bandicoots. Green sea turtles also nest between November and January on the largest of the group – Rabbit island. There are 2 km of walking tracks on Newry Island leading through rainforest and open forest to elevated viewpoints.

Cape Hillsborough National Park

Although positively petite compared to most of Queensland's other mainland national parks, Hillsborough is no less impressive, boasting some superb coastal habitats, views and beaches. It is also particularly famed for its tame, beach loving wildlife such as kangaroos, the aptly named pretty-faced wallabies and the distinctly more ugly scrub turkeys. There are four diverse walking tracks ranging from 1.2 km to 2.6 km in length, including the Juipera Plant Trail, which highlights the food plants once utilized by the Juipera Aboriginal people.

Eungella National Park and Pioneer Valley

The 80-km inland excursion from Mackay via the Pioneer Valley to Eungella (pronounced 'young-galah') offers an excellent diversion from the coast and access to what the aboriginal people once called 'the land of the clouds'. Whether shrouded in mist or gently baking under

Beware the endangered – and very large – cassowary, Mission Beach

the midday sun, Eungella and its exquisite national park possess a magic as special as the wildlife that lives there and the aboriginals who once did.

Immediately west of Mackay, the Mackay-Eungella Road branches off the Peak Downs Highway and follows the southern bank of the Pioneer River to the small sugar cane town of **Marian**. In **Mirani**, 10 km further west of Marian, you can find out why the two were so called, and if they were indeed sisters, at the small museum on Victoria Street. Just beyond Mirani is the **Illawong Fauna Sanctuary** ⓘ *T4959 1777, 0930-1730, $12, child $6*. It's a fairly low-key affair but worth stopping to see all the unusual suspects. Included is a walk through enclosures full of emus, wallabies and roos. The sanctuary also has accommodation, a café and its own tour company, **Gem Tours**.

A further 29 km past Mirani, beyond the small hamlet of Gargett and 1 km east of Finch Hatton Township, is the turn-off to the **Finch Hatton George section** of the Eungella National Park. In the dry season the 10-km road is suitable for 2WD, but in the wet, when several creek crossings are subject to flooding, the final 6-km gravel road often requires 4WD. At the gorge there is a private bush camp (see below), picnic site and access to the memorable **Wheel of Fire Falls** (5-km return) and **Araluen Falls walks** (3-km return).

Back on the main highway, the road head towards the hills before climbing dramatically, 800 m up to the small, pretty township of **Eungella**. At the crest of the hill, past a few worrying gaps in the roadside barriers, is the historic **Eungella Chalet**, with its spacious lawns, swimming pool and views to blow your wig off. As well as being an ideal spot for lunch, it is also a popular launch pad for hang-gliders.

From the chalet the road veers 6 km south, following the crest of the hill, before arriving at Broken River. Here you will find a picnic area, QPWS campsite and the **Eungella National Park Ranger Station** ⓘ *T49584552, open 0800-0900, 1130-1230, 1530-1630*. They will give you all the necessary detail on the numerous excellent short walks in the vicinity. There is also a platypus viewing platform nearby but bear in mind they can only be seen around daybreak. The park is also home to a host of other unique species including the Eungella honeyeater, the brown thornbill and the infinitely wonderful Eungella gastric brooding frog. The latter, as its name suggests, has the unenviable habit of incubating its eggs in the stomach before spitting the young out of its mouth.

Travellers' tales

If you wallaby my lover

Our best roo encounter (well wallaby actually) came while on our honeymoon, camping in the Hillsborough National Park in Queensland. Most campsites in Australia (even those in urban areas) have resident animals eager to share your lunch, but with our friendly wallaby this went a step further. While we were having dinner and being given the eye by our furry, flirting friend, a sudden heavy shower came over. Quickly, we erected our flysheet over our tiny tent and ducked inside. Nothing unusual in that of course and climbing into our sleeping bags we felt both snug and smug.
"Where's the wallaby?" I asked.
"Probably eating your meatballs!" replied my wife.
A few moments later a large, hairy bottom appeared next to my head and in an instant one side of the tent was flattened. The wallaby had sidled under the flysheet and was sitting peering out at the rain. Lord knows what it must have looked like from a far but from inside it was a scene of utter hilarity.
"Can I pat his bum?" asked my wife.
"By all means, if you want to collect the tent in Townsville", I replied.
Thankfully the shower passed quickly and my intimate encounter with the marsupial's nether regions was a brief one. But I swear that wallaby winked at me as we left the following day.

Murdo and Rowan McLeod, Portree, Scotland.

Airlie Beach *pp330-344.*

From a sleepy coastal settlement, Airlie Beach and its neighbouring communities of Cannonvale and Shute Harbour (known collectively as Whitsunday) have developed into the principal gateway to the Whitsunday Islands. With over 74 islands, many idyllic resorts and a long list of beaches, including Whitehaven, which is often hailed as among the world's best, it comes as no surprise that little Airlie has seen more dollars spent in the name of tourism in recent years than almost anywhere else in the State. With all the offerings of the Whitsunday Islands lying in wait offshore, most people use Airlie simply as an overnight stop but the town itself can be a great place to party or just relax and watch the tourist world go by.

Ins and outs

Getting there and around The nearest airports are at Proserpine and Hamilton Island. Long-distance bus services run from Cairns and Sydney, stopping at all major centres and cities along the way. Both north and south services run three times weekly. The train station is at Proserpine. The main centre is small and easily explored on foot. See page 337 for tours to the Whitsundays and below for tourist information details. *p341.*

Sights

Right in the heart of town, and the focus for many, is the new and glorious **lagoon** development. In the absence of a proper beach (and the accompanying threat of marine stingers between October and May) it has to be said that the local authorities have created a fine (and safe) substitute. A scary wildlife experience can be had at **Barefoot Bushman's Wildlife Park** ⓘ *T4946 1480, 7 km west of Airlie on Shute Harbour Rd, 0900-1630, $20, child $10, snake show 1100, croc-feeding 1200, 1400*, in Cannonvale, a fairly non-descript settlement just north of Airlie Beach. Here you can acquaint yourself with a wide array of nasty natives. The park is home to Rob – 'the barefoot bushman'– who is not as instrusive as the 'poke it, jump on it and annoy it' Crocodile Hunter, Steve Irwin. To spot wildlife for yourself, you can always take a quiet walk in a section of the **Conway National Park** between Airlie and Shute Harbour. There is a self-guided 6.5-km circuit walk through mangrove forest on the way to a lookout on the summit of Mount Rooper offering a slightly obscured view of Hamilton, Dent, Long and Henning Islands.

Whitsunday Islands ›› pp330-344.

With over 70 sublime, sun-soaked islands, the Whitsundays are not only the largest offshore island chain on the east coast of Australia but the biggest tourist draw between Brisbane and Cairns. It is hardly surprising. Many of the islands are home to idyllic resorts, from the luxurious Hayman and Hamilton to the quieter, more affordable, South Molle, as well as a plethora of beautiful, pristine beaches. Here, for once, the term paradise is not merely tourist board hyperbole.

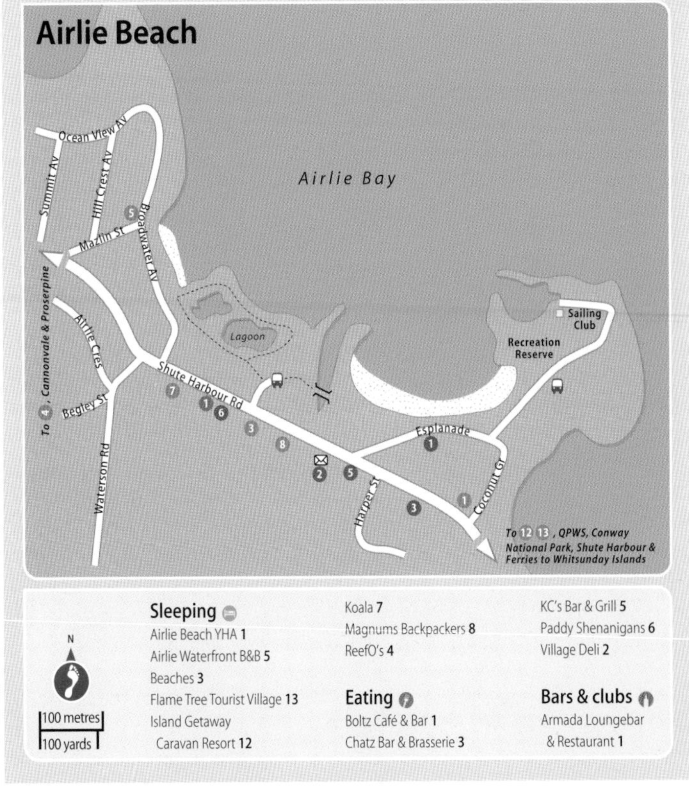

Ins and outs

Tourist information Whitsunday VIC ⓘ *Bruce Highway, Proserpine, T4945 3711, www.whitsundaytourism. com*, is the main accredited VIC for the islands. **QPWS office** ⓘ *corner of Shute Harbour Rd and Mandalay St, Airlie Beach, T4946 7022, www.epa.qld.gov.au, Mon-Fri 0900-1700, Sat 0900-1300*, is very helpful. They can supply all camping information and issue permits. Note, to obtain a permit you must have proof of return transportation. **Island Camping Connections**, T4946 5255, offers independent transportation by water taxis and hire out camping gear. Shute Harbour scheduled ferry services stop on most major island resorts. ⊖ ⏩ *p341*.

South Molle Island

South Molle (405 ha) is one of three little Molles (South, Mid and North) sitting about 8 km from Shute Harbour. Being in such close proximity to the mainland, and therefore relatively cheap to reach, South Molle is popular with day-trippers. With its varied habitats and hilly topography, the island offers some excellent walking and sublime views. The best of these is undoubtedly the 6-km **Spion Kop walk** that climbs through forest and over open grassland to some superb viewpoints across to the outer islands. The resort on the island is both pleasant and casual (see Sleeping page 332 for more details).

Long Island

Aptly named Long Island is the closest island to the mainland and runs parallel with the uninhabited coastal fringes of the Conway National Park. A national park in its own right, much of its 2,000 acres of dense rainforest is inaccessible, save for a loose network of tracks that connect a number of pretty beaches near the major resorts at the northern end.

Daydream Island

One of the smallest of the Whitsunday Islands - with a name almost as nauseating as the staff's shirts - Daydream is one of the closest islands to the mainland (just 5 km away) and most accessible. As such its congenial, if compact, surrounds and newly renovated resort have become a popular holiday venue. On offer for guests are a host of activities including sail boarding, jet-skiing, parasailing, reef fishing, diving, snorkelling, tennis and even

The Whitsundays are one of the Queensland coast's greatest attractions

croquet. Don't expect too many walking tracks, other the very short variety to the bar. Walking on little Daydream is like circling a small buffet table trying to decide what to choose. It is best just to sit back by the pool, shade your eyes from the staff's shirts and, well…daydream.

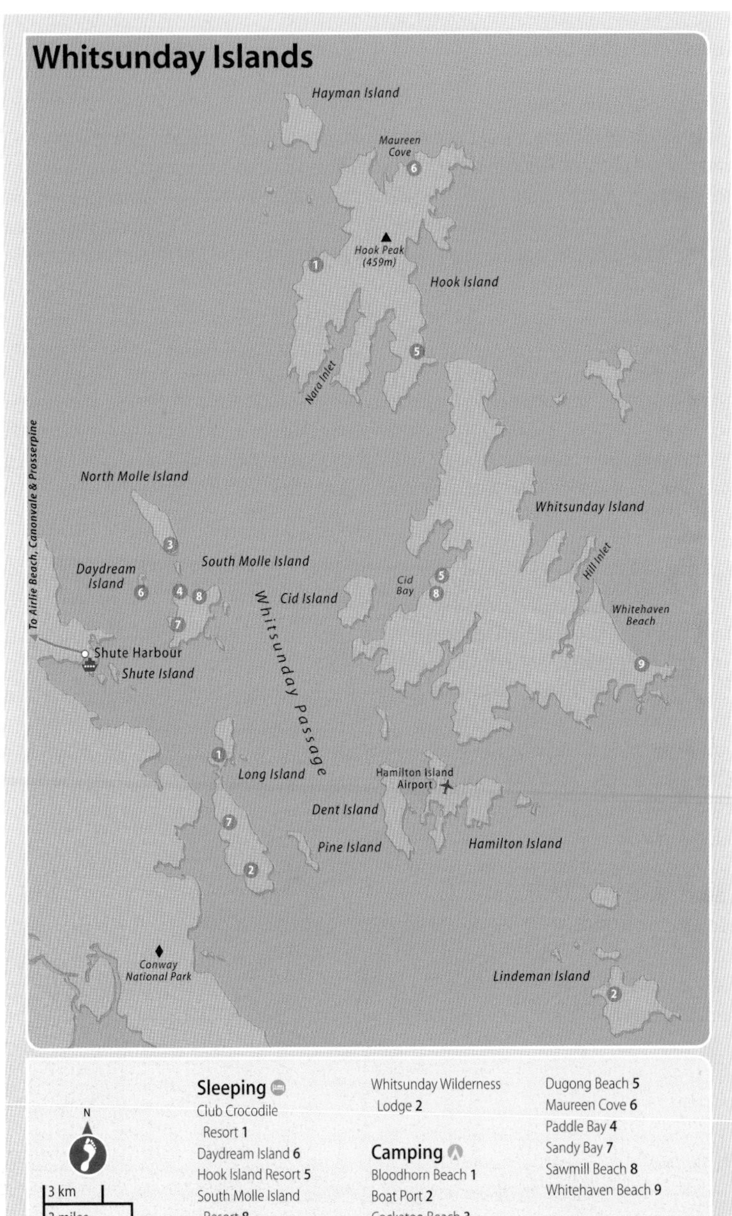

Whitsunday Island

At over 100 sq km, Whitsunday Island is the biggest in the group, boasting perhaps their biggest attraction – the 6-km white silica sands of **Whitehaven Beach**. Aerial views of this magnificent beach and the adjoining Hill Inlet repeatedly turn up in the pages of glossy magazines and on postcards as the epitome of the term 'tropical paradise'. Though best seen from the air, the beach is easily accessed by numerous day trips and island cruises, though in many ways this is its downfall. Thankfully uninhabited and without a resort, Whitsunday's only available accommodation comes in the form of eight QPWS campsites scattered around its numerous bays and inlets.

Hook Island

Hook is the second largest island in the group and the loftiest, with Hook Peak (459m) being the highest point of all the islands. Like the others it is densely forested, its coastline puntuated with picturesque bays and inlets. The most northerly of these, **Maureen Cove**, has a fringing reef that offers excellent snorkelling. Lovely Nara Inlet, on the island's south coast, has caves that support evidence of early Ngalandji Aboriginal occupation. It is also a popular anchorage for visiting yachties.

Lindeman Island

Lindeman Island, 20 sq km, is one of the most southerly of the Whitsunday group and the most visited of a cluster that make up the **Lindeman Island National Park**. It offers all the usual natural features of beautiful inlets and bays and has over 20 km of walking tracks that take you through rainforest and grassland to spectacular views from the island's highest peak, Mount Oldfield (7 km return, 212 m). The island has seven beaches, with Gap Beach providing the best snorkelling.

Townsville » *pp330-344.*

Considered the capital of Queensland's north coast and the second largest city in the state, Townsville had, until recently, shunned the tourist trappings of its northerly neighbour, Cairns. Recently, however, Townsville has started to make an effort to attract visitors and this is clearly working. Beyond the city centre, with its drab mall and bizarre 'sugar dispenser' tower block, the waterfront has been transformed into one of the most attractive in Australia. What it may still lack in aesthetics, it more than makes up for with its tropical climate, friendliness and huge range of activities on offer, not to mention the considerable attraction of the aptly-named Magnetic Island lying offshore.

Ins and outs

Tourist information The main **VIC** ⓘ *T4778 3555, 0900-1700,* is several kilometres south of town on the Bruce Highway. Also an information booth in the Flinders Mall ⓘ *T4721 3660, Mon-Fri 0900-1700, Sat-Sun 0900-1300,* can also be of assistance. Alternatively see www.townsvilleonline.com.au. **QPWS** ⓘ *Marlow St, T4796 7777.* » *p342.*

Sights

SS Yongala is a passenger ship that sank with all 121 crew – and a racehorse called Moonshine – during a cyclone in 1911. Located about 17 km off Cape Bowling Green, it is often touted as one of Australia'a best dives, offering diverse habitats and a huge range of species, including enormous manta rays, colourful coral gardens and even the odd human bone. Since the wreck sits at a depth of 29 m and is subject to strong currents, the dive presents a challenge and requires an above average level of competency. See Activities and tours, page 339 for details.

The long-established **Reef HQ** ⓘ *2-68 Flinders St East, T4750 0800, www.reefHQ.org.au, 0930-1700, $21.50, child $10.50, family $54*, is due for a multi-million dollar refurbishment and, though it's not on a par with Sydney Aquarium's remarkable Reef Exhibit, it still provides an excellent introduction to the reef. The centrepiece is a huge 750,000-litre 'Predator Exhibit', complete with genuine wave action, a part replica of the famous (local) *Yongala* wreck, an 'interactive island' and myriad colourful corals, fish and the obligatory sharks. Feeding takes place on most days at 1500, but equally interesting is the 'Danger Trail', a guided presentation (daily at 1300) that introduces some of the most deadly and dangerous creatures on the reef, such as the downright nasty box jellyfish (see the Safety section in Essentials for more on this charming creature). The star of the show, however, has to be the stonefish, which has to be the ugliest fish on the planet.

Next door to Reef HQ, the newly renovated **Museum of Queensland** ⓘ *Flinders St East, T4726 0606, www.mtq.qld.gov.au, 0930-1700, $10, child $6, family $26.50*, provides an impressive insight into the region's maritime history, with the story of *HMS Pandora*, the British 17th-century tall ship that is closely linked with that of the better known *HMS Bounty*. It was the *Pandora* that was dispatched by the British Admiralty in 1790 to bring the Bounty mutineers to justice, but her own voyage to the South Pacific proved no less notorious.

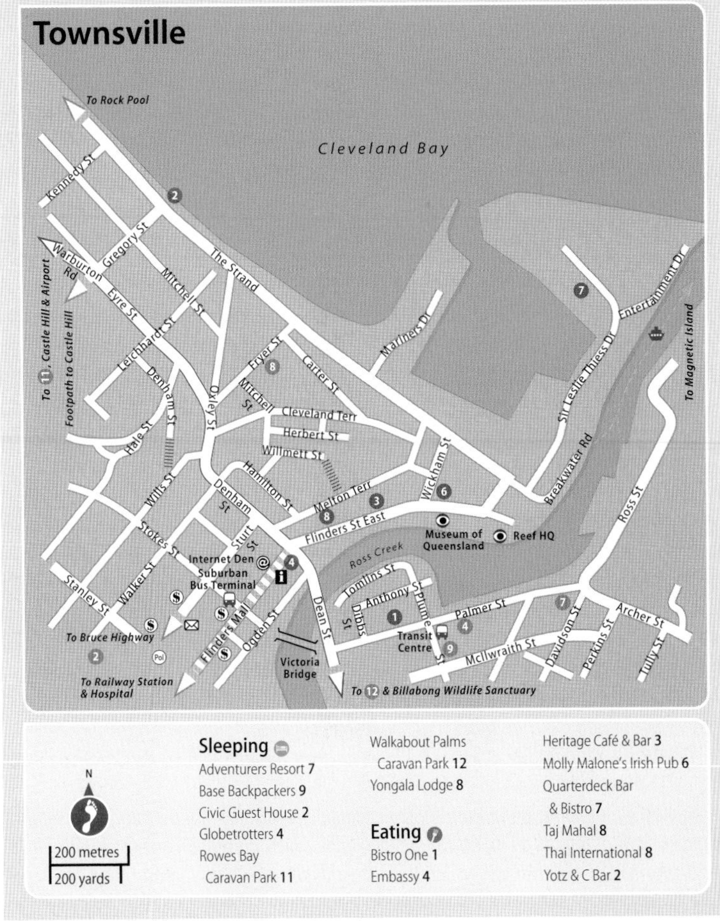

(Left) Koalas spend much of their time asleep; (Right) A wild roo enjoys an afternoon siesta

Having captured 14 of the mutineers on the island of Tahiti and then going in search of those who remained on the *Bounty*, the *Pandora* ran aground on the Barrier Reef, with the loss of 31 crew. The wreck was rediscovered near Cape York in 1977 resulting in a frenzy of archaeological interest and the many exhibits and artefacts are on show in the museum today. There is an interactive science centre to keep the less nautically inclined suitably engaged. The café has fine views across the river.

Fringing the shoreline east of the city centre is **The Strand**, which, along with the Museum of Queensland, is the new 'showpiece' of the city and part of its recent multi-million pound facelift. Said by some to be the most attractive public waterfront development in Australia, it provides an ideal spot to soak up the rays, take a stroll or break a leg on rollerblades. It is also designed to serve as protection against cyclones, but you won't find any signs advertising the fact. One of the most attractive features of the Strand are the 50-year old Bunyan Fig Trees that look like columns of melted wax. At its westerly terminus – **Kissing Point** – there is a man-made rock pool, which provides safe swimming year round and complete protection from the infamous 'marine stingers'. There is also a popular fish and chip shop and seafood restaurant next to the pool, but unless you want an enforced hunger strike while you wait in line, it is best avoided. For rollerblades hire, see page 337.

As well as the enigmatic 'sugar shaker' building, Townsville's skyline is dominated by **Castle Hill**, which glows orange in the rays of the rising sun. If you cannot drag yourself out of bed to see for yourself, then you can always make the climb to the summit by car or on foot and take in the memorable views, day or night. Access by car is at the end of Burk Street, off Warburton Street. The aptly named 'Goat Track' to the summit is off Stanton Street, at the end Gregory Street, also off Warburton.

Billabong Wildlife Sanctuary ⓘ *17 km south of the city, next to the Bruce Highway, T4778 8344, www.billabongsanctuary.com.au, 0800-1700, $25, child $14, family $74*, is undoubtedly one of the best in Queensland. Fringing an authentic billabong (water hole or stagnant pool), it houses an extensive collection of natives, from the leggy cassowary to the sleepy wombat. There are many tame roos and emus lazing on paths around the park, as well more dangerous individuals such as crocs and poisonous snakes. Various shows and talks throughout the day give you an opportunity to learn about the animals and if you wish, to handle the more docile serpents and baby crocs. Don't miss the smelly fruit bat colony next to the lake. If you do not have your own transport, **Billabong Tours**, T4724 1335, offer twice daily shuttles to Billabong (from $38, child $19, returning at 0900 and 1400).

Magnetic Island pp330-344.

Magnetic Island is Townsville's biggest tourist attraction and the most easily accessible 'tropical island escape' on the reef. Lying only 8 km offshore and baking in over 320 days of sunshine a year, 'Maggie' has always been a popular holiday spot, but its discreet permanent population also adds charm and an authenticity lacking in most of the resort-style islands. In fact, it is considered by many in the region as the most desirable suburb in Townsville. With its amenities concentrated in the eastern and northeastern fringes of the island, Maggie boasts a much larger area of wild and fairly inaccessible terrain giving an overall impression of wilderness and escape. With over half the island given over to national park, encompassing over 40 km of walking tracks, 20 picture-postcard bays and beaches, as well as a wealth of activities and some great budget accommodation, not to mention a resident population of koalas, the island certainly does earn its name in the number of visitors it attracts, though the real derivation is from Captain Cook (who else?) whose compass had a small fit as he passed by in 1770.

Ins and outs

Getting there and around There are regular ferry services from Townsville to Nelly Bay. The best way to explore the island is to hire a 4WD or moke. The four main villages spread along its eastern coastline are served by public transport. Tours are also available. p342.

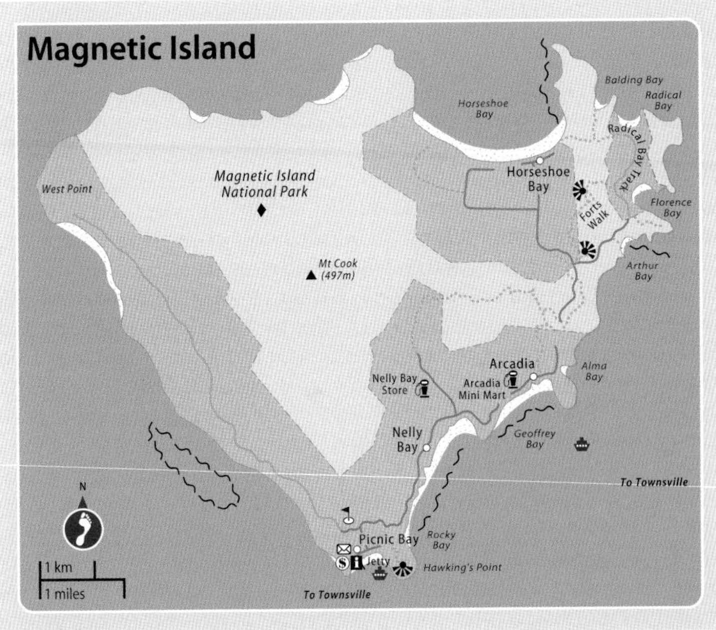

Hinchinbrook is the largest island national park in the world and one of the most unspoilt

Tourist information VIC ⓘ *Shop 1, Nelly Bay, T4758 1862, www.magneticisland info.com, 0800-1630*, is a short walk from the ferry. They offer transportation, accommodation and activity bookings.

Sights

With over 20 beaches to choose from there are plenty of places to set up camp and just relax. Although there is excellent swimming and some good snorkelling spots – most notably the left side of Arthur Bay – care must be taken during the stinger season from October to May, when you are advised to swim only in the netted areas at Picnic Bay and Horseshoe Bay. The most popular beaches are **Rocky Bay**, between Picnic Bay and Nelly Bay, and **Alma Bay**, just north of Arcadia, though the most secluded and most beautiful are **Arthur Bay**, **Florence Bay**, **Radical Bay** and **Balding Bay**, at the northeast corner of the island. All four are accessed via the unsealed Radical Bay Track, 8 km north of Picnic Bay (but note that all vehicle hire companies place restrictions on unsealed roads, so you may have to walk). Beyond these bays is **Horseshoe Bay**, the biggest on the island and a popular spot for swimming and watersports.

There are many excellent walking tracks on the island with the two most notable being the **Horseshoe Bay to Arthur Bay track** (3 km, two hours one way) and in the same vicinity, the **Forts Walk** (2 km, 1½ hours return). The Horseshoe Bay to Arthur Bay track can be tackled in either direction and takes in all the secluded bays and some low lying bush. Many allow themselves extended stops at one of the beaches since it can be very difficult to drag yourself away. The Forts Walk starts at the Radical Bay turn-off and follows the ridge past some old gun emplacements to the old observation tower lookout. This track is also one of the best places to observe koalas. Late afternoon (when they are awake and feeding) is the best time to see them. Another short walk to **Hawking's Point lookout** above Picnic Bay is also worthwhile. It starts at the end of Picnic Street (600 m, 30 minutes). To visit the more remote areas on the south and west coast requires your own 4WD, a boat or a very long trek. The unsealed track west starts from Yule Street, Picnic Bay, beside the golf course. Sadly, the island's highest peak Mount Cook (497 m) is inaccessible to anything other than the local

> From the moment you first see it, Hinchinbrook Island casts its irresistible spell. Even from afar, the green rugged peaks possess a dramatic air of wilderness.

wildlife. Magnetic Island is a superb and relatively cheap venue to learn to dive. There are also some excellent dive sites around the island, including the wreck of the *Yongala*. ▸▸ *p337.*

Hinchinbrook Island National Park ▸▸ *pp330-344.*

From the moment you first see it, Hinchinbrook Island casts its irresistible spell. Even from afar, the green rugged peaks possess a dramatic air of wilderness. Heading north from Townsville, the Bruce Highway passes Ingham before crossing the Herbert River and climbing to reach the breathtaking lookout across to Hinchinbrook, its mountainous outline and velvety green cloak of rainforest seeming almost connected to the mainland by the huge expanse of impenetrable mangrove swamps and smaller islands.

Ins and outs

The beachside town of **Cardwell** is jumping off point for Hinchinbrook. It is fast developing into a tourist resort and provides a welcome stop on the route north. The lengthy main drag, Victoria Street, hosts most amenities, accommodation and numerous operators offering fishing, cruising, flightseeing or wildlife watching activities, as well as the **QPWS Rainforest and Reef Centre** ⓘ *by the jetty, T4066 8601, www.epa.qld.gov.au, 0830-1630,* which provides local tourist information, details of seasonal eco-cruises operations and issues permits for Hinchinbrook Island National Park.

Around the island

At almost 40,000 ha, Hinchinbrook is the largest island national park in the world and, having changed little since white settlement in Australia, remains one of the most unspoilt. Crowned by the 1142 m peak of Mount Bowen, it is a wonderland of sheer cliffs, forested slopes and pristine beaches inhabited with some of the state's weirdest and most dangerous wildlife. And unlike many of its peers along the Queensland coast, Hinchinbrook presents more of a challenge than a relaxing excursion. Most who choose to visit the island do so for a day, but you can stay longer at one of two designated campsites, or in the lap of luxury at its one and only (expensive) resort (see box on page 331). For true explorers, though, there is only one mission – the famed **Thorsborne Trail**. This 32-km, 4-day (minimum) bushwalk, also known as the East Coast Trail, is one of best in the country and takes in a wide range of habitats along the east coast, from Ramsay Bay in the north to George Point in the south. Given its obvious popularity, only 40 intrepid souls are allowed on the track at any one time and you must book, sometimes up to a year in advance. The best time to do it is from April to September, which avoids the very wet and the very dry, but the topography of Hinchinbrook can create inclement weather at any time. The track is not graded and in some areas is rough and hard to traverse and insect repellent is an absolute must. QPWS provide detailed information on the track and issue the relevant camping permits (Ins and outs above). Their excellent broadsheet Thorsborne Trail is a fine start.

The beach at Dunk Island

Mission Beach and Dunk Island » pp330-344.

Taking its name from a former Aboriginal Mission established in the early 1900s, Mission Beach is the loose term given to an idyllic 14-km stretch of the Queensland coast from Bingil Bay in the north to the mouth of the Hull River to the south. The area is not only noted as the main tourist centre between Townsville and Cairns, but for the importance of its rainforest biodiversity, being home to many unique plants and animals. These include the umbrella-like Licuala Palm and the rare cassowary. There is plenty to see and do here, but it is as much a place to relax from the rigours of the road, as it is to explore its many natural delights. The superb offshore resort of Dunk Island, is no exception.

Ins and outs

Tourist information Mission Beach VIC ⓘ *El-Arish-Mission Beach Rd, Porter Promanade, T4068 7099, www.missionbeachtourism.com, 0900-1700*, is a powerhouse of information, fuelled with the management and volunteers' great enthusiasm. The area is hard to navigate, so be sure to secure the free Street and Business Directory. » *p343.*

Mission Beach

Wet Tropics Environmental Centre ⓘ *next door to the VIC, 1000-1700*, offers a fine introduction to the rainforest ecology and habitats of the region. If you plan on doing any rainforest walks, this is the place to get directions and all the relevant details. The centre also acts as a nursery for rainforest plants, collected, by all accounts, from cassowary droppings! Also of note are the records kept of the great bird's all-too-frequent disagreements with local automobiles. Before leaving this area, take a look at the large tree just to the south of the VIC and Environmental Centre. It is the seasonal home to a large colony of metallic starlings and in spring (August) becomes a hive of activity when the birds return to their own extensive and exclusive piece of real estate, in the form of countless, beautifully woven nests.

The main tracts of accessible rainforest are to be found in the **Tam O'Shanter State Forest** that dominates the region and contains one of the largest tracts of coastal lowland rainforest in northern Queensland. There are a number of excellent walks on offer, but take plenty of insect repellent. The best and the most moderate of these is the **Licuala Walk**,

The distinctive licuala palm trees dominate the rainforest at Mission Beach

accessed and signposted off the Tully-Mission Beach Road. It's a 1.2-km stroll under the canopy of the rare and beautiful Licuala Palms. On a hot day the torn lily pad-like leaves offer a cool and quiet sanctuary. There is also a special 350-m section designed for kids, where they can 'follow the cassowary footprints' to find a surprise at the end of the walk. If you are fit for a longer walk the 7-km/2-hour, **Licuala-Lacey Creek Track** also starts at the car park. This track cuts through the heart of the Tam O'Shanter Forest and links Licuala with Lacey Creek, taking in a the upper Hull River, a giant fig and lots of mosquitoes on the way. At Lacey Creek there is another short rainforest walk (1.1-km, 45-minutes), accessed and signposted off the El-Arish-Mission Beach Road. Just north of Mission Beach and Clump Point is the 4-km/2-hour **Bicton Hill Track**. It is a stiff, yet pleasant climb to the summit though views are rather disappointing once you get there. Yet another option is the historic, 8-km/4-hour return **Kennedy Track** (named after local explorer Edmund Kennedy), which heads from South Mission Beach to the mouth of the Hull River.

Other than the rainforest and Dunk Island, the big attractions in these parts are the beaches. There are over 65 to choose from, blending together into one 14-km long stretch of glorious, soft sand backed by coconut palms. While sunbathing here might be heavenly enough, you may also be tempted into the water to swim and to snorkel. But if your visit is between October to May , play it safe and stick within the netted areas off Mission and South Mission beaches, in order to avoid 'stingers'.

Dunk Island

Once named (far more aptly) 'Coonanglebah' by the Aboriginals meaning 'The Island of Peace and Plenty', this island was renamed Dunk by Captain James Cook in 1770 after Lord Dunk, First Lord of the Admiralty. But whatever its official label, this 730-ha national and marine park, lying less than 5 km off Mission Beach, certainly offers plenty and is one of the most beautiful island parks and resorts north of the Whitsundays. What is perhaps most attractive for the visitor is the fact that it is so easily accessible.

Whether staying at the resort or as day visitors, the vast majority come to relax big style, but if you can drag yourself away from the beautiful stretch of palm-fringed beach either side of the wharf in **Brammo Bay**, you can experience the island's rich wildlife or sample some of the many activities on offer. The island has 13 km of walking tracks and the reception in the

Queensland Outback

The former gold-mining settlement of Charters Towers, 132 km west of Townsville, offers a great outback experience and is only two hours away, via the sealed Flinders Highway. This was the second largest city in Queensland at the turn of the 20th Century - a place known as 'The World', where people's wildest dreams of wealth could come true. In its heyday, its gold mines yielded over six million ounces ($25 million) of the precious metal. Nowadays its better known for its beef production than its mineral resources, but is a fascinating example of a quintessential outback town.

With the help of the National Trust Charters Town has made some sterling efforts in the restoration of its heritage buildings and mining relics. The 'Ghosts of Gold Heritage Trail' begins at the **VIC** ⓘ *74 Mosman St, T4752 0314, www.charterstowers.qld.gov.au, 0900-1700*, which is housed in the former band hall building between the former Stock Exchange and City Hall. It covers a number of venues throughout the city and helps to bring to life the colourful stories, legends, incredible feats and the characters of the gold rush.

The trail includes the old Stock Exchange Building 0900-1500, built originally as a shopping arcade in 1888 and converted into a stock exchange in 1890 before being fully restored in 1970. Next door is the magnificent, former 1892 Australian Bank of Commerce building. The unusually named Ay Ot Lookout, on the corner of Hodkingson and the High Street, was built in 1896 and reflects the architectural excellence of the era. Guided tours of the interior are conducted throughout the week, 0800-1500, for $5. The **Zara Clark Folk Museum** ⓘ *1000-1500, $5, child $2.20*, houses a fascinating collection of photographs and memorabilia mostly donated by local residents.

On the outskirts of the city, east via Gill Street and Millchester Road, are the remains of the **Venus Battery Mill** ⓘ *0930-1630, guided tours on the hour, $11, child $5*, the largest surviving battery relic in Australia. Interactive displays tell the story of how the battery was used to extract the precious metal, and as you wander around its eight huge stampers and former cyanide ponds it certainly stirs the imagination back to the days when it was in full production. Just south of the city on the Flinders Highway are the Dalrymple Sale Yards, one of the largest stock sale yards in the state with countless head of beef cattle transported in by monstrous road trains – a true reminder that you are now in real outback country.

Nearby, Towers Hill provides excellent views across the city and beyond, especially at sunrise or sunset. It also serves as the last piece of the Heritage Trail incorporating an open-air amphitheatre, where in the evening you can once again watch the 'Ghosts of Gold' unfold before you, this time on film. Access by foot or by car is from the south end of Mosman Street, off Black Jack Road. Film tickets from the VIC. **Gold City Bush Safari Tours** is run by long-term local Geoff Philips. He provides an excellent day tour of the city with plenty of entertaining insight into Charters Towers old and new, from $20. Multi-day trips and adventures in remote outback areas are also a speciality. Book through the VIC.

Sleeping

A-D **York St B&B**, 58 York St, Charters Towers, T4787 1028, yorkstreetbb@httech.com.au, is an old, spacious Queenslander with welcoming hosts, offering doubles, singles and backpacker units and a pool. Recommended.
Charters Towers is the stepping-stone to popular outback stations offering comfortable accommodation mixed with the quintessential outback experience. Charters Towers VIC has full details.
A **Rosegreen Station**, 104 km north of Cloncurry, T4742 5995, rosegreen@bigpond.com.au, offers an outback station experience with activities including, fossil hunting, wildlife spotting, or kick-back and do nothing.
A-D **Bluff Downs**, T4770 4084, Rhonda@bluffdowns.com.au, is a historic 40,000 ha working cattle station, set around the spectacular deep water lagoons of the Basalt River, 80 km north of the city. It offers a range of activities from mustering to fossil hunting and accommodation ranging from a/c backpackers quarters to homestead rooms and a self-contained cottage.

Transport

Daily **Greyhound** bus service to/from Townsville, 1 hr 40 mins, from $29. The Inlander train service operates twice weekly services from Townsville to Mount Isa Sun and Wed from $24. The station is on the corner of Gill St and Enterprise Rd, T132232, www.traveltrai.com.au. **Travel Experience**, 13 Gill St, Charters Towers, T4787 2622, acts as bus and rail booking agents.

 main resort building can offer free maps and information. There are plenty of options, from the short 15-minute stroll to see **Banfield's Grave** at the eastern end of the resort complex, to a complete Island Circuit (9.2 km, three hours) which takes in the remote **Bruce Arthur's Artists Colony/Gallery** ⓘ *Mon-Thu 1000-1300, $4*. The energetic may also like to attempt the stiff climb (5.6 km, three hours return) to the summit of Mount Kootaloo (271 m), the island's highest peak.

The resort itself offers a day visitor's package that includes lunch and access to the bar, some sports facilities and the very attractive **Butterfly Pool** (from $30, child $19), tickets available at **Watersports**, next to the wharf. If you really want to push the pampering boat out, book a session at the heavenly **Spa of Peace and Plenty** where you can choose from a wide-range of alluring treatments, with such evocative names as the 'Floral Rain' or 'Taste of Tahiti'. Also book at **Watersports**.

Sleeping

Mackay and around *p313, map p313*

L-B **Broken River Mountain Retreat**, Broken River (for Eungella National Park), T4958 4528, www.brokenrivermr.com.au. Has a range of studio, 1- and 2-bedroom self-contained cabins, restaurant (open to the public) and an exciting range of in-house activities from night spotting to canoeing. There is also a delightful pet kangaroo.

A **Breakfree Ko Huna Beach** Griffin Ave, Bucasia, T4969 7575, www.kohuna beach.com. North of Mackay, in Bucasia, next to the beach, is this new option offering attractive self-contained apartments, in-house restaurant, pool and spa.

A-D **Historic Eungella Chalet**, Eungella, T4958 4509. As well as the magnificent views it has a wide range of options, from self-contained cabins with open fires to motel rooms and backpacker (weekday only) beds, an à la carte restaurant, public bar and swimming pool.

B-E **Beach Tourist Park**, 8 Petrie St, Illawong Beach, Mackay, T49574021, www.beachtour istpark.com.au. In the south, 4 km to the city centre, this 4-star motor park offers villas, cabins, powered and non-powered sites, a good camp kitchen and internet. It is beachside but don't expect to go swimming at low tide or you'll have a 3-km walk to reach the water!

B-E **Larrikin Lodge YHA**, 32 Peel St (200 m south of the bus terminal), Mackay, T4951 3728, larrikin@mackay.net.au. Backpackers will find a warm welcome here, the city's budget mainstay for some time now. It offers standard dorms, doubles and one family room with all the usual facilities in a traditional 'Queenslander'. Internet and entertaining in-house tours to Eungella National Park from $59.

B-F **Bucasia Beachfront Caravan Park**, 2 Esplanade, Bucasia Beach, T4954 6375. Some 10 km north of the city, this is one of several good motor parks in the area. It has 3-stars and offers self-contained villas, cabins, powered and non-powered sites and memorable views across to the Whitsunday Islands.

B-F **Cape Hillsborough Nature Resort**, Casuarina Bay in Cape Hillsborough National Park, T4959 0152, www.capehills borough resort.com.au. Has beachfront cabins, motel units or powered and non-powered sites. Fires permitted. There is a small store, pool, restaurant and bar lounge with internet.

B-F **Eungella Holiday Park**, North St (take the first right beyond the chalet), Eungella, T4958 4590, www.eungella-holidaypark.com.au. Has a self-contained cabin, powered and non-powered sites.

D-F **Platypus Bush Camp**, Finch Hatton Gorge Rd (for Eungella National Park), T4958 3204, www.bushcamp.net. Offers a superb and authentic bush camping experience. Created and maintained by a friendly and laid-back

Budget busters

Eco-friendly tropical island hideaways

LL-L **Hinchinbrook Island Wilderness Lodge**, Hitchinbrook Island, T4066 8270, www.hinchinbrookresort.com.au. This exclusive place offers an excellent, though somewhat expensive, sanctuary for those with enough cash to splash, with eco-friendly surroundings and all mod cons. Don't expect a party atmosphere or a place overrun with activities, this is a resort proudly in tune with the wilderness and environment that surrounds it. All in all a very nice place at which to indulge, relax and pamper yourself.

LL **Whitsunday Wilderness Lodge**, Long Island, T4946 9777, www.southlongisland. com.au. In almost perfect isolation on the island's western side, this is an architect's dream realized. It strives very successfully to create a relaxing eco-friendly retreat with a focus on the place rather than the amenities. Although basic and expensive, visitors very rarely leave disappointed. The accommodation is in comfortable en suite beachfront units. The hosts are very professional and friendly and there is a moody, yet enchanting pet kangaroo. The lodge has its own yacht which is part of an optional, and comprehensive, daily activities schedule.

bushman called 'Wazza', it features a characterful collection of basic open-air huts and campsites, set amongst the bush and beside the river. The huts range from single, through doubles to the notably more distant 'Honeymoon Hut', with its exclusive platypus-spotting opportunities. Other camp features include an open-air communal kitchen a sauna (all constructed from local cedar wood) and a fine swimming hole. Campfires are also authorized.

QPWS campsites At **Broken River** (for Eungella National Park), with toilets, drinking water, showers and gas BBQs, permits available at the Ranger Station (T4958 4552) which has a small food kiosk attached. Also at **Newry Island** and **Outer Newry Island**. The latter has a hut (maximum of 10 at any one time). **Rabbit Island** has a QPWS campsite with toilets and a seasonal water tank. Also available at **Smalley's Beach** at the western end of Cape Hillsborough National Park, T4944 7800, limited fresh water. There's a basic site at **Carlisle Island**, all supplies must be imported, seasonal water tank but a back-up supply should be taken anyway. Basic bush campsites are also on Goldsmith, Scawfell, Cockermouth, Keswick and St Bee's Islands. Permits and fees apply to all sites. Book ahead with the QPWS, Wood St, Mackay,T4944 7800.

Airlie Beach *p316, map p317*

Despite having numerous smart resorts, apartments and backpackers aplenty, Airlie can hardly keep pace with its own popularity and you are advised to book ahead. Many backpackers offer accommodation and activity combo deals, often booked from afar, but though these can be attractive in price, they can severely limit your choice.

L-A **Airlie Waterfront B&B**, corner of Broadwater St and Mazlin St, T4946 7631, www.airliewaterfrontbnb.com.au. This one of the best B&Bs in the region and certainly the best located for all amenities.

B-F Flame Tree Tourist Village, Shute Harbour Rd, T4946 9388, www.flametreevillage.com.au. Further east near the airfield, low-key in a quiet bush setting, with a camp kitchen and within easy reach of the ferry terminal.

B-F Island Getaway Caravan Resort, a short walk east of the town centre (corner of Shute Harbour Rd and Jubilee Pocket Rd), T4946 6228. This 4-star motor park is a popular option offering value units, cabins, camp-o-tels and powered and non-powered sites. Good camp kitchen and very tame possums.

C-E Airlie Beach YHA, 394 Shute Harbour Rd, T4946 6312. YHA members will get the usual discounts at this friendly and motel-style option.

C-E Beaches, 362 Shute Harbour Rd, T4946 6244, **C-F Koala**, Shute Harbour Rd, T4946 6001, and **C-E Magnums Backpackers**, 366 Shute Harbour Rd, T4946 6266, are the main players when it comes to the major party-oriented backpackers located right in the heart of the town. In many ways they are the heart of the town! At the end of the day (or night) they are all pretty similar and certainly fiercely competitive, always trying to outdo each other on the small details. But in essence they all have the full range of dorms, singles and doubles, boast lively bars, nightclubs, a pool, good-value eateries and internet. They can also advise on the best activities and trips (though this advice will not be completely objective).

C-E Bush Village Backpackers Resort, 2 St Martins Rd, Cannonvale, T4946 6177, www.bushvillageback packers.com. For a little bit of peace and quiet this is an excellent option. It is friendly with tidy and spacious self-catering cabins with a/c, en suite doubles, dorms, pool and a regular shuttle into town.

C-F ReefO's, 147 Shute Harbour Rd, T4946 6137, www.reeforesort.com.au. For sheer value for money this spacious and tidy place cannot be beaten. Dorm beds go for $16, with breakfast, en suite cabins with a/c and TV for $59. There is a bar/restaurant and small communal kitchen on site, as well as an excellent (and honest) tour/activities desk. Its only drawback is the walk into town but regular shuttles are available.

Whitsunday Islands *p317, map p319*

L-B Club Crocodile Resort, Long Island, T4946 9400, www.clubcroc.com.au. Offering its guests the perfect arrival point in Happy Bay, both atmosphere and amenities are casual but stylish.

L-B South Molle Island Resort, South Molle Island, T4946 9433, www.southmolleisland.com.au. A pretty relaxed offering all the usual mod cons to in-house guests and allowing day-trippers access to the pool, bar/bistro and some activities. It is also noted for its evening entertainment.

B-E Daydream Island, T4948 8488, www.daydreamisland.com. Daydream is the closest island to the mainland and one of the smallest, making it a popular base. The resort is modern and well facilitated offering attractive multi-night package deals, a luxury spa, open-air cinema and organized activities.

B-E Hook Island Resort, Hook Island, T4946 9380, www.hookislandresort.com. Located towards the southeastern end of the island, this is a low key resort, popular with budget travellers. It offers en suite cabins, standard cabins and dorms along with numerous activities, an underwater observatory, café-bar, pool and spa.

QPWS campsites Whitsunday Island There are 8 QPWS campsites here. The most popular is Whitehaven Beach, southern end. It can accommodate up to 60 and has toilets, but no water supply. The only campsites with water are Sawmill Beach and Dugong Beach, both of which fringe Cid Bay on the island's western side. They are connected by a 1-km walking track. There are 5 QPWS campsites on **Hook Island** with Maureen Cove and Bloodhorn Beach (Stonehaven Bay) being the most popular. None has a water supply. The only campsite on **Lindeman Island** is at Boat Port, with toilets but no water. **Long island** has a campsite on the western side of the island at Sandy Bay. It is a fine, secluded spot backed by rainforest, through which there is a track allowing you to explore and reach viewpoints overlooking the other islands. There are toilets but no water supply. **South Molle** has 2 campsites, at Sandy Bay and Paddle Bay with toilets but no water supply. There are 2 other sites on small offshore islands and at Cockatoo Beach on North Molle, but if the resort cannot offer you a lift in one of its vessels, independent access must be arranged. Cockatoo Beach site has seasonal water supplies.

Townsville *p320, map p321*

C **Yongala Lodge**, off the Strand on Fryer St, T4772 4633, www.historicyongala.com.au. Named after the famous local shipwreck, offers a range of basic motel units from single to 2-bedroom, has a pleasant Greek/ international restaurant and is a stone's throw from the waterfront.
B-E **Rowes Bay Caravan Park**, west of the Strand on Heatley's Parade, T4771 3576. Close to town, offering villas, cabins, powered and un-powered sites and is close to the beach, but no camp kitchen.
B-E **Walkabout Palms Caravan Park**, 6 University Rd, Wulguru, T4778 2480. This 4-star park is well facilitated and connected to the 24-hr petrol station. Although not central to the city it is in a good position for the transitory visitor right on the main north-south highway.
C-E **Base Backpackers**, corner of Palmer and Plume St, South Townsville, T1800-628836, www.basebackpackers.com. The most recent addition to the raft of backpackers here is this newly renovated and spotlessly clean option. Conveniently located above the transit centre and near trendy Palmer St, it offers the full range of rooms, all with a/c and some with en suite, good kitchen facilities, cable TV, fast internet, spa and the ubiquitous tours desk.
C-E **Civic Guest House**, 262 Walker St, T4771 5381, www.backpackersinn.com.au. A little less conveniently situated, but the pick of the bunch. It has a wide range of rooms (some with TV and a/c), good general facilities, a spa and interesting in-house trips.
C-E **Globetrotters**, 45 Palmer St, T4771 3242. Smaller and more intimate.
D-E **Adventurers Resort**, 79 Palmer St, T4721 1522, large and well facilitated with a rooftop pool. Attractive weekly rates.

Hitchinbrook Island National Park *p325*

There are as yet limited accommodation options in Cardwell. Hitchinbrook VIC can help with finding accommodation (see page 325 for details).
A-E **Kookaburra Holiday Park and Hinchinbrook Hostel (YHA)**, 175 Bruce Highway (north of the jetty), Cardwell, T4066 8648, www.kookaburraholiday park.com.au. YHA affiliated, this has everything from self-catering villas to campsites as well as dorms, doubles and twins in the well-facilitated hostel section. Pool, tours and activities bookings, internet and free bike hire for guests.
Camping Facilities on Hitchinbrook Island are at Scraggy Point (The Haven), on the island's northwest coast, and Maucushla Bay, near the resort. Toilets and gas fireplaces. **Bush camping sites** on Hitchinbrook Island have been established along the Thorsborne Trail with Zoe Bay offering toilets and water. Open fires are not allowed and you will require a gas stove and water containers. Camping permits for all sites must be obtained from the QPWS Rainforest and Reef Centre, see page 325, for contact details, or email to hinchinbrook.camp@env.qld.gov.au.

Magnetic Island *p323, map p323*

Picnic Bay, the main arrival point, offers many amenities but most of the accommodation is evenly spread down the east coast. There is plenty of choice, from luxury poolside apartments to a hammock, and most are virtually self-contained. For full listings contact the VIC and for budget accommodation, and during school and public holidays, book ahead.

L-C **Magnetic Island Tropical Resort**, Yates St, Nelly Bay, T4778 5955, www.magnetic islandresort.com. An excellent choice, has en suite chalet-style cabins with restaurant/bar, pool and spa, amidst a bush setting.

A **Beaches B&B**, 39 Marine Parade, Arcadia, T4778 5303. A small and pleasant beachside cottage in a quiet location, ideal for couples.

B-C **Marshall's B&B**, 3-5 Endeavour Rd, Arcadia, T4778 5112, www.moonshine.com.au. This eco-friendly option, next door to Magnetic North Apartments, offers basic, but good value singles and doubles in a traditional Queenslander house and is surrounded by spacious gardens with the odd friendly wallaby for company. Fans. Free night stand-by special (ie buy 2, get 3) from Oct-Jun.

B-F **Arcadia Hotel Resort** ('Arkies'), 7 Marine Parade, Arcadia, T4778 5177, www.arkiesonmagnetic.com. A busy, sprawling place with 30 a/c motel-style units (including dorms) close to all local amenities. Pool, spa, restaurant/bar and bistro. Internet.

A-E **Maggie's Beach House**, 1 Pacific Dr, Horseshoe Bay, T4778 5144, www.maggiesbeachhouse.com.au. A modern, purpose-built facility next to the beach and although the most remote and expensive of the backpackers it is, deservedly, the most popular. It offers a wide range of rooms, from en suites to dorms, has a pool, bar and internet café.

C-F **Bungalow Bay (YHA)**, 40 Horseshoe Bay Rd, Horseshoe Bay, T4778 5577, www.bungalowbay.com.au. Newly renovated and set in spacious grounds, offering everything from a/c chalets (some en suite) and en suite multi-share to camp and powered sites with camp kitchen. Regular, mass lorikeet feeding. Lively place with popular late night bar and bistro, pool, spa and internet but a little further away from the beach.

C-E **Base Backpackers**, 1 Nelly Bay Rd, Nelly Bay, T4778 5777, www.basebackpackers.com. South of Nelly Bay on the beach, this newly branded backpackers is regaining popularity after renovations. It has an interesting range of accommodation options from dorms to ocean-view *bures* (traditional South Pacific thatched huts). Modern facilities, in-house café, dive shop and home to the notorious 'Full Moon Parties'.

Mission Beach and Dunk Island *p326*

Although there is a smattering of resorts in the area, the many excellent and characterful B&Bs and self-contained accommodation are recommended.

LL-A **Sejala**, 1 Pacific St, Mission Beach, T4088 6699, www.sejala.com.au. Offers 5-star luxury in the form of a stunning beachfront villa with private pool or a choice of three very arty, self-contained beach huts with shared plunge pool.

LL-B **Dunk Island Resort**, Brammo Bay, Dunk Island, T4068 8199, www.poresorts.com.au. This 4-star resort offers a delightful range of units and suites, excellent amenities and a wealth of activities and sports on offer. Book well ahead. Children welcome.

L-F **Beachcomber Coconut Caravan Village**, Kennedy Esplanade, Mission Beach South, T4068 8129. There are several motor parks in the area including this very tidy and recommended beachside option.

L-F **Hideaway Holiday Village**, 60 Porters Prom, Mission Beach village, T4068 7104, www.missionbeachhideaway.com. This motor park is a little sterile but well facilitated and certainly handy for the beach and village amenities. Pool, camp kitchen and internet.

B **Missions**, corner of Banfield Rd and Wongaling Beach Rd, Wongaling Beach, T4068 8433. For a very modern and stylish motel option look no further than the new stand alone units here.

B-C **Licuala Lodge**, 11 Mission Circle, Mission Beach, T4068 8194, www.licualalodge.com.au. Excellent award-winning, pole house B&B with doubles, singles, and a memorable 'jungle pool' and spa. Dinner available on request.
B-C **Sanctuary Retreat**, 72 Holt Rd, Bingil Bay, T4088 6064, www.sanctuaryatmission.com. An interesting eco-retreat, wildlife enthusiasts will love it. The minimalist and secluded forest huts are in a setting designed to nurture and attract the local wildlife rather than scare it away. Restaurant, internet and pick-ups. Good value.
B-C **Dragonheart B&B Resort**, Bingil Bay, T4068 7813, www.dragonheartbnb.com. Offers a friendly welcome and separate accommodation in Balinese style cottages (with en suite) set in the rainforest. It also has a pool. A good choice and good value.
C-D **Treehouse YHA**, Bingil Bay Rd, Bingil Bay, T4068 7137, treehouse.yha@znet.net.au. Always popular, this pole house has doubles, twins and dorms a pool and all the usual amenities. Its only drawback is its distance from the beach but shuttle buses regularly ply the route.
C-E **Beach Shack**, 86 Porter Promenade, 1 km north of Mission Beach village, T4068 7783, www.missionbeachshack.com. This new complex is a colourful two-storey house opposite the beach and within walking distance to the village centre. It offers tidy dorms and doubles, 2 kitchens, spas and a relaxed, friendly atmosphere.
C-E **Bingil Bay Backpackers**, Cutten St, Bingil Bay, T4068 7208, www.nomadsworld.com.au. A/c motel style units in an elevated position with good views a pool and lively bar/bistro.
C-E **Mission Beach Backpackers Lodge**, 28 Wongaling Beach Rd, Wongaling Beach, T4068 8317, www.missionbeachbackpacker.com. Although nothing special to look at, it's a popular place with a social atmosphere, offering 10, 8 and 4 bed dorms and separate doubles with fans or a/c, a well-equipped kitchen. It is also close to the happening bar in the **Mission Beach Resort** and the main shopping complex.
C-E **Scotty's Beachouse Hostel**, 167 Reid Rd, Wongaling Beach, T4068 8676, www.scottysbeachouse.com.au. Closer to the beach than **Mission Beach Backpackers Lodge**, this is a well established and popular place, offering a range of unit style dorms and doubles surrounding a fine pool, a very relaxed atmosphere, restaurant and reputedly the best bar in town.
QPWS camping ground, Dunk Island, is discreetly located next to the resort. Permits can be purchased from Watersports on the island. BBQs and showers.

Eating

Mackay and around *p313, map p313*

¥¥ **Angelo's**, 29 Sydney St, T4953 5111. Open for lunch and dinner Wed-Sun from 1130. Probably the best Italian restaurant in town, though the good people at **Sorbello's** (166B Victoria St, T4957 8300) would disagree.
¥¥-¥ **Café La De Da**, 70 Wood St, T4944 0203. New establishment offering good quality and value.
¥ **Kate O'Reilley's Irish Pub**, 38 Sydney St, T4953 3522. The best for pub grub.
¥ **Eimeo Hotel**, Mango Ave, Dolphin Heads, 12 km away, T4954 6106. Daily 1200-2000. Cheap counter meals with spectacular views over Eimeo Beach and the Whitsunday Islands.
¥ **Hideaway Café**, just beyond the chalet, Eungella, T4958 4533. Daily 0800-1700. Well worth a stop. The delightful Suzanna has single handedly created her own little piece of paradise, with spacious gardens, home-made pottery and a wishing well. Take a tour of the imaginative and truly international menu while supping a coffee and soaking up the views across the valley.

Airlie Beach *p316, map p317*

¥¥-¥ **KC's Bar and Grill**, 382 Shute Harbour Rd, T4946 6320. Popular for seafood and meat dishes and has live entertainment most nights until 0300.

ŸŸ-Ÿ **Magnums** and **Beaches Backpackers** (see Sleeping above), have popular bar/bistros offering a wide variety of good-value dishes (including the obligatory 'roo burgers') and have a lively atmosphere. The two for one pizzas in the Magnums complex are also a bargain. Both are open for lunch and dinner.

ŸŸ-Ÿ **Paddy Shenanigans**, 352 Shute Harbour Rd, T4946 5055. This Irish pub also offers good value bar meals and is a fine place to remain for a night out.

Ÿ **Boltz Café and Bar**, 7 Beach Plaza, The Esplanade, T4946 7755. Daily 0700-late. Offers a varied Mediterranean lunch and dinner menu in modern surroundings and is also open for breakfast.

Ÿ **Chatz Bar and Brasserie**, at the eastern end of Shute Harbour Rd, T4946 7223. Daily until 0200. Good value lunches and dinners.

Ÿ **Village Deli**, 366 Shute Harbour Rd, T4946 5745. Tucked away at the back of the shopping complex, opposite the post office, good coffee, healthy snacks, fruit smoothies and breakfast in peaceful surroundings.

Townsville *p320, map p321*

There are reputable, upmarket restaurants in most of the major hotels and motels. Palmers St has now taken over from Flinders St East as the preferred venue of the local gourmand offering a wide range of international, mid-range options.

ŸŸ **Bistro One**, 30-34 Palmer St, T4771 6333. Popular, especially for seafood.

ŸŸ **The Embassy**, corner of Denham St and Sturt St, T4724 5000. Where meat lovers can attempt to conquer a 1000 g Mofo (reputedly Australia's biggest steak) at this delightfully cool (as in temperature) venue.

ŸŸ **Molly Malone's Irish Pub**, corner of Wickham and Flinders St East, T4771 3428. For pub grub, tidy surroundings and congenial atmosphere.

ŸŸ **Quarterdeck Bar and Bistro**, overlooking the marina, off Sir Leslie Theiss Dr, T4722 2261. It offers good-value seafood dishes in a nice setting, with live jazz on Sun from 1600-2000.

ŸŸ **Taj Mahal**, 2/235 Flinders Street East, T4772 3422. Good Indian cuisine.

ŸŸ **Yotz Restaurant and the CBar**, Gregory St Headland, T4724 5488, www.yotz.com. Daily for lunch and dinner. Fine venue for seafood and in the perfect spot overlooking the ocean.

ŸŸ **Thai International**, 235 Flinders St, T4771 6242. Daily 0530-late. Offer a takeaway service. Locally recommended.

Ÿ **Heritage Café and Bar**, 137 Flinders St East, T4771 2799. Nice atmosphere, varied and good-value blackboard of dishes.

Magnetic Island *p323, map p323*

The restaurants and cafés on Maggie tend to be very casual affairs and close early. Most of the major resorts and backpackers have cafés, bistros, or à la carte restaurants all open to the public. Self-caterers will find grocery stores in all the main centres mostly open daily until about 1900.

ŸŸ-Ÿ **Man Friday**, 37 Warboys St, Nelly Bay, T4778 5658. Wed-Mon from 1800. Mexican, traditional Australian and International dishes with vegetarian options.

Ÿ **Bannister's Seafood Restaurant**, 22 McCabe Cr, Arcadia, T4778 5700. Daily until 2000. Claims to offer the best fish and chips on the island.

Ÿ **Café Africa**, in the Mall, Picnic Bay, T4758 1119. Has an extensive blackboard menu and does good breakfasts and coffee.

Ÿ **Noodies**, on the waterfront, Horseshoe Bay, T4778 5786. Another place offering fine seafood and overlooking the beach.

Mission Beach *p326*

Most eateries are concentrated in and around the Village Green Shopping Complex on Porter Promenade in Mission Beach village, but between here and Wongaling Beach you won't be short of choice.

ŸŸŸ **Missions**, corner of Banfield Rd and Wongaling Beach Rd, Wongaling Beach,

T4068 8433. Daily for dinner except Wed. For fine dining with an international menu try this new and classy joint. Cleverly designed in typical, though modern, Queenslander style, on poles and open plan, it is stylish with food to match. Recommended.

ŸŸ **Raymond's on the Beach**, corner of Webb St and Banfield Parade, T4068 8177. Tue-Sun from 1100. Perfect for a quiet romantic dinner.

Ÿ **Café Geko**, Shop 6, The Hub, Porter Promenade, T4068 7390. Daily 0900-1700. Seems to change management regularly but maintains quality when it comes to a caffeine fix.

Ÿ **Scotty's Beachhouse Bar and Grill**, 167 Reid Rd, off Cassowary Drive, Wongaling. This place has a lively atmosphere and offers budget bistro meals.

Bars and clubs

Airlie Beach *p316, map p317*

Armada Lounge bar and restaurant, 350 Shute Harbour Rd, T4948 1600. The more discerning traveller might like to enjoy a sophisticated approach over cocktails.

Magnums and **Beaches Backpackers** have streetside bars which are popular and the best place to meet others for the obligatory wild night out.

M@ss, at **Magnums**, is a nightclub that rips it up well into the wee hours (sometimes quite literally, with wet tee-shirt competitions and foam parties).

Magnetic Island *p323, map p323*

The major backpackers provide most of the island's entertainment and have late bars.

Arkie's Resort, Arcadia (see Sleeping), has live bands most nights and full-on pool competitions every Thu.

Picnic Bay Hotel (see Sleeping), has pool competitions every Tue.

Activities and tours

Mackay and around *p313, map p313*

Jungle Johno Tours, T4951 3728, larrikin@ mackay.net.au. A popular option, offering entertaining ecotours and camping trips to Eungella National Park and the Finch Hatton Gorge. Platypus spotting is a speciality. Full to half-day from $59.

Mackay Reeforest Tours, T4959 8360, www.reeforest.com. Wider range of day tours to Hillsborough and Eungella National Parks and the Moranbah open cast coal mine, from $105, child $64, family $295.

Mackay Water Taxi and Adventures, T0417-073969. Snorkelling, deep-sea fishing and reef trips, full-day from $155.

Pro Dive Mackay, Shop 6, 34 Sydney St, T4951 1150, www.prodivemackay.com. Offers a range of courses, day and multi-day dive trips from $150.

Airlie Beach *p316, map p317*

With numerous dive shops, umpteen cruise operators, over 74 islands and almost as many vessels, the choice of water-based activities and trips is mind blowing. The two most popular trips are Whitehaven Beach and Fantasea's floating 'Reefworld' pontoon, which offers the chance to dive, snorkel or view the reef from a semi-submersible or underwater observatory. Note that these two options are also the most commercial and most crowded. The main ferry companies also offer island transfers and island 'day-tripper' specials with South Molle being a popular and good value choice.

Cruises

All offer a wide array of day cruises to the islands, the outer reef, or both. A day cruise will cost from $85-200.

Fantasea (Blue Ferries) Cruises, T4946 5111, www.fantasea.com.au. The major player with fast catamarans.

Budget busters

Scenic flights from Airlie Beach

There are several options for scenic flights from Airlie Beach. Most of the operators are based at the airfield between Airlie and Shute Harbour. Helicopter flight are also offered from the waterfront in Airlie; a 10-minute scenic flight around the bay costs from $69. In general a flight of 5-20 minutes of the town and inner islands (South Mole, Long and Daydream islands) will cost from $60-100. A scenic trip to Whitehaven with no stopover will cost around $180, while a 40-minute Whitehaven Beach flight with 2-hour stopover will cost from $225. Extended trips to the outer reef with stopovers will cost up to $500.
HeliReef Whitsunday, T4946 9102, www.av ta.com.au, offers a range of flight-seeing options by helicopter, fixed-wing and floatplane. **Air Whitsunday**, T4946 9111, www.airwhit sunday.com.au, and **Island Air**, T4946 9120, www.avta.com.au, both have a fleet of fixed- wing land and seaplanes and offer both tours and island transfers, from $69-499.

Whitehaven Express, T4946 7172, www.whitehavenxpress.com.au. Well established operator offering day trips to Whitehaven from $99.

Diving

The outer reef offers the clearest water and most varied marine life. There are numerous options with all local dive shops and most of the larger cruise companies offering day or multi-day trips and courses.
Reef Dive, Shute Harbour Rd, T4946 6508, www.reefdive.com.au. Offers 2-day/ 2-night packages from $295 and 3-day/ 3-night packages and certification from $440. Snorkellers are also catered for.
Oceania Dive, 257 Shute Harbour Rd, T4946 6032, www.oceaniadive.com.au. Offers 5-day open water course from $550 and 10 dive certified diver trip from $525).
Pro Dive, 344 Shute Harbour Rd, T4948 1888, www.prodivewhitsundays.com.au. Offers a 5-day Open Water Course from $545.
Reefjet, Shop 2, Abel Point Marina, T4946 5366, www.reefjet.com.au. Excellent day cruise to the Bait Reef (outer reef) and Whitehaven Beach with dive and snorkelling options from $138/$105 (snorkel only).
Tallarook, 4/1 Esplanade, T4946 4777, www.tallarookdive.com.au. Also hires dive equipment for independent divers, snorkelling gear and stinger suits.

Fishing

MV Jillian, T4948 0999. Offers entertaining half/full-day trips from the Abel Point Marina at 0900, from $85.
MV Moruya, T4946 7127. Another popular option, from $100, child $50.

Kayaking

Salty Dog Sea Kayaking, T4946 1388, www.saltydog.com.au. Half-day guided trips from $58, full-day from $115, 3- (from $395) or 6-day (from $1190), island camping adventures and independent kayak hire from $50 per day. The trips guarantee plenty of beautiful scenery as well as a spot of island bush walking and snorkelling.

Ocean rafting

Ocean Rafting, T4946 6848, www.ocean rafting.com.au. Runs a 6½-hr fast cruise around the islands and Whitehaven Beach on board their rigid inflatable. Includes snorkelling, guided rainforest and aboriginal cave walk from $79, child $47, family $234.

Quad biking

Whitsunday Quad Bike Bush Adventures, T4946 1998, www.bushadventures.com.au. Not only a lot of fun but great views, wildlife and history, 1 hr quad biking from $70, 2 hrs from $115. Mountain biking 6-hr from $80. Good wet weather activity.

Sailing

Again the choices are mind-boggling. A whole host of vessels from small dinghies to world-class racing yachts are available for day, night or multi-day adventures. Depending on the vessel type, accommodation and food, a day cruise will cost about $100 while a 2-day/2-night will cost from $285-$500; a 3-day/2-night trip around $375-$650 and a 3-day/3-night from $500-$900.

Townsville *p320, map p321*

Cruises

Sunferries, T1800-447333, www.sunferries.com.au. Full-day trip to John Brewer Reef with plenty of snorkelling, lunch inclusive from $139, child $74. Novice or experienced diving optional. Departs via Townsville and Magnetic Island at 0830.

Diving

There are several companies in Townsville or on Magnetic Island (which is often the preferred location) offering a wide variety of trips for certified divers wishing to experience the *Yongala*. It's best to shop around.

Diving Dreams, 252 Walker St, T4721 2500, www.divingdreams.com.au. Reputable 2-5 day trips from $445 and a day-trip to the *Yongala* from $175.

Sightseeing tours

Townsville Tropical Tours, T4721 6489, www,townsvilletropicaltours.com.au. Range of tours including entertaining full-day trips to the Paluma National Park and Charters Towers from $130.

Magnetic Island *p323, map p323*

Cruises/sailing

Jazza's Sailing Tours, 90 Horseshoe Bay Rd, T4778 5530, www.jazza.com.au. Good value, 6-hr cruise aboard the 12-m *Jazza* from $95, child $50 (includes lunch).

Magnetic Palm Islands Rent-A-Yacht, T4772 4773, www.miray.com.au. Hire of yachts from $440 per night and day sailing trips from Townsville.

Reef Rafting, based at the Nelly Bay Marina, T4758 1364. Offers 3-hr reef visits with snorkelling from $69, departing at 1300. Also land-based wildlife safari with koala-tracking the highlight, 3-hr from $49. Departs 0900, free pick-ups.

Diving

Magnetic Island Bus Service, T4778 5130. Offers 3-hr guided tours from Nelly Bay, 0900 and 1300 from $35, child $18, family $88.

Dive Shack, T4778 5690, www.diveshack.com.au. Multi-day PADI Open Water Courses and Advanced courses culminating with a trip to the *SS Yongala* from $449.

Golf

Magnetic Island has a small 9-hole golf course in Picnic Bay, visitors welcome, $15, T4778 5188.

Horse trekking

Bluey's Ranch, 38 Gifford St, Horseshoe Bay, T4778 5109. Horse treks from 1 hrs to half-day, from $75.

Sightseeing tours

Tropicana Tours, 2/26 Picnic St, T4758 1800, www.tropicanatours.com.au. Excellent and highly entertaining 9-hr '7 Days in 1' adventure around the island, from $135. Book ahead. See also Reef Rafting above for wildlife tours.

Watersports

Watersports, T4758 1336, www.jazza.com.au. Based at Horseshoe Bay, offers a range of activities from parasailing (from $60) to waterskiing (from $25). Closed Tue.

Magnetic Island Sea Kayaks, Horseshoe Bay, T4778 5424, www.seakayak.com.au. Half-day sea kayaking adventures from $59 which also includes a beach breakfast.

Hinchinbrook Island National Park

p325

Hinchinbrook Explorer Fishing and Eco-Tours, Mission Beach, T4088 6154, www.hexplorer.com. Full day national park or estuary fishing trips from $130 and night wildlife (croc) spotting trips up the Hull River from $50. See also Transport page 343 for cruises with Hinchinbrook island Ferries.

Mission Beach and Dunk Island *p326*

Many of the Mission Beach operators incorporate Dunk Island in their kayak and jet ski tours. Snorkelling on Dunk is poor compared to the reef.

Horse trekking

Bush 'n' Beach, T4068 7893. Offers 1½ to half-day rides along the beach from $50.

Skydiving

Skydive Mission Beach, T4052 1822, www.jumpthebeach.com. Great value tandem jumps on to Mission Beach or Dunk Island, 10000ft from $219, 14,000 from $270.

Paul's Parachuting, based in Cairns, T1800-005006, www.paulsparachuting. Com.au. Tandems with landings on Mission Beach at similar prices.

Watersports

Calypso Dive and Snorkle, T4068 8432, www.calypsodive.com. Has its own purpose-built dive centre in Mission Beach and as well as the full range of courses it offers wreck dives and a blast around Dunk Island in their rigid inflatable from $55.

Coral Sea Kayaking, T4068 9154, www.coralseakayaking.com. Full-day sea kayaking voyages to Dunk Island with plenty of time to explore and a fine lunch from $93 (half-day coastal exploration $60).

Dunk Jet Sports, T1800-688632, www.dunkjetsports.com. Offers a 2-hr circumnavigation of Dunk Island on jet ski, with lunch inclusive. Plenty of time is allowed after the tour to relax and explore Dunk itself. From $194. Departs South Mission Beach 0830.

Watersports, next to the wharf on Dunk Island, offers independent day visitors a host of equipment and water-based activities from a mask and snorkel hire to windsurfing, waterskiing and parasailing.

Wildlife night spotting

River Rats, T4068 8018, www.riverrat cruises.com. Fascinating evening eco-cruises up the Hull River from $42, child $22 and bird watching cruises from $34, child $18. See also **Hinchinbrook Explorer Fishing and Eco-Tours** above.

Transport

Mackay and around *p313, map p313*

There is no public transport to Eungella, though it is possible to make arrangements with local tour operators (see Activities and tours above).

Air

Mackay Airport, T4957 0255, is 2 km south of the city centre, along Sydney St and is served by **Qantas**, T131313, **Jet Star**, T131538, and **Virgin Blue**, T136789, www.virginblue.com.au. All have daily services throughout Queensland and New South Wales. **Whitsunday Island Air Taxis**, T49469933, has shuttle services to **Proserpine** and **Hamilton Island**. Taxis meet all flights and cost about $12 into town.

For **Brampton and Carlisle islands**, local companies also fly to and from Hamilton Island (see below) and daily to and from

Mackay. A launch service for resort guests is available from Thu-Mon, at 1130 from Mackay Marina, T4951 4499. Campers can take a scheduled launch and walk to the QPWS campsite or, alternatively arrange to be ferried directly to the island through the resort. **Qantas** flies to Brampton from Australian state capitals. For more information contact the QPWS office, Mackay.

Boat

For the Newry Islands, **Seaforth Fishing Tours**, Seaforth, T4959 0318, has transfers.

Bus

Local **Mackay Transit**, Casey Ave, T4957 3330, www.mackaytransit.com.au, is a hail 'n' ride bus service to Northern Beaches (Mon-Fri, route 7) and Mirani (route 11). Day Rover tickets are available.
Long distance **Greyhound**, T131499, stop at the terminal on Milton St, between Victoria and Gordon St, T4951 3088.

Taxi

Mackay Taxis (24 hrs), T131008.

Train

The station is 5 km southwest of the city centre on Connor's Rd, between Archibald St and Boundary Rd off the Bruce Highway. **Queensland Rail**, T132332. Taxis meet most trains and cost $15 in to the centre. Regular buses leave from Nebo Rd (Bruce Highway).

Airlie Beach *p316, map p317*

Air

The nearest airports are in Proserpine, 36 km west, and Hamilton Island in the Whitsunday Islands. Both are served by **Qantas**, T131313, and **Island Air Taxis**, T4946 8249, www.avta.com. au, who provide local island transfers by fixed wing or helicopter from **Mackay**, **Proserpine** or **Shute Harbour**. **Whitsunday Transit** buses meet flights in Proserpine.

Bus

Local **Whitsunday Transit**, T4946 1800, www.whitsundaytransit.com.au, offers daily buses from **Proserpine** to **Shute Harbour** (through Airlie) from $15.40 one-way. Buses between **Cannonvale** and **Shute Harbour** operate daily between 0600- 1845, from $5 one way. Day pass, $8.50.
Long-distance Buses stop beside the lagoon in the heart of town or next to the Sailing Club in the Recreation reserve. Either way most accommodation is within walking distance or you will be met by private shuttle. **Greyhound**, T131499, run regular daily services.

Taxi

Whitsunday Taxis, T131008.

Train

The nearest station is in Proserpine, 36 km west of Airlie, with 8 trains weekly including the Brisbane-Cairns Tilt Train. For bookings **Queensland Rail**, T132232. The station is served by **Whitsunday Transit**, T4946 1800, linking Proserpine with Airlie Beach and Shute Harbour and meets all arrivals.

Whitsunday Islands *p317, map p319*

Air

Proserpine Airport, 36 km west of Airlie Beach, on the mainland, and Hamilton Island Airport, provide air access. Both are serviced by **Qantas**, T131313. **Lindeman** is the only other island with an airfield.

Island Air Taxis, T4946 9102, www.avta.com.au, provides local island transfers by fixed-wing or helicopter from **Mackay**, **Proserpine** or **Shute Harbour**. **Air Whitsunday**, T4946 9111, www.airwhitsunday.com.au, also offers fixed-wing and seaplane services. All local fixed-wing, helicopter and seaplane companies also offer scenic flights (see box on page 338).

Boat

Shute Harbour, east of Airlie Beach, is the main departure point for ferry services to the Whitsunday islands. **Blue Ferries (Fantasea)**, T4946 5111, www.fantasea.com.au, offers daily services to **Hamilton** (6 per day, from $46 return), **South Molle/Daydream** (6 per day, from $34 return) and **Long Island** (3 per day, from $34 return). A range of 'Day-tripper' and adventure cruises that include use of resort facilities and lunch are also on offer from $50-70. Their main office is at the ferry terminal, with another office at Shop 10, Whitsunday Village, Shute Harbour Rd, Airlie Beach, T4948 2300. Ferry schedules are available at VICs. **Whitehaven Express**, T4946 6922, www.whitehavenxpress.com.au, runs a daily trip to Whitehaven Beach from Abel Point Marina (Cannonvale) from $99, child $55, family $295. **Kookaburra**, T4946 5299, www.airlie beach.com, runs a similar day trip. **Island Camping Connections**, T4946 5255, is based at the ferry terminal and offers island transfers for campers by water taxi, from $45-150. Book ahead.

Bus

Whitsunday Transit, T4946 1800, www.whit sundaytransit.com.au, has regular daily services from **Proserpine** to **Shute Harbour** (through Airlie Beach).

Townsville *p320, map p321*

Air

Townsville is serviced from all major cities by **Qantas**, **Jet Star**, and **Virgin Blue**. **Macair**, T4035 9722, www.macair.com.au, service several locations including **Cairns**, **Cooktown** and **Dunk Island**. The airport, T4727 3211, is about 5 km west of the city in the suburb of Garbutt.

Bus

Local Townsville's Sunbus, T4725 8482, www.sunbus.com.au, runs regular daily suburban services. Fares are from $2.50, Day Pass from $10.

Long-distance Premier Motor **Services**, T133410, and **Greyhound**, T131499. Westbound destinations include **Charters Towers**. The transit centre is at the corner of Palmer and Plume St, T4772 5100. Open daily 0430-2000.

Car

Main companies at the airport. **Townsville Car Rentals**, 12 Palmer St, South Townsville, T4772 1093.

Train

The station, Blackwood St, just south of the Flinders Mall, next to the river, has a travel centre, T4772 8358 (confirmations and timetable), T132232 (bookings), www.traveltrain.qr.com. au. *The Sunlander* and *Tilt Train* operate regular services between **Brisbane** and **Cairns**; *The Spirit of the Tropics* operates a twice-weekly service from **Brisbane** to **Townsville** and *The Inlander* run twice-weekly services to **Mount Isa**.

Magnetic Island *p323, map p323*

The island speed limit is a strict 60 kph. Fuel is available around the island.

Bus

Interstate buses stop in the centre of **Cardwell** off the Bruce Highway on Brasenose St.

Magnetic Island Bus Service, T4778 5130, runs up and down the east coast, between Picnic Bay to Horseshoe Bay every hour or so from 0600-2340. Tickets are sold on the bus from $2. One-day ($11) and two-day ($13) unlimited passes are generally the preferred option. They also offer 3-hr guided tours from Picnic Bay at 0900 and 1300 from $34, child $18.

Cycle and scooter hire

Magnetic Island Photos, Picnic Bay Mall, T4778 5411, rents bikes. **Road Runner Scooter Hire**, 64 Kelly St, T4778 5222, scotters from $35 per day. Bikes can also be hired from some hostels.

Ferry

Passenger ferries arrive at the Nelly Bay wharf. Vehicular ferries arrive at Geoffrey Bay, Arcadia. **Magnetic Island Car and Passenger Ferries**, Ross St, Townsville South, T4772 5422, www.magnetic-island.com.au, have regular sailings to Geoffrey Bay (Arcadia) Mon-Fri 0600-1720, Sat 0745-1540, Sun 0745-1720, from $123 (vehicle with up to 6 passengers), return. **Sunferries Magnetic Island**, T4771 3855, www.sunferries.com.au, offers regular daily sailings from both the Flinders St Ferry Terminal and Bayswater Terminal to Nelly Bay from 0550-1855 and from $23, child $12, return.

Moke and 4WD

One of the highlights of Maggie is exploring the island by mini-moke or toy-like 4WDs. **Moke Magnetic**, based at the Nelly Bay Marina, T4778 5377, www.mokemagnetic.com, hires mokes and vehicles seating up to 8 from $65 per day, with 60 km of fuel for free. Deposit $200. **MI Wheels**, 13 Pacific Dr, Horseshoe Bay, T4778 5491, hire mokes on a sliding scale rate for about the same rate as above. **Tropical Topless Car Rentals**, 138 Sooning St, T4758 1111, has a fleet of colourful (and topless) 4WD, comfortable, good value and economical, from $65 per day, flat rate, unlimited km. Credit card deposit.

Hinchinbrook Island *p325*

Hinchinbrook Island Ferries, Cardwell, T4066 8270, www.hinchinbrookferries.com.au, is the main operator in Cardwell and provides the northerly access to the island (including the resort, $60). It also offers day cruises from $90, child $45. Irregular schedule Nov-May. **Hinchinbrook Wilderness Safaris** (Bill Pearce) T4777 8307, or **Lucinda Reef and Island Charters**, T4777 8200, provide southerly access from Lucinda (from $50), east of Ingham, and a range of day tours and cruises. Most people doing the Thorsborne Trail attempt it from north to south using **Hinchinbrook Island Ferries** for the northerly drop-off and **Hinchinbrook Wilderness Safaris** for southerly pick up. Sailings vary according to season.

Mission Beach and Dunk Island *p326*

Air

Dunk has its own airport and regular flights are available from major Australian cities. **Qantas Link** from Cairns 4 times daily with **Macair**, T1800-622247, www.macair.com.au.

Boat

Dunk Island Ferry and Cruises (*MV Kavanagh*), T4068 7211, www.dunkferry.com.au, leaves Clump Point for **Dunk** twice daily at 0830 and 1030, from $32, child $16 return, but given the fierce competition fares are often reduced. Their Dunk Day Tour, which includes the use of facilities and lunch at the resort, costs as little as $32. It also offers cruise options to Bedarra Island and Barrier Reef with diving, snorkelling and boom netting. **Dunk Island Express**, T4068 8310, departs from the beach opposite their office on Banfield Parade, Wongaling Beach, 5 times daily, from $22, child $13 return ($26 if overnight). **Dunk Island Ferry and Cruises** and **Dunk Island Express** offer local courtesy pick-ups.

Quickcat, T4068 7289, leaves Clump Point for **Dunk** daily at 0930 and 1630, from $34, child $17 return. Quickcat also visit the outer reef and Beaver Cay which is a beautiful spot offering much better snorkelling than Dunk Island, from $150. Quickcat offers coach pick-ups from Cairns. Prices vary, so shop around.

Bus

Mission Beach Bus and Coach, T4068 7400, run the daily **Bingil Bay** to **South Mission Beach** service, single fare $1.50, day ticket $10, child $5. **Greyhound**, **Premier Motor Services** and **Coral**

Coaches have regular daily services from north and south stopping outside the post office on Porter Promenade in Mission Beach. **Mission Beach Connections**, T4059 2709, offers daily shuttles from **Cairns** (departing 0730 arriving at 0925 and departing **Mission Beach** 0730 arriving **Cairns** 0945 from $32 single. They link up with the *Tilt Train* in Tully from $9.

Directory

Mackay and around *p313, map p313*
Banks Branches at Victoria St and Sydney St. **Hospital** Mackay Base Hospital, Bridge Rd, T4968 6000. **Internet** Hong Kong Importers Bazaar, 128 Victoria St, T4953 3188, Mon-Fri 0845-1715, Sat-Sun 0900-1400, or Easy Internet, 22 Sydney St, T4953 3331, Mon-Fri 0830-1730, Sat 0800-1300. **Pharmacy** Night and Day, Sydney St (next door to the post office). 0800-2100. **Post** 69 Sydney St. Open Mon-Fri 0800-1700. Postcode 4740. **Useful numbers** Police, Sydney St, T4968 3444.

Airlie Beach *p316, map p317*
Banks Most (with ATMs) on Shute Harbour Rd in Airlie and Cannonvale. Currency exchange at Magnums Backpackers. **Medical services** Whitsunday Medical Centre, 400 Shute Harbour Rd, T4946 6275 (24 hrs). Whitsunday Doctors Service, Shute Harbour Rd, T4946 6241. **Pharmacy** Night and Day, Shute Harbour Rd, Airlie, T4946 7000. **Post** Shop 6A/366-370 Shute Harbour Rd, T4946 6515. Mon-Fri 0900-1700. **Useful numbers** Police, 8 Altmann Ave, Cannonvale, T4946 6445.

Townsville *p320, map p321*
Banks Most in and around the Flinders Mall. Currency exchange at Westpac Bank, 337 Flinders Mall. **Hospital** Townsville Hospital, 100 Agnes Smith Dr, T4796 1111. **Internet** Internet Den, 265 Flinders Mall, T4721 4500, Mon-Fri 0900-2100, Sat-Sun 1000-2000. **Post** Sturt St, T4760 2020, Mon-Fri 0830-1730. **Useful numbers** Police, corner of Sturt and Stanley sts, T4759 7777. RACQ, 202 Ross River Dr, T4725 5677.

Magnetic Island *p325, map p323*
Banks The post office, Nelly Bay, acts as Commonwealth Bank agents. There are ATMs at Picnic Bay Hotel, Arkie's Resort and Horseshoe Bay Store. **Internet** VIC, Nelly Bay, free with bookings and in Picnic Bay at most backpackers. **Medical services** At Sooning St, Nelly Bay, T4778 5614. **Pharmacy** Magnetic Island Pharmacy, Shopping Centre, Nelly Bay, T4778 5375, Mon-Fri 0900-1730, Sat 0900-1300. **Post** 43 Sooning St, Nelly Bay. Mon-Fri 0830-1700, Sat 0900-1100. Postcode 4819. **Useful numbers** Police, T4778 5270.

Mission Beach and Dunk Island *p326*
Bank/Post Post office, Porter Promenade, Mission Beach, is Commonwealth Bank Agent. ATMs in the Mission Beach Supermarket and at Comfort Resort Mission Beach. **Internet** Piccalo Paradiso, Village Green Complex, Mission Beach, and Mission Beach Information Station, shop 4, Mission Beach Resort Shops, Wongaling Beach. **Medical services** Medical Centre, Cassowary Dr, Mission Beach, T4068 8174. **Useful numbers** Police, corner of Cassowary Dr and Web Rd, Mission Beach, T4068 8422.

Far North Queensland

Far North Queensland offers more to see and do than any other region in Australia. The bustling tourist centre of Cairns is the gateway to the Great Barrier Reef and Wet Tropics Rainforest which, between them, offer a seemingly endless choice of activities, from world-class diving to wilderness outback tours. West of Cairns the lush, green plateau of the Atherton Tablelands is a cool retreat from the coast, while to the north, Cape Tribulation and Port Douglas are popular excursions. Few venture beyond Port Douglas but those adventurous souls who try will experience the very best that 4WD has to offer, and be exposed to some of Australia's true wilderness.

Getting there International and interstate flights (Cairns); interstate and regional bus networks. Rail from Brisbane.
Getting around Local bus network, local or regional tour companies or hire car/campervan.
Time required 7-8 days.
Weather Hot, humid and wet in summer. Warm and dry in winter.
Sleeping Good hostels and motor camps. Resorts on some reef islands.
Eating Good range in Cairns and Port Douglas.
Activities and tours Reef cruising, sailing, diving, outback tours and snorkelling.
★ **Don't miss** Diving the reef ▸▸ *p351*.

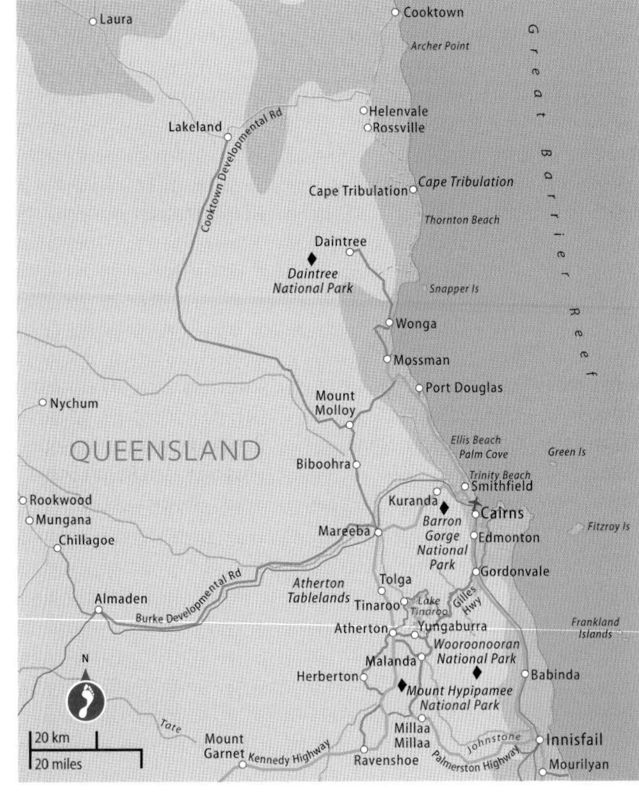

Cairns pp364-380.

Wedged between rolling hills to the west, the ocean to the east and thick mangroves swamps to the north and south, Cairns is the second most important tourist destination in Australia, only after Sydney. With the phenomenal Great Barrier Reef on its doorstep, Cairns was always destined to become a major tourist hot-spot, but the attractions don't end there. With the ancient rainforest of Daintree National Park just to the north, this is one of the very few places on earth where two such environmentally rich and diverse World Heritage listed national parks meet.

Ins and outs

Getting there Many hotels and hostels provide shuttle services to and from the airport, on the northern outskirts of the town. **Coral Reef Coaches**, T4098 2800, www.coralreefcoaches.com.au offers regular services to and from the city and throughout the region, from $12. **Cairns City Airporter** (Australia Coach), T4048 8355, offers services to the city and to/from Port Douglas, Cape Tribulation and Mission Beach. A taxi costs about $15, T131008. The interstate coach terminal is in the CBD, beside Trinity Wharf. Cairns Railway Station is located beside Cairns Central Shopping Complex. Coach and rail services from all major towns nearby, Brisbane and beyond. *p378.*

Getting around The centre of Cairns is compact and easily negotiable on foot. The attractive waterfront with its new lagoon complex serves as the social focus of the city during the day along with the many hostels, hotels, shops and restaurants along the Esplanade and in the CBD. South of the CBD, the new Lagoon and Trinity Pier complex gives way to Trinity Inlet and Trinity Wharf, where the reef ferry and interstate coach terminals are based. Local bus operators serve the outskirts of the city. Bike hire is readily available. Maps are available from **Absells Map Shop**, Andrew Jecks Arcade off Lake Street (55), T4041 2699.

Tourist information The number of independent 'commission based' information centres and operators in Cairns is famously out of control. For objective information and advice on accommodation and especially activities, look no further than the accredited **Tourism Tropical North Queensland** ⓘ *The Gateway Discovery Centre, 51 The Esplanade, T4051 3588, www.tropicalaustralia.com.au, 0830-1730.* **QPWS office** ⓘ *1 Moffat St, T4053 4533, www.env.qld.gov.au, Mon-Fri 0830-1630,* has detailed information on national parks and the Barrier Reef Islands, including camping permits and bookings. Other useful websites include www.wettropics.gov.au and www.great barrierreef.aus.net.au.

Sights

The majority of tourist activities in Cairns are focussed on the Great Barrier Reef. The choice is simply vast and includes diving and snorkelling, cruising, sailing, kayaking and flightseeing. On land the choices are no less exciting with everything from bungee jumping to ballooning. See page 371 for details. The city itself, however, does offer a number of colourful attractions.

The impressive **Lagoon Complex**, which overlooks the mudflats of Trinity Bay, is without doubt the city's biggest attraction and its new social hub. Cleverly designed and with shades of the hugely popular Brisbane and Airlie Beach urban lagoons, it is now the place to see and be seen and to watch the cosmopolitan comings and goings. Café and changing rooms on site.

The **Cairns Regional Art Gallery** ⓘ *corner of Abbott St and Shields St, T4046 4800, www.cairnsregionalgallery.com.au, Mon-Sat 1000-1700, Sun 1300-1700, $5, child free,* is housed in the former 1936 Public Curators Offices. Since 1995 the gallery has been an excellent showcase for mainly local and regional art as well as national visiting and loan

(Left) Fishy sculptures at the hugely popular Cairns Lagoon complex; (Right) A decorated telephone exchange box, typical of the street art in Cairns

exhibitions. The new **Centre for Contemporary Arts (CoCA)** ⓘ *T4050 9401, www.coca.org.au, Tue-Sun 1100-1700, café and bar from 1100-late, free*, intruigingly guarded on the outside by five man-sized Jelly Babies, is home to three resident arts companies and is never short of artistic programmes. Visiting international exhibitions also feature. Also worth a visit is the **Tanks Art Centre** ⓘ *46 Collins St, T4032 2349, Mon-Fri 1100-1600*, on the northern outskirts of the city. These former diesel storage tanks are now used as a dynamic exhibition and performance space for the local arts community.

The new **Rainforest Dome** ⓘ *T4031 7250, www.cairnsrainforestdome.com.au 0700-1800, $22, child $11*, housed in the glass rooftop dome of the **Reef Hotel Casino**, is a strange mix of hotel, casino and small zoo, but once inside the dome itself, it soon proves a very enjoyable experience and a far better bet than $20 on the card tables downstairs. There are over 100 creatures, from the ubiquitous koalas to 'Goliath' the salty croc. For some divine inspiration head for **St Monica's Cathedral** ⓘ *183 Abbott St, entry by donation*, to see the unique stained glass windows known as the 'Creation Design'. The huge and spectacularly colourful display even includes the Great Barrier Reef, complete with tropical fish. Leaflets are on hand to guide you through the design.

If you know very little about the reef and its myriad fascinating and colourful inhabitants, and especially if you are going snorkelling or are a first-time reef diver, you would greatly benefit from an appointment with **Reef Teach** ⓘ *14 Spence St, T4031 7794, www.reefteach.com.au, Mon-Sat show at 1815, $13.* Hosted by the rather over-animated Irish marine biologist and diver Paddy Cowell and his equally enthusiastic staff, it offers an entertaining two-hour lecture on the basics of the reef's natural history, conservation and fish/coral identification.

Skyrail Rainforest Cableway and Kuranda Scenic Railway

Skyrail: ⓘ *T4038 1555, www.skyrail.com.au. Daily 0800-1700. $36 one-way, child $18, return $52, child $26, price excludes Cairns transfers.* **Kuranda Scenic Railway**: ⓘ *T4031 3636, departs Cairns 0830 and 0930 (except Sat), departs Kuranda 1400 and 1530 (except Sat), $35 single, child $17.*

The award winning Skyrail Rainforest Cableway, 15 mins north of Cairns on the Captain Cook Highway, is highly recommended in both fine or wet weather and is perhaps best combined with a day tour package to Kuranda via the Kuranda Scenic Railway (see below). The once

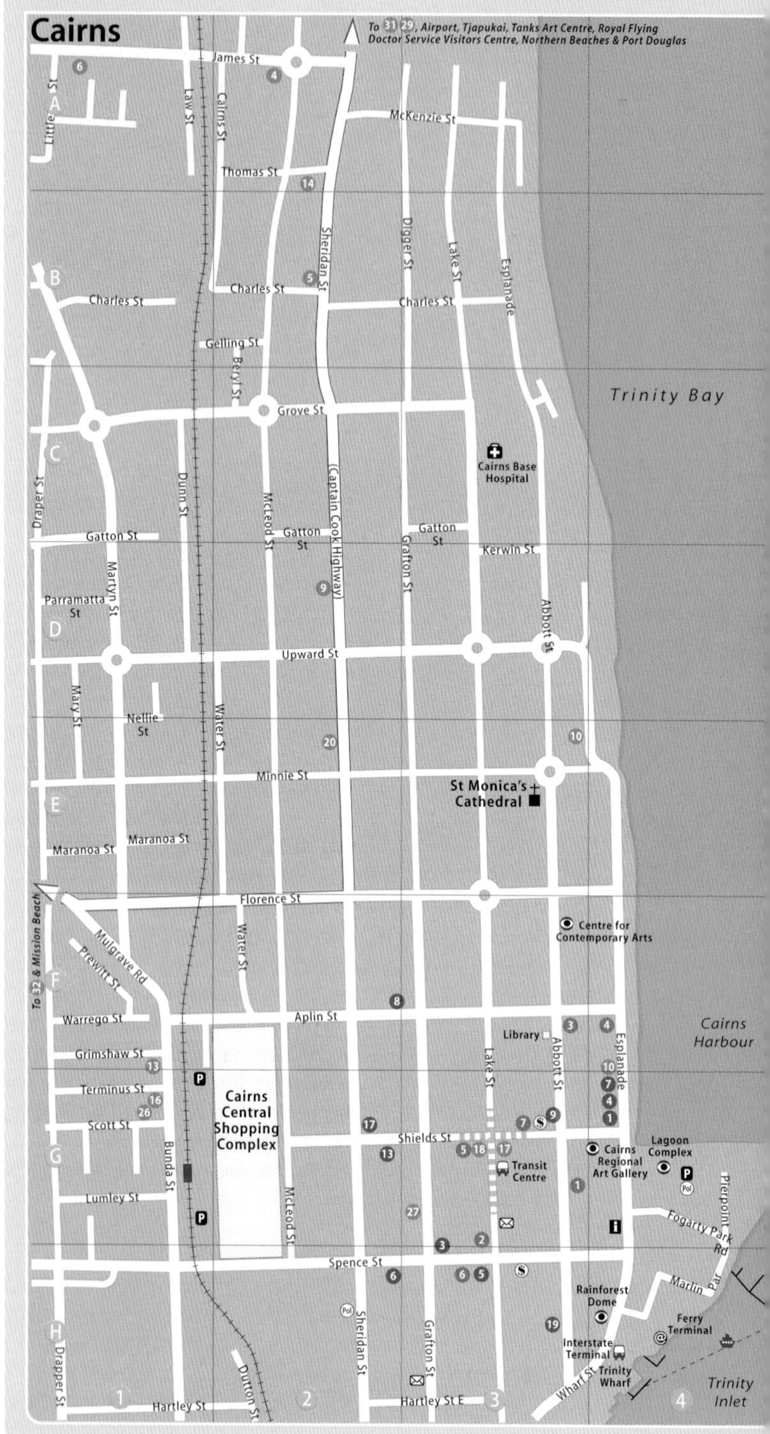

Cairns
To 31 29, Airport, Tjapukai, Tanks Art Centre, Royal Flying Doctor Service Visitors Centre, Northern Beaches & Port Douglas
James St
Little St
Law St
Cairns St
McKenzie St
Thomas St
Sheridan St
Digger St
Lake St
Esplanade
Charles St
Gelling St
Beryl St
Grove St
Trinity Bay
Cairns Base Hospital
Draper St
Dunn St
Mcleod St
(Captain Cook Highway)
Gatton St
Grafton St
Kerwin St
Martyn St
Parramatta St
Abbott St
Upward St
Mary St
Nellie St
Water St
Minnie St
St Monica's Cathedral
Maranoa St
Florence St
To 32 & Mission Beach
Mulgrave Rd
Prewitt St
Centre for Contemporary Arts
Warrego St
Aplin St
Library
Cairns Harbour
Grimshaw St
Terminus St
Cairns Central Shopping Complex
Scott St
Shields St
Bunda St
Transit Centre
Cairns Regional Art Gallery
Lagoon Complex
Lumley St
Pierpoint Rd
Fogarty Park Rd
Spence St
Marlin Par
Rainforest Dome
Ferry Terminal
Interstate Terminal
Trinity Wharf
Wharf St
Dutton St
Hartley St
Hartley St E
Trinity Inlet

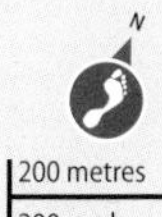

Sleeping
Bohemia Resort **4** *A2*
Cairns Beach House **5** *B2*
Cairns City Caravan Park **6** *A1*
Cairns Coconut Caravan Resort **32** *F1*
Cairns Rainbow Inn **9** *D2*
Carravella Hostels **10** *E4, F4*
Dreamtime Travellers Rest **13** *G1*
Fig Tree Lodge & Willie McBride's **14** *A2*
Geckos **16** *G1*
Gilligans Backpackers Resort **27** *G3*
Global Palace **17** *G3*
Hides **18** *G3*
Inn the Tropics **20** *E2*
Kookas B&B **29** *A2*
Travellers Oasis **26** *G1*
Trinity Beach Holiday Park **31** *A2*

Eating
Barnacle Bills **1** *G4*
Café China **3** *H3*
Coffee Club **4** *G4*
Dundee's **5** *H3*
Gaura Nitai's Vegetarian **6** *H3*
Inbox **9** *G3*
International Food Court **7** *G4*
Red Ochre Grill **13** *G3*
Verdi's **17** *G2*
Yamagen Japanese **19** *H3*
Yanni's Taverna **8** *F2*

Bars & clubs
Embassy **1** *G4*
Frog & Firkin **2** *G3*
Johno's Blues Bar **3** *F3*
P J O'Briens **5** *G3*
Sporties **6** *H3*
The Chapel **4** *F4*
Tropos **2** *G3*
Woolshed **7** *G3*

highly controversial Skyrail Gondola project was completed in 1995 and at 7.5 km is the longest cable-gondola ride in the world. It gives visitors the unique opportunity to glide quietly above the pristine rainforest canopy and through the heart of the World Heritage listed Barron Gorge National Park. From the outset the mere prospect of such an intrusion into the ancient forest caused international uproar. Conservationists and botanists the world over were immediately up in arms and high profile local demonstrations took place. But for once, all the fears and protestations proved groundless and now Skyrail has proved a highly impressive project that effectively encompasses both environmental sensitivity and education, with a generous dash of fun thrown in for good measure.

The journey includes two stops: one to take in the views and guided rainforest boardwalk from Red Peak Station (545 m) and another at Barron Falls Station where you can look around the entertaining Rainforest Interpretive Centre before strolling down to the lookouts across the Barron River Gorge and Barron Falls. The interpretative centre offers a range of displays and some clever computer software depicting the sights and sounds of the forest both day and night, while the short walkway to the falls lookout passes some rather unremarkable remains of the 1930s Barron Falls hydro-electric scheme construction camp. One word of warning here – prepare to be disappointed. Ignore the postcards or promotional images you see of thunderous, 'Niagara-like' falls. They only look like that after persistent heavy rain and/or during the wet season. Sadly for much of the year – from April to December – the falls are little more than a trickle. From the Barron Falls Station you then cross high above the Barron River before reaching civilization again at the pretty Kuranda Terminal. When you are crossing the rainforest you may be lucky enough to see the unmistakable Ulysses butterfly, which has become a fitting mascot of the North Queensland rainforest.

Mangrove trees at sunrise

The Kuranda Scenic Railway wriggles its way down the Barron Gorge to Cairns and provides an ideal way to reach the pretty village of Kuranda. To add to the whole experience, you are transported in a historic locomotive, stopping at viewpoints along the way (which provides respite from the rambling commentary). Skyrail can be combined with the Kuranda Scenic Railway for around $71, child $35.50. Tickets available on the web, from travel agents, tour desks, hotels, motels, caravan parks and at the VIC.

Tjapukai

ⓘ *T4042 9999, www.tjapukai.com.au, 0900-1700, day rates $30, child $15, night rates $84, child $42.*

Tjapukai, pronounced 'Jaboguy', is an award-winning, multi-million dollar Aboriginal Cultural Park lauded as one of the best its kind in Australia. It is the culmination of many years of quality performance by the local Tjapukai tribe. The 11-ha site, located next to the Skyrail terminal in Smithfield, offers an entertaining and educational insight into Aboriginal mythology, customs and history and, in particular, that of the Tjapukai. The complex is split into various dynamic theatres that explore dance, language, storytelling and history and there is also a mock up camp where you can learn about traditional tools, food and hunting techniques. For many, the highlight is the opportunity to learn how to throw a boomerang or to play a didgeridoo properly without asphyxiating. To make the most of the experience give yourself at least half a day. Tjapukai also offers a new 'Tjapukai by Night' experience' which begins at 1930 with an interactive, traditional and dramatic *corroboree* ritual, followed by an impressive buffet of regional foods and an entertaining stage show. Transfers are readily available for an extra charge and there's a quality restaurant and shop on site. Breakfast from $16, buffet lunch from $24.

Other excursions

North of the airport the thick mangrove swamps give way to the more alluring northern beaches and the expensive oceanside resorts of **Trinity Beach** and **Palm Cove**. Both make an attractive base to stay outside the city, or a fine venue in which to swing a golf club or to catch some rays. The VIC has listings. Other than Trinity Beach and Palm Cove the most northerly of the beaches, **Ellis Beach** is recommended. The northern beaches are also home to the **Cairns Tropical Zoo** ⓘ *Clifton Beach, 22 km, T4055 3669, www.cairnstropical zoo.com.au, 0830-1700, $26, child $13*, which houses crocs, snakes, wombats, etc, as well as a range of species unique to tropical North Queensland. It is very 'touchy-feely' and there are various shows on offer with everybody's favourite – the 'Cuddle a Koala Photo Session' – taking place daily at 1100 and 1430, $14 extra. Night Zoo kicks off at 1900 from Monday to Thursday and Saturday and combines a look at the many nocturnal animals in the zoo with a traditional Aussie BBQ and entertainment including the inevitable singalong around a campfire. Bookings are a must.

Some 40 km north of Cairns, on the road to Port Douglas, is **Hartley's Crocodile Adventures** ⓘ *T4055 3576, www.crocodileadventures.com, 0830-1700, $26, child $13*, one of the best wildlife attractions in the region. Long-term resident and near octogenarian croc 'Charlie', was, until his death in September 2000, the star exhibit. Despite his demise, the park has been greatly enhanced by a recent relocation and impressive renovations, and still hosts plenty of heavyweights (fed daily at 1100 and 1500). There are plenty of other animals in evidence, including the ubiquitous koala, wallabies and cassowaries. There's also a restaurant and shop. Just north of Hartley's Creek is the Rex Lookout from where you can get your first glimpse of Port Douglas and the forested peaks of the Daintree National Park and Cape Tribulation in the distance.

Northern Great Barrier Reef islands pp364-380.

Cairns is the principal access point to the some of the top attractions of the Great Barrier Reef. The GBR is sometimes referred to as the largest single living entity on earth and is certainly the largest coral reef on the planet, stretching 2,000 km from Cape York to the Tropic of Capricorn and up to 250 km at its widest point. Diving is the great attraction here, but if that's not your thing, then you should at least take a day-cruise to one of the islands to sample the good life and go snorkelling. If you seek solitude there are also a number of islands that can be visited independently and where camping is permitted, but all transportation must be arranged independently. Bookings and permits are essential. For information contact the QPWS Office in Cairns.

Green Island

Once you arrive in Cairns it won't take long before you see postcards of Green Island, a small outcrop of lush vegetation, fringed with white sand and surrounded by azure and green reefs. The island, named after Charles Green, the chief observer and astronomer on board Captain Cook's ship, *Endeavour*, is a text book 'coral cay' formed by dead coral and will fulfil most people's fantasy of a tropical island. Only 45 minutes (27 km) away by boat, and part of the inner reef, it is the closest island to Cairns and, at 15 ha, one of the smallest islands on the reef. It is home to an exclusive resort but is designed more for the day tripper in mind, with concrete pathways leading to food outlets, bars, dive and souvenir shops, a pool and, of course, some well trodden beaches.

Despite its size, you can still grab a snorkel and mask and find a quiet spot on the bleached white sand. The best place to snorkel is by the pier itself, where the fish love to congregate around the pylons. Here you may see what appears to be a large shark. It is, in fact, a shark ray or 'bucket mouth', a charming and congenial bottom feeder and totally harmless. Another fine set of dentures can be seen at the **Marineland Melanesia** ⓘ *T4051 4032, 0900-1600, $11.50*, in the heart of the island, with its small collection of aquariums and marine artefacts, all presided over by 'Cassius' a crocodile with plenty of attitude. If you are unable to go diving or snorkelling, you can still experience the vast array of colourful fish and corals from a glass-bottom boat or a small underwater observatory ($6)

Green Island is the epitome of a fantasy tropical island

both located by the pier. Although nothing remarkable, it was reputedly the first underwater observatory in the world.

There are a number of tour options for Green Island, giving you the opportunity to combine, diving and/or snorkelling to the outer islands with a few hours exploring the Island. Alternatively you may just want to pay the ferry fare and use the island's facilities, go snorkelling, or laze on the beach. You can also walk right round the island (1.5 km) in 20 minutes.

Fitzroy Island

Fitzroy, part of the inner reef, just 6 km off the mainland and 25 km south of Cairns, is a large 339-ha continental island surrounded by coral reef. It is mountainous and offers more of an escape than the others, with pleasant walking tracks through dense eucalyptus and tropical rainforests rich in wildlife. One of the most popular walks is a 4 km circuit to the island's highest point, 269 m, with its memorable views and modern lighthouse. A scattering of quiet beaches provide good snorkelling and diving. The best beach is **Nudey Beach** which is not, as the name suggests, a base for naturists. It can be reached in about 20 minutes from the island's resort. Fitzroy was used by the Gunghandji Aboriginal people as a fishing base for thousands of years and in the 1800s by itinerants harvesting bêche-de-mer, or sea cucumber. It is named after the Duke of Grafton who was the British Prime Minister when the *Endeavour* left England.

Frankland Islands

A further 20 km south of Fitzroy Island are the Frankland Group, a small cluster of continental islands of which 77 ha are national park. They are covered in rainforest and fringed with white sand beaches and coral reef. The islands offer a wonderfully quiet retreat in comparison to the larger, busier islands. There are QPWS camping areas on Russell and High Islands. Permits and bookings through the QPWS in Cairns. See page 371 for tours.

Atherton Tablelands pp364-380.

The Atherton Tablelands extend inland in a rough semi-circle from the Cairns coast to the small mining settlements of Mount Molloy in the north, Chillagoe in the west and Mount Garnet in the south: in total an area about the size of Ireland. At an average height of over 800 m, and subsequently the wettest region in Queensland, the Atherton Tablelands are most extraordinary: here, you'll find lush fields and plump cattle, tropical forests busting with birdsong, huge brimming lakes, high, and at times thunderous, waterfalls, and even kangaroos that live in trees (see page 358). The further west you go the drier it gets until, at the edge of the Great Divide Range, the vast emptiness of the 'outback' takes over. Given its inherent beauty, the Tablelands, especially the small and pretty settlements like Yungaburra, are the favourite retreat of Queensland's coastal dwellers, as well as tourists in search of peace and quiet, greenery and, above all, cooler temperatures.

Ins and outs

Getting there and around If you are short of time the best way to see the region is as part of a tour from Cairns. Otherwise, the Tablelands are best explored using your own transport. There are four access roads from the coast: from the south via Palmerston Highway (north of Innisfail) through the scenic tropical rainforests of Wooroonooran National Park and Millaa Millaa; from Cairns, south via Gordonvale and the steeply climbing Gillies Highway; north via Smithfield, the Kuranda Range Road and Kuranda; and from Port Douglas via the Rex Range Road and Kennedy Highway. **Whitecar Coaches**, Trinity Wharf Terminal, Cairns, provide daily services to Atherton, Yungaburra, Mareeba and Kuranda. To arrive via Kuranda Scenic Railway or Skyrail Gondola, see page 347. *p379.*

Tourist information Research the region from the VIC in Cairns. **Tropical Tableland Promotion Bureau** ⓘ *T4091 4222, www.athertontableland.com*, is the principal accredited regional body. For parks information contact the QPWS office in Cairns. **Kuranda VIC** ⓘ *Centenary Park, Therwine St, T4093 9311, www.kuranda.org.au, 1000-1600*, has maps and accommodation, tours and activities details.

Kuranda

The small, arty settlement of Kuranda has become the main tourist attraction in the Atherton Tablelands, thanks to its proximity to Cairns, its scenic railway and its markets. But while there's no doubting its appeal, particularly the spectacular means of access, Kuranda has, to a large extent, become a victim of its own popularity. The town was first put on the map in 1891 with the completion of the railway, providing a vital link between the Hodgkinson Gold Fields and the coast.

Kuranda's main attraction is its permanent markets. **Heritage Markets** are just off Veivers Drive (daily from 0900-1500), while the **Original Markets** are nearby on Therwine Street (open from 0900-1500 Wednesday to Sunday). Other stalls and permanent shops are also strung along the village's main drag, **Coondoo Street**. The emphasis is on souvenirs, with much of it being expensive and tacky, but there are some artists and craftsmen producing pieces that are both unusual and good quality, so shop around. Although not actually part of the markets themselves, the **Australis Gallery**, at 26 Coondoo Street, is worth a look, showcasing some fine work by local artists.

Below the Heritage Markets is **Koala Gardens** ⓘ *T4093 9953, 0900-1600, $15, child $7.50*, which offers the inevitable photo sessions for $15 on top of the admission price. Also next to the Heritage Markets is **Birdworld** ⓘ *T/F4093 9188, www.birdworldkuranda.com.au, 0900-1600, $12,child $5, family $29*, which is a free-flight complex showcasing some of Australia's most

The Atherton Tablelands are a green and pleasant escape from the heat and humidity of the coast

colourful (and audible) avian species. There is much emphasis on the endangered cassowary, though the numerous parrots and lorikeets will provide the best photo opportunities.

Another wildife attraction is the **Australian Butterfly Sanctuary** ⓘ *8 Veivers Drive, T4093 7575, www.australianbutterflies.com.au, 1000-1600, $13, child $6.50*. It is reputedly the world's largest and houses about a dozen of the country's most brilliant and beautiful 'Lepidoptera' in a huge free-flight enclosure nicely landscaped like a rainforest complete with stream and waterfalls. A bright red or white hat is recommended.

To complete the tour of all things winged and wonderful you could also consider a visit to **Batreach** ⓘ *T4093 8858, www.batreach.cairns.tc, Tue-Fri and Sun 1030-1430, entry by donation*, an independent wild bat rescue and rehabilitation hospital at the far end of Barang Street. Here you will get close up and personal with a number of species, most notably, the huge flying fox – a sort of startled looking dog on a hang-glider. Those who think bats are vicious creatures, invented by witches and horror movie makers, will have their ideas changed here. There is a large local colony of flying foxes in the **Jum Rum Creek Park**, off Thongon Street. Follow the noise – and the unmistakable musty smell.

The award-winning **Rainforestation Nature Park** ⓘ *T4085 5008, www.rainforest.com.au, 0900-1600, attractions $34, child $17, transportation and tours extra*, is located a few kilometres east of Kuranda on the Kuranda Range Road. Set amidst a rainforest and orchard setting it offers yet another chance to experience aboriginal culture and mingle with captive native animals. There is also an exhilarating one-hour tour of the complex and rainforest in an amphibious army vehicle.

If you did not arrive in Kuranda via the Skyrail or railway and it is the wet season then take a look at the **Barron Falls**, which can be accessed via Barron Falls Road (Wrights Lookout) south of the town. In 'the wet' the floodgates are opened above the falls and the results can be truly spectacular.

Lake Tinaroo and Danbulla Forest

Barron River Tinaroo Dam was completed in 1958 creating a vast series of flooded valleys that now make up Lake Tinaroo and provide the region with essential irrigation. The lake itself has an astonishing 200 km of shoreline and is a popular spot for watersports, especially barramundi fishing. Indeed, some say the lake contains the biggest 'barra' in Australia. The Danbulla Forest that fringes its northern bank is bisected by 28-km of unsealed scenic road that winds its way from the dam slipway, at Tolga, to Boar Pocket Road, northeast of Yungaburra.

Other than the various campsites, viewpoints and short walks on offer, highlights include **Lake Euramoo**, a picturesque 'double explosion' crater lake, **Mobo Creek Crater**, something of a geological odyssey, and the unmissable **Cathedral Fig**. Signposted and reached by a 5-minute walk, this superb example of the strangler fig species is indeed a sight to behold. The tree – though it is hard to see it as such – is 500-years-old, over 50 m

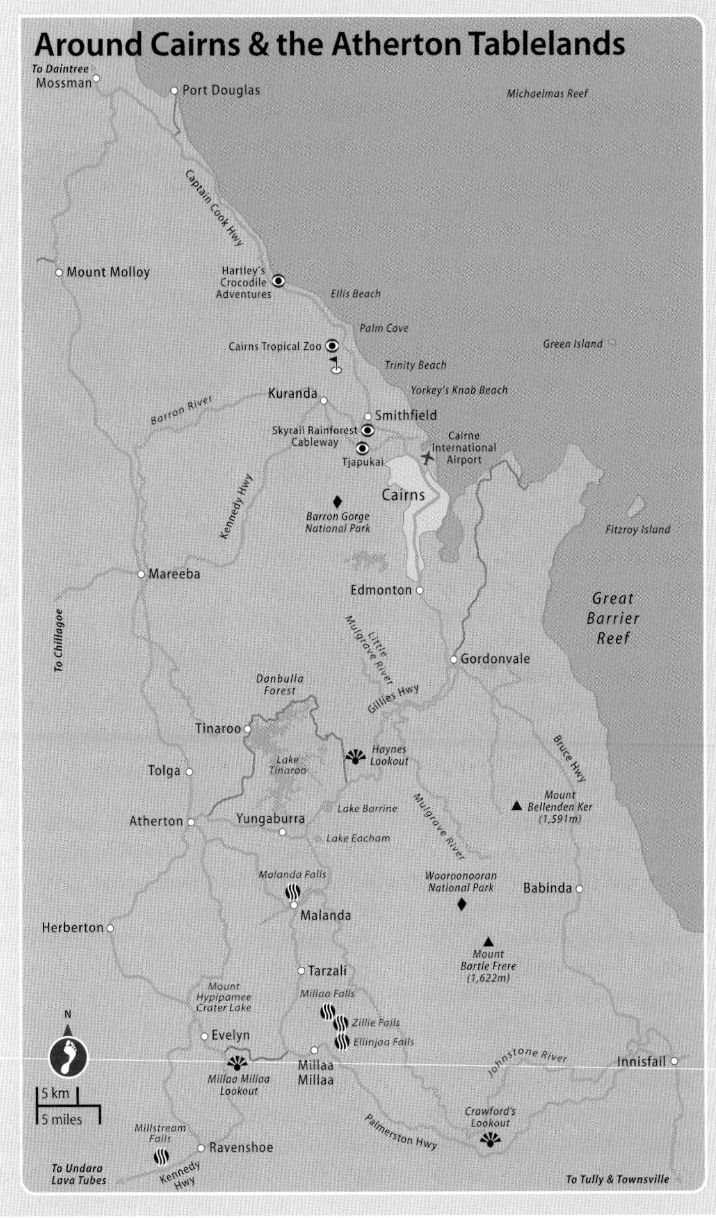

Going further

Undara Lava Tubes

The Undara Lava Tubes, on the edge of the Undara Volcanic National Park, 150 km south of Ravenshoe via Mount Surprise, is an amazing 190,000-year-old volcanic feature and well worth the journey. There are regular guided tours available, also available from Cairns, as well as a licensed restaurant, pool and a range of accommodation from charming train carriages to a swag tent village and powered sites, YHA affiliated. **Undara Experience,** T4097 1900, www.undara.com.au. offer day trips and excellent multi-day package deals by coach, self-drive or rail to see the lava tubes with additional activities and accommodation in their unique railway carriages or swag-tent village. Day-trip from $135, 2-day coach, from $428 and 3-day rail, from $654.

tall and 40 m around the base and is worth visiting at dawn, when its many avian inhabitants are full of chatter. Several types of nocturnal possum also inhabit the tree and are best seen with a torch after dark.

From the Cathedral Fig you emerge from the forest onto Boar Pocket Road. The short diversion to the **Haynes Lookout**, left on Boar Pocket Road, heading from the forest towards Gillies Highway, is worthy of investigation. The track itself passes through some beautiful woodland before emerging at the edge of the mountain and the memorable views across the **Mulgrave River Valley** and **Bellenden Ker Range**. When the winds are right the site is often used by hang-gliders. Check out the message written on the launch pad.

For more information on the Danbulla Forest scenic drive and self-registration campsites ($2) contact the **QPWS** at 83 Main Sreet, Atherton, T4091 1844, or their Tinaroo Office (T4095 8459). The area is best explored in your own vehicle or a regional tour.

Yungaburra and around

While Kuranda may be the most visited and high profile town in the Atherton Tablelands, sleepy little Yungaburra is without doubt the main event. Formerly called Allumba, it has changed little in over a century and offers a wonderful combination of history, alternative lifestyle and a cool and tranquil retreat from the coast. As well as an impressive gathering of listed historical buildings it has good places to stay, eat and shop and is surrounded by some of the best scenery in the Tablelands. Lakes Tinaroo, Barrine and Eacham, see below, are all within a short drive and provide the focal point for a number of walks, scenic drives and water-based activities. The most spectacular way to reach Yungaburra is via the Gilles Highway and Mulgrave River Valley just south of Cairns. From the valley floor the road climbs almost 800 m up to the top of the Gilles Range.

Most of the listed historical buildings were built from local wood, between 1910 and 1920. Two of the finest examples are **St Mark's and St Patrick's churches**, on Eacham Road. Other fine examples are evident on Cedar Street, next to the **Lake Eacham Hotel**. Look out for the Yungaburra Heritage Village leaflet, available from the VICs in Cairns and Atherton, or from most local businesses. Just a few minutes southwest of the village, on Curtain Fig Tree Road, is the 800-year old **Curtain Fig Tree**, another impressive and ancient example of the strangler species (Yungaburra is Aboriginal for 'fig tree').

Yungaburra is also one of the best, and most accessible, places in country in which to see that surreal quirk of nature, the duck-billed platypus. **Peterson Creek**, which slides gently past the village, is home to several pairs. The best place to see them is from the bottom and north of Penda Street, at the end of Cedar Street, and the best time is around dawn or sometimes at dusk. Sit quietly beside the river and look for any activity in the grass that fringes the river or on its surface. They are generally well submerged but once spotted are fairly obvious. Provided you are quiet they will generally go about their business, since their eyesight is fairly poor.

A few kilometres east of the village are two volcanic lakes, **Lake Barrine** and **Lake Eacham**. Lake Barrine is the largest and has been a tourist attraction for over 80 years. It's fringed with rainforest and circled by a 6-km walking track. Two lofty and ancient kauri pines, amongst Australia's largest species, are located at the start of the track. The long-established **Lake Barrine Rainforest Cruise and Tea House** (T4095 3847) is nestled on the northern shore and offers 40-minute trips on the lake ($10, child $5.50). Just south of Lake Barrine and accessed off the Gilles Highway, or from the Malanda Road, is Lake Eacham. Once again it is surrounded by rainforest and a 3.5-km walking track and is a favourite spot for a picnic and a cool dip. The most southerly fingers of Lake Tinaroo can also be accessed northeast of the village via Barrine Road. There is currently no official visitor information centre in the village, however the locals are always glad to help. There is also a useful website, www.yungaburra.com. The local **QWPS** office at Lake Eacham (T4095 3786), provides information about campsites and all things environmental.

Malanda and Millaa Millaa

The little village of Malanda marks the start of the famous Tablelands waterfalls region. Malanda has its own set of falls but they are actually amongst the least impressive in the group and the village is more famous for milk than water. Dairying has always been the raison d'être in Malanda. The first herds of cattle were brought by foot from the north of NSW – a journey that took a gruelling 16 months. Today, there are over 190 farmers in the region producing enough milk to make lattes and shakes from here to Alice Springs. The main attraction, other than a cool dip in the swimming hole below the falls, is the neighbouring **Malanda Falls Environmental Centre and Visitors Information** ⓘ *T4096 6957, 1000-1600*, which has some interesting displays on the geology, climate and natural history of the Tablelands.

A further 24 km south of Malanda is the sleepy agricultural service town of Millaa Millaa, which also has its own waterfalls and is surrounded by fields of black and white Friesian cattle. The **Millaa Millaa Falls** are the first of a trio – the others being the **Zillie Falls** and **Ellinjaa Falls** – which can be explored on a 16-km circuit accessed (and signposted) just east of the town on the **Palmerston Highway**, which links with the Bruce Highway just north of Innisfail. There are a few lesser-known waterfalls on the way and Crawford's lookout, on the left, with its dramatic view through the forest to the North Johnstone River – a favourite spot for rafting.

The **Millaa Millaa Lookout** (at 850 m) just to the west of Millaa Millaa on the recently upgraded East Evelyn Road, is said to offer the best view in North Queensland. On a clear day you can see 180 degrees from the Tablelands to the coast, interrupted only by the Bellenden Ker Range and the two highest peaks in Queensland, Mount Bartle Frere (1,622 m) and Mount Bellenden Ker (1,591 m).

Mount Hypipamee National Park

Mount Hypipamee National Park is a small pocket of dense rainforest with a volcanic crater lake, waterfalls and some very special wildlife. During the day the trees are alive with the

Going further

Chilled out in Chillagoe

Given its isolation, yet easy access from Cairns, the former mining settlement of Chillagoe presents and ideal opportunity to experience the 'outback' proper, without having to embark on a long and difficult 4WD journey from the coast. It's a fascinating little place, somewhat out of character with the rest of the Atherton Tablelands, and combines mining history with natural limestone caves and Aboriginal rock paintings. Chillagoe was formerly a cattle station before the discovery of gold in the late 1880s dramatically transformed both the settlement and the landscape. The establishment of rail link in 1900 led to a sharp increase of incomers and for the next 40 years the area produced almost 10 tonnes of gold and 185 tonnes of silver, as well many more tonnes of copper and lead. Those boom days are long gone and the population has declined dramatically but it retains a hint of its former importance in the sun-baked mining relics that remain.

The Hub Interperative Centre ⓘ *Queen St, T4094 7111, chillagoehubinfo@bigpond.com, 0800-1700*, is the best source of local information and offers the best introduction to the settlement's mining history and can provide directions to the most obvious mining relics. **QPWS**, on the corner of Cathedral and Queen Street, offer guided tours of three of the local limestone caves. Details the Hub. There are more caves and old copper mines about 10 km west of the town at Mungana which is also the location of the Aboriginal rock paintings.

sound of many exotic birds such as the tame Lewin's honeyeaters, but it is at night that it really comes into its own. Armed with a torch and a little patience (preferably after midnight) you can see several of the 13 species of possum that inhabit the forest, including the coppery brush tail, the green ringtail, and the squirrel glider who leaps and flies from branch to branch. If you are really lucky you may also encounter the park's most famous resident the Lumholtz's tree kangaroo, one of only two species of kangaroo that live in trees.

The 95,000-year-old **Crater Lake** – which is, in fact, a long, water-filled volcanic pipe blasted through the granite – is a 10-minute walk from the car park. With its unimaginable depths, algae-covered surface and eerie echoes it is quite an unnerving spectacle, like some horrific natural dungeon. The park has picnic facilities but no camping.

Port Douglas and The Daintree » *pp364-380.*

Almost since their inception the coastal ports of Cairns and Port Douglas, just 70 km apart, have slugged it out as to who is the most important. Although Cairns has gone on to become a world-famous tourist heavyweight, lesser known Port Douglas has always known that it's a classier option, with its boutiques, fine restaurants and upmarket accommodation. Given its proximity to the Barrier Reef, the Mossman Gorge, Daintree and Cape Tribulation, Port Douglas has never had a problem attracting tourist dollars, though the building of massive developments and multi-million dollar resorts will result in it losing its village feel and much of its charm.

Port Douglas

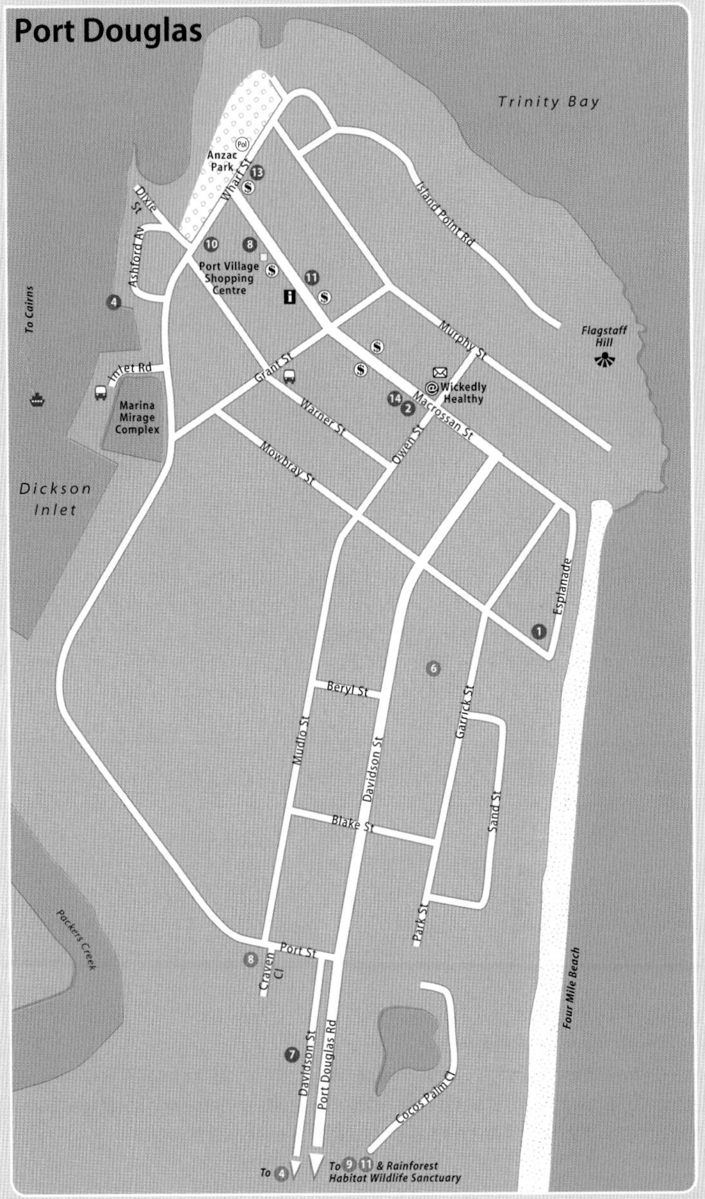

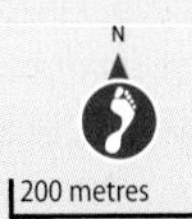

Sleeping
Dougie's Nomads Backpackers **4**
Glengarry Caravan Park **9**
Marae B & B **11**
Tropic Breeze Van Village **6**
YHA Port 'O' Call **8**

Eating
2 Fish **10**
Beaches Café **1**
Café Ecco **2**
Combined Club **4**
Gone Bananas **7**
Iron Bar **8**
Michael Angelo's **11**
Sassi Cucina **13**
Table 41 **14**

Patchwork quilt on sale at a market in Port Douglas

Ins and outs

Port Douglas Tourist Information Centre ⓘ *23 Macrossan St, T4099 5599, www.pddt.com.au, 0830-1800*. The nearest QPWS office is in Mossman ⓘ *1 Front St, T4098 2188, www.epa.qld.gov.au*. **Daintree Tourist Information Centre** ⓘ *Stewart St, T4098 6120, www.daintree village.asn.au*. For Daintree and local walks information also contact the QPWS office in Cairns (T4046 6600), or visit www.port-douglas-daintree.com.

Port Douglas

Like Cairns, Port Douglas places great emphasis on reef and rainforest tours with only a few attractions in the town itself pulling in the crowds. See page 371 for details of the activities available in the area. About 6 km from the centre of town, at the junction of Captain Cook Highway and Port Douglas Road, the **Rainforest Habitat** ⓘ *T4099 3235, www.rainforest habitat.com.au, 0800-1730, $28, child $14*, is well worth a visit, offering a fine introduction to the region's rich biodiversity and natural habitats. There are over 180 species housed in three main habitat enclosures – 'wetlands', 'rainforest' and 'grassland' with many of the tenants being tame and easily approachable. 'Breakfast with the Birds' (0800-1100, $39, child $20) is an enjoyable way to start the day, while 'Habitat After Dark' (see Eating, page 370) offers a truly unique dining experience.

Port Douglas is rather proud of its lovely **Four Mile Beach**, which attracts cosmopolitan crowds of topless backpackers and the more conservative resort clients. Many water-based activities are on offer for those not satisfied with merely sunbathing or swimming. A net is placed just offshore to ward off box jellyfish and other stingers and lifeguards are usually in attendance (always swim between the flags). Before picking your spot on the sand you might like to enjoy the picture-postcard view of the beach from Flagstaff Hill, turn right at the bottom of Mossman Street, then follow Wharf Street on to Island point Road. **Anzac Park** hosts a market every Sunday. It is a colourful affair and offers everything from sarongs to freshly squeezed orange juice. More expensive permanent boutiques are housed in the delightfully cool **Marina Mirage** Complex, Wharf Street. For further information, see www.marinamiragepd.com.au.

Mossman River

Mossman Gorge and the Daintree Wilderness National Park

Built on the back of the sugar cane industry in the 1880s, **Mossman** sits on the banks of the Mossman River and has one of the world's most exotic tropical gardens on its back door in the form of the Daintree Wilderness National Park. Although the 80 year-old, fern covered, Tall Raintrees that form a cosy canopy on its northern fringe are a sight in themselves it is the Mossman Gorge, some 5 km west of the town that is its greatest attraction. Here, the Mossman River falls towards the town, fringed with rainforest and networked with a series of short walks. Many combine a walk with another big attraction – the cool swimming holes. Although the walks are excellent, you should also try following the river upstream for about 2 km – if you are fit. This will give you an ideal opportunity to see the region's most famous mascot – the huge Ulysses blue butterfly.

The tiny, former timber town of Daintree sits at the end of the Mossman-Daintree Road, sandwiched between the western and eastern blocks of the Daintree National Park. The village exudes a quaint and original charm and consists of an enormous model barramundi fish, a general store, **Bushman's Lodge**, a small timber museum, a couple of restaurants, a school and a caravan park. At the edge of the village is the biggest local attraction – the croc infested Daintree River. Visitors can embark on a leisurely cruise on the river in search of these gargantuan saltwater crocodiles – or salties, as they are better known. There are several cruise operators to choose from, all of whom ply the river from Daintree village to the coast several times a day. You can either pick up the cruise near the village itself or at various points south to the Daintree/Cape Tribulation ferry crossing, but most people arrive on pre-organized tours. For independent choice and bookings call in at the general store (T4098 6146).

Cape Tribulation » *pp364-380.*

Although Cape Tribulation is the name attributed to a small settlement and headland that forms the main tourist focus of the region, the term itself is loosely used to describe a 40-km stretch of coastline within Daintree National Park and the start of the Bloomfield Track to Cooktown. It was Captain Cook who bestowed the name, just before his ship *Endeavour* ran aground here in 1770. The name 'Tribulation', and others such as Mount Sorrow, Mount Misery and Darkie's Downfall, are indeed fitting for a place of such wild and, at times, inhospitable beauty. People come to this remote wilderness not only to witness a rainforest rich in flora and fauna, but also to experience nature in the raw.

Ins and outs

Tourist information Detailed information can be obtained from the **VIC**s in Port Douglas or Cairns. Local information is available from Daintree Discovery Centre or Bat House (see below). For walks information contact the **QPWS** office in Cairns (T4046 6600). Australian Rainforest Foundation website, www.wettropics.com.au, is also useful.

Sights

Five kilometres beyond the ferry crossing, the Cape Tribulation Road climbs steadily over the densely forested Waluwurriga Range to reach **Mount Alexandra Lookout**, offering the first glimpse of the coast and the mouth of the Daintree River. Turning back inland and 2 km past

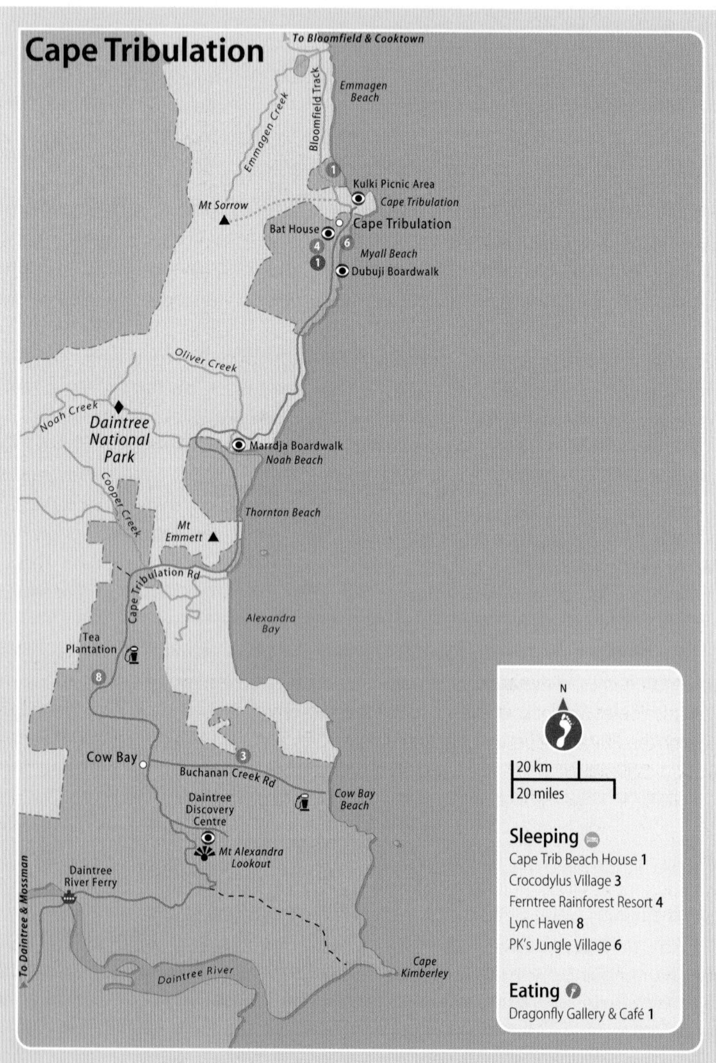

(Left) A baby gecko seeks shelter from the sun beneath a leaf in the rainforest, Queensland; (Right) The rugged and remote coastline viewed from the Bloomfield Track, Cape Tribulation

the lookout, is the turn-off (east) to the **Daintree Discovery Centre** ⓘ *T4098 9171, www.daintree-rec.com.au, 0830-1700, $15, child $7.50*, with excellent displays on the local flora and fauna, and added attraction of a 400-m boardwalk where guided walks are available and a 25-m canopy tower offers a bird's-eye view of the forest canopy. There's also a very nice café on site from which to sit back and let the forest wildlife pervade the senses. Back on Cape Tribulation Road and just beyond the centre, is the settlement of **Cow Bay** with its attractive bay and beach that can be reached by road 6 km to the east on Buchanan Creek Road.

Continuing north you are then given another interesting reminder of being in the tropics by passing a well-manicured tea plantation before crossing Cooper Creek and hitting the coast below Mount Emmett. Oliver Creek then sees the first of a duo of excellent boardwalks, which provide insight into the botanical delights of the forest and mangrove swamps. **Marrdja boardwalk** takes about 45 minutes and is well worth a look. From here it is about 9 km before you reach the settlement of Cape Tribulation. Here, too, is the second and equally interesting 1.2-km **Dubuji** boardwalk, taking about 45 minutes.

The headland at Cape Tribulation is also well worthy of investigation, as are its two beautiful beaches – **Emmagen** and **Myall** – that sit either side like two golden bookends. The Kulki picnic area and lookout is at the southern end of Emmagen Beach and is signposted just beyond the village. Just beyond that the Kulki turn-off, 150 m, is the start of the **Mount Sorrow track**, a challenging 3.5-km ascent rewarded with spectacular views from the 650-m summit.

While in Cape Tribulation be sure to visit the **Bat House** ⓘ *T4098 0063, Tue-Sun, 1030-1530, $2 donation at least*, opposite **PK's Backpackers**. Although you won't encounter the saviour of Gotham City, you will find the saviours of the local bat population, in the form of volunteers who tend the needs of injured and orphaned flying foxes. A range of interesting wildlife displays are also to hand.

Beyond Cape Tribulation the road gradually degenerates to form the notorious, controversial blot on the landscape known as **Bloomfield Track**. From here you are entering real 'Tiger Country' and 4WD is essential. A 2WD will only get you as far as Emmagen Creek, which offers a limited incursion into the fringes of the dense rainforest and some good swimming holes, thankfully, too clear and too shallow for local crocodiles.

Sleeping

Cairns *p346, map p348*
There is plenty of choice and something to suit all budgets. Most of the major hotels and countless backpackers are in the heart of the city, especially along The Esplanade, while most motels are located on the main highways in and out of town. If you are willing to splash out, want access to a proper beach and wish to escape the city, ask at the VIC about the numerous apartment and resort options at Palm Beach and other northern beach resorts (about 20 mins north of the city). Prices fluctuate according to season, with some going through the roof at peak times (May-Sep). Prices are often reduced and special deals are offered through 'the Wet' (Jan-Mar). Despite the wealth of accommodation pre-booking is still advised. **Cairns and TNQ Accommodation Centre**, corner of Sheridan St and Alpin St, T4051 4066, www.accomcentre.com.au, can also be of assistance.

B&Bs

A **Kookas B&B**, 40 Hutchinson St, Edge Hill, T4053 3231, www.kookas-bnb.com.au. Some 10 km from city centre. A traditional modern home in an elevated position, 3 en suites tastefully decorated, friendly owners lots of visiting kookaburras.

B-C **Fig Tree Lodge**, 253 Sheridan St, T4041 0000, www.figtreelodge.com.au. More like a motel than a lodge, but offers fine facilities, a warm Irish welcome and a bar.

Backpackers

There is plenty of choice of backpackers with over 30 establishments, almost all within easy reach of the city centre. Most people gravitate towards The Esplanade where a string of places sit, virtually side by side, but you are advised to look into other options too. Another small cluster of quieter hostels lies just west of the railway station. All offer the usual facilities and range of dorms, twins/ doubles. Look for rooms with a/c or at least a powerful fan and windows that open, and check for approved fire safety regulations.

C-D **Gilligan's Backpackers Hotel and Resort**, 57 Grafton St, T4041 6566, www.gilligansbackpackers.com.au. Causing something of a stir in backpacking circles, it is one of a new breed, pitched somewhere between a backpackers and modern 3-star hotel. There is no doubting its class or its range of facilities. It has a large pool, internet café, chic bar with dance floor and big screen TV. Rooms vary from tidy spacious doubles with TV and futon lounge to traditional dorms.

D-E **Global Palace**, corner of Lake St and Shields St, T4031 7921, www.globalpalace.com.au. Another hostel more like a modern boutique motel than a traditional backpackers. It has great facilities including a rooftop pool and large deck from which to watch the world go by. The only criticism is that most of the a/c rooms do not have windows and can feel a bit claustrophobic. Otherwise it gets a big thumbs-up.

C-E **Carravella Hostels**, at 77 The Esplanade, T4051 2159, and 149 The Esplanade, T4051 2431, www.caravella.com.au. Both are modern, well facilitated with good a/c doubles and free meals.

D-E **Bohemia Resort**, 231 McLeod St, T4041 7290, www.bohemiaresort.com.au. A little further out of the centre is this modern, excellent option. It is more like a tidy modern motel with great doubles and a pool. Regular shuttles to town.

D-E **Inn The Tropics**, 141 Sheridan St, T4031 1088, www.cairns.net.au/~innthetropics. A quality option with single rooms, good motel style doubles. Also suited for families.

D-E **Cairns Beach House**, 239 Sheridan St, T40414116, www.cairnsbeachhouse.com.au. North of the centre is this popular option with all the usual facilities, it is especially noted for its pool,

Budget busters

Far North Queensland sleeping

LL **Allumbah Pocket Cottages**, 24-26 Gillies Highway, Yungaburra, T40953023, www.allumbahpocketcottages.com.au, is a cluster of new, spacious and well-appointed, 1-bedroom and fully self-contained cottages complete with spa. The friendly and welcoming owners also offer two other exceptional 2-bedroom cottages, at 7/9 Pine St, ideal for the romantic couple.

LL **Daintree Eco Lodge and Spa**, 20 Daintree Rd, 3 km south of the village, T40986100, www.daintree-ecolodge.com.au. This is a multi-award winner and enjoys a good reputation offering 15 luxury, serviced villas set in the rainforest, a specialist spa, aboriginal and eco-based activities and a top class restaurant.

LL **Silky Oaks Lodge**, north of Mossman, T40981666, www.poresorts.com.au. The most upmarket place in the immediate area. It offers 60 excellent freestanding ensuite chalets doubles (some with spa) and a fine restaurant. Complimentary activities and pick-ups are also available.

beer/bistro garden and party atmosphere. Courtesy coach in to town.

D-E **Dreamtime Travellers Rest**, 4 Terminus St, T40316753, www.dreamtimetravel.com.au. Homely and friendly with a great atmosphere, well equipped facilities and a great pool and spa, as well as proper beds, not bunks. Ask about their sister hostel in Yungaburra and the Tablelands tour package.

D-E **Geckos**, 187 Bunda St, T4031 1344, www.geckosbackpackers.com.au. Relatively new, rambling and spacious Queenslander with good facilities, caring staff and 2 great dogs, Digger and Ruby. Rooms have fans not a/c but they are well ventilated. Good for doubles. Free meals at The Woolshed.

D-E **Travellers Oasis**, 8 Scott St, T4052 1377, www.travoasis.com.au. A large place that still maintains a nice quiet atmosphere, offering a good range of a/c rooms including value singles ($30) and pool.

Motels, motor parks and apartments

There are endless motel and apartment options, with the vast majority offering the standard clean, spacious rooms and usual facilities, including the almost obligatory tropical flower paintings and palm-tree fringed swimming pools. Most motels are located on the main drag in and out of town (Sheridan St). If you are looking for a caravan park you are advised to base yourself in the northern beaches.

L-F **Cairns Coconut Caravan Resort**, on the Bruce Highway (about 6 km south, corner of Anderson Rd), T4054 6644, www.coconut. com.au. Offering sheer class and with all mod cons, this is one of the best in the country.

A **Hides**, corner of Lake St and Shields St, T4051 1266, www.clubcroc.com.au. Historical and well placed apartments offering budget options with shared facilities.

A-B **Cairns Rainbow Inn**, 179 Sheridan St, T40511022. A colourful motel with standard room options, restaurant, pool and spa.

C-E Cairns City Caravan Park, corner of James St and Little St, T4051 1467. If you prefer to be in the city this is the best placed for sheer convenience but is very basic.

C-E Trinity Beach Holiday Park, 116 Trinity Beach Rd, T4055 6306. A fine choice, spacious with an excellent camp kitchen and a smart bathroom block with individual shower rooms. There is also plenty of resident wildlife including stone curlews and cockatoos.

Atherton Tablelands *p353, map p355*

Although Kuranda attracts the tourist hordes like bees to honey, once the last train leaves and peace returns it can be a wonderful place to stay away from the usual coastal haunts. However there aren't too many options and for something more luxurious you have to look further afield than Kuranda.

LL-A Fur 'n' Feathers Rainforest Tree Houses, between Malanda and Millaa Millaa (2.5 km on Hogan Road east of Tarzali), T4096 5364, www.rainforesttreehouses.com.au. A trio of charming, fully self-contained pole houses set in the bush offering real peace and quiet and all mod cons including a spa. There is also a separate, fully self-contained, semi-detached cottage.

L-E Liberty Resort, 3 Greenhills Rd, Kuranda, T4093 7556, www.libertyresort.com.au. Just 2 km southwest of the village, this attractive new resort offers a fine range of villas, a self-contained apartment and a multi-share budget option. Very well facilitated with a gym, spa, pool and in-house massage therapies and a fine restaurant.

A Curtain Fig Motel, 16 Gilles Highway, Yungaburra, T4095 3168, www.curtainfig.com.au. Good value, spacious self-contained units and one large fully self-contained apartment in the heart of the village.

C Pteropus House B&B corner of Carrington Rd and Hutton Rd, Atherton, T4091 2683, www.athertontablelands.com/bats. An excellent and unusual place to say (provided you love bats). Kind host Jenny Mclean runs not only a quality B&B with two tidy self-contained apartments, but a (separate) working fruit bat hospital. There is also the opportunity to see some of the patients and sometimes assist in their care.

A-E Kuranda Rainforest Accommodation Park, 88 Kuranda Heights Rd, Kuranda, T4093 7316. This 3-star place has cottages, cabins, powered and non powered sites. Facilities include kitchen and pool.

D-E Kuranda Backpackers Hostel, 6 Arara St, Kuranda, T4093 7355, www.kurandaback packershostel.com. Near the train station, this renovated 1907 traditional Queenslander is a fine retreat with dorms, doubles, singles and good facilities. Pool, bike rental and pick-ups from Cairns.

D-F On the Wallaby Backpackers, 34 Eacham Rd, Yungaburra, T4050 0650, www.onthewallaby.com.au. The best budget option is this excellent little backpackers offering dorms, doubles and camping for $10 (pair $15). The decor is all wood and stone giving it a cosy ski-lodge feel, very different to the bustling modern places in Cairns. Plenty of activities are on offer including an exciting range of wildlife and day/night canoeing tours on Lake Tinaroo from $25. Mountain bikes for hire. Two-day/1-night package with tour, canoeing and mountain biking for $155. Pick-ups from Cairns daily.

C-E Lake Eacham Caravan Park, Lakes Drive, 1 km south of Lake Eacham, T4095 3730. The nearest motor park to Yungaburra. Basic but good value, it has cabins, powered and non-powered sites.

C-E Millaa Millaa Tourist Park, Malanda Rd, T4097 2290. Recently upgraded to 3-star, with cabins, powered and non-powered sites, pool, camp kitchen and café.

Going further

Lizard Island

Lizard Island is home to Australia's most northerly, and most exclusive, reef island resort. The island lies 270 km north of Cairns, 27 km off Cooktown and is almost 1,000 ha, with the vast majority of that being national park. Tranquil and pristine with fantastic diving and snorkelling, it makes for a great trip. All the delights of the other popular islands are on offer without the hordes of tourists. There are over 24 tranquil beaches, backed by lush forests, mangroves and bush, all abundant in wildlife, while just offshore, immaculate, clear water reefs offer superb diving and snorkelling. The famous Cod Hole is considered one of the best dive sites on the reef and the island is also a popular base for big game fishermen in search of the elusive Black Marlin. A delightful walking track leads to Cook's Look, which at 359 m is the highest point on the island and the place where Captain Cook stood in 1770 trying to find passage through the reef. The island was named by Joseph Banks, the ship's naturalist, who must have kept himself busy searching for lizards as Cook struggled to find a way back out to the ocean.

LL **Lizard Island Resort**, T8296 8010, www.lizardisland.com.au, offers some of the state's best views. The resort accommodation is in lodges and chalets but pick of the lot is the superb (and very expensive) Pavilion Suite, with its plunge pool and four-poster Daybed. The resort also boasts a 5-star restaurant and an exciting range of guest complimentary activities from windsurfing to guided nature walks.

Port Douglas and The Daintree

p358, map p359

There is plenty of choice in Port Douglas and though the emphasis is on 4-star resorts and apartments, budget travellers are also well catered for with a number of good backpackers, cheap motels and motor parks. Rates are naturally competitive and more expensive in the high season but at any time you are advised to shop around for special rates, especially in the 'wet' (Dec-Mar).

B-C Marae B&B, Lot 1, Ponzo Rd, Shannonvale, T4098 4900, www.marae.com.au. This B&B provides an ideal sanctuary, yet is still within reach (15 km north) of Port Douglas. It is a beautiful eco-friendly place offering 3 very comfortable en suite rooms (2 king and 1 double).

B-C Red Mill House, T/F4098 6233, www.red millhouse.com.au. One of a few good B&Bs in the heart of town is this very pleasant and friendly option offering well-appointed rooms, some with shared facilities and some with en suites (separate from the main house). Overall the place has a wonderfully peaceful atmosphere with lovely gardens and plenty of wildlife that you can watch from the deck. Good value.

B-F Glengarry Caravan Park, Mowbray River Rd, just short of Port Douglas, off the captain Cook Highway, T4098 5922, www.glengarry park.com.au. This motor park has fully self-contained en suite cabins, powered/ non-powered sites, with a good camp kitchen and a pool.

C-E Tropic Breeze Van Village, 24 Davidson St, closer to the centre of town, and only a short stroll from Four Mile Beach, T4099 5299. A 3-star motor park, it offers cabins, powered/non-powered sites and a camp kitchen.

D-E YHA Port 'O' Call, Port St, just off Davidson St, T4099 5422, www.portcall.com.au. One of 2 good backpackers in town. Motel-style with en suite doubles/twins, budget dorms and a fine restaurant/bar, pool and internet. Free pick-ups from Cairns.

D-F Daintree Riverview Caravan Park, 2 Stewart St, T4098 6119, www.daintree riverview.com. Has en suite cabins, powered and non-powered sites right in the heart of the village. Modern amenities block.

D-F Dougie's Nomads Backpackers, 111 Davidson St, T4099 6200, www.dougies.com. au. The other good backpacker in town, this one has a/c doubles/twins, dorms and van/campsites, bar, bike hire, internet. Free pick-ups from Cairns.

Cape Tribulation *p361, map p362*

There is a wide range of accommodation in and around the Cape, though prices are well above the norm for north Queensland.

A-F Lync Haven, T4098 9155, www.lync haven.com.au. Some 4 km north of Cow Bay Village, this park is very eco-friendly with plenty of wildlife around and also has a reputable restaurant.

C-D Ferntree Rainforest Resort, Camelot Close, T4098 0000, www.ferntreeresort.com.au. Just to the south of Cape Tribulation, this large 3-star complex, with fine facilities and, for a resort, a pleasantly quiet and intimate feel. The wide range of rooms, villas and suites are well appointed, the restaurant and bar is a fine place to relax and the pool is truly memorable. Occasional good deals on offer and budget accommodation with full access to facilities.

D-E Crocodylus Village, near Cow Bay Village along Buchanan Creek Rd and the beach, T4098 9166, crocodylus capetrib.com. YHA affiliated backpacker. By far the most ecologically 'in tune', it is essentially a glorified bush camp, with an interesting array of huts (some en suite) centred around a large communal area and a landscaped pool. The only drawback is the 3-km distance from the beach. Regular shuttle buses are run, as are regular daily Cairns and Port Douglas transfers, tours and activities including local canoe trips.

A-E Cape Trib Beach House, Cape Tribulation Rd, T4098 0030, www.capetribbeach.com.au. At the top end of Cape Tribulation is this new and very congenial option. It offers a range of modern cabins (some en suite) from dorm to 'beachside'. The most attractive aspects are the bush setting, its quiet atmosphere, the communal bar and bistro (with internet) all right next to the beach. A wide range of activities and tours are also available. The only drawback is the inability to park your vehicle near the cabins. This is definitely the best budget option for couples.

B-D **PK's Jungle Village**, Cape Tribulation Rd, in Cape Tribulation village, T4098 0040, www.pksjunglevillage.com.au. This is a well-established, mainstream hostel, popular with the social and party set. It offers all the usual facilities including a lively bar, restaurant, pool and a host of activities.

Eating

Cairns *p346, map p348*

There's a huge choice. Many of the mid-range eateries best suited for day or early evening dining are found along The Esplanade. Don't forget the options on offer in the major hotels and in the Pier Complex. Seafood or Australian cuisine is generally recommended. The International Food court on The Esplanade has a number of cheap outlets. See also under Bars and clubs below for cheap pub grub.

YYY **Red Ochre Grill**, 43 Shields St, T4051 0100. Daily for lunch and dinner. An award-winning Australian restaurant, offering the best of Australian 'game' fare including kangaroo, crocodile and local seafood favourites.

YY **Barnacle Bills**, 103 The Esplanade, T4051 2241. Another well-established seafood favourite.

YY **Café China**, corner of Spence St and Grafton St, T4041 2828. Daily from 1030. Considered the best of the Chinese restaurants.

YY **Dundee's**, 29 Spence St, T0417-605982. Well-established favourite offering good-value Australian cuisine in a relaxed atmosphere. Meat lovers will love the buffalo, roo, croc and barramundi combos. The seafood platters are also excellent.

YY **Verdi's**, corner of Shields St and Sheridan St, T4052 1010. Mon-Fri 1200-2300, Sat-Sun 1100. Good Italian cuisine.

YY **Yamagen Japanese**, in the **Cairns International Hotel**, 17 Abbott St, T4031 1300. Daily from 1700. Recommended for Asian fare.

YY **Yanni's Taverna**, corner of Alpin St and Grafton St, T4041 1500. Good Greek place offering attractive discounts between 1800 and 1900.

Y **Coffee Club**, The Esplanade, T4041 0522. Popular café serving up a good breakfast and light lunches for about $12.

Y **Gaura Nitai's Vegetarian**, 55 Spence St, T4031 2255. Mon-Fri 1100-1430, 1800-2100, Sat 1800-2100. A lively wee place that offers imaginative and value vegetarian selections.

Y **Inbox**, 119 Abbott St, T4041 4677, www.inboxcafe.com.au. Daily 0730-late, Fri-Sat till 0200. A new and very cool café with an easygoing atmosphere, good music and fast internet.

Y **Willie McBride's**, in the **Fig Tree Lodge**, corner of Sheridan St and Thomas St, T4041 0000. Daily from 1800. For value pub grub in a quieter Irish atmosphere.

Atherton Tablelands *p353, map p355*

Kuranda is awash with affordable cafés and eateries and Yungabarra also has a fair selection. Elsewhere the choice are limited.

YY **Monsoon Rainforest Kitchen**, at the **Liberty Resort**, see page 366, near Kuranda, T4093 7556. Come here if you want to escape the crowds or are staying in or around the village. It's a fine venue for lunch or dinner.

YY **Nick's Swiss-Italian Restaurant**, on Gillies Highway, Yungaburra, T4095 3330, www.nicksrestaurant.com.au. Tue-Sun for lunch and dinner 1130-2300. Stylish with live music at the weekends.

YY **Rainforest View Restaurant**, 28 Coondoo St, Kuranda, T4093 9939. Wide range of dishes and views of the rainforest but it does get packed with tour groups.

YY-Y **Kuranda Hotel**, corner of Coondoo St and Arara St, Kuranda, T4093 7206. Another option with generous pub meals and a pleasant laid-back atmosphere.

Ÿ **Flynn's Internet Café**, beside the food market on Eacham Rd, Yungaburra, T4095 2235. Thu-Tue 0700-1700. Good coffee and a good-value breakfast.
Ÿ **Frogs**, Kuranda, T4093 7405, in the heart of Coondoo St. Daily 0900-1600. The most popular café with the locals.

Port Douglas and The Daintree

p358, map p359

There are plenty of options in Port Douglas, mostly centred along Macrossan St.
ŸŸŸ **Rainforest Habitat Wildlife Sanctuary**, T4099 3235. Jul-Oct. For wildlife of a different nature why not consider dinner here. It offers an entertaining 'Habitat after Dark' dining experience under the gaze of creatures of the night, from $85,child $35. Bookings essential.
ŸŸ **Gone Bananas**, 87 Davidson St, T4099 5400. Daily 1800. Aptly named and highly entertaining. The owner is a true eccentric and it will almost certainly prove to be a memorable experience.
ŸŸ **Michael Angelo's**, Saltwater, 26 Macrossan St, T4099 4663. Daily from 1800. Italian and modern Australian with a cool atmosphere, retro fittings and elevated position overlooking the main street.
ŸŸ **Table 41**, 41 Macrossan St, T4099 4244; and ŸŸ **2 Fish**, 20 Wharf St, T4099 6350, are both excellent for atmosphere and seafood
ŸŸ **Sassi Cucina**, corner of Macrossan St and Wharf St, T4099 6100. Daily from 1800. Well regarded for its elegance and Italian or Japanese fare.
Ÿ **Beaches Café**, on The Esplanade, over looking Four Mile Beach, T4099 4998. Daily from 0700. For a good value breakfast and lots of tropical atmosphere.
Ÿ **Café Ecco**,Shop 1, 43 Macrossan St, T4099 4056. Excellent for healthy lunches and a good breakfast.
Ÿ **The Combined Club**, Wharf St, T4099 5553. This place is unbeatable for the waterfront view and for value.
Ÿ **Iron Bar**, 5 Macrossan St, T4099 4776. Well known for its imaginatively named and generous Australian dishes.

Cape Tribulation *p361, map p362*

See also Sleeping. Most resorts and backpackers listed above have their own restaurants or bistros, for breakfast lunch and dinner.
Ÿ **Dragonfly Gallery and Café**, T4098 0121, www.dragonflycapetrib.com. Daily 1000-late. Across the road from Ferntree Resort, in Cape Tribulation, is licensed, offers tasty lunches and diners with the added attraction of local artworks and an internet loft.

Bars and clubs

Cairns *p346, map p348*

With so many backpackers descending on the city the nightlife is very much geared to the get dressed up (or down), get drunk and fall over mentality. Finding somewhere to have a few good beers and a good conversation can be more difficult.

Bars

There is a good range of pubs in the town from the traditional Aussie corner hotels to sports bars and, of course, the ubiquitous pseudo Irish joints.
PJ O'Brien's, 87 Lake St, T4031 5333. Daily 1000-0300. The best of the Irish pubs is this popular spot. It offers live music most nights and is not too shabby in the food department either.
Frog and Firkin, corner of Spence St and Lake St, T4031 5305. Nicely laid-back, offers live music, a bistro and has a good balcony overlooking the main street.
Embassy Bar, in the former courthouse on Abbott St, T4031 4166. For something a little classier try the cool (as in temperature) atmosphere here. It is great during the heat of the day or for a little more decorum and offers live Jazz on Sunday nights and al fresco dining. Open daily until late.

Clubs

The Chapel, 91 The Esplanade, T4041 4222. Offers meals during the day, but at night the congregation flock here for cocktails and shooters. Open until 0200.

Club Trix, 53 Spence St, T4051 8223. Essentially a gay bar, but it welcomes both straight and gay and has highly entertaining drag shows.
Johno's Blues Bar, corner of Abbott St and Alpin St, T4051 8770.
Long established and popular live music venue. Entry is free before 2100 and on Sun there is the opportunity to show off your talents at the **Talent Quest** or on Mon the chance to win best didgeridoo player competition worth a cool $100.
Playpen, Lake St, T4051 8211. Has 3 separate bars offering various levels of mayhem and a huge dance floor.
Sporties, 33 Spence St, T4041 2533. Also lures in the younger crowds with cheap drink and has live bands from Thu-Sat.
Tropos, corner of Lake and Spence St, T4031 2530. Well-established this venue offers regular theme nights and is open until 0500.
Woolshed, 24 Shields St, T4031 6304. Very much backpacker-oriented, very cheap drinks are offered and it generally goes off well into the wee hours.

Shopping

Cairns *p346, map p348*
Cairns offers some excellent shopping. The renovated Pier offers everything from opals to art works.
Aussie Bush Hats and Oilskins, Bellview Centre, 85 The Esplanade, T4037 0011. Australiana and traditional attire.
City Palace Disposals, corner of Shields St and Sheridan St, is one of several outlets selling camping equipment.
Cairns Night Markets, 54-60 Abbott St, T4051 7666. Open daily 1630-2300. Over 100 stalls selling a rather predictable array of arts, crafts, clothing, food and souvenirs.
Peter Lik's Wilderness Gallery, 4 Shields St, T4031 8177, www.peterlik.com.au. For classy colourful panoramic photographs don't miss the works of Peter Lik at his original award-winning gallery (one of four in Australia).
Rusty's Bazaar, between Grafton St and Sheridan St. Open Fri evening and Sat-Sun morning. An eclectic conglomerate of colourful consumables.

Atherton Tablelands *p353, map p355*
Yungaburra markets, on the 4th Sat of the month, 0700-1200, have a good reputation for homemade arts, home-grown produce and odd farm animal.

Activities and tours

Cairns *p346, map p348*
With literally hundreds of operators in the city vying (sometimes quite aggressively) for your tourist dollar, you are advised to seek unbiased information at the official and accredited VIC. Then shop around before choosing a specific activity, trip, or tour (or combination thereof) to suit your desires, your courage and your wallet.

Bungee jumping

AJ Hackett, McGregor Rd, Smithfield, T4057 7188, www.ajhackett. com.au. Daily 1000-1700. Kiwi bungee jumping guru AJ Hackett has created an attractive jump complex in Smithfield 15 mins north of Cairns. It offers a 50-m jump and also the popular jungle swing, a sort of half free-fall/half swing that makes what you did when you were a toddler in the park seem awfully tame. Better yet is the newest addition to the adrenaline arsenal – a 150m Parasail or Jetski ride from $60. Standard Bungee $125, Swing $45. Pick-ups.

Adrenaline junkies should ask about the **Awesome Foursome** deals which combine such adventures as an island visit, a rafting trip, a bungee jump and a skydive for around $500 (saving about $60), T4057 7188 for details.

Cruises

There are many companies offering half, full or multi-day cruise options that concentrate on sailing, diving or just plain relaxing, with various islands stops and other water-based activities thrown in. In general, for a basic Inner Reef Island trip without extras, expect to pay anywhere between $60-90. For an Outer Reef Cruise with snorkelling, anything from $90-200. For an Outer Reef Cruise with introductory dive from $120-200 and for a luxury 3-day cruise with accommodation, meals and all activities included about $450-1000. It all boils down to the type of vessel, its facilities, numbers, optional extras and the actual time allowed on the reef. Generally speaking the smaller sailing companies do offer the most attractive rates and perhaps more peace and quiet, but lack the speed, convenience and razzmatazz of the fast, modern catamarans.

Big-Cat Green Island Reef Cruises, Reef St Terminal, 1 Spence St, T4051 0444, www.bigcat-cruises.com.au; **Great Adventures**, Reef St Terminal, T4044 9944, www.great adventures.com.au; **Reef Magic**, T4031 1588, www.reefmagic cruises.com.au; and **Sunlover Cruises**, T1800-810512, www.sun lover.com.au; are the main cruise operators in Cairns and like all the main operators are based at the new Reef Fleet Terminal on Spence St. They offer a range of tour options to Green Island, and beyond that, include certified dives, introductory dives, snorkelling, sightseeing and other water-based activities.

Great Adventures, based in Cairns, and **Quicksilver**, T4087 2100, www.quick silver-cruises.com.au, based in Port Douglas, both have huge floating pontoons moored on the outer reef where you can dive, snorkel, view the reef from a glass-bottom boat or with a very fetching looking gold-fish bowl on your head (you had better believe it), or simply sunbathe or watch the underwater world go by.

Compass, T4031 7217, www.reeftrip.com. Offers an attractive alternative with a good value trip on board a modern vessel to Michaelmas and Hastings Reef, both on the outer reef. Also offered is free snorkelling, boom netting and optional dive extras, from $60. Two-day, one-night trips are good value at $290.

Falla, T4041 3000. A charming, former Pearl Lugger that allows 4-hr on Upolo Reef 30 km from Cairns, with free snorkelling. Departs 0900, returns 1730, $79, child $49 (introductory dives available).

Passions of Paradise, T4051 9505, www.pass ionsofparadise.com.au. Large, modern catamaran that goes to Upolo Cay and Paradise Reef. From $99 (introductory dive $60). Departs daily 0800, returns 1800.

Ecstasea, T4041 3055, www.reef-sea-charters .com.au. A 60-ft luxury yacht that also visits Upolo Cay with free snorkelling, from $99 (Introductory dive $70).

Ocean Spirit, T4031 2920, www.ocean spirit .com.au. An even more luxurious trip to Michaelmas Cay on the outer reef is offered on this beautiful vessel. All mod cons though you pay for the extra at $175, (introductory dive $95).

Diving

Cairns is an internationally renowned base for diving and there are dozens of dive shops, operators and schools. It is also an ideal place to learn though certainly not the cheapest (from $300 for the most basic courses with no accommodation up to between $500-1500 for an all-inclusive liveaboard course). Shop around and choose a reputable company with qualified instructors. The best diving is to be had on the outer reef where the water is generally clearer and the fish species bigger. The following are just a sample and are not necessarily recommended above the many other operators. Almost all offer competitive rates and options for certified divers and snorkellers. Also check out www.divingcairns.com.au.

Cairns Dive Centre, 121 Abbott St, T4051 0294, www.cairnsdive.com.au, offers certification from $319-594 and

Budget busters

Scenic flights from Cairns

Cairns Heli Scenic, T4031 5999, www.cairns-heliscenic.com.au. 10 mins from $98.
Daintree Air Services, T4034 9300, www.daintreeair.com.au. 30 mins fixed wing flight from $165.
Reefwatch Air Tours, T4035 9808, www.reefwatch.com.au. Fixed wing flights over the reef and surrounding islands.
Sunlover Helicopters, T4035 9669, www.sunloverheli.com.au. 30mins ($279) to reef or rainforest from $449.

Champagne Balloon Flights, T4058 1688, www.champagne balloons.com.au, **Raging Thunder**, T4030 7990, www.raging thunder.com.au, and **Hot Air**, T4039 2900, www.hotair.com.au, all offer similar hot air balloon trips from $155.
Cairns Tiger Moth, T4035 9400, 20 mins from $120. For a more unusual flight experience you might also like to try this.

a day long introductory dive cruise with 2 dives from $120.
Down Under Dive, 287 Draper St, T4052 8300, www.downunderdive.com.au. Offers 4-day/2-night certification from $320.
ProDive, corner of Abbott St and Shields St, T4031 5255, www.prodive-cairns.com.au. Offers a range of trips including a 3-day/ 2-night certification with 11 dives from $595, 1-day Introductory dive from $180.
Reef Encounter, 100 Abbott St, T4050 0688, www.reeftrip.com. Offers a 3-day/ 2-night certification with 10 dives from $560.

Fishing

Cairns has been a world-class big game fishing venue for many years and as a result there are many excellent charters with experienced guides. Black Marlin are the biggest species, capable of reaching weights of over 1,000 lb, which must be a bit like landing a pair of irate sumo wrestlers. Another commonly caught species is the Wahoo, whose name is surely derived from the noise you make while catching it.
Cairns Reef Charter Services, T4031 4610, www.ausfish.com/crcs. One of the best charter companies, it has a fleet of ocean-going vessels and also offers an exciting range of multi-day ocean and inland trips to catch game fish or the famed barramundi.
Cairns Travel and Sports fishing, T4031 6016. Another reputable company offering a wide range of fishing trips including both salt and freshwater. Around $85 per half-day.
VIP, T4031 4355. Offers a wide range of fishing trips targeting both salt and freshwater. Prices start at about $85 for a half-day and $225 a day per person for big game fishing. Crabbing is also popular and especially fun for kids.

Horse trekking and mountain biking

Most of these companies offer combination packages with other activities or attractions.
Bandicoot Bike Tours, 153 Sheridan St, T4041 0100. Offers a good day trip in the Atherton Tablelands with a flexible hop-on hop-off escort should you prefer to do some sightseeing, from $109 including lunch and pick up.
Blazing Saddles, T4059 0955, www.blazingsaddles.com.au.

Runs a half-day trek suitable for beginners, from $90, child $70. They also offer entertaining half-day ATV safaris from $110.

Dan's Mountain Biking, T4032 0066, www.cairns.aust.com/mtb. Half-day trips to the rainforested Mulgrave Valley from $75.

General/sightseeing tours

There are numerous trips on offer that combine the Scenic Railway and Skyrail Gondola (see page 347). Others include deductions in to the major sights. Ask at the VIC. One-day 4WD tours to Daintree and Cape Tribulation generally leave Cairns at about 0700 and return about 1800 and cost in the region of $140-175.

Billy Tea Bush Safaris, T4032 0077, www.billytea.com.au. Has friendly, entertaining guides, day tour from $139, child $95.

Cairns Discovery Tours, T4053 5259. Half-day tour of city sights including the Botanical Gardens, Flying Doctor Service Visitors Centre and Northern Beaches, from $56, child $28.

Jungle Tours, T4032 5600, www.jungle tours.com.au. Offer good value day-trips from $130 and overnight trips and combination adventure packages from $250, staying at the Cape's various backpacker establishments.

Tropical Horizons, T4058 1244, www.tropicalhorizonstours.com.au. Offer very comfortable, quality, small group tours, of up to 11 hrs from $130.

Trek North, T4051 4328, www.treknorth. com.au. Takes small groups to Daintree and Mossman Gorge and includes a cruise on the Daintree River. Good value, from $115, child $69 (Cape Tribulation from $145).

Tropic Wings, 278 Hartley St, T4041 9400, www.tropicwings.com.au. Offers an excellent tour to Kuranda combining the Kuranda Scenic Railway and Skyline Gondola with the addition of many exciting diversions and activities, from $175, child $88.

Northern Experience Eco Tours, T4041 4633, www. cairnstours.com. Another good company offering a wildlife edge to their day tour, from $99, child $71.

Wooroonooran Rainforest Safaris, T4051 5512, www.wooroonooran-safaris. com.au. Sightseeing and trekking trips with in the beautiful Wooroonooran National Park south of Cairns, from $149.

Rafting

Fancy tackling a 'Double D-Cup,' opting for the 'Corkscrew,' or going headfirst into the 'Wet and Moisty'? Well, you can with various rafting companies who have christened various rapids with such 'exotic' names. Cairns is the base for some excellent rafting with a wide range of adrenaline pumping trips down the Barron, North Johnstone and Tully Rivers. It is all mighty fun, but watch out for the 'Doors of Deception'. The minimum age for rafting is usually 13 years.

Raging Thunder, T4030 7990, www.ragingthunder.com.au. Half, full, and multi-day trips, as well as heli-trips and many other activity combos. Half-day Barron River from $98, full-day Tully River, $155.

R'n'R, Abbott St, T4051 7777, www.raft.com. au. A similar outfit offering full-day trips down the Tully for $145, half-day on the Barron for $98.

Foaming Fury, 19-21 Barry St, T4031 3460, www.foamingfury.com.au. Tackles the Barron, half-day from $81 and also offer something a bit different with a full-day 2-man 'sports rafting' experience on the Russell River, from $125. They are also recommended for families.

Watersports

Skii-Mee Tours, T4034 1907, www.skiimee.com.au. A small and friendly family owned operation offering good value waterskiing or wakeboarding tours and instruction from $99, full day from $159.

Cooktown

Like Cairns and Port Douglas, Cooktown has grown in stature as an attractive lifestyle proposition and a popular tourist destination. There is plenty to see and do here, with the **James Cook Museum** the undeniable highlight. A good place to start is from the Grassy Hill Lighthouse, which is reached after a short climb at the end of Hope Street, north of the town centre. Here you can take in the views of the coast and town from the same spot Captain Cook reputedly worked out his safe passage back through the reef to the open sea. The old corrugated iron lighthouse that dominates the hill was built in England and shipped to Cooktown in 1885. For decades it served local and international shipping before being automated in 1927 and becoming obsolete in the 1980s. From Hope Street it is a short walk to the **James Cook Museum**, at the corner of Furneaux Street and Helen Street ⓘ*T4069 5386, Apr-Jan 0930-1600 (reduced hours Feb-Mar), $7, child $2*, housed in a former convent built in 1889 and touted as one of the most significant museums in Australia. The museum is not dedicated solely to Cook and also houses interesting displays covering the town's colourful and cosmopolitan history. Other sites of historical interest include the Cooktown Cemetery, at the southern edge of town along Endeavour Valley Road, where many former pioneers died.

As well as the obvious historical attraction Cooktown offers a number of activities from self-guided local walks and historic town tours to reef fishing, cruising and snorkelling. **Cookshire Council,** T4069 5444, and **Cooktown Travel Centre**, T4069 5446, cooktown travel@bigpond.com, cover visitor information services. Many tour operators in Cairns and Port Douglas offer day or multi-day trips to Cooktown some combining road travel with a scenic return flight. **Skytrans Airlines**, T4069 5446/1800-818405, www.skytrans.com.au, offers regular transfers to Cairns from $91 one-way (with 3-day advance purchase). If you are not joining an tour operation from Cairns or Port Douglas contact **Cooktown Travel**, T4069 5446, for the latest information on scheduled bus services.

Sleeping

L-A **Sovereign Resort Hotel**, on the corner of Charlotte St and Green St, T4069 5400, www.sovereign-resort.com.au, is the most upmarket place in town offering modern 2 bedroom apartments, deluxe and standard units. It also has a reputable à la carte restaurant and a fine pool.

C-E **Pam's Place YHA**, on the corner of Charlotte St and Boundary St, T4069 5166, www.cooktownhostel.com.au, is the main backpackers in town. It offers dorms, singles and doubles and has all the usual facilities including a pool, tour desk and bike hire.

Wildscapes Safaris, T4057 6272, www.wildscapes-safaris.com.au. For specialist wildlife trips:

Northern Great Barrier Reef Islands

p351

Big Cat Green Island Reef Cruises, Reef Fleet Terminal, T4051 0444, www.bigcat-crui ses.com.au. This is one of the two main operators to Green Island. It offers half and full-day cruises with optional extras from, $59, child $34. **Dive Shop** ($12) has snorkel, mask and fins for hire. It also offers introductory dives to non-guests (30 mins) from around $100. Pool access costs $5 for those with children or an inability to stray too far from the well-stocked bar.

Frankland Islands Cruise and Dive, T4031 6300, www.franklandislands. com.au. Full day trip with activities from $129 and camp transfers from $199. Also on offer is certified/ introductory diving (full package) from $175 and a range of combo multi sight/tour package deals. The ferry departs daily from Cairns.

Great Adventures, The Wharf, Cairns, T4044 9944, www.greatadventures. com.au. There are two main tour operators to Green Island. This one offers basic transfers from $58, child $29, and a wide range of tour options with activity inclusions and optional extras, full day $98, child $49. Additionally there is a Green Island and Outer Reef (pontoon) tour from $182, child $94. Added extras include snorkel tour from $25, intro dive from $110.

Raging Thunder Fitzroy Resort, T4124 9943, www.ozhorizons.com.au. Offers introductory dive trips on Fitzroy Island with 3-day certification from $395 and snorkel hire from $12. Other watersports are also available including a 2-day kayaking trip around the island from $176. These activities come as part of the resort accommodation packages, but are also offered to independent visitors.

Atherton Tablelands *p353, map p355*

Carrawong Fauna Sanctuary, Kuranda, T4093 7287, www.australiawildlife tours.com. A local company offering wildlife night spotting tours from $98. .

On The Wallaby Tablelands Tours, T4050 0650, www.tropic days.com.au. Offers entertaining guided tours of the Tablelands sights with excellent wildlife canoeing trips as a further option. Their 2-day/1-night accommodation/ activity package based at their hostel in Yungaburra is good value and recommended (see Sleeping section). Offers excellent backpacker-oriented wildlife and day/night canoeing.

Wildscapes Safaris, Yungaburra, T4057 6272, www.wildscapes-safaris. com.au. Wildlife tours and specializes in platypus spotting.

Port Douglas and The Daintree

p358, map p359

Cultural tours

Kuku-Yalanji Tours, T4098 3437. Just short of the Mossman gorge car park is this operation. It offers excellent 2- to 3-hr Aboriginal cultural awareness walks that will enlighten you on the use of certain plants for medicinal purposes and traditional hunting methods, from $10. There is also a shop, gallery open daily 0900-1600.

Diving and snorkelling

All the major reef operators are based at the Marina Mirage Wharf, Wharf St. Almost all of the Cairns based companies listed on page 371 also provide transfers from Port Douglas. The vast majority combine cruising with snorkelling and/or diving with others being dive specialists. Those listed below are recommended but this does not imply that those not listed are not reputable.

Discover Dive School, 6 Grant St, T4099 5544, www.discoverdiveschool.com.

Quicksilver, T4087 2100, www.quicksilver-cruises.com.au. This is the main operator in Port Douglas. Long-established and highly

professional, it will shuttle tourists out to their own pontoon on the edge of Agincourt Reef, where you can spend the day (5 hrs) diving, snorkelling or sunbathing. The basic day-cruise with a buffet lunch costs $189, child $95. Diving and snorkelling is an added option and there are cruise/scenic flight combos from $375. Departs daily 0930. They also operate a smaller luxury dive vessel the *Quicksmart*, www.quicksilverdive.com.au, which visits the Agincourt Reef with introductory dives from $204, certified dives from $194, and snorkelling from $142. Departs 0830 daily. Also in the fleet is the modern sailing catamaran, the *Wavedancer* which visits the Low Isles on the inner reef where independent (or guided) snorkelling and guided beach walks are available. Day package from $132, child $66, lunch included. Departs 0930 daily.
Tech Dive Academy, 1/18 Macrossan Street, Port Douglas T4099 6880, www.tech-dive-academy.com.
Undersea Explorer, PO Box 615, Port Douglas, T4099 5911, www.undersea.com.au. Large vessel which runs unique trips combining adventure diving with the focus on conservation, education and scientific exploration.

Fishing

There are a posse of charter boats available to take you fishing. **Hooker Too**, T4099 5136, **Crystal Blue**, T0428-466522 (good fishing and snorkel package) and the compact **Dragon Lady**, T0418-298412. A full day will cost around $175. To hire your own pontoon boat or dinghy contact **Port Douglas Boat Hire**, T4099 6277, or **Out 'n' About**, T4098 5204, from $20 per hr.

Horse trekking

Wonga Beach Equestrian Centre, T4098 7583. Entertaining rides along Wonga Beach, 20 km north, including Port Douglas transfers from $110, 3 hr.

Parasailing and jet ski

Extra Action Water Sports, based on the first jetty north of the Marina Mirage Complex, T4099 3175. Offer 'fast' half-day trips to the Low Isles and the wonderfully quiet Snapper Island from $140, parasailing and jet bike hire from around $75 (30 mins). Combination packages are also available.

Spas

Daintree Eco Lodge and Spa, T4098 6100, www.daintree-ecolodge.com.au. Offer a 30-min 'Milkanga Kaday' (aboriginal for 'Come Back to the Mind') from $65, plus numerous other attractive options. Book ahead.

Wildlife and sightseeing tours

Fine Feather Tours, T4094 1199, www.fine feathertours.com.au. Operated by enthusiastic locals Del and Pat offer full day birding tours in Mossman Gorge, one of which includes a Daintree River Cruise from $155.
Reef and Rainforest Connections, 8/40 Macrossan St, Port Douglas, T4099 5599, www.reefandrain forest.com.au. Offers a wide range to Kuranda, Mossman Gorge, Daintree/Cape Tribulation and Cooktown.
Native Guide Safari Tours, T4098 2206, www.nativeguidesafaritours.com.au. For a personalized, authentic and informative look at the Mossman Gorge through aboriginal eyes contact Hazel. Full-day from $130, child $80 ($140 includes ferry transfer from Cairns).
On the Daintree River The search for crocs has become something of a cruise fest and there are dozens of operators. Pick-ups and day tours from Cairns or Port Douglas are available.
Crocodile Express, T4098 6120, is the largest and longest serving operator. It offers two cruises. The most popular is their 1½-hr River Cruise that departs from the village on the hour from 1030-1600, from $20, child $7. The second is a 2½-hr Estuary Cruise that explores the lower reaches and the mouth of river.

Chris Dahlberg's River Tours, T4098 7997, www.daintreerivertours.info. Offers an excellent dawn cruise (departs 0600 Nov-Mar and 0630 Apr-Oct), with an emphasis on bird spotting, from $45. **Daintree Wildlife Safari**, based at the General Store in Daintree, T4098 6146, offers 1½-hr Croc Spot cruises on the hour from 0930-1530, from $20, child $7 and 1-hr cruises on the hour from 1000-1600, from $17, child $6. Cruise and walk options, 0800-1000 or 1600-1800, cost from $30, child $20.

Cape Tribulation *p361, map p362*

There are many activities on offer in the region, including crocodile spotting, sea kayaking, horse riding, reef cruising with diving or snorkelling – even candlelit dinners deep in the rainforest. These are best arranged through the main backpackers such as **The Cape Trib Beach House** (see page 368). See also Cairns and Port Douglas based tour operators. Some do not operate in the wet season (Dec-Mar) when access can be severely affected. Also consult the VICs in Cairns or Port Douglas.
Jungle Adventures T4098 0090, www.jungleadventures capetrib.com.au, and **Mason's Tours**, T4098 0070, www.masonstours.com.au, offer guided rainforest walks and are recommended. Their night walk spotting the doe-eyed possums is a well worthwhile (from $32). A 4WD day trip exploring the Bloomfield Track with **Mason's Tours** costs from $185. **Jungle Adventures** also offer a spot of 'rainforest canopy surfing' which is essentially a series of flying fox cables allowing the opportunity to do the inevitable 'Tarzan', from $75.

Transport

Cairns *p346, map p348*

Air

Cairns International Airport is 6 km north of the city centre, on the Captain Cook Highway, www.cairnsport.com.au. International, domestic and state air carriers are all represented, including **Qantas**, T131313, **Air New Zealand**, T131223, **Cathay Pacific**, T131747, **Malaysia Airlines**, T132627, **Virgin Blue**, T136789, **Jetstar**, T131538, **Air Niugini** (Papua New Guinea). Other local charter flight companies also provide inter-island services throughout the Great Barrier Reef and to the Whitsunday Islands including **Macair**, T131313, **Skytrans**, T4046 2462, and **Daintree Air Services**, T4043 9300.

Bus

The main suburban bus operator is **Sunbus**, T4057 7411, www.sunbus.com.au, offers regular services north as far as Palm Cove and south as far as Gordonvale. Day/week passes available. The bus transit centre is on Lake St (City Place) where schedules are posted. The interstate coach terminal is at Trinity Wharf, Wharf St (open daily 0600-0100). Some services also drop off at the new Marina Complex which is nearby. **Greyhound**, T131499, www.mccaffertys.com.au, have an office within the terminal and operate regular daily services south to Brisbane and beyond (including onward connections to Darwin from Townsville). **Premier Motor Service**, T133410, www.premierms.com.au, also operates daily services to Brisbane and beyond. Cairns to Brisbane takes about 28 hrs. **Coral Reef Coaches**, T4098 2800, www.coralreefcoaches.com.au, runs regular local services to the Airport, Port Douglas, Mossman, Daintree and Cape Tribulation. **Whitecar Coaches**, T4091 1855, services the Atherton Tablelands including Kuranda daily.

Car

The wet road conditions around Cairns and far north Queensland can be, in a word, aquatic. For up-to-date conditions and flood warnings, T131111.
Car rental at the airport and Abbott St and Lake St in the city have most outlets.

Avis, Airport, T4035 9100; **Budget**, 153 Lake St, T1327227; **All Day Rentals**, 151 Lake St, T1800-246869; **Delta**, 403 Sheridan St, T4032 2000; **MiniCar Rentals**, 150 Sheridan St, T4051 6288; **4WD Hire**, 440 Sheridan St, T4032 3094. For a standard car and 7-day hire expect to pay from $50 a day. Some of the larger companies like Avis also offer 4WD hire from around $150 per day.

For **campervan rentals and purchase** (second-hand), **Travellers Auto Barn**, 123-125 Bunda St, T4041 3722, www.travellers-autobarn.com.au. They offer guaranteed buy-backs in Sydney. **Car servicing**, 4WD second-hand vans and genuine advice at **Mac's Workshop**, Shed 1, 8-10 West St, Manunda, T4032 0122. For RACQ road conditions report T1300-130595.

Train

The station is on Bunda St. Travel centre is open Mon-Fri 0900-1700, Sat 0800-1200, T4036 9250. For other long-distance enquiries, T132232, 24 hr, www.traveltrain.qr.com.au. There are 3 coastal train services to/from **Brisbane** and beyond, ranging in standards of luxury and price. The most popular is the fast *Tilt Train* (departs Brisbane Mon and Fri, Cairns Sun and Wed), or alternatively there is the *The Sunlander* (departs Brisbane 0835, Tue, Sat, Sun and Thu). There is one 'Outback' service, *The Gulflander*, that shuttles between **Croydon** and **Normanton**. A local scenic service also operates to **Kuranda**, from $35, child $17 ($50 return). Ask about the various holiday and 'Discoverer Passes', for price reductions and packages.

Northern Great Barrier Reef Islands

p351

For **Green Island**, ferries leave the Reef Fleet Terminal on waterfront , Cairns with additional transfers from Palm Beach (Northern Beaches) and Port Douglas.

For **Fitzroy Island**, Fitzroy Island Ferry, T4030 7907, and **Sunlover Cruises**, T4050 1333, both service Fitzroy departing Cairns, from $36, child$18.

For **Lizard Island**, there are various regional air operators and vessel charter companies but prices and times vary. VIC in Cooktown is the best place to enquire for the most up-to-date options. **Daintree Air Services**, T4034 9300, www.daintreeair.com. au, offers a day-trip package from $550, from Cairns. **Skytrans Airlines**, T4046 2462, www.skytrans. com.au, also offers air charters from Cairns or Cooktown.

Atherton Tablelands *p353, map p355*

Most visitors to **Kuranda** make the village part of a day-tour package from Cairns, with the highlight actually accessing it via the Barron Gorge and the Skyline Gondola, the Scenic Railway or both. See above for operators in Cairns. Prices and schedules for the **Skyrail**, T4038 1555, and **Scenic Railway**, T4031 3636, are also listed on page 347. **Kuranda Shuttle**, T0402-032085, and **Whitecar Coaches**, Trinity Wharf Terminal, T4091 1855, share services to Kuranda at the most competitive price, sometimes for as little as a $2. 'D' stop in the Cairns City Terminal, daily 0900, 1100, 1300 and 1500, Wed, Thu, Fri and Sun.

Whitecar Coaches, Trinity Wharf Terminal, T4091 1855, runs daily services to **Yungaburra**.

Port Douglas *p358, map p359*

Air

Port Douglas is accessed from Cairns International Airport. **Airport Shuttle**, T4099 5950, offers services at least every hour daily from 0630-1630, $22, child $11.

Bus

Coral Reef Coaches, Port Douglas Local Shuttle, T4098 2800, www.coralreefcoaches.com.au, runs regular local bus services to the **Cairns City**, (from $23), **Cairns Airport**, **Mossman**, **Daintree** and **Cape Tribulation** (from $55). The main bus

State phone codes and time difference

There are no area phone codes. Use a state code if calling outside the state you are in. These are: 02 for ACT/NSW (08 for Broken Hill), 03 for VIC and 07 for QLD. Note that NSW operates daylight saving, which means that clocks go forward one hour from October and March.

stops are on Grant St and at the Marina Mirage (Wharf) Complex. They also have an office in Mossman at 37 Front St, T4098 2800.

Cycling/scooter

Bike and Hike, 6/42 Macrossan St, T4099 4000, hires out bikes for half-day from $10, full-day from $15, week from $50. Scooter hire from **Port Motor Bike and Scooter Hire**, T4099 4000.

Taxi

Port Douglas Taxis, 45 Warner St, T40995345, 24 hrs.

Cape Tribulation *p361, map p362*

Bus

Coral Reef Coaches, 37 Front St, Mossman, T4098 2800, offers daily scheduled services and tour packages from Cairns and Port Douglas, from $32, one-way (Cairns), tours from $55.

Car

Self-drive is recommended but all roads in the area can be treacherous in the wet season (Dec-Mar). For road information, T4051 6711.

Daintree River Ferry, 15 km southeast of Daintree village, runs daily from 0600-2400, pedestrian $4 return, vehicle $20 return. Beyond Cape Tribulation (36 km), the road degenerates into the strictly 4WD Bloomfield Track that winds its precarious 120 km way to Cooktown. Fuel is available 4 km east of Cow Bay village and 6 km north at the Rainforest Village Store. In the event of breakdown contact the RACQ (Cow Bay), T4098 2848.

Directory

Cairns *p346, map p348*

Banks All the major banks have branches in the city centre especially at the intersection of Shields St and Abbott St. **Library** Cairns City Public Library, 151 Abbott St, T4044 3720. Free internet. **Medical services** Cairns Base Hospital, Esplanade (north), T4050 6333. Cairns City 24-hr Medical centre, corner of Florence St and Grafton St, T4052 1119. After Hours, 29B Shields St, T4051 2466. Open 0800-2100. **Post** 13 Grafton St, T131318. Open Mon-Fri 0830-1700. **Useful numbers** Police, emergency T000, 5 Sheridan St, T4030 7000.

Port Douglas *p358, map p359*

Banks Macrossan St or Port Village Centre. **Internet** Wickedly Healthy, corner Macrossan and Owen St, T4099 5568. Open daily 0900-2200. **Medical services** Mossman, T4098 2444. Port Village Medical Centre, Shop 17, shopping centre, Macrossan St, T4099 5043, 24 hrs. **Post** 5 Owen St,T4099 5210. Open Mon-Fri 0900-1700, Sat 0900-1200. Postcode 4877. **Pharmacy** Macrossan St Pharmacy, 13/14 Port Village Centre, T4099 5223. **Useful numbers** Police, Wharf St, T4099 5220.

Index

Credits

Footprint credits

Editor: Alan Murphy
Editorial assistants: Emma Bryers, Angus Dawson
Map editor: Sarah Sorensen
Picture editor: Kevin Feeney

Publisher: Patrick Dawson
Editorial: Sophie Blacksell, Sarah Thorowgood, Claire Boobbyer, Felicity Laughton, Nicola Jones
Cartography: Robert Lunn, Claire Benison, Kevin Feeney
Sales and marketing: Andy Riddle
Advertising: Debbie Wylde
Finance and administration: Sharon Hughes, Elizabeth Taylor

Photography credits

Front cover: Alamy (Bondi Beach surf mural)
Inside: Darroch Donald, Shaun Tierney, Photolibrary, Powerstock, Travel-Ink
Back cover: Darroch Donald (Cassowary road sign)

Print

Manufactured in Italy by Eurografica
Pulp from sustainable forests

Footprint feedback

We try as hard as we can to make each Footprint guide as up to date as possible but, of course, things always change. If you want to let us know about your experiences – good, bad or ugly – then don't delay, go to www.footprintbooks.com and send in your comments.

Darroch would like to thank the staff and representatives of the many VICs for their assistance. Also thanks to Tony and Brigitte Robinson and a special thanks to Grace and Rebecca for their encouragement and support.

Publishing information

Footprint East Coast Australia
2nd edition

December 2005
ISBN 1 904777 57 0
CIP DATA: A catalogue record for this book is available from the British Library
® Footprint Handbooks and the Footprint mark are a registered trademark of Footprint Handbooks Ltd

Published by Footprint

6 Riverside Court
Lower Bristol Road
Bath BA2 3DZ, UK
T +44 (0)1225 469141
F +44 (0)1225 469461
discover@footprintbooks.com
www.footprintbooks.com

Distributed in the USA by

Publishers Group West

Neither the black and white nor colour maps are intended to have any political significance.

Every effort has been made to ensure that the facts in this guidebook are accurate. However, travellers should still obtain advice from consulates, airlines etc about travel and visa requirements before travelling. The authors and publishers cannot accept responsibility for any loss, injury or inconvenience however caused.